ELEMENTS OF
COMPUTATIONAL
SYSTEMS BIOLOGY

Wiley Series on
Bioinformatics: Computational Techniques and Engineering

Bioinformatics and computational biology involve the comprehensive application of mathematics, statistics, science, and computer science to the understanding of living systems. Research and development in these areas require cooperation among specialists from the fields of *biology*, computer science, mathematics, statistics, physics, and related sciences. The objective of this book series is to provide timely treatments of the different aspects of bioinformatics spanning theory, new and established techniques, technologies and tools, and application domains. This series emphasizes algorithmic, mathematical, statistical, and computational methods that are central in bioinformatics and computational biology.

Series Editors: **Professor Yi Pan** and **Professor Albert Y. Zomaya**
pan@cs.gsu.edu   zomaya@it.usyd.edu.au

ELEMENTS OF COMPUTATIONAL SYSTEMS BIOLOGY

Edited by

Huma M. Lodhi
Stephen H. Muggleton

Imperial College London, London, UK

WILEY

A John Wiley & Sons, Inc., Publication

Published by John Wiley & Sons, Inc., Hoboken, New Jersey
Published simultaneously in Canada.

For general information on our other products and services or for technical support, please contact our Customer Care Department within the United States at (800) 762-2974, outside the United States at (317) 572-3993 or fax (317) 572-4002.

Wiley also publishes its books in a variety of electronic formats. Some content that appears in print may not be available in electronic formats. For more information about Wiley products, visit our web site at www.wiley.com.

Library of Congress Cataloging-in-Publication Data:

Lodhi, Huma M.
  Elements of computational systems biology / Huma M. Lodhi, Stephen H. Muggleton.
    p. cm.
  Includes bibliographical references and index.
  ISBN 978-0-470-18093-8 (cloth)
  1. Systems biology. 2. Computational biology. I. Muggleton, Stephen.   II. Title.
  QH324.2.L64 2010
  570.285–dc22   2009028768

10 9 8 7 6 5 4 3 2 1

CONTENTS

PART III   BIOLOGICAL NETWORK INFERENCE

7   Reconstruction of Biological Networks by Supervised Machine Learning Approaches   165

Jean-Philippe Vert

8   Supervised Inference of Metabolic Networks from the Integration of Genomic Data and Chemical Information   189

Yoshihiro Yamanishi

9   Integrating Abduction and Induction in Biological Inference Using CF-Induction

Yoshitaka Yamamoto, Katsumi Inoue, and Andrei Doncescu

10   Analysis and Control of Deterministic and Probabilistic Boolean Networks

Tatsuya Akutsu and Wai-Ki Ching

PART IV   GENOMICS AND COMPUTATIONAL SYSTEMS BIOLOGY

PREFACE

Recently there has been a huge interest in the development of computational methodologies for modeling and simulating biological processes. The book facilitates the design of effective and efficient techniques by introducing key elements of the emerging field of computational systems biology. It gives an in-depth description of core subjects including biological network modeling, analysis, and inference. It presents a measured introduction to foundational topics such as genomics and describes state-of-the-art software tools.

The collaborations between experts from highly diverse areas ranging from biology to computer science are crucial for the progress in computational systems biology. The book is aimed at fostering close collaborations between biologists, chemists, physicists, mathematicians and computer scientists by providing ground-breaking research. It provides an inspiration and basis for the future development and applications of novel computational and mathematical methods to solving complex and unsolved problems in biology.

The book is intended for researchers and scientists from the fields of biology, chemistry, mathematics, physics, and computer science who are interested in computational systems biology or focused on developing, refining, and applying computational and mathematical approaches to solving biological problems. It is organized in a way so that the experts from the industry such as biotechnology and pharmaceutical companies will find it very useful and simulating. The book is accessible to students and provides knowledge that he/she requires.

We wish to thank Wiley for the support and help in the processing of the book. We would also like to thank Yanqing Zhang, Bart Bijnens, Antti Honkela, Zhongming Zhao, Nicos Angelopoulos, Roman Rosipal, Jae-Hyung Lee, Zhaolei Zhang, Ying Liu, Wenyuan Li, Dong Xu, Giovani Gomez Estrada, Li Liao, Leming Zhou, and Etienne Birmele for their help in the reviewing process.

H. M. Lodhi and S. H. Muggleton

Feburary, 2009

CONTRIBUTORS

Tatsuya Akutsu, Kyoto University, Kyoto, Japan

Panayiotis V. Benos, Departments of Computational Biology and Biomedical Informatics, School of Medicine, University of Pittsburgh, Pittsburgh, PA, USA

Alessandra Carbone, Génomique Analytique, Université Pierre et Marie Curie–Paris 6, FRE3214 CNRS-UPMC, 15 rue de l'Ecole de Médecine, 75006 Paris, France

Carsten Carlberg, Life Sciences Research Unit, University of Luxembourg, Luxembourg, UK

Matteo Cavaliere, The Microsoft Research - University of Trento, CoSBi, Trento, Italy

Wilbur E. Channels, Department of Electrical and Computer Engineering, The Johns Hopkins University, Baltimore, MD, USA

Wai-Ki Ching, University of Hong Kong, Hong Kong, China

Kwang-Hyun Cho, Department of Bio and Brain Engineering, Korea Advanced Institute of Science and Technology (KAIST), Daejeon, 305–701 Korea

Sang-Mok Choo, School of Electrical Engineering, University of Ulsan, Ulsan, Korea

Vincent Danos, University of Edinburgh, Edinburgh, UK

Andrei Doncescu, LAAS-CNRS, Avenue du Colonel Roche, Toulouse, France

Jérôme Féret, ENS-INRIA-CNRS, Paris, France

Duncan Gillies, Department of Computing, Imperial College London, London, UK

Jeremy Gunawardena, Department of Systems Biology, Harvard Medical School, Boston, MA, USA

Jörg Hakenberg, Computer Science and Engineering, Arizona State University, Tempe, AZ, USA

Russell Harmer, CNRS-Paris-Diderot, Paris, France

Merja Heinäniemi, Life Sciences Research Unit, University of Luxembourg, Luxembourg

Pablo A. Iglesias, Department of Electrical and Computer Engineering, The Johns Hopkins University, Baltimore, MD, USA

Katsumi Inoue, Department of Informatics, The Graduate University for Advanced Studies and National Institute of Informatics, Chiyoda-ku, Tokyo, Japan

Tae-Hwan Kim, Department of Bio and Brain Engineering, Korea Advanced Institute of Science and Technology (KAIST), Daejeon, 305–701 Korea

Jean Krivine, Harvard University, Cambridge, MA, USA

Ulf Leser, Knowledge Management in Bioinformatics, Humboldt-Universität zu Berlin, Berlin, Germany

Huma M. Lodhi, Department of Computing, Imperial College London, London SW7 2AZ, UK

Anthony Mathelier, Génomique Analytique, Université Pierre et Marie Curie–Paris 6, FRE3214 CNRS-UPMC, 15 rue de l'Ecole de Médecine, 75006 Paris, France

Itay Mayrose, Department of Cell Research and Immunology, George S. Wise Faculty of Life Sciences, Tel Aviv University, Tel Aviv, Israel

Tommaso Mazza, The Microsoft Research - University of Trento, CoSBi, Trento, Italy

Alok Mishra, Department of Computing, Imperial College London, London, UK

Elaine Murphy, University of Edinburgh, Edinburgh, UK

Conrad Plake, Biotechnological Centre, Technische Universität Dresden, Dresden, Germany

Tal Pupko, Department of Cell Research and Immunology, George S. Wise Faculty of Life Sciences, Tel Aviv University, Tel Aviv, Israel

Sung-Young Shin, Department of Bio and Brain Engineering, Korea Advanced Institute of Science and Technology (KAIST), Daejeon, 305–701 Korea

Alain B. Tchagang, Department of Computational Biology, School of Medicine, University of Pittsburgh, Pittsburgh, PA, USA

Jean-Philippe Vert, Mines ParisTech – Institut Curie, Paris, France

Stephen T. C. Wong, The Center for Biotechnology and Informatics, The Methodist Hospital Research Institute and Department of Radiology, The Methodist Hospital Weill Cornell Medical College, Houston, TX, USA

Ling-Yun Wu, The Center for Biotechnology and Informatics, The Methodist Hospital Research Institute and Department of Radiology, The Methodist Hospital Weill Cornell Medical College, Houston, TX, USA

Yoshitaka Yamamoto, Department of Informatics, The Graduate University for Advanced Studies, Chiyoda-ku, Tokyo, Japan

Yoshihiro Yamanishi, Mines ParisTech - Institut Curie, Paris, France

Xiaobo Zhou, The Center for Biotechnology and Informatics, The Methodist Hospital Research Institute and Department of Radiology, The Methodist Hospital Weill Cornell Medical College, Houston, TX, USA

I

OVERVIEW

1

ADVANCES IN COMPUTATIONAL SYSTEMS BIOLOGY

Huma M. Lodhi

Department of Computing, Imperial College London, London, SW7 2AZ, UK

1.1 INTRODUCTION

Computational systems biology, a rapidly evolving field, is at the interface of computer science, mathematics, physics, and biology. It endeavors to study, analyze, and understand complex biological systems by taking a coordinated integrated systems view using computational methodologies. From the middle of the twentieth century till present, we have been witnessing breakthrough discoveries in biology that range from molecular structure of deoxyribonucleic acid (DNA) to the generation of the sequence of the euchromatic portion of the human genome. There have also been recent advances in sophisticated computational methodologies, high-throughput biotechnologies, and computational power. The stunning developments in diverse disciplines such as biology and computer science are playing a key role in the fast progression of the emerging field. Computational systems biology provides a point of convergence for genomics, proteomics, metabolomics, and computational modeling. It is characterized by its focus on experimental data, computational techniques, and hypotheses testing [1–3].

Open and unsolved problems in biology range from understanding structure and dynamics of biological systems to prediction and inference in the complex systems.

Elements of Computational Systems Biology   Edited by Huma M. Lodhi and Stephen H. Muggleton
Copyright © 2010 John Wiley & Sons, Inc.

In the postgenomic era, systems-based approaches may provide a solution to such unsolved problems. It is believed that some answer to the question "what is life" may be obtained by taking a broader, integrated view of biology [4]. However, applications of systems-based techniques to biology are not new. Such methods and frameworks have been applied to analyze biological processes since early twentieth century [5, 6]. Norbert Wiener's groundbreaking work [7] is a well-known example of these applications.

The purpose and objective of this chapter is to review cutting-edge and long-ranging research in the field of computational systems biology in the recent years. However, the review is not meant to be exhaustive. We briefly describe novel methodologies to build multiscale biological models in Section 1.2. In Section 1.3, we present an overview of the applications of proteomics techniques to study biological processes. We then summarize computational systems biology methods to examine and understand aging in Section 1.4. Section 1.5 describes systems-based techniques for drug design, where such methods are revolutionizing the process of drug discovery. Efficient software tools and infrastructure are crucial to solving complex biological problems. In Section 1.6, we review tools for systems biology.

1.2 MULTISCALE COMPUTATIONAL MODELING

In the postgenomic era, researchers seek to focus their attention to studying and analyzing biological networks and pathways by the use of multiscale computational modeling techniques. A model can be viewed as a representation of a biological system, where the representation can comprise a set of differential equations [8], a set of first-order logic clauses [9], and so on. Biological models that incorporate multiple scales such as time and space or multiple timescales may be viewed as multiscale models [10]. Chapter 2 gives an in-depth account of mathematical and computational models in systems biology.

Development of efficient and effective computational methodologies to perform modeling, simulation, and analysis of complex biological processes is a challenging task. Traditionally, mathematical and computational models have been developed by considering a single scale. However, it is now feasible to incorporate multiple scales in the process of model building due to recent advances in computational power and technology. Generally, multiscale models are constructed by using sophisticated techniques including numerical methods and integration approaches. Multiscale model of the heart [11, 12] is a well-known example of an application of these modeling techniques.

Multiscale computational modeling and simulation methods are showing promising results in the field of oncology. The development of three-dimensional multiscale brain tumor model by Zhang et al. [13] is an attempt in this direction. The dynamics of tumor growth were simulated by using an agent-based multiscale model where microscopic scale, macroscopic scale, and molecular scale were incorporated in the *in silico* model. In micro-macroscopic environment, a virtual brain tissue block was represented by points in three-dimensional lattice. The lattice was divided into four cubes that illustrated the behavior of chemotactically acting tumor cells. The chemotaxis distribution of transforming growth factor alpha (TGFα), glucose, and oxygen tension were illustrated in a set of mathematical equations. It was observed that the amount of TGFα and glucose was chemoattractant, and diffusion of glucose occurred at a constant rate. In order to incorporate molecular scale, epidermal growth factor receptor (EGFR) gene–protein interaction network model [14] was used in conjunction with cell cycle module. The authors used a simplified EGFR network that comprised of EGFR and TGFα genes. The mathematical model of EGFR gene–protein network was represented as a set of differential equations. The authors utilized the cell cycle model presented in Tyson and Novak [15] and Alacron et al. [16]. The implementation of the software systems was carried out by combining in-house code with an agent-based software tool, namely, MASON (http://cs.gmu.edu/ eclab/projects/mason/). In order to study and analyze tumor growth and spread, 10 simulations were performed. The results demonstrated an increase in tumor volume with respect to time, where the relationship between tumor volume and time was not linear. There was a sharp increase in volume growth at later time intervals. The study found that migrating and proliferating cells exhibited a dynamic behavior with respect to time. Furthermore, the cells caused spatiotemporal tumor growth. The results showed that the number of migrating cells was greater than the number of proliferating cells over time, where the high concentration of phospholipase C gamma (PLCγ) might be the key factor behind the phenomenon. In summary, the study demonstrated a successful construction of multiscale computational model of the complex multifaceted biological process. However, the approach is not free from shortcomings as described below:

- A simple EGFR network was used.
- Clonal heterogeneity within tumor was not examined.

It has been found that the distribution of tumor cells is not homogeneous, and the cells exhibit heterogeneous patterns. Techniques that account for clonal heterogeneity of tumor cell populations can be vital to analyze and study the development of cancerous diseases. Furthermore, clonal heterogeneity can strongly impact the design of effective therapeutic strategies. Therefore, many studies examined heterogeneity in tumors [17, 18]. Zhang et al. [19] extended their multiscale computational modeling technique [13] to investigate the clonal heterogeneity by incorporating genetic instability. The extended model included doubling time of cell and cell cycle. Other parameters such as cell–cell adhesion were also considered so that the strength of the chemoattractants' (TGFα, oxygen tension, and glucose) impact on cancer cells adhesion and rate of cell migration could be investigated. The authors used Shannon's entropy for the quantification of tumor heterogeneity. Shannon entropy in this context can be calculated as follows: Let c_i denote the occurrence of clone i in the tumor, the entropy is given by $\sum_i c_i \ln(c_i)$, where the higher values of Shannon's entropy represent more clonal heterogeneity.

The results of the study showed an increase in tumor total volume over time, where the tumor was categorized into three regions on the basis of the distance between it and the nutrient source. It was observed that there was a general increase in the values of Shannon's entropy for all the three regions. However, there was highest clonal heterogeneity in the region closest to the nutrient source at early time stages where the region exhibited a homogeneous pattern at later stages. The study inferred that cancer could spread faster due to clonal heterogeneity as compared to homogeneous cell populations in tumor.

The complexity of the mechanisms of development and morphogenesis establishes a need to design effective and efficient computational techniques to investigate and analyze the biological process. In a recent study, Robertson et al. [20] presented a multiscale computational framework to investigate morphogenesis mechanisms in *Xenopus laevis*. Mammalian cells share similarities with *X. laevis* in terms of signaling network and cell behavior. A multiscale model was constructed by integrating an intercellular signaling pathway model with the multicellular model of mesendoderm migration. The authors implemented Wnt/β-catenin signaling pathway model that was presented by Lee et al. [21], whereas an agent-based approach was applied to build mesendoderm migration model. In order to simulate mesendoderm cells' migration, it was viewed that each cell comprised of nine sections, where each section was modeled as an agent. Mesendoderm migration was facilitated by the use of fibronectin extracellular matrix substrate. The study found that fibronectin gradient was a key factor behind the cellular movement. It was also observed that polarity signals [22] might be important for mesendoderm migration and morphogenesis. The simulations also demonstrated the importance to keep the cadherin binding strength in balance with the integrin binding strength. Although the study establishes the efficacy of multiscale computational methodologies to studying morphogenesis, the proposed approach may not be computationally attractive for large-scale simulations.

Physiome project [12] is well known for the development of multiscale modeling infrastructures. Given that standard modeling languages are useful for sharing biological data and models, three markup languages, namely, CellML (http://www.cellml.org/), FieldML, and ModelML, have been developed in the project. CellML [23] is characterized by its ability to capture three-dimensional information regarding cellular structures. It can also incorporate mathematical knowledge and metadata. FieldML, a related language, is known for its incorporation of spatial information. The third systems biology modeling language, namely, ModelML, is characterized by its ability to encode physical equations that illustrate complex biological processes. The efficacy of the languages was established by building multiscale heart models [12].

It has been found that same input, to constituent parts of a system, can produce different outputs. Such variations may be produced by factors including alterations in the concentration of system's components. It is desirable to design techniques and methods that can provide robustness to variations. Shinar et al. [24] presented a robust method by exploiting molecular details. The authors coined the term "input–output relation" for the association between input signal strength and output. The study investigated the input–output relation in bacterial signaling systems.

1.3 PROTEOMICS

Proteomics, the study of proteins, is viewed crucial to analyze and understand biological systems, as protein is the building block of life. Mass spectrometry (for details see Chapter 17) is a well-known proteomics technology that is showing a huge impact on the development of the field of computational systems biology. Several recent studies have identified the significant role of proteomics techniques in solving complex biological problems [25–27].

Proteomics methods and data can be useful for the reconstruction of biological networks. Recently, Rho et al. [28] presented a computational framework to reconstruct biological networks. The framework is based on the use of proteomics data and technologies to build and analyze computational models of biological networks. It is termed as integrative proteomic data analysis pipeline (IPDAP). IPDAP incorporates a number of network modeling and analysis tools. The component tools of IPDAP can be applied to reconstruct biological networks by fusing different types of proteomics data. The successful application of IPDAP to different cellular and tissue systems demonstrated the efficacy and functionality of the framework.

In another study, Zhao et al. [29] investigated signal transduction by applying techniques from optimization theory and exploiting proteomics and genomics data. They formulated the network identification problem as an integer linear programming problem. The proteomics (protein–protein interaction) data were represented as weighted undirected graph, where the nodes and the edges represented proteins and interaction between pair of proteins, respectively. The results of the study confirmed the efficacy of the approach in searching optimal signal transduction networks from the data.

Cell cycle comprises a series of ordered events by which cell replication and division take place. Studying cell cycle regulation provides useful insights in cancer growth and spread. The relationship between cell cycle and cancer has been a focus of many studies [30, 31]. In Sigal et al. [32], a proteomics approach was applied to investigate cell cycle mechanisms. The approach is based on the use of time-lapse microscopy to study protein dynamics. The study identified cell cycle-dependent changes in protein localization, where 40 percent of the investigated nuclear proteins demonstrated cell cycle dependence. Another challenging problem is to find patterns of polarized growth in cells where such growth is viewed as an important process in organisms. In order to investigate the biological problem, Narayanaswamy et al. [33] conducted a study by using budding yeast as the model system. The proposed computational method is based on the use of microarray image analysis and a machine learning technique, namely, naive Bayes algorithm. The study found 74 localized proteins including previously uncharacterized proteins and observed novel patterns of cell polarization in budding yeast.

In a recent study [34], a computational technique is presented for predicting peptide retention times. The method is at the intersection of two machine learning approaches, namely, neural networks and genetic algorithms. In order to predict the retention times, an artificial neural network is trained and the predicted values are further optimized by using a genetic algorithm. The method was successfully applied to *Arabidopsis* proteomics data.

1.4 COMPUTATIONAL SYSTEMS BIOLOGY AND AGING

Aging is a complex phenomenon that has not been well understood. In aging, we witness gradual diminishing/decreasing functions at different levels, including organs and tissues. Cell division has been viewed as a key process in aging since long [35, 36]. Recently, de Magalhaes and Faragher [37] have elucidated that aging might be affected by variations in cell division. Hazard rates and nutrition may be the key factors that influence the longevity of cellular organisms [38]. There are a number of theories that describe how aging occurs. Kirkwood [38] listed five different theories that are as follows:

- Somatic mutation theory
- Telomere loss theory
- Mitochondrial theory
- Altered proteins and waste accumulation theory
- Network theory

Aging has been extensively studied in *Caenorhabditis elegans* (nematode), mice, humans, and fruit flies. A number of genes that extend organisms' life span have been discovered. Several studies on aging found that genetic mutations could increase longevity [39–41]. Furthermore, aging genes with their associated pathways may influence the variations in aging between different species but may not have any affect on the differences in aging within a particular specie [42]. Gene expression and pathway analysis can provide useful means to identify aging-related similarities and differences between various species [43], where the efficacy of DNA microarray technology, in studying aging, is significant [44]. In a recent study on aging, DNA microarray experiments were utilized to show that aging in *C. elegans* is influenced by GATA transcriptional circuit [45].

Advances in computational systems biology have led to the development of tools and methods for solving highly complex problem of aging. For example, Xue et al. [46] addressed the key issue regarding aging by applying an analytic method to human/fruit fly protein–protein interaction network, namely, NP analysis [47]. The method is based on the identification of active modules in network, where the chosen module comprised of protein–protein interaction subnetwork between genes that show (positive or negative) correlation during aging. The application of the method to human brain aging identified four modules. Among these modules, the two showed transcriptionally anticorrelation with each other. The other two modules comprised of immunity genes and translational genes, respectively. In order to study correlation between genes in other species during aging, the method was applied to fruit fly interactome. The results of the study showed that in addition to two transcriptionally anticorrelated genes modules, there were two other modules that demonstrated such anticorrelation. On the basis of these findings, the authors suggest that only a few modules are associated with aging. The other key result of the study is the identification of the influence of module connecting genes on aging.

In another study, Garan et al. [48] presented a computational systems biology framework for studying neuroendocrine aging. The framework allows fusion of heterogeneous data from different disciplines such as endocrinology, cell biology, genetics, and so on. The method can be effective in identifying underlying relationship between the components that define aging.

Machine learning provides useful approaches and techniques to conduct studies on aging. In Swindell et al. [49], a number of machine learning methods were used to predict mouse life span. Twenty-two learning algorithms were applied to the problem, where the results demonstrated usefulness of support vector machines (SVMs), stabilized linear discriminant analysis, and nearest shrunken centroid in solving the problem, hence establishing the efficacy of machine learning technique for aging research. Agent-based modeling techniques have also been used to understand the biological processes of aging. The study published by Krivenko and Burtsev [50] is indicative of the success of such approaches for aging related studies. The authors applied their technique to simulate evolution and studied important factors including kin recognition and aggression.

Analysis of pathways for aging can also facilitate the understanding of complex diseases such as cancer. The probability of the occurrence of a cancer can be substantially lowered by downregulating the aging pathways [39]. Recently, Bergman et al. [51] investigated longevity genes. They conducted an extensive study by using more than 1200 subjects. On the basis of system-based analysis, the authors recommend that the investigation of genetic pathways can lead to the development of strategies that may regulate age-related diseases and disorders.

1.5 COMPUTATIONAL SYSTEMS BIOLOGY IN DRUG DESIGN

Millions of people are suffering from fatal diseases such as cancer, AIDS, and many other bacterial and viral illnesses. Computational systems biology approaches can provide a solution to the key issue that is how to design lifesaving and cost-effective drugs so that the diseases can be cured and prevented. Pharmaceutical companies view that systems-based computational techniques will be highly useful in designing effective therapeutic drugs [52–54]. Furthermore, advanced and sophisticated methods will accelerate drug discovery and development. In 2007, FDA approved only 17 new drugs [55] and approximately 50 drugs in 2008 (http://www.fda.gov/).

It is believed that the association between systems-based biological methods and drug design is age-old. Herbal drugs were developed by observing the diseases; hence, today's drug design has been (directly/indirectly) influenced by such early attempts [56]. Computational systems biology approaches may revolutionize therapeutic intervention in clinical medicine [2]. Effective systems-based drug design techniques can be developed by exploiting the knowledge of the robustness of biological systems [57].

An overview of a number of computational methods' (Petri nets, cellular automata techniques, hybrid methods, pi calculus, agent systems, and differential equations-based methods) application to the task of drug design can be found in Materi and Wishart [52].

Identification of novel drug targets in diseases is a key problem. In order to solve such problems, Chu and Chen [58] recently presented a systems-based approach for the identification of apoptosis drug targets. The selection of the drug targets by utilizing the approach can be viewed as a multistage discovery process. In the first stage, a protein–protein interaction network is constructed by a number of datasets and online interactome databases. In the second stage, a stochastic model of protein–protein interactions is constructed. In order to refine the model, false protein interactions are removed by utilizing an information theoretic measure, namely, Akaike's information criterion to microarray data. Finally, drug targets are identified by conducting a network-level comparison between normal and cancer cells.

Transcription factors-based methods can play an important role in devising an effective therapeutic and preventive interventions strategy for diseases. In Rosenberger et al. [59], the role of activating transcription factor 3 (ATF3) was investigated for murine cytomegalovirus (MCMV) infection. Mouse was used as the model system. The study demonstrated negative regulation of interferon-gamma (IFN-γ) expression caused by ATF3 in natural killer cells. The mice that had zero ATF3 exhibited high resistance to MCMV infection.

In another study, Nelander et al. [60] introduced a computational systems biology methodology for the prediction of pathway responses to combinatorial drug perturbations or drug combinations. The method is based on the use of multiple input–output model. Given that the linear models are not able to capture crucial information required for the task at hand, the authors presented nonlinear multiple input–output model. The approach was applied to analyze perturbations in MCF7 human breast carcinoma cells, where a number of compounds including rottlerin, rapamycin, and and so on were selected as perturbants. The leave-one-out cross-validation results showed the efficacy of the method.

Genetic causes of diseases can provide information that is crucial to design effective therapeutic approaches. A network that illustrates the association between diseases and their related genes can be highly informative. The human disease network presented in Goh et al. [61] is an attempt in this direction. The graph theoretic framework is based on the construction of a network to analyze and investigate the association between phenotypes and disease genes. In the constructed bipartite graph, one set of nodes represents genetic disorders and the second set denotes known disease genes in human genome. The edge between the disease and a gene represents the mutation in gene caused by the disease. The network provides a means to study novel patterns of gene disease associations.

Screening toxic compounds is a key issue in drug design and development. In Amini et al. [62], a novel computational methodology was introduced as an accurate means of predicting toxicity of compounds. The technique integrates two machine learning approaches, namely, SVMs [63] and inductive logic programming (ILP), and is termed support vector inductive logic programming (SVILP). The method works by obtaining a set of rules from an ILP system, hence mapping the compounds into relational ILP space. The induced rules are then applied to compute the similarity between two compounds by the use of a novel kernel function. The function, given by an inner product in relational ILP space, is a weighted sum over all the common hypothesized rules. The ILP kernel is used in conjunction with SVMs to compute toxicity. The authors applied their method to a diverse and broad ranging toxicity dataset, namely, DSSTox [64]. The effectiveness of the method was established by using a cross-validation experimental methodology to predict the toxicity of the compounds. The results of the study confirmed the efficacy of the method for drug design and development. In Lodhi et al. [65], the method is extended to classify mutagens and recognize protein folds. The extended method learns a multiclass classifier by using a divide-and-conquer reduction strategy that divides multiclasses into binary groups and solves each individual problem by inducing an SVILP. The extended multiclass SVILP was successfully applied to classify compounds.

The database storing detailed kinetic knowledge can be a useful resource as it can provide information that is required to build models of biological processes. In order to provide such a knowledge base, a database of kinetic data, namely, KDBI, has been developed [66]. The database contains various types of data, including protein–protein interactions and protein–small molecule interactions. It includes 19,263 records, where 2635 entries belong to protein–protein interactions and 11,873 records contain information regarding protein–small molecule interactions. The database also comprises ordinary differential equations-based pathways models.

1.6 SOFTWARE TOOLS FOR SYSTEMS BIOLOGY

In this section, we will very briefly describe software tools that are designed for modeling, simulating, and analyzing complex biological processes. Bioconductor is a project that provided a number of useful tools for conducting systems biology-based studies. The design of effective infrastructure is crucial for the development of efficient and user-friendly tools. Software infrastructures may be developed by using only a basic computer language and generator (a software tool) [67]. Chapter 15 provides an in-depth description of a text mining tool for systems biology. Table 1.1 summarizes a number of software packages for studying and investigating biological systems.

SQUAD [68] is an example of modeling tools for systems biology. It constructs dynamic models of signaling networks, where the unavailability of kinetic data do not hinder its performance. The underlying methodology of the systems is based on the integration of Boolean and continuous modeling techniques. The implementation is written in Java, whereas C++ has been used to code algorithms for the computation of steady states. SQUAD supports a number of input formats, including NET (text file), MML (xml file), and SMBL (systems biology markup language). The system performs simulations as follows: It takes as input a directed graph representing the structure of the network. The steady states of the graph are identified by

Table 1.1   Software tools for systems biology

Tools	Biological systems	Input format	Platform
	Modeling		
SQUAD	Signaling and regulatory networks	XML, MML, and NET	Windows and Linux
CellNetAnalyzer	Metabolic, signaling, and regulatory networks	Network Composer and ASCII	All platforms (approximately)
BioTapestry	Signaling and regulatory networks	CSV and tabular	Linux, Mac, and Windows
	Sensitivity Analysis		
SBML-SAT	Signaling, regulatory and metabolic network	SBML	Linux, Mac, and Windows
	Visualization		
Cytoscape	Molecular interaction networks	MS Excel, SIF, and so on	All platforms (approximately)
CellProfiler	Cell images	DIB	Linux, Mac, and Windows

using a Boolean algorithm. Then, a dynamic model is constructed. Finally, a user can perform simulations. SQUAD has a user-friendly graphical interface and can be downloaded from `http://www.enfin.org/dokuwiki/doku.php?id=squad:start`.

CellNetAnalyzer [69] is a related software tool for modeling and analyzing biological process. It can be applied to analyze signaling, regulatory, and metabolic networks. The software tool is implemented in MATLAB, and C has been used to code some underlying techniques. The input data can be provided to CellNetAnalyzer by using Network Composer or ASCII file. It is available at `http://www.mpi-magdeburg.mpg.de/projects/cna/cna.html`.

BioTapestry [70] is another biological modeling tool. It can perform analysis and modeling of large biological networks. Linux, Windows, and Mac are supported platforms. BioTapestry is available at `http://www.biotapestry.org/`.

Sensitivity analysis is an important aspect of computational modeling for systems biology. SBML-SAT [71] performs sensitivity analysis of biological systems, and the systems are represented in the form of ordinary differential equations. It incorporates and implements a number of well-known sensitivity analysis techniques. Windows, Mac, and Linux are supported platforms. SBML-SAT is implemented in MATLAB, where the input data need to be coded in SBML format. It is available at `http://sysbio.molgen.mpg.de/SBML-SAT/`.

We now briefly describe Cytoscape [72] that facilitates the visualization and analysis of biological networks. It also allows data integration. The supported input formats are delimited text files, MS Excel, SIF (simple interaction format), SMBL, GO (gene association), and so on. It enables the identification of active modules in biological networks. Cytoscape also allows export of network structures as images in different formats. Cytoscape is available at http://www.cytoscape.org/.

The development of CellProfiler [73, 74] is an attempt to study complex biological processes by using image analysis software packages. The tool comprises two components, namely, CellProfiler and CellProfiler Analyst. The images are processed by using CellProfiler. CellProfiler Analyst is applied to analyze the processed data produced by CellProfiler. The tool can analyze hundreds and thousands of images. It is characterized by its capability of recognizing nonmammalian cells and quantification of phenotypes. It supports processing and analysis of multidimensional images and can perform illumination correction and cell identification by using standard and advanced methods. The tool is implemented in MATLAB and is available for Windows, Unix, and Mac platforms. The software tool is available at http://www.cellprofiler.org/.

1.7 CONCLUSION

The review presented in the chapter shows that computational systems biology encompasses a range of complex problems and methodologies. We are witnessing a rapid development in the field that will revolutionize and give answers to unsolved questions in biology. Biotechnology will be on the forefront due to the influence of systems-based approaches on medicine, agriculture, and so on [75, 76]. We believe that the growing popularity of systems-based computational techniques to studying and analyzing biological processes will foster collaboration between researchers from diverse disciplines and will lead to significant development and progress in the field of computational systems biology.

REFERENCES

1. P. K. Sorger. A reductionist's systems biology: opinion. *Curr. Opin. Cell Biol.*, 17(1):9–11, 2005.

2. E. Klauschen, B. R. Angermann, and M. Meier-Schellersheim. Understanding disease by mouse click: the promise and potential of computational approaches in systems biology. *Clin. Exp. Immunol.*, 149:424–429, 2007.

3. H. Kitano. Computational systems biology. *Nature*, 420:206–210, 2002.

4. D. Noble. *The Music of Life*. Oxford University Press, 2006.

5. H. Kitano. Systems biology: a brief overview. *Science*, 295:1662–1664, 2002.

6. O. Wolkenhauer. Systems biology: the reincarnation of systems theory applied in biology. *Brief. Bioinform.*, 2(3):258–270, 2001.

7. N. Wiener. *Cybernetics: or Control and Communication in the Animal and the Machines*. MIT Press, 2000 (first edition 1948).

8. A. Bellouquid and M. Delitala. *Mathematical Modeling of Complex Biological Systems: A Kinetic Theory Approach*. Birkhauer, 2006.

9. H. Lodhi and S. Muggleton. Modelling metabolic pathways using stochastic logic programs-based ensemble methods. In V. Danos and V. Schachter, editors. *Second International Conference on Computational Methods in System Biology (CMSB-04)*, LNCS. Springer, 2004, pp. 119–133.

10. J. Southern, J. Pitt-Francis, J. Whiteley, D. Stokeley, H. Kobashi, R. Nobes, Y. Kadooka, and D. Gavaghan. Multi-scale computational modelling in biology and physiology. *Prog. Bio. Mol. Biol.*, 96:60–89, 2008.

11. D. Noble. Modeling the heart. *Physiology*, 19(4):191–197, 2004.

12. P. J. Hunter, E. J. Crampin, and P. M Nielsen. Bioinformatics, multiscale modeling and the IUPS Physiome Project. *Brief. Bioinform.*, 9(4):333–343, 2008.

13. L. Zhang, C. A. Athale, and T. S. Deisboeck. Development of a three-dimensional multi-scale agent–based tumor model: simulating gene-protein interaction profiles, cell phenotypes and multicellular patterns in brain cancer. *J. Theor. Biol.*, 244(1):96–107, 2007.

14. C. Athale, Y. Mansury, and T. Deisboeck. Simulating the impact of a molecular 'decision-process' on cellular phenotype and multicellular patterns in brain tumors. *J. Theor. Biol.*, 233(4):469–481, 2005.

15. J. J. Tyson and B. Novak. Regulation of the eukaryotic cell cycle: molecular antagonism, hysteresis, and irreversible transitions. *J. Theor. Biol.*, 210(2):249–263, 2001.

16. T. Alacron, H. M. Byrne, and P. K. Maini. A mathematical model of the effects of hypoxia on the cell-cycle of normal and cancer cells. *J. Theor. Biol.*, 229(3):395–411, 2004.

17. J. Mora, N. K. Cheung, and W. L. Gerald. Genetic heterogeneity and clonal evolution in neuroblastoma. *Br. J. Cancer*, 85(2):182–189, 2001.

18. S. A. Hill, S. Wilson, and A. F. Chambers. Clonal heterogeneity, experimental metastatic ability, and p21 expression in H-ras-transformed NIH 3T3 cells. *J. Natl. Cancer Inst.*, 80(7):484–490, 1988.

19. L. Zhang, C. G. Strouthos, Z. Wang, and T. S. Deisboeck. Simulating brain tumor heterogeneity with a multiscale agent-based model: linking molecular signatures, phenotypes and expansion rate. *Math. Comput. Model.*, 49(1–2):307–319, 2009.

20. S. H. Robertson, C. K. Smith, A. L. Langhans, S. E. McLinden, M. A. Oberhardt, K. R. Jakab, B. Dzamba, D. W. DeSimone, J. A. Papin, and S. M. Peirce. Multiscale computational analysis of *Xenopus laevis* morphogenesis reveals key insights of systems-level behaviour. *BMC Syst. Biol.*, 1(46), 2007.

21. E. Lee, A. Salic, R. Kruger, R. Heinrich, and M. W. Kirschner. The roles of APc and Axin derived from experimental and theoretical analysis of the Wnt pathway. *PLoS Biol.*, 1:116–132, 2003.

22. M. Nagel, E. Tahinci, K. Symes, and R. Winklbauer. Guidance of mesoderm cell migration in the *Xenopus gastrula* requires PDGF signalling. *Development*, 131:2727–2736, 2004.

23. A. C. Cuellar and P. Lloyd. An overview of CellML 1.1, a biological model description language. *Simulation: Trans. Soc. Model. Simul. Int.*, 79(12):740–747, 2003.

24. G. Shinar, R. Milo, M. R. Martinez, and U. Alon. Input–output robustness in simple bacterial signaling systems. *Proc. Natl. Acad. Sci. USA*, 104(50):19931–19935, 2007.

25. R. Aebersold and D. R. Goodlett. Mass spectrometry in proteomics. *Chem. Rev.*, 101(2):269–295, 2001.

26. A. D. Weston and L. Hood. Systems biology, proteomics and the future of health care: toward predictive, preventative and personalized medicine. *J. Proteome Res.*, 3(2):179–196, 2004.

27. X. Feng, K. Liu, Q. Luo, and B.-F. Liu. Mass spectrometry in systems biology: an overview. *Mass Spectrom. Rev.*, 27(6):635–660, 2008.

28. S. Rho, S. You, and D. Hwang. From proteomics towards systems biology: integration of different types of proteomics data into network models. *BMB Rep.*, 41(3):184–193, 2008.

29. X-M. Zhao, R-S. Wang, L. Chen, and K. Aihara. Uncovering signal transduction networks from high-throughput data by integer linear programming. *Nucleic Acids Res.*, 36(9):e48, 2008.

30. K. Collins, T. Jacks, and N. P. Pavletich. The cell cycle and cancer. *Proc. Natl. Acad. Sci. USA*, 94:2776–2778, 1997.

31. M. Macaluso, G. Russo, C. Cinti, V. Bazan, N. Gebbia, and A. Russo. Ras family genes: an interesting link between cell cycle and cancer. *J. Cell. Physiol.*, 192:125–130, 2002.

32. A. Sigal, R. Milo, A. Cohen, N. Geva-Zatrosky, I. Alaluf, N. Swerdlin, N. Perzov, T. Danon, Y. Liron, T. Raveh, A. E. Carpenter, G. Lahav, and U. Alon. Dynamic proteomics in individual human cells uncovers widespread cell-cycle dependence of nuclear proteins. *Nat. Methods*, 3(7):525–531, 2006.

33. R. Narayanaswamy, E. K. Moradi, W. Niu, G. T. Hart, M. Davis, K. L. McGray, A. D. Ellington, and E. M. Marcotte. Systematic definition of protein constituents along the major polarization axis reveals an adaptive reuse of the polarization machinery in pheromone-treated budding yeast. *J. Proteome Res.*, 8:6–19, 2009.

34. K. Shinoda, M. Tomita, and Y. Ishihama. Aligning LC peaks by converting gradient retention times to retention index of peptides in proteomic experiments. *Bioinformatics*, 24(14):1590–1595, 2008.

35. L. Hayflick. *How and Why We Age*. Ballantine Books, 1994.

36. J. Campisi. Replicative senescene: an old lives' tale. *Cell*, 84:497–500, 1996.

37. J. P. de Magalhaes and R. G. A. Faragher. Cell divisions and mammalian aging: integrative biology insights from genes that regulate longevity. *Bioessays*, 30(6):567–578, 2008.

38. T. B. L. Kirkwood. Understanding the odd science of aging. *Cell*, 120, 2005.

39. V. D. Longo, M. R. Leiber, and J. Vijg. Turning anti-aging genes against cancer. *Mol. Cell Biol.*, 9:903–910, 2008.

40. V. D. Longo and C. E. Finch. Evolutionary medicine: from dwarf model systems to healthy centenarians. *Science*, 299:1342–1346, 2003.

41. C. Kenyon. The plasticity of aging: insights from long-lived mutant. *Cell*, 120(4):449–460, 2005.

42. J. P. de Magalhaes and G. M. Church. Analyses of human–chimpanzee orthologous gene pairs to explore evolutionary hypotheses of aging. *Mech. Ageing Dev.*, 128:355–364, 2007.

43. S. K. Kim. Common aging pathways in worms, flies, mice and humans. *J. Exp. Biol.*, 210(9):1607–1612, 2007.

44. S. K. Kim. Genome-wide views of aging gene networks. *Molecular Biology of Aging*. Cold Spring Harbor Laboratory Press, 2008.

45. Y. V. Budovskaya, K. Wu, L. K. Southworth, M. Jiang, P. Tedesco, and T. E. Johnson. An elt-3/elt-5/elt-6 GATA transcription circuit guides aging in *C. elegans*. *Cell*, 134:1–13, 2008.

46. H. Xue, B. Xian, D. Dong, K. Xia, S. Zhu, Z. Zhang, L. Hou, Q. Zhang, Y. Zhang, and J.-D. J. Han. A modular network model of aging. *Mol. Syst. Biol.*, 3(147), 2007.

47. K. Xia, D. Dong, H. Xue, S. Zhu, J. Wand, Q. Zhang, L. Hou, H. Chen, R. Tao, Z. Huang, Z. Fu, Y. G. Chen, and J. D. Han. Identification of the proliferation/differentiation switch in the cellular network of multicellular organisms. *PLoS Comput. Biol.*, 2(11):e145, 2006.

48. S. A. Garan, W. Freitag, V. Caspo, P. Chrysler, B. Rizvi, and N. Shewaramani. A computational systems biology approach to neuroendocrine aging: initial results. *Exp. Gerontol.*, 42:142, 2007.

49. W. R. Swindell, J. M. Harper, and R. A. Miller. How long will my mouse line? Machine approaches for prediction of mouse life span. *J. Gerontol.*, 63A(9):895–906, 2008.

50. S. Krivenko and M. Burtsev. Simulation of the evolution of aging: effects of aggression and kin-recognition. In *Advances in Artificial Life, 9th European Conference, ECAL. Notes in Computer Science* 4648, 2007, pp. 84–92.

51. A. Bergman, G. Atzmon, K. Ye, T. MacCarthy, and N. Barzilai. Buffering mechanisms in aging: a systems approach toward uncovering the genetic component of aging. *PLoS Comput. Biol.*, 3(8):e170, 2007.

52. W. Materi and S. Wishart. Computational systems biology in drug discovery and development: methods and applications. *Drug Discov. Today*, 12(7–8):295–303, 2007.

53. C. R. Cho, M. Labow, M. Reinhardt, J. van Oostrum, and M. C. Peitsch. The application of systems biology to drug discovery. *Curr. Opin. Chem. Biol.*, 10(4):294–302, 2006.

54. N. Kumar, B. S. Hendriks, K. A. Janes, D. de Graaf, and D. A. Lauffenburger. Applying computational modeling to drug discovery and development. *Drug Discov. Today*, 11(17–18):806–811, 2006.

55. M. L. Billingsley. Druggable targets and targeted drugs: enhancing the development of new therapeutics. *Pharmacology*, 82:239–244, 2008.

56. E. C. Butcher, E. L. Berg, and E. J. Kunkel. Systems biology in drug discovery. *Nat. Biotechnol.*, 22(10):1253–1259, 2004.

57. H. Kitano. A robustness-based approach to systems-oriented drug design. *Nat. Rev. Drug Discovery*, 6:202–210, 2007.

58. L.-H. Chu and B.-S. Chen. Construction of a cancer-perturbed protein–protein interaction network for discovery of apoptosis drug targets. *BMC Syst. Biol.*, 2(56), 2008.

59. C.M. Rosenberger, A. E. Clark, P. M. Treuting, C. D. Jhonson, and A. Aderem. ATF3 regulates MCMV infection in mice by modulating IFN-γ expression in natural killer cells. *Proc. Natl. Acad. Sci. USA*, 105(7):2544–2549, 2008.

60. S. Nelander, W. Wang, B. Nilsson, C. Pratilas Q.-B. She, N. Rossen, and P. Gennemark. Models from experiments: combinatorial drug perturbations of cancer cells. *Mol. Syst. Biol.*, 4(216), 2008.

61. K.-II. Goh, M. C. Cusick, D. Valle, B. Childs, M. Vidal, and A.-L Barabasi. The human disease network. *Proc. Natl. Acad. Sci. USA*, 104(21):8685–8690, 2007.

62. A. Amini, S. Muggleton, H. Lodhi, and M.J.E. Sternberg. A novel logic-based approach for quantitative toxicology prediction. *J. Chem. Inform. Model.*, 47(3):998–1006, 2007.

63. V. Vapnik. *The Nature of Statistical Learning Theory*. Springer, New York, 1995.

64. A.M. Richard and C.R. Williams. Distributed structure-searchable toxicity (DSSTox) public database network: a proposal. *Mutat. Res.*, 499:27–52, 2000.

65. H. Lodhi, S. Muggleton and M. J. E Sternberg. *Learning Large Margin First Order Decision Lists for Multi-Class Classification*. In J. Gama, V. S. Costa, A. M. Jorge and P. B. Brazdil, editors. Discovery Science (DS) 2009, LNCS (LNAI) 5808, Springer, 168–183, 2009.

66. P. Kumar, B. C. Han, Z. Shi, J. Jia, Y. P. Wang, Y. T. Zhang, L. Liang, Q. F. Liu, Z. L. Ji, and Y. Z. Chen. Update of KDBI: kinetic data of bio-molecular interaction database. *Nucleic Acids Res.*, 37:D636–D641, 2009.

67. M. A. Swertz and R. S. Jansen. Beyond standardization: dynamic software infrastructure for systems biology. *Nat. Rev. Genet.*, 8:235–243, 2007.

68. A. D. Cara, A. Garg, G. D. Micheli, I. Xenarios, and L. Mendoza. Dynamic simulation of regulatory networks using SQUAD. *BMC Bioinform.*, 8(462), 2007.

69. S. Klamt, J. Saez-Rodriguez, and E. D. Gilles. Structural and functional analysis of cellular networks with CellNetAnalyzer. *BMC Syst. Biol.*, 1(2), 2007.

70. W. J. Longabaugh, E. H. Davidson, and H. Bolouri. Computational representation of developmental genetic regulatory networks. *Dev. Biol.*, 283(1):1–16, 2005.

71. Z. Zi, Y. Zheng, A. E. Rundell, and E. Klipp. SBML-SAT: a systems biology markup language (SBML) based sensitivity analysis tool. *BMC Bioinform.*, 9(342), 2008.

72. M. S. Cline, et al. Integration of biological networks and gene expression data using Cytoscape. *Nat. Protocols*, 2(10):2366–2382, 2007.

73. A. E. Carpenter, T. R. Jones, M. R. Lamprecht, C. Clarke, I. H. Kang, O. Friman, D. A. Guertin, J. H. Chang, R. A. Lindquist, J. Moffat, P. Golland, and D. M. Sabatini. CellProfiler: image analysis software for identifying and quantifying cell phenotype. *Genome Biol.*, 7(R:100), 2006.

74. M. P. Lamprecht, D. M. Sabatini, and A. E. Carpenter. CellProfiler: free, versatile software for automated biological image analysis. *Biotechniques*, 42(1):71–75, 2007.

75. T. Ideker, T. Galitski, and L. Hood. A new approach to decoding life: systems biology. *Annu. Rev. Genomics Hum. Genet.*, 2:343–372, 2001.

76. A. Aderem. Systems biology: its practices and challenges. *Cell*, 121:511–513, 2005.

II

BIOLOGICAL NETWORK MODELING

2

MODELS IN SYSTEMS BIOLOGY: THE PARAMETER PROBLEM AND THE MEANINGS OF ROBUSTNESS

Jeremy Gunawardena

Department of Systems Biology, Harvard Medical School, Boston, MA, USA

With four parameters I can fit an elephant and with five I can make him wiggle his trunk.
— told by Enrico Fermi to Freeman Dyson and
attributed to John von Neumann [1].

2.1 INTRODUCTION

I coteach a graduate course at Harvard called *An Introduction to Systems Biology*. It covers some of the mathematical methods used to build mechanistic models of molecular and cellular systems. Beginning students tend to ask two kinds of questions. Those with a biological background say "Why do I need to use mathematical models? What can they tell me that conventional biological methods cannot?", while those from the physical sciences (mathematics, physics, and engineering) or computer science

Elements of Computational Systems Biology   Edited by Huma M. Lodhi and Stephen H. Muggleton
Copyright © 2010 John Wiley & Sons, Inc.

say "I know how to model. Why is biology any different from physics or engineering?" Broadly speaking, everyone wants to know, from very different perspectives, "How do I do systems biology?" Students are usually under the misapprehension that the person standing in front of them knows the answers to such questions. In my case, I was only marginally less ignorant than the students themselves. It was their curiosity and skepticism, along with a realization that the field lacks a shared foundation for discussing such questions, that forced me to think more deeply about the issues.

This paper is the first of at least two in which I review some tentative conclusions. It sets out a framework for thinking about models in which I try to rise above the partisan assertions that are sometimes made—"my kind of model is better than yours"—and point to some of the broader themes and open problems. It should be obvious that this can be no more than a report of work in progress and is neither complete nor definitive. The next paper will discuss, among other things, why models are being used in systems biology and what we should expect from them [2]. Ideally, this should not be treated separately, but I found it difficult to do justice to everything in the bounds of a single paper.

For our purposes, systems biology may be defined as the emerging discipline that asks how physiology and phenotype emerge from molecular interactions [3, 4]. Mathematical models are being used in support of this, continuing a long tradition inherited from genetics [5, 6], physiology [7, 8], biochemistry [9–11], evolutionary biology [12, 13], and ecology [14]. Models, however, mean different things to physicists, mathematicians, engineers, and computer scientists, not to mention to biologists of varying persuasions. These different perspectives need to be unraveled and their advantages distilled if model building is to fulfill its potential as an explanatory tool for studying biological systems. I begin in Section 2.2 by pointing out that most mechanistic models (as opposed to those arising from "omics") can be thought of as some form of dynamical system. This provides a unified framework in which to compare different kinds of models. Mechanistic models are often complex, in the sense of having many undetermined parameters, and the parameter problem emerges as one of the central difficulties in the field. Different disciplines provide sharply contrasting approaches to this, as I discuss in Section 2.3, and this has tended to obscure the problem in the literature. Attempts are sometimes made to resolve the parameter problem by making assertions of "robustness." This is generally regarded as a desirable feature—who could doubt that biology is robust? However, its wide usage is often uncorrelated with precise definition. I identify in Section 2.5 four kinds of robustness that arise in the dynamical systems framework and review some previous studies in terms of this classification. Section 2.4 outlines the qualitative view of dynamical systems that forms the basis for this discussion.

Parameters and robustness are concepts that have been widely studied in mathematics, engineering, and statistics. My intention here is not to review this material, for which there are many standard texts—see, for instance, Varma et al. [15] and Walter and Pronzato [16]—but rather to show how these concepts are being used, and sometimes abused, in systems biology and to draw attention to some of the scientific issues that arise from that.

2.2   MODELS AS DYNAMICAL SYSTEMS

Two broad directions have emerged in systems biology. The first, "omics," initiated by new technologies such as the microarray [17], relies on inferring causality from correlation in large datasets (see, for instance, Sieberts and Schadt [18]). To the extent that models are used, they are statistical in character. The second direction, which might be called "mechanistic" systems biology, has been less visible but has deeper historical roots [7–11]. The resulting models specify molecules, cells, and tissues and their interactions based on what is known or believed to be true. It is with the latter type of model that we will be concerned here. The subtleties of causal analysis are well discussed elsewhere [19].

Most mechanistic models in systems biology can be regarded as some form of *dynamical system*. A dynamical system describes the *states* of a biological system and how these states change in time. It can be abstractly visualized as in Figure 2.1 as a *state space*, upon which is imposed a temporal dynamics: Given a particular state as an *initial condition*, the dynamics define the *trajectory* taken over time from that starting point. Not all models take this form. For instance, constraint-based models represent systems at steady state and have no explicit representation of time [20]. We focus here on models that do.

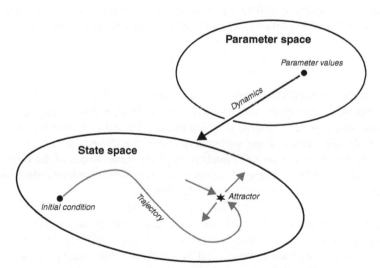

Figure 2.1   Dynamical system. A point in parameter space, given by a set of parameter values, defines the dynamics on the state space. If the system is prepared in an initial condition, then the dynamics typically lead to an attractor, pictured here as a star. Common attractors are steady states or periodic orbits but they can be much more complex [46]. Note that some trajectories leave the attractor, indicating that it is unstable, as discussed in Section 2.4.1. The parameter and state spaces are pictured as abstract sets. For ODE models, they usually correspond to Euclidean spaces, $\mathbb{R}^k$, of some dimension k but for other kinds of models the state space can be infinite dimensional (PDEs or stochastic models) or not have any linear structure (discrete models).

Dynamical systems usually depend on parameters. In abstractly visualizing a dynamical system, therefore, one should always keep in mind the *parameter space* that accompanies the state space, as in Figure 2.1. The dynamics on the state space cannot be defined without first specifying the parameter values, thereby fixing a point in parameter space. As this point varies, so do the dynamics.

2.2.1 Continuous Models

A type of model that is frequently used is one in which the state of a molecular component, x, is its concentration in some cellular compartment (cytoplasm, plasma membrane, etc.), which we will also denote by x and treat as a function of time, $x(t)$. The temporal dynamics are then described by an ordinary differential equation (ODE) for the net rate of production of x. This is how the biochemistry of enzymes has been modeled [21], which provides a foundation for models of molecular networks [22, 23]. As an example, if x is produced at a (zero order) rate of a molar per second and consumed at a (first order) rate of b per second, then

$$\frac{dx}{dt} = a - bx. \tag{2.1}$$

In this case, the dynamical system has a one-dimensional state space, consisting of the single state variable x, and a two-dimensional parameter space, consisting of the two parameters a and b. Since (2.1) is linear, it can be readily solved [24]:

$$x(t) = \frac{a}{b} - \left(\frac{a}{b} - x_0\right) \exp(-bt), \tag{2.2}$$

where x_0 is the initial condition from which the system starts at time $t = 0$: $x(0) = x_0$. We see that no matter where the system is started from, it relaxes exponentially to the unique steady state, $x = a/b$, at which production and consumption are exactly balanced. As the values of the parameters a and b change, the steady state also changes but the dynamics remain "qualitatively" the same. Much of the difficulty in comprehending nonlinear, higher dimensional systems lies in understanding how this very simple picture has to be refined; see Section 2.4.

Example (2.1) is unusual in that it is explicitly solvable in a closed form in which the parameters appear as symbols. Most dynamical systems arising in systems biology are nonlinear and cannot be solved in this way (except possibly at steady state; see Section 2.4.2.3). They have to be studied by simulation, for which parameter values must be specified. The difficulties with this—the parameter problem—are discussed in Section 2.3.

Several kinds of differential equation models have proved useful in systems biology, reflecting the emergence of new experimental techniques. Fluorescent sensors have revolutionized cell biology, making it possible to image specific proteins in individual living cells in real time and revealing extraordinary dynamical complexity. Ionic calcium, Ca^{2+}, for instance, exhibits sparks, puffs, oscillations, and traveling waves in certain cell types [25], reflecting its role as a second messenger linking external signals (first messengers) to a spectrum of cellular responses. To model this, spatial compartments need to be represented as two- or three-dimensional geometries, rather than as unstructured entities like "cytoplasm" and "membrane," and the dynamics need to be described by partial differential equations, often of reaction–diffusion type, with the compartment geometry entering into the boundary conditions [26].

The same fluorescent technology has more recently made it possible to measure noise in individual cells, revealing the impact of both molecular stochasticity ("intrinsic noise") and cell-to-cell variability ("extrinsic noise") [27, 28]. Extrinsic noise can sometimes be modeled as a probability distribution on the initial conditions of a deterministic model or by adding external noise terms, as in the Langevin approach [29]. Molecular stochasticity, however, requires some form of stochastic master equation in which the state of a component is described by the probability distribution of the number of molecules of component x, as a function of time, and the dynamics are described by stochastic differential equations [29].

2.2.2 Discrete Models

Differential equation models of the kinds discussed above are familiar in the physical sciences, biochemistry, and physiology. Biologists, however, often find it convenient to describe gene expression in terms of discrete states—on/off or low/high—and the development of microarray technology allows mRNA levels to be quantified into multiple discrete levels, as in the familiar heat maps. Genetic manipulations also lead naturally to causal inferences expressed in Boolean logic: "in the absence of X, Y becoming low leads to high Z." These kinds of data and reasoning can be modeled by dynamical systems with discrete states, where the temporal dynamics are given by discrete transitions between states, rather than being parameterized by a global clock, t, that marks the passage of time. When states are composed of many discrete variables (e.g., many genes), state transitions may take place synchronously, with each variable being updated simultaneously, or asynchronously, with variables being updated independently of each other.

Discrete models often permit abstraction from the mechanistic details [30]. Such abstraction may lead to an absence of visible parameters, which is sometimes touted as an advantage of discrete models over continuous models. Such assertions should be treated skeptically. Parameters are usually insidiously hiding in the unstated assumptions that accompany a discrete model. For instance, for states composed of many discrete variables, the assumption of asynchronous timing gives equal opportunity to each interleaved sequence of updates. In reality, each variable may have its own rate of change and a model that took these rates into account as parameters would select some interleaved sequences in preference to others. Such distinctions are beyond the scope of unparameterized discrete models but may sometimes have serious biological implications.

Discrete models have a long history in biology [31, 32], prior to the recent resurgence of interest in them via computer science [33]. Theoretical computer scientists view discrete models as computing machines [34]. A Turing machine, for instance, is a discrete state/transition system coupled to a read/write memory. Computer scientists are concerned, among other issues, with methods for constructing such machines, for instance, for building complex machines out of simpler ones. This introduces a syntactic capability that is lacking from the physical science perspective but which becomes important in building models [35, 36].

One way to construct a complex model is to regard it as emerging from the collective interactions of independent agents, each of which has its own internal state and can undertake computations based on rules about its state and the state of other agents in the system [35, 37, 38]. For instance, each individual molecule could be an agent and the computations undertaken by agents could represent chemical reactions between molecules. Such agent-based systems capture molecular fluctuations and can reproduce stochastic models but their syntactic structure permits additional forms of analysis such as model checking or abstract interpretation, which have been important in computer science [33, 39].

This last example illustrates the limitations of Figure 2.1. In an agent-based system, the state space may unfold with the dynamics and is then no longer a static entity. More generally, cells produce new cells, organisms produce new organisms; one of the characteristic features of biology is its capability for self-reproduction. There exists no general mathematical framework for dynamical systems in which the dynamics reconstruct the state space as they progress. Hybrid models, which combine discrete and continuous dynamics, provide only a partial kludge [40].

Thinking in terms of dynamical systems draws attention to the state of the system. Deciding how the state should be represented, whether coarsely as Boolean levels or at fine grain in an agent-based description or somewhere in between as concentrations, and how time and space should be modeled, should depend not on the disciplinary prejudices of the modeler but on the nature of the experimental data and the kinds of biological questions that are being asked. No one type of model is best for all purposes.

2.3   THE PARAMETER PROBLEM

Biological systems have many "moving parts," whose collective interactions produce the physiology or phenotype of interest. Two general strategies have emerged to model this complexity. One seeks to bring the model's assumptions close to reality by embracing the details of components and interactions. The resulting models are *thick*, with many states and more parameters. The other strategy moves in the opposite direction and seeks to abstract the essentials from the details, giving rise to *thin* models with fewer parameters. Despite parochial assertions to the contrary, both strategies have provided biological insight; their pros and cons are discussed in the companion paper to this [2]. In both cases, but most especially with thicker models, the problem arises of determining parameter values in a way that maintains credibility in a model's conclusions. The importance of this problem has tended to be obscured in the literature for several reasons. On the one hand, it is easier to assert (particularly to an experimental audience) "This model accounts for the data" than "This model, with these parameter values, accounts for the data." The latter formulation invites awkward questions as to why those parameter values were chosen and not others. (One might have included "initial conditions" along with parameter values but since the initial conditions are values of state variables, they share the same level of measurability and are, therefore, usually easier to determine than parameter values.) Even if editors and reviewers are aware of the problem—and it seems they are mostly not—they are generally disinclined to ferret about in the Supplementary Information, to which graveyard such technical details are usually consigned. Finally, such a variety of approaches have something to say about the problem that it is hardly surprising to find confusion as to best practice. Here, we emphasize the significance and centrality of the parameter problem by contrasting different disciplinary perspectives of it.

2.3.1 Parameterphobia

Parameters are anathema to physicists, who take the view expressed in the quotation from von Neumann that, with enough parameters, any behavior can be modeled. Of course, von Neumann was joking: a weighted sum of increasing functions with positive weights (parameters) can never fit a decreasing function, no matter how many parameters are used. (See Section 2.4.2.1 for a more relevant example.) However, the truth behind the joke distills a long tradition of modeling the inanimate world on the basis of the fundamental laws of physics. Biology, while founded entirely upon these laws, is not modeled in terms of them. Molecular or cellular behavior is not deduced from Schrödinger's equation. At best, a model may be based on chemical principles such as the law of mass action. At worst, it may rely on some ad hoc guess that is only tenuously related to specific biological knowledge, let alone an underlying molecular mechanism. We have, in such cases, no systematic methodology for avoiding parameters.

While physicists are familiar with parameters and keep them firmly in their place, computer scientists (at least those of a theoretical disposition) are less acquainted with them. The discrete models used in theoretical computer science, like finite automata or Turing machines, have no parameters [34]. (They may have labels but these are passive adornments that do not effect the rate of state transitions.) When discrete models are parameterized, they transmogrify into Markov chains, whose properties are more commonly studied elsewhere than in computer science. In consequence, computer science has had little to say about the parameter problem.

2.3.2 Measuring and Calculating

Ideally, parameter values should be independently measured. In practice, our limited ability to make quantitative measurements of molecular states makes this difficult if not impossible for many parameters. Even when parameters have been measured, the conditions may have been sufficiently different as to raise doubts as to the relevance of the measurements. *In vitro* values, for instance, may differ substantially from those *in vivo*, while *in vivo* measurements themselves may require very careful interpretation [41]. Nevertheless, such measurements as do exist are often useful for initial analysis. Molecular dynamics (MD) calculations—arising from atomic-scale models—can now provide illuminating explanations of intramolecular behavior [42]. Certain kinds of parameters, such as binding constants, might be calculated from such MD models. Since these calculations are limited largely by computational power, it would be unwise to bet against them in the long run, but it seems unlikely that they will yield a systematic approach anytime soon. They will, in any case, be limited to only certain kinds of parameters and to molecules whose atomic structures are well understood.

2.3.3 Counter Fitting

Engineers are accustomed to building thick models with many parameters—of chemical reactors or combustion chambers, for instance—and determining parameter values by fitting to quantitative data [16]. This is the strategy most widely adopted in systems biology when sufficient data of the right kind are available. The development of nonlinear optimization algorithms has made parameter fitting easy to undertake but has also concealed its dangers. These take several forms. The structure of a model may render it nonidentifiable *a priori*: It may not be possible, even in principle prior to any data fitting, to determine certain parameter values. Even if a model is identifiable, the fitting process itself may need to be carefully examined. The reported optimum may be only local. Even if a global optimum is found, there may be several parameter sets that yield roughly similar optimal values. In other words, the energy landscape underlying the optimization may be undulating with many optimal valleys rather than a broad funnel leading to a single optimum. A classic example is that of fitting a sum of two exponentials; see, for instance, Figure 4.6 of Lakowicz [43].

The second and more serious danger in model fitting brings us back to the broader significance of von Neumann's quip. How is a model to be rejected? The answer "when there are no parameter values that fit the data" would not have satisfied von Neumann because, in his view, a model that is complex enough may fit all manner of data. In other words, the rejection criterion is inadequate. As we will see in Section 2.4.2.1, the behavior of biochemical models is more subtle than this: models with arbitrary many parameters may sometimes have the simple qualitative behavior shown by Eq. (2.2). The core issue may be restated in terms of explanatory power. A model does not explain the data to which it is fitted; the process of fitting already incorporates the data into the model.

Of course, parameter fitting is widely used in other areas of science. An X-ray crystal structure, for instance, is obtained by fitting an atomic model to diffraction data, with many free parameters (bond angles, bond lengths, etc.). In such cases, independent cross-validation is used [44]. The data are partitioned into two sets: "test" data and "working" data. Parameters are determined by fitting on the working data. Having been fitted, they are used to account for the test data. If they do, the model is accepted; if not, it is rejected. Hodgkin and Huxley used a similar strategy for their famous model of the action potential in the squid giant axon [8]. The parameters were fitted in independent experiments on each of the three ion channels. Once fitted, the model, with those parameter values, was shown to numerically reproduce the time course of the action potential. Another strategy is to use wild-type data as working data and mutant data to test it by computationally mimicking the effect of the mutation [45]. As these examples make clear, a model's explanatory power comes from being able to account for data to which it has not been fitted.

Merely showing that quantitative data can be accounted for with some choice of parameter values can be such an effort, particularly with thick models, that it is often regarded as sufficient in itself. While this is easy to get away with, at least at present, it is not a good foundation for a new discipline.

2.3.4 Beyond Fitting

Determining a specific set of parameter values and accounting for novel data is only part of the parameter problem. We have a general suspicion of models that are fine-tuned, for which some parameters require precise values. They are not "robust." (Much the same argument is made about unstable steady states; see Section 2.4.1.) Robustness is a good feature, so the argument goes, because there are always errors, often substantial errors, in measuring and fitting data. Related systems might also be expected to show qualitatively similar behavior but not have quite the same parameter values. If a model can be shown to be robust to changes in parameter values, then one can be more confident in drawing conclusions from it despite such uncertainties. There may also be properties of a model that are robust to variation in certain parameter values, like temperature compensation in circadian oscillators. Identifying such properties may yield biological insight; see Section 2.5.3. Aside from such robustness, which we will discuss further in Section 2.5, there may not always be sufficient quantitative data, or data of the right type, to fit all parameter values. The available data may, for instance, not be numerical but qualitative, as in developmental patterns. Finally, models can also be used in an exploratory way to understand how to think about a system in the first place, prior to any determination of parameter values. In all these cases, it becomes important to know how the model's behavior varies as a function of parameter values. This is the broader aspect of the parameter problem. To address it, a more qualitative view of dynamical systems becomes necessary.

2.4 THE LANDSCAPES OF DYNAMICS

2.4.1 Qualitative Dynamics

Although the general ideas outlined in this section apply to most forms of dynamical system, they are best understood for ODE models [23, 46]. Figure 2.2 illustrates, in a simple case, the kind of behavior to be expected of a model similar to example (2.1), in which

$$\frac{dx}{dt} = f(x; a), \tag{2.3}$$

where $x \in \mathbb{R}^n$ is a vector of state variables, $a \in \mathbb{R}^m$ is a vector of parameters, and $f : \mathbb{R}^n \to \mathbb{R}^n$ is the vector rate function expressing the balance between production

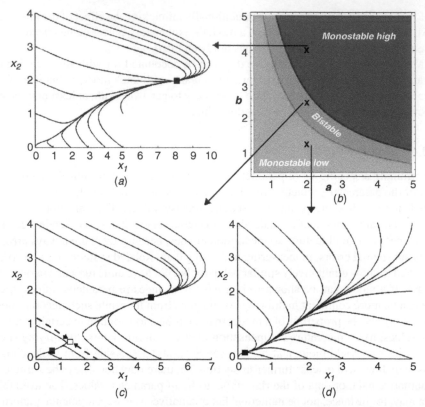

Figure 2.2 Qualitative dynamics. Panels (a), (c), and (d) show different patterns of trajectories on the state space—the nonnegative quadrant of $\mathbb{R}^2$—of the ODE model $dx_1/dt = bx_2 - x_1$, $dx_2/dt = a(1 + x_1^3)/(10 + x_1^3) - x_2$, adapted from Ozbudak et al. [52]. Each figure shows the trajectories starting from the initial conditions with integer coordinates on the boundary of the box defined by the origin and $(5, 4)$. Note that the vertical axis is the same in each figure but the horizontal axis varies. Black square denotes a stable steady state, open square an unstable saddle point. Some trajectories go to the state with high x_1 value, others to the state with low x_1 value. Panels (a) and (d) have only a single basin of attraction leading to a stable state. Panel (c) has three basins of attraction corresponding to bistability. The dashed line marks the approximate location of the (one-dimensional) basin of attraction of the saddle point, which provides the boundary between the two larger (two-dimensional) basins leading to the stable states. Panel (b) shows the parameter space for the two parameters a and b divided into regions corresponding to parameter values with qualitatively similar dynamics. Note the bifurcations—creation or destruction of steady states—that arise as the boundaries of regions are crossed, a behavior that was absent in example (2.1). Both basins of attraction and parameter regions can be much more complex than in this simple example, particularly in higher dimensions.

and consumption of each x_i. Biological state variables are frequently non-negative (concentrations, for instance) and the state space may then be taken to be the non-negative orthant of $\mathbb{R}^n$. For any given set of parameter values, the trajectory starting from a given initial condition will typically converge upon an *attractor*: a limited region of the state space within which trajectories become confined. For instance, the trajectory may reach a steady state, as in example (2.1), or a periodic orbit, as in models of the cell cycle [23], circadian rhythms [47], or developmental clocks [48]. Chemical systems can also have more complex attractors and exhibit behaviors like bursting and chaos [49], which may have some biological role in the excitable tissues found in cardiac and neural systems [50]. A dynamical system may have several different attractors for a given set of parameter values. A familiar instance in systems biology is bistability [23, 51, 52], in which a dynamical system has three attractors, consisting of two stable steady states and one unstable steady state (Figure 2.2(c)). In this case, different initial conditions may reach different attractors and each attractor will have its own *basin of attraction* consisting of those initial conditions that lead to it. The state space breaks up into multiple disjoint basins of attraction, each leading to a unique attractor.

The geometry of a basin of attraction reveals something of the dynamics leading to the corresponding attractor. For instance, a steady state is stable if its basin of attraction has the same dimension as that of the ambient state space (dimension 2 for the two stable states in Figure 2.2(c)). If its dimension is lower, then moving away from the attractor along one of the missing dimensions leads outside the basin of attraction and toward some other attractor. This is the case for the saddle point in Figure 2.2(c) for which the basin of attraction has dimension 1. The argument is made that an unstable steady state is never found experimentally because random perturbations ("noise") would destabilize it. Stable states are "robust" to such perturbation. Consequently, a steady state of a model that is claimed to represent some observed behavior should always be checked to be stable. However, if only a few dimensions among hundreds are missing from a basin of attraction, then it may be possible for the system to linger in the corresponding steady state for an appreciable time, relative to the noise timescales in the system, before becoming destabilized. Our experience of high-dimensional systems is still too limited to know how significant this might be.

The dynamics may also satisfy constraints, which complicate the above picture. We will return to this in Section 2.5.2.

The dimension of a basin of attraction can often be estimated in the local vicinity of an attractor. For instance, the Hartman–Grobman theorem [53] tells us that for a reasonable ("nondegenerate") steady state, $x = x^*$, the local dynamics are qualitatively the same as those of the linearized system, in which the full dynamics represented by $f(x)$ is replaced by the linearized dynamics

$$\frac{dx}{dt} = J(x^*)x, \qquad (2.4)$$

where $J(x)$ is the $n \times n$ matrix of first partial derivatives (the Jacobian), $J_{i,j}(x) = \partial f_i / \partial x_j$. Since linear equations are solvable, (2.4) gives considerable information about the local vicinity of steady states, including the (local) dimension of the basin of attraction [24]. In contrast, rather little is known, in general, about the global geometry of basins of attraction. Are they large or small and is their shape long and thin or short and squat? A characteristic difficulty in dynamical systems derived from differential equations is that local behavior may be accessible (a derivative is a

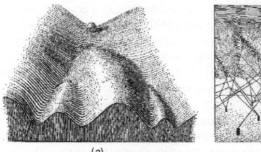 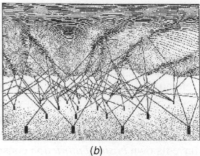

(a)   (b)

Figure 2.3 Waddington's epigenetic landscapes. As he put it, "A multidimensional phase space is not very easy for the simple-minded biologist to imagine or to think about." [56, p. 27]. (He refers to the state space by its alternative name of "phase" space.) (a) Waddington abstracted dynamics on the high-dimensional state space of a developing embryo into a picture of a ball rolling down an inclined landscape into a branching fan of valleys and coming to rest at the end of one of them [56, Figure 4]. The end points represent different attractors, corresponding to different differentiation states of the organism. (b) Waddington's analogy for the action of genes on development shows the underside of the landscape being maintained by guy ropes in tension [56, Figure 5]. Each peg represents a gene that can have multiple effects and each attachment point can have multiple genes influencing it. Changes to a single gene may sometimes have little effect on the dynamics, depending on the background of the other genes.

measure of local slope) but global behavior can be very challenging to analyze. For new developments in this direction see, in particular, GutenKunst et al. [54] and Rand [55].

Systems biology forces us to confront the subtleties of global dynamics in high-dimensional spaces. This was already apparent to Conrad Waddington over 50 years ago [56]. His "epigenetic landscape" (Figure 2.3(a)) was an attempt to create a visualizable analogy for the complex dynamics through which an egg gives rise to an adult organism. (Sewall Wright's earlier "adaptive landscape" had a similar heuristic intent for the dynamics of genotypes during evolution but lacked the moving parts [57].) The epigenetic landscape continues to provide a conceptual basis for thinking about biological dynamics in high dimensions [58]. While many biologists are now familiar with the ball rolling down the valleys, fewer are aware of the mathematical models that Waddington used to arrive at this analogy [56, Chapter 2].

The picture of trajectories in state space holds for a given set of parameter values. If we now imagine moving through the parameter space, the pattern of trajectories will change (Figure 2.2(b)). In general, the parameter space itself also falls into disjoint regions. Within each region, the pattern of trajectories remains qualitatively ("topologically") similar. It is as if the trajectories were inscribed on rubber and the rubber is stretched: While distances change, the connectivities remain the same. Different parameter regions, however, exhibit qualitatively different patterns (Figure 2.2(b)). In moving between regions, attractors may appear or disappear or change their dynamical characteristics, for instance, from stable to unstable, and the trajectories may reorganize themselves accordingly. Such *bifurcations* are usually key features of the overall behavior [46].

Waddington was well aware of the role of parameters and illustrated them through the use of guy ropes, representing genes with pleiotropic effects (Figure 2.3(b)). While this gives a vivid illustration of systems behavior, it is less satisfactory in giving a sense of the landscape of parameter space. Waddington was a remarkable scientist, who, more than any other, anticipated modern systems biology [59] and dismantled some of the barriers between biology and mathematics—see Section 2.5.4. He was marginalized in his own time partly because he was so far ahead of it in thinking about development, genetics, and evolution as an integrated system. It is good to see his reputation restored for a modern audience [60].

For a given dynamical system, it would be useful to know, at least, the number of parameter regions and, for each region, the number of attractors and their types. No general methods are known for eliciting such details but some partial insights have come from different mathematical approaches.

2.4.2 Steady State Attractors of ODE Models

2.4.2.1 *Chemical Reaction Network Theory* Example (2.1) has only a single parameter region and only a single attractor—a stable steady state—for all parameter values in that region. Remarkably, more complex models may still exhibit similar behavior. This emerges from Feinberg's chemical reaction network theory (CRNT) [61]; see Gunawardena [62] for an overview and other references. CRNT applies to the ODE model coming from a network of chemical reactions by applying the principle of mass action. It associates with such a network a nonnegative integer called the "deficiency", which does not depend on the values of the parameters but only on the underlying network of reactions. The deficiency is the dimension of a certain linear subspace, reflecting one of the key insights of CRNT: Behind the nonlinearity of mass-action kinetics, there exists a remarkable degree of hidden linearity [62]. Under reasonable conditions, deficiency zero networks behave like example (2.1): Provided constraints are respected (see Section 2.5.2 for an explanation of constraints), there is a single parameter region and only a single stable steady state for all parameter values in that region [61, 62]. This theorem is important because it shows that thick models, with many parameters, may nevertheless have simple qualitative dynamics. One cannot always fit an elephant! Having said that, the "deficiency zero theorem" is too restricted to be widely used in systems biology, where parameter values have typically been found to influence the qualitative dynamics. Recent developments in CRNT may be more relevant [63] and the full implications of CRNT for systems biology remain to be worked out.

2.4.2.2 *Monotone Systems* The dependence of the qualitative dynamics on the parameters can often be calculated for ODE models with only two state variables. The method of nullclines provides a geometric guide to the existence of steady states and there are mathematical theorems, like that of Poincaré–Bendixson, that help identify more complex attractors like periodic orbits [46]. Such methods are strictly limited to two-dimensional systems. Sontag and others have shown, nevertheless, that the steady states of certain high-dimensional ODE systems, with many state variables

and parameters, correspond to those of an associated two-dimensional system [64]. There are several requirements for this method to work; among the most crucial is that the high-dimensional system is *monotone*, meaning, roughly speaking, that its dynamics preserve an underlying order on the state space (for full details, see Angeli et al. [64]). Powerful mathematical results are known for such monotone systems, upon which is based the reduction from many dimensions to 2. For a model that satisfies the requirements, monotone theory shows that the steady state behavior and its parameter dependence is no more complex than would be expected for the associated two-dimensional model. This can be a useful tool when it can be applied.

If an enzymatic reaction is modeled in the standard biochemical manner [21], with an enzyme–substrate complex and mass-action kinetics, then it is not monotone. It becomes monotone in the quasi-steady-state approximation, which leads to the familiar Michaelis–Menten rate function. While continuing to be widely used in complex models, the Michaelis–Menten function is suspect for at least two reasons. First, in the context of a single enzyme acting on a single substrate, it emerges through a singular perturbation based on a separation of timescales, which is only known to be accurate under certain conditions on the enzyme and substrate [65, 66]. Second, because the enzyme–substrate complex is removed from the dynamics (which is what makes the perturbation singular), the approximation cannot capture enzyme sequestration when there are many substrates present. This can readily lead to errors. The "total quasi-steady-state" approximation appears safer in both respects [67]. It would be interesting if a separation of timescales argument could be found that was broadly accurate and also resulted in monotonicity.

2.4.2.3 *Algebraic Geometric Methods*   As the previous discussion suggests, there is much to be said for constructing a model directly from a network of chemical reactions using the principle of mass action. This is a systematic procedure that allows the biochemistry to be modeled in a realistic form. (Of course, the sheer complexity of biology may make this infeasible in general.) Mass action has one other consequence, which has, until recently, been largely overlooked. If the rate function $f(x; a)$ in Eq. (2.3) comes from some network of chemical reactions by mass action, then it is always a polynomial function of the state variables, $x_1, \ldots, x_n$. Accordingly, the steady states of the system, at which $dx/dt = 0$, correspond to an *algebraic variety* [68]. One of the interesting features of algebraic geometry, which it shares with linear algebra, is that it can be undertaken over an arbitrary coefficient field. In particular, the set of steady-state solutions, $\{f_i(x; a) = 0\}$, can be regarded as an algebraic variety over the field $\mathbb{R}(a)$ of real rational functions in the parameters, $a_1, \ldots, a_m$. In other words, the parameters can be treated as uninterpreted symbols, rather than as actual numbers, to which can be applied, nevertheless, all the usual arithmetic operations of addition, subtraction, multiplication, and division.

While this possibility is evident, it has not previously been exploited because there appeared to be nothing one could say about the geometric structure of the steady-state variety. Recently, we have shown that for multisite phosphorylation systems, the steady-state variety forms a *rational algebraic curve* over $\mathbb{R}(a)$ [69, 70]. Rationality provides an explicit description of the steady states, which, together with the ability to roam algebraically over the parameter space, leads to unexpected insights. We show that such systems can have a parameter region with multiple stable steady states, whose maximum number increases with the number of sites, suggesting that multisite phosphorylation, which plays a key regulatory role in most cellular processes, can implement complex information processing [70]. The method also yields stringent quantitative predictions that, nevertheless, do not require parameter values to be known or estimated [69]. While these results are currently limited to post-translational modification [71], they suggest that algebraic geometric methods may have wider application to the parameter problem in systems biology.

The freedom to treat parameters as algebraic symbols applies only to the steady state; the dynamics, which depend upon derivatives and infinitesimal procedures, are fundamentally nonalgebraic. It remains an interesting question, however, to what extent other attractors, such as periodic orbits, can also be analyzed symbolically.

2.5 THE MEANINGS OF ROBUSTNESS

Robustness is one of the themes to have emerged in systems biology [72–75] and it is particularly relevant to the parameter problem. Unfortunately, it is also one of those concepts whose wide usage has not been matched by precise definition. Robustness means, broadly, that some property of the system remains the same under perturbation. To make this precise, it is necessary to say what the property is, in what sense it remains the same, and what kinds of perturbations are being considered. The property might be the overall qualitative dynamics of a system, in which case "remaining the same" could mean that the number and type of attractors and the connectivity and shape of the trajectories remain the same under perturbation. Alternatively, the property could be a quantitative function evaluated on an attractor, like the period of a periodic orbit. In this case, "remaining the same" could mean that the property remains quantitatively unchanged under perturbation ("exact robustness") or that it only changes by a limited amount ("approximate robustness"). As for perturbations, at least three different kinds can be distinguished: changes to parameter values, changes to initial conditions, and changes to the functional form that describes the dynamics (i.e., the f in Eq. (2.3) for an ODE model). These perturbations have distinct mathematical and biological implications. We will discuss the first two as preparation for reviewing some influential studies of robustness and then return to the third.

2.5.1 Parameter Biology

Consider an ODE model derived by the principle of mass action from a network of biochemical reactions. In this case, the parameters are rate constants of various kinds: association rates, disassociation rates, catalytic rates, and so on. Such rates are, hopefully (see the next paragraph), intrinsic features of the corresponding proteins and would not be expected to change except through alterations to their amino acid sequences. This could happen on an evolutionary timescale, so that different species may have different parameter values, but this would not be expected to happen in different cells of the same organism or tissue or clonal population of cells in cell culture. The situation could be different in a polyclonal population, such as a tumor or a natural population of outbred organisms, in which there could be substantial genetic polymorphism. Depending on which loci exhibit polymorphism and how it affects protein function, this genetic variation could give rise to rate constant variation between different cells or different organisms.

(A caveat is essential here. Rate constants are not solely determined by intrinsic features of a protein. They also depend on the ambient conditions in the cell—temperature, pH, and other ionic strengths—as well as, potentially, posttranslational modifications such as disulfide bridges or glycosylations, or the presence of accessory molecules such as chaperones or scaffolds, none of which might have been included in a model. The reductionist approach commonly used in systems biology, in which the properties of a system are deduced from its components, is always at risk of the system biting back: The properties of the components may depend on that of the system [2]. To put it another way, the boundary of a system has to be drawn somewhere, with the implicit assumption that what is outside the boundary is irrelevant to the behavior inside. Such assumptions tend to be taken for granted until they fail.)

Models are not always deduced from mass action. For instance, separation of timescales is often convenient, if not essential, in reducing complexity. Whether this is achieved through the suspect "quasi-steady state" or the safer "total quasi-steady state," approximations discussed in Section 2.4.2.2, it necessarily leads to parameters that are no longer rate constants. Similarly, models of allosteric enzymes [76, 77] or rate functions for gene expression in terms of transcription factor binding [78] are also based on separation of timescales and lead to rational algebraic rate functions resembling the ubiquitous Hill functions. (Despite their very wide usage, Hill functions are not derived from any approximation and have no well-founded mechanistic interpretation [21].) The basic issues can be discussed for the Michaelis–Menten formula

$$\frac{rx}{k+x}, \tag{2.5}$$

in which r, the maximal rate, and k, the Michaelis–Menten constant, are the two parameters. Of these, k is derived from rate constants [21] and may hence be assumed to vary only under the same conditions. Notice, however, that this depends on the underlying mechanistic derivation of (2.5) and on the assumptions behind it. As for r, it is, in terms of the usual derivation [21], a product of a catalytic rate and an enzyme concentration. The enzyme is not formally part of the dynamics but its concentration can change on multiple timescales. On a physiological timescale, the concentration is set by the balance between synthesis and degradation and could readily vary from cell to cell within a single organism, tissue, or clonal population through differences in cell volumes, intrinsic noise in transcription/translation, and stochastic partitioning of molecules during cell division. In polyclonal populations, genetic variation or gene copy number variation could introduce additional variation in concentration levels. These factors would also play a role on a longer evolutionary timescale. As we see, the biological interpretation of changes to parameter values depends both on the model and the nature of its parameters and on the biological context that is being modeled.

2.5.2 Robustness to Initial Conditions

If the property thought to be robust is associated with an attractor, such as a steady state, then its robustness to initial conditions would seem to follow from the stability of the attractor, in the sense discussed in Section 2.4.1. However, it is often the case that the dynamics satisfy additional constraints. For instance, an enzyme suffers no net change in concentration in any reaction that it catalyzes. If it is not being otherwise synthesized or degraded, then its total concentration remains constant at all times. Similarly, if a substrate exists in many states of modification—multisite phosphorylation, for instance—and is also not synthesized or degraded, then its total concentration remains constant. (Note that these constraints are linear in the state variables; nonlinear constraints may also be possible.) If there are k independent constraints, they confine the dynamics to lie within a subspace of dimension $d = n - k$, where n is the dimension of the ambient space. The state space thereby becomes divided into "slices" of dimension d, each corresponding to a set of constraint values (Figure 2.4). Within each slice, the dynamics behave as they did in Figure 2.1, with attractors, basins of attraction and stability, as appropriate to an ambient space of dimension d (not n). However, its qualitative character can change with the constraint values. Hence, the constraint space also becomes divided into regions, within each of which the dynamics in the corresponding slices remain qualitatively similar (Figure 2.4).

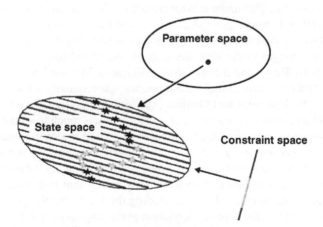

Figure 2.4 Dynamical system with constraints. The state space becomes divided into "slices," represented by the straight lines, each slice corresponding to a set of constraint values, represented by a point in the space of constraints. Note that if the invariants are nonlinear, then the slices may be curved spaces. The dynamics are confined within the slices. If an initial condition is chosen within a slice, then the trajectory remains within that slice for all time; trajectories never cross between slices. The dynamics within a slice can have attractors, represented by stars, and other features as described in Figure 2.1 but their qualitative character can change as the constraints vary, as illustrated by the appearance and disappearance of attractors.

Unlike variation of parameters, rather little seems to be known about variation of constraints. Parameters and constraints are mathematically distinct. Parameters can be chosen independently of initial conditions, while constraints cannot. Parameters define the dynamics; constraints confine the dynamics. The biological implications of the two forms of robustness can be quite distinct; see Section 2.5.3.

In summary, for properties associated with an attractor, robustness to initial conditions may take two forms. If initial conditions are varied within the same set of constraint values, then it corresponds to stability of the attractor and the dimension and shape of the basin of attraction in state space (with respect to the effective ambient space of dimension d) provide measures of it. If constraint values are varied, then robustness goes beyond stability and the dimension and shape of the appropriate region in constraint space become relevant.

2.5.3 Robustness in Reality

With this background, let us review some particularly interesting and influential demonstrations of robustness in different biological systems.

Signaling in bacteria is typically implemented by two-component systems consisting of a sensor kinase coupled to a response regulator protein [79]. The sensor autophosphorylates in response to a signal, using ATP as the phosphate donor. It then transfers the phosphate to the response regulator, which initiates the signaling response, by, for instance, stimulating gene transcription. In some two-component systems involved in homeostasis—such as the EnvZ/OmpR system that regulates osmolarity in *Escherichia coli*—the sensor also catalyzes the dephosphorylation of the response regulator. This unusual bifunctional mechanism has been studied in several models [80–82], whose general conclusion is that the mechanism enables the amount of phosphorylated response regulator at steady state to be constraint robust with respect to changes in the total amounts of sensor and response regulator. The initial analysis by Russo and Silhavy using Michaelis–Menten kinetics [81], which provided the first indication of this robustness, was subsequently refined using mass-action kinetics by Batchelor and Goulian [80]. Their analysis showed approximate constraint robustness when the amount of sensor kinase is much less than the amount of response regulator, which, indeed, corresponds well to *E. coli's* normal operating regime. In their accompanying experimental analysis, they varied the total amounts of EnvZ and OmpR and found good agreement with their model. Shinar et al. incorporated a further element into the mechanism by noting that in certain bifunctional two-component systems [82, Table 1], including the EnvZ/OmpR system in *E. coli*, ATP acts as a cofactor in the dephosphorylation of the response regulator. Their model for this shows exact constraint robustness of the amount of phosphorylated response regulator, with respect to changes to the total amounts of sensor, response regulator, and ATP, provided the amount of response regulator remains above a threshold. These predictions were also borne out by experiment.

E. coli has also been a model bacterium for the study of chemotaxis. It moves by rotating its multiple flagella. Rotation in one direction brings the flagella into alignment, allowing the bacterium to "run" in a straight line. Rotation in the other direction drives the flagella apart, causing the bacterium to "tumble" and randomly reorient its direction. By regulating its tumbling frequency, the bacterium can efficiently seek out nutrients and escape poisons (chemotaxis) in environments that lie outside its control. Because *E. coli* is so small, it has to sense changes in ligand concentration over time, not space. It has been found to adapt its sensitivity to such changes across a remarkably broad range of background concentrations. Unraveling the mechanism behind this has been a triumph of systems biology [83].

Barkai and Leibler [84] studied robustness of the precision of adaptation in *E. coli* by simulation of an ODE model. For a given chemotactic ligand concentration, the system appears to reach a steady state, presumably stable, irrespective of the other parameter values. To measure the precision of adaptation, the activated state of the receptor was evaluated at steady state for zero ligand and for a fixed saturating concentration of ligand (1 mM), and the ratio of the latter to the former, denoted by p, was taken as a measure of the precision of adaptation. If $p = 1$, the adaptation is "perfect." There are three constraints in the model, corresponding to the total amounts of the receptor and the two chemotactic enzymes CheR and CheB, which implement adaptation by methylating and demethylating the receptor. The constraints and the parameters were randomly sampled and it was shown that the precision of adaptation remains close to 1 despite substantial perturbation around a reference model with physiologically realistic parameters and constraints.

This analysis reveals both constraint robustness and parametric robustness. In his commentary on Barkai and Leibler [84], Hartwell invoked them both (implicitly) by suggesting that the robustness explains why chemotactic behaviors are buffered against the extensive polymorphism seen in outbred natural populations [85]. This is an attractive argument but it would be bolstered by knowing how much the genes in the chemotactic network are specifically affected by this polymorphism. How much of this variation contributes to variation in rate constants and how much to variation in concentration levels? Is the robustness in the model consistent with the actual level of variation seen in natural populations? Because of the implications for human physiology and disease, there are increasing data on polymorphisms in human populations [86] but few studies on how this affects the function of specific molecular systems or even individual proteins (see, for instance, Tiseo et al. [87]). In a subsequent paper by Alon et al. [88], only constraint robustness was experimentally verified. Concentrations of chemotactic proteins were varied and the precision of adaptation was measured in individual bacteria. In these circumstances, each bacterium in a clone would be expected to have different concentrations of proteins through intrinsic noise in the transcriptional machinery and stochastic partitioning between daughter cells. The precision of adaptation was found to be very close to 1 [88, Table 1]. The experimental data are well explained by constraint robustness. However, since the parameters are all rate constants, the data are not at all explained by parametric robustness. We see that these two types of robustness are distinct both mathematically and experimentally.

Morphogens are spatial signals that direct patterning in embryonic development [89]. They have been found to exhibit remarkable levels of robustness between different embryos [90, 91]. In a series of penetrating studies in *Drosophila*, Barkai and others used robustness as a design principle to identify molecular mechanisms that implemented it [91, 92]; for overviews, see Barkai and others [73, 93] and Alon [3, Chapter 9]. They assumed a network of molecular interactions based on what was known in the literature and that the concentrations of the network components could vary between embryos because of polymorphisms in the population. By sampling points in parameter space ("numerical screening"), they identified regions in which the spatial profile of the morphogen exhibited robustness to changes in initial concentration levels of the network components. While these parametric regions were tiny (<1 percent of the sampled points), they could be interpreted as particular kinds of mechanisms. The underlying models in these spatial studies are PDEs rather than ODEs but the qualitative framework of Section 2.4 can be used in much the same way and we see that the robustness here is to changes in the state space rather than the parameter space.

It would be interesting to know whether robustness to changes in the state space on a physiological timescale arises from the same mechanisms as robustness to changes in the parameter space on an evolutionary timescale, or whether different aspects of the molecular circuitry are responsible. As Waddington recognized [56], physiological robustness may lay the foundation for evolutionary adaptation ("genetic assimilation" as he put it); see also Kirschner and Gerhart [94]. The different types of robustness discussed here may provide a framework for studying such questions.

2.5.4 Structural Stability

Robustness with respect to functional variation—perturbing the f in Eq. (2.3)—has not been as widely utilized as the kinds of robustness described above. However, it was the basis for a remarkable historical episode that still has resonance for us today. Waddington's distillation of biological dynamics inspired the distinguished French pure mathematician René Thom to develop a mathematical framework for describing it [95]. Thom made two general assumptions. First, that the dynamics arose from descending down a gradient, so that $f(x; a) = -\nabla g(x; a)$, where $\nabla = \sum_{i=1}^{n} \partial/\partial x_i$ is the gradient operator. Waddington's epigenetic landscape has just such a gradient dynamics but for Thom the assumption arose from technical necessity rather than analogy and, in his case, the parameters play a key role. In gradient dynamics, steady states correspond to minima of the gradient function, g, which provides a crucial simplification. Second, Thom assumed that, in the absence of detailed knowledge about the underlying molecular mechanisms that gives rise to g, it was reasonable to focus on *structurally stable* behaviors; that is, those behaviors that remained qualitatively the same if the function g was perturbed, $g \to g + h$, where h is "small." Under these assumptions, Thom proved that, for small numbers of parameters ($m \leq 5$), there were only finitely many—in fact, just 11—different types of structurally stable bifurcations [96, Chapter 7]. Note that the state space can be of any dimension. Furthermore, most bifurcations that have been studied tend to depend on only a few parameters, with the others playing only a background role. Hence, in practice, the restriction to $m \leq 5$ is not limiting.

The subtitle to Thom's book, *An Outline of a General Theory of Models* [97], reflects the broad view he took of the scope of these results. The theory remains deep and difficult. Thom was himself a Fields medallist but could only guess parts of the argument and had to enlist the help of other mathematicians to complete the details. Later work filled in some gaps and clarified its place within mathematics, where it is now largely absorbed into bifurcation theory and singularity theory [53, 98]. Poston and Stewart remains the most accessible account [96]. Thom's own book [97] "transcends the world of numbers," as the back cover puts it.

What is important about Thom's theorem is that it gives the first hint that even very complex dynamics may still be composed of only a small finite number of key "motifs." At the same time, from our vantage point, the difficulties with Thom's assumptions become much clearer. First, the dynamics arising from molecular networks are rarely of gradient type. Second, it is not reasonable to perturb f in an arbitrary way, since the resulting perturbed function may not have arisen from any molecular network. What is required, instead, is a restricted notion of structural stability in which perturbations are confined to a biochemically realistic subclass.

We unwittingly undertook a computational study of this in the context of developmental patterning in the *Drosophila* embryo [36]. In an influential paper, von Dassow et al. had found that the segment polarity gene regulation network was parametrically robust [99] (using the language developed here) and the evolutionary implications of this were widely cited [89]. However, their model was based on a regular hexagonal lattice of cells, which is far from the normal structure of an epithelium [100]. Moreover, because cellularization in *Drosophila* takes place late in embryonic development, the segment polarity network has to operate without knowing in advance which lattice of cells has emerged. If the cellular lattice is changed, the effect on the model is to change f in a biochemically realistic manner, through alterations in cell-to-cell communication. Hence, robustness to lattice variation is a form of restricted structural stability. Our paper was concerned with computational infrastructure for building models rather than with structural stability (the relevance of which was unclear at the time), but our limited analysis suggested that the segment polarity network was structurally unstable despite being parametrically robust. We speculated that small changes to the underlying molecular network might render it robust to lattice variation but were unable to pursue this further.

In our analysis, the robustness operates on the physiological and not the evolutionary timescale. However, molecular networks can be reorganized during evolution, which can change both nodes and links, as well as parameter values and expression levels. Restricted structural stability might be the appropriate type of robustness with which to study this.

We see from this that Thom's ideas remain relevant, despite being largely forgotten. His approach came to be called "catastrophe theory" and garnered great celebrity, being compared to Newton's theory of gravitation and mechanics. The resulting fall from grace was predictably brutal [101, 102]; for a more balanced perspective, see Arnold et al. [98] and Zeeman et al. [103]. While most of those who know of it think it dead and buried, I think, in contrast, that it has merely been dormant, waiting for systems biology to provide a more fertile landscape for Thom's ideas to germinate again.

2.5.5 Classifying Robustness

One reason why robustness has attracted such attention is that it may be a biological design principle [74]. This is an appealing idea, but to make sense of it, robustness needs to be precisely defined and grounded in the kind of careful experiments discussed in Section 2.5.3. As we have shown, there are different types of robustness, which may be classified according to which aspect of the dynamical system is changed.

- *Type I: Dynamical Stability.* Robustness to change of initial conditions within a fixed set of constraint values.
- *Type II: Constraint Robustness.* Robustness to change of constraint values.
- *Type III: Parametric Robustness.* Robustness to change of parameter values.
- *Type IV: Structural Stability.* Robustness to change of the dynamical function.

No doubt there are others. As noted in Section 2.5.1, the interpretation of these mathematical properties depends crucially on the biological context that is being modeled. Robustness could be quantified if we could estimate the size and shape of various regions in high-dimensional spaces: basins of attraction, constraint regions, and parameter regions. Many studies can be seen as attempts to do this by random sampling [84, 99]. Lack of space precludes a discussion of robustness trade-offs [74, 104] and new methods of global sensitivity analysis [54, 55]. Kitano has remarked on the need for a theory of biological robustness [105]. The dynamical systems framework outlined here may provide a basis for this.

2.6 CONCLUSION

One of the difficulties for students of systems biology is to make sense of the many different concepts and techniques that are coming into the subject from the physical sciences and computer science. Those of us who have been trained in these other disciplines necessarily take a particular perspective (as will be evident to readers of this paper), and it is ultimately our students who bear the burden of harmonizing this cacophony. Steven Pinker tells the story [106] of indentured laborers from different language groups being brought together on some remote island under colonial occupation. The first generation cobbles together a form of communication—a "pidgin"—which suffices for getting along on an everyday basis. It is the second generation who, spontaneously and magically, creates a full-fledged natural language, a "creole." It should be evident that this paper is written in systems biology pidgin. Let us hope that, in time, our students will teach us how to write systems biology creole.

I thank the students of MCB195, SB101, and SB200 for their questioning enthusiasm, which prompted this paper; Uri Alon for many helpful and perceptive comments; an anonymous reviewer for pointing out some issues of scope that needed clarification; Rebecca Ward for her unerring editorial eye; and the editors for their patience. They bear no responsibility for any of the paper's remaining mistakes, obscurities, or omissions, for which I alone must apologize.

REFERENCES

1. F. Dyson. A meeting with Enrico Fermi. *Nature*, 427:297, 2004.
2. J. Gunawardena. Some fallacies about systems biology. In preparation.
3. U. Alon. *An Introduction to Systems Biology: Design Principles of Biological Circuits.* Chapman and Hall/CRC, 2006.
4. M. Kirschner. The meaning of systems biology. *Cell*, 121:503–504, 2005.
5. S. E. Luria and M. Delbrück. Mutations of bacteria from virus sensitivity to virus resistance. *Genetics*, 28:491–511, 1943.
6. G. Mendel. Versuche über Pflanzen-Hybriden. *Verhandlungen des naturforschenden Vereines, Abhandlungen, Brünn*, 4:3–47, 1866.
7. A. C. Guyton, T. G. Coleman, and H. J. Granger. Circulation: overall regulation. *Annu. Rev. Physiol.*, 34:13–44, 1972.
8. A. L. Hodgkin and A. F. Huxley. A quantitative description of membrane current and its application to conduction and excitation in nerve. *J. Physiol.*, 117:500–544, 1942.
9. R. Heinrich and T. A. Rapoport. A linear steady-state treatment of enzymatic chains. General properties, control and effector strengths. *Eur. J. Biochem.*, 42:89–95, 1974.
10. H. Kacser and J. A. Burns. The control of flux. *Biochem. Soc. Trans.*, 23:341–366, 1995. Reprint of 1973 paper in *Symp. Soc. Exp. Biol.*
11. M. A. Savageau. *Biochemical Systems Analysis: A Study of Function and Design in Molecular Biology.* Addison-Wesley, 1976.
12. R. A. Fisher. *The Genetical Theory of Natural Selection.* Clarendon Press, Oxford, 1930.
13. M. A. Nowak. *Evolutionary Dynamics: Exploring the Equations of Life.* Belknap Press, 2006.
14. R. May. *Stability and Complexity in Model Ecosystems.* Princeton University Press, 1973.
15. A. Varma, M. Morbidelli, and H. Wu. *Parametric Sensitivity in Chemical Systems.* Cambridge University Press, 2005.
16. E. Walter and L. Pronzato. *Identification of Parametric Models from Experimental Data.* Springer, 1997.
17. M. Schena, D. Shalon, R. W. Davis, and P. O. Brown. Quantitative monitoring of gene expression patterns with a complementary DNA microarray. *Science*, 270:467–470, 1995.
18. S. K. Sieberts and E. E. Schadt. Moving towards a system genetics view of disease. *Mamm. Genome*, 18:389–401, 2007.
19. J. Pearl. *Causality: Models, Reasoning and Inference.* Cambridge University Press, Cambridge, UK, 2000.
20. B. Ø. Palsson. *Systems Biology: Properties of Reconstructed Networks.* Cambridge University Press, New York, 2006.
21. A. Cornish-Bowden. *Fundamentals of Enzyme Kinetics*, 2nd edition. Portland Press, London, 1995.
22. B. B. Aldridge, J. M. Burke, D. A. Lauffenburger, and P. K. Sorger. Physicochemical modelling of cell signalling pathways. *Nat. Cell Biol.*, 8:1195–1203, 2006.
23. J. J. Tyson, K. Chen, and B. Novak. Network dynamics and cell physiology. *Nature Rev. Mol. Cell Biol.*, 2:908–916, 2001.

24. M. W. Hirsch and S. Smale. *Differential Equations, Dynamical Systems and Linear Algebra. Pure and Applied Mathematics.* Academic Press, San Diego, CA, 1974.

25. G. Dupont, S. Swillens, C. Clair, T. Tordjmann, and L. Combettes. Hierarchical organization of calcium signals in hepatocytes: from experiments to models. *Biochim. Biophys. Acta*, 1498:134–152, 2000.

26. B. M. Slepchenko, J. C. Schaff, J. H. Carson, and L. M. Loew. Computational cell biology: spatiotemporal simulation of cellular events. *Annu. Rev. Biophys. Biomol. Struct.*, 31: 423–441, 2002.

27. M. B. Elowitz, A. J. Levine, E. D. Siggia, and P. S. Swain. Stochastic gene expression in a single cell. *Science*, 297:1183–1186, 2002.

28. J. Paulsson. Summing up the noise in gene networks. *Nature*, 427:415–418, 2004.

29. N. G. van Kampen. *Stochastic Processes in Physics and Chemistry.* Elsevier, Amsterdam, The Netherlands, 1992.

30. S. Li, S. M. Assmann, and R. Albert. Predicting essential components of signal transduction networks: a dynamic model of guard cell abscisic acid signaling. *PLoS Biol.*, 4:e312, 2006.

31. S. A. Kauffman. Metabolic stability and epigenesis in randomly constructed genetic nets. *J. Theor. Biol.*, 22:437–467, 1969.

32. R. Thomas and R. D'Ari. *Biological Feedback.* CRC Press, Boca Raton, FL, 1990.

33. J. Fisher and T. Henzinger. Executable cell biology. *Nat. Biotechnol.*, 25:1239–1249, 2007.

34. J. E. Hopcroft, R. Motwani, and J. D. Ullman. *Introduction to Automata Theory, Languages, and Computation.* Addison-Wesley, Boston, MA, 2006.

35. W. S. Hlavacek, J. R. Faeder, M. L. Blinov, R. G. Posner, M. Hucka, and W. Fontana. Rules for modeling signal-transduction systems. *Sci. STKE*, 344:re6, 2006.

36. A. Mallavarapu, M. Thomson, B. Ullian, and J. Gunawardena. Programming with models: modularity and abstraction provide powerful capabilities for systems biology. *J. R. Soc. Interface*, 6:257–270, 2009.

37. W. Fontana. Algorithmic chemistry. In C. G. Langton, C. Taylor, J. D. Farmer, and S. Rasmussen, editors, *Artificial Life II.* Addison-Wesley, Redwood City, CA, 1992.

38. A. Regev, W. Silverman, and E. Shapiro. Representation and simulation of biochemical processes using the pi-calculus process algebra. *Pac. Symp. Biocomput.*, 459–470, 2001.

39. V. Danos, J. Feret, W. Fontana, and J. Krivine. Abstract interpretation of cellular signalling networks. In *Proceedings VMCAI 2008*, Vol. 4905 of *Lecture Notes in Computer Science.* Springer, 2008.

40. A. R. A. Anderson, A. M. Weaver, P. T. Cummings, and V. Quaranta. Tumor morphology and phenotypic evolution driven by selective pressure from the microenvironment. *Cell*, 127:905–915, 2006.

41. B. L. Sprague, R. L. Pego, D. A. Stavreva, and J. G. McNally. Analysis of binding reactions by fluorescence recovery after photobleaching. *Biophys. J.*, 86:3473–3495, 2004.

42. E. Tajkhorshid, P. Nollert, M. O. Jensen, L. J. Miercke, J. O'Connell, R. M. Stroud, and K. Schulten. Control of the selectivity of the aquaporin water channel family by global orientational tuning. *Science*, 296:525–530, 2002.

43. J. A. Lakowicz. *Principles of Fluorescence Spectroscopy.* 2nd edition. Kluwer Academic, New York, 1999.

44. A. Brünger. Free R value: a novel statistical quantity for assessing the accuracy of crystal structures. *Nature*, 355:472–475, 1992.

45. J. G. Albeck, J. M. Burke, B. B. Aldridge, M. Zhang, D. A. Lauffenburger, and P. K. Sorger. Quantitative analysis of pathways controlling extrinsic apoptosis in single cells. *Mol. Cell*, 30:11–25, 2008.

46. S. H. Strogatz. *Nonlinear Dynamics and Chaos: With Applications to Physics, Biology, Chemistry and Engineering*. Perseus Books, 2001.

47. A. Mehra, C. I. Hong, M. Shi, J. J. Loros, J. C. Dunlap, and P. Ruoff. Circadian rhythmicity by autocatalysis. *PLoS Comput. Biol.*, 2:0816–0823, 2006.

48. J. Lewis. Autoinhibition with transcriptional delay: a simple mechanism for the Zebrafish somitogenesis oscillator. *Curr. Biol.*, 13:1398–1408, 2003.

49. E. Di Cera, P. E. Phillipson, and J. Wyman. Limit cycle oscillations and chaos in reaction networks subject to conservation of mass. *Proc. Natl. Acad. Sci. USA*, 86:142–146, 1989.

50. C. Koch. *Biophysics of Computation: Information Processing in Single Neurons*. Oxford University Press, 1999.

51. J. E. Ferrell. Self-perpetuating states in signal transduction: positive feedback, double-negative feedback and bistability. *Curr. Opin. Chem. Biol.*, 6:140–148, 2002.

52. E. M. Ozbudak, M. Thattai, H. N. Lim, B. I. Shraiman, and A. van Oudenaarden. Multistability in the lactose utilization network of *Escherichia coli*. *Nature*, 427:737–740, 2004.

53. M. Demazure. *Bifurcations and Catastrophes*. Universitext. Springer, 2000.

54. R. N. Gutenkunst, J. J. Waterfall, F. P. Casey, K. S. Brown, C. R. Myers, and J. P. Sethna. Universally sloppy parameter sensitivities in systems biology models. *PLoS Comput. Biol.*, 3:1871–1878, 2007.

55. D. A. Rand. Mapping the global sensitivity of cellular network dynamics: sensitivity heat maps and a global summation law. *J. R. Soc. Interface*, 5 Suppl 1:S59–S69, 2008.

56. C. H. Waddington. *The Strategy of the Genes: A Discussion of Some Aspects of Theoretical Biology*. George Allen & Unwin Ltd., London, 1957.

57. S. Wright. The roles of mutation, inbreeding, crossbreeding and selection in evolution. In *Proceedings of the 6th International Conference on Genetics*, Vol. I, 1932, pp. 356–366.

58. S. Huang and D. E. Ingber. A non-genetic basis for cancer progression and metastasis: self-organizing attractors in cell regulatory networks. *Breast Dis.*, 26:27–54, 2006-2007.

59. G. Mitchison. Theory in biology. Happy days here again? *Curr. Biol.*, 14:R97–R98, 2004.

60. J. M. W. Slack. Conrad Hal Waddington: the last Renaissance biologist. *Nat. Rev. Genet.*, 3:889–895, 2002.

61. M. Feinberg. Chemical reaction network structure and the stability of complex isothermal reactors I. The deficiency zero and deficiency one theorems. *Chem. Eng. Sci*, 42(10):2229–2268, 1987.

62. J. Gunawardena. Chemical reaction network theory for *in-silico* biologists. Lecture Notes, Harvard University, 2003, http://vcp.med.harvard.edu/papers/crnt.pdf.

63. G. Craciun, Y. Tang, and M. Feinberg. Understanding bistability in complex enzyme-driven reaction networks. *Proc. Natl. Acad. Sci. USA*, 103:8697–8702, 2006.

64. D. Angeli, J. E. Ferrell, and E. D. Sontag. Detection of multistability, bifurcations, and hysteresis in a large class of biological positive-feedback systems. *Proc. Natl. Acad. Sci. USA*, 101:1822–1827, 2004.

65. L. Segel. On the validity of the steady-state assumption of enzyme kinetics. *Bull. Math. Biol.*, 50:579–593, 1988.

66. R. A. Tzafriri. Michaelis-Menten kinetics at high enzyme concentration. *Bull. Math. Biol.*, 65:1111–1129, 2003.

67. A. Ciliberto, F. Capuani, and J. J. Tyson. Modeling networks of coupled enzymatic reactions using the total quasi-steady state approximation. *PLoS Comput. Biol.*, 3:e45, 2007.

68. D. Cox, J. Little, and D. O'Shea. *Ideals, Varieties and Algorithms*, 2nd edition. Springer, 1997.

69. A. Manrai and J. Gunawardena. The geometry of multisite phosphorylation. *Biophys. J.*, 95:5533–5543, 2008.

70. M. Thomson and J. Gunawardena. Unlimited multistability in multisite phosphorylation systems. *Nature*, 460:274–277, 2009.

71. M. Thomson and J. Gunawardena. The rational parameterisation theorem for multisite post-translational modification systems. *J. Theor. Biol*, doi:10.1016/j.jtbi.2009.09.003, 2009.

72. I. Amit, R. Wides, and Y. Yarden. Evolvable signalling networks of receptor tyrosine kinases: relevance of robustness to malignancy and cancer therapy. *Mol. Syst. Biol.*, 3:151, 2007.

73. N. Barkai and B.-Z. Shilo. Variability and robustness in biomolecular systems. *Mol. Cell*, 28:755–760, 2007.

74. H. Kitano. Biological robustness. *Nat. Rev. Genet.*, 5:826–837, 2004.

75. J. Stelling, U. Sauer, Z. Szallasi, F. J. Doyle III, and J. Doyle. Robustness of cellular functions. *Cell*, 118:675–685, 2004.

76. D. E. Koshland, G. Nemethy, and D. Filmer. Comparison of experimental binding data and theoretical models in proteins containing subunits. *Biochemistry*, 5:365–385, 1966.

77. J. Monod, J. Wyman, and J. P. Changeux. On the nature of allosteric transitions: a plausible model. *J. Mol. Biol.*, 12:88–118, 1965.

78. G. K. Ackers, A. D. Johnson, and M. A. Shea. Quantitative model for gene regulation by lambda phage repressor. *Proc. Natl. Acad. Sci. USA*, 79:1129–1133, 1982.

79. A. H. West and A. M. Stock. Histidine kinases and response regulator proteins in two-component signaling systems. *Trends Biochem. Sci.*, 26:369–376, 2001.

80. E. Batchelor and M. Goulian. Robustness and the cycle of phosphorylation and dephosphorylation in a two-component regulatory system. *Proc. Natl. Acad. Sci. USA*, 100:691–696, 2003.

81. F. D. Russo and T. J. Silhavy. The essential tension: opposed reactions in bacterial two-component regulatory systems. *Trends Microbiol.*, 1:306–310, 1993.

82. G. Shinar, R. Milo, M. R. Martínez, and U. Alon. Input–output robustness in simple bacterial signaling systems. *Proc. Natl. Acad. Sci. USA*, 104:19931–19935, 2007.

83. H. C. Berg. *E. coli in Motion*. Springer, New York, 2004.

84. N. Barkai and S. Leibler. Robustness in simple biochemical networks. *Nature*, 387:913–917, 1997.

85. L. Hartwell. A robust view of biochemical pathways. *Nature*, 387:855–857, 1997.

86. The International Hap Map Consortium. The international HapMap project. *Nature*, 426:789–796, 2003.

87. M. Tiseo, M. Capelletti, G. De Palma, V. Franciosi, A. Cavazzoni, P. Mozzoni, R. R. Alfieri, M. Goldoni, M. Galetti, B. Bortesi, C. Bozzetti, M. Loprevite, L. Boni, R. Camisa, G. Rindi, P. G. Petronini, and A. Ardizzoni. Epidermal growth factor receptor intron-1 polymorphism predicts gefitinib outcome in advanced non-small cell lung cancer. *J. Thorac. Oncol.*, 3:1104–1111, 2008.

88. U. Alon, M. G. Surette, N. Barkai, and S. Leibler. Robustness in bacterial chemotaxis. *Nature*, 397:168–171, 1999.

89. L. Wolpert. *Principles of Development*. Oxford University Press, 2001.

90. B. Houchmandzadeh, E. Wieschaus, and S. Leibler. Establishment of developmental precision and proportions in the early *Drosophila* embryo. *Nature*, 415:798–802, 2002.

91. A. Eldar, R. Dorfman, D. Weiss, H. Ashe, B.-Z. Shilo, and N. Barkai. Robustness of the BMP morphogen gradient in *Drosophila* embryonic patterning. *Nature*, 419:304–308, 2002.

92. A. Eldar, D. Rosin, B.-Z. Shilo, and N. Barkai. Self-enhanced ligand degradation underlies robustness of morphogen gradients. *Dev. Cell*, 5:635–646, 2003.

93. A. Eldar, B.-Z. Shilo, and N. Barkai. Elucidating mechanisms underlying robustness of morphogen gradients. *Curr. Opin. Genet. Dev.*, 14:435–439, 2004.

94. M. W. Kirschner and J. C. Gerhart. *The Plausibility of Life*. Yale University Press, 2005.

95. C. H. Waddington, editor. *Towards a Theoretical Biology. 1. Prolegomena*. Edinburgh University Press, 1968.

96. T. Poston and I. Stewart. *Catastrophe Theory and Its Applications*. Dover Publications, 1996.

97. R. Thom. *Structural Stability and Morphogenesis*. W. A. Benjamin, Inc., Reading, MA, 1975. English translation of the 1972 French edition.

98. V. I. Arnold, V. F. Afrajmovich, Yu. S. Il'yashenko, and L. P. Shil'nikov. *Bifurcation Theory and Catastrophe Theory. Encyclopedia of Mathematical Sciences*. Springer, 1999.

99. G. von Dassow, E. Meir, E. M. Munro, and G. M. Odell. The segment polarity network is a robust developmental module. *Nature*, 406:188–192, 2000.

100. M. C. Gibson, A. B. Patel, R. Nagpal, and N. Perrimon. The emergence of geometric order in proliferating metazoan epithelia. *Nature*, 442:1038–1041, 2006.

101. G. Kolata. Catastrophe theory: the emperor has no clothes. *Science*, 196:287–351, 1977.

102. R. S. Zahler and H. J. Sussmann. Claims and accomplishments of applied catastrophe theory. *Nature*, 269:759–763, 1977.

103. E. C. Zeeman, R. Bellairs, B. Goodwin, M. R. Mackley, I. Stewart, M. Berry, J. Guckenheimer, and A. E. R. Woodcook. In support of catastrophe theory. *Nature*, 270:381–384, 2005.

104. M. E. Csete and J. C. Doyle. Reverse engineering of biological complexity. *Science*, 295:1664–1669, 2002.

105. H. Kitano. Towards a theory of biological robustness. *Mol. Syst. Biol.*, 3:137, 2007.

106. S. Pinker. *The Language Instinct: How the Mind Creates Language*. William Morrow and Co., 1994.

3

IN SILICO ANALYSIS OF COMBINED THERAPEUTICS STRATEGY FOR HEART FAILURE

Sung-Young Shin, Tae-Hwan Kim, and Kwang-Hyun Cho*

Department of Bio and Brain Engineering, Korea Advanced Institute of Science and Technology (KAIST), Daejeon, Korea

Sang-Mok Choo

School of Electrical Engineering, University of Ulsan, Ulsan, Korea

3.1 INTRODUCTION

In failing cardiac myocytes, chronic stimulation of β-adrenergic receptor (β-AR) due to the high level of circulating catecholamine secreted by activation of the sympathetic nervous system leads to desensitization and impaired β-AR responsiveness [1]. Furthermore, chronic activation of β-adrenergic signaling pathway may result in altered expression and functional activity of β-AR, G-protein, adenylyl cyclase (AC), and G-protein receptor kinase [2]. The alteration of this pathway makes the β-AR-mediated cardiac response substantially blunt and ultimately delivers adverse biological signals [3]. These molecular and biochemical alterations of the β-AR signaling pathway are common to the failing hearts despite the varying etiologies [4]. Therefore, restoring the altered signaling pathway is a generally accepted notion to treat

*Corresponding author: Kwang-Hyun Cho (ckh@kaist.ac.kr)

Elements of Computational Systems Biology   Edited by Huma M. Lodhi and Stephen H. Muggleton
Copyright © 2010 John Wiley & Sons, Inc.

heart failure (HF), and actually, new therapeutic strategies have been developed based on this notion [5]. Among those new therapeutic strategies, β-AR-blocking agent (β-blocker) is conceived as a standard therapy for patients with mild-to-moderate HF [6]. The diastolic function of such patients gets worsened with decreasing cardiac performance. This results in shortened diastolic filling time, which is insufficient for the ventricle to properly prepare for the next heartbeat. In such a case, β-blocker can be used to elongate the diastolic filling time by reducing the heart rate. However, the tolerance for the β-blocker therapy is limited due to its possibility of syncopes caused by a too low heart rate, resulting in a too big drop in overall blood pressure. Moreover, since β-blocker intrinsically decreases cardiac contractility, the β-blocker therapy to the patients with severely impaired cardiac function may further decompensate failing cardiac myocytes, eventually leading to lethal results [3]. In such cases, β-blocker should be administered with inotropic agents to prevent further deterioration of cardiac functioning [6]. In fact, it was reported that some combined therapies with β-blocker and inotropic agents have reduced the rehospitalization rate and the mortality of patients with severe HF [6]. However, little is known about the fundamental effect of the combined therapies at the molecular and cellular levels.

In this chapter, we show an integrative mathematical model of the β-AR signaling pathway and the underlying excitation–contraction coupling mechanism of the cardiac myocytes to quantitatively analyze the different effects of the selected drugs (β-blocker, β-AR inhibitor (β-ARKI), and phosphodiesterase inhibitor (PDEI)) and their combined therapies. Extensive in silico simulations showed that β-blocker significantly decreases the Ca^{2+} transient (potentially leading to a negative inotropic effect), while inotropes (β-ARKI and PDEI) increase the Ca^{2+} transient (potentially leading to a positive inotropic effect) [3]. For the combined therapy, PDEI showed remarkably increased cAMP and receptor phosphorylation, which could possibly lead to a strong positive inotropic effect with the risk of a lethal result for long-term use. On the other hand, although β-ARKI showed potentially moderate positive inotropic effect compared with PDEI, the relatively lower cAMP concentration and decreased receptor phosphorylation might be advantageous in the long-term use. The mathematical modeling and in silico simulation analysis proposed in this chapter can provide a useful guideline for designing new pharmacotherapeutics and developing an optimal pharmacological treatment protocol for HF.

3.2 MATERIALS AND METHODS

3.2.1 Model Construction and Validation

We have developed an integrative mathematical model of the β-AR signaling pathway and the underlying excitation–contraction coupling mechanism of the cardiac myocytes. The model is comprised of a cardiac myocyte physiological part and a β-AR signaling pathway part (see Figure 3.1 and Appendix 3A.1.2). The cardiac myocyte physiological part is composed of 15 ion channels (mediating Ca^{2+}, Na^+,

K^+, and Cl^- current flows) and four compartments (subspace (dyadic space), cytoplasm, junctional sarcoplasmic reticulum (JSR), and network sarcoplasmic reticulum (NSR)) as shown in Figure 3.1. This model was developed by introducing the post-translational modification (PTM) effects of cyclic AMP-dependent protein kinase (PKA) and Ca^{2+}/calmodulin-dependent protein kinase II (CaMKII) (i.e., the regulation of L-type Ca^{2+} channel (LTCC), ryanodine receptor (RyR), phospholamban (PLB), and sarco(endo)plasmic reticulum Ca^{2+} ATPase (SERCA) by these protein kinases) into the previously published model [7]. In addition, the proposed model explicitly describes the regulation of the intracellular Ca^{2+} transient by calcineurin (CaN) and CaMKII. Note that CaN is activated by Ca^{2+} increase and plays a crucial role in inhibiting the PKA function through dephosphorylating inhibitor 1 (I1) and PLB. CaMKII is also activated by Ca^{2+} increase like CaN, but it phosphorylates LTCC, RyR, PLB, and troponin I (TnI), resulting in increase of the intracellular Ca^{2+} transient, which ultimately contributes to a positive inotropic effect [8]. It turns out that our simulation results are in well accord with the previous experimental data, qualitatively and quantitatively (see Appendix 3A.1.1). The β-AR signaling pathway part describes the β-AR signal transduction mechanism ranging from ligand (β-agonist such as catecholamine and isoproterenol) binding to β-AR and activation of Gs-proteins to cAMP generation by active AC and PKA activation (Figure 3.1). There have been some attempts to develop a mathematical model of this signaling pathway, but only a partial model was developed and the multiple feedback loops in this pathway were not considered [9, 10]. We note, however, that the multiple negative feedback loops should be considered to properly investigate the hidden system dynamics and drug effects, since such feedback loops may play crucial roles in overall regulations. Hence, in this chapter, we have introduced all of the six negative feedback loops (i.e., β-AR → β-ARK⊣ β-AR, β-AR → PKA⊣ β-AR, AC → cAMP → PKA⊣ AC, AC → cAMP → PKA → Ca^{2+}⊣ AC, PDE⊣ cAMP → PKA → PDE, PDE⊣ cAMP → PKA → Ca^{2+} → PDE) into the mathematical model based on experimental evidences [11, 12]. Most of the reaction parameters used in the mathematical model were obtained from literature of experimental measurements, and those parameters not available from literature were estimated through iterative simulations and fitting such that they are consistent with other indirect experimental evidences (see Appendix 3A.1.1 and 3A.1.2).

3.2.2   Classification of Different Heart Failure Cases

HF has numerous etiologies, including myocardial infarction, hypertension, and valvular disease, which usually have functional alterations in the β-AR signaling pathway or ion channels of cardiac myocytes. For instance, it was reported that the expression and functional activity of β-AR, AC, and Gs-protein became decreased, while those of β-ARK and Gi-proteins got increased in the failing heart [4]. It was also reported that some components of cardiac myocytes such as SERCA, NCX, RyR,

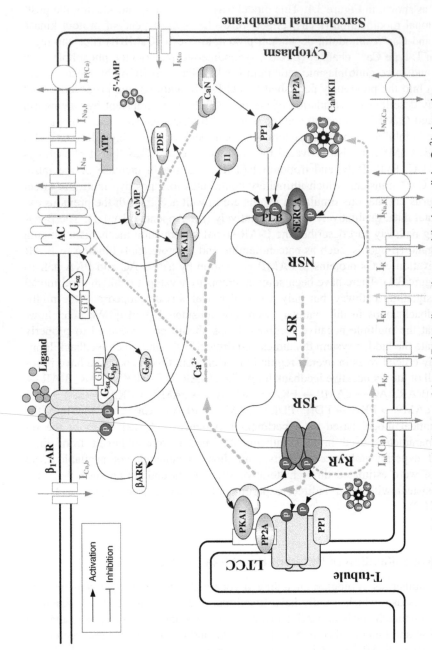

Figure 3.1 A schematic diagram of the β-AR signaling pathway and the intracellular Ca^{2+} dynamics representing the electrophysiological mechanism in mouse ventricular myocytes, where solid lines denote protein interactions and dashed lines indicate ion flows.

Table 3.1   Possible morphological changes in failing heart. HFC-1 and HFC-2 are primarily characterized by alterations in the signaling pathway, and HFC-3 is mainly characterized by ion channel remodeling*

Component	HFC-1	HFC-2	HFC-3
β-AR	10% ($\downarrow$)[21]	50% ($\downarrow$)[22]	20% ($\downarrow$)[21]
β-ARK	200% ($\uparrow$)[16]	50% ($\uparrow$)[23]	50% ($\uparrow$)[23]
AC	20% ($\downarrow$)[24]	20% ($\downarrow$)[24]	20% ($\downarrow$)[24]
G-proteins	–	–	10% ($\downarrow$)[21]
RyR	–	–	30% ($\downarrow$)[13]
LTCC	–	–	30% ($\downarrow$)[13]
SERCA	–	–	50% ($\downarrow$)[25]
NCX	–	–	200% ($\uparrow$)[26]
Na^+/K^+ pump	–	–	30% ($\downarrow$)[27]
K^+ channel	–	–	IKr 40% ($\downarrow$)[28], IKur 40 ($\downarrow$)[26], Itof 50% ($\downarrow$)[26]

*The symbols ($\downarrow$) and ($\uparrow$) denote down- and upregulation of the corresponding protein, respectively. "–" means that the expression and functional activity of the protein showed no change in failing heart. IKr, IKur, and Itof denote the rectifier, the ultrarapidly activating delayed rectifier, and the transient outward K^+ current, respectively.

LTCC, and potassium channels got remarkably changed in HF [13]. Drug effects might be considerably different depending on such intracellular molecular changes. To systematically analyze the drug effects, we classify the molecular changes of HF into three types by focusing on down-regulation of β-AR, up-regulation of β-ARK, and ion channel remodeling (see Table 3.1). We refer to these types as heart failure cases (HFCs) throughout the remaining part of this chapter.

We analyze the effects of individual drugs and combined treatments for the three different HFCs with respect to the following four system responses: the intracellular Ca^{2+} transient, the membrane action potential (AP), the phosphorylation of β-AR, and the cAMP accumulation. The intracellular Ca^{2+} transient and the membrane action potential are typical physiological responses of cardiac myocytes at the cellular level, therefore important factors in determining the hemodynamics of heart. In addition, β-AR and cAMP play a crucial regulatory role in the β-AR signaling pathway at the molecular level. Figure 3.2 shows the variation of the intracellular Ca^{2+} transient and action potential with respect to isoproterenol (Iso) stimulation (50 nM) for each HFC and the normal cardiomyocyte (control). In all HFCs, the Ca^{2+} transient peak did not change to Iso stimulation, while it became remarkably increased in the control. The half-decay time (i.e., the period of time taken for decrease from the peak to its 50 percent) of the Ca^{2+} transient was significantly prolonged in the control but not in the three HFCs. It is typical in failing heart that the Ca^{2+} transient does not increase in spite of the strong stimulation [14]. Such HF patients might intrinsically have fully stimulated inotropic systems in a way that all the receptors are activated. As shown in Figure 3.2, the 90 percent and 50 percent depolarization of AP (APD90 and APD50, respectively) did not show any significant change in all the cases. However, it should be noted that APDs were more prolonged in HFC-3.

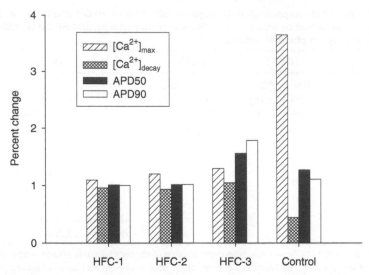

Figure 3.2   The simulation result for percent changes of cellular responses (Ca^{2+} transient and APDs) to Iso (50 nM) stimulation. The percent change of the Ca^{2+} transient was remarkably blunt in all the HFCs compared to the control.

3.2.3   Simulation Protocol

The equations of the integrated mathematical model (Appendix 3A.1.2) were coded in Matlab, and the full set of ordinary differential equations was solved on three HP workstations (xw-8200) by using a Runge–Kutta–Merson numerical integration algorithm. The software package Matlab (V7.0, R14) was utilized while developing/solving equations of individual components. To trigger an action potential, we used a 0.5-ms 80 pA/pF stimulus current with a frequency of 0.83 Hz (the pacing period is 1200 ms). The effects of drug intervention on the system responses were observed at steady-state beats obtained after a train of 200 stimulus pulses.

3.3   RESULTS

3.3.1   β-Adrenergic Receptor Antagonists

It is widely known that the cardiac functioning might be temporarily but significantly decreased in failing heart by the β-blocker therapy as it is intrinsically a β-AR antagonist, but this impaired cardiac function might also be restored in long-term use by reverse remodeling of cardiac myocytes [3]. However, we note that this temporary effect of the β-blocker therapy can cause severe cardiac malfunctioning. Figure 3.3 illustrates the effect of the β-blocker therapy in short-term use that might differ from HFCs. β-Blocker (propranolol) significantly decreased the Ca^{2+} transient as expected from the previous experiment [15]. The Ca^{2+} transient decreased to 12 percent for

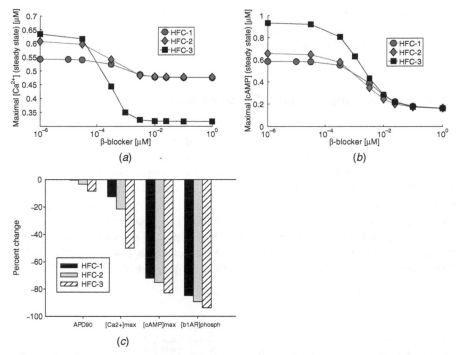

Figure 3.3 The simulation result of cellular responses for β-blocker therapy. (a) The intracellular Ca²⁺ transient peaks. (b) The maximal concentration of cAMP. (c) The percent change of the cellular responses at the maximal dose. The system responses for the smallest drug concentration $[10^{-6} (\mu M)]$ are similar to those without β-blocker administration.

HFC-1 and 21 percent for HFC-2 at the maximal dose of the drug. It remarkably decreased to 50 percent for HFC-3 (Figure 3.3(a) and (c)). APD90 did not significantly change except 8 percent decrease for HFC-3 (Figure 3.3(c)). cAMP decreased to 72 percent for HFC-1, 73 percent for HFC-2, and 83 percent for HFC-3 (Figure 3.3(b) and (c)). The receptor phosphorylation also decreased to 85 percent for HFC-1, 90 percent for HFC-2, and 94 percent for HFC-3 after the drug administration (Figure 3.3(c)).

It is interesting that the Ca²⁺ transient of HFC-3 most significantly decreased along with an increase of the β-blocker dose, even if it was larger than the others before the β-blocker administration. This is because HFC-3 implies having defects in both the β-AR signaling pathway and ionic channels. It seems that the Ca²⁺ transient decreased first by the β-blocker treatment and then further aggravated by the remodeled ion channels. This result suggests that the β-blocker therapy for patients having complex defects like HFC-3 might induce severe impairment of cardiac muscle contractility due to the rapidly decreased Ca²⁺ transient and eventually lead to lethal results. It is also interesting that the receptor phosphorylation decreased along with an increase of the β-blocker dose in all HFCs. This is because the activity of β-ARK was remarkably attenuated for the decreased number of agonist-bound receptors due to the β-blocker—β-blocker competes with β-agonist (Iso) for the same binding site. Although PKA contributes to receptor phosphorylation, this effect seems negligible compared with that of β-ARK.

3.3.2 β-Adrenergic Receptor Kinase Inhibitor

It was reported that the activity of β-ARK significantly increased in failing heart [16]. In addition, the receptor phosphorylation increased, and thereby the accumulation of cAMP also decreased in failing heart due to the functional decoupling of β-AR [17]. From these reports, it turns out that the cardiac muscle contractility becomes impaired by β-ARK, and therefore, the inhibition of β-ARK can be one promising way of restoring the impaired cardiac muscle contractility [1]. In our simulations, β-ARKI (hepalin) increased the Ca^{2+} transient for all HFCs as shown in Figure 3.4(a) and (c) (210 percent for HFC-1, 87 percent for HFC-2, and 59 percent for HFC-3 at the maximal drug dose). cAMP also significantly increased to 174 percent for HFC-1, 50 percent for HFC-2, and 48 percent for HFC-3 (Figure 3.4(b) and (c)). As expected

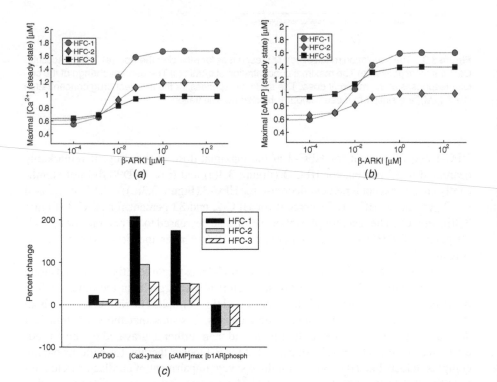

Figure 3.4   The simulation result of cellular responses for β-ARKI treatment. The system responses for the smallest drug concentration [10^{-5} (μM)] are similar to those without β-ARKI administration.

from the role of β-ARKI, the receptor phosphorylation decreased for all HFCs as shown in Figure 3.4(c) (62 percent for HFC-1, 58 percent for HFC-2, and 52 percent for HFC-3). On the other hand, APD90 was slightly prolonged (Figure 3.4(c)). Although cAMP concentration of HFC-3 was larger than that of HFC-2 for the maximal β-ARKI, the Ca^{2+} transient of HFC-3 was less than that of HFC-2 (Figure 3.4(a) and (b)). This result suggests that the effect of β-ARKI might be quite limited in the failing heart caused by ion channel remodeling. For full administration of β-ARKI, the receptor phosphorylation was not completely depleted, but the depletion level was proportional to the level of cAMP. This implies that PKA considerably inhibits the receptor activation by increased cAMP. In other words, the negative feedback formed through PKA contributes to suppressing the drug effect.

3.3.3 Phosphodiesterase Inhibitor

The PDE families are activated by PKA phosphorylation and Ca^{2+}/CaM binding. The activated PDE hydrolyzes cAMP to $5'$-AMP, and this again suppresses the activity of PKA and the increase of Ca^{2+}. This negative feedback loop seems to keep the homeostasis of cAMP for abnormally increased external stimuli such as hormones or neurotransmitters, including catecholamine and forskoline. PDEI is a typical inotropic drug agent that improves the impaired cardiac functioning of failing heart [18] by ultimately ablating the PKA-mediated negative feedback. In our simulations, PDEI (IBMX) dramatically increased the Ca^{2+} transient compared with β-ARKI therapy. The Ca^{2+} transient increased to 262 percent for HFC-1, 222 percent for HFC-2, and 97 percent for HFC-3 at the maximal dose (Figure 3.5(a) and (c)). Moreover, the increment of cAMP was surprising. It was augmented to 8520-fold for HFC-1, 7940-fold for HFC-2, and 7500-fold for HFC-3 at the maximal dose (Figure 3.5(b) and (c)). However, the receptor phosphorylation was not significantly changed despite the overwhelming increase of cAMP and PKA activation (Figure 3.5(c)). APD90 was prolonged to 33 percent for HFC-1 and HFC-2, and 28 percent for HFC-3 in proportion to the Ca^{2+} transient increment (Figure 3.5(c)). Note that the PDEI effect on the Ca^{2+} transient of HFC-3 seems very limited compared with that of HFC-1 or HFC-2, since HFC-3 has defects in both the signaling pathway and ion channels. Hence, this result shows that the decreased Ca^{2+} transient by remodeling of ion channels may not be fully restored by PDEI, although the PDEI effect on the Ca^{2+} transient was strong enough. The PDEI effect on the Ca^{2+} transient was similar to that of β-ARKI (Figure 3.4(c)), except for the receptor phosphorylation. PDEI increased the receptor phosphorylation, since the activity of PKA due to cAMP was significantly increased after the PDEI administration, although some of the receptors were already phosphorylated due to the increased β-ARK. The most interesting result we obtained is that cAMP was abnormally increased as the PDEI dose increased beyond a certain threshold (about 50 μM). We can explain this phenomenon as follows. Below the threshold, the drug effect might mostly be compensated by the negative feedback effect of PDE, although the activity of PDE was suppressed in proportion to the drug dose. In other words, the decreased activity of PDE by PDEI is compensated by the increased PKA, since PDE is activated by PKA. On the other hand, there is

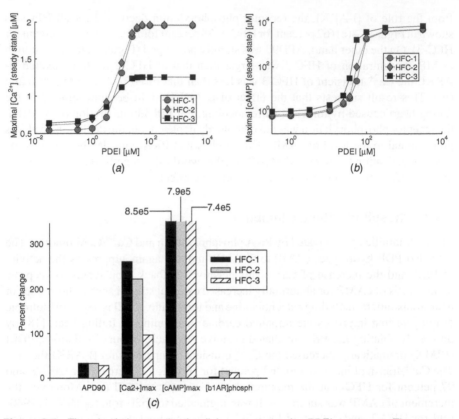

Figure 3.5 The simulation result of cellular responses for PDEI treatment. The system responses for the smallest drug concentration [10^{-2} (μM)] are similar to those without PDEI administration.

no longer a negative feedback effect of PDE if PDEI can completely inhibit PDE. Hence, beyond the threshold, cAMP became increased along with the drug dose. From this result, we found that if the dynamics of the system is dominantly regulated by a negative feedback and a drug perturbs this negative feedback loop, then the drug dose–response curve shows a switch-like behavior as shown in Figure 3.5(a) and (b).

3.3.4 Combined Therapies

The combined therapy of β-blocker and inotropic drug agents for patients with severely impaired cardiac functioning is a desirable therapeutics for HF [6]. We have analyzed the combined therapeutic effects of β-blocker and positive inotropic agents by varying their administration from a low to high dose and found reasonable therapeutic strategies to treat HF. The Ca^{2+} transient (Figure 3.6(a)–(c)) and cAMP

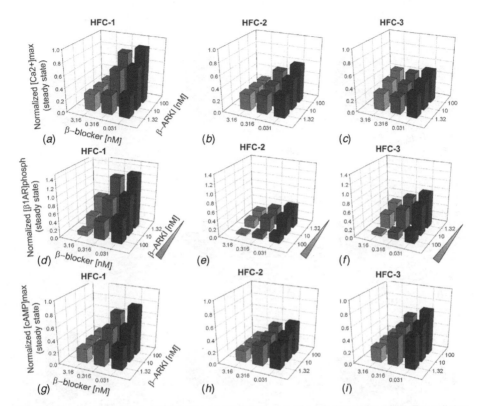

Figure 3.6 The simulation result for the combined therapy of β-blocker and β-ARKI. The cellular responses to the combined therapy were normalized with respect to their controls (i.e., the system responses of nonfailing heart for Iso stimulation (50 nM)).

(Figure 3.6(g)–(i)) became increased along with the increase of β-ARKI, whereas the receptor phosphorylation (Figure 3.6(d)–(f)) became significantly decreased in the combined therapy of β-blocker and β-ARKI. However, such effects of β-ARKI were almost diminished for a high dose of β-blocker. The effects of β-ARKI on the Ca^{2+} transient and cAMP were most significant for HFC-1, while they were minimal for HFC-3. This combined therapy, however, does not show any remarkable effect on APD irrespective of HFCs (data not shown). Although β-ARKI improved the Ca^{2+} transient in this combined therapy, the effect of β-ARKI was not enough to increase the Ca^{2+} transient to an extent as much as in the control. In particular, this effect was significantly limited for HFC-3. The Ca^{2+} transient (Figure 3.7(a)–(c)) and cAMP (Figure 3.7(g)–(i)) became significantly increased along with the increase of PDEI. The PDEI effect in the combined therapy was more significant than the β-ARKI effect in Figure 3.6, while the receptor phosphorylation (Figure 3.7(d)–(f)) did not change much with PDEI variations unlike β-ARKI. Such PDEI effects on the Ca^{2+} transient and cAMP were remarkably decreased for a high dose of β-blocker.

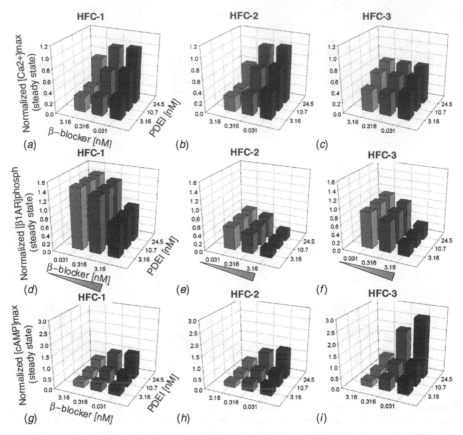

Figure 3.7 The simulation result for the combined therapy of β-blocker and PDEI.

The effect of the PDEI therapy in HFC-3 was interesting in that the Ca^{2+} transient increased and the receptor phosphorylation was insignificant at a high dose of β-blocker (Figure 3.7(c) and (f)), while cAMP greatly increased (Figure 3.7(i)). This implies that the PDEI effect might be significantly limited for the failing heart with the dual defects.

In summary, the β-ARKI therapy in the combined therapy showed significant increases in the Ca^{2+} transient and cAMP, potentially leading to a positive inotropic effect, while the receptor phosphorylation decreased for a high dose of β-ARKI. This suggests the long-term use of β-ARKI for combined therapy without much adverse effect. On the other hand, the PDEI therapy in the combined therapy greatly increased the Ca^{2+} transient and cAMP. Since an excessive increase of cAMP might lead to lethal results [19], the long-term use of PDEI could induce serious adverse effect. Moreover, the highly increased receptor phosphorylation in HFC-1 can cause receptor internalization and degradation, resulting in the attenuation of β-AR signaling.

3.4 DISCUSSION

In this chapter, we have analyzed various drug effects for HF treatment. As well known, β-blocker showed a negative inotropic effect that significantly decreased the Ca^{2+} transient and cAMP, whereas both β-ARKI and PDEI showed a positive inotropic effect. These effects were, however, rather different depending on HFCs. Moreover, we have analyzed the effects of β-ARKI and PDEI in the combined therapy with β-blocker to compensate the temporary decrease of cardiac functioning caused by β-blocker. β-ARKI increased the Ca^{2+} transient and cAMP by decreasing the receptor phosphorylation. However, these effects were more significant in the combined therapy with PDEI. In particular, the receptor became highly phosphorylated for HFC-1 irrespective of the PDEI dose. From these simulation results, we can evaluate the two combined therapies as follows: Although the inotropic effect of β-ARKI was less significant than PDEI, potential adverse effect of the β-ARKI therapy with respect to the receptor phosphorylation was much lower, and that with respect to cAMP was moderate even for a high dose of β-ARKI. On the other hand, although the cardiac inotropic effect was obvious in the PDEI therapy, the PDEI dose should be limited to a moderate range to prevent potential adverse effect.

The Ca^{2+} transient decreased more significantly in HFC-3 than other HFCs after β-blocker administration. This result suggests that responses to the same drug can be quite different depending on HFCs, even if the hemodynamics of all HFCs are similar before the drug administration. The major cause for the remarkable decrease of the Ca^{2+} transient in HFC-3 seems to be the synergistic effect of the cAMP decrease by β-blocker and the ion channel remodeling. This also implies that it might be difficult to restore the cardiac functioning by targeting only one of the multiple morphological and biochemical alterations as in HFC-3. In addition to modulating the Ca^{2+} transient for HF treatment, modulating the dynamics of Ca^{2+} binding to the contractile elements or the dynamics of the Ca^{2+} uptake by the SR might be other measures.

Mathematical modeling and *in silico* simulations have emerged as a useful tool for therapeutics in the context of systems biology [20]. Throughout this approach, we can systematically integrate various clinical data, disease information, and experimental data. Moreover, it helps us to establish a fundamental understanding of the disease–drug interaction mechanism. On the basis of this, we can predict probable adverse effects and investigate an optimal dosage and treatment schedules. In this chapter, we have focused on a therapeutic strategy to improve the impaired cardiac functioning caused by β-blocker, but the proposed approach can also be applied to other pharmacotherapeutics.

ACKNOWLEDGMENT

This work was supported by the National Research Foundation of Korea (NRF) grant funded by the Korea Ministry of Education, Science & Technology (MEST) through the BRL (Basic Research Laboratory) grant (2009-0086964), the Systems Biology grant (20090065567), and the Nuclear Research grant (M20708000001-07B0800-00110).

3A.1   APPENDIX

3A.1.1   Model Validation

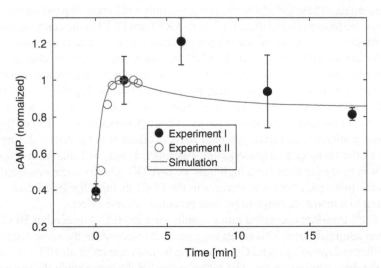

Figure 3A.1   The transient response of cAMP accumulation for Iso (isoproterenol) stimulation. The simulation result is consistent with previous experimental data (empty circle [29]; filled circle [30]).

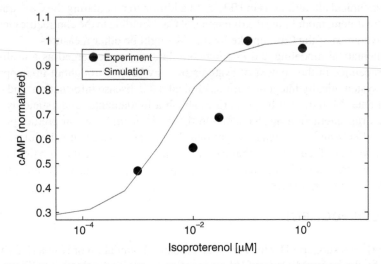

Figure 3A.2   The cAMP accumulation with respect to Iso. The simulation result is consistent with previous experimental data [30].

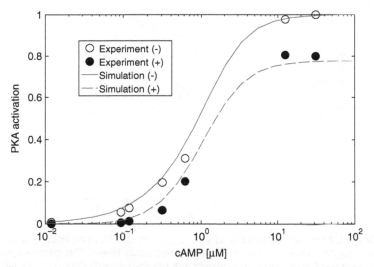

Figure 3A.3   The PKA activation with respect to cAMP with PKI (+)/without PKI (−). The simulation results are consistent with previous experimental data [31].

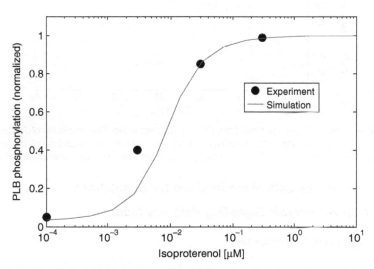

Figure 3A.4   The PLB phosphorylation with respect to Iso. The simulation result is consistent with previous experimental data [32].

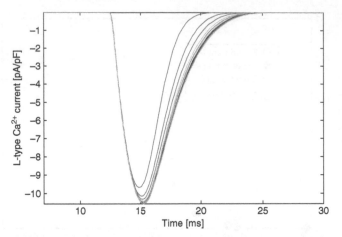

Figure 3A.5 L-type Ca^{2+} current (ICaL) with respect to Iso. The amplitude of ICaL gets increased along with Iso from 0 nM to 50 nM, and the half-decay time of ICaL becomes prolonged. This simulation result is qualitatively consistent with previous experimental data [33, 34].

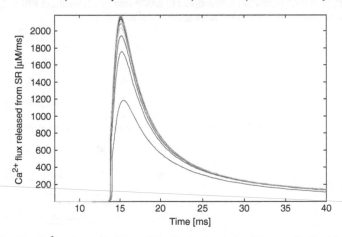

Figure 3A.6 The Ca^{2+} release (Jrel) from SR with respect to Iso. The amplitude of Jrel becomes dramatically increased along with Iso from 0 nM to 50 nM, and the half-decay time of Jrel becomes shortened. This simulation result is qualitatively consistent with previous experimental data [33].

3A.1.2 The Mathematical Model Used for Simulations

3A.1.2.1 β-Adrenergic Signaling Pathway Model

β-Adrenergic Receptor Module

$$\frac{d[\beta_1 AR_{\_p_1}]}{dt} = [LR_{\text{tot}}]\left(k_{a\_\beta ARK}[\beta_1 ARK^*] \right.$$

$$\left. - \frac{k_{d\_\beta ARK}[\beta_1 AR_{\_p_1}]}{k_{m\_\beta ARK} + [LR_{\text{tot}}]} \frac{k_{i\_\beta ARK}^3}{k_{i\_\beta ARK}^3 + [\beta_1 ARK^*]^3} \right), \quad (3A.1)$$

where $[\beta_1 ARK^*] = \dfrac{k_{i\_b_1 ARKI}[\beta_1 ARK]}{k_{i\_b_1 ARKI} + [\beta_1 ARKI]}.$

$$\frac{d[\beta_1 AR\_p_2]}{dt} = k_{PKA+}[PKAC_I][\beta_1 AR_{act}] - k_{PKA-}[\beta_1 AR\_p_2]. \qquad (3A.2)$$

$$[\beta_1 AR_{act}] = [\beta_1 AR] + [LR] + [LRG] + [RG] + [DR] + [DRG]. \qquad (3A.3)$$

$$[\beta_1 AR_{tot}] = [\beta_1 AR_{act}] + [\beta_1 AR\_p_1] + [\beta_1 AR\_p_2]. \qquad (3A.4)$$

$$[LR_{tot}] = [LR] + [LRG]. \qquad (3A.5)$$

$$[Gs_{tot}] = [RG] + [LRG] + [DRG] + [Gs_{\beta\gamma}] + [Gs]. \qquad (3A.6)$$

where $[RG] = [\beta_1 AR][G_S]/K_C$, $[LR] = [L][\beta_1 AR]/K_L$,
$[LRG] = [L][\beta_1 AR][G_S]/(K_L \cdot K_R)$, $[DR] = [Blocker][\beta_1 AR]/K_{DR}$,
$[DRG] = [Blocker][\beta_1 AR][G_S]/(K_{DR} \cdot K_R)$.

$[\beta_1 AR]$

$$= \frac{-(A_1 B_2 + B_3 - A_2 B_1) + \sqrt{(A_1 B_2 + B_3 - A_2 B_1)^2 + 4 B_1 B_3 A_2}}{2 B_1 B_3} \quad (3A.7)$$

where $A_1 = [Gs_{tot}] - [Gs_{\beta\gamma}]$, $A_2 = [\beta_1 AR_{tot}] - ([\beta_1 AR\_p_1] + [\beta_1 AR\_p_2])$,

$$B_1 = \frac{1}{K_C} + \frac{[L]}{K_L \cdot K_R} + \frac{[Blocker]}{K_{DR} \cdot K_R}, \quad B_2 = \frac{[L]}{K_L \cdot K_R} + \frac{1}{K_C} + \frac{[Blocker]}{K_{DR} \cdot K_R},$$

$$B_3 = 1 + \frac{[L]}{K_L} + \frac{[Blocker]}{K_{DR}}.$$

$$[Gs] = \frac{[Gs_{tot}] - [Gs_{\beta\gamma}]}{1 + [\beta_1 AR]\left(\frac{1}{K_C} + \frac{[L]}{K_L \cdot K_R} + \frac{[Blocker]}{K_{DR} \cdot K_R}\right)} \qquad (3A.8)$$

Parameter	Value	Unit	Reference	Parameter	Value	Unit	Reference
K_L	0.285	μM	[35]	k_{PKA-}	$0.62 k_{a\_PKA}$	s^{-1}	[35]
K_R	6.2e–2	μM	[36]	$k_{m\_\beta ARK}$	4.0e–4	μM	[36, 40]
K_C	33.0	μM	[35]	$k_{i\_\beta ARK}$	3.0	μM	[39, 40]
K_{DR}	4.1	nM	[38]	βARK	1.0	μM	[39, 40]
$k_{a\_\beta ARK}$	1.1e–3	μM^{-1} s^{-1}	[35]	Gs_{tot}	3.83	μM	[35]
$k_{d\_\beta ARK}$	$2 k_{a\_\beta ARK}$	s^{-1}	[35]	$\beta_1 AR_{tot}$	1.32e–2	μM	[35]
k_{PKA+}	3.6e–3	μM^{-1} s^{-1}	[35]	L	0~500	nM	[35]

Gs Activation Module

$$\frac{d[Gs_\alpha GTP_{tot}]}{dt} = k_{gact}([RG] + [LRG]) - k_{hyd}[Gs_\alpha GTP_{tot}]. \qquad (3A.9)$$

$$\frac{d[Gs_{\beta\gamma}]}{dt} = k_{\text{gact}} ([RG] + [LRG]) - k_{\text{reassoc}}[Gs_{\alpha}GDP][Gs_{\beta\gamma}] \qquad (3A.10)$$

$$\frac{d[Gs_{\alpha}GDP]}{dt} = k_{\text{hyd}}[Gs_{\alpha}GTP_{\text{tot}}] - k_{\text{reassoc}}[Gs_{\alpha}GDP][Gs_{\beta\gamma}] \qquad (3A.11)$$

where $[Gs_{\alpha}GTP_{\text{tot}}] = [Gs_{\alpha}GTP] + [Gs_{\alpha}GTP : AC]$, $[AC_{\text{tot}}] = [Gs_{\alpha}GTP/AC] + [AC]$, and $[Gs_{\alpha}GTP/AC] = [Gs_{\alpha}GTP][AC]/KGs_{\alpha}$.

$$[AC] = \frac{\begin{array}{c} KGs_{\alpha}[AC_{\text{tot}}] - (KGs_{\alpha}^2 + KGs_{\alpha}[Gs_{\alpha}GTP_{\text{tot}}]) \\ +\sqrt{ \left(KGs_{\alpha}^2 + KGs_{\alpha}[Gs_{\alpha}GTP_{\text{tot}}] - KGs_{\alpha}[AC_{\text{tot}}] \right)^2 + 4KGs_{\alpha}^3[AC_{\text{tot}}] } \end{array}}{2KGs_{\alpha}}$$

$$(3A.12)$$

Parameter	Value	Unit	Reference	Parameter	Value	Unit	Reference
k_{gact}	16	s^{-1}	[35]	KGs_{α}	0.315	μM	[35]
k_{hyd}	0.8	s^{-1}	[35]	AC_{tot}	0.0497	μM	[35]
k_{reassoc}	1.2e3	$\mu M^{-1} s^{-1}$	[35]				

cAMP Activation and PDE Modulation

$$\frac{d[cAMP_{\text{tot}}]}{dt} = \frac{k_{AC-\text{basal}}[AC][ATP]}{k_{m-\text{basal}} + [ATP]}$$
$$+ \frac{k_{AC-Gs_{\alpha}GTP}\Psi_{AC}[AC : Gs_{\alpha}GTP][ATP]}{k_{m-Gs_{\alpha}GTP} + [ATP]}$$
$$- \frac{k_{c-PDE}\Psi_{PDE}[cAMP][PDE]}{(k_{m-PDE} + [cAMP])\frac{k_{i-IBMX}+IBMX}{k_{i-IBMX}}} \qquad (3A.13)$$

$$\Psi_{PDE} = \frac{[Ca^{2+}]}{k_{m-PDE-Ca} + [Ca^{2+}]} + \frac{[PKAC_I]}{k_{m-PDE-PKA} + [PKAC_I]}. \qquad (3A.14)$$

$$\Psi_{AC} = 0.5\psi_{AC5} + 0.5\psi_{AC6}, \qquad (3A.15)$$

$$\psi_{AC5} = \frac{0.25k_{m-AC5-Ca-\text{high}}}{k_{m-AC5-Ca-\text{high}} + [Ca^{2+}]} + \frac{0.25k_{m-AC5-Ca-\text{low}}}{k_{m-AC5-Ca-\text{low}} + [Ca^{2+}]}$$
$$+ \frac{0.5k_{m-AC-PKA}}{k_{m-AC-PKA} + [PKAC_I]}, \qquad (3A.16)$$

$$\psi_{AC6} = \frac{0.25 k_{m-AC6-Ca-\text{high}}}{k_{m-AC6-Ca-\text{high}} + [Ca^{2+}]} + \frac{0.25 k_{m-AC6-Ca-\text{low}}}{k_{m-AC6-Ca-\text{low}} + [Ca^{2+}]}$$

$$+ \frac{0.5 k_{m-AC-PKA}}{k_{m-AC-PKA} + [PKAC_I]}. \tag{3A.17}$$

Parameter	Value	Unit	Reference	Parameter	Value	Unit	Reference
ATP	5.0e3	μM	[41]	$k_{AC-basal}$	0.2	s^{-1}	[35]
$k_{m-AC5-Ca-\text{high}}$	7.9e-2	μM	[41]	$k_{m-basal}$	1.03e3	μM	[35]
$k_{m-AC5-Ca-\text{low}}$	58.0	μM	[41]	$k_{AC-Gs_\alpha GTP}$	8.5	s^{-1}	[35]
$k_{m-AC6-Ca-\text{high}}$	0.15	μM	[41]	$k_{m-Gs_\alpha GTP}$	315.0	μM	[35]
$k_{m-AC5-Ca-\text{low}}$	60.0	μM	[41]	k_{c-PDE}	1.67	s^{-1}	[35]
$k_{m-AC-PKA}$	5.0e-2	μM	[42]	k_{m-PDE}	1.3	μM	[35]
$k_{m-PDE-PKA}$	3.0e-2	μM	[43]	k_{i-IBMX}	16.0	μM	[45]
$k_{m-PDE-Ca}$	8.01e-2	μM	[44]				

PKA Activation Module

$$[ARC_I] = \frac{[cAMP][RC_I]}{K_A}, \tag{3A.18}$$

$$[A2RC_I] = \frac{[cAMP]^2[RC_I]}{K_A K_B} = \frac{[PKAC_I][A2R_I]}{K_D}, \tag{3A.19}$$

$$[A2R_I] = \frac{K_D [cAMP]^2 [RC_I]}{K_A K_B [PKAC_I]}, \tag{3A.20}$$

$$[PKAC_I/PKI] = \frac{[PKAC_I][PKI_{tot}]}{K_{PKI} + [PKAC_I] + [PKAC_{II}]}, \tag{3A.21}$$

$$[PKA_{Itot}] = [RC_I] + \frac{[cAMP][RC_I]}{K_A} + \frac{[cAMP]^2[RC_I]}{K_A K_B}$$

$$+ \frac{K_D [cAMP]^2 [RC_I]}{K_A K_B [PKAC_I]}, \tag{3A.22}$$

$$[RC_I] = \frac{[PKA_{Itot}]}{1 + \frac{[cAMP]}{K_A} + \frac{[cAMP]^2}{K_A K_B} + \frac{K_D [cAMP]^2}{K_A K_B [PKAC_I]}}, \tag{3A.23}$$

$$[PKA_{Itot}] = [RC_I] + [ARC_I] + [A2RC_I] + [PKAC_I]$$

$$+ [PKAC_I/PKI], \tag{3A.24}$$

$$[PKAC_I] =$$

$$\frac{1}{2K_AK_B}\left\{-\left(K_AK_B[PKA_{\mathrm{Itot}}] + \frac{K_D[cAMP]^2}{C_1} - K_AK_B([PKA_{\mathrm{Itot}}] - [PKI_{\mathrm{tot}}])\right)\right.$$

$$\left. + \sqrt{\begin{aligned}&\left(K_AK_B[PKA_{\mathrm{Itot}}] + \tfrac{K_D[cAMP]^2}{C_1} - K_AK_B([PKA_{\mathrm{Itot}}] - [PKI_{\mathrm{tot}}])\right)^2 \\ &+4K_AK_B\left(\tfrac{K_D[cAMP]^2([PKA_{\mathrm{Itot}}]-[PKI_{\mathrm{tot}}])}{C_1}\right)\end{aligned}}\right\}, \quad (3A.25)$$

$$[PKAC_{II}] = \frac{1}{2K_AK_B}\left\{-\left(K_AK_B[PKA_{\mathrm{Itot}}] + \frac{K_D[cAMP]^2}{C_1} - K_AK_B[PKA_{\mathrm{IItot}}]\right)\right.$$

$$\left. + \sqrt{\begin{aligned}&\left(K_AK_B[PKA_{\mathrm{Itot}}] + \tfrac{K_D[cAMP]^2}{C_1} - K_AK_B[PKA_{\mathrm{IItot}}]\right)^2 \\ &+4K_AK_B\tfrac{K_D[cAMP]^2[PKA_{\mathrm{IItot}}]}{C_1}\end{aligned}}\right\}, \quad (3A.26)$$

Parameter	Value	Unit	Reference	Parameter	Value	Unit	Reference
K_A	9.14	μM	[35]	PKA_{Itot}	0.59	μM	[35]
K_B	1.64	μM	[35]	PKA_{IItot}	2.5e-2	μM	[35]
K_D	4.375	μM	[35]	PKI_{tot}	0.18	μM	[35]
K_{PKI}	2e-4	μM	[35]				

I1 and PP1 Module

$$\frac{d[I1^*]}{dt} = \frac{k_{c\_I1\_PKACI}[PKAC_I][I1]}{k_{m\_I1\_PKACI} + [I1]} - \frac{k_{c\_I1^*\_PP2A}[PP2A][I1^*]}{k_{m\_I1^*\_PP2A} + [I1^*]}$$

$$- \frac{k_{c\_I1^*\_CaN^*}[CaN^*][I1^*]}{k_{m\_I1^*\_CaN^*} + [I1^*]} - \frac{k_{c\_I1^*\_CaN^{**}}[CaN^{**}][I1^*]}{k_{m\_I1^*\_CaN^{**}} + [I1^*]},$$

$$-k_{a\_I1^*\_PP1}[I1^*][PP1] + k_{d\_I1^*\_PP1}[I1^*/PP1]. \quad (3A.27)$$

$$\frac{d[I1^*/PP1]}{dt} = k_{a\_I1^*\_PP1}[I1^*][PP1] - k_{d\_I1^*\_PP1}[I1^*/PP1]$$

$$- \frac{k_{c\_I1^*PP1\_PP2A}[PP2A][I1^*/PP1]}{k_{m\_I1^*PP1\_PP2A} + [I1^*/PP1]}$$

$$- \frac{k_{c\_I1^*PP1\_CaN^{**}}[CaN^{**}][I1^*/PP1]}{k_{m\_I1^*PP1\_CaN^{**}} + [I1^*/PP1]}, \quad (3A.28)$$

$$\frac{d[I1/PP1]}{dt} = \frac{k_{c\_I1^*PP1\_PP2A}[PP2A][I1^*/PP1]}{k_{m\_I1^*PP1\_PP2A} + [I1^*/PP1]}$$

$$+ \frac{k_{c\_I1^*PP1\_CaN^{**}}[CaN^{**}][I1^*/PP1]}{k_{m\_I1^*PP1\_CaN^{**}} + [I1^*/PP1]}$$

$$- k_{d\_I1PP1}[I1/PP1], \quad (3A.29)$$

$$[I1_{tot}] = [I1] + [I1^*] + [I1/PP1] + [I1^*/PP1], \tag{3A.30}$$

$$[PP1_{tot}] = [PP1] + [I1/PP1] + [I1^*/PP1], \tag{3A.31}$$

$$[CaN^*] = \frac{[CaN][Ca^{2+}]^{2.8}}{k_{m\_Ca\_CaN}^{2.8} + [Ca^{2+}]^{2.8}}, \tag{3A.32}$$

$$[CaN^{**}] = \frac{[CaN][Ca^{2+}]^{2.8}}{k_{m\_CaM\_CaN}^{2.8} + [Ca^{2+}]^{2.8}}, \tag{3A.33}$$

$$[CaN_{tot}] = [CaN] + [CaN^*] + [CaN^{**}]. \tag{3A.34}$$

Parameter	Value	Unit	Reference	Parameter	Value	Unit	Reference
$k_{c\_I1\_PKACI}$	7.5	$\mu M^{-1} s^{-1}$	[46]	$k_{m\_I1^*PP1\_PP2A}$	6	μM	[46]
$k_{m\_I1\_PKACI}$	9	μM	[46]	$k_{c\_I1^*PP1\_CaN^{**}}$	4.97	$\mu M^{-1} s^{-1}$	[46]
$k_{c\_I1^*\_PP2A}$	7.83	$\mu M^{-1} s^{-1}$	[46]	$k_{m\_I1^*PP1\_CaN^{**}}$	0.34	μM	[46]
$k_{m\_I1^*\_PP2A}$	6	μM	[46]	k_{d_I1PP1}	1	s^{-1}	[46]
$k_{c\_I1^*\_CaN^*}$	4.97	$\mu M^{-1} s^{-1}$	[46]	$k_{m\_Ca\_CaN}$	1.3	μM	[47]
$k_{m\_I1^*\_CaN^*}$	0.034	μM	[46]	$k_{m\_CaM\_CaN}$	0.6	μM	[47]
$k_{c\_I1^*\_CaN^{**}}$	4.97	$\mu M^{-1} s^{-1}$	[46]	$PP2A$	0.12	μM	[46]
$k_{m\_I1^*\_CaN^{**}}$	0.34	μM	[46]	CaN_{tot}	1	μM	[46]
$k_{a\_I1^*\_PP1}$	18.47e3	$\mu M^{-1} s^{-1}$	[46]	$I1_{tot}$	1.8	μM	[46]
$k_{d\_I1^*\_PP1}$	0.1	s^{-1}	[46]	$PP1_{tot}$	1.8	μM	[46]
$k_{c\_I1^*\_PP1\_PP2A}$	7.83	$\mu M^{-1} s^{-1}$	[46]				

PLB

$$[PLB]_{tot} = [PLB] + [PLBp]. \tag{3A.35}$$

$$[CaN]_{act} = [CaN^*] + [CaN^{**}]. \tag{3A.36}$$

$$\frac{d[PLBp]}{dt} = \frac{k_{c-PKA-PLB}NPKE_1[PLB]}{k_{m-PKA-PLB} + [PLB]}$$
$$- \frac{k_{c-PP1-PLB}([PP1] + [CaN^*])[PLBp]}{k_{m-PP1-PLB} + [PLBp]} \tag{3A.37}$$

where $NPKE_1 = \dfrac{PK_{tot\_1}}{k_{m-npke} + PK_{tot\_1}}$ and $PK_{tot\_1} = CaMKII_{act} + \dfrac{[PKAC_1]}{[PKA_{Itot}]}$.

Parameter	Value	Unit	References	Parameter	Value	Unit	References
$k_{c-PKA-PLB}$	54	s^{-1}	[35]	$k_{m-PP1-PLB}$	7.0	μM	[35]
$k_{m-PKA-PLB}$	21	μM	[35]	k_{m-npke}	0.4	–	Estimated
$k_{c-PP1-PLB}$	8.5	s^{-1}	[35]	PLB_{tot}	106	μM	[35]

CaMKII

$$\frac{dW_B}{dt} = k_{ib}[Ca^{2+}/CaM]W_I - k_{bi}W_B - V_A + k_{\text{dephos}}W_P, \tag{3A.38}$$

$$\frac{dW_P}{dt} = V_A - k_{pt}W_P + k_{tp}[Ca^{2+}]^4 W_T - k_{\text{dephos}}W_P, \tag{3A.39}$$

$$\frac{dW_T}{dt} = k_{pt}W_P - k_{tp}[Ca^{2+}]^4 W_T - k_{ta}W_T + k_{at}[CaM]W_A - k_{\text{dephos}}W_T, \tag{3A.40}$$

$$\frac{dW_A}{dt} = k_{ta}W_T - k_{at}[CaM]W_A - k_{\text{dephos}}W_A, \tag{3A.41}$$

$$W_I = 1 - (W_B + W_P + W_T + W_A), \tag{3A.42}$$

$$V_A = K_A W_{tot}\left((c_B W_B)^2 + (c_B W_B)(c_P W_P) + (c_B W_B)(c_T W_T) + (c_B W_B)(c_A W_A)\right) \tag{3A.43}$$

where $T_w = W_B + W_P + W_T + W_A$ and $K_A = K'_A \left(a \cdot T_w + b \cdot T_w^2 + c \cdot T_w^3\right)$,

$$[Ca^{2+}/CaM] = \frac{[Ca^{2+}]_i^{h\_cmk}}{k_{m\_CaCaM}^{h\_cmk} + [Ca^{2+}]_i^{h\_cmk}}, \tag{3A.44}$$

$$CaMKII_{\text{act}} = c_A W_A + c_P W_P + c_T W_T + c_A W_A. \tag{3A.45}$$

Parameter	Value	Unit	Reference	Parameter	Value	Unit	Reference
k_{ib}	10e-3	μM^{-1} ms^{-1}	[48]	h_cmk	5.0	–	[48]
k_{bi}	0.8e-3	ms^{-1}	[48]	a	0.22	–	[48]
k_{pt}	1e-3	ms^{-1}	[48]	b	1.83	–	[48]
k_{tp}	1e-3	μM^{-1} ms^{-1}	[48]	c	0.8	–	[48]
k_{ta}	0.8e-6	ms^{-1}	[48]	c_B	0.75	–	[48]
k_{at}	10e-3	μM^{-1} ms^{-1}	[48]	c_P	1.0	–	[48]
k_a^p	5.8e-2	ms^{-1}	[48]	c_T	0.8	–	[48]
k_{m_CaCaM}	0.55	μM^{-1} ms^{-1}	[49]	c_A	0.8	–	[48]
k_{dephos}	5.0e-4	ms^{-1}	Estimated				

3A.1.2.2   Cardiac Myocyte Physiological Model

Membrane Potential

$$-C_m \frac{dV}{dt} = I_{CaL} + I_{p(Ca)} + I_{NaCa} + I_{Cab} + I_{Na} + I_{Nab} + I_{NaK} + I_{Kto,f}$$
$$+ I_{Kto,s} + I_{K1} + I_{Ks} + I_{Kur} + I_{Kss} + I_{Kr} + I_{Cl,Ca} + I_{\text{stim}} \quad (3A.46)$$

Calcium Dynamics

$$\frac{d[Ca^{2+}]_i}{dt} = B_i \left\{ J_{\text{leak}} + J_{\text{xfer}} - J_{\text{up}} - J_{\text{trpn}} - (I_{Cab} - 2I_{NaCa} + I_{p(Ca)}) \frac{A_{cap} C_m}{2 V_{myo} F} \right\},$$
$$(3A.47)$$

$$\frac{d[Ca^{2+}]_{ss}}{dt} = B_{ss} \left\{ J_{rel} \frac{V_{JSR}}{V_{SS}} - J_{xfer} \frac{V_{myo}}{V_{SS}} - I_{CaL} \frac{A_{cap} C_m}{2 \cdot V_{myo} F} \right\}, \quad (3A.48)$$

$$\frac{d[Ca^{2+}]_{JSR}}{dt} = B_{JSR}(J_{tr} - J_{rel}), \quad (3A.49)$$

$$\frac{d[Ca^{2+}]_{NSR}}{dt} = (J_{\text{up}} - J_{\text{leak}}) \frac{V_{myo}}{V_{NSR}} - J_{tr} \frac{V_{JSR}}{V_{NSR}}, \quad (3A.50)$$

$$B_i = \left\{ 1 + \frac{[CMDN]_{tot} K_m^{CMDN}}{\left(K_m^{CMDN} + [Ca^{2+}]_i \right)^2} \right\}^{-1}, \quad (3A.51)$$

$$B_{ss} = \left\{ 1 + \frac{[CMDN]_{tot} K_m^{CMDN}}{\left(K_m^{CMDN} + [Ca^{2+}]_{ss} \right)^2} \right\}^{-1}, \quad (3A.52)$$

$$B_{JSR} = \left\{ 1 + \frac{[CSQN]_{tot} K_m^{CSQN}}{\left(K_m^{CSQN} + [Ca^{2+}]_{JSR} \right)^2} \right\}^{-1}. \quad (3A.53)$$

$$J_{\text{rel}} = v_1 (P_{O1} + P_{O2})([Ca^{2+}]_{JSR} - [Ca^{2+}]_{SS}) P_{RyR}, \quad (3A.54)$$

$$J_{\text{tr}} = \frac{[Ca^{2+}]_{NSR} - [Ca^{2+}]_{JSR}}{\tau_{tr}}, \quad (3A.55)$$

$$J_{\text{xfer}} = \frac{[Ca^{2+}]_{ss} - [Ca^{2+}]_i}{\tau_{xfer}}, \quad (3A.56)$$

$$J_{\text{leak}} = v_2([Ca^{2+}]_{NSR} - [Ca^{2+}]_i), \tag{3A.57}$$

$$J_{\text{up}} = \frac{v_3(1 + A_{CMK})[Ca^{2+}]_i^2}{[Ca^{2+}]_i^2 + (K_{m,up}(1 - K_{plb}))^2} \tag{3A.58}$$

where $A_{CMK} = \dfrac{P_{\text{max}-CaMKII}\,CaMKII_{act}}{k_{m-\text{ser}38} + CaMKII_{act}}$ and $K_{plb} = \dfrac{P_{\text{max}-PLB}[PLBp]}{k_{m-PLBp} + [PLBp]}.$

Parameter	Value	Unit	Reference	Parameter	Value	Unit	Reference
C_m	1.0	μF/cm^2	[50]	τ_{tr}	20.0	ms	[50]
A_{cap}	1.534e-4	cm^2	[50]	τ_{xfer}	8.0	ms	[50]
V_{myo}	25.84e-6	μl	[50]	$K_{m,up}$	0.5	μM	[50]
V_{JSR}	0.12e-6	μl	[50]	k_{m-PLBp}	40	μM	Estimated
V_{NSR}	2.098e-6	μl	[50]	$k_{m-\text{ser}38}$	0.3	–	Estimated
V_{SS}	1.485e-6	μl	[50]	$P_{\text{max}-PLB}$	0.5	–	Estimated
$[K_+]_0$	5400	μM	[50]	$P_{\text{max}-CaMKII}$	0.75	–	Estimated
$[Na^+]_0$	140,000	μM	[50]	v_1	4.5	ms^{-1}	[50]
$[Ca^{2+}]_0$	1,800	μM	[50]	v_2	1.74e-5	ms^{-1}	[50]
K_m^{CMDN}	0.238	μM	[50]	v_3	0.45	μM ms^{-1}	[50]
K_m^{CSQN}	800	μM	[50]				

$$J_{trpn} = k_{ht}^+[Ca^{2+}]_i([HT]_{tot} - [HTCa]) - k_{ht}^-[HTCa] + k_{lt}^+[Ca^{2+}]_i([LT]_{tot}$$
$$-[LTCa]) - k_{lt}^-[LTCa], \tag{3A.59}$$

$$\frac{dP_{RyR}}{dt} = -0.2NPKE_2\left(0.4P_{RyR} + \frac{I_{CaL}}{I_{CaL,\text{max}}}e^{-(V-5.0)^2/648.0}\right), \tag{3A.60}$$

$$\frac{d[HTCa]}{dt} = k_{ht}^+[Ca^{2+}]_i([HT]_{tot} - [HTCa]) - k_{ht}^-[HTCa], \tag{3A.61}$$

$$\frac{d[LTCa]}{dt} = k_{lt}^+[Ca^{2+}]_i([LT]_{tot} - [LTCa]) - k_{lt}^-[LTCa], \tag{3A.62}$$

where $NPKE_2 = \dfrac{PK_{\text{tot}\_2}}{k_{m-npke} + PK_{\text{tot}\_2}}$ and $PK_{\text{tot}\_2} = CaMKII_{act} + \dfrac{[PKAC_{II}]}{[PKA_{IItot}]}.$

$$P_{C_1} = 1 - (P_{C_2} + P_{O_1} + P_{O_2}), \tag{3A.63}$$

$$\frac{dP_{O_1}}{dt} = k_a^+[Ca^{2+}]_{ss}^n P_{C_1} - k_a^- P_{O_1} - k_b^+[Ca^{2+}]_{ss}^m P_{O_1} + k_b^- P_{O_2} - k_c^+ P_{O_1} + k_c^- P_{C_2}, \tag{3A.64}$$

$$\frac{dP_{O_2}}{dt} = k_b^+[Ca^{2+}]_{ss}^m P_{O_1} - k_b^- P_{O_2}, \tag{3A.65}$$

$$\frac{\mathrm{d}P_{C_2}}{\mathrm{d}t} = k_c^+ P_{O_1} - k_c^- P_{C_2},$$ (3A.66)

$$I_{CaL} = G_{CaL}\, O(V - E_{Ca,L}),$$ (3A.67)

$$\frac{\mathrm{d}O}{\mathrm{d}t} = \alpha C_4 - 4\beta O + K_{pcb}I_1 - \gamma O + 0.001(\alpha I_2 - K_{pcf}O),$$ (3A.68)

$$C_1 = 1 - (O + C_2 + C_3 + C_4 + I_1 + I_2 + I_3),$$ (3A.69)

$$\frac{\mathrm{d}C_2}{\mathrm{d}t} = 4\alpha C_1 - \beta C_2 + 2\beta C_3 - 3\alpha C_2,$$ (3A.70)

$$\frac{\mathrm{d}C_3}{\mathrm{d}t} = 3\alpha C_2 - 2\beta C_3 + 3\beta C_4 - 2\alpha C_3,$$ (3A.71)

$$\frac{\mathrm{d}C_4}{\mathrm{d}t} = 2\alpha C_3 - 3\beta C_4 + 4\beta O - \alpha C_4 + 0.01(4\beta K_{pcb}I_1 - \alpha\gamma C_4)$$
$$+ 0.002(4\beta I_2 - K_{pcf}C_4) + 4\beta K_{pcb}I_3 - \gamma K_{pcf}C_4,$$ (3A.72)

$$\frac{\mathrm{d}I_1}{\mathrm{d}t} = \gamma O - K_{pcb}I_1 + 0.001(\alpha I_3 - K_{pcf}I_1) + 0.01(\alpha\gamma C_4 - 4\beta K_{pcb}I_1),$$ (3A.73)

$$\frac{\mathrm{d}I_2}{\mathrm{d}t} = 0.001(K_{pcf}O - \alpha I_2) + K_{pcb}I_3 - \gamma I_2 + 0.002(K_{pcf}C_4 - 4\beta I_2),$$ (3A.74)

$$\frac{\mathrm{d}I_3}{\mathrm{d}t} = 0.001(K_{pcf}I_1 - \alpha I_3) + \gamma I_2 - K_{pcb}I_3 + \gamma K_{pcf}C_4 - 4\beta K_{pcb}I_3,$$ (3A.75)

$$\alpha(V_p) = \frac{0.4(0.1V_p + 1.2)\left[1 + 0.7e^{-0.1(V_p+40.0)^2} - 0.75e^{-0.0025(V_p+20.0)^2}\right]}{1 + 0.12e^{0.1(V_p+12.0)}},$$
(3A.76)

$$\beta(V_p) = 0.05e^{-0.0769(V_p+12.0)},$$ (3A.77)

$$K_{pcf} = 13.0\left(1 - e^{(-0.01(V_p+14.5)^2)}\right),$$ (3A.78)

$$\gamma = \frac{K_{pc,\max}[Ca^{2+}]_{ss}}{K_{pc,\mathrm{half}} + [Ca^{2+}]_{ss}} \quad \text{where} \quad V_p = V + 10NPKE_2.$$ (3A.79)

Parameter	Value	Unit	Reference	Parameter	Value	Unit	Reference
k_{ht}^+	2.37e–3	$\mu M^{-1} ms^{-1}$	[50]	k_c^-	0.8e–3	Ms^{-1}	[50]
k_{ht}^-	3.2e–5	Ms^{-1}	[50]	n	4.0	–	[50]
k_{lt}^+	3.27e–2	$\mu M^{-1} ms^{-1}$	[50]	m	3.0	–	[50]
k_{lt}^-	1.96e–2	ms^{-1}	[50]	G_{CaL}	0.173	$mS/\mu F$	[50]
k_a^+	6.08e–3	$\mu M^{-4} ms^{-1}$	[50]	$E_{Ca,L}$	63.0	mV	[50]
k_a^-	7.13e–2	Ms^{-1}	[50]	K_{pcb}	0.5e–3	Ms^{-1}	[50]
k_b^+	4.05e–3	$\mu M^{-3} ms^{-1}$	[50]	$K_{pc,max}$	0.23	ms^{-1}	[50]
k_b^-	0.965	Ms^{-1}	[50]	$K_{pc,half}$	20.0	μM	[50]
k_c^+	0.9e–2	Ms^{-1}	[50]	$I_{CaL,max}$	7.0	pA/pF	[50]

$$I_{p(Ca)} = I_{p(Ca)}^{max} \frac{[Ca^{2+}]_i^2}{K_{m,p(Ca)}^2 + [Ca^{2+}]_i^2}. \tag{3A.80}$$

$$I_{NaCa} = k_{NaCa} \frac{1}{K_{m,Na}^3 + [Na^+]_o^3} \frac{1}{K_{m,Ca} + [Ca^{2+}]_o} \frac{1}{1 + k_{sat} e^{(\eta-1)VF/RT}}$$
$$\left(e^{\eta VF/RT} [Na^+]_i^3 [Ca^{2+}]_o - e^{(\eta-1)VF/RT} [Na^+]_O^3 [Ca^{2+}]_i \right) \tag{3A.81}$$

$$I_{Cab} = G_{Cab}(V - E_{CaN}), \tag{3A.82}$$

$$E_{CaN} = \frac{RT}{2F} \ln \left(\frac{[Ca^{2+}]_o}{[Ca^{2+}]_i} \right). \tag{3A.83}$$

Parameter	Value	Unit	Reference	Parameter	Value	Unit	Reference
k_{sat}	0.1	–	[50]	T	298	K	[50]
k_{NaCa}	2.93e2	$pA\,pF^{-1}$	[50]	$I_{p(Ca)}^{max}$	1.0	$pA\,pF^{-1}$	[50]
η	0.35	–	[50]	$K_{m,p(Ca)}$	0.5	μM	[50]
G_{Cab}	3.67e–4	$mS\,\mu F^{-1}$	[50]	$K_{m,Ca}$	1.38e3	μM	[50]
F	96.5	$C\,mmol^{-1}$	[50]	$K_{m,Na}$	8.75e4	μM	[50]
R	8.31	$J\,mol^{-1}\,K^{-1}$	[50]				

Na⁺ Dynamics

$$\frac{d[Na^+]_i}{dt} = -(I_{Na} + I_{Nab} + 3I_{NaCa} + 3I_{NaK}) \frac{A_{cap} C_m}{V_{myo} F}, \tag{3A.84}$$

$$I_{Na} = G_{Na} O_{Na}(V - E_{Na}), \tag{3A.85}$$

$$E_{Na} = \frac{RT}{F} \ln \left(\frac{0.9[Na^+]_o + 0.1[K^+]_o}{0.9[Na^+]_i + 0.1[K^+]_i} \right), \tag{3A.86}$$

$$C_{Na3} = 1 - (O_{Na} + C_{Na1} + C_{Na2} + IF_{Na} + I1_{Na} + I2_{Na} + IC_{Na2} + IC_{Na3}),$$

$$(3A.87)$$

$$\frac{dC_{Na2}}{dt} = \alpha_{NaI1} C_{Na3} - \beta_{NaI1} C_{Na2} + \beta_{NaI2} C_{Na1} - \alpha_{NaI2} C_{Na2} + \alpha_{NaI3} IC_{Na2}$$

$$-\beta_{Na3} C_{Na2}, \qquad (3A.88)$$

$$\frac{dC_{Na1}}{dt} = \alpha_{NaI2} C_{Na2} - \beta_{NaI2} C_{Na1} + \beta_{NaI3} O_{Na} - \alpha_{NaI3} C_{Na1} + \alpha_{NaI3} IF_{Na}$$

$$-\beta_{Na3} C_{Na1}, \qquad (3A.89)$$

$$\frac{dO_{Na}}{dt} = \alpha_{NaI3} C_{Na1} - \beta_{NaI3} O_{Na} + \beta_{Na2} IF_{Na} - \alpha_{Na2} O_{Na}, \qquad (3A.90)$$

$$\frac{dIF_{Na}}{dt} = \alpha_{Na2} O_{Na} - \beta_{Na2} IF_{Na} + \beta_{Na3} C_{Na1} - \alpha_{Na3} IF_{Na} + \beta_{Na4} I1_{Na}$$

$$-\alpha_{Na4} IF_{Na} + \alpha_{NaI2} IC_{Na2} - \beta_{NaI2} IF_{Na}, \qquad (3A.91)$$

$$\frac{dI1_{Na}}{dt} = \alpha_{Na4} IF_{Na} - \beta_{Na4} I1_{Na} + \beta_{Na5} I2_{Na1} - \alpha_{Na5} I1_{Na}, \qquad (3A.92)$$

$$\frac{dI2_{Na}}{dt} = \alpha_{Na5} I1_{Na} - \beta_{Na5} I2_{Na}, \qquad (3A.93)$$

$$\frac{dIC_{Na2}}{dt} = \alpha_{NaI1} IC_{Na3} - \beta_{NaI1} IC_{Na2} + \beta_{NaI2} IF_{Na} - \alpha_{NaI2} IC_{Na2} + \beta_{Na3} C_{Na2}$$

$$-\alpha_{Na3} IC_{Na2}, \qquad (3A.94)$$

$$\frac{dIC_{Na3}}{dt} = \beta_{NaI1} IC_{Na2} - \alpha_{NaI1} IC_{Na3} - \beta_{Na3} C_{Na3} - \alpha_{Na3} IC_{Na3}, \qquad (3A.95)$$

where

$$\alpha_{NaI1} = \frac{3.802}{0.1027 e^{-(V+2.5)/17.0} + 0.2 e^{-(V+2.5)/150.0}},$$

$$\alpha_{NaI2} = \frac{3.802}{0.1027 e^{-(V+2.5)/15.0} + 0.23 e^{-(V+2.5)/150.0}},$$

$$\alpha_{NaI3} = \frac{3.802}{0.1027 e^{-(V+2.5)/12.0} + 0.25 e^{-(V+2.5)/150.0}},$$

$$\beta_{NaI1} = 0.1917e^{-(V+2.5)/20.3},$$

$$\beta_{NaI2} = 0.2e^{-(V-2.5)/20.3}, \ \beta_{NaI3} = 0.22e^{-(V-7.5)/20.3},$$

$$\alpha_{Na3} = 7.0 \times 10^{-7}e^{-(V+7.0)/7.7}, \ \beta_{Na3} = 0.0084 + 0.00002(V+7.0),$$

$$\alpha_{Na2} = \frac{1.0}{0.188495e^{-(V+7.0)/16.6} + 0.393956}, \ \beta_{Na2} = \frac{\alpha_{NaI3} \cdot \alpha_{NaI3} \cdot \alpha_{Na3}}{\beta_{NaI3} \cdot \beta_{Na3}},$$

$$\alpha_{Na4} = \frac{\alpha_{Na2}}{1000}, \ \beta_{Na4} = \alpha_{Na3}, \alpha_{Na5} = \frac{\alpha_{Na2}}{95000}, \ \text{and} \ \ \beta_{Na5} = \frac{\alpha_{Na3}}{50}.$$

$$I_{Nab} = G_{Nab}(V - E_{Na}). \tag{3A.96}$$

Parameter	Value	Unit	Reference	Parameter	Value	Unit	Reference
G_{Na}	13.0	mS μF^{-1}	[50]	G_{Nab}	0.0026	mS μF^{-1}	[50]

K⁺ Dynamics

$$\frac{d[K^+]_i}{dt} = -(I_{Kto,f} + I_{Kto,s} + I_{K1} + I_{Ks} + I_{Kss} + I_{Kur} + I_{Kr} - 2I_{NaK})\frac{A_{cap}C_m}{V_{myo}F}. \tag{3A.97}$$

$$I_{Kto,f} = G_{Kto,f}a_{to,f}^3 i_{to,f}(V - E_K), \tag{3A.98}$$

$$E_K = \frac{RT}{F}\ln\left(\frac{[K^+]_O}{[K^+]_i}\right), \tag{3A.99}$$

$$\frac{da_{to,f}}{dt} = \alpha_a(1 - a_{to,f}) - \beta_a a_{to,f}, \tag{3A.100}$$

$$\frac{di_{to,f}}{dt} = \alpha_i(1 - i_{to,f}) - \beta_i i_{to,f} \tag{3A.101}$$

where $\alpha_a = 0.18064e^{0.03577(V+30.0)}$, $\beta_a = 0.3956e^{-0.06237(V+30.0)}$,

$$\alpha_i = \frac{0.000152e^{-(V+13.5)/7.0}}{0.067083e^{-(V+33.5)/7.0} + 1}, \ \ \text{and} \ \ \beta_i = \frac{0.00095e^{(V+33.5)/7.0}}{0.051335e^{(V+33.5)/7.0} + 1}.$$

$$I_{Kto,s} = G_{Kto,s}a_{to,s}i_{to,s}(V - E_K), \tag{3A.102}$$

$$\frac{da_{to,s}}{dt} = \frac{a_{ss} - a_{to,s}}{\tau_{ta,s}}, \tag{3A.103}$$

$$\frac{di_{to,s}}{dt} = \frac{i_{ss} - i_{to,s}}{\tau_{ti,s}} \tag{3A.104}$$

where $a_{ss} = \dfrac{1}{1 + e^{-(V+22.5)/7.7}}$, $i_{ss} = \dfrac{1}{1 + e^{-(V+45.2)/5.7}}$,

$\tau_{ta,s} = 0.493e^{-0.0629V} + 2.058$ and $\tau_{ti,s} = 270 + \dfrac{1050}{1 + e^{(V+45.2)/5.7}}$.

$$I_{K1} = 0.2938 \left(\frac{[K^+]_o}{210 + [K^+]_o} \right) \left[\frac{V - E_K}{1 + e^{0.0896(V - E_K)}} \right]. \qquad (3A.105)$$

$$I_{Ks} = G_{Ks}n_{Ks}^2(V - E_K), \qquad (3A.106)$$

$$\frac{dn_{Ks}}{dt} = \alpha_n(1 - n_{Ks}) - \beta_n n_{Ks} \qquad (3A.107)$$

where $\alpha_n = \dfrac{0.00000481333(V + 26.5)}{1 + e^{-0.128(V+26.5)}}$ and $\beta_n = 0.0000953333e^{-0.038(V+26.5)}$.

$$I_{Kur} = G_{Kur}a_{ur}i_{ur}(V - E_K), \qquad (3A.108)$$

$$\frac{da_{ur}}{dt} = \frac{a_{ss} - a_{ur}}{\tau_{aur}}, \qquad (3A.109)$$

$$\frac{di_{ur}}{dt} = \frac{i_{ss} - i_{ur}}{\tau_{iur}}, \qquad (3A.110)$$

where $\tau_{aur} = 0.493e^{-0.0629V} + 2.058$ and $\tau_{iur} = 12000 - \dfrac{170}{1 + e^{(V+45.2)/5.7}}$.

$$I_{Kss} = G_{Kss}a_{Kss}i_{Kss}(V - E_K), \qquad (3A.111)$$

$$\frac{da_{Kss}}{dt} = \frac{a_{ss} - a_{Kss}}{\tau_{Kss}}, \qquad (3A.112)$$

$$\frac{di_{Kss}}{dt} = 0 \qquad (3A.113)$$

where $\tau_{Kss} = 39.3e^{-0.0862V} + 13.17$.

$$I_{Kr} = O_kG_{Kr} \left[V - \frac{RT}{F}\ln\left(\frac{0.98[K^+]_O + 0.02[Na^+]_O}{0.98[K^+]_i + 0.02[Na^+]_i} \right) \right], \qquad (3A.114)$$

$$C_{K0} = 1 - (C_{K1} + C_{K2} + O_K + I_K), \qquad (3A.115)$$

$$\frac{dC_{K1}}{dt} = \alpha_{a0}C_{K0} - \beta_{a0}C_{K1} + k_bC_{K2} - k_fC_{K1}, \qquad (3A.116)$$

$$\frac{dC_{K2}}{dt} = k_fC_{K1} - k_bC_{K2} + \beta_{a1}O_k - \alpha_{a1}C_{K2}, \qquad (3A.117)$$

$$\frac{dO_k}{dt} = \alpha_{a1}C_{K2} - \beta_{a1}O_k + \beta_iI_K - \alpha_kO_K, \qquad (3A.118)$$

$$\frac{dI_k}{dt} = \alpha_i O_K - \beta_i I_K, \tag{3A.119}$$

where $\alpha_{a0} = 0.022348e^{0.01176V}$, $\beta_{a0} = 0.047002e^{-0.0631V}$,

$\alpha_{a1} = 0.013733e^{0.038198V}$, $\beta_{a1} = 0.0000689e^{-0.04178V}$,

$\alpha_i = 0.090821e^{0.02339(V+5.0)}$,   and $\beta_i = 0.006497e^{-0.03268(V+5.0)}$.

$$I_{NaK} = I_{NaK}^{max} f_{NaK} \frac{1}{1 + (K_{m,Nai}/[Na^+]_i)^{3/2}} \frac{[K^+]_o}{K_{m,Ko} + [K^+]_o} \tag{3A.120}$$

where $f_{NaK} = \dfrac{1}{1 + 0.1245e^{-0.1VF/RT} + 0.0365\sigma e^{-VF/RT}}$ and

$\sigma = \dfrac{1}{7}(e^{[Na^+]_o/67300} - 1).$

Cl⁻ Dynamics

$$I_{Cl,Ca} = G_{Cl,Ca} O_{Cl,Ca} \frac{[Ca^{2+}]_i}{K_{m,Cl} + [Ca^{2+}]_i} (V - E_{Cl}), \tag{3A.121}$$

where $O_{Cl,Ca} = \dfrac{0.2}{1 + e^{-(V-46.7)/7.8}}.$

Parameter	Value	Unit	Reference	Parameter	Value	Unit	Reference
$G_{Kto,f}$	0.47	mS μF^{-1}	[50]	G_{Kr}	7.8e–2	mS μF^{-1}	[50]
$G_{Kto,f}$	7.98e–2	mS μF^{-1}	[50]	I_{NaK}^{max}	2.38e–2	pA pF^{-1}	[50]
G_{Ks}	5.75e–3	mS μF^{-1}	[50]	$G_{Cl,Ca}$	3.67e–2	mS μF^{-1}	[50]
$G_{Kto,s}$	0.0	mS μF^{-1}	[50]	E_{Cl}	−40.0	mV	[50]
G_{Kur}	0.16	mS μF^{-1}	[50]	$K_{m,Cl}$	10.0	μM	[50]
G_{Kss}	0.05	mS μF^{-1}	[50]	$K_{m,Nai}$	2.1e4	μM	[50]
$G_{Kto,s}$	6.9e–2	mS μF^{-1}	[50]	$K_{m,Ko}$	1.5e3	μM	[50]
G_{Kur}	9.5e–2	mS μF^{-1}	[50]	k_f	2.38e–2	ms^{-1}	[50]
G_{Kss}	3.4e–2	mS μF^{-1}	[50]	k_b	3.68e–2	ms^{-1}	[50]

Initial Values

Variable	Control (Iso 50 nM)	HFC-1	HFC-2	HFC-3	Unit
V	−81.58	−81.71	−81.61	−81.74	mV
C_{Na2}	2.17e–2	2.16e–2	2.12e–2	2.15e–2	–
C_{Nal}	3.22e–4	3.15e–4	3.2e–4	3.13e–4	–
O_{Na}	9.19e–7	8.85e–7	9.1e–7	8.75e–7	–
IF_{Na}	1.97e–4	1.9e–4	1.95e–4	1.88e–4	–
$I1_{Na}$	1.13e–6	1.03e–6	1.08e–6	1.15e–6	–
$I2_{Na}$	4.59e–6	3.3e–6	3.41e–6	9.03e–6	–
IC_{Na2}	1.33e–2	1.3e–2	1.32e–2	1.29e–2	–
IC_{Na3}	0.367	0.36	0.37	0.36	–

O	1.2e–12	2.62e–13	2.99e–13	5.54e–13	–
C_2	3.55e–4	1.43e–4	1.6e–4	2.14e–4	–
C_3	7.37e–8	7.75e–9	9.66e–9	1.75e–8	–
C_4	1.76e–8	2.62e–11	3.62e–11	2.12e–10	–
I_1	2.73e–8	2.19e–8	2.27e–8	3.12e–8	–
I_2	4.93e–7	2.71e–10	4.22e–10	3.54e–9	–
I_3	2.44e–5	3.72e–8	5.14e-8	3.02e–7	–
$a_{to,f}$	2.88e–3	2.85e–3	2.87e–3	2.84e–3	–
$i_{to,f}$	1.0	1.0	1.0	1.0	–
$a_{to,s}$	4.66e–4	4.58e–4	4.63e–4	4.56e–4	–
$i_{to,s}$	0.98	0.98	0.98	0.97	–
n_{Ks}	8.31e–4	7.62e–4	7.72e–4	1.07e–3	–
a_{ur}	4.66e–4	4.58e–4	4.63e–4	4.56e–4	–
i_{ur}	1.0	1.0	1.0	1.0	–
a_{Kss}	0.73	0.75	0.74	0.77	–
i_{Kss}	1.0	1.0	1.0	1.0	–
C_{K1}	1.057e–3	1.047e–3	1.054e–3	1.04e–3	–
C_{K2}	6.88e–4	6.8e–4	6.84e–4	6.84e–4	–
O_k	2.85e–4	2.55e–4	2.6e–4	3.63e–4	–
I_k	5.47e–5	4.86e–5	4.97e–5	6.93e–5	–
$[Na^{2+}]_i$	1.67e4	1.66e4	1.66e4	1.71e4	μM
$[K^+]_i$	1.36e5	1.36e5	1.36e5	1.35e5	μM
$[Ca^{2+}]_i$	9.65e–2	0.11	0.1	0.1	μM
$[Ca^{2+}]_{ss}$	9.65e–2	0.11	0.1	0.1	μM
$[Ca^{2+}]_{JSR}$	3.11e3	1.47e3	1.64e3	1.16e3	μM
$[Ca^{2+}]_{NSR}$	3.11e3	1.47e3	1.64e3	1.16e3	μM
$[HTC_a]$	128.60	127.84	127.87	128.31	μM
$[LTC_a]$	9.7	10.62	10.258	10.08	μM
P_{O_1}	1.94e–3	1.47e–3	1.5c–3	1.44e–3	–
P_{O_2}	7.32e–9	7.59e–9	6.8e–9	6.14e–9	–
P_{C_2}	0.19	0.15	0.15	0.14	–
P_{RyR}	2.34e–16	2.8e–17	0	7.42e–17	–
W_B	4.54e–2	2.44e–2	2.9e–2	3.54e–2	–
W_P	1.21e–2	3.46e–4	6.77e–4	1.46e–3	–
W_T	3.21e–2	9.66e–4	1.91e–3	4.072e–3	–
W_A	5.13e–8	1.54e–9	3.05e–9	6.51e–9	–
$[\beta_1AR\_p_1]$	3.49e–3	8.7e–3	2.81e–3	4.21e–3	μM
$[\beta_1AR\_p_2]$	2.77e–3	4.37e–4	5.8e–4	1.28e–3	μM
$[Gs_\alpha GTP_{tot}]$	0.13	4.96e–2	5.79c–2	9.06e–2	μM
$[Gs_{\beta\gamma}]$	1.33e–3	2.41e–4	2.99e–4	6.25e–4	μM
$[Gs_\alpha GDP]$	6.28e–2	0.14	0.13	9.67e–2	μM
$[cAMP_{tot}]$	1.82	0.59	0.67	0.93	μM
$[I1^*]$	1.75e–5	6.32e–6	7.54e–6	1.06e–5	μM
$[I1^*:PP1]$	0.92	0.5	0.57	0.71	μM
$[I1:PP1]$	0.14	8.99e–2	9.97e–2	0.12	μM
$[PLBp]$	101.82	5.11	14.68	87.5	μM

REFERENCES

1. H. Tachibana, S. V. Naga Prasad, R. J. Lefkowitz, W. J. Koch, and H. A. Rockman. Level of beta-adrenergic receptor kinase 1 inhibition determines degree of cardiac dysfunction after chronic pressure overload-induced heart failure. *Circulation*, 111: 591–597, 2005.

2. M. J. Lohse, S. Engelhardt, and T. Eschenhagen. What is the role of beta-adrenergic signaling in heart failure? *Circ. Res.*, 93:896–906, 2003.

3. M. R. Bristow. Beta-adrenergic receptor blockade in chronic heart failure. *Circulation*, 101:558–569, 2000.

4. J. R. Keys and W. J. Koch. The adrenergic pathway and heart failure. *Recent Prog. Horm. Res.*, 59:13–30, 2004.

5. D. G. Tilley and H. A. Rockman. Role of beta-adrenergic receptor signaling and desensitization in heart failure: new concepts and prospects for treatment. *Expert Rev. Cardiovasc. Ther.*, 4:417–432, 2006.

6. M. R. Bristow, S. F. Shakar, J. V. Linseman, and B. D. Lowes. Inotropes and beta-blockers: is there a need for new guidelines? *J. Card. Fail.*, 7:8–12, 2001.

7. V. E. Bondarenko, G. P. Szigeti, G. C. Bett, S. J. Kim, and R. L. Rasmusson. Computer model of action potential of mouse ventricular myocytes. *Am. J. Physiol. Heart Circ. Physiol.*, 287:H1378–H1403, 2004.

8. M. E. Anderson. Calmodulin kinase signaling in heart: an intriguing candidate target for therapy of myocardial dysfunction and arrhythmias. *Pharmacol. Ther.*, 106:39–55, 2005.

9. J. J. Saucerman, L. L. Brunton, A. P. Michailova, and A. D. McCulloch. Modeling beta-adrenergic control of cardiac myocyte contractility in silico. *J. Biol. Chem.*, 278:47997–48003, 2003.

10. D. J. Roberts and M. Waelbroeck. G protein activation by G protein coupled receptors: ternary complex formation or catalyzed reaction? *Biochem. Pharmacol.*, 68:799–806, 2004.

11. D. M. Cooper, Regulation and organization of adenylyl cyclases and cAMP. *Biochem. J.*, 375:517–529, 2003.

12. F. Rochais, G. Vandecasteele, F. Lefebvre, C. Lugnier, H. Lum, J. L. Mazet, D. M. Cooper, and R. Fischmeister. Negative feedback exerted by cAMP-dependent protein kinase and cAMP phosphodiesterase on subsarcolemmal cAMP signals in intact cardiac myocytes: an in vivo study using adenovirus-mediated expression of CNG channels. *J. Biol. Chem.*, 279:52095–52105, 2004.

13. A. A. Armoundas, R. Wu, G. Juang, E. Marban, and G. F. Tomaselli. Electrical and structural remodeling of the failing ventricle. *Pharmacol. Ther.*, 92:213–230, 2001.

14. X. H. Wehrens and A. R. Marks. Novel therapeutic approaches for heart failure by normalizing calcium cycling. *Nat. Rev. Drug Discov.*, 3:565–573, 2004.

15. Y. Takuwa, N. Takuwa, and H. Rasmussen. The effects of isoproterenol on intracellular calcium concentration. *J. Biol. Chem.*, 263:762–768, 1988.

16. G. Iaccarino, P. C. Dolber, R. J. Lefkowitz, and W. J. Koch. Beta-adrenergic receptor kinase-1 levels in catecholamine-induced myocardial hypertrophy: regulation by beta- but not alpha1-adrenergic stimulation. *Hypertension*, 33:396–401, 1999.

17. S. Chakraborti, T. Chakraborti, and G. Shaw. Beta-adrenergic mechanisms in cardiac diseases: a perspective. *Cell Signal.*, 12:499–513, 2000.

18. B. D. Lowes, et al. Rationale and design of the enoximone clinical trials program. *J. Card. Fail.*, 11:659–669, 2005.

19. M. A. Movsesian, Altered cAMP-mediated signalling and its role in the pathogenesis of dilated cardiomyopathy. *Cardiovasc. Res.*, 62:450–459, 2004.

20. P. Rajasethupathy, S. J. Vayttaden, and U. S. Bhalla. Systems modeling: a pathway to drug discovery. *Curr. Opin. Chem. Biol.*, 9:400–406, 2005.

21. O. E. Brodde, M. C. Michel, and H. R. Zerkowski. Signal transduction mechanisms controlling cardiac contractility and their alterations in chronic heart failure. *Cardiovasc. Res.*, 30:570–584, 1995.

22. M. R. Bristow, et al. Decreased catecholamine sensitivity and beta-adrenergic-receptor density in failing human hearts. *N. Engl. J. Med.*, 307:205–211, 1982.

23. X. Wang, and N. S. Dhalla. Modification of beta-adrenoceptor signal transduction pathway by genetic manipulation and heart failure. *Mol. Cell. Biochem.*, 214:131–155, 2000.

24. N. Bouanani, A. Corsin, N. Gilson, and B. Crozatier. Beta-adrenoceptors and adenylate cyclase activity in hypertrophied and failing rabbit left ventricle. *J. Mol. Cell. Cardiol.*, 23:573–581, 1991.

25. G. Hasenfuss and B. Pieske. Calcium cycling in congestive heart failure. *J. Mol. Cell. Cardiol.*, 34:951–969, 2002.

26. D. Qin, Z. H. Zhang, E. B. Caref, M. Boutjdir, P. Jain, and N. el-Sherif. Cellular and ionic basis of arrhythmias in postinfarction remodeled ventricular myocardium. *Circ. Res.*, 79:461–473, 1996.

27. K. Kjeldsen, P. Bjerregaard, E. A. Richter, P. E. Thomsen, and A. Norgaard. Na+, K+-ATPase concentration in rodent and human heart and skeletal muscle: apparent relation to muscle performance. *Cardiovasc. Res.*, 22:95–100, 1988.

28. D. J. Beuckelmann, M. Nabauer, and E. Erdmann. Alterations of K+ currents in isolated human ventricular myocytes from patients with terminal heart failure. *Circ. Res.*, 73:379–385, 1993.

29. M. Zaccolo and T. Pozzan. Discrete microdomains with high concentration of cAMP in stimulated rat neonatal cardiac myocytes. *Science*, 295:1711–1715, 2002.

30. M. G. Vila Petroff, J. M. Egan, X. Wang, and S. J. Sollott. Glucagon-like peptide-1 increases cAMP but fails to augment contraction in adult rat cardiac myocytes. *Circ. Res.*, 89:445–452, 2001.

31. J. A. Beavo, P. J. Bechtel, and E. G. Krebs. Activation of protein kinase by physiological concentrations of cyclic AMP. *Proc. Natl. Acad. Sci. U S A*, 71:3580–3583, 1974.

32. L. Vittone, C. Mundina-Weilenmann, M. Said, and A. Mattiazzi. Mechanisms involved in the acidosis enhancement of the isoproterenol-induced phosphorylation of phospholamban in the intact heart. *J. Biol. Chem.*, 273:9804–9811, 1998.

33. D. M. Bers. *Excitation-Contraction Coupling and Cardiac Contractile Force* (Developments in Cardiovascular Medicine), Springer, 2001.

34. S. Viatchenko-Karpinski and S. Gyorke. Modulation of the Ca(2+)-induced Ca(2+) release cascade by beta-adrenergic stimulation in rat ventricular myocytes. *J. Physiol.*, 533:837–848, 2001.

35. J. J. Saucerman, L. L. Brunton, A. P. Michailova, and A. D. McCulloch. Modeling beta-adrenergic control of cardiac myocyte contractility in silico. *J. Biol. Chem.*, 278:47997–48003, 2003.

36. N. S. Roth, P. T. Campbell, M. G. Caron, R. J. Lefkowitz, and M. J. Lohse. Comparative rates of desensitization of beta-adrenergic receptors by the beta-adrenergic receptor kinase and the cyclic AMP-dependent protein kinase. *Proc. Natl. Acad. Sci. U S A*, 88:6201–6204, 1991.

37. M. J. Lohse, J. L. Benovic, M. G. Caron, and R. J. Lefkowitz. Multiple pathways of rapid beta 2-adrenergic receptor desensitization. Delineation with specific inhibitors. *J. Biol. Chem.*, 265:3202–3211, 1990.

38. M. R. Bristow. beta-adrenergic receptor blockade in chronic heart failure. *Circulation*, 101:558–569, 2000.

39. N. J. Freedman, S. B. Liggett, D. E. Drachman, G. Pei, M. G. Caron, and R. J. Lefkowitz. Phosphorylation and desensitization of the human beta 1-adrenergic receptor. Involvement of G protein-coupled receptor kinases and cAMP-dependent protein kinase. *J. Biol. Chem.*, 270:17953–17961, 1995.

40. S. Pippig, S. Andexinger, K. Daniel, M. Puzicha, M. G. Caron, R. J. Lefkowitz, and M. J. Lohse. Overexpression of beta-arrestin and beta-adrenergic receptor kinase augment desensitization of beta 2-adrenergic receptors. *J. Biol. Chem.*, 268:3201–3208, 1993.

41. J. L. Guillou, H. Nakata, and D. M. Cooper. Inhibition by calcium of mammalian adenylyl cyclases. *J. Biol. Chem.*, 274:35539–35545, 1999.

42. Y. Chen, et al., Adenylyl cyclase 6 is selectively regulated by protein kinase A phosphorylation in a region involved in Galphas stimulation. *Proc. Natl. Acad. Sci. U S A*, 94:14100–14104, 1997.

43. C. Sette and M. Conti. Phosphorylation and activation of a cAMP-specific phosphodiesterase by the cAMP-dependent protein kinase. Involvement of serine 54 in the enzyme activation. *J. Biol. Chem.*, 271:16526–16534, 1996.

44. R. Kakkar, R. V. Raju, and R. K. Sharma. Calmodulin-dependent cyclic nucleotide phosphodiesterase (PDE1). *Cell. Mol. Life. Sci.*, 55:1164–1186, 1999.

45. X. Pan, E. Arauz, J. J. Krzanowski, D. F. Fitzpatrick, and J. B. Polson. Synergistic interactions between selective pharmacological inhibitors of phosphodiesterase isozyme families PDE III and PDE IV to attenuate proliferation of rat vascular smooth muscle cells. *Biochem. Pharmacol.*, 48:827–835, 1994.

46. U. S. Bhalla and R. Iyengar. Emergent properties of networks of biological signaling pathways. *Science*, 283:381–387, 1999.

47. P. M. Stemmer and C. B. Klee. Dual calcium ion regulation of calcineurin by calmodulin and calcineurin B. *Biochemistry*, 33:6859–6866, 1994.

48. G. Dupont, G. Houart, and P. De Koninck. Sensitivity of CaM kinase II to the frequency of Ca^{2+} oscillations: a simple model. *Cell Calcium*, 34:485–497, 2003.

49. B. B. Olwin and D. R. Storm. Calcium binding to complexes of calmodulin and calmodulin binding proteins. *Biochemistry*, 24:8081–8086, 1985.

50. V. E. Bondarenko, G. P. Szigeti, G. C. Bett, S. J. Kim, and S. J. Rasmusson. Computer model of action potential of mouse ventricular myocytes. *Am. J. Physiol. Heart Circ. Physiol.*, 287:H1378–H1403, 2004.

4

RULE BASED MODELING
AND MODEL REFINEMENT

Elaine Murphy and Vincent Danos

University of Edinburgh, Edinburgh, UK

Jérôme Féret

ENS-INRIA-CNRS, Paris, France

Jean Krivine

Harvard University, Boston, Massachusetts, USA

Russell Harmer

CNRS-Paris-Diderot, Paris, France

Rule-based modeling is an effective way of handling the explosive combinatorics of biological networks. The use of partial objects in describing molecular interactions means that only the necessary conditions for a rule are specified and not the complete chemical entities taking part in a reaction. This leads to descriptions that are easier to set up and more compact. Networks of substantial scale can be described without having to reduce the combinatorics of the system—as other approaches must.

An important aspect of the rule-based approach is its agility, as one can easily modify rules to incorporate new knowledge or test different assumptions. A special and rather frequent case is when one wishes to replace a rule with ones imposing

Elements of Computational Systems Biology   Edited by Huma M. Lodhi and Stephen H. Muggleton
Copyright © 2010 John Wiley & Sons, Inc.

stronger conditions. This process is called *refinement*, and we approach it in this study both from the practical and the theoretical point of view.

There are various reasons why one would like to use refinement:

- One wants to understand how the activity of a rule varies with its application contexts
- One realizes that more conditions are necessary than previously thought
- One more subtly wishes to evolve the behavior of the current system

The notion of behavior-preserving, or neutral, refinement commands an analysis of the possible symmetries of partial complexes. Here, we need a rigourous algebraic theory to see through the intricacies caused by symmetries. Incidentally, the problem of neutral refinement is one of a family of problems that is well-studied in the theory of concurrent systems, usually under the catch phrase of "behavioral equivalence." The form of equivalence we are looking for here is especially strong, since it should hold irrespective of the other rules defining the dynamics of the model.

The material is organized as follows. We begin with a brief introduction to the Kappa language (Section 4.1). Next, we present several examples (Section 4.2) of refinements. We have, in particular, a somewhat lengthy example that shows how refinements can be used to evolve complex behavior from simple systems. By introducing mutant variants of agents that alter the behavior of a single rule, it is possible to change dramatically and in unexpected ways the outcome of a pathway (Section 4.2.2).

Once we are reassured that the notion of refinement is actually useful, we turn to the second part, namely, the mathematical development of rule refinement. An algebraic version of (a mild simplification of) Kappa is introduced (Section 4.3). This is framed in basic category theory, which allows us to make use of existing mathematical techniques. Previous work in this area developed a framework for homogeneous rule refinement, where agents of the same type had the same sets of sites [1]. The framework developed here is much more general and introduces the notion of addresses to access specific agents in partial complexes (Section 4.4). This enables us to model a much larger class of rule refinements, and an example is given of a model that could not have been dealt with previously. We end by deriving a general formula for neutral refinement and show that the stochastic transition system underlying the rule set is unchanged.

The following is self-contained. Nevertheless, readers might want to consult earlier Kappa references on a concrete example of the agility of rule-based modeling [2], the use of debugging methods based on abstract interpretation [3], the development of techniques for large-scale stochastic simulation [4], or the study of statistical asymptotic properties of simple Kappa networks [5].

4.1 KAPPA, BRIEFLY

The realm of protein–protein interactions commands a picture that is substantially different from the traditional closed biochemical world of metabolic networks. The innumerable combinations that noncovalent binding brings about all but forbid an extensional view of protein networks. An analogy with group theory might help. Even when a group is finite, its multiplication table might be so large that no extensional description is possible. Yet, in some favorable cases, one can handle such groups using generators and relations. Accordingly, in Kappa and other rule-based languages such as BNG [6], agents do not represent species (aka complexes) but their elementary components, that is, to say proteins. Agents are used as generators, and rules specify how more complex objects can be assembled from them. This does not preclude simulation, and one can even simulate systems with an infinite number of possible complexes (supposing agents are available in infinite numbers of course). For unconditional rule sets, by using simple statistical mechanics techniques, one can derive conditions on the affinities and copy numbers of agent types for the set of possible unique complexes to become infinite in the limit of infinite populations; so to some extent, one can predict where traditional enumerative methods cease to apply [5].

Throughout this study, we will use the rather generic term "agent" to designate our basic entitities, but in most applications, these are indeed idealizations of proteins. Agents have sites that can be used to bind to other sites and can also hold an internal state. Binding via sites accounts for the formation of domain-mediated complexes, while internal states account for posttranslational modifications such as phosphorylation. (Syntactically, as we will soon see in the examples below, the binding of two sites is represented by a common superscript, while the internal state of a site is indicated as a subscript.) Different types of atomic events can be combined in a rule such as binding, unbinding, modification of an internal state, and addition or deletion of an agent. A binding rule requires two distinct free sites, and hence, at any given time, it is not possible for a site to be bound more than once, although an agent may be bound simultaneously on different sites.

A Kappa model consists of (1) a rule set specifying how the initial solution may evolve, with each rule being given a rate and (2) an initial state that declares the names, sites, and copy numbers of all agents present in the system at the outset. Each rule in the rule set has a likelihood attached to it, which gives the model a stochastic behavior. This likelihood is proportional to the number of ways in which the rule can be applied to the current state of the system multiplied by its rate. This rate is a measure of how efficient a rule is at turning a chance encounter of reagents into an actual reaction. In the case where agents have no sites at all, a model boils down to a Petri net, and the dynamics is the same as the mass action law put in Gillespie form [7].

4.2 REFINEMENT, PRACTICALLY

4.2.1 A Simple Cascade

In order to introduce our notation for rules and agents and demonstrate the notion of refinement in a first simple case, we start with an elementary cascade. This type of biological circuitry occurs frequently in actual pathways (e.g., see [8]).

In our example, we have one kinase S, covalently modifying another kinase X, which, in turn, modifies some third agent Y. Each agent type is supposed to have a single site, and the sites of X and Y hold an internal state of either u (unphosphorylated) or p (phosphorylated); one says, X and Y are active when they are phosphorylated. To keep things simple, the model does not include any mechanism to deactivate X or Y.

4.2.1.1   *The Rules*   The interactions between S and X are defined by the following rules:

$$S(i), X(s_u) \rightarrow S(i^1), X(s_u^1),$$

$$S(i^1), X(s^1) \rightarrow S(i), X(s),$$

$$S(i^1), X(s_u^1) \rightarrow S(i^1), X(s_p^1).$$

In this rule set, a binding is represented by a shared exponent, for example, $S(i^1)$, $X(s^1)$ represents a binding between the S and the X agents via their respective i and s sites. The first rule in the triplet specifies the conditions for such a binding to take place: one needs the sites i and s to be free and one also needs the site s to have a specific internal state u, indicated as a subscript s_u. One might say that S is 'smart' in so far as it does not bind a target that is already modified, that is, of the form $X(s_p)$. The second rule represents the unbinding of the two molecules. Contrary to the first one, this rule does not depend on the s site of X being in a particular internal state. The ability to not have to specify the entirety of the context in which an event can be triggered—which we alluded to earlier, and which is sometimes called the "don't care, don't write" convention—already shows here in a very simple form. The third rule represents the activation of X, that is, the change of X's internal state from u to p.

A second and similar rule triplet defines the interactions of X and Y:

$$X(s_p), Y(s_u) \rightarrow X(s_p^1), Y(s_u^1),$$

$$r := X(s^1), Y(s^1) \rightarrow X(s), Y(s),$$

$$X(s^1), Y(s_u^1) \rightarrow X(s^1), Y(s_p^1).$$

This rule set differs from the previous one only in that the X agent is required to have a phosphorylated s site in order to bind a Y agent, as stipulated in the first rule. This ensures that the first half of the cascade happens before the second and, in particular, that Y cannot be activated if there is no S signal.

4.2.1.2   *On The Importance of Being Off*   To complete the definition of our model and define a proper stochastic system, we need to choose rates for the above rules and to define an initial state. We will assume that all rates are 1, except the rate k of the rule r, whereby X and Y detach. In fact, we want to ask a classical cascade

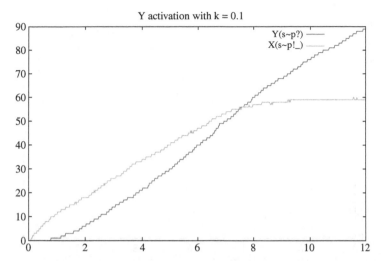

Figure 4.1   Simulation with $k = 0.1$ (sticky case): Y's rise time is approximately 8 (higher curve), at which time about 100% Xs are active and bound (lower curve).

question, namely, how the overall rate of production of the active (phosphorylated) form of Y depends on k. (One could ask the same for the rate at which S and X detach.) Intuitively, if k is too low, X will tend to remain attached to Y for long periods of time after Y has been activated and during which it will be unable to interact with any other Y; moreover, this also potentially prevents Y to which it is attached from further propagating the signal. On the other hand, if k is too high, X will detach from Y before it has had a chance to activate it. The performance of the cascade is, therefore, a nonmonotonic function of k, and somehow, an efficient activation of Y needs to strike the right balance between binding too loosely and too tightly.

Let us demonstrate this numerically by varying k. Suppose one starts with an initial state of $15 * S(i) + 60 * X(s_u) + 120 * Y(s_u)$, so as to have significantly more Ys than Xs (otherwise the stickiness effect will be largely invisible). As expected, the activation of Y is rather slow when $k = 0.1$ (Figure 4.1), becomes faster for $k = 10$ (Figure 4.2), and slows again when $k = 100$ (Figure 4.3).[1]

Specifically, the Y's rise times, defined as the time where half of the Ys are active, are respectively and approximately 8, 5, and 7. A closer numerical examination of the rise time of Y as a function of k would reveal the boundaries of the control area, which produces the optimal behavior of the rule. With the above set of parameters, and for k within $[1, 50]$, one has a rise time below 6. Outside of this interval, the production slows down either because binding is too sticky or too liquid. We make a mental note that there is a rather large interval k where the cascade operates fast; how large of course will depend on all the other parameters as well.

---

[1] Simulations are obtained with the Kappa factory, an implementation of the Kappa language, which includes a graphical interface, is free for academic usage and can be obtained at `support@plectix.com`.

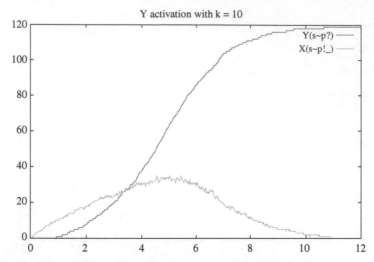

Figure 4.2   Simulation with $k = 10$ (near optimum): Y's rise time is about 5 (higher curve), at which time about 50% of Xs are active and bound (lower curve).

4.2.1.3   *Refinement of The Off Rule* However, there is another method to optimize the behavior of this rule without having to investigate the effect of varying the rate parameter to probe the control area. In this system, the rule r regarding the detachment of X from Y given above is applied regardless of the internal state of Y. A natural strategy to optimize the cascade is to make r depend on Y's internal state,

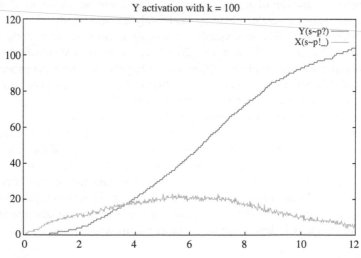

Figure 4.3   Simulation with $k = 100$ (liquid case): Y's rise time is about 7 (higher curve), at which time less than 30% of Xs are active and bound (lower curve).

and split it into two subcases with respective rates k_1 and k_2:

$$r_1 := X(s^1), Y(s_u^1) \rightarrow X(s), Y(s_u),$$

$$r_2 := X(s^1), Y(s_p^1) \rightarrow X(s), Y(s_p).$$

The substitution of r with r_1, r_2 is an example of a rule refinement. If one sets $k_1 := k_2 := k$, the behavior of the system will remain unchanged. Such a case where a refinement does not alter the dynamics of a system is what we have called earlier "a neutral refinement." On the other hand, if one sets $k_1 := 0$, so that X never detaches if the Y site has not been activated and $k_2 := \infty$, that is, X detaches as soon as activation has occurred, one will clearly accelerate the activation of Y. In effect, in this example, splitting r is exactly what one needs to make Y's rise time a monotonic function of both k_1 (decreasing) and k_2 (increasing), whereas before, as we have seen above, it was not a monotonic function of k. It follows that the optimal assignment for k_1 and k_2 is as above. This definitely changes the dynamics and constitutes what we have called a kinetic refinement.

4.2.2 Another Cascade

Here is another two-tiered cascade:

$$S(i), X(s_u) \rightarrow S(i^1), X(s_u^1),$$

$$r := S(i^1), X(s^1) \rightarrow S(i), X(s),$$

$$S(i^1), X(s_u^1) \rightarrow S(i^1), X(s_p^1).$$

$$r' := X(s_p^?, y), Y(s_u) \rightarrow X(s_p^?, y^1), Y(s_u^1),$$

$$X(y^1), Y(s^1) \rightarrow X(y), Y(s),$$

$$X(y^1), Y(s_u^1) \rightarrow X(y^1), Y(s_p^1).$$

The first rule triplet is identical to that in the first example. However, the second rule triplet has an important difference. First, X now has two sites s and y, one to bind S, and the other to bind Y, respectively. Second, the X/Y association rule r' does not require X to detach from S to attach to a Y. The superscript ? on the s in X precisely expresses that the X, Y association rule does not care whether the X agent is free or bound on its other site s. The rule does, however, ask X to be activated as in the first example.

These rules are also more solid examples of the "don't care, don't write" convention of which we have seen simple examples earlier (Section 4.2.1.1). The left-hand sides of rules are partial complexes containing only the conditions that are necessary for the rule to be activated. For example, in the fifth rule, the s site of the X molecule is not mentioned because we do not care which internal or binding state it is in. Every such rule embodies a regularity assumption that may or may not hold. One use of refinements is to allow one to revise such assumptions and admit in the dynamics less regularity, viz, more dependence on the context of a rule than hitherto assumed. However, with this second example, we wish to explore another aspect of refinement, namely, that it enables complex behavior to evolve from simple systems. We are going to perform a series of refinements of the above cascade and obtain rather surprising behaviors.

4.2.2.1   *Neutral Refinements*   Our first refinement concerns r, the S/X dissociation rule, which we replace with the following:

$$r_1 := S(i^1, s_1), X(s^1) \rightarrow S(i, s_1), X(s),$$
$$r_2 := S(i^1, s_2), X(s^1) \rightarrow S(i, s_2), X(s).$$

This refinement has the effect of adding a new site s to S with an internal state that can be either of 1 or 2. As there are no rules that modify this internal state, the refinement can be seen as defining a variant of S. To use a more biological terminology, we will say that $S(i, s_1)$ and $S(i, s_2)$ are isoforms, sometimes simply written as S_1, S_2 hereafter.

Our second refinement concerns r', the X/Y association rule, which we replace with the following:

$$r'_1 := X(s_p^?, y), Y(s_u, y_1) \rightarrow X(s_p^?, y^1), Y(s_u^1, y_1),$$
$$r'_2 := X(s_p^?, y), Y(s_u, y_2) \rightarrow X(s_p^?, y^1), Y(s_u^1, y_2).$$

This time, we have introduced isoforms of the Y agent, using the new site y, which we again write simply Y_1, Y_2.

For our final refinements, we pick r'_1 and r'_2 and make a distinction based on whether the s site of the X agent is bound or free:

$$r'_{11} := X(s_p^-, y), Y(s_u, y_1) \rightarrow X(s_p^-, y^1), y(s_u^1, y_1),$$
$$r'_{12} := X(s_p, y), Y(s_u, y_1) \rightarrow X(s_p, y^1), Y(s_u^1, y_1),$$
$$r'_{21} := X(s_p^-, y), Y(s_u, y_2) \rightarrow X(s_p^-, y^1), Y(s_u^1, y_2),$$
$$r'_{22} := X(s_p, y), Y(s_u, y_2) \rightarrow X(s_p, y^1), Y(s_u^1, y_2).$$

Here, the s^- superscript carried by s means that it is bound, but the rule does not care what it is bound to. In fact, in this simple example, s at X can only be bound to one of the two S isoforms, so this is just a convenient abbreviation, and one could equivalently write for example:

$$r'_{21} := S(i^1), X(s_p^1, y), Y(s_u, y_2) \rightarrow S(i^1), X(s_p^1, y^2), Y(s_u^2, y_2).$$

This begs the remark that a left-hand side can have any number of agents in any configuration. The important thing to notice is that neither r'_{11} nor r'_{21} knows which isoform of S it is dealing with.

Applying these four successive refinements gives us a new rule set, where r is replaced with r_1, r_2, and r' with $r'_{11}, r'_{12}, r'_{21}$, and r'_{22}. We now have two inputs, S_1, S_2, and two outputs, Y_1, Y_2, that we can manipulate independently. The question we ask now is another classical cascade question, namely, we wish to understand the range of input/output dependencies one can attain with our cascade.

4.2.2.2   *Kinetic Refinements*   If all refined rules were to inherit the original rule rates, this would be a neutral refinement, all our isoforms would be indistinguishable, and there would be no interesting dependency created by our rule set. We need to alter some of the rule rates to obtain a kinetic refinement with an interesting behavior. This is what we do now.

We first set r_2 to have a lower rate and r_1 to have a higher rate than the original rule r. All other rates being equal, this has the effect of making S_2 stickier and S_1 more liquid. As S_1's dissociation rate is high, it is less likely to stay bound to X at s. So, with only S_1s in the system, one would expect to see higher numbers of s-free active Xs compared with the neutral refinement. Conversely, the S_2 variant is more likely to stay bound to X at s, and one would expect to see higher numbers of s-bound active Xs, with only S_2s in the system. Furthermore, as we have seen in the first example (Section 4.2.1.2), for well-chosen values of the various cascade parameters, one has a large window of efficient dissociation rates (our numerical study concerned the dissociation rate of the second tier of the cascade, but the same holds for the first one). So, our variant signals S_1 and S_2 may well be equally efficient, and in fact nearly optimal in their activation of Ys. They only differ in style or in their degree of liquidity.

Now, we can take advantage of this difference in the transient behavior of our signal isoforms by setting the rates of r'_{11} and r'_{22} to 0. This amounts to requiring that an s-bound active X can attach only to the Y_2 variant, whereas s-free active X can attach only to the Y_1 variant.

With this second kinetic refinement in place and following the informal argument above, one would now expect S_1 to activate primarily Y_1, and S_2, Y_2. To confirm this, we can run simulations varying the numbers of S_1, S_2:

$$15 * S(i, s_1) + 0 * S(i, s_2) + 50 * X(s_u) + 120 * Y(s_u, y_1) + 120 * Y(s_u, y_2),$$

$$0 * S(i, s_1) + 15 * S(i, s_2) + 50 * X(s_u) + 120 * Y(s_u, y_1) + 120 * Y(s_u, y_2),$$

In the first case, one has only the S_1 isoform, and this has the effect of mainly producing active Y_1s (Figure 4.4), while in the second one (Figure 4.5), one has only the S_2 isoform, and this has the effect of mainly producing active Y_2s. As we have no rule for the deactivation of Xs, all Xs eventually become free at s (because the S/X association rule tests for the internal state of X), which explains why some active Y_1 is also produced in the second case. However, this happens at a much slower rate

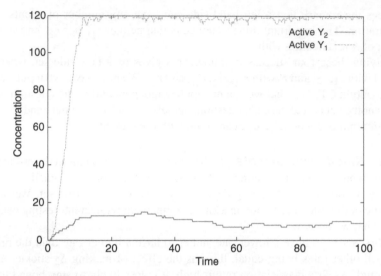

Figure 4.4 Simulation with only S_1: Y_1 gets activated and not Y_2. Here, and in the following, rules for spontaneous inactivation of X, Y at a rate of 0.01 were added.

than the production of active Y_2. Were we to include deactivation rules for X or Y, we would see a low production of active Y_1 at all times. The design we obtain successfully establishes a specific input/output relation, whereby S_1 only activates Y_1, and S_2 only Y_2, despite the fact that both cascades share a component, namely, X.

Of course, if one reflects on the design, there is no magic, as it hinges on the shared component reflecting its binding status upstream in its behavior downstream (the role of the second kinetic refinement). The subtle point is that it does so without sensing

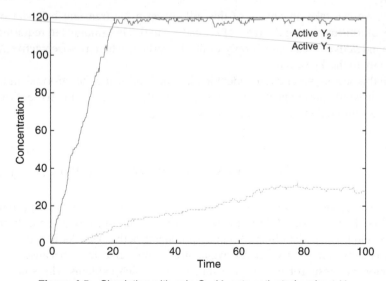

Figure 4.5 Simulation with only S_2: Y_2 gets activated and not Y_1.

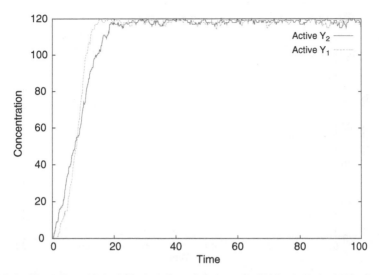

Figure 4.6 Simulation with both S_1 and S_2 and an excess of X: both Y_1 and Y_2 get activated at the same rate.

the upstream isoform it is bound to—the information is contained only in the different residency times of the two signal isoforms (the role of the first kinetic refinement). This *in numero* experiment shows that there is "plenty of room" at the relevant time scales (to paraphrase a famous quote from Feynman).

4.2.2.3 Signal Integration Thus, and so far, the results of our numerical experiment are as one would expect given the rule set. It is when one asks what happens if both signal isoforms of S are present in the system at the same time that one gets a surprise. If there is an excess of available X, both active Y_1 and Y_2 are produced at approximately even rates, and the system behaves as two independent juxtaposed pathways (Figure 4.6). However, if one has a limited number of Xs as in

$$15 * S(i, s_1) + 15 * S(i, s_2) + 10 * X(s_u) + 120 * Y(s_u, y_1) + 120 * Y(s_u, y_2),$$

the S_2 to Y_2 pathway takes over, and despite the presence of S_1, only active Y_2 is significantly produced (Figure 4.7). The behavior of the system in this case can be seen to be analogous to that of a transistor, whereby S_2 can completely override S_1. To summarize the situation, and despite the fact that it is always tricky to give Boolean representations of biological circuitry, one could say that the final design behaves as the Boolean function $Y_1, Y_2 = S_1 \wedge \neg S_2, S_2$. Note, however, that the amount of control exerted by S_2 can be modulated by the amount of the shared component X, as when X is in excess, the mapping becomes simply the identity (Figure 4.6).

4.2.2.4 Discussion One can easily imagine that such a 'transistor' circuit, as we have just derived, could be useful for cellular decision-making. Of course, this prompts

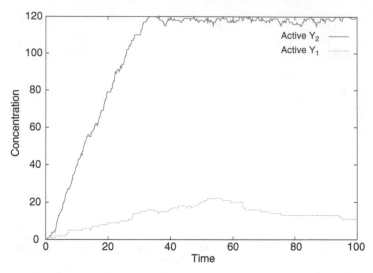

Figure 4.7 Simulation with both S_1 and S_2 and few Xs: S_2 overrides S_1, as only Y_1 gets significantly activated.

the fascinating question of whether it can be implemented, and more specifically, whether a variation in a real protein cascade, mimicking our derivation of the said circuit, can be engineered by varying the code of the various relevant proteins. This is one of a set of questions that is being actively researched in the new and exciting engineering field of synthetic biology (see [9] for a recent review). One might soon be able to answer this kind of question, but at the moment, the technology of synthetic protein networks is far less advanced than that of transcriptional circuits.

Our design also raises the intriguing possibility of encoding information in the transient assembly of complexes, a mode of information processing that is unique to the world of protein interactions, and which needs a language where binding is a primitive operation to be comfortably dealt with. From the specific point of view of this study, it is also an example of the explanatory power of refinements, as they make the design particularly transparent, whereas presumably, it would be rather difficult to understand it without resorting to refinements.

This second extended example concludes the motivational and methodological part of our refinement study. By now, hopefully, the reader will have a good intuition of refinements and their use. So, we turn now to other, less biologically motivated examples, no longer meant to show the usefulness of refinements but rather to anticipate some of the mathematical challenges we will need to address later and prepare the ground for the algebraic treatment that constitutes the core of this study, and which comes next (Section 4.3 onward).

4.2.3   The SSA Convention

The previous examples show how natural and intuitive refinement can be, but have maybe given the (mistaken) impression that obtaining a neutral refinement is a fairly straightforward matter. In fact, this is far from being the case in general, and there are several subtleties that we need to take into account.

Let us begin examining this by considering a straightforward binding rule, $r :=$ $A(x), A(x) \to A(x^1), A(x^1)$ between agent type A (with at least one site x) and itself, with stochastic rate constant k_r. Now, in the case where rule r is actually a reaction, that is, A has just the one site x with no internal state, it is usual, during stochastic simulation, to calculate the activity of the rule as $k_r n(n-1)/2$, where n is the number of As currently unbound on site x [7]. In this convention, call it the SSA convention, an event is the identification of a multiset, here an unordered pair of As, and there are $^nC_2$ such unordered pairs not $n(n-1)$.

The SSA convention works well for reactions (aka Petri nets or multiset rewriting) because any application of a reaction preserves the reaction symmetries (as expressed in its multiset representation). This is no longer true with our richer notion of rewriting, where the local symmetries of a rule may increase or decrease depending on its application context. So, we shall use another convention, where an event is an injection of the rule's left-hand side, and one does not attempt at quotienting those injections by the automorphisms of the rule (aka symmetries).

To understand this better, let us examine a concrete case where r is not a reaction. This means that the rule can instantiate as several distinct reactions. For example, let us suppose that the site x actually has an internal state, blue or red, that the rule does not mention. Intuitively, the result of firing r is the creation of either a red–red, a red–blue, or a blue–blue pair of As. We can make this explicit with the following refinement of r into the three subcases:

$$r_1 := A(x_R), A(x_R) \to A(x_R^1), A(x_R^1),$$

$$r_2 := A(x_R), A(x_B) \to A(x_R^1), A(x_B^1),$$

$$r_3 := A(x_B), A(x_B) \to A(x_B^1), A(x_B^1).$$

Let us assume that these three refined rules are actually reactions, that is, we have now revealed everything about A's sites and states. Notice that r_2, unlike the other two refinements, breaks the symmetry of the original rule r. This has a significant consequence on how we calculate its activity; unlike r_1 and r_3 that follow the above pattern, that is, $k_{r_1} n_R(n_R - 1)/2$ and $k_{r_3} n_B(n_B - 1)/2$, r_2's activity is $k_{r_2} n_R n_B$. The total combined SSA activity of r_1, r_2, and r_3 is the same as that of r:

$$k_r n(n-1)/2 = k_r n_R(n_R - 1)/2 + k_r n_B(n_B - 1)/2 + k_r n_R n_B,$$

where $n = n_R + n_B$. In other words, setting $k_{r_1} := k_{r_2} := k_{r_3} := k_r$ defines a neutral refinement.

Now, what about the other convention, where one does not take into account a rule's apparent local symmetry when calculating its activity, that is, does not divide by the number of automorphisms (in r's case, 2). Obviously, we have to divide r's rate constant by the number of automorphisms in order to recover the original behavior, in our case assigning $k_r/2$ to r. This keeps the activity of r unchanged, $k_r/2n(n-1)$, and we readily calculate that

$$(k_r/2)n(n-1) = (k_r/2)n_R(n_R-1) + (k_r/2)n_B(n_B-1) + (2k_r/2)n_R n_B,$$

so that this time we need the assignment $k_{r_1} := k_{r_3} := k_r/2$ and $k_{r_2} := k_r$ to get a neutral refinement. It seems here we need a non uniform assignment of rate constants in order to obtain a neutral refinement, and the reader might think the SSA convention is more natural. It is not. The nonuniform rate assignment is an optical illusion, since one can rewrite the above as:

$$(k_r/2)n(n-1) =$$
$$(k_r/2)n_R(n_R-1) + (k_r/2)n_B(n_B-1) + (k_r/2)n_R n_B + (k_r/2)n_R n_B,$$

where all rates are now equal, and one has two copies of the assymmetric refined rule r_2. These copies are associated with the two nonisomorphic injections of the original r left-hand side in r_2's. The subtle point is that although the injections are not isomorphic (since they map the first A either to a red or a blue type; see also the discussion in Sections 4.3.4, and 4.4.1), the obtained rules are. Likewise, one can inject r's left-hand side in two ways in r_1's and r_3's, but this time, the injections are isomorphic (meaning they are conjugated by an automorphism of their joint target), since both extensions preserve r's automorphisms. So, in these two latter cases, there is no need for a copy. This point of view leads indeed to our main technical result (Th. 1, Section 4.4.3), where all rates are kept equal to the original rule—provided one uses our convention, not the SSA one.

In summary, in a rule-based setting, we can either rely on the SSA convention (underlying Gillespie's stochastic simulation algorithm) or the one presented above. The calculation of the rate constants required to obtain a neutral refinement will be affected. Our choice is more natural in that it brings a general result of a simpler form. In this red–blue example, both conventions seem to be on a par, and the next example will show a case where the SSA convention is less natural.

4.2.4 A Less Obvious Refinement

Let us consider a final example that should demonstrate the full subtlety of determining the appropriate rate constants for a neutral refinement. To this end, consider two agent types B and C, again each with only one site x, and define a family of systems $x(n_1, n_2)$ consisting of n_1-free $C(x)$ and n_2 dimers $C(x^1)$, $B(x^1)$.

Consider the rule $r := C(), B() \rightarrow C()$ with rate 1. Note, that r does not mention x at all. This means that r can be applied irrespective of the binding of B and C. Whatever the bindings are, the effect of the rule will be, provided $n_2 > 0$, to delete a B and to bring $x(n_1, n_2)$ to a new state $x(n_1 + 1, n_2 - 1)$. If $n_2 = 0$, then there are no Bs left in the system, and the rule cannot be applied, in which case we say that the system is in a deadlock.

We would like to refine r into mutually exclusive subcases depending on the bindings between B and C. Specifically, we want to use the following three refined rules.

$$r_1 := C(x^1), B(x^1) \rightarrow C(x),$$

$$r_2 := C(x^1), B(x^1), C(x^2), B(x^2) \rightarrow C(x^1), B(x^1), C(x),$$

$$r_3 := C(x), C(x^1), B(x^1) \rightarrow C(x), C(x).$$

Note, that by deleting the agent B, we implicitly also delete all bonds emanating from that B, so, in particular, the previously bound C becomes free. Each of these is a particular case of r in the sense that their left-hand sides embed, sometimes in more than one way, that of r. Intuitively, r_1 is the case where B and C are bound together, r_2 is the case where B and C are both bound but not to each other, and r_3 is the case where B is bound but C is free. Given the family of systems we are working with, these are the only relevant subcases and are mutually exclusive.

Recall that the activity of a rule is defined as the number of ways in which it is possible to apply the rule multiplied by the rule rate. This determines the likelihood that the rule is applied next and only depends on the current state of the system. We have not yet chosen rates for the refined rules above. In the cascade examples, it was the case that simply assigning each new rule the same rate as the original rule resulted in a neutral refinement. Even in the preceding red/blue example, under the SSA convention (Section 4.2.3), where the stochastic simulator implicitly deals with automorphisms (which is the case of the implementation in the Kappa factory), the same uniform assignment of rates gives a neutral refinement.

However, if we assume this is true in this case and run a simulation of the system before and after the rule refinement with an initial state of $x(0, 100)$ and plot the activities of the rules, we see that such rate choices are not appropriate, as the sum of the activities of the refined rules is clearly different from the activity of the original rule r (Figure 4.8). So, setting each refined rule rate to be equal to the original does not result in a neutral refinement in this case.

When we look at the refined rules, we see that the problem most likely lies with r_2 whose left-hand side contains symmetries that should increase the ways in which it can be applied to x but which are ignored by the simulation algorithm. The question we wish to answer is how do these factors contribute to the dynamics and how, in general, do we choose rates for refined rules. The stochastic semantics of the system is determined by the joint activities of all the rules in the rule set over all states of the system. In order to preserve this stochastic semantics, we need to preserve the global activity. Intuitively, this means we must ensure that the joint activities of the rules we are adding to the system are equal to the activity of the rule we are replacing. Below, we derive a general formula to choose the refined rules such that the global activity is preserved. We will return to this example when we have a general solution.

This concludes our series of examples, where hopefully we have shown how natural and useful refinements are. As seen in the last couple of examples, choosing rates even for a neutral refinement is not necessarily as simple as one might imagine. Moreover,

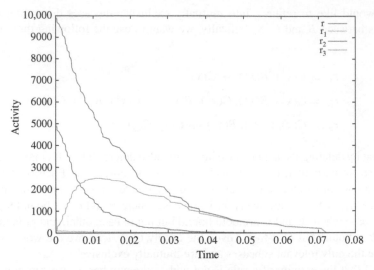

Figure 4.8   Graph of all rule SSA activities with initial state $x(0, 100)$.

the cascade examples, particularly the 'transistor,' illustrate just how subtle (and useful) the effects of kinetic refinement can be. In order to fully understand how refined rules contribute to the dynamics of the system, we have developed a formal mathematical framework to study the Kappa modeling language and rule refinements. The following sections (Sections 4.3 and 4.4) present the technical aspects of this work and derive a general formula for choosing rule rates for neutral refinements that generalizes the homogeneous framework developed in Danos et al. [1]. This gives us a baseline reference for subsequently modulating the behavior of a rule set with kinetic refinements, a process that is otherwise difficult to design and justify.

4.3   RULE-BASED MODELING

The modeling approach we have explained informally (Section 4.1), and illustrated with examples (Section 4.2), we shall now make precise using a simple categorical language, where

- The state of a system is seen as an object x
- The various ways a rule r may apply to x are seen as arrows from r's left-hand side to x.

To make this presentation easier, we simplify the Kappa syntax in two respects. The first is that we assume agents have no internal states. There is no loss of generality here, since internal states can be modeled as sites that can bind to specific unary nodes. The second simplification is that wildcard bindings (as in Section 4.2.2.1) are not used, for example, expressions such as $A(x^-)$, meaning that x is bound to an unspecified agent, are not considered. However, for a given set of rules, it is easy to compute a syntactic super-approximation of all possible bindings (in effect, defining the contact map associated with the rule set, defined below), and wildcards can be replaced with all possible concrete bindings agents they may correspond to. So, this again does not lose generality.

4.3.1 Notation

We will use a certain number of basic notations hereafter. If given a family of sets $(A_i; i \in I)$, we write $\sum_{i \in I} A_i$ for their disjoint sum. We write $A \setminus B$ for the set of elements of A that are not in B, $\wp(A)$ for the set of subsets of A. If an equivalence relation $\simeq$ on a set A is given, we write $A/\simeq$ for the set of equivalence classes and $A/\simeq^* \subseteq A$ for a generic selection of representatives. If f, g are maps to a partial order, then $f \leq g$ means that f is pointwise below g. If f is a partial map on A, we write $dom(f) \subseteq A$ for its domain of definition. Finally, we define a partial pairing on a set A as an irreflexive symmetric binary relation on A such that an element of A is in relation with at most one (other) element of A.

We suppose we are given a set $\mathbb{A}$ of agent names and a set $\mathbb{S}$ of site names. A signature is a map from agent names $\mathbb{A}$ to sets of sites $\wp(\mathbb{S})$.

4.3.2 Objects and Arrows

Definition 4.1 (objects)   *An object is a quadruple $(V, \lambda, \sigma, \pi)$ where*

- *V is a finite set of nodes,*
- *$\lambda \in \mathbb{A}^V$ assigns agent names to nodes,*
- *$\sigma \in \mathcal{P}(\mathbb{S})^V$ assigns sets of site names to nodes, and*
- *π is a partial pairing over the disjoint sum $\sum_{v \in V} \sigma(v)$.*

The pairing π represents bindings, or edges, between sites. Because π is a pairing, any given site can be bound at most once, but a node can be bound many times via different sites.

The simplest nonempty objects are single nodes with no sites (and therefore no binding).

We define $(u, a) \in \pi$ as shorthand for $\exists(v, b) : (u, a, v, b) \in \pi$, and say (u, a) is *free* when $(u, a) \notin \pi$ and *bound* when $(u, a) \in \pi$.

Definition 4.2 (arrows)   *An arrow from x to y is a map $f : V_x \to V_y$ such that*

- *(1) f preserves names: $\lambda_y f = \lambda_x$,*
- *(2) f preserves sites: $\sigma_y f \supseteq \sigma_x$,*
- *(3a) f preserves edges: $(u, a, v, b) \in \pi_x \Rightarrow (f(u), a, f(v), b) \in \pi_y$,*
- *(3b) f reflects edges: $(f(u), a) \in \pi_y, a \in \sigma_x(u) \Rightarrow (u, a) \in \pi_x$,*
- *(4) f is injective.*

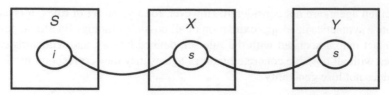

Figure 4.9   The contact map of the simple cascade given in section 4.2.1.

The category **S** of site graphs has objects and arrows (aka morphisms) as above. We write $[x, y]$ for the set of arrows from x to y. We say that y embeds x, or that x is embedded in y when $[x, y] \neq \varnothing$. Rules, defined below, will use arrows to recognize a partial configuration and rewrite it. Importantly, the existence of an arrow in $[x, y]$ is not enough information to apply a rule, since there are many ways in which y can embed x. This is why we have to keep track of arrows. In particular, the set $[x, x]$ of automorphisms of x (aka symmetries) might contain more than the identity map, and this brings subtle aspects in rule refinement.

Our **S** lives naturally in a larger category of contact maps, where one relaxes both the definition of objects and arrows:

- Objects are as above with π any symmetric relation (no longer necessarily a partial pairing)
- Arrows are only asked to satisfy clauses (1), (2), and (3a) (no longer (3b) or (4)).

An example of a contact map is shown in Figure 4.9, which sums up all possible pairings that the simple cascade given in Section 4.2.1 can form. Note, in particular, that X's unique site s is linked twice, so π is indeed not a pairing.

One has an obvious forgetful functor from site graphs (and contact maps as well) to the category of graphs and graph morphisms—one simply forgets sites. However, from the point of view of graphs, the reflectivity condition (3b) above does not really make sense, and one really needs sites to express edge reflection.

If $f \in [x, y]$, we write $f(x)$ for y the target object of f not to be confused with the image of f, $f(V_x) \subseteq V_y$. We also define the site image of f in y as $Im(f) := \{(f(v), a); v \in V_x, a \in \sigma_x(v)\}$. This is a subset of $\sum_{v \in V_x} \sigma_y(f(v))$, and only sites in $Im(f)$ are mentioned in the arrow-defining clauses above.

Conditions (2) and (3a) and the notion of pairing alone already severely constrain arrows:

Lemma 4.1 (rigidity)   *Suppose x is connected, then any nonempty partial injection f from V_x to V_y extends to at most one morphism in $[x, y]$.*

Proof: If f is strictly partial, that is, if $V_x \setminus dom(f)$ is not empty, pick $v \in V_x$ such that for some node $w \in dom(f)$, and some sites $a, b, (w, a, v, b) \in \pi_x$. This is always possible because x is connected. Then, either $(f(w), a, v', b) \in \pi_y$ for some $v' \in V_y$, and by (3a) one must extend f as $f(v) = v'$, or there is no such extension.   □

4.3.3   Extensions

Our theory of refinement (Section 4.4) relies entirely on choosing appropriate sets of extensions of a given s up to isomorphism, so it is worth examining a few basic properties thereof.

It is easy to see that an arrow is injective if and only if it is a mono, but there are more epis than surjections.

Lemma 4.2 (epis)   *A map $h \in [x, y]$ is an* epi *if and only if every connected component of y intersects $f(V_x)$; that is to say for all connected component $c_y \subseteq y$, $h^{-1}(c_y) \neq \varnothing$.*

Proof: Suppose $f_1 h = f_2 h$ for $h \in [x, y]$, $f_i \in [y, z]$, and let $c_y \subseteq y$ be a connected component of y such that $h^{-1}(c_y) \neq \varnothing$. Pick u such that $h(u) \in c_y$, then $f_1(h(u)) = f_2(h(u))$ and by Lemma 4.1 $f_1/c_y = f_2/c_y$. $\qquad\square$

We write $[x, y]^e \subseteq [x, y]$ for the epis from x to y.

Definition 4.3 (extensions)   *The category $\mathbf{S}(s)$ of extensions of an object s is defined as*

- *objects are epis $\phi \in [s, x]^e$ for some x, and*
- *an arrow $\psi : \phi_1 \to \phi_2$ is an arrow in $\mathbf{S}$ such that $\psi\phi_1 = \phi_2$.*

If $\psi\phi_1 = \phi_2$, then ψ is an epi, because ϕ_2 is one; ψ is also a unique such arrow because ϕ_1 is an epi. The category of extensions of s is, therefore, a simple graph (meaning there is at most one arrow between any two objects); however, it is not a partial order, and two extensions ϕ_1, ϕ_2 may be isomorphic.

We write $\phi_1 \simeq_{\mathbf{S}(s)} \phi_2$ when ϕ_1 and ϕ_2 are isomorphic. It is easy to see that this is the case if and only if

- *there are ψ, ψ' such that $\psi\phi_1 = \phi_2$ and $\psi'\phi_2 = \phi_1$ or*
- *there is ψ such that $\psi\phi_1 = \phi_2$ and $\sigma_{\phi_2(s)}\psi = \sigma_{\phi_1(s)}$.*

One has to be careful that $\phi_1 \simeq_{\mathbf{S}(s)} \phi_2$ is a stronger statement than saying that their targets $\phi_1(s)$, $\phi_2(s)$ are isomorphic in $\mathbf{S}$ (as site graphs). Consider the simple example, where $s = A(a), A(a)$, and $t = A(a), A(a, b^1), B(a^1)$; one has two maps ϕ_1, ϕ_2 in $[s, t]$, and their targets are isomorphic, since they are equal; however, they are not isomorphic as objects of $\mathbf{S}(s)$. We will return to this example later.

4.3.4   Actions and Rules

To complete our presentation of Kappa, we need to explain rules. A rule is seen as an object, an action thereon, and a rate at which the rule applies.

An atomic action on s is one of the following:

- an edge addition $+u, a, v, b$,
- an edge deletion $-u, a, v, b$,
- an agent addition $+A, \sigma$ with A a name, σ a set of free sites, and
- an agent deletion $-u$,

with $u, v \in V_s, a \in \sigma_s(u)$, and $b \in \sigma_s(v)$. Edge additions and deletions are symmetric. An atomic action α on s is defined:

- if $\alpha = +u, a, v, b$, when both (u, a) and (v, b) are free in s or
- if $\alpha = -u, a, v, b$, when $(u, a, v, b) \in \pi_s$.

An action on s is a finite sequence of atomic actions on s. The notion of definedness extends recursively to nonatomic actions. We consider only defined actions hereafter.

Definition 4.4 (rules) *A rule is a triple $r = s, \alpha, \tau$, where s is an object, α is an action defined on s, and τ is a rate (a positive real number).*

We write $\alpha \cdot s$ for the result of the action α on s (usually called the right hand side). Given $f \in [s, x]$, and α one defines $f(\alpha)$ the transport of an atomic α along f as:

- $f(\pm u, a, v, b) = \pm f(u), a, f(v), b$,
- $f(+A, \sigma) = +A, \sigma$, and
- $f(-u) = -f(u)$.

This can be extended to nonatomic actions.
Conditions (3a) and (3b) entail that $f(\alpha)$ is defined on x when α is defined on s.
Given an $f \in [s, s']$ and a rule $r = s, \alpha, \tau$, one can define the image rule $f(r) = s', f(\alpha), \tau$.

4.3.5   Events and Probabilities

A rule set R defines a quantitative labeled transition system on objects.

Definition 4.5 (transitions) *Let $r = s, \alpha, \tau$ be a rule, R be a set of rules, and x be an object.*
Define:

- *the set of events in x associated to r as $\mathcal{E}(x, r) := \{r\} \times [s, x]$,*
- *the set of events in x associated to R as $\mathcal{E}(x) = \sum_{r \in R} \mathcal{E}(x, r)$,*
- *the activity of r at x as $\mathbf{a}(x, r) := \tau |[s, x]|$, and*
- *the activity of R at x as $\mathbf{a}(x) := \sum_{r \in R} \mathbf{a}(x, r)$.*

This defines a labeled continuous Markov chain on objects:

$$x \longrightarrow^r_f f(\alpha) \cdot x, \tag{4.1}$$

where $f \in [s, x]$ and the event r, f has probability $\tau/\mathbf{a}(x)$ if $\mathbf{a}(x) > 0$, and the subsequent time advance is an exponential random variable $\delta t(x)$ such that $p(\delta t(x) > t) := e^{-\mathbf{a}(x)t}$.

As long as the quantitative structure of the transition system is determined by the activities of its rules, our analysis of refinements holds; the exact form of the dependency does not matter.

We say r, r' are isomorphic rules, written $r \simeq r'$, if there is an isomorphism $\theta \in [s, s']$ such that $r' = \theta(r)$. If that is the case, then r and $\theta(r)$ have isomorphic transitions:

$$x \longrightarrow^r_f f(\alpha) \cdot x \Leftrightarrow x \longrightarrow^{\theta(r)}_{f\theta^{-1}} f\theta^{-1}(\theta(\alpha)) \cdot x$$

and, in particular, the same events and activities $\mathbf{a}(r, x) = \mathbf{a}(\theta(r), x)$. These rules are, therefore, indistinguishable.

To define activities, one can use the alternate SSA convention and define $\mathbf{a}(x, r) := \tau|[s, x]|/|[s, s]|$. As discussed earlier (Section 4.2.3), this convention is natural in the special case of Petri nets because siteless objects have simple automorphisms, and rule application uses simpler contexts. In particular, two injections in $[s, x]$ that are conjugated by an autorphism of s will define transitions to isomorphic states. This is no longer true with the richer contexts offered by site graphs, as the context can easily be made to distinguish conjugate injections by breaking their symmetry. The convention we choose to follow, that is, to consider each injection (of each rule) as a distinct event, is more natural in our context.

4.4 REFINEMENT, THEORETICALLY

Now that we have our basics in place, we turn first to the question of what constitutes a refinement of a rule r. Intuitively, it is a set of extensions (in the sense of Section 4.3.3) that will partition the various ways in which a rule can be applied. To capture this notion, we introduce now the concept of growth policy.

4.4.1 Growth Policies

The idea of a growth policy for an object s is to state explicitly which sites need to be present along each extension of s. We start with a mathematical definition. Later, we will investigate practical ways to obtain growth policies.

Let s be a fixed object in $\mathbf{S}$, and G be a family of maps $G(\phi)$ from $V_{\phi(s)}$ to $\wp(\mathbb{S})$ indexed by s's extensions $\mathbf{S}(s)$. Define $\mathbf{S}(s, G)$ as the subcategory of $\mathbf{S}(s)$ obtained by restricting oneself to objects ϕ such that $\sigma_{\phi(s)} \leq G(\phi)$. Objects not in $\mathbf{S}(s, G)$ correspond to overgrown extensions, where one has more sites than asked for.

Definition 4.6 (growth policy) *One says G is a growth policy for s if for all $\psi\phi \in$ $S(s, G)$, and for all $u \in V_{\phi(s)}$:*

$$G(\phi)(u) = G(\psi\phi)(\psi(u)).$$

The above condition is called the faithful condition and ensures that any sites that are asked for over an extension are also asked for over further extensions.

Given a growth policy G, the set of extensions we wish to use as refinements are those that have grown fully under G, that is, for all nodes in $\phi(s)$, all and only the sites asked for by G are present.

Definition 4.7 (refinement) *Given a rule $r = s, \alpha, \tau$, and a growth policy G for s, one defines the refinement of s and r via G:*

$$G(s) := \{\phi \in S(s) \mid \sigma_{\phi(s)} = G(\phi)\}/ \simeq_{S(s)},$$

$$G(r) := \{\phi(r) \mid \phi \in G(s)^*\},$$

where $G(s)^*$ stands for a particular selection of representatives in $G(s)$.

There are a few comments worth making about this definition.

First, the resulting $G(r)$ does not depend on the selection. Evidently, if $\phi_1 \simeq_{S(s)} \phi_2$, then the associated refined rules $\phi_1(r)$ and $\phi_2(r)$ are equivalent. As discussed earlier (Section 4.2.3), the rates are unchanged, as all the clever accounting is hidden in the quotient under the equivalence $\simeq_{S(s)}$.

This begs the second remark, namely, that $G(r)$ can contain equivalent rules, since one is only selecting up to $\simeq_{S(s)}$, and as we have noticed earlier, this is a more stringent condition than having isomorphic targets. To illustrate this, consider again the example where $s = A(a), A(a)$, $t = A(a), A(a, b^1), B(a^1)$, and one has two nonisomorphic extensions ϕ_1, ϕ_2 in $G_\Sigma(s)$. Suppose, the rule action is $A(a), A(a) \rightarrow A(a^1), A(a^1)$, then $\phi_1(r) \simeq \phi_2(r)$, since this action is stable under the automorphism of s that swaps the two As. This is entirely similar to the red–blue example (Section 4.2.3).

Third, there is no reason why $G(s)^*$ should be finite or even computable. As said, ours is a purely mathematical definition.

4.4.2 Simple Growth Policies

An example is the empty growth policy $G_\emptyset$ defined as:

$$G_\emptyset(\phi)(u) = \begin{cases} \sigma_s(v) & \text{if } u = \phi(v), \\ \emptyset & \text{if } u \notin \phi(V_s). \end{cases}$$

The faithful condition on growth policies is satisfied, as only sites that exist in s are asked for over any (and all) extensions. Furthermore, $G_\emptyset(s) = [s, s]/ \simeq_{S(s)}$ contains only the identity map (up to selection), and $G_\emptyset(r) = r$ for any r of the form s, α, τ.

This is as expected, one asks for no new sites in $G_\varnothing$ and, therefore, the original rule is its own refinement.

A simple way to obtain further growth policies is to let the growth requirement of a node depend only on the node's name. This leads to what we call homogeneous or name-based refinements.

Specifically, given a signature Σ, one can define:

$$G_\Sigma(\phi)(u) := \Sigma(\lambda_{\phi(s)}(u)).$$

Obviously, G_Σ satisfies the faithful condition, since by condition (1), $\lambda_{\psi\phi(s)}(\psi(u)) = \lambda_{\phi(s)}(u)$.

The associated refinement is given by

$$G_\Sigma(s) := \{\phi \mid \sigma_{\phi(s)} = \Sigma\}/\simeq_{S(s)}.$$

This set is not empty as soon as $\sigma_s \le \Sigma \circ \lambda_s$. It can well be infinite. Suppose for example, that $s = A()$, $\Sigma(A) = \{a, b\}$, $\Sigma(B) = \varnothing$ for $A \ne B$, then $G_\Sigma(s)$ consists of all pointed chains and cycles one can form with each node being of type A and having a, b as sites. Even after selection, the resulting $G_\Sigma(s)^*$ is clearly infinite.

4.4.3 Neutral Refinements

We can now obtain our first general result, which expresses the fact that the refined rules $G(r)$ decompose unambiguously r.

4.4.3.1 Injectivity

Theorem 4.1 (injectivity)   *Let $r = s, \alpha, \tau$ be a rule, G be a growth policy for s, and x an object: the composition map from $\mathcal{E}(x, G(r))$ to $\mathcal{E}(x, r)$ is injective.*

Proof: We want to prove that the map from $\sum_{\phi \in G(s)^*}[\phi(s), x]$ to $[s, x]$ mapping (ϕ, γ) to $\gamma\phi$ is injective.

So, let us suppose given two factorizations $\gamma_1\phi_1 = \gamma_2\phi_2$ as in the diagram below:

We want to show that $\phi_1 = \phi_2$ and $\gamma_1 = \gamma_2$. It is enough to prove that $\phi_1 = \phi_2$ because ϕ_1 is an epi, so it is enough to prove $\phi_1 \simeq_{S(s)} \phi_2$, since one selects one representative only per class in $G(s)$. But then it is enough to prove that there is an epi α such that $\alpha\phi_1 = \phi_2$, since by symmetry, there will also be an α' such that $\phi_1 = \alpha'\phi_2$, and this implies the above ($\phi_1 = \alpha'\alpha\phi_1 \Rightarrow \alpha'\alpha = Id$). So, consider the partial injective map from V_{t_1} to V_{t_2} defined by $\alpha := \gamma_2^{-1}\gamma_1$, we are going to prove that this map is total and an epi such that $\alpha\phi_1 = \phi_2$.

Pick $v_1 \in V_{t_1}$; we wish to prove that $\gamma_2^{-1}\gamma_1(v_1)$ is defined. Since ϕ_1 is an epi, there is $u \in V_s$, such that there is a path p that connects $u_1 := \phi_1(u)$ to v_1, and γ_1 being an arrow, there is an image path in x that connects $v := \gamma_1(u_1) = \gamma_2(u_2)$ to $\gamma_1(v_1)$. Pick along this image path the node that immediately precedes the first node (if any) that is not in $Im(\gamma_2)$ (i.e., where γ_2^{-1} is undefined). Call that node e (as exit), this is the node via which one exits $Im(\gamma_2)$, call a the site of e used to exit $Im(\gamma_2)$, write $e_i := \gamma_i^{-1}(e)$, and call p' the path p up to e_1. Because γ_2 is an arrow, it must be that e_2 does not have a as a site.

Consider now the object t obtained from s by grafting p' and the associated extension $\phi \in [s, t]$. Since p' is connected to s, ϕ is indeed an epi. Also, by construction, there are (epis) β_1 and β_2 such that $\beta_i\phi = \phi_i$.

We are in a position to apply the condition on G, since all our objects ϕ, ϕ_1, ϕ_2 are in $\mathbf{S}(s, G)$, which combined with the fact that ϕ_1, ϕ_2 are in $G(s)$ gives:

$$a \in \sigma_{t_1}(e_1) = G(\phi_1)(e_1) = G(\phi)(\beta_1^{-1}(e_1)) = G(\phi_2)(\beta_2\beta_1^{-1}(e) = e_2) = \sigma_{t_2}(e_2),$$

which means e_2 has a as a site, after all. Therefore, the image path of p along γ_1 wholly lies in $Im(\gamma_2)$, γ_2^{-1} is defined at $\gamma_1(v_1)$, and α is total. It is easy to verify that α is an arrow. Trivially, $\alpha\phi_1 = \phi_2$, and α is, hence, an epi (since it is the suffix of ϕ_2). $\square$

4.4.3.2 *Surjectivity*   It is time to tackle the question of refinement surjectivity.

Given $f \in [s, x]$, and G a growth policy for s, f can be decomposed as $f = \gamma\phi$, where ϕ is maximal in $\mathbf{S}(s)$ such that $\sigma_{\phi(s)} \leq G(\phi)$. Such a ϕ is called the G-factorization of f in x. We say x is G-decomposable, if for all f, its G-factorization is in $G(s)$.

We can illustrate this definition with a growth policy we have already considered: $s = A()$, $\Sigma(A) = \{a, b\}$, $\Sigma(B) = \varnothing$ for $A \neq B$, and $G = G_\Sigma$.

Here are some examples:

- $x = A(a)$, then $\phi = f \notin G_\Sigma(s)$, and x is not G_Σ-decomposable.
- $x = A(a, b^1)$, $B(a^1)$, then $Im(\phi) = \{A(a)\}$, so again $\phi \notin G_\Sigma(s)$ and x is not G_Σ-decomposable.
- $x = A(a, b^1)$, $A(a^1, b)$, $A(a, b)$, then it is easy to see that x is G_Σ-decomposable.

In the first case, x does not have enough sites, while in the second, it has too many. In the third, x is G_Σ-decomposable because it is itself obeying signature Σ.

Theorem 4.2   *Let $r = s, \alpha, \tau$ be a rule, G be a growth policy for s, and x be G-decomposable, the composition map from $\mathcal{E}(x, G(r))$ to $\mathcal{E}(x, r)$ is bijective.*

Proof: We already know that the composition map is injective, so all there remains to prove is that it is surjective. But since x is G-decomposable, any $f \in [s, x]$ factorizes as $\gamma\phi$ with $\phi \in G(s)$. $\square$

Given R a rule set, r a rule in R, we write $R[r\backslash G(r)]$ for the rule set obtained by replacing r with $G(r)$.

We have just seen that $\mathcal{E}(x, G(r))$ and $\mathcal{E}(x, r)$ are in bijection. In other words, each event $f \in [s, x]$ associated to rule $r = s, \alpha, \tau$ has a unique matching refined event γ associated to some unique rule $\phi(r) = \phi(s), \phi(\alpha), \tau$. Since $\gamma\phi = f$, both events have the same effect on x.

This establishes the following corollary.

Corollary 4.1 *Let R be a rule set and G be a growth policy, R and $R[r\backslash G(r)]$ determine the same stochastic transition system on G-decomposable states.*

4.4.4 Example Concluded

We can now conclude our pending example where we had $s := C(), B()$, and:

$$t_1 := C(x^1), B(x^1),$$
$$t_2 := C(x^1), B(x^1), C(x^2), B(x^2),$$
$$t_3 := C(x^1), B(x^1), C(x).$$

Observe that the above refinements are definable by a name-based growth policy, where: $\Sigma(B) = \Sigma(C) = \{x\}$, and Σ is empty on all other names. The set $G_\Sigma(s)$ contains many more extensions (e.g., $C(x^1), C(x^1), B(x))$, but these have no matches on the states $x(n_1, n_2)$ considered here (see 4.2.4).

Now, although we have $|[s, t_2]^e| = 2$ (recall that epis must have images in all connected components), these two extensions are actually isomorphic, so the refinement of r via t_2 only contributes one rule to $G(r)$ according to Definition 4.7. This means that by giving r_1, r_2, and r_3 uniformly the same rate, that of the original rule, k_r, their activities will add up exactly to that of r.

However, our simulation engine follows the SSA convention (where a rule's activity is modulated by dividing by the number of automorphisms of its left hand side). So, in the only case of refinement r_2, which has two automorphisms, we need to multiply k_{r_2} by a factor of 2 to get from the SSA activity to ours. To numerically verify this, we ran a simulation of the refined system with $x(0, 100)$ as the initial state. Figure 4.10 shows the simulation run, and we can see that at all times the refined activities add up to the original one (the top curve)—unlike in Figure 4.8.

4.4.5 Growth Policies, Concretely

We turn now to the question of how one can define concrete nonhomogeneous growth policies. To do this, we introduce a notion of address, which is a way to designate a node in an extension of s by a path that connects it to the image of a node in s.

Let us define $\mathbb{S}^{2\star}$ as the set of formal paths, that is, the set of finite even-length sequences with values in $\mathbb{S}$, the set of sites.

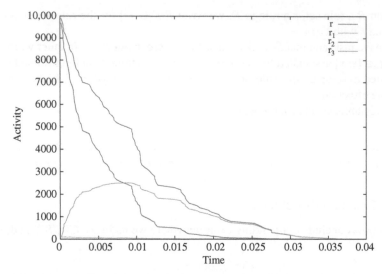

Figure 4.10   The activities of the refined rules r_1, r_2, and r_3 add up exactly to r's (top curve).

Definition 4.8 (addresses)   *Given $\phi \in S(s)$, $u \in V_s$, $v \in V_{\phi(s)}$, p a formal path, one says that (u, p) is an* address *for $v \in V_{\phi(s)}$ in ϕ, written $v = [\![u, p]\!]_\phi$, if p defines in $\phi(s)$ a path starting from $\phi(u)$ and ending at v.*

One says that v is addressable *if it has an address; one says u, p is* valid *in ϕ if it addresses some v.*

Clearly, for a given ϕ, an address uniquely identifies $v \in V_\phi(s)$, and because ϕ is an epi, every v can be addressed in this way. However, a v can be addressed in different ways. For instance, if $s = A(a^1)$, $B(b^1)$, then $A = [\![A, \varnothing]\!]_{Id} = [\![B, b, a]\!]_{Id}$, where we have written $\varnothing$ for the empty path.

Now, we want to define our growth policy for a given node in an extension based on its address, and we need only specify this for nodes that we actually want to see in a refinement. To do this, we introduce the notion of formal growth and allow it to be only a partial assignment of sets of sites to addresses.

Definition 4.9 (formal growth)   *A partial map g from $V_s \times \mathbb{S}^{2\star}$ to $\wp(\mathbb{S})$ is said to be a formal growth on s if for all $u \in V_s$, $(u, \varnothing) \in dom(g)$, and for all $\phi \in S(s)$:*

$$[\![u, p]\!]_\phi = [\![u', p']\!]_\phi, \ (u, p), \ (u', p') \in dom(g) \Rightarrow g(u, p) = g(u', p').$$

Given a formal growth, one defines:

$$G_g(\phi)(v) := \begin{cases} g(u, p) & \text{if } v = [\![u, p]\!]_\phi \text{ and } (u, p) \in dom(g), \\ \varnothing & \text{else.} \end{cases}$$

The condition of Definition 4.9 ensures that $G_g(\phi)(v)$ does not depend on the choice of an address in the domain of g.

Lemma 4.3   *If g is a formal growth, then G_g is a growth policy.*

Proof: To see this, pick a $\psi(v)$ in a $\psi\phi \in \mathbf{S}(s, G_g)$.

Suppose, $G_g(\phi)(v) = g(u, p)$ as in the first case of the definition above. Then by definition $[\![u, p]\!]_\phi = v$, and $(u, p) \in dom(g)$; certainly, $[\![u, p]\!]_{\psi\phi} = \psi(v)$, so $G_g(\psi\phi)(\psi(v)) = g(u, p)$.

Suppose, now one is in the second case, and v has no address in $dom(g)$. Again by definition, $G_g(\phi)(v) = \varnothing$, and since $\phi \in \mathbf{S}(s, G_g)$, this forces $\sigma_{\phi(s)}(v) = \varnothing$, which ϕ being an epi is only possible if $v = \phi(u)$ for $u \in V_s$, but then an address for v is simply $(u, \varnothing) \in dom(g)$.   □

A similar argument shows readily that all nodes in a $\phi \in \mathbf{S}(s, G_g)$ have an address in $dom(g)$, and $G_g(s)$ is the set of extensions of s, where all nodes are addressable within $dom(g)$ and have all the required sites.

We will call such growth policies address-based, or also sometimes weakly homogeneous.

It is easily seen that a name-based growth policy G_Σ is a particular type of address-based growth policy. We may safely assume to simplify notations that sites can only belong to one node type (else the notion of a formal path can incorporate the name of the nodes visited as well as the sites). An address u, p along any ϕ will, therefore, always lead to a node of the same type, namely, the type of the last site of p, or that of u if $p = \varnothing$, and, therefore, G_Σ assigns nodes with the same address to the same growth.

Likewise, it is easy to verify that the empty growth policy $G_\varnothing$ is address based: just define $g(u, \varnothing) = \sigma_s(u)$ for $u \in V_s$. But, of course, the point of this new notion is that it is more flexible, and we shall now see an example of a weakly homogeneous refinement, which is not homogeneous.

4.4.6   A Weakly Homogeneous Refinement

Let us consider a system with three agent types: a receptor R with two sites a and x, a messenger M with one site y, and an adaptor A with two sites r and m. The system contact map summarizing all the bindings one is interested in is shown in Figure 4.11.

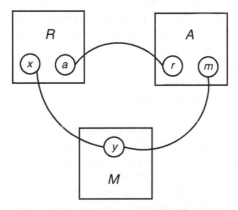

Figure 4.11   Contact map for RAM system.

We have a rule, say for the activation of M, with left hand side $s := My^-$, that is, the rule requires that M is bound via the y site, but does not care what it is bound to. We wish to refine the rule into the following extensions:

$$t_1 = M(y^1), A(m^1, r),$$
$$t_2 = M(y^1), A(m^1, r^2), R(a^2),$$
$$t_3 = M(y^1), R(x^1).$$

In each case, there is clearly a unique extension in $[s, t_i]$, so it is enough to specify the target of the extension.

A concrete motivation for this refinement would be the need to express the fact that the activation of M is impossible in the case t_1, and faster when it is directly connected to the receptor as in t_3. However, t_2 and t_3 both mention a node of type R with different binding sites, so the desired refinement cannot be homogeneous, meaning that there is no Σ such that the above t_is are jointly in $G_\Sigma(s)$.

So, let us define a finite formal growth g as follows:

$$g(M, \varnothing) = \{y\},$$
$$g(M, ym) = \{m, r\},$$
$$g(M, ymra) = \{a\},$$
$$g(M, yx) = \{x\},$$

where other pairs (M, p) are assumed not in $dom(g)$.

We have to verify that g is a formal growth (as in Definition 4.9). There are two conditions. The first holds trivially. The second also does because no two addresses in the domain of g can address the same node. Indeed, suppose (M, p), (M, q) belong to the domain of g, and address the same node in some extension ϕ; just by the type of their end nodes, one sees that the only nontrivial possibility is $p = yx, q = ymra$, where the end node is of type R; but $M, yx, M, ymra$ cannot both be valid in ϕ, since y can only be paired with one of x and m.

The diagram below shows $\mathbf{S}(s, G_g)$ and $G_g(s)$ (Figure 4.12), and one can observe that all extensions shown there project to the contact map (Figure 4.11).

As said, the formal growth we have constructed can address any node in at most one way. In other words, if $[\![u, p]\!]_\phi = [\![u', p']\!]_\phi$, and both (u, p), (u', p') are in $dom(g)$, then in fact $u, p = u', p'$. This is an easy way to satisfy the constraint of Definition 4.9, and it might be that this suffices in practice, at least when s is connected.

It is also worth noticing that a formal growth with finite domain defines a finite $G(s)$. This is general. For any extension $\phi \in G(s)$, $|V_{\phi(s)}| \leq |dom(g)|$, since each node is addressable at least once within $dom(g)$. Therefore, if $dom(g)$ is finite, refinements are uniformly bounded in size, and $G(s)$ is finite, that is, in sharp constrast with name-based growth policies, which are in general defining infinite refinements (as the earlier example of chains and rings).

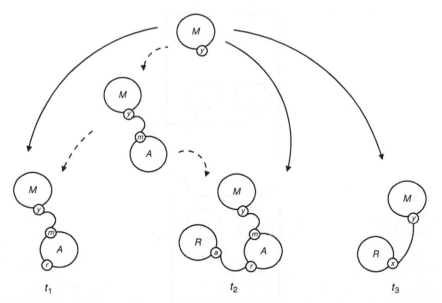

Figure 4.12   The refinement $G_g(s)$ of s via G_g for the *RAM* system (solid arrows); intermediate extensions in S(s, G_g) are shown too (dotted arrows).

4.4.7   Non-homogeneous Growth Policies

There are obviously ways for objects to grow that do not obey the constraints of the above examples. In order to see this, let us consider another example.

We are given $s := B()$ and the following contact map (see Figure 4.13).

Clearly, the following t_i define each a unique extension of s, which we will call ϕ_i:

$$t_1 = B(x, y),$$
$$t_2 = B(x^1, y), A(x^1),$$
$$t_3 = B(x, y^1), A(y^1),$$
$$t_4 = B(x^1, y^2), A(x^1), A(y^2),$$
$$t_5 = B(x^1, y^2), A(x^1, y^2).$$

There is a valid growth policy to describe this, namely:

$$G(\phi_1)([\![B, \varnothing]\!]_{\phi_1}) = G(\phi_2)([\![B, \varnothing]\!]_{\phi_2}) = \cdots = G(\phi_5)([\![B, \varnothing]\!]_{\phi_5}) = \{x, y\},$$
$$G(\phi_2)([\![B, xx]\!]_{\phi_2}) = \{x\},$$
$$G(\phi_3)([\![B, yy]\!]_{\phi_3}) = \{y\},$$
$$G(\phi_4)([\![B, xx]\!]_{\phi_4}) = \{x\}, G(\phi_4)([\![B, yy]\!]_{\phi_4}) = \{y\},$$
$$G(\phi_5)([\![B, xx]\!]_{\phi_5}) = \{x, y\},$$

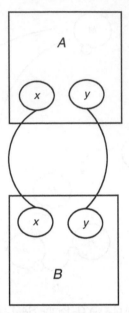

Figure 4.13   Contact map for the $A(x, y)$, $B(x, y)$ system.

where all other extensions, which are not intermediates of the above, are assigned uniformly $G(\phi) = \varnothing$. (Note that we have used the address notation, which is convenient even for general growth policies.)

The refinements associated with G are shown in Figure 4.14. It is not an address-based growth policy, as its formal growth would have to verify the contradictory assignments $g(B, xx) = \{x\} = \{x, y\}$ because of extensions ϕ_2 and ϕ_5, respectively.

An interesting thing to note is that if we relax the injectivity requirement in our ambient category **S** (condition (4) in Definition 4.2), the above is no longer a valid growth policy at all. With this requirement lifted, there is an arrow h from t_4 to t_5 mapping

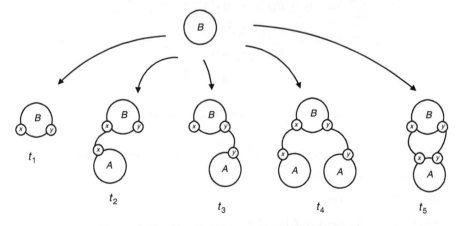

Figure 4.14   Growth diagram for the cyclic AB system.

the two As to the unique A in t_5, which has sites $\{x, y\}$; this h violates the faithful condition. This shows that G being a growth policy depends on the ambient category, and may also suggest that one has a simpler refinement theory without condition (4).

4.5 CONCLUSION

We have presented a notion of refinement for rule based modeling.
   Specifically, we have

- Proposed a notion of growth policy to manage the growth of objects and produce refined rules
- Characterized situations where these refinements preserve the original behavior.

The somewhat technical treatment of these concepts is justified by the fact that, unlike in the case of simpler rewriting frameworks such as Petri nets, the solution to this problem needs a thorough understanding of symmetries.

Our refinements as they stand under this approach are a lot more flexible than in our previous work [1]. However, they still do not allow full flexibility. For example, it would be beneficial if we were able to use the wild card binding where we say that an agent is bound to a site not in a growth policy, but we do not care what the site is. This would extend the validity of the surjectivity argument that establishes that a set of refined rules covers all cases. There is no real mathematical difficulty here, but the needed notations could prove daunting.

Another question that we have not addressed is how to generate growth policies. The growth policies used in our examples were informally generated using the contact map to keep track of possible bindings that should be added to extensions. An interesting future direction for this work would be to develop a formal theory of how to generate refinements starting with a possibly restricted notion of formal growth. This would have an evident utility in a modeling environment, in that it could guarantee a user that his refinements are neutral, without him having to sit down and do the kind of calculations we have done here in a few examples.

Talking about which, we have shown on the more practical side, how refinement can be used to derive models. This of course is the main motivation for our study. This sort of approach might offer a structured top–down approach to navigate the space of parameters of a given model for data fitting. Indeed, every time one refines a rule, more parameters are made available to optimization. This line of thought is pursued further in the recent study [10], where one derives a biological repair scheme from a very simple initial model solely by means of successive refinements.

Finally, on the more conceptual side, one wonders whether refinements could provide some interesting grammatical substrate, with a measure of biological plausiblity, that one could use to investigate the plasticity of existing pathways and study their evolution.[2]

---

[2]The first author was the principal contributor to this study, others have contributed equally.

REFERENCES

1. V. Danos, J. Feret, W. Fontana, R. Harmer, and J. Krivine. Rule-based modelling, symmetries, refinements. *FMSB 2008*. Springer vol. 5054 of *LNBI*, 2008, pp. 103–122.
2. V. Danos, J. Feret, W. Fontana, and J. Krivine. Abstract interpretation of cellular signalling networks. In F. Logozzo, et al., editor. *VMCAI'08*, vol. 4905 of *LNCS*, Springer, 2008, pp. 83–97.
3. V. Danos. Agile modelling of cellular signalling. *Computation in Modern Science and Engineering, Volume 2, Part A*, 963:611–614, Sep 2007.
4. V. Danos, J. Feret, W. Fontana, and J. Krivine. Scalable simulation of cellular signaling networks. In Z. Shao, editor, *Proceedings of APLAS 2007*, volume 4807 of *LNCS*, Nov 2007, pp. 139–157.
5. V. Danos and L. Schumacher. How liquid is biological signalling? *TCS A*, Sep 2008.
6. W. S. Hlavacek, J. R. Faeder, M. L. Blinov, R. G. Posner, M. Hucka, and W. Fontana. Rules for modeling signal-transduction systems. *Science's STKE*, 2006(344), 2006.
7. D. T. Gillespie. Exact stochastic simulation of coupled chemical reactions. *J. Phys. Chem*, 81:2340–2361, 1977.
8. C. Y. F. Huang and J. E. Ferrell. Ultrasensitivity in the mitogen-activated protein kinase cascade. *Proc. Natl. Acad. Sci.* USA, 93(19):10078–10083, 1996.
9. R. P. Bhattacharyya, A. Remenyi, B. J. Yeh, and W. A. Lim. Domains, motifs, and scaffolds: the role of modular interactions in the evolution and wiring of cell signaling circuits. *Annu. Rev. Biochem.*, 75:655–680, 2006.
10. V. Danos, J. Feret, W. Fontana, R. Harmer, and J. Krivine. Investigation of a biological repair scheme. In G. Paun, editor, *Proceedings of WMC'09*, volume 5391 of *LNCS*. Springer, Jan 2009.

5

A (NATURAL) COMPUTING PERSPECTIVE ON CELLULAR PROCESSES

Matteo Cavaliere and Tommaso Mazza

The Microsoft Research - University of Trento, CoSBi, Trento, Italy

5.1 NATURAL COMPUTING AND COMPUTATIONAL BIOLOGY

Natural computing is a fast growing field of interdisciplinary research driven by the idea that natural processes can be used for implementing computations, constructing new computing devices, and to get inspirations for new computational paradigms. Moreover, natural computing can also be understood as abstracting biological processes in form of computational processes to allow the use of computational tools for analyzing biologically relevant properties. The field is growing very fast (see, the journals in the area, e.g., [1] and [2]). This chapter is constructed on the same double vision: In the first part of the chapter, we recall a computational model inspired by the structure and the functioning of living cells, called membrane system, and we show how one can abstract biologically relevant properties and study them by using tools coming from theoretical computer science. In the second part of the chapter, we show how the paradigm can be extended and adapted in order to describe and simulate the mechanisms underlying cell cycle and breast tumor growth.

Elements of Computational Systems Biology   Edited by Huma M. Lodhi and Stephen H. Muggleton
Copyright © 2010 John Wiley & Sons, Inc.

5.2   MEMBRANE COMPUTING

An important research direction in natural computing concerns computations in living cells. An abstract computational model inspired by the structure and the functioning of living cells is a membrane system, introduced in 1998 by Păun [3]. Since their introduction, a large number of membrane systems models have been introduced in the literature. Several of them have been proved to be computationally complete and useful for solving hard computational problems in an efficient way (see, for instance the introductory monograph [4]). In 2003, Thomson Institute for Scientific Information, ISI, has nominated membrane computing as fast emerging research front in computer science with the initial paper considered fast breaking paper.

Most of the work done in the membrane systems community concerns the computational power of the system (for an updated bibliography, the reader can consult the Web page [5], where also preprints can be downloaded). Currently, a handbook of membrane computing is in preparation (it was scheduled to appear at the end of 2008).

More recently, membrane systems have been applied to systems biology and several models have been proposed for simulating biological processes (e.g., see the monograph dedicated to membrane systems applications [6]).

In the original definition, membrane systems are composed of a hierarchical nesting of membranes that enclose regions in which floating objects exist. Each region can have associated rules for evolving these objects (called evolution rules, modeling the biochemical reactions present in cell regions) and/or rules for moving objects across membranes (called symport/antiport rules, modeling some kinds of transport mechanism present in cells). Recently, inspired by brane calculus [7], a model of membrane systems, having objects attached to the membranes, was introduced in Cardelli and Păun [8]. A more general approach, considering both free-floating objects and objects attached to the membranes, has been proposed and investigated in Brijder et al. [9]. The idea of these models is that membrane operations are moderated by the objects (proteins) attached to the membranes. However, in all these models, objects are associated with an atomic membrane, which has no concept of inner or outer surface. In reality, many biological processes are driven and controlled by the presence of specific proteins on the appropriate sides of a membrane. For instance, endocytosis, exocytosis, and budding in cells are processes in which the existence and locality of membrane proteins is crucial (see, e.g. [10]).

In general, the compartments of a cell are in constant communication, with molecules being passed from a donor compartment to a target compartment, mediated by membrane proteins. Once transported to the correct compartment, the substances are often then processed by means of local biochemical reactions.

Motivated by this, an extended model has been investigated in Cavaliere and Sedwards [11, 12] by combining some basic features found in biological cells: (i) evolution of objects (molecules) by means of multiset rewriting rules associated with specific regions of the systems (the rules model biochemical reactions); (ii) transport of objects across the regions of the system by means of rules associated with the membranes of the system and involving proteins attached to the membranes (on one or possibly both sides); and (iii) rules that take care of the attachment/detachment of objects to/from the sides of the membranes. Moreover, since we want to distinguish the functioning of different regions, we also associate with each membrane a unique identifier (a label).

We review the basic paradigm and show how one can, in this way, abstract and investigate biologically relevant properties such as reachability of a certain state of the system.

In particular, we are interested in finding classes of membrane systems, where one can provide algorithms (possibly, efficient) to check interesting and biologically relevant properties. In computability theory, it is well-known that not all problems can be algorithmically solved (problems for which algorithms exist are called decidable). Moreover, for some problems, only inefficient algorithms are known. For these topics, the reader can consult standard books in computability theory as in Hopcroft and Ullman [13].

In this respect, we investigate the proposed model by defining two classes of systems based on two different ways of applying the rules: These two ways correspond to two different ways of abstracting the applications of biochemical rules in cellular compartments (a third possible way, less abstract and closer to biochemistry, is to associate kinetic rates with the rules: This possibility is presented only in the second part of the chapter when cellular pathways are modeled).

The first way is based on free parallelism: At each step of the evolution of the system, an arbitrary number of rules may be applied. We prove that, in this case, there are algorithms that can be used to check important properties like reachability of a certain configuration (state) even in the presence of cooperative evolution and transport rules (intuitively, cooperative means that several objects/molecules are needed for starting a biochemical or transport rule).

We also consider a maximal parallel evolution: In this case, if a rule can be applied then it must be applied, with alternative possible rules being chosen nondeterministically. This strategy models, for example, the behavior in biology, where a process takes place as soon as resources become available. In this case, we show that there is no algorithm that can be used to check whether or not a system can reach a certain configuration, when the systems use noncooperative evolution rules coupled with cooperative transport rules. However, several other cases where algorithms are possible are also presented.

The model presented follows the philosophy of a well-known model in the area of membrane computing, called evolution–communication model, introduced in Cavaliere [14], where the system evolves by evolution of the objects and transport of objects by means of symport/antiport rules that are essentially synchronized exchanges of objects. However, in the model presented here, the transport of objects may depend on the presence of particular proteins attached to the internal and external surfaces of the membranes. Clearly, the model presented is an abstraction whose main purpose is to produce a cellular-inspired model of computation; the model needs to be complemented with "real-life" details (e.g., as done in the second part of this chapter). However, we believe that even such abstract computational paradigm could give a different view on cellular processes and on the types of problems that one could and should address.

Sections 5.4 and 5.5 are based on the the work presented in Cavaliere and Sedwards [11, 12] (the reader can find there details concerning the definitions and the proofs of the presented results). A survey of the models of membrane systems that consider proteins on the membranes is given in Cavaliere et al. [15].

5.3   FORMAL LANGUAGES PRELIMINARIES

Membrane systems are based on formal languages theory and multiset rewriting, two well-known tools in theoretical computer science. We briefly recall the basic theoretical notions used in this chapter. For more details, the reader can consult standard books in the area, such as those by Hopcroft and Ullman [13] and Salomaa [16] and the corresponding chapters of the handbook by Rozenberg and Salomaa [17].

Given the set A, we denote by $|A|$ its cardinality and by $\varnothing$ the empty set. We denote by $\mathbb{N}$ and by $\mathbb{R}$ the set of natural and real numbers, respectively.

As usual, an alphabet V is a finite set of symbols. By V^*, we denote the set of all strings (sequences of symbols) over V. By V^+, we denote the set of all strings over V excluding the empty string. The empty string is denoted by λ (it is the string with zero symbols). The length of a string v is denoted by $|v|$. The concatenation of two strings $u, v \in V^*$ is written uv.

The number of occurrences of the symbol a in the string w is denoted by $|w|_a$.

Suppose $V = \{a, b\}$. Then a string is $w = aaba$, then $|w| = 4$ and $|w|_a = 3$.

A multiset is a set where each element may have a multiplicity. Formally, a multiset over a set V is a map $M : V \to \mathbb{N}$, where $M(a)$ denotes the multiplicity of the symbol $a \in V$ in the multiset M.

For multisets M and M' over V, we say that M is *included in* M' if $M(a) \leq M'(a)$ for all $a \in V$. Every multiset includes the empty multiset, defined as M where $M(a) = 0$ for all $a \in V$.

The *sum* of multisets M and M' over V is written as the multiset $(M + M')$, defined by $(M + M')(a) = M(a) + M'(a)$ for all $a \in V$. The difference between M and M' is written as $(M - M')$ and defined by $(M - M')(a) = \max\{0, M(a) - M'(a)\}$ for all $a \in V$. We also say that $(M + M')$ is obtained by adding M to M' (or vice-versa), while $(M - M')$ is obtained by removing M' from M. For example, given the multisets $M = \{a, b, b, b\}$ and $M' = \{b, b\}$, we can say that M' is included in M, that $(M + M') = \{a, b, b, b, b, b\}$ and that $(M - M') = \{a, b\}$.

If the set V is finite, for example, $V = \{a_1, \ldots, a_n\}$, then the multiset M can be explicitly described as $\{(a_1, M(a_1)), (a_2, M(a_2)), \ldots, (a_n, M(a_n))\}$. The support of a multiset M is defined as the set $\text{supp}(M) = \{a \in V \mid M(a) > 0\}$. A multiset is empty (hence finite) when its support is empty (also finite).

A compact notation can be used for finite multisets: If $M = \{(a_1, M(a_1)), (a_2, M(a_2)), \ldots, (a_n, M(a_n))\}$ is a multiset of finite support, then the string $w = a_1^{M(a_1)} a_2^{M(a_2)} \ldots a_n^{M(a_n)}$ (and all its permutations) precisely identifies the symbols in M and their multiplicities. Hence, given a string $w \in V^*$, we can say that it identifies a finite multiset over V, written as $M(w)$, where $M(w) = \{a \in V \mid (a, |w|_a)\}$. For instance, the string bab represents the multiset $M(w) = \{(a, 1), (b, 2)\}$, which is the multiset $\{a, b, b\}$. The empty multiset is represented by the empty string λ.

5.4 MEMBRANE OPERATIONS WITH PERIPHERAL PROTEINS

In the membrane systems field, it is usual to represent a membrane (that represents a biological membrane) by a pair of square brackets [ ]. To each topological side of a membrane, we associate the multisets u and v (over a particular alphabet V), and this is denoted by $[\ _u]_v$. We say that the membrane is marked by u and v; v is called the external marking and u the internal marking; in general, we refer to them as markings of the membrane. The objects of the alphabet V are called proteins or, simply, objects. An object is called free if it is not attached to the sides of a membrane, so is not a part of a marking.

Each membrane encloses a region, and the contents of a region can consist of free objects and/or other membranes (we also say that the region contains free objects and/or other membranes).

Moreover, each membrane has an associated label that is written as a superscript of the square brackets. If a membrane is associated with the label i, we call it membrane i. Each membrane encloses a unique region, so we also say region i to identify the region enclosed by membrane i. The set of all labels is denoted by Lab.

For instance, in the system $[abbbbc[abb\ _{ba}]_b^2\ _{ab}]_{ab}^1$, the external membrane, labeled by 1, is marked by ab (internal and external marking). The contents of the region enclosed by the external membrane is composed of the free objects a, b, b, b, b, c, and the membrane $[abb\ _{ba}]_b^2$. The system is graphically represented in Figure 5.1.

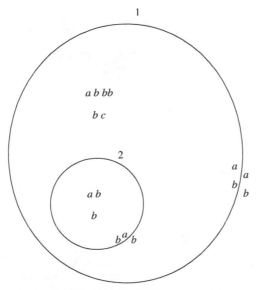

Figure 5.1 Graphical representation of the membrane system $[abbbbc[abb\ _{ba}]_b^2\ _{ab}]_{ab}^1$. It has a multiset of floating molecules and proteins attached to the membranes.

We consider rules that model the attachment of objects to the sides of the membranes.

$$\text{attach} : [a_u]_v^i \rightarrow [ua]_v^i, \quad a[u]_v^i \rightarrow [u]_{va}^i,$$

$$\text{detach} : [ua]_v^i \rightarrow [a_u]_v^i, \quad [u]_{va}^i \rightarrow [u]_v^i a,$$

with $a \in V$, $u, v \in V^*$, and $i \in$ Lab.

The semantics of the attachment rules (attach) is as follows.

For the first case, the rule is applicable to the membrane i if the membrane is marked by multisets containing the multisets u and v on the appropriate sides, and region i contains an object a. In the second case, the rule is applicable to membrane i if it is marked by multisets containing the multisets u and v, as before, and is contained in a region that contains an object a. If the rule is applicable, we say that the objects defined by u, v, and a can be assigned to the rule (so that it may be executed).

In both cases, if a rule is applicable and the objects given in u, v, and a are assigned to the rule, then the rule can be executed (applied) and the object a is added to the appropriate marking in the way specified. The objects not involved in the application of a rule are left unchanged in their original positions.

The semantics of the detachment rule (detach) is similar, with the difference that the attached object a is detached from the specified marking and added to the contents of either the internal or external region. An example of the application of an attachment rule is shown in Figure 5.2.

As it is biologically relevant, we also consider rules associated with the membranes that control the passage of objects across the membranes. Precisely

$$\text{move}_{\text{in}} : a[\ _u]_v^i \rightarrow [\ a\ _u]_v^i,$$

$$\text{move}_{\text{out}} : [\ a\ _u]_v^i \rightarrow a[\ _u]_v^i,$$

with $a \in V$, $u, v \in V^*$, and $i \in$ Lab.

The semantics of the rules is as follows.

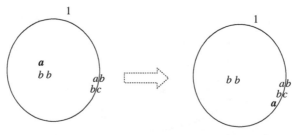

Figure 5.2 Graphical representation of the attach rule $[a\ _b]_{cb}^1 \rightarrow [\ _{ba}]_{cb}^1$.

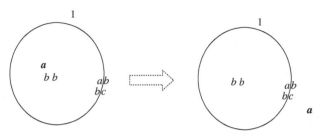

Figure 5.3 Graphical representation of the move$_\text{out}$ rule $[a\ {}_{b}]^1_{cb} \rightarrow a[\ {}_{b}]^1_{cb}$.

In the first case, the rule is applicable to membrane i if it is marked by multisets containing the multisets u and v, on the appropriate sides, and the membrane is contained in a region containing an object a. The objects defined by u, v, and a can thus be assigned to the rule.

If the rule is applicable and the objects a, u, and v are assigned to the rule, then the rule can be executed (applied) and, in this case, the object a is removed from the contents of the region surrounding membrane i and added to the contents of region i.

In the second case, the semantics is similar, but here, the object a is moved from region i to its surrounding region.

An example of the execution of a movement rule (move$_\text{out}$) is shown in Figure 5.3.

The rules of attach, detach, move$_\text{in}$, and move$_\text{out}$ are generally called membrane rules (denoted collectively as mem$_\text{rul}$) over the alphabet V and the set of labels Lab.

Membrane rules for which $|uv| \geq 2$, we call cooperative membrane rules (in short, coo$_\text{mem}$). Membrane rules for which $|uv| = 1$, we call noncooperative membrane rules (in short, ncoo$_\text{mem}$). Membrane rules for which $|uv| = 0$ are called simple membrane rules (in short, sim$_\text{m}$).

We also introduce evolution rules that involve objects but not membranes. These can be considered to model the biochemical reactions that take place inside the compartments of the cell. They are evolution rules over the alphabet V and set of labels Lab, and they follow the definition that can be found in evolution–communication P systems [14]. We define

$$\text{evol} : [u \rightarrow v]^i,$$

with $u \in V^+$, $v \in V^*$, and $i \in$ Lab. An evolution rule is called cooperative (in short, coo$_\text{e}$) if $|u| > 1$, otherwise the rule is called noncooperative (ncoo$_\text{e}$).

The *rule is* applicable to region i if the region contains a multiset of free objects that includes the multiset u. The objects defined by u can thus be assigned to the rule.

If the rule is applicable and the objects defined by u are assigned to the rule, then the rule can be executed. In this case, the objects specified by u are subtracted from the contents of region i, while the objects specified by v are added to the contents of the region i. An example of the application of an evolution rule is shown in Figure 5.4.

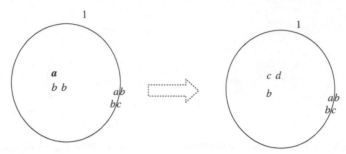

Figure 5.4 Graphical representation of the evolution rule $[ab \to cd]^1$.

5.5 MEMBRANE SYSTEMS WITH PERIPHERAL PROTEINS

We can now define a membrane system having membranes marked with multisets of proteins on both sides of the membrane, free objects, and using the operations introduced in Section 5.4.

Formally, a membrane system with peripheral proteins (in short, a P_{pp} system) and n membranes is a construct

$$\Pi = (V, \mu, (u_1, v_1), \ldots, (u_n, v_n), w_1, \ldots, w_n, R, R^m),$$

where

- V is a finite, nonempty alphabet of objects (proteins).
- μ is a membrane structure with $n \geq 1$ membranes, injectively labeled by $1, 2, \ldots, n$.
- $(u_1, v_1), \ldots, (u_n, v_n) \in V^* \times V^*$ are the markings associated, at the beginning of any evolution, with the membranes $1, 2, \ldots, n$, respectively. They are called initial markings of Π; the first element of each pair specifies the internal marking, while the second one specifies the external marking.
- $w_1, \ldots, w_n$ specify the multisets of free objects contained in regions $1, 2, \ldots, n$, respectively, at the beginning of any evolution and they are called initial contents of the regions.
- R is a finite set of evolution rules over V and the set of labels $\text{Lab} = \{1, \ldots, n\}$.
- R^m is a finite set of membrane rules over the alphabet V and set of labels $\text{Lab} = \{1, \ldots, n\}$.

5.5.1 Dynamics of The System

A configuration (state) of a membrane system Π consists of a membrane structure, the markings of the membranes (internal and external), and the multisets of free objects present inside the regions. In what follows, configurations are denoted by writing the markings as subscripts (internal and external) of the parentheses, which identify the membranes. The labels of the membranes are written as superscripts, and the contents of the regions as string, for example,

$$[\ [\ _{aa}]^4_{ab} \ [aaa \ _{aa}]^2_b \ [\ b \ ]^3_{bb} \ a \ ]^1_a$$

The initial configuration consists of the membrane structure μ, the initial markings of the membranes, and the initial contents of the regions; the environment is empty at the beginning of the evolution.

We denote by $\mathbb{C}(\Pi)$ the set of all possible configurations of Π.

We assume the existence of a clock that marks the timing of steps (single transitions) for the whole system.

A transition from a configuration $C \in \mathbb{C}(\Pi)$ to a new one is obtained by assigning the objects present in the configuration to the rules of the system and then executing the rules as described in Section 5.4.

As we were mentioning earlier, we define two possible ways of assigning the objects to the rules: free-parallel and maximal-parallel. These two ways conceptualize two ways of abstracting the application of biochemical reactions. As we will see, the obtained predictive results are different according to the considered abstraction.

- *Free-parallel evolution*
  In each region and for each marking, an arbitrary number of applicable rules is executed (membrane and evolution rules have equal precedence). A single object (free or not) may only be assigned to a single rule.

  This implies that in one step, no rule, one rule, or as many applicable rules as desired may be applied.

  We call a single transition performed in a free-parallel way a free-parallel transition.

- *Maximal-parallel evolution*
  In each region and for each marking, to the applicable rules, chosen in a non-deterministic way, are assigned objects, chosen in a nondeterministic way, such that after the assignment no further rule is applicable using the unassigned objects. As with free-parallel evolution, membrane and evolution rules have equal precedence, and a single object (free or not) may only be assigned to a single rule.

  We call a single transition performed in a maximal-parallel way a maximal-parallel transition.

A sequence of free-parallel [maximal-parallel] transitions, starting from the initial configuration, is called a free-parallel [maximal-parallel, respectively] evolution.

A configuration of a P_{pp} system Π that can be reached by a free-parallel [maximal-parallel] evolution, starting from the initial configuration, is called free-parallel [maximal-parallel, respectively] reachable. A pair of multisets (u, v) is a free-parallel [maximal-parallel] reachable marking for Π if there exists a free-parallel [maximal-parallel, respectively] reachable configuration of Π that contains at least one membrane marked internally by u and externally by v.

We denote by $\mathbb{C}_R(\Pi, \mathit{fp})$ [$\mathbb{C}_R(\Pi, \mathit{mp})$] the set of all free-parallel [maximal parallel, respectively] reachable configurations of Π and by $\mathbb{M}_R(\Pi, \mathit{fp})$ [$\mathbb{M}_R(\Pi, \mathit{mp})$] the set of all free-parallel [maximal-parallel, respectively] reachable markings of Π.

Moreover, we denote by $\mathbb{P}_{pp,m}(\alpha, \beta)$, $\alpha \in \{\mathrm{coo}_e, \mathrm{ncoo}_e\}$, $\beta \in \{\mathrm{coo}_{mem}, \mathrm{ncoo}_{mem}, \mathrm{sim}_m\}$ the class of all possible membrane systems with peripheral proteins, evolution rules of type α, membrane rules of type β, and m membranes (m is changed to $*$ if the number of membranes is not bounded). We omit α or β from the notation if the corresponding types of rules are not allowed. We also denote by V_Π the alphabet V of the system Π.

5.5.2   Reachability in Membrane Systems

One of the main goal of having a formal model is to provide a way to abstract and analyze relevant properties. In our case, we use tools from theoretical computer science, in particular coming from formal languages theory, to investigate biologically relevant properties of the defined membrane systems.

In particular, a rather natural question concerns whether or not a biological system can reach a particular specified configuration/state. Hence, it would be useful to construct models having such qualitative properties to be decidable.

In the described model, one can prove that when the evolution is free-parallel, it is possible to decide, for an arbitrary membrane system with peripheral proteins and an arbitrary configuration, whether or not such a configuration is reachable by the system. Formally, the following theorem holds (results presented in these sections can be found in Cavaliere and Sedwards [11, 12]). Notice that the number of membranes is not relevant for the obtained results (the symbol $*$ is used).

Theorem 5.1   *It is decidable whether or not for any P_{pp} system Π from $\mathbb{P}_{pp,*}(\mathrm{coo}_e, \mathrm{coo}_{mem})$ and any configuration C of Π, $C \in \mathbb{C}_R(\Pi, \mathit{fp})$.*

It is decidable whether or not for any P_{pp} system Π from $\mathbb{P}_{pp,*}(\mathrm{coo}_e, \mathrm{coo}_{mem})$ and any pair of multisets (u, v) over V_Π, $(u, v) \in \mathbb{M}_R(\Pi, \mathit{fp})$.

We can now suppose that a membrane system evolves in a maximal-parallel way; in this case, one can prove that the reachability of a specified configuration is decidable when the evolution rules used are noncooperative and the membrane rules are simple or when the system uses only membrane rules (including cooperative membrane rules).

Moreover, one can also show that it is undecidable whether or not an arbitrary configuration can be reached by an arbitrary system working in the maximal-parallel way and using noncooperative evolution rules coupled with cooperative membrane rules.

We first consider systems where only membrane rules are present.

Theorem 5.2   *It is decidable whether or not for an arbitrary P_{pp} system Π from $\mathbb{P}_{pp,*}(\mathrm{coo}_{mem})$ and an arbitrary configuration C of Π, $C \in \mathbb{C}_R(\Pi, \mathit{mp})$.*

It is decidable whether or not for an arbitrary P_{pp} system Π from $\mathbb{P}_{pp,*}(\text{coo}_{\text{mem}})$ and an arbitrary pair of multisets u, v over V_{Π}, $(u, v) \in \mathbb{M}_R(\Pi, mp)$.

For systems having noncooperative evolution and simple membrane rules, the following theorem holds.

Theorem 5.3   *It is decidable whether or not for an arbitrary P_{pp} system Π from $\mathbb{P}_{pp,*}(\text{ncoo}_e, \text{sim}_m)$ and an arbitrary configuration C of Π, $C \in \mathbb{C}_R(\Pi, mp)$.*
  It is decidable whether or not for any P_{pp} system Π from $\mathbb{P}_{pp,*}(\text{ncoo}_e, \text{sim}_m)$ and any pair of multisets (u, v) over V_{Π}, $(u, v) \in \mathbb{M}_R(\Pi, mp)$.

Another possibility is to consider systems having noncooperative evolution rules and cooperative membrane rules; in this case, the reachability of an arbitrary configuration becomes an undecidable problem and, as mentioned before, this means that, in general, there is no algorithm that can be found to solve such a problem.

Theorem 5.4   *It is undecidable whether or not for an arbitrary P_{pp} system Π from $\mathbb{P}_{pp,*}(\text{ncoo}_e, \text{coo}_{\text{mem}})$ and an arbitrary configuration C of Π, $C \in \mathbb{C}_R(\Pi, mp)$.*

It is known that membrane proteins can cluster and form more complex molecules whose activity is very distinct from the original components; moreover, proteins can cross sides of a membrane, and proteins on opposite sides can influence each other in a "synchronized" manner. To capture all these aspects, we can extend the considered paradigm by admitting evolution rules also for the proteins embedded in the membranes.

This can be done in a rather natural manner, since membrane proteins are represented as multisets of objects, and then we can still use multiset rewriting rules to represent these membrane processes.

Precisely, we can define a membrane-evolution rule

$$\text{mem} - \text{evol} : \ [\,u\,]_v^i \rightarrow [\,u'\,]_{v'}^i,$$

with $u, v, u', v' \in V^*$, and $i \in \text{Lab}$; if $u = \lambda$ or $v = \lambda$ then $u' = \lambda$ or $v' = \lambda$, respectively.

The rule is applicable to membrane i if the internal marking of the membrane contains the multiset of proteins u and the external marking contains the multiset v. The proteins defined by u and v can thus be assigned to the rule. If the rule is applicable and the objects defined by u and v are assigned to the rule, then the rule can be executed. In this case, the objects specified by u are subtracted from the internal marking of membrane i, the objects specified by v are subtracted from the external marking of membrane i, while the objects specified by u' are added to the internal marking of membrane i, and the objects specified by v' are added to the external marking of membrane i. An example of the application of an internal membrane-evolution rule is shown in Figure 5.5.

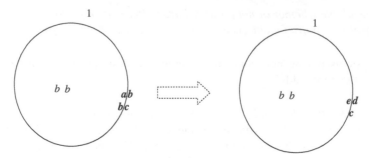

Figure 5.5   Graphical representation of the membrane-evolution rule $[\,_{ab}]_b^1 \to [\,_{e}]_d^1$.

As we will see in the next section, such extension will be extremely useful to describe cellular processes that involve membrane receptors.

Looking into the details of the proof of Theorem 6.2 as presented in Cavaliere and Sedwards [12], it is easy to extend the result and prove that is possible to check the reachability of arbitrary configurations and markings for membrane systems with peripheral proteins and membrane-evolution rules, with the systems working in a free-parallel manner (the idea, as used in Cavaliere and Sedwards [12], is that attached objects can be indexed in a special manner to separate from floating objects; membrane-evolution rules can be then seen as cooperative evolution rules acting only on attached objects).

However, from a computational point of view, it is not clear if the inclusion of membrane-evolution rules leads to higher complexity algorithms. A more detailed computational study of membrane systems with peripheral proteins and membrane evolution-rules is then left as a research topic. The proposed membrane evolution rules can also be seen as a generalization of the protein rules used in Păun and Popa [18], where only one single protein can be rewritten on one side of the membrane. Moreover, similar types of rules have been included in the stochastic simulator presented in Cavaliere and Sedwards [19]: in that case, the attachment of an object can allow the rewriting of the multiset of embedded proteins.

5.6   CELL CYCLE AND BREAST TUMOR GROWTH CONTROL

In this section, we show how the computational paradigm introduced in Section 5.5 can be adapted in order to model important cellular processes. In particular, we show how it is possible to model the processes concerning cell cycle and breast tumor growth.

It is well-known that the life of human beings is marked by the cycling life of its constitutive cells. It goes through four repetitive phases: Gap 1 (G1), S, Gap 2 (G2), and M. G1 is in between mitosis and DNA replication and is responsible for cell growth. The transition occurring at the restriction point (called R) during the G1 phase commits a cell to the proliferative cycle. If the conditions that enforce this transition are not present, the cell exits the cell cycle and enters a nonproliferative phase (called G0) during which cell growth, segregation, and apoptosis occur. Replication of DNA takes place during the synthesis phase (called S). It is followed by a second gap phase responsible for cell growth and preparation for division. Mitosis and production of two daughter cells occur in the M phase. Switches from one phase to the next one are critical checkpoints of the basic cyclic mechanism, and they are under constant investigation [20, 21].

Passage through these four phases is regulated by a family of cyclins[1] that act as regulatory subunits for the cyclin-dependent kinases (Cdks). Cyclins' complex activates Cdks, with the aim to promote the next phase transition. Such activation is due to sequential phosphorylations and dephosphorylations[2] of the key residues mostly located on each Cdk complex subunit. Therefore, the activity of the various cyclin-Cdk complexes results to be controlled by the synthesis of the appropriate cyclins during each specific phase of the cell cycle.

5.6.1 Cell Cycle Progression Inhibition in G1/S

Episodes of DNA damage during G1 pose a particular challenge because replication of damaged DNA can be deleterious and because no other chromatid is present to provide a template for recombinational repair. Besides, by considering that cyclins operate as promoting factors for mitosis and that typical cancer evolutions act as suppressors of certain members of the cyclins family, in case of DNA damage, the desired (healthy) state is identified by the G0 phase. Hence, in this context, we are interested to understand where and why G0 is reached.

5.6.1.1 p53-Dependent Checkpoint Pathway   There are several proteins that can inhibit the cell cycle in G1 but, whenever a DNA damage occurs, p53[3] is the protein that gets accumulated in the cell and that induces the CyclinE_cdk2 p21-mediated inhibition. It can be activated by different proteins that, in turn, can be activated by different genotoxic or nongenotoxic stimuli. The role of this transcription factor is to induce the transcription of genes that encode proteins involved in apoptosis, of genes that encode proteins in charge to stop the cell cycle, and of proteins involved in the DNA repair machinery. When a damage is detected, p53 allows a cell a unique possibility for survival by starting the repair machinery. If this process fails, the cell is destined to die. In particular, whenever the DNA double strand is broken, p53 is activated by the ATM protein kinase. The oncoprotein Mdm2[4] binds the transcription

---

[1]Cyclins are a family of proteins involved in the progression of cells through the whole cell cycle. They are so named because their concentrations vary in a cyclical fashion. They are produced or degraded as needed in order to drive the cell through the different phases of its life cycle.

[2]In eukaryotes, protein phosphorylation is probably the most important regulatory event. Many enzymes and receptors are switched on or off by phosphorylation and dephosphorylation. Phosphorylation is catalyzed by various specific protein kinases, whereas phosphatases dephosphorylate.

[3]p53 is a key regulator of cellular responses to genotoxic stresses; for this reason, it is named: the guardian of the genome [29].

[4]Mdm2 is the pivotal negative regulator of p53.

factor and blocks its activity through a dual mechanism: It conceals the p53 transactivation domain and promotes the p53 degradation after ubiquitination[5] [22]. ATM activates p53 preventing the Mdm2 binding, so its inhibitory effect cannot occur. This action allows p53 to shuttle to the nucleus. Here, it can promote the transcription of different target genes; one of them is a cyclin-dependent kinase inhibitor: p21. p21 is in charge to suppress the CyclinE_Cdk2 kinase activity, thereby resulting in G1 arrest [23].

This mechanism has been formalized using membrane systems and simulated in Mazza and Nocera [24]. In particular, we have extended the corresponding Reactome[6] [25] model (written in the Systems Biology Markup Language, SBML [26]). Moreover, we have translated the model into the membrane system framework [27] and have simulated its dynamics. The obtained membrane system model is described in Figure 5.6.

In addition to the described pathway, we have provided some extra rules with the aim to reduce any possible pathways cross-talk effects (in fact, very often, chemicals are involved in more than one living function and hence, they are involved in different pathways). Moreover, we have added an interaction rate to the rules, as described in Sedwards and Mazza [28], and we have used Cyto-Sim[7] to simulate the model.

We have initially employed the same quantitative initial configurations (except for Cyclin_Cdk2, which we set one-tenth of the others with the aim both to accelerate the degradation of p21 and to better qualitatively depict the arrest process) and same rate constants (except for the last two degradations and for the p21 binding, merely for complying qualitatively the well-known behaviors of the chemicals under examination).

As already mentioned before, we have added to the model some extra feedback rules in order to avoid pathways cross-talks issues. In particular, we have added a fictitious rule (r_9) that causes the consumption of the sequestered complex CyclinE_Cdk2 by p21 (r_8). In this way, we can monitor and temporize the cycle arrest process. Moreover, because damage, ATM, p53, and Mdm2 undergo phosphorylation and the corresponding ATMphospho, p53phospho, and Mdm2phospho are endlessly created, we have introduced three simple degradation rules (r_{10-12}) to take into account their balancing processes (that are, possibly, envisaged by other

---

[5]Ubiquitin-mediated proteolysis of regulatory proteins controls a variety of biological processes. A protein molecule doomed for destruction is marked with a chain of ubiquitin molecules. Proteins displaying this ubiquitin death tag are promptly destroyed by the proteosome.

[6]Reactome is a knowledgebase of biological pathways. It offers significant literature references and pictorial representations of reactants and reactions. (Part of) the pathway under investigation is available in numerous data formats.

[7]Cyto-Sim [28] is a stochastic simulator of biochemical processes in hierarchical compartments that may be isolated or may communicate via peripheral and integral membrane proteins. It is available online as a Java applet [30] and as a standalone application. It works fully and correctly, although the functionalities of the applet have been reduced for security issue. It is possible to model and simulate in a stochastic and deterministic manner, (i) interacting species, (ii) compartmental hierarchies, (iii) species localizations inside compartments and membranes, and (iv) rules (and correlated velocity formulas that govern the dynamics of the system to be simulated) in the form of chemical equations.

$\Pi = (O, \mu, w_c, w_n, (u_c, v_c), (u_n, v_n), R^m, R)$, where

$O = \{damage, ATMdimer, ATMphospho, Mdm2, Mdm2\_p53, Mdm2phospho, p53phospho,$

$\quad p21, CyclinE\_Cdk2, p21\_CyclinE\_Cdk2\}$,

$\mu = [c[n]n]c$,

$w_c = \lambda$,

$w_n = damage^{1000}\ ATM\_dimer^{1000}\ Mdm2^{1000}\ p53^{1000}\ Cyclin\_Cdk2^{1000}$,

$u_c = \lambda;\ v_c = \lambda;\ u_n = \lambda;\ v_n = \lambda$,

$R^m = \{r_1: [Mdm2\_p53]^n \rightarrow [\ ]^n\ Mdm2\_p53\}$ $\qquad\qquad$ $rate(r_1) = 1$,

$R =$

$\{$

$\quad r_2: [damage + ATMdimer \rightarrow ATMphospho^2]^n$ $\qquad$ $rate(r_2) = 1$,

$\quad r_3: [Mdm2 + p53 \rightarrow Mdm2\_p53]^n$ $\qquad\qquad$ $rate(r_3) = 1$,

$\quad r_4: [Mdm2\_p53 \rightarrow \lambda]^c$ $\qquad\qquad\qquad\qquad$ $rate(r_4) = 1$,

$\quad r_5: [ATMphospho + Mdm2 \rightarrow ATMphospho + Mdm2phospho]^n$ $\quad$ $rate(r_5) = 1$,

$\quad r_6: [ATMphospho + p53 \rightarrow ATMphospho + p53phospho]^n$ $\quad$ $rate(r_6) = 1$,

$\quad r_7: [p53phospho \rightarrow p53phospho + p21]^n$ $\qquad$ $rate(r_7) = 1$,

$\quad r_8: [p21 + CyclinE\_Cdk2 \rightarrow p21\_CyclinE\_Cdk2]^n$ $\qquad$ $rate(r_8) = 0.8$,

$\quad r_9: [p21\_CyclinE\_Cdk2 \rightarrow \lambda]^n$ $\qquad\qquad$ $rate(r_9) = 1$,

$\quad r_{10}: [ATMphospho \rightarrow \lambda]^n$ $\qquad\qquad\qquad$ $rate(r_{10}) = 1$,

$\quad r_{11}: [p53phospho \rightarrow \lambda]^n$ $\qquad\qquad\qquad$ $rate(r_{11}) = 0.6$,

$\quad r_{12}: [Mdm2phospho \rightarrow \lambda]^n$ $\qquad\qquad\qquad$ $rate(r_{12}) = 0.6$

$\}$

Figure 5.6 p53-dependent G1/S arrest. The membrane system is written in the style described in Section 5.5. However, with the aim to be closer to biochemistry, we use the symbol "+" to represent multiset concatenation (instead of just writing them by concatenating the symbols, as is usually done in the membrane systems area and as presented in Section 5.3). For instance, here a rule $[u_1 u_2 \rightarrow v_1 v_2]^1$ is written as $[u_1 + u_2 \rightarrow v_1 + v_2]^1$. Moreover, the labels used are short notations for the following cellular compartments: $s =$ system, $c =$ cytoplasm, and $n =$ nucleoplasm.

pathways). When the modeled pathway is not perturbed by a DNA damage, the Mdm2_p53 complex is rapidly created (r_3) and quickly shuttled to cytoplasm (r_1), where it is degradated (r_{12}) (Figure 5.7). But when a damage occurs (r_2), the accumulation of Mdm2_p53 into the nucleus is quickly blocked (reducing its shuttling) and the accumulation of p53phospho is promptly triggered (r_6). After the damage, the quantity of Mdm2_p53 shuttled decreases (from 270 to 370 complexes), and the accumulated p53phospho molecules transcriptionally activate p21 (r_7) that accumulates and sequesters CyclinE_Cdk2 (r_8) for G1/S arrest (Figure 5.8).

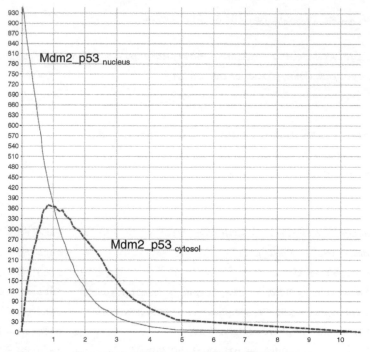

Figure 5.7   p53-dependent G1/S progression.

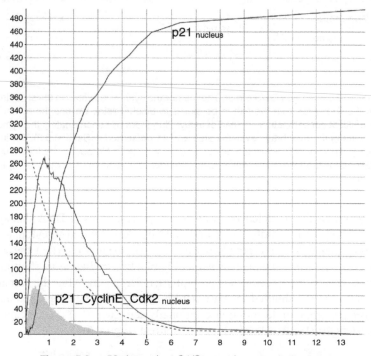

Figure 5.8   p53-dependent G1/S arrest in response to stress.

$\Pi = (O, \mu, w_c, w_n, (u_c, v_c), (u_n, v_n), R^m, R)$, where

$O = \{damage, ChkX, Cdc25A, Cdc25Aphospho, CyclinE\_Cdk2phospho\}$,

$\mu = [c[n]n]c$,

$w_c = \lambda$,

$w_n = Cdc25A^{1000} CyclinE\_Cdk2phospho^{1000}$,

$u_c = \lambda, v_c = \lambda$,

$u_n = \lambda, v_n = \lambda$,

$R^m = \{r_1: [Cdc25Aphospho]^n \rightarrow [\ ]^n Cdc25Aphospho\}$ $rate(r_1) = 1$

$R =$

$\{$

  $r_2 : [damage \rightarrow ChkX]^n$ $rate(r_2) = 10000$,

  $r_3 : [ChkX + Cdc25A \rightarrow Cdc25Aphospho]^n$ $rate(r_3) = 1$,

  $r_4 : [Cdc25Aphospho \rightarrow \lambda]^c$ $rate(r_4) = 1$,

  $r_5 : [Cdc25A + CyclinE\_Cdk2phospho \rightarrow CyclinE\_Cdk2]^n$ $rate(r_5) = 1$,

  $r_6 : [CyclinE\_Cdk2 \rightarrow TRANSITION]^n$ $rate(r_6) = 10000$

$\}$

Figure 5.9   p53-independent G1/S arrest.

5.6.1.2 *p53-Independent Checkpoint Pathway* There is an alternative way
where the inhibition of Cdk2[8] in response to DNA damage can occur even in cells
lacking p53 or p21. In such case, the elimination of Cdc25A evokes a cell-cycle
arrest, promotes repair of the DNA cross-links and protects cells from DNA strand
breaks. Here, we have explored the response of human cells to phosphorylation of
Cdc25A by Chk1 or Chk2[9] due to ultraviolet light (UV) or ionizing radiation (IR) [31].
Indeed, upon exposure to UV or IR, the abundance and activity of Cdc25A rapidly
decreases. The destruction of Cdc25A prevents the entry into S-phase by maintaining the CyclinE_Cdk2 complexes phosphorylated and inactive. Such a degradation
takes place within the cytosol[10] and is mediated by the 'endopeptidase activity' of
26S proteosome. This process has been fully described in Franco et al. [32] and
here is summarized by the membrane system in Figure 5.9.

"Unfortunately," between 16 and 24 h after exposure to UV, cells resume DNA
replication and progression through the cell cycle, indicating that the UV-induced cell
cycle arrest is then reversible. Using simulations, we have discovered that the source

---

[8]Cdk2 is the kinase (complexed with cyclinE) activated by Cdc25A.
[9]Chk1 is activated in response to DNA damage due to UV. Chk2 is activated by IR.
[10]Cytosol is the fluid portion of the cytoplasm, exclusive of organelles and membranes.

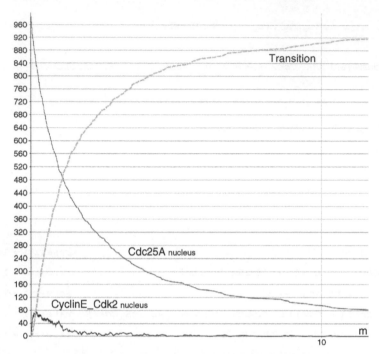

Figure 5.10   p53-independent G1/S progression.

of reversibility is the Cdc25A–Cdc25Aphospho interplay. These are in charge of the arrest and of triggering the cell cycle, respectively, by activating or disabling the CyclinE_Cdk2 complex. Whenever the cycle stops, the degradation activity becomes low and both species exhibit permanent oscillations due to their peer competition. Oscillations are influenced by complementary cross-talk pathways. They interfere with the unstable Cdc25A–Cdc25Aphospho interplay and stimulate the cell cycle restarting.

Moreover, we have emulated the system evolution with normal degradation levels as well. In Figure 5.10, we have shown that cell cycle progression quickly takes place whenever no DNA damage occurs. The dashed line represents the G1/S progression trend (r_6). Its behavior is strongly correlated to the CyclinE_Cdk2 dephosphorylation process (r_5). On the other hand, in Figure 5.11, we have reproduced an artificial DNA damage (square caps line). In accordance to the damage type, Chk1/2 (it is named ChkX into the corresponding membrane system) quickly accumulates (r_2). Chk1/2 phosphorylates Cdc25A (r_3) and blocks the CyclinE_Cdk2 dephosphorylation process (r_5). Consequently, cycle progression results are significantly reduced (550 vs. 1000) and slower (Figure 5.11).

5.6.2   Cell-Cycle Progression Inhibition in G2/M

14-3-3_σ, also known as stratifin, is a p53-inducible gene that inactivates mitotic-Cdk$_s$ by cytoplasmatic sequestration [33, 34]. Since the accumulation of mitotic-Cdk$_s$

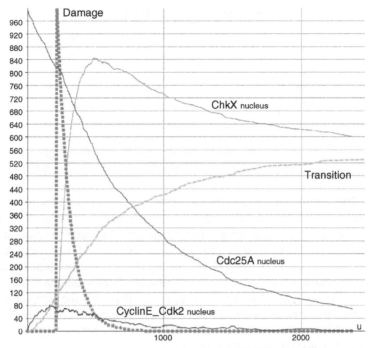

Figure 5.11   p53-independent G1/S arrest in response to stress.

is required for mitotic entry, the overexpression of $14-3-3_\sigma$ leads to cycle arrest in G2. On the other hand, the inhibitory effect of $14-3-3_\sigma$ is usually balanced by the $14-3-3_\sigma$-Efp[11] binding, which results in ubiquination of $14-3-3_\sigma$, enhanced turnover of $14-3-3_\sigma$ by the proteosome and cycle progression [35, 36]. BRCA1[12] balances the Efp-mediated cycle progression-enhancing activity by monitoring the regulatory effects of the estrogen receptor ER_α. It inhibits the ER_α signaling cascade and blocks its AF-2 transcriptional activation [35, 37]. Moreover, in presence of wild-type p53, BRCA1 induces $14-3-3_\sigma$. Loss of this control may contribute to tumorigenesis.

Estrogens are a group of steroid compounds that are the primary female sex hormone. They are involved in cell cycle progression and generation/promotion of tumors such as breast, uterus, and prostate cancers. Estrogen actions are assumed to be mediated by estrogen receptors, which are found in different ratios in the different tissues

---

[11]Efp (estrogen responsive finger protein) gene is predominantly expressed in female reproductive organs (uterus, ovary and mammary glands). It acts as one of the primary estrogen responsive genes in Er_α- and/or Er_β-positive breast tumor and would mediate estrogen functions such as cell proliferation. Efp controls ubiquitin-mediated destruction of a cell-cycle inhibition and may regulate a switch from hormone-dependent to hormone-independent growth of breast tumors.

[12]BRCA1 belongs to a class of genes known as tumor suppressors. The multifactorial BRCA1 protein product is involved in DNA damage repair, ubiquitination, transcriptional regulation, and other functions. Variations in the gene are implicated in a number of hereditary cancers, namely breast, ovarian, and prostate. The majority (70%) of BRCA1-related breast cancers are negative for ER_α.

Table 5.1   Estrogenic compound binding affinity

	ER_α	ER_β
17-beta estradiol	x	x
Estron	x	
Raloxifen	x	
Estriol		x
Genistein		x

of the body and which regulate the transcription of some target genes. A certain stimulation of Efp by estrogen has been shown to promote genetic instability.

5.6.2.1   *The Role of Estrogen Receptors*   Receptors are proteins located on the cell membrane or within the cytoplasm or cell nucleus that bind to specific molecules (ligands[13]) and initiate the cellular responses. Estrogen receptors are intracellular proteins present both on the cell surface membrane and in the cytosol. Those localized within the cytosol have a DNA-binding domain and can function as transcription factors to regulate the production of proteins. Their signaling effects depend on several factors: (i) the structure of the ligand or drug, (ii) the receptor subtype, (iii) the gene regulatory elements, and the (iv) cell-type specific proteins. There are two different ER proteins produced from ESR1 and ESR2 genes: ER_α and ER_β. ERs are widely distributed throughout the human body

- ER_α: endometrium, breast cancer cells, ovarian stroma cells, and hypothalamus.
- ER_β: kidney, brain, bone, heart, lungs, intestinal mucosa, prostate, and endothelial cells.

ERs actions can be selectively enhanced or disabled by some estrogen receptor, modulators, in accordance with the binding affinities level of each estrogenic compound (see Table 5.1). In particular, in many breast cancers, tumor cells grow in response to estradiol, the natural hormone that activates both ERs [38]. Estradiol ("female" hormone, but also present in men) represents the major estrogen in humans. Although estrogen is a well-known promoting factor of sporadic breast carcinoma (because the estrogen–ER binding stimulates the proliferation of mammary cells with the resulting increase in cell division and DNA replication), its effects on risk modification about hereditary breast cancers are still not clear.

5.6.2.2   *G2/M Transition Control*   In healthy conditions, DNA damages induce the increase of p53 levels. p53 promotes transcription of Cdk inhibitors (e.g., $14\text{-}3\text{-}3_\sigma$), which recruit CyclinB–Cdk complexes leading to cell cycle arrest and DNA repair. We have modeled the proteolysis of $14\text{-}3\text{-}3_\sigma$ modulated by Efp. The

---

[13]Ligands introduce changes in the behavior of the receptor proteins, resulting in physiological changes and constituting their biological actions.

$\Pi = (O, \mu, w_s, w_c, w_n, (u_s, v_s), (u_c, v_c), (u_n, v_n), R^m, R)$, where

$O = \{damage, p53, BRCA1, stratifin, estrogen, ER, ER\_estrogen, ER\_act, Efp, Cdc2\_CyclinB,$
$stratifin\_Cdc2\_CyclinB, stratifin\_Cdc2\_CyclinB\_ub, TRANSITION\}$,

$\mu = [s[c[n]n]c]s$,

$w_s = estrogen^{1000}$,

$w_c = Cdc2\_CyclinB^{1000}$,

$w_n = BRCA1^{1000}$,

$u_s = \lambda, v_s = \lambda, u_c = \lambda, v_c = ER^{1000}, u_n = \lambda, v_n = \lambda$,

$R^m =$
$\{$

$r_1 : [\ ]^c\ ER\_act \to [ER\_act]^c$	$rate(r_1) = 1,$
$r_2 : [ER\_act]^c \to [ER\_act]^c$	$rate(r_2) = 1,$
$r_3 : [stratifin]^n \to [\ ]^n\ stratifin$	$rate(r_3) = 1,$
$r_4 : [\ ]^n\ ER_{act} \to [ER_{act}]^n$	$rate(r_4) = 1,$
$r_5 : [Efp]^n \to [\ ]^n\ Efp$	$rate(r_5) = 1,$
$r_6 : [\ ]^n\ Cdc2\_CyclinB \to [Cdc2\_CyclinB]^n$	$rate(r_6) = 1$

$\}$

$R =$
$\{$

$r_7 : [\ ]^c_{ER} + estrogen \to [\ ]^c_{ER\_estrogen}$	$rate(r_7) = 1$
$r_8 : [\ ]^c_{ER\_estrogen} \to [\ ]^c_{ER\_act}$	$rate(r_8) = 1$
$r_9 : [\ stratifin + Cdc2\_CyclinB \to stratifin\_Cdc2\_CyclinB]^c$	$rate(r_9) = 1$
$r_{10} : [Efp + stratifin\_Cdc2\_CyclinB \to stratifin\_Cdc2\_CyclinB\_ub]^c$	$rate(r_{10}) = 1$
$r_{11} : [stratifin\_Cdc2\_CyclinB\_ub \to Cdc2\_CyclinB]^c$	$rate(r_{11}) = 1$
$r_{12} : [damage \to p53]^n$	$rate(r_{12}) = 1000$
$r_{13} : [p53 + BRCA1 \to stratifin]^n$	$rate(r_{13}) = 1$
$r_{14} : [ER\_act \to Efp]^n$	$rate(r_{14}) = 1$
$r_{15} : [ER\_act \to \lambda]^n$	$rate(r_{15}) = 1$
$r_{16} : [Cdc2\_CyclinB \to TRANSITION]^n$	$rate(r_{16}) = 1$
$r_{17} : [damage + BRCA1 + ER_{act} \to BRCA1 + ER + damage]^n$	$rate(r_{17}) = 1$

$\}$

Figure 5.12   G2/M transition control.

degradation of 14-3-3_σ is subsequently followed by the protein dissociation of the cyclinb–Cdk complexes, leading to cell cycle progression and tumor growth. Finally, we have considered the compensative role of BRCA1 in (i) suppressing any estrogen-dependent transcriptional pathway and in (ii) inducing 14-3-3_σ. To test whether altered checkpoints can modulate sensitivity to treatment *in vivo*, we have constricted a model for this signaling pathway. The corresponding model is reported in Figure 5.12.

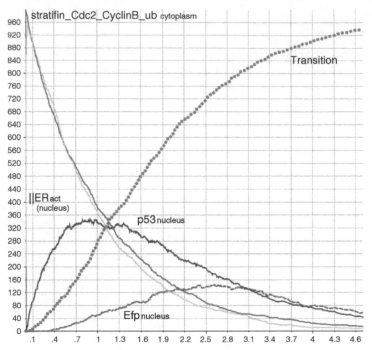

Figure 5.13   Healthy G2/M phase transition.

Whenever a healthy cell divides, its free `Cdc2_CyclinB` dimers shuttle to the nucleus (r_6) and induce the G2/M transition (r_{16}). When we have simulated such situation, we have monitored the accumulation of `Efp` into the nucleus (r_{14}) and its migration to the cytoplasm (r_5) (dashed line in Figure 5.13) caused by the activation of the ERs (r_{7-8}) and the consequent migration into the nucleus ($r_{1-2,4}$). `Cdc2_CyclinB` complexes accumulate into the nucleus and promote entry in mitosis (square caps line). On the other hand (see Figure 5.14), when a DNA damage occurs, `p53` starts to accumulate (r_{12}). `p53` and `BRCA1` coinduce $14\text{-}3\text{-}3_\sigma$ (r_{13}), which is free to migrate out to the cytoplasm (r_3). Here, it sequesters the `Cdc2_CyclinB` complexes (r_9) and prevents their shuttling to the nucleus. Consequently, the cell stops its cycle. Therefore, to allow cell-cycle progression, estrogens stimulate production of `Efp` (see Figure 5.15). This is obtained by enabling the ERs placed on the cell surface (because of the interaction with the estrogens hormones (r_{7-8}) and then by moving the receptors into the nucleus ($r_{1-2,4}$)). Here, the receptors can bind DNA and enhance the `Efp` production (r_{14}). `BRCA1` balances this process by disabling the receptors moved into the nucleus and then controlling their `Efp` induction (r_{17}). The level of `Efp` in Figure 5.15 is significantly lower than that in Figure 5.13. This is due to the `BRCA1` inhibitory control. The resulting `Efp` is free to shuttle to the cytoplsm (r_5) and bind $14\text{-}3\text{-}3_\sigma$ for ubiquination (r_{10}). $14\text{-}3\text{-}3_\sigma$ marked with ubiquitin chains is recognized and destroyed by the proteosome (r_{11}). Released `Cdc2_CyclinB` dimers can then escape into the nucleus

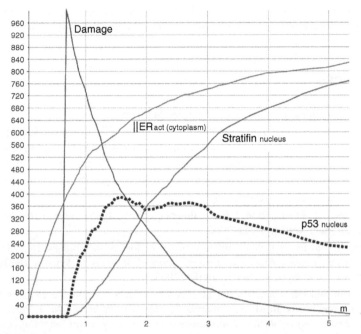

Figure 5.14 Stratifin induction by p53 accumulation and ERs activation and migration into the cytoplasm in response to stress.

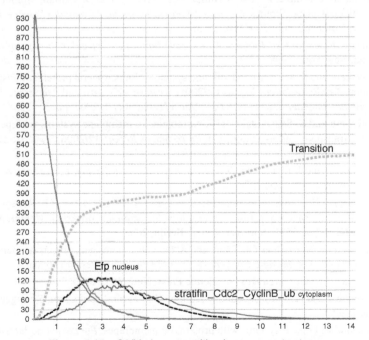

Figure 5.15 G2/M phase transition in response to stress.

(r_6) and promote mitotic entry (r_{16}). Finally, the transition process of Figure 5.15 results to be slower and less effective than that of the healthy system in Figure 5.14.

REFERENCES

1. *Natural Computing*, An International Journal. Springer.

2. *IEEE Transactions on Evolutionary Computing (TEC)*. IEEE Computer Society.

3. Gh. Păun. Computing with membranes. *Journal of Computer and System Sciences*, Vol. 61, 1, 2000, pp. 108–143. (First circulated as TUCS Research Report No 28, 1998).

4. Gh. Păun. *Membrane Computing—An Introduction*. Springer-Verlag, Berlin, 2002.

5. http://ppage.psystems.eu.

6. G. Ciobanu, Gh. Păun, and M. J. Pérez-Jiménez, editors. *Applications of Membrane Computing*. Springer-Verlag, Berlin, 2006.

7. L. Cardelli and Brane Calculi. Interactions of biological membranes. In V. Danos and V. Schächter, editors. *Proceedings Computational Methods in Systems Biology 2004*. LNCS, Vol. 3082, Springer-Verlag, Berlin, 2005.

8. L. Cardelli and Gh. Păun. An universality result for a (mem)brane calculus based on mate/drip operations. In M. A. Gutiérrez-Naranjo, Gh. Păun, and M. J. Pérez-Jiménez, editors. *Proceedings of the ESF Exploratory Workshop on Cellular Computing (Complexity Aspects)*. *International Journal of Foundations of Computer Science*, Vol. 17, Fénix Ed., Seville, Spain, 2006, pp. 49–68.

9. R. Brijder, M. Cavaliere, A. Riscos-Núñez, G. Rozenberg, and D. Sburlan. Membrane systems with marked membranes. *Electronic Notes in Theoretical Computer Science, ENTCS*, Vol. 171, Number 2, July 2007, pp. 25–36.

10. B. Alberts. *Essential Cell Biology. An Introduction to the Molecular Biology of the Cell*. Garland, New York, 1998.

11. M. Cavaliere and S. Sedwards. Membrane systems with peripheral proteins: transport and evolution. *CoSBi Technical Report* 04/2006, www.cosbi.eu, and *Electronic Notes in Theoretical Computer Science, ENTCS*, Vol. 171, Number 2, 2007, pp. 37–53.

12. M. Cavaliere and S. Sedwards. Decision problems in membrane systems with peripheral proteins, transport, and evolution. *CoSBi Technical Report* 12/2006, www.cosbi.eu, and *Theoretical Computer Science*, to appear.

13. J. E. Hopcroft and J. D. Ullman. *Introduction to Automata Theory, Languages, and Computation*. Addison-Wesley, 1979.

14. M. Cavaliere. Evolution–communication P systems. In Gh. Păun, G. Rozenberg, A. Salomaa, and C. Zandron, editors. *Proceedings International Workshop Membrane Computing*, LNCS, Vol. 2597, Springer-Verlag, Berlin, 2003.

15. M. Cavaliere, S. N. Krishna, Gh. Păun, and A. Păun. P systems with objects on membranes. *The Handbook of Membrane Computing*, Oxford University Press, to appear.

16. A. Salomaa. *Formal Languages*. Academic Press, New York, 1973.

17. G. Rozenberg and A. Salomaa, editors. *Handbook of Formal Languages*. Springer-Verlag, Berlin, 1997.

18. A. Păun and B. Popa. P systems with proteins on membranes. *Fundamentae Informaticae*, Vol. 72, Number 4, 2006, pp. 467–483.

19. M. Cavaliere and S. Sedwards. Modelling cellular processes using membrane systems with peripheral and integral proteins. *Proceedings Computational Methods in Systems Biology*, Trento, 2006, LNCS–LNBI, Vol. 4210, Springer, Berlin, 2006, pp. 108–126.

20. R. E. Shackelford, W. K. Kaufmann, and R. S. Paules. Cell cycle control, checkpoint mechanisms, and genotoxic stress. *Environmental Health Perspectives Supplements*, Vol. 107, Number S1, 1999, pp. 5–24.

21. B. Novák, J. C. Sible, and T. T. Tyson. Checkpoints in the cell cycle. *Encyclopedia of Life Sciences*, Nature Publishing Group, London, 2002, pp. 1–8.

22. Y. Haupt, R. Maya, A. Kazaz, and M. Oren. Mdm2 promotes the rapid degradation of p53. *Nature*, 387:296–299, 1997.

23. A. L. Gartel and A. L. Tyner. The role of the cyclin-dependent kinase inhibitor p21 in apoptosis. *Mol. Cancer Ther.*, 1(8):639–649, 2002.

24. T. Mazza and A. Nocera. A formal lightweight view of the p53-dependent G1/S checkpoint control. In *Proceedings of Prague International Workshop on Membrane Computing*, 2008, pp. 35–46.

25. I. Vastrik, P. D'Eustachio, E. Schmidt, G. Joshi-Tope, G. Gopinath, D. Croft, B. de Bono, M. Gillespie, B. Jassal, S. Lewis, L. Matthews, G. Wu, E. Birney, and L. Stein. Reactome: a knowledge base of biologic pathways and processes. *Genome Biol.*, 8(3):R39, 2007.

26. M. Hucka and A. Finney, et al. The systems biology markup language (SBML): a medium for representation and exchange of biochemical network models. *Bioinformatics*, 5(19):524–531, 2003.

27. T. Mazza. Towards a complete covering of SBML functionalities. In *Proceedings of the Eightn Workshop on Membrane Computing (WMC8)*, LNCS, Vol. 4860, 2007, pp. 425–444.

28. S. Sedwards and T. Mazza. Cyto-Sim: a formal language model and stochastic simulator of membrane-enclosed biochemical processes. *Bioinformatics*, 20(23):2800–2802, 2007.

29. D. P. Lane. p53, guardian of the genome. *Nature*, 358(6381):15–16, 1992.

30. Cyto-Sim web site. http://www.cosbi.eu/Rpty_Soft_CytoSim.php.

31. N. Mailand, J. Falck, C. Lukas, R. G. Syljuasen, M. Welcker, J. Bartek, and J. Lukas. Rapid destruction of human cdc25a in response to dna damage. *Science*, 288(5470):1425–1429, 2000.

32. G. Franco, P. H. Guzzi, T. Mazza, and V. Manca. Mitotic oscillators as MP graphs. In *Proceedings of the Seventh Workshop on Membrane Computing (WMC7)*, LNCS, Vol. 4361, 2006, pp. 382–394.

33. H.-Y. Yang, Y.-Y. Wen, C.-H. Chen, G. Lozano, and M.-H. Lee. 14-3-3sigma positively regulates p53 and suppresses tumor growth. *Mol. Cell. Biol.*, 23(20):7096–7107, 2003.

34. A. Benzinger, N. Muster, H. B. Koch, J. R. 3rd Yates, and H. Hermeking. Targeted proteomic analysis of 14-3-3 sigma, a p53 effector commonly silenced in cancer. *Mol. Cell. Proteom.*, 4(6):785–795, 2005.

35. K. Ikeda, A. Orimo, Y. Higashi, M. Muramatsu, and S. Inoue. Efp as a primary estrogen-responsive gene in human breast cancer. *FEBS Lett.*, 472(1):9–13, 2000.

36. T. Urano, T. Saito, T. Tsukui, M. Fujita, T. Hosoi, M. Muramatsu, Y. Ouchi, and S. Inoue. Efp targets 14-3-3 sigma for proteolysis and promotes breast tumour growth. *Nature*, 417(6891):871–875, 2002.

37. T. Ouchi, A. N. A. Monteiro, A. August, S. A. Aaronson, and H. Hanafusa. BRCA1 regulates p53-dependent gene expression. *Proc. Natl. Acad. Sci. USA*, 95(5):2302–2306, 1998.

38. D. Zivadinovic, B. Gametchu, and C. S. Watson. Membrane estrogen receptor-alpha levels in MCF-7 breast cancer cells predict cAMP and proliferation responses. *Breast Cancer Res.*, 7(1):R101–R112, 2005.

6

SIMULATING FILAMENT DYNAMICS IN CELLULAR SYSTEMS

Wilbur E. Channels and Pablo A. Iglesias

*Department of Electrical and Computer Engineering,
The Johns Hopkins University, Baltimore, MD, USA*

6.1 INTRODUCTION

Increasingly, there is an appreciation of the importance of computational models in biology. These models of biological systems have principally been used to show the level of quantitative understanding of the systems in terms of how well they produce previously observed behavior or more importantly produce a "testable hypothesis relevant to important problems" [1].

Computational models provide two significant benefits. First, they help to test conceptual models of how signaling networks interact. This is particularly important when the number of interacting components is large or when the network topology is complex—for example, containing numerous feedback loops or cross-talk between different pathways. Second, computational models provide testable hypotheses that can lead to new insight into the function of biological systems.

Most computational models in biology are based on ordinary differential equation implementations of molecular wiring diagrams [2]. The states that are updated by these equations represent the concentrations of biochemical species. Standard techniques are then used to translate the nature of the interactions (e.g., Michaelis–Menten

Elements of Computational Systems Biology   Edited by Huma M. Lodhi and Stephen H. Muggleton
Copyright © 2010 John Wiley & Sons, Inc.

kinetics to describe enzymatic reactions) into the correct equations. As the scope of systems being modeled increases from reacting chemical species to reaction diffusion systems to force interaction systems, the complexity of the model and the computational demand increase.

However, there are situations in which we are interested in factors beyond the concentrations of the individual species. One particular case is where we consider the role of intracellular filaments in generating force. As an example, consider the formation of the mitotic spindle [3, 4]. Here, individual microtubule filaments interact with their associated motors to create a distinctive morphology. To test whether the interaction gives rise to a mitotic spindle, these structures must be modeled individually.

In this chapter, we outline some of the computational issues necessary for modeling cytoskeletal filament systems. In particular, we focus on the components necessary to simulate microtubule filaments under the influence of motor complexes.

6.2   BACKGROUND: THE ROLES OF FILAMENTS WITHIN CELLS

Eukaryotic cells contain three main types of filaments: actin filaments, intermediate filaments (IFs), and microtubules (MTs). All three play vital roles within cells; they facilitate intracellular protein transport, cellular motility, chromosome movement, vesicle transport, and help maintain the structural integrity of the cell. In all three cases, cytoskeletal filaments form through polymerization of subunits.

6.2.1   The Actin Network

The actin filament network contributes structural support for the cell and is the major cytoskeletal system driving cell motility [5] and cytokinesis [6].

Actin, an approximately 42-kDa globular protein, is one of the most highly conserved proteins in nature. In nature, it is found as a pool of monomers (so-called G-actin) at high concentrations and as a directed semiflexible rod-like filament (F-actin). Actin filaments have the structure of a two-start right-handed helix spanning 36 nm for every 13 actin monomers; thus, every new actin monomer extends the filament a distance of roughly 2.7 nm [7] (Figure 6.1). Actin is an ATPase, using energy

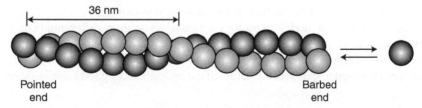

Figure 6.1   Actin filaments are polarized. Though actin monomers can bind at either end, the rate of binding at the front end is considerably higher, which means that most of the growth comes at this end.

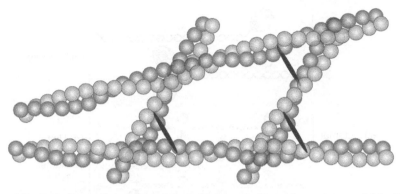

Figure 6.2 Actin filaments are cross-linked. Single actin filaments are long and thin. Cross-linking greatly increases their stiffness and resistance to bending forces. Common cross-linking proteins are α-actinin, filamin, cortexillin and fimbrin.

from ATP hydrolysis to assemble into filaments [8]. However, because small actin dimers and trimers are highly unstable, nucleators (the Arp2/3 complex and formins) are needed for filaments to appear [9]. Once these filaments are formed, however, their growth is rapid, approximately 0.3 μm/s [5].

Single actin filaments are thin (7 nm) and long. Recently, three-dimensional electron microscope tomograms were used to determine an average filament length of approximately 100 nm [10]. Thus, alone they would not provide much support to the cell. However, a number of proteins (e.g. α-actinin, filamin, cortexillin, fimbrin) have evolved that cross-link individual filaments (Figure 6.2), creating a dense meshwork or interconnected filaments [11]. While individual actin filaments are less rigid than MTs [12], networks of actin filaments are more rigid than those consisting of MTs or IFs, but cannot sustain as much force as intermediate filaments [13].

6.2.2 Intermediate Filaments

IFs are formed from a heterogeneous family of proteins. The filaments are around 10 nm in diameter and derive their name from their intermediate thickness between that of actin and MT filaments [14]. The filaments are extremely difficult to break but bend easily [13].

Though IFs vary greatly, they can be divided into several main groups: types I–VI. Keratins, which form types I and II, give epithelial cells in the outer layers of animal skin their resistance to mechanical stress. One of the type III IFs, neurofilaments, which lines the axon of neurons, is involved in the neurodegenerative amyotrophic lateral sclerosis when the filaments do not properly form in motor neuron cells [16]. Type V IFs, lamins, form a fibrous network found on the inner surface of the nucleus and may also serve an important fuction during spindle assembly [17]. In humans, mutations in lamin cause premature ageing (Hutchinson Gilford progeria syndrome) [18].

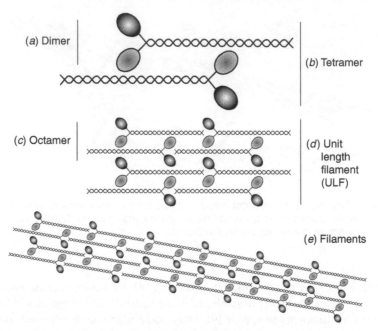

Figure 6.3 Formation of intermediate filaments. Intermediate filaments form parallel, coiled-coil heterodimers (a). A tetramer is formed by two of these heterodimers in a staggered, over-lapping fashion (b). These tetramers become octamers (c), two of which then join to form the basic Unit Length Filament (ULF) (d). (e). Longer filaments are formed by the addition of multiple ULFs. Adapted from [15].

Unlike the other two classes of filaments, IFs are not polar. Instead, parallel coiled-coil dimers come together to form tetramers and two of these will assemble into an octamer known as a unit length filament (Figure 6.3) [15].

6.2.3   Microtubules

MTs are primarily known for their role in forming the mitotic spindle, which separates the chromosomes during cell division in eukaryotes [19]. MTs also form the flagella and cilia in eukaryotic cells [20]. Flagella give spermatazoa their motility [21]. Cilia allow the transport of fluid past stationary cells such as the transport of mucus along the respiratory tract [22]. MTs are also used for intracellular transport such as dispersing or condensing pigment granules in chromatophores allowing fish to camouflage themselves. Viruses, such as HIV, have also taken advantage of MT filaments with aster arrays to guide themselves toward the nucleus, so that they can inject their DNA into that of their host cell [23].

MTs nucleate from gamma tubulin ring complexes (γ-TuRC), upon which α-tubulin and β-tubulin heterodimers join together longitudinally to form protofilaments (Figure 6.4). Thirteen such protofilaments bind together laterally via weak noncovalent interactions to form a hollow microtubule, with an outer diameter of 25 nm [24] and lengths capable of exceeding 10 μm [25].

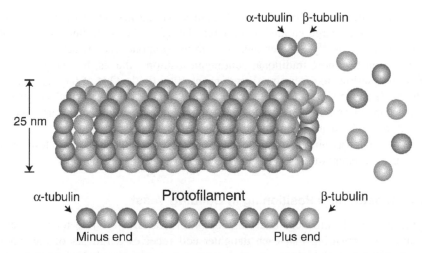

Figure 6.4 Microtubule protein formation. A heterodimer, consisting of α- and β-tubulin subunits, forms the basic building block. Chains of these dimers are said to form a protofilament. A microtubule is formed as a hollow cylinder, 25 nm in diameter, of parallel connections of 13 protofilaments.

Each end of the protofilament is characterized by the appearance of either α-tubulin or β-tubulin. Both of these ends display different dynamic behaviors. The more dynamic end, where β-tubulin is exposed, is known as the plus end; the less dynamic end is the minus end.

MTs exhibit highly dynamic behavior, referred to as dynamic instability, in which they transition between growing and shrinking states [24]. A transition from the growing to the shrinking state is termed a catastrophe, and a transition from the shrinking to the growing state is a rescue. This transition comes about because of the different states that β-tubulin subunits can acquire. In the guanosine diphosphate (GDP)-bound state, β-tubulin rapidly depolymerizes. On the other hand, if the β-tubulin subunits at the plus end are bound to guanosine triphosphate (GTP) then the plus end is stabilized allowing MT growth to occur. Thus, whether the plus end is in the growing or shrinking state is determined by the presence of a GTP end cap.

6.3 EXAMPLES OF FILAMENT SIMULATIONS

To date, filament simulations have demonstrated the plausibility of hypotheses, where direct validation through biological experimentation is difficult to attain. Here, we present several examples. The principle benefit of these simulations is that they produce quantitative results that can be compared with experimental results.

6.3.1 Actin-Based Motility in *Listeria*

The bacterium *Listeria monocytogenes* moves by highjacking its host's actin network and producing a dense comet tail of actin. Alberts and Odell [26] developed a detailed three-dimensional model of the actin dynamics driving *Listeria* propulsion. In this multiscale model, large entities (e.g., actin filaments, the bacterium) are modeled and treated individually. Smaller, more numerous components (e.g., actin monomers) are treated in the more traditional continuum fashion—that is, by using reaction–diffusion equations to determine their concentration fields. One of the keys features of the model is the simulation of the nucleation of actin dynamics, which is a process for which much biophysical data are known [5]. In the model, filaments are modeled as rigid rods, which are subject to Brownian forces.

This model was able to produce saltatory motion at the nanoscale level while producing persistent motion at larger scales as observed experimentally.

6.3.2   Kinetochore Positioning in Budding Yeast

During mitosis, kinetochore microtubules (kMTs) are responsible for segregating chromosomes ensuring that each daughter cell receives a full set of the mother cell's genetic material. Sprague et al. used a filament-based model to simulate kinetochore positioning in fission yeast [27]. Modeling the action of individual kMTs in budding yeast is particularly appropriate, as there is only one MT per kinetochore.

In these simulations, kMTs were modeled as one-dimensional rigid rods that undergo catastrophes and rescue under a variety of regulatory schemes. Simulation results were quantified by determining the plus end distributions and comparing these to biological images. Interestingly, to make this comparison possible, the simulation data were blurred using the point spread function of the microscope that was used to obtain the experimental images

Using the model, it was found that dynamic instability alone could not reproduce the spatial distribution of kMT plus ends nor could tension-dependent rescues of sister kMTs reproduce the experimentally obtained distribution. However, it was possible to recreate the distribution using either polar ejection forces to rescue shrinking kMTs or a chemical gradient centered on the spindle equator promoting catastrophe in the kMTs as they get closer to the spindle equator. This model demonstrates the role of filament simulations as a means of rejecting competing hypotheses.

6.3.3   Spindle Positioning in *Caenorhabditis Elegans* Embryos

Kozlowski et al. used three-dimensional simulations to determine how the interaction between MTs and the cell cortex can determine the position of intracellular organelles [28].

The simulation models several intracellular components of the *Caenorhabditis elegans* embryo. MT asters are nucleated by centrosomes with a fixed number of MT nucleation sites. MTs act as rigid rods that grow and shrink according to the dynamic instability state. All MTs are acted on by Brownian motion forces. When one of the MTs comes into contact with the cortex, its growth/shrinkage rates change. The cell cortex is modeled by a cylinder capped by two hemispheres. To ensure that MTs stay inside the cell, a confinement force that is proportional to the extent by which a MT protrudes outside the volume is used.

Using this model, simulations suggest that pulling forces are generated at the cortex by force generators that remain attached to depolymerizing MT ends. The interaction between the resultant spindle motion and MT dynamics and the force-dependent release of cortical force generators acts as a positive feedback loop that can explain experimentally observed oscillations in the position of the spindle poles [29].

6.3.4 Other Examples

The number of computational models that capture the dynamic behavior of individual cellular filaments is growing. There are several models explaining spindle formation, either the requirement for heterodimer motors [3], the need for spatial regulation of MT motor parameters [4], or the role of nucleation—the so-called slide and cluster model [30]. Other models explain the assembly of the contractile ring during cytokinesis [31] and microtubule aster organization [32].

Interesting, we see that models in all one, two, and three dimensions. While less than three-dimensional representations may represent an oversimplification of the geometry of many problems, useful results can still be generated by these simpler models that can then be compared with biological observations. Through these comparisons, one can then obtain a minimal model consistent with observed behavior.

6.4 OVERVIEW OF FILAMENT SIMULATION

In this section, we provide an overview of the different steps required to simulate the behavior of a filamental network. Details will be provided below.

To simulate the dynamics and force interactions of large filament systems, we model each filament as a sequence of rigid rods that can bend at each rod junction (Figure 6.5). A filament consisting of n rods is represented by a vector

$$\mathbf{m}(t) = [x_0 \, y_0 \, \cdots \, x_i \, y_i \, \cdots \, x_n \, y_n]^T,$$

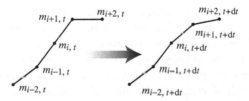

Figure 6.5 In dynamic simulations, individual filaments are represented by rigid rods that can bend at each interconnecting node, $M_{i,t}$. The evolution of these nodes is determined by the forces acting on the rod.

where $m_{i,t} = (x_i, y_i)(t)$ for $i > 0$ is the end point of the ith node at time t and $(x_0, y_0)(t)$ is the location of the initial point of the filament, which for actin and MTs would be the minus end. To simulate multiple filaments $\mathbf{m}_1, \ldots, \mathbf{m}_N$, their vector representations are concatenated into a larger vector:

$$\mathbf{M}(t) = [\mathbf{m}_1(t) \cdots \mathbf{m}_N(t)]^T.$$

While we do not account for the individual molecular interactions of the subunits making up the filaments, we do account for filament growth and shrinkage.

For MTs, growth and shrinkage occur via dynamic instability, in which transitions between the growing and the shrinking state are random events characterized by rescue and catastrophe frequencies. As the plus ends of MTs are the most dynamic ends, we model the minus end as static and allow growth and shrinkage to occur only at the plus end. This can be achieved by several different methods.

The simplest approach is to add an additional rod of fixed length at the end of the filament at each time step. The problem with this method is that at a growth rate of 0.1–0.2 μm/s [33] and at a time step of 0.01 s, the segment lengths would have to be 2 nm, which means that a 10 μm filament would consist of 5000 rods. This is computationally infeasible if many filaments are to be simulated at once. We could allow larger rods or add them less frequently, but this would produce long stationary periods followed by an abrupt filament.

Alternatively, we can allow variable length rods and have the ones at the plus end to be much smaller for smoother growth while having the rest of the segments be considerably larger to reduce the computational load per filament. The problem with allowing neighboring segments to have different lengths is that it complicates the curvature calculation for bent filaments (Section 6.6.2). The quickest way to calculate the forces on a bent rod is if each rod is of the same length. Thus, within a given filament, we would like to have all segment lengths be the same.

As we can now vary the segment lengths arbitrarily by changing the number of segments making up each filament, we would like to have a large segment length to have as few segments as possible to reduce the computational load. We also want this length to be sufficiently small so that a sharply bent filament appears smoothly curved. As a compromise, we select a target segment length of 1 μm and adjust the number of segments to keep the actual segment length as close as possible to this (as explained in Section 6.5.1).

After filament growth and shrinkage have been accounted for, we need to apply external forces to the filament. We consider forces arising from Brownian motion, linked motor complexes attached to two filaments, and straightening forces acting on bent filaments. Because the filaments are stored as a series of segment end points, we need to determine how the positions of these points should change at each time step in response to the applied forces. As the mass of the filament section corresponding to each rod is negligible when compared to the viscous damping that the filament section would be subjected to, the velocities of rod end points will be proportional to the forces acting on the end points.

Thus, the filament positions will be calculated by solving a differential equation, which, in a simplified form, and when discretized, can be expressed as:

$$\frac{d\mathbf{M}}{dt} = \Gamma\mathbf{F} \Longrightarrow \mathbf{M}(t + dt) \approx \mathbf{M}(t) + dt\,\Gamma\,\mathbf{F}, \tag{6.1}$$

where $\mathbf{M}(t)$ is a vector of all filament points at time t, Γ is a diagonal mobility matrix expressing the proportionality constant between each segment velocity and the forces acting on it, and $\mathbf{F}$ is a vector of net forces acting on the filaments points. The latter is a function of the stochastic Brownian forces as well as a function of $\mathbf{M}$. Also, if the filaments are considered inelastic, the forces acting on the filaments should not be able to stretch the filaments. Thus, forces parallel to the direction of the segments must be removed. This contrainst will be enforced through virtual work [34] and is described in the Section 6.7 on imposing constraints.

As shown in Section 6.7.4, the difference equation (6.1) can be rewritten in the form of a linear system of equations:

$$\mathbf{Ax} = \mathbf{b},$$

where $\mathbf{x}$ is the position of the filaments at the next time step. At this point, a solver is needed to obtain $\mathbf{x}$. Owing to the nonsymmetric nature of the matrix $\mathbf{A}$, the biconjugate gradient-stabilized method is used to solve the equation [35].

In summary, the steps that are needed at each step in time are

(1) Change filament length.
(2) Apply forces from filament stiffness, attached motor complexes, and Brownian diffusion.
(3) Impose constraints using virtual work.
(4) Apply biconjugate gradient solver.

Below, we consider each of the steps in detail.

6.5 CHANGING FILAMENT LENGTH

To grow and shrink the filaments by small amounts requires extending or retracting the endpoint by a small amount and repositioning the points to achieve equal segment lengths. Over time, the segments lengths will deviate far from the desired segment length. This will require that we resegment the filament by adding or removing a segment, and that we recalculate the end point positions of the filaments.

6.5.1 Resegmenting Filament

At each time step, we are presented with a filament of a given length L, which may have grown longer and needs to be resegmented. That is, we need to determine the number of segments n that the filament should be divided into.

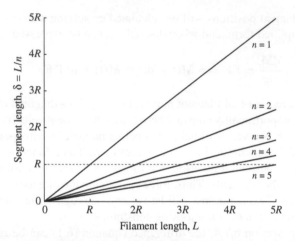

Figure 6.6 Segment lengths as a function of the number of segments n and filament length L, where L is expressed relative to the desired segment length R.

Given a desired segment length R, which should be small enough to portray a bent filament smoothly and small enough to represent the shortest filaments with a single segment, but not so small that we have an inordinate number of segments, we would like to achieve a segment length $\delta = L/n$ as close as possible to R (Figure 6.6).

Suppose that we have too few segments ($\delta > R$). We increase n (decrease δ) until $|R - \delta|$ is minimized (Figure 6.7). If $L \leq R$, then we set $\delta = L$. Otherwise, if $L > R$, then, when n is small, $\delta = L/n$ will be larger than R and n can continue being

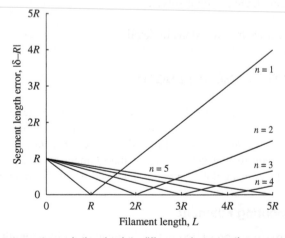

Figure 6.7 The segment error is the absolute difference between the segment length δ and the desired segment length R. The number of segments n is chosen according to which segmentation has the lowest segment error.

increased as long as

$$\frac{L}{n} - R > R - \frac{L}{n+1}$$

holds, that is, until the next increment produces a segment length $\delta = L/(n+1)$ whose error is larger than or equal to the error before it $(L/n - R)$. We use $R - L/(n+1)$, which will be negative and thus allow an increment in n until the first δ is obtained that is smaller than R.

At this point, there is no reason to increase n further as this would decrease δ below R even more. This procedure would thus pick the number of segments necessary to minimize the absolute error between the segment length and the target segment length $|\delta - R|$ (Figure 6.7). The end points of segments for the new segmentation can then be determined by following the path of the previous segmentation based on the path length from the endpoints.

6.6 FORCES ON FILAMENTS

We now outline which forces act on the filaments and how these are simulated.

6.6.1 Brownian Forces

Filaments and other objects (such as diffusing molecules) are subject to Brownian motion. In a two-dimensional simulation, this Brownian motion gives rise to a mean-square displacement $(\langle ||x||^2 \rangle)$ equal to

$$\langle ||x||^2 \rangle = 4D\,dt,$$

where dt is the time step of the simulation and D is the diffusion coefficient, which can be related to the drag coefficient (γ) using Einstein's relation [8]:

$$D = \frac{k_B T}{\gamma}.$$

For a sphere, the drag coefficient is obtained using Stokes's law:

$$\gamma_{sphere} = 6\pi\eta r,$$

where η is the viscosity and r is the radius of the particle. This formula needs to be adjusted for the rod-like filaments. In particular, for an ellipsoid that is moving at random with long axis L and radius r, the drag coefficient is given [36] by:

$$\gamma_{ellipsoid} = \frac{6\pi\eta L}{\ln(2L/r)}.$$

It remains to compute the formula describing the force. In particular, the force and velocity are related by the drag coefficient:

$$F = \gamma \dot{x} \approx \gamma \frac{x}{dt}.$$

Thus,

$$\langle ||F||^2 \rangle = \frac{\gamma^2 \langle ||x||^2 \rangle}{(dt)^2}$$

$$= \frac{4k_B T}{\text{mob}_{\text{avg}}\, dt},$$

where $\text{mob}_{\text{avg}} = 1/\gamma$ is the average mobility and equals the inverse of the drag coefficient [3].

6.6.2 Straightening Force

For the purpose of calculating the restoring force, we model the filament as a rod with an external bending force. To calculate the force on a bent rod, we follow the treatment given in Feynman [37], which we now explain.

As seen in Figure 6.8, when a rod is bent, its outer portion is stretched and its inner portion compressed. There is a cross-section through the middle that is neither stretched nor compressed (assuming that the rod is undergoing bending forces only and there is no net elongation of the rod). The increase in length, ΔL, of a slice due to stretching should then be proportional to the slice's height (y) above the unstretched

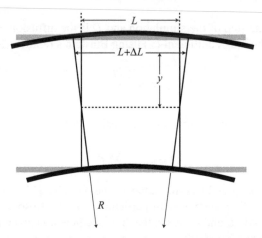

Figure 6.8 The increase in length ΔL of a slice due to stretching should then be in proportion to the slice's height y above the unstretched neutral slice. R is the radius of curvature. Adapted from [37].

neutral slice. Denoting the radius of curvature by R, we conclude that

$$\frac{\Delta L}{L} = \frac{y}{R}.$$

If we model the rod as elastic, then the strain $\Delta L/L$ is proportional to the stress $\Delta F/\Delta A$, where the ratio is Young's modulus Y,

$$\frac{\Delta F}{\Delta A} = Y \frac{\Delta L}{L}.$$

If we integrate the product of ΔF with its moment arm y over a cross-section of the rod, then we get the bending moment about the neutral axis

$$\mathscr{M} = \frac{Y}{R} \int y^2 \, dF = \frac{Y}{R} I,$$

where I is the second moment of area about the neutral axis. Thus, if an external force F is bending a rod, then the straightening torque required to put the rod in equilibrium is equivalent to $\mathscr{M}$.

To calculate the value of $\mathscr{M}$, we need an estimate of Young's modulus Y and the second moment of area I for the filament. More importantly, we need to calculate the curvature $1/R$. More formally, the curvature $k(s)$ is

$$|\alpha''(s)|,$$

where $\alpha(s)$ is the curve parameterized by arc length

$$s(t) = \int_0^t |\alpha'(\tau)| \, d\tau,$$

where $\alpha(\tau)$ is any differentiable parameterized curve without singular points, and the double prime refers to the second derivative. For the discrete representation of the filament, we need to be able to approximate the second derivative of a parameterization by arc length. Parameterizing by arc length is used, so that the second derivative is only measuring changes in the tangent vector $\alpha'(s)$ in the form of changes in direction. Parameterizing by arc length makes the change in magnitude of the tangent vector zero, as increasing the parameter of the curve by one unit corresponds to increasing the distance covered along the curve by one unit, and this will be valid for the entire length of the parameterized curve.

We can achieve the constant tangent vector magnitude by making each segment of the filament the same length δ, in which case the second derivative becomes:

$$\frac{1}{R} = |\alpha''(s)| = \left| \frac{1}{\delta} \left(\frac{m_{i+1} - m_i}{\delta} - \frac{m_i - m_{i-1}}{\delta} \right) \right|.$$

Thus, the bending moment should be

$$\mathcal{M} = \frac{YI}{\delta^2}\left(m_{i+1} - 2m_i + m_{i-1}\right).$$

Because the straightening forces are applied at the ends of each segment, we assume that the straightening force is acting with a moment arm of one segment length δ and is directed along the change in the tangent vectors. That is, the straightening force F is:

$$F = \frac{\mathcal{M}}{\delta} = \frac{YI}{\delta^3}\left(m_{i+1} - 2m_i + m_{i-1}\right).$$

Forces equal to $-F$ are applied at both the m_{i+1} and m_{i-1} nodes, and $2F$ is applied at the m_i rod.

6.6.3   Forces from Motor Complexes

When a motor complex connects two filaments, or a filament and another structure, (such as the membrane) it exerts a force on both. This force needs to be applied at the end points of the segment to which the motor complex is attached. To distribute this force F acting on a filament at postion p, we need to consider p as a linear combination of the end points of the segment on which it lies, that is, we write it as

$$p = \alpha m_i + (1 - \alpha)m_{i+1},$$

where $\alpha \in [0, 1)$. We can then apply the force αF at m_i and the force $(1 - \alpha)F$ at m_{i+1}.

6.7   IMPOSING CONSTRAINTS

6.7.1   Motivation

For running simulations, it is often the case that simulated objects are confined to follow certain constraints. For example, to simulate experiments on molecular motor processivity in microtubule gliding assays [38] where the motors are anchored to a substrate, we would constrain the motors to fixed locations on the substrate.

One way of satisfying position constraints is through the use of springs to impose forces. For example, if the motor was to deviate far from its original position, then a fictitous spring would pull it back toward the initial position. The problem with this approach is that to enforce the constraint, the spring coefficient must be large so that small deviations from the position produce strong forces pulling it back to the substrate location. This produces large differences in the relaxation times in the system of ordinary differential equations being solved, which dramatically increase the time it takes the solver to finish.

Thus, rather than calculating what forces are necessary to impose these constraints while simultaneously allowing the molecular motor to obey Newton's laws, we employ a method known as virtual work [34]. Virtual work is the method for finding the forces necessary to cancel out those forces that would cause a constraint to be violated, and in the case of the example, it would find the forces necessary to cancel out those forces that would cause the motor to move from its initial location. As applied to simulating filaments, the constraint is that the filaments can bend but cannot be stretched longitudinally. So, any forces that are applied that would cause the filament to stretch get cancelled out automatically by applying virtual work.

6.7.2   Derivation

Here we follow [34]. We express the constraints of our model by defining valid positions of elements as those that satisfy

$$\mathbf{C}(\mathbf{x}) = 0, \tag{6.2}$$

where the positions of our model elements are stored in the vector $\mathbf{x}$ and $\mathbf{C}(\mathbf{x})$ is a system of equations, with one equation for each constraint. Because Eq. (6.2) must hold at all times, taking the first and second derivatives with respect to time leads to

$$\dot{\mathbf{C}} = 0 \quad \text{and} \quad \ddot{\mathbf{C}} = 0.$$

Specifically,

$$\dot{\mathbf{C}} = \frac{\partial \mathbf{C}}{\partial \mathbf{x}} \dot{\mathbf{x}} = 0.$$

To simplify the notation, define $\mathbf{J} = \partial \mathbf{C}/\partial \mathbf{x}$, which is the Jacobian of $\mathbf{C}$. Then, for the second derivative

$$\ddot{\mathbf{C}} = \dot{\mathbf{J}}\dot{\mathbf{x}} + \mathbf{J}\ddot{\mathbf{x}} = 0,$$

where $\dot{\mathbf{J}}$ refers to $\partial\dot{\mathbf{C}}/\partial\mathbf{x}$. Note that Eq. (6.3) yields:

$$\mathbf{J}\ddot{\mathbf{x}} = -\dot{\mathbf{J}}\dot{\mathbf{x}}. \tag{6.3}$$

We also construct a mass matrix $\mathbf{M}$ with the masses of each particle along the diagonal. We then have the external forces $\mathbf{F}$ and the virtual forces $\hat{\mathbf{F}}$, which we need to solve so as to cancel out the constraint violating forces within $\mathbf{F}$. In particular,

$$(\mathbf{F} + \hat{\mathbf{F}}) = \mathbf{M}\ddot{\mathbf{x}}.$$

Thus,

$$\ddot{\mathbf{x}} = \mathbf{M}^{-1}(\mathbf{F} + \hat{\mathbf{F}}). \tag{6.4}$$

Multiplying Eq. (6.4) by $\mathbf{J}$ and substituting Eq. (6.3) leads to

$$\mathbf{J}\mathbf{M}^{-1}\hat{\mathbf{F}} = -\dot{\mathbf{J}}\dot{\mathbf{x}} - \mathbf{J}\mathbf{M}^{-1}\mathbf{F}. \tag{6.5}$$

We have two unknowns, $\dot{\mathbf{x}}$ and $\hat{\mathbf{F}}$, and only one equation. We use virtual work to obtain a second equation.

For the virtual forces $\hat{\mathbf{F}}$ to do no work on the particles we must have:

$$\hat{\mathbf{F}} \cdot \dot{\mathbf{x}} = 0$$

for all $\dot{\mathbf{x}}$ satisfying $\mathbf{J}\dot{\mathbf{x}} = 0$. This condition holds if and only if

$$\hat{\mathbf{F}} = \mathbf{J}^T\lambda, \tag{6.6}$$

where λ has the same dimensions as $\mathbf{C}$. Substituting Eq. (6.6) into Eq. (6.5), we obtain

$$\mathbf{J}\mathbf{M}^{-1}\mathbf{J}^T\lambda = -\dot{\mathbf{J}}\dot{\mathbf{x}} - \mathbf{J}\mathbf{M}^{-1}\mathbf{F}. \tag{6.7}$$

We can now solve for λ and find $\hat{\mathbf{F}}$ using Eq. 6.6. We can then use $\ddot{\mathbf{x}} = \mathbf{M}^{-1}(\mathbf{F} + \hat{\mathbf{F}})$ and integrate to obtain the position.

6.7.3 Implementation

For simulating unstretchable filaments in two dimensions with a segment length s, we define our constraints to be

$$C_0 = (x_0 - x_1)^2 + (y_0 - y_1)^2 - s^2$$
$$C_1 = (x_1 - x_2)^2 + (y_1 - y_2)^2 - s^2$$
$$\vdots$$
$$C_{n-2} = (x_{n-2} - x_{n-1})^2 + (y_{n-2} - y_{n-1})^2 - s^2$$

and construct

$$\mathbf{C} = \begin{bmatrix} C_0 \\ \vdots \\ C_{n-2} \end{bmatrix} \quad \text{and} \quad \mathbf{x} = \begin{bmatrix} x_0 \\ y_0 \\ \vdots \\ x_{n-1} \\ y_{n-1} \end{bmatrix}, \tag{6.8}$$

where $\mathbf{x}$ corresponds to our filament vector $\mathbf{m}$ from Section 6.4, we then obtain $\mathbf{J} = \partial \mathbf{C}/\partial \mathbf{x}$, which is a $(n-1) \times 2n$ matrix. For our model, we only need to use the first derivative of $\mathbf{C}$:

$$\dot{\mathbf{C}} = \frac{\partial \mathbf{C}}{\partial \mathbf{x}}\dot{\mathbf{x}}, \tag{6.9}$$

as the filaments are more influenced by viscous forces than inertial forces. Using the virtual forces:

$$\hat{\mathbf{F}} = \mathbf{J}^T \lambda, \tag{6.10}$$

we have $\dot{\mathbf{x}} = \gamma(\mathbf{F} + \hat{\mathbf{F}})$. Solving for λ using Eqs. (6.9) and (6.10), we obtain

$$\lambda = -(\mathbf{J}\mathbf{J}^T)^{-1}\mathbf{J}\mathbf{F},$$

causing the net force

$$\mathbf{F}_{\text{net}} = \mathbf{F} + \hat{\mathbf{F}}$$

to be

$$\mathbf{F}_{\text{net}} = (\mathbf{I} - \mathbf{J}^T(\mathbf{J}\mathbf{J}^T)^{-1}\mathbf{J})\mathbf{F},$$

where $\mathbf{F}$ is the sum of the external forces. These include the straightening forces, the forces due to motor complexes, and Brownian motion forces. We define the projection matrix

$$\mathbf{P} = \mathbf{I} - \mathbf{J}^T(\mathbf{J}\mathbf{J}^T)^{-1}\mathbf{J},$$

so that $\mathbf{F}_{\text{net}} = \mathbf{P}\mathbf{F}$.

6.7.4 State Equation

Storing the filament positions in the vector $\mathbf{x}$ as in Eq. (6.8), we then use

$$\dot{\mathbf{x}} = \gamma \mathbf{F}_{\text{net}},$$

where γ is a diagonal mobility matrix to set up our update equation.

$$\mathbf{x}(t + dt) = \mathbf{x}(t) + \gamma\, dt\mathbf{P}(\mathbf{B} - \mathbf{G}\mathbf{x}(t + dt)),$$

where $\mathbf{B}$ includes the Brownian forces and $\mathbf{G}\mathbf{x}(t + dt)$ are the forces due to motor complexes and straightening forces on bent filaments. Rearranging, we obtain

$$(\mathbf{I} + \gamma\, dt\mathbf{P}\mathbf{G})\mathbf{x}(t + dt) = \mathbf{x}(t) + \gamma\, dt\mathbf{P}\mathbf{B},$$

which is now in the form $\mathbf{Ax} = \mathbf{b}$ with

$$\mathbf{A} = \mathbf{I} + \gamma \, dt \mathbf{PG} \tag{6.11}$$

and

$$\mathbf{b} = \mathbf{x}(t) + \gamma \, dt \, \mathbf{PB},$$

which we can apply a solver to find $\mathbf{x}$.

6.8 SOLVER

There are a number of solvers that can be applied to large systems of the form $Ax = b$, where A is a sparse matrix. If A is symmetric and positive definite, the conjugate gradient method is generally considered as an ideal choice among iterative methods [39]. When A is not symmetric, other methods such as biconjugate gradient (Bi-CG) [40], conjugate gradient squared (CG-S) [39], or biconjugate gradient stabilized (Bi-CGSTAB) [41] can be applied.

CG-S and Bi-CGSTAB are both variants of Bi-CG. CG-S converges roughly twice as fast as Bi-CG, but the rate of convergence becomes erratic as one moves closer to the solution [39, 41]. Bi-CGSTAB has a convergence rate similar to CG-S but without the erratic convergence rate [35]. As the matrix A in Eq. (6.11) is not symmetric (due to applying motor complex forces in $\mathbf{G}$ in proportion to the attachment distance to the nearest filament segment end points), we cannot apply the conjugate gradient method. Instead, we use the biconjugate gradient-stabilized method.

The preconditioned biconjugate gradient-stabilized method as given in Barrett et al. [35] is reproduced in Algorithm 6.1. If we let the preconditioner matrix M be the identity, then the residual $r^{(i)}$ reduces to

$$r^{(i)} = (r_{(i-1)} - \alpha_i A p^{(i)})(I - \omega_i A).$$

The first factor, $(r_{(i-1)} - \alpha_i A p^{(i)})$, corresponds to the recurrence relation for the residual in the conjugate gradient, where $p^{(i)}$ is the search direction along which the next iterate $x^{(i)}$ would be found. The residual, defined as $r^{(i)} = b - Ax^{(i)}$, has the desirable property of being the negative gradient of the function

$$f(x) = \tfrac{1}{2} x^T A x - x^T b.$$

evaluated at $x^{(i)}$, when A is symmetric. And when A is positive definite, the global minimum of $f(x)$ occurs at the solution of $Ax = b$. What we have lost in our case, because A is not positive definite, is that minimizing f no longer implies we have solved $Ax = b$. The second factor in the computation of $r^{(i)}$, that is, $(I - \omega_i A)$, is what smooths the convergence over CG-S.

Algorithm 6.1   Bi-CGSTAB

```
1{
    Compute r⁽⁰⁾ = b − Ax⁽⁰⁾ for some initial guess x⁽⁰⁾.
    Choose r̃ for example r̃ = r⁽⁰⁾.
    for i ∈ {1, 2, ...}
    {
```

$$\rho_{i-1} = \tilde{r}^T r^{(i-1)}$$

```
        if (ρᵢ₋₁ = 0)
                Method fails
        else if (i = 1)
```

$$p^{(i)} = r^{(i-1)}$$

```
        else {
```

$$\beta_{(i-1)} = \frac{\rho_{i-1}}{\rho_{i-2}} \frac{\alpha_{i-1}}{\omega_{i-1}}$$

$$p^{(i)} = r^{(i-1)} + \beta_{i-1}(p^{(i-1)} - \omega_{i-1}v^{(i-1)})$$

```
        }
        solve Mp̂ = p⁽ⁱ⁾
```

$$v^{(i)} = A\hat{p}$$

$$\alpha_i = \rho_{i-1}/(\tilde{r}^T v^{(i)})$$

$$s = r^{(i-1)} - \alpha_i v^{(i)}$$

```
        check norm of s;
            if small enough:    set x⁽ⁱ⁾ = x⁽ⁱ⁻¹⁾ + αᵢp̂ and stop
        solve Mŝ = s
```

$$t = A\hat{s}$$

$$\omega_i = t^T s/(t^T t)$$

$$x^{(i)} = x^{(i-1)} + \alpha_i \hat{p} + \omega_i \hat{s}$$

$$r^{(i)} = s - \omega_i t$$

```
        check convergence; continue if necessary
        for continuation it is necessary that ωᵢ ≠ 0
    }
}
```

6.9 CONCLUSION

In large systems with many types of chemical and force interactions, it can be difficult to explore the consequences of each type of interaction, especially for those interactions that have multiple roles at different levels within the system, where a biological knockdown might only reveal the maximum upstream interaction in the system. Such systems are optimal grounds for computational modeling, where each hypothesized mechanism can be implemented and its consequences measured and compared to experimental results.

There are limitations, though to the complexity of the system, which can be modeled. Whether it be individual atoms in protein conformation problems or molecular motors diffusing and interacting with thousands of filaments within the cytoplasm, simulations that track individual components and their interactions can take much longer to complete than simulations that track just their bulk properties. The feasability of obtaining results and the validity of those results depend on finding the right level of model complexity. The model must be simple enough to simulate in a reasonable amount of time while still encapsulating the relevant biological mechanisms. As our understanding of these mechanisms improves, so will our ability to model systems that build upon them, and as these models improve so too will our biological understanding.

REFERENCES

1. R. Levins. The strategy of model building in population biology. *Am. Sci.*, 54:421–431, 1966.

2. E. D. Conrad and J. J Tyson. Modeling molecular interaction networks with nonlinear ordinary differential equations. In Z. Szallasi, J. Stelling, and V. Periwal, editors. *System Modeling in Cellular Biology*, Chapter 6. MIT Press, Cambridge, MA, 2006.

3. F. Nédélec. Computer simulations reveal motor properties generating stable antiparallel microtubule interactions. *J. Cell Biol.*, 158:1005–1015, 2002.

4. W. E. Channels, F. J. Nédélec, Y. Zheng, and P. A. Iglesias. Spatial regulation improves antiparallel microtubule overlap during mitotic spindle assembly. *Biophysical J.*, 94:2598–2609, 2008.

5. T. D. Pollard and G. G. Borisy. Cellular motility driven by assembly and disassembly of actin filaments. *Cell*, 112(4):459–65, 2003.

6. E. M. Reichl, J. C Effler, and D. N Robinson. The stress and strain of cytokinesis. *Trends Cell Biol.*, 15(4):200–206, 2005.

7. K. C. Holmes, D. Popp, W. Gebhard, and W. Kabsch. Atomic model of the actin filament. *Nature*, 6(347):44–49, 1990.

8. J. Howard. *Mechanics of Motor Proteins and the Cytoskeleton*. Sinauer Associates, Sunderland, MA, 2001.

9. T. D. Pollard. Regulation of actin filament assembly by Arp2/3 complex and formins. *Annu. Rev. Biophys. Biomol. Struct.*, 36:451–477, 2007.

10. E. M. Reichl, Y. Ren, M. K. Morphew, M. Delannoy, J. C. Effler, K. D. Girard, S. Divi, P. A. Iglesias, S. C. Kuo, and D. N. Robinson. Interactions between myosin and actin crosslinkers control cytokinesis contractility dynamics and mechanics. *Curr. Biol.*, 18:471–480, 2008.

11. T. M. Svitkina, A. B. Verkhovsky, K. M. McQuade, and G. G. Borisy. Analysis of the actin-myosin II system in fish epidermal keratocytes: Mechanism of cell body translocation. *J. Cell Biol.*, 139:397–415, 1997.

12. F. Gittes, B. Mickey, J. Nettleton, and J. Howard. Flexural rigidity of microtubules and actin filaments measured from thermal fluctuations in shape. *J. Cell Biol.*, 120:923–934, 1993.

13. P. A. Janmey, U. Euteneuer, P. Traub, and M. Schliwa. Viscoelastic properties of vimentin compared with other filamentous biopolymer networks. *J. Cell Biol.*, 113:155–160, 1991.

14. E. Fuchs and K. Weber. Intermediate filaments: Structure, dynamics, function, and disease. *Annu. Rev. Biochem.*, 63:345–382, 1994.

15. R. D. Goldman, B. Grin, M. G. Mendez, and E. R. Kuczmarski. Intermediate filaments: versatile building blocks of cell structure. *Curr. Opin. Cell Biol.*, 20:28–34, 2008.

16. Z. Xu, L. C. Cork, J. W. Griffin, and D. W. Cleveland. Involvement of neurofilaments in motor neuron disease. *J. Cell Sci.*, 17:101–108, 1993.

17. M. Y. Tsai, S. Wang, J. M. Heidinger, D. K. Shumaker, S. A. Adam, R. D. Goldman, and Y. Zheng. A mitotic lamin B matrix induced by RanGTP required for spindle assembly. *Science*, 311:1887–1893, 2006.

18. B. Liu and Z. Zhou. Lamin A/C, laminopathies and premature ageing. *Histol. Histopathol.*, 23:747–763, 2008.

19. T. Wittmann, A. Hyman, and A. Desai. The spindle: a dynamic assembly of microtubules and motors. *Nat. Cell Biol.*, 3:28–34, 2001.

20. L. T. Haimo and J. L. Rosenbaum. Cilia, flagella, and microtubules. *J. Cell Biol.*, 91(3): 125–130, 1981.

21. K. Inaba. Molecular architecture of the sperm flagella: molecules for motility and signaling. *Zoologic. Sci.*, 20:1043–1056, 2003.

22. M. A. Sleigh, J. R, Blake, and N. Liron. The propulsion of mucus by cilia. *Am. Rev. Respir. Dis.*, 137:726–741, 1988.

23. D. McDonald, M. A. Vodicka, G. Lucero, T. M. Svitkina, G. G. Borisy, M. Emerman, and T. J. Hope. Visualization of the intracellular behavior of HIV in living cells. *J. Cell Biol.*, 159:441–452, 2002.

24. A. Desai and T. J. Mitchison. Microtubule polymerization dynamics. *Annu. Rev. Cell Develop. Biol.*, 13:83–117, 1997.

25. M. Kirschner and T. Mitchison. Beyond self-assembly: from microtubules to morphogenesis. *Cell*, 45:329–342, 1986.

26. J. B. Alberts and G. M. Odell. In silico reconstitution of Listeria propulsion exhibits nano-saltation. *PLoS Biol.*, 2:e412, 2004.

27. B. L. Sprague, C. G. Pearson, P. S. Maddox, K. S. Bloom, E. D. Salmon, and D. J. Odde. Mechanisms of microtubule-based kinetochore positioning in the yeast metaphase spindle. *Biophysical J.*, 84:3529–3546, 2003.

28. C. Kozlowski, M. Srayko, and F. Nedelec. Cortical microtubule contacts position the spindle in C. elegans embryos. *Cell*, 129:499–510, 2007.

29. E. Munro. The microtubules dance and the spindle poles swing. *Cell*, 129:457–458, 2007.

30. K. S. Burbank, T. J. Mitchison, and D. S. Fisher. Slide-and-cluster models for spindle assembly. *Curr. Biol.*, 17:1373–1383, 2007.

31. D. Vavylonis, J. Q. Wu, S. Hao, B. O'Shaughnessy, and T. D. Pollard. Assembly mechanism of the contractile ring for cytokinesis by fission yeast. *Science*, 319:97–100, 2008.

32. A. Chakravarty, L. Howard, and D. A. Compton. A mechanistic model for the organization of microtubule asters by motor and non-motor proteins in a mammalian mitotic extract. *Mol. Biol. Cell*, 15:2116–2132, 2004.

33. M. Piehl and L. Cassimeris. Organization and dynamics of growing microtubule plus ends during early mitosis. *Mol. Biol. Cell*, 14:916–925, 2003.

34. A. Witkin. *An Introduction to Physically Based Modeling: Constrained Dynamics*, 1997.

35. R. Barrett, M. Berry, T. F. Chan, J. Demmel, J. Donato, J. Dongarra, V. Eijkhout, R. Pozo, C. Romine, and H. Van der Vorst. *Templates for the Solution of Linear Systems: Building Blocks for Iterative Methods*, 2nd edition, SIAM, Philadelphia, PA, 1994.

36. H. C. Berg. *Random Walks in Biology*, Expanded Edition. Princeton University Press, Princeton, NJ, 1993.

37. R. Feynman. *The Feynman Lectures on Physics*, Vol. 2, Addison Wesley, Reading, MA, 1989.

38. W. O. Hancock and J. Howard. Processivity of the motor protein kinesin requires two heads. *J. Cell Biol.*, 140:1395–1405, 1998.

39. P. Sonneveld. CGS, a fast Lanczos-type solver for nonsymmetric linear systems. *SIAM J. Sci. Statistic. Comput.*, 10(1):36–52, 1989.

40. R. Fletcher. Conjugate gradient methods for indefinite systems. In A. Dodd and B. Eckmann, editors. *Numerical Analysis*, Vol. 506 of Lecture Notes in Mathematics, Springer, Berlin, 1976, pp. 73–89.

41. H. A. van der Vorst. BI-CGSTAB: a fast and smoothly converging variant of BI-CG for the solution of nonsymmetric linear systems. *SIAM J. Sci. Statistic. Comput.*, 13(2):631–644, 1992.

BIOLOGICAL NETWORK INFERENCE

III

BIOLOGICAL NETWORK INFERENCE

7

RECONSTRUCTION OF BIOLOGICAL NETWORKS BY SUPERVISED MACHINE LEARNING APPROACHES

Jean-Philippe Vert

Mines ParisTech - Institut Curie, Paris, France

7.1 INTRODUCTION

In this review chapter, we focus on the problem of reconstructing the structure of large-scale biological networks. By biological networks, we mean graphs whose vertices are all or a subset of the genes and proteins encoded in a given organism of interest, and whose edges, either directed or undirected, represent various biological properties. As running examples, we consider the three following graphs, although the methods presented below may be applied to other biological networks as well.

- *Protein–protein interaction (PPI) network*. This is an undirected graph with no self-loop, which contains all proteins encoded by an organism as vertices. Two proteins are connected by an edge if they can physically interact.
- *Gene regulatory network*. This is a directed graph that contains all genes of an organism as vertices. Among the genes, some called transcription factors (TFs) regulate the expression of other genes through binding to the DNA. The edges of the graph connect TFs to the genes they regulate. Self-loops are possible

Elements of Computational Systems Biology Edited by Huma M. Lodhi and Stephen H. Muggleton
Copyright © 2010 John Wiley & Sons, Inc.

if a TF regulates itself. Moreover, each edge may in principle be labeled to indicate whether the regulation is a positive (activation) or negative (inhibition) regulation.

- *Metabolic network.* This graph contains only a subset of the genes as vertices, namely, those coding for enzymes. Enzymes are proteins whose main function is to catalyze a chemical reaction, transforming substrate molecules into product molecules. Two enzymes are connected in this graph if they can catalyze two successive reactions in a metabolic pathway, that is, two reactions, such that the main product of the first one is a substrate of the second one.

Deciphering these networks for model organisms, pathogens, or human is currently a major challenge in systems biology, with many expected applications ranging from basic biology to medical applications. For example, knowing the detailed interactions possible between proteins on a genomic scale would highlight key proteins that interact with many partners, which could be interesting drug targets [1], and would help in the annotation of proteins by annotation transfer between interacting proteins. The elucidation of gene regulatory networks, especially in bacteria and simple eukaryotes, would provide new insights into the complex mechanisms that allow an organism to regulate its metabolism and adapt itself to environmental changes and could provide interesting guidelines for the design of new functions. Finally, understanding, in detail, the metabolism of an organism and clarifying which proteins are in charge of its control, would give a valuable description of how organisms have found original pathways for degradation and synthesis of various molecules, and could help again in the identification of new drug targets [2].

Decades of research in molecular biology and genetics have already provided a partial view of these networks, in particular, for model organisms. Moreover, recent high-throughput technologies such as the yeast two-hybrid systems for PPI provide large numbers of likely edges in these graphs, although probably with a high rate of false positives [3, 4]. Thus, much work remains to be done in order to complete (adding currently unknown edges) and correct (removing false-positive edges) these partially known networks. To do so, one may want to use information about individual genes and proteins such as their sequence, structure, subcellular localization, or level of expression across several experiments. Indeed, this information often provides useful hints about the presence or absence of edges between two proteins. For example, two proteins are more likely to interact physically if they are expressed in similar experiments and localized in the same cellular compartment, or two enzymes are more likely to be involved in the same metabolic pathway if they are often coexpressed and if they have homologs in the same species [5–7].

Following this line of thought, many approaches have been proposed in the recent years to infer biological networks from genomic and proteomic data, most of them attempting to reconstruct the graphs *de novo*. In *de novo* inference, the data about individual genes and proteins are given and edges are inferred from these data only, using a variety of inference principles. For example, when time series of expression data are used, regulatory networks have been reconstructed by fitting various dynamical system equations to the data [8–14]. Bayesian networks have also been used to infer *de novo* regulatory networks from expression data, assuming that direct regulation can be inferred from the analysis of correlation and conditional independence between expression levels [15]. Another rationale for *de novo* inference is to connect genes or proteins that are similar to each other in some sense [5, 6]. For example, coexpression networks or the detection of similar phylogenetic profiles are popular ways to infer "functional relationships" between proteins, although the meaning of the resulting edges has no clear biological justification [16]. Similarly, some authors have attempted to predict gene regulatory networks by detecting large mutual information between expression levels of a TF and the genes it regulates [17, 18].

In contrast to these *de novo* methods, in this review, we present a general approach to reconstruct biological networks using information about individual genes and proteins based on supervised machine learning algorithms, as developed through a recent series of articles [19–26]. The graph inference paradigm we follow assumes that, besides the information about individual vertices (genes or proteins) used by *de novo* approaches, the graph we wish to infer is also partially known, and known edges can be used by the inference algorithm to infer unknown edges. This paradigm is similar to the notion of supervised inference in statistics and machine learning, where one uses a set of input/output pairs (often called the training set) to estimate a function that can predict the output associated with new inputs [27, 28]. In our paradigm, we give us the right to use the known edges of the graph to supervise the estimation of a function that could predict whether a new pair of vertices is connected by an edge or not, given the data about the vertices. Intuitively, this setting can allow us to automatically learn what features of the data about vertices are the most informative to predict the presence of an edge between two vertices. In a sense, this paradigm leads to a problem much simpler than the *de novo* inference problem, since more information is used as an input, and it might seem unfair to compare *de novo* and supervised methods. However, as already mentioned, in many real-world cases of interest, we already partially know the graph we wish to infer. It is, therefore, quite natural to use as much information as we can in order to focus on the real problem, which is to infer new edges (and perhaps delete wrong edges), and, therefore, to use as an input both the genomic and proteomic data, on the one hand, and the edges already known, on the other.

In a slightly more formal language, we, therefore, wish to learn a function that can predict whether an edge exists or not between two vertices (genes or proteins), given data about the vertices (e.g., expression levels of each gene in different experimental conditions). Technically, this problem can be thought of as a problem of binary classification, where we need to assign a binary label (presence or absence of an edge) to each pair of vertices, as explained in Section 7.2.1. From a computational point of view, the supervised inference paradigm we investigate can, in principle, benefit from the availability of a number of methods for supervised binary classification, also known as pattern recognition [28]. These methods, as reviewed in Section 7.2.2, are able to estimate a function to predict a binary label from data about patterns, given a training set of (pattern, label) pairs. The supervised inference problem we are confronted with, however, is not a classical pattern/label problem because the data are associated with individual vertices (e.g., expression profiles are available for each individual gene), while the labels correspond to pairs of vertices. Before applying out-of-the-box state-of-the-art machine learning algorithms, we, therefore, need to clarify how our problem can be transformed as a classical pattern recognition problem (Section 7.2.3). In particular, we show that there is not a unique way to do that, and present in Sections 7.2.4 and 7.2.5, two classes of approaches that have been proposed recently. Both classes involve a support vector machine (SVM) as a binary classification engine, but follow different avenues to cast the edge inference problem as a binary classification problem. In Section 7.3, we provide experimental results that justify the relevance of supervised inference and show that a particular approach, based on local models, performs particularly well on the reconstruction of PPI and regulatory and metabolic networks. We conclude with a rapid discussion in Section 7.4.

7.2 GRAPH RECONSTRUCTION AS A PATTERN RECOGNITION PROBLEM

In this section, we formally define the graph reconstruction problem considered and explain how to solve it with pattern recognition techniques.

7.2.1 Problem Formalization

We consider a finite set of vertices $V = (v_1, \ldots, v_n)$ that typically correspond to the set of all genes or proteins of an organism. We further assume that for each vertex $v \in V$, we have a description of various features of v as a vector $\phi(v) \in \mathbb{R}^p$. Typically, $\phi(v)$ could be a vector of expression levels of the gene v in p different experimental conditions, measured by DNA microarrays, a phylogenetic profile that encodes the presence or absence of the gene in a set of p sequenced genomes [6], a vector of p sequence features, or a combination of such features. We wish to reconstruct a set of edges $E \subset V \times V$ that defines a biological network. While in *de novo* inference, the goal is to design an algorithm that automatically predicts edges in E from the set of vertex features $(\phi(v_1), \ldots, \phi(v_n))$, in our approach, we further assume that a set of pairs of vertices known to be connected by an edge or not is given. In other words, we assume given a list $S = ((e_1, y_1), \ldots, (e_N, y_N))$ of pairs of vertices $(e_i \in V \times V)$ tagged with a label $y_i \in \{-1, 1\}$ that indicate whether the pair e_i is known to interact ($y_i = 1$) or not ($y_i = -1$). In an ideal noise-free situation, where the labels of pairs in the training set are known with certainty, we thus have $y_i = 1$ if $e_i \in E$, and $y_i = -1$ otherwise. However, in some situations, we may also have noise or errors in the training set labels, in which case, we could only assume that pairs in E tend to have a positive label, while pairs not in E tend to have a negative label.

The graph reconstruction problem can now be formally stated as follows: Given the training set S and the set of vertex features $(\phi(v_1), \ldots, \phi(v_n))$, predict for all pairs not in S whether they interact (i.e., whether they are in E) or not. This formulation is illustrated in Figure 7.1.

Stated this way, this problem is similar to a classical pattern recognition problem, for which a variety of efficient algorithms have been developed over the years. Before highlighting the slight difference between the classical pattern recognition framework

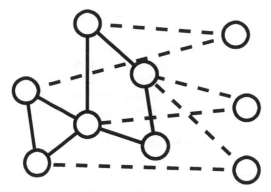

Figure 7.1   We consider the problem of inferring missing edges in a graph (dotted edges), where a few edges are already known (solid edges). To carry out the inference, we use attributes available about individual vertices such as vectors of expression levels across different experiments if vertices are genes.

and ours, it is, therefore, worth recalling this classical pattern recognition paradigm and mentioning some algorithms adapted to solve it.

7.2.2   Pattern Recognition

Pattern recognition, of binary supervised classification, is a well-studied problem in statistics and machine learning [27, 28]. In its basic setup, a training set $\mathcal{T} = \{(u_1, t_1), \ldots, (u_N, t_N)\}$ of labeled patterns is given, where $u_i \in \mathbb{R}^q$ is a vector and $t_i \in \{-1, 1\}$ is a binary label, for $i = 1, \ldots, N$. The goal is then to infer a function $f : \mathbb{R}^q \rightarrow \{-1, 1\}$ that is able to predict the binary label t of any new pattern $u \in \mathbb{R}^q$ by $f(u)$.

Many methods have been proposed to infer the labeling function f from the training set $\mathcal{T}$, including, for example, nearest neighbor classifiers, decision trees, logistic regression, artificial neural networks, or SVMs. Although any of these methods can be used in what follows, we will present experiments carried out with an SVM, which we briefly describe below, mainly for three reasons:

- It is now a widely used algorithm, in particular, in computational biology, with many public implementations [29, 30].
- It provides a convenient framework to combine heterogeneous features about the vertices such as the sequence, expression, and subcellular localization of proteins [19, 31, 32].
- Some methods developed so far for graph inference, which we describe below, are particularly well-adapted for a formalization in the context of SVM and kernel methods [22, 24].

Let us, therefore, briefly describe the SVM algorithm and redirect the interested reader to various textbooks for more details [33–35]. Given the labeled training set $\mathcal{T}$, an

SVM estimates a linear function $h(u) = w^\top u$ for some vector $w \in \mathbb{R}^q$ (here $w^\top u$ represents the inner product between w and u) and then makes a label prediction for a new pattern u that depends only on the sign of $h(u)$: $f(u) = 1$ if $h(u) \geq 0$, $f(u) = -1$ otherwise. The vector w is obtained as the solution of an optimization problem that attempts to enforce a correct sign with large absolute values for the values $h(u_i)$ on the training set while controlling the Euclidean norm of w. The resulting optimization problem is a quadratic program for which many specific and fast implementations have been proposed.

An interesting property of SVM, particularly for the purpose of heterogeneous data integration, is that the optimization problem only involves the training patterns u_i through pairwise inner products of the form $u_i^\top u_j$. Moreover, once the classifier is trained, the computation of $h(u)$ to predict the label of a new point u also involves only patterns through inner products of the form $u^\top u_i$. Hence, rather than computing and storing each individual pattern as a vector u, we just need to be able to compute inner products of the form $u^\top u'$ for any two patterns u and u' in order to train an SVM and use it as a prediction engine. This inner product between patterns u and u' is a particular case of what is called a kernel and denoted $K(u, u') = u^\top u'$ to emphasize the fact that it can be seen as a function that associates a number to any pair of patterns (u, u'), namely, their inner product. More generally, a kernel is a function that computes the inner product between two patterns u and u' after possibly mapping them to some vector space with inner product by a mapping ϕ, that is, $K(u, u') = \phi(u)^\top \phi(u)'$.

Kernels are particularly relevant when the patterns are represented by vectors of large dimensions, whose inner products can nevertheless be computed efficiently. They are also powerful tools to integrate heterogeneous data. Suppose, for example, that each pattern u can be represented as two different vectors $u^{(1)}$ and $u^{(2)}$. This could be the case, for example, if one wanted to represent a protein u either by a vector of expression profile $u^{(1)}$ or by a vector of phylogenetic profile $u^{(2)}$. Let now K_1 and K_2 be the two kernels corresponding to inner products for each representation, namely, $K_1(u, u') = u^{(1)\top} u^{(1)'}$ and $K_2(u, u') = u^{(2)\top} u^{(2)'}$. If we now want to represent both types of features into a single representation, a natural approach would be, for example to concatenate both vectors $u^{(1)}$ and $u^{(2)}$ into a single vector, which we denote by $u^{(1)} \oplus u^{(2)}$ (also called the direct sum of $u^{(1)}$ and $u^{(2)}$). In order to use this joint representation in an SVM, we need to be able to compute the inner products between direct sums of two patterns to define a joint kernel K_{joint}. Interestingly, some simple algebra shows that the resulting inner product is easily expressed as the sum of the inner products of each representation, that is:

$$
\begin{aligned}
K_{\text{joint}}(u, u') &= \left(u^{(1)} \oplus u^{(2)} \right)^\top \left(u^{(1)'} \oplus u^{(2)'} \right) \\
&= \begin{pmatrix} u^{(1)} \\ u^{(2)} \end{pmatrix}^\top \begin{pmatrix} u^{(1)'} \\ u^{(2)'} \end{pmatrix} \\
&= u^{(1)\top} u^{(1)'} + u^{(2)\top} u^{(2)'} \\
&= K_1(u, u') + K_2(u, u').
\end{aligned}
\tag{7.1}
$$

Consequently, the painstaking operation of concatenation between two vectors of potentially large dimension is advantageously replaced by simply doing the sum between two kernels. More generally, if k different representations are given, corresponding to k different kernels, then summing together the k kernels results in a joint kernel that integrates all different representations. The sum can also be replaced by any convex combination (linear combination with nonnegative weights) in order to weight differently the importance of different features [32].

7.2.3 Graph Inference as a Pattern Recognition Problem

Let us now return to the graph reconstruction problem, as presented in Section 7.2.1. At first sight, this problem is very similar to the general pattern recognition paradigm recalled in Section 7.2.2: Given pairs of vertices with positive and negative labels, infer a function f to predict whether a new pair has a positive label (i.e., is connected) or not. An important difference between the two problems, however, is that the features available in the graph reconstruction problem describe properties of individual vertices v and not of pairs of vertices (v, v'). Thus, in order to apply pattern recognition techniques such as the SVM to solve the graph reconstruction problem, we can follow one of the two possible avenues.

(1) Reformulate the graph reconstruction problem as a pattern recognition problem, where binary labels are attached to individual vertices (and not to pairs of vertices). Then pattern recognition methods can be used to infer the label of vertices based on their features.

(2) Keep the formulation as the problem of predicting the binary label of a pair of vertices, but find a way to represent as vectors (or as a kernel) pairs of vertices, while we initially only have features for individual vertices.

Both directions are possible and have been investigated by different authors, leading to different algorithms. In Section 7.2.4, we present an instantiation of the first idea, which rephrases graph reconstruction as a combination of simple pattern recognition problems at the level of individual vertices. In Section 7.2.5, we present several instantiations of the second strategies, which amount to defining a kernel for pairs of vertices from a kernel for individual vertices.

7.2.4 Graph Inference with Local Models

In this section, we describe an approach that was proposed by Bleakley et al. [25] for the reconstruction of metabolic and PPI networks and successfully applied by Mordelet and Vert [26] for regulatory network inference. The basic idea is very simple and can be thought of as a "divide-and-conquer" strategy to infer new edges in a graph. Each vertex of the graph is considered in turn as a seed vertex, independently from the others, and a "local" pattern recognition problem is solved to discriminate the vertices that are connected to this seed vertex against the vertices that are not connected to it. The local model can then be applied to predict new edges between the seed vertex and other vertices. This process is then repeated with other vertices as seed to obtain edge prediction throughout the graph. More precisely, the "local model" approach can be described as follows:

(1) Take a seed vertex v_{seed} in V.
(2) For each pair (v_{seed}, v') with label y in the training set, associate the same label y with the individual vertex v'. This results in a set of labeled vertices $\left\{ (v'_1, t_1), \ldots, (v'_{n(v_{seed})}, t_{n(v_{seed})}) \right\}$, where $n(v_{seed})$ is the number of pairs starting with v_{seed} in the training set. We call this set a local training set.
(3) Train a pattern recognition algorithm on the local training set designed in step 2.
(4) Predict the label of any vertex v' that has no label, that is, such that (v_{seed}, v') is not in the training set.
(5) If a vertex v' has a positive predicted label, then predict that the pair (v_{seed}, v') has a positive label (i.e., is an edge).
(6) Repeat steps (1)–(5) for each vertex v_{seed} in V.
(7) Combine the edges predicted at each iteration together to obtain the final list of predicted edges.

This process is illustrated in Figure 7.2. Intuitively, such an approach can work if the features about individual vertices provide useful information about whether or not they share a common neighbor. For example, the approach was developed by Mordelet and Vert [26] to reconstruct the gene regulatory network, that is, to predict whether a transcription factor v regulates a gene v', using a compendium of gene expression

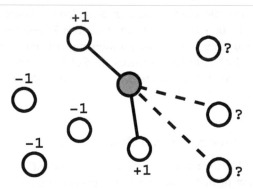

Figure 7.2 Illustration of one binary classification problem that is generated from the graph inference problem of Figure 7.1, with the local model approach. Taking the shaded vertex as seed, other vertices in the training set are labeled as +1 or −1 depending on whether they are known to be connected or to be not connected to the shaded vertex. The goal is then to predict the label of vertices not used during training. The process is then repeated by shading each vertex in turn.

levels across a variety of experimental conditions as features. The paradigm seems particularly relevant in that case. Indeed, if two genes are regulated by the same TF, then they are likely to behave similarly in terms of expression level; conversely, if a gene v' is known to be regulated by a TF v and if the expression profile of another gene v'' is similar to that of v', then one can predict that v'' is likely to be regulated by v. The pattern recognition algorithm is precisely the tool that automatizes the task of predicting that v'' has a positive label, given that v' has itself a positive label and that v' and v'' share similar features.

We note that this local model approach is particularly relevant for directed graphs such as gene regulatory networks. If our goal is to reconstruct an undirected graph, such as the PPI graph, then one can follow exactly the same approach, except that (i) each undirected training pair $\{v, v'\}$ should be considered twice in step (2), namely as the directed pair (v, v') for the local model of v and as the directed pair (v', v) for the directed model of v', and (ii) in the prediction step for an undirected pair $\{v, v'\}$, the prediction of the label of the directed pair (v, v') with the local model of v must be combined with the prediction of the label of the directed pair (v', v) made by the local model of v'. In Bleakley et al. [25], for example, in the prediction step, the score of the directed pair (v, v') is averaged with the score of the directed pair (v', v) to obtain a unique score for the undirected pair $\{v, v'\}$.

In terms of computational complexity, it can be very beneficial to split a large pattern recognition problem into several smaller problems. Indeed, the time and memory complexities of pattern recognition algorithms such as SVM are roughly quadratic or worse in the number of training examples. If a training set of N pairs is split into s local training sets of roughly N/s patterns each, then the total cost of running s SVM to estimate local models will, therefore, be of the order of $s \times (N/s)^2 = N^2/s$. Hence, if a local model is built for each vertex ($s = n$), one can expect a speedup of the algorithm of up to a factor of n over an SVM that would work with N pairs as training patterns. Moreover, the local problems associated with different seed vertices being independent from each others, one can trivially benefit from parallel computing architectures by training the different local models on different processors.

On the other hand, an apparently important drawback of the approach is that the size of each local training set can become very small if, for example, a vertex has few or even no known neighbors. Inferring accurate predictive models from few training examples is known to be challenging in machine learning, and in the extreme case, where a vertex has no known neighbor during training, then no new edge can ever be predicted. However, the experimental results, reported by Bleakley et al. [25] and Mordelet and Vert [26] and in Section 7.3, show that one can obtain very competitive results with local models in spite of this apparent difficulty.

7.2.5 Graph Inference with Global Models

Splitting the training set of labeled pairs to make independent local models, as presented in Section 7.2.4, prevents any sharing of information between different local models. Using a slightly different inference paradigm, one could argue that if a pair

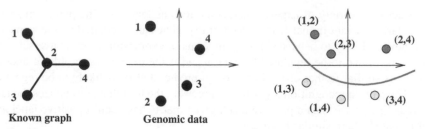

Known graph   Genomic data

Figure 7.3 With global models, we want to formulate the problem of edge prediction as a binary classification problem over pairs of vertices. A pair can be connected (label +1) or not connected (label −1). However, the data available are attributes about each individual vertices (central picture). Hence, we need to define a representation for pairs of vertices, as illustrated on the right-hand picture, in order to apply classical pattern recognition methods to discriminate between interacting and noninteracting pairs in the graph shown in the left-hand picture.

(v, v') is known to be connected, and if both v is similar to v'' and v' is similar to v''' in terms of features, then the pair (v'', v''') is likely to be connected as well. Such induction principle is not possible with local models, since the pair (v, v') is only considered by the local model of v, while (v'', v''') is only considered by the local model of v''.

In order to implement this inference paradigm, we need to work directly with pairs of vertices as patterns, and in particular, to be able to represent any pair $(u, v) \in V \times V$ by a feature vector that we denote $\psi(u, v)$. As we originally have only data to characterize each individual protein v by a vector $\phi(v)$, we, therefore, need to clarify how to derive a vector for a pair $\psi(u, v)$ from the vectors $\phi(u)$ and $\phi(v)$ that characterize u and v. This problem is illustrated in Figure 7.3.

As suggested in Section 7.2.2, kernels offer various useful tricks to design features, or equivalently kernels, for pairs of vertices starting from features for individual vertices. Let us consider, for example, a simple, although not very useful, trick to design a vector representation for a pair of vertices from a vector representation of individual vertices. If each vertex v is characterized by a vector of features $\phi(v)$ of dimension p, we can choose to represent a pair of vertices (u, v) by the concatenation of the vectors $\phi(u)$ and $\phi(v)$ into a single vector $\psi_{\oplus}(u, v)$ of size $2p$. In other words, we could consider their direct sum defined as follows:

$$\psi_{\oplus}(u, v) = \phi(u) \oplus \phi(v) = \begin{pmatrix} \phi(u) \\ \phi(v) \end{pmatrix}. \tag{7.2}$$

If the dimension p is large, one can avoid the burden of computing and storing large-dimensional vectors by using the kernel trick. Indeed, let us denote by K_V the kernel for vertices induced by the vector representation ϕ, namely, $K_V(v, v') = \phi(v)^{\top}\phi(v')$ for any pair of vertices (v, v'), and let us assume that $K_V(v, v')$ can be easily computed. Then the following computation, similar to (7.1), shows that the kernel $K_{\oplus}$ between two pairs of vertices (a, b) and (c, d) induced by the vector representation

$\psi_\oplus$ is easily computable as well:

$$K_\oplus\left((a, b), (c, d)\right) = \psi_\oplus(a, b)^\top \psi_\oplus(c, d)$$

$$= \begin{pmatrix} \phi(a) \\ \phi(b) \end{pmatrix}^\top \begin{pmatrix} \phi(c) \\ \phi(d) \end{pmatrix} \tag{7.3}$$

$$= \phi(a)^\top \phi(c) + \phi(b)^\top \phi(d)$$

$$= K_V(a, c) + K_V(b, d).$$

Hence, the kernel between pairs is here simply obtained by summing individual kernels, and an algorithm like an SVM could be trained on the original training set of labeled pairs to predict the label of new pairs not in the training set. Although attractive at first sight, this formulation has an important limitation. Training an SVM (or any linear classifier) means that one estimates a linear function in the space of direct sums, that is, a function for pairs of the form: $h(u, v) = w^\top \psi_\oplus(u, v)$. The vector w (of size $2p$) can be decomposed as a concatenation of two parts w_1 and w_2 of size p, that is, $w = w_1 \oplus w_2$. We can then rewrite the linear function as:

$$h(u, v) = (w_1 \oplus w_2)^\top (\phi(u) \oplus \phi(v)) = w_1^\top \phi(u) + w_2 \top \phi(v).$$

Hence, any linear classifier $h(u, v)$ in the space defined by the direct sum representation decomposes as a sum of two independent functions:

$$h(u, v) = h_1(u) + h_2(v),$$

with $h_i(v) = w_i^\top v$ for $i = 1, 2$. This is, in general, an unfortunate property, since it implies, for example, that whatever the target vertex u, if we sort the candidate vertices v that can interact with u according to the classifier (i.e., if we rank v according to the value of $h(u, v)$), then the order will not depend on u. In other words, each vertex v would be associated with a particular score $h_2(v)$ that could be thought of as its general propensity to interact, and the prediction of vertices connected to a particular vertex u would only depend on the scores of the vertices tested, not on u itself. This clearly limits the scope of the classification rules that linear classifiers can produce with the direct sum representations, which suggests that this approach should not be used in general.

A generally better alternative to the direct sum $\psi_\oplus(u, v)$ is to represent a pair of vertices (u, v) by their direct product:

$$\psi_\otimes(u, v) - \phi(u) \otimes \phi(v). \tag{7.4}$$

If $\phi(u)$ and $\phi(v)$ each has a dimension p, then the direct product $\psi_\otimes(u, v)$ is by definition a vector of dimension p^2 whose entries are all possible products between a feature of $\phi(u)$ and a feature of $\phi(v)$. An interesting property of the direct product is that it encodes features that are characteristic of the pair (u, v), and not merely of u and v taken separately. For example, let us assume that $\phi(u)$ and $\phi(v)$ contain binary features that indicate the presence or absence of particular features in u and v. Then, because the product of binary features is equivalent to a logical AND, the vector $\psi_\otimes(u, v)$ contains binary features that indicate the joint occurrence of particular pairs of features in u and v. As a result, contrary to the direct sum representation $\psi_\oplus(u, v)$, linear classifiers in the space defined by $\psi_\otimes(u, v)$ could predict that a is more likely to interact with u than b, while b is more likely to interact with v than a for two different target vertices u and v.

The price to pay in order to obtain this large flexibility is that the dimension of the representation, namely p^2, can easily get very large. Typically, if an individual gene is characterized by a vector of dimension 1000 to encode expression data, phylogenetic profiles, and/or subcellular localization information, then the direct product representation has 1 million dimensions. Such large dimensions may cause serious problems in terms of computation time and memory storage for practical applications. Fortunately, if one works with kernel methods like SVM, a classical trick allows to compute efficiently the inner product between two tensor product vectors from the inner products between individual vectors:

$$
\begin{aligned}
K_\otimes\left((a, b), (c, d)\right) &= \psi_\otimes(a, b)^\top \psi_\otimes(c, d) \\
&= \left(\phi(a) \otimes \phi(b)\right)^\top \left(\phi(c) \otimes \phi(d)\right) \\
&= \phi(a)^\top \phi(c) \times \phi(b)^\top \phi(d) \\
&= K_V(a, c) \times K_V(b, d),
\end{aligned}
\tag{7.5}
$$

where the third line is a classical result easily demonstrated by expanding the inner product between tensor product vectors. Hence, one obtains the kernel between two pairs of vertices by just multiplying together the kernel values involving each vertex of the first pair and the corresponding vertex of the second pair.

The direct sum (7.2) and product (7.4) representations correspond to representations of ordered paired, which usually map a pair (u, v) and its reverse (v, u) to different vectors. For example, the concatenation of two vectors $\phi(u)$ and $\phi(v)$ is generally different from the concatenation of $\phi(v)$ and $\phi(u)$, that is, $\psi_\oplus(u, v) \neq \psi_\oplus(v, u)$, except when $\phi(u) = \phi(v)$. Hence, these representations are well-adapted to the prediction of edges in directed graphs, where an ordered pair (u, v) can represent an edge form u to v and the pair (v, u) then represents the different edge from v to u. When the graph of interest is not directed, then it can be advantageous to also represent an undirected pair $\{u, v\}$. An extension of the tensor product representation was, for example, proposed by Ben-Hur and Noble [22], with the following tensor product pairwise kernel (TPPK) representation for undirected pairs:

$$
\psi_{\text{TPPK}}\left(\{u, v\}\right) = \psi_\otimes(u, v) + \psi_\otimes(v, u).
\tag{7.6}
$$

This representation is the symmetrized version of the direct product representation, which makes it invariant to a permutation in the order of the two vertices in a pair.

The corresponding kernel is easily derived as follows:

$$
\begin{aligned}
K_{\text{TPPK}}(\{a, b\}, \{c, d\}) &= \psi_{\text{TPPK}}(\{a, b\})^{\top} \psi_{\text{TPPK}}(\{c, d\}) \\
&= (\psi_{\otimes}(a, b) + \psi_{\otimes}(b, a))^{\top} (\psi_{\otimes}(c, d) + \psi_{\otimes}(d, c)) \\
&= \psi_{\otimes}(a, b)^{\top} \psi_{\otimes}(c, d) + \psi_{\otimes}(a, b)^{\top} \psi_{\otimes}(d, c) \qquad (7.7) \\
&\quad + \psi_{\otimes}(b, a)^{\top} \psi_{\otimes}(c, d) + \psi_{\otimes}(b, a)^{\top} \psi_{\otimes}(d, c) \\
&= 2 \{K_V(a, c) K_V(b, d) + K_V(a, d) K_V(b, c)\} .
\end{aligned}
$$

Once again, we see that the inner product in the space of the TPPK representation is easily computed from the values of kernels between individual vertices, without the need to compute explicitly the p^2 dimension TPPK vector. This approach is, therefore, again, particularly well-suited to be used in combination with an SVM or any other kernel method.

An alternative and perhaps more intuitive justification for the TPPK kernel (7.7) is in terms of similarity or distance between pairs induced by this formulation. Indeed, when a kernel K_V is such that $K_V(v, v) = 1$ for all v, which equivalently means that all vectors $\phi(v)$ are normalized to unit norm, then the value of the kernel $K_V(u, v)$ is a good indicator of the "similarity" between u and v. In particular, we easily show in that case that:

$$
K_V(u, v) = \phi(u)^{\top} \phi(v) = 1 - \frac{||\phi(u) - \phi(v)||^2}{2},
$$

which shows that $K_V(u, v)$ is "large" when $\phi(u)$ and $\phi(v)$ are close to each other, that is, when u and v are considered "similar." An interesting point of view to define a kernel over pairs in this context is then to express it in terms of similarity: When do we want to say that an unordered pair $\{a, b\}$ is similar to a pair $\{c, d\}$, given the similarities between individual vertices? One attractive formulation is to consider them similar if either (i) a is similar to c and b is similar to d or (ii) a is similar to d and b is similar to c. Translating these notions into equation, the TPPK kernel formulation (7.7) can be thought of as an implementation of this principle [22].

At this point, it is worth mentioning that although the tensor product (7.4) for directed pairs, and its extension (7.6) for undirected pairs, can be considered as "natural" default choices to represent pairs of vertices as vectors from representations of individual vertices, they are by no means the only possible choices. As an example, let us briefly mention the construction by Vert et al. [24] who propose to represent an undirected pair as follows:

$$
\psi_{\text{MLPK}}(u, v) = (\phi(u) - \phi(v))^{\otimes 2} = (\phi(u) \quad \phi(v)) \otimes (\phi(u) - \phi(v)). \qquad (7.8)
$$

The name MLPK stands for metric learning pairwise kernel. Indeed, Vert et al. [24] show that training a linear classifier in the representation defined by the MLPK vector (7.8) is equivalent, in some situations, to estimating a new metric in the space of individual vertices $\phi(v)$ and classifying a pair as positive or negative depending on whether or not the distance between $\phi(u)$ and $\phi(v)$ (with respect to the new metric) is below a threshold or not. Hence, this formulation can be particularly relevant in cases where connected vertices seem to be "similar," in which case a linear classifier coupled with the MLPK representation can learn by itself the optimal notion of "similarity" that should be used in a supervised framework. For example, if a series of expression values for genes across a range of experiments is available, one could argue that proteins coded by genes with "similar" expression profiles are more likely to interact than others, and, therefore, that a natural way to predict interaction would be to measure a "distance" between all pairs of expression profiles and threshold it above some value to predict interactions. The question of how to chose a "distance" between expression profiles is then central, and instead of choosing *a priori* a distance such as the Euclidean norm, one could typically let an SVM train a classifier with the MLPK representation to mimic the process of choosing an optimal way to measure distances in order to predict interactions.

An interesting property of the MLPK representation (7.8) is that, as for the tensor product and TPPK representation, it leads to an inner product that can easily be computed without explicitly computing the p^2-dimensional vector $\phi_{\text{MLPK}}(a, b)$:

$$
\begin{aligned}
K_{\text{MLPK}}(\{a, b\}, \{c, d\}) &= \psi_{\text{MLPK}}(a, b)^\top \psi_{\text{MLPK}}(c, d) \\
&= \left[(\phi(a) - \phi(b))^{\otimes 2} \right]^\top \left[(\phi(c) - \phi(d))^{\otimes 2} \right] \\
&= \left[(\phi(a) - \phi(b))^\top (\phi(c) - \phi(d)) \right]^2 \qquad (7.9) \\
&= \left[\phi(a)^\top \phi(c) - \phi(a)^\top \phi(d) - \phi(b)^\top \phi(c) + \phi(b)^\top \phi(d) \right]^2 \\
&= \left[K_V(a, c) - K_V(a, d) - K_V(b, c) + K_V(b, d) \right]^2 .
\end{aligned}
$$

7.2.6 Remarks

We have shown how the general problem of graph reconstruction can be formulated as a pattern recognition problem (Sections 7.2.1–7.2.3) and described several instances of this idea: either by training a multitude of local models to learn the local structure of the graph around each node (Section 7.2.4), which boils down to a series of pattern recognition problems over vertices, or by training a single global model to predict whether any given pair of vertices interacts or not, which requires the definition of a vector representation (or equivalently of a kernel) for pairs of vertices (Section 7.2.5). Our presentation has been fairly general in order to highlight the general ideas behind the approach and the main choices one has to make in order to implement it. Now, we discuss several important questions that one must also address to implement the idea on any particular problem.

- *Directed or undirected graph.* As pointed out in the introduction, some biological networks are better represented by undirected graphs (e.g., the PPI network), while others are more naturally viewed as directed graphs (e.g., a gene regulatory network). In the course of our presentation, we have shown that some methods are specifically adapted to one case or the other. For example, the MLPK and TPPK kernel formulations to learn global models (Eqs. (7.7) and (7.9)) are specifically tailored to solve problems over undirected pairs, that is, to reconstruct undirected graphs. On the other hand, the local models (Section 7.2.4) or the global models with the direct product kernel (7.5) are naturally suited to infer interactions between directed pairs, that is, to reconstruct directed graphs. However, one can also use them to reconstruct undirected graph by simply counting each undirected pair $\{u, v\}$ as two directed pairs (u, v) and (v, u). In the training step, this means that we can replace each labeled undirected pair (i.e., undirected edge known to be present or absent) by two directed pairs labeled by the same label. In the prediction step, this means that one would get a prediction for the pair (u, v) and another prediction for the pair (v, u) that have no reason to be consistent between each other to predict whether the undirected pair $\{u, v\}$ is connected or not. In order to reconcile both predictions, one typically can take the average of the prediction scores of the classifiers for both directed pairs in order to make a unique prediction score for the undirected pair.

- *Different types of edges.* Some biological networks are better represented by graphs with edges having additional attributes such as a label among a finite set of possible labels. For example, to describe a gene regulatory network, it is common to consider two types or regulations (edges), namely, activation or inhibition. In terms of prediction, this means that we not only need to predict whether two vertices are connected or not, but also by what type of edges they are connected. A simple strategy to extend the pattern recognition paradigm to this context is to see the problem not as a binary classification problem, but more generally as a multiclass classification problem. In the previous example, one should, for example, assign each pair (u, v) to one of the three classes (no regulation, activation, inhibition). Luckily, the extension of pattern recognition algorithms to the multiclass setting is a well-studied field in machine learning for which many solutions exist [27, 28]. For example, a popular approach to solve a classification problem with k classes is to replace it by k binary classification problems, where each binary problem discriminates versus data in one of the k classes and the rest of the data. Once the k classifiers are trained, they can be applied to score each new candidate point, and the class corresponding to the classifier that outputs the largest score is predicted. Other approaches also exist besides this scheme, known as the one-versus-all strategy. Overall, they show that the pattern recognition formulation can easily accommodate the prediction of different edge types just by using a multiclass classification algorithm.

- *Negative training pairs.* While most databases store information about the presence of edges and can be used to generate positive training examples, few, if any, negative interactions are usually reported. This is an important problem since, as we formulated it in Section 7.2.2, the typical pattern recognition formalism requires positive as well as negative training examples. In order to overcome this obstacle, several strategies can be pursued. A first idea would be to refrain from focusing exclusively on pattern recognition algorithms, which are not adapted to the lack of negative examples, and use instead algorithms specifically designed to handle only positive examples. For example, many methods in statistics for density estimation or outlier detection are designed to estimate a small region that contains all or most of the positive training points. If such a region of "positive examples" is found around pairs known to be connected, then a new pair of vertices can be predicted to be connected if it also lies in the region. An algorithm like the one-class SVM [36] is typically adapted to this setting and can accommodate all the kernel formulations we presented so far. A second idea would be to keep using algorithms for binary classification and generate negative examples. Perhaps, the simplest way to do this is to randomly sample pairs of vertices, among the ones not known to be connected, and declare that they are negative examples. As the graph is usually supposed to be sparse, most pairs of vertices randomly picked by this process indeed do not interact and are correctly labeled as negative. On the other hand, the few pairs that would be wrongly labeled as negative with this procedure, namely, the pairs that interact, although we do not know it yet, are precisely the one we are interested to find. There may then be a danger that by labeling them as negative and training a classifier based on this label, we could have more difficulties finding them. To overcome this particular issue of generating false-negative examples in the training set, one may again consider two ideas. First, try to reduce the quantity of wrongly labeled negative training pairs by, for example, using additional sources of informations to increase the likelihood that they do not interact. For example, if one wants to choose pairs of proteins that are very unlikely to interact, he may restrict himself to proteins known to be located in different subcellular localization, which in theory prevent any possibility of physical interaction. While this may increase the size of the training set, there is also a danger to bias the training set towards "easy" negative examples [37]. The second idea is to accept the risk of generating false-negative training examples, but then to be careful at least that the predictive models never predict the label of a pair that was used during its training. This can be achieved, for example, by splitting the set of candidate negative pairs (i.e., those not known to interact) into k disjunct subsets, train a classifier using $k - 1$ of these subsets as negative training examples, and using the resulting classifier to predict the labels of pairs in the subset that was left apart. Repeating this procedure k times leads to the possibility of predicting the labels for the k subsets, without ever predicting the label of a negative example that was used during training. This strategy was, for example, used in Mordelet and Vert [26].

- *Presence or absence of errors in the training data.* Besides the lack of known negative examples, one may also be confronted with possible errors in the positive training examples, that is, false positives in the training set. Indeed, many databases of biological networks contain both certain interactions and interactions believed to be true based on various empirical evidences but that could be wrong. This is particularly true, for example, for PPI networks when physical interactions have been observed with high-throughput technologies such as the yeast two-hybrid system, which is known to be prone to many false-positive detections. In that case, we should not only be careful when using the data as positive training examples, but also we may even consider the possibility of using the predictive algorithms to remove wrong positive annotations from the training set. Regarding the problem of training models with false-positive training examples, this may not be a major obstacle since one of the strengths of statistical pattern recognition methods is precisely to accept "noise" or errors in the data. On the other hand, if one wants to further use the models to correct the training data, then a specific procedure could be imagined, for example, similar to the procedure described in the previous paragraph to predict the label of false-negative examples.

7.3 EXAMPLES

Recently, the different approaches surveyed in Section 7.2 have been extensively tested and compared with other approaches in several publications. In this section, we review the main findings of these publications, focusing on our three running examples of biological networks.

7.3.1 Reconstruction of a Metabolic Network

The reconstruction of metabolic networks has been among the first applications that motivated the line of research surveyed in this Chapter [19–21, 25]. We consider here the problem of inferring the metabolic gene network of the yeast *S. cerevisiae* with the enzymes represented as vertices, and an edge between two enzymes when the two enzymes catalyze successive reactions. The dataset, proposed by Yamanishi et al. [21], consists of 668 vertices (enzymes) and 2782 edges between them, which were extracted from the KEGG database of metabolic pathways [38]. In order to predict edges in these networks, Bleakley et al. [25] used various genomic datasets and compared different inference methods. Following Yamanishi et al. [21], the data used to characterize enzymes comprise 157 expression data measured under different experimental conditions [39, 40], a vector of 23 bits representing the localization of the enzymes (found or not found) in 23 locations in the cell determined experimentally [41], and the phylogenetic profiles of the enzymes as vectors of 145 bits denoting the presence or absence of the enzyme in 145 fully sequenced genomes [38]. Each type of data was processed and transformed into a kernel as described in Yamanishi et al. and Kato et al. [21, 42], and all matrices were summed together to produce a single kernel integrating heterogeneous data.

On a common five-fold cross-validation setting, Bleakley et al. [25] compared different methods including local models (Section 7.2.4), the TPPK and MLPK kernels (Section 7.2.5) as well as several other methods: a direct *de novo* approach, which only infers edges between similar vertices, an approach based on kernel canonical correlation analysis (KCCA) [19], and a matrix completion algorithm based on an

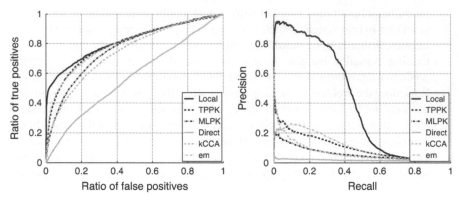

Figure 7.4 Performance of different methods for the reconstruction of metabolic networks (from Bleakley et al. [25]): ROC (left) and precision/recall (right) curves.

em procedure [42, 43]. On each fold of the cross-validation procedure, each method uses the training set to learn a model and makes predictions on pairs in the test set. All methods associate a score with all pairs in the test set, hence by thresholding this score at different levels, they can predict more or less edges. Results were assessed in terms of average ROC curve (which plots the percentage of true positives as a function of the percentage of false positives, when the threshold level is varied) and average precision/recall curve (which plots the percentage of true positives among positive predictions, as a function of the percentage of true positives among all positives). In practical applications, the later criterion is a better indicator of the relevance of a method than the former one. Indeed, as biological networks are usually sparse, the number of negatives far exceeds the number of positives, and only large precision (over a recall as large as possible) can be tolerated if further experimental validations are expected.

Figure 7.4 shows the performance of the different methods on this benchmark. A very clear advantage for the local model can be seen. In particular, it is the only method tested that can produce predictions at more than 80 percent precision. There is no clear winner among the other supervised methods, while the direct approach, which is the only *de novo* method in this comparison, is clearly below the supervised methods.

7.3.2 Reconstruction of a PPI Network

As a second application, we consider the problem of inferring missing edges in the PPI network of the yeast *S. cerevisiae*. The gold standard PPI graph used to perform a cross-validation experiment is a set of high-confidence interactions supported by several experiments provided by Von Mering et al. [44] and also used in Kato et al. [42]. After removal of proteins without interactions, we end up with a graph involving 2438 interactions (edges) among 984 proteins (vertices). In order to reconstruct missing edges, the genomic data used are the same as those used for the reconstruction of the

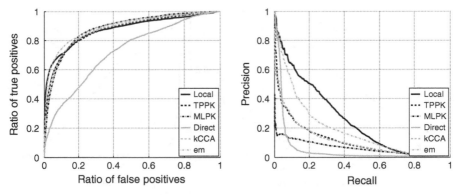

Figure 7.5 Performance of different methods for the reconstruction of the PPI network (from Bleakley et al. [25]): ROC (left) and precision/recall (right) curves.

metabolic network in Section 7.3.1, namely, gene expression, protein localization, and phylogenetic profiles, together with a set of yeast two-hybrid data obtained from Uetz et al. [3] and Ito et al. [4]. The later was converted into a positive definite kernel using a diffusion kernel, as explained in Kato et al. [42]. Again, all datasets were combined into a unique kernel by adding together the four individual kernels.

Figure 7.5 shows the performances of the different methods, using the same experimental protocol as the one used for the experiment with metabolic network reconstruction in Section 7.3.1. Again, the best method is the local model, although it outperforms the other methods with a smaller margin than for the reconstruction of the metabolic network (Figure 7.4). Again, the ROC curve of the *de novo* direct method is clearly below the curves of the supervised methods, although this time it leads to a large precision at low recall. This means that a few interacting pairs can very easily be detected because they have very similar genomic data.

7.3.3 Reconstruction of Gene Regulatory Networks

Finally, we report the results of an experiment conducted for the inference of a gene regulatory network by Mordelet and Vert [26]. In that case, the edges between transcription factors and the genes they regulate are directed; therefore, only the local model of Section 7.2.4 is tested. It is compared with a panel of other state-of-the-art methods dedicated to the inference of gene regulatory networks from a compendium of gene expression data, using a benchmark proposed by Faith et al. [18]. More precisely, the goal of this experiment is to predict the regulatory network of the bacteria *Escherichia coli* from a compendium of 445 microarray expression profiles for 4345 genes. The microarray was collected under different experimental conditions such as pH changes, growth phases, antibiotics, heat shock, different media, varying oxygen concentrations, and numerous genetic perturbations. The goal standard graph used to assess the performance of different methods by cross-validation consists of 3293 experimentally confirmed regulations between 154 TF and 1211 genes, extracted from the RegulonDB database [45].

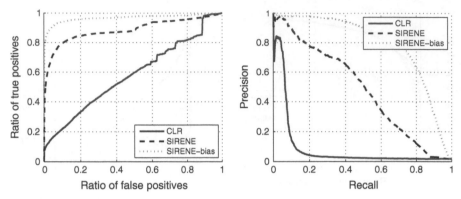

Figure 7.6 Comparison of the CLR method and the local pattern recognition approach (called SIRENE) on the reconstruction of a regulatory network: ROC (left) and precision/recall (right) curves. The curve SIRENE-bias corresponds to the performance of SIRENE with a cross-validation procedure, which does not take into account the organization of genes in operons, thus introducing an artificial positive bias in the result.

In Faith et al. [18], this benchmark was used to compare different algorithms, including Bayesian networks [15], ARACNe [46], and the context likelihood of relatedness (CLR) algorithm [18], a new method that extends the relevance networks class of algorithms [17]. They observed that CLR outperformed all other methods in prediction accuracy and experimentally validated some predictions. CLR can, therefore, be considered as the state-of-the-art among methods that use compendia of gene expression data for large-scale inference of regulatory networks. However, all the methods compared in Faith et al. [18] are *de novo*, and the goal of Mordelet and Vert [26] was to compare the supervised local approach to the best *de novo* method on this benchmark, namely, the CLR algorithm. Using a three-fold cross-validation procedure (see details in Mordelet and Vert [26]), they obtained the curves in Figure 7.6. We can observe that the local supervised approach (called SIRENE for Supervised Inference of REgulatory NEtwork) strongly outperforms the CLR method on this benchmark. The recall obtained by SIRENE, that is, the proportion of known regulations that are correctly predicted, is several times larger than the recall of CLR at all levels of precision. More precisely, Table 7.1 compares the recalls of SIRENE, CLR, and several other methods at 80 percent and 60 percent precision. The other methods reported are relevance network [17], ARACNe [46], and a Bayesian network [15] implemented by Faith et al. [18].

This experiment also highlights the special care that must be taken when performing a cross-validation procedure, in particular, to make sure that no artificial bias is introduced. The curve called SIRENE-bias in Figure 7.6 corresponds to a normal k-fold cross-validation procedure, where the set of genes is randomly split into k folds, and each fold is used in turn as a test set. In the case of regulation in bacteria like *E. coli*, however, it is known that TFs can regulate groups of genes clustered together on the genome called operons. Genes in the same operons are transcribed in the same messenger RNA and have, therefore, very similar expression values across

Table 7.1   Recall of different gene regulation prediction algorithms at different levels of precision (60% and 80%)

Method	Recall at 60%	Recall at 80%
SIRENE	44.5%	17.6%
CLR	7.5%	5.5%
Relevance networks	4.7%	3.3%
ARACNe	1%	0%
Bayesian network	1%	0%

Source: From Ref. 26.

different experiments. If two genes within the same operon are split in a training and test set during cross-validation, then it will be very easy to recognize that the one in the test set has the same label as the one in the training set, which will artificially increase the accuracy of the method. Hence, in this case, it is important to make sure that, during the random split into k subsets, all genes within an operon belong to the same fold. The curve named SIRENE in Figure 7.6 has been obtained with this unbiased procedure. The important difference between both curves highlights the importance of the bias induced by splitting operons in the cross-validation procedure.

7.4   DISCUSSION

We reviewed several strategies to cast the problem of graph inference as a classical supervised classification problem, which can be solved by virtually any pattern recognition algorithm. Contrary to *de novo* approaches, these strategies assume that a set of edges is already known and use the data available about vertices and known edges to infer missing edges. On several experiments involving the inference of metabolic, PPI, and regulatory networks from a variety of genomic data, these methods were shown to give good results compared with the state-of-the-art *de novo* methods, and a particular implementation of this strategy (the local model) consistently gave very good results on all datasets.

In a sense, the superiority of supervised methods over *de novo* methods observed in the experiments is not surprising because supervised methods use more informations. As this additional information is available in many real-world applications, it suggests that supervised methods may be a better choice than *de novo* ones in many cases. It should be pointed out, though, that some of the methods we classified as *de novo*, for example, Bayesian networks, could easily be adapted to the supervised inference scenario by putting constraints or prior distribution on the graph to be inferred. On the other hand, the strength of supervised methods depends critically on the availability of a good training set, which may not be available in some situations such as inferring the structure of smaller graphs.

We observe that there is not a single way to cast the problem as a binary classification problem, which suggests that further research is needed to design optimally adapted methods. In particular, the local method, which performs best in the three benchmark experiments, has obvious limitations such as its inability to infer new edges for vertices with no edge already known. The development of new strategies that keep the performance of the local methods for vertices with enough known edges, but borrow some ideas from, for example, the global models of Section 7.2.5 to be able to infer edges for vertices with few or no known edge, is thus a promising research direction.

REFERENCES

1. H. Jeong, S. P. Mason, A.-L. Barabási, and Z. N. Oltvai. Lethality and centrality in protein networks. *Nature*, 411:41–42, 2001.

2. S. Okamoto, Y. Yamanishi, S. Ehira, S. Kawashima, K. Tonomura, and M. Kanehisa. Prediction of nitrogen metabolism-related genes in anabaena by kernel-based network analysis. *Proteomics*, 7(6):900–909, 2007.

3. P. Uetz, L. Giot, G. Cagney, T. A. Mansfield, R. S. Judson, J. R. Knight, D. Lockshon, V. Narayan, M. Srinivasan, P. Pochart, A. Qureshi-Emili, Y. Li, B. Godwin, D. Conover, T. Kalbfleish, G. Vijayadamodar, M. Yang, M. Johnston, S. Fields, and J. M. Rothberg. A comprehensive analysis of protein-protein interactions in *Saccharomyces cerevisiae*. *Nature*, 403:623–627, 2000.

4. T. Ito, T. Chiba, R. Ozawa, M. Yoshida, M. Hattori, and Y. Sakaki. A comprehensive two-hybrid analysis to explore the yeast protein interactome. *Proc. Natl. Acad. Sci. U S A*, 98(8):4569–4574, 2001.

5. E. M. Marcotte, M. Pellegrini, H.-L. Ng, D. W. Rice, T. O. Yeates, and D. Eisenberg. Detecting protein function and protein-protein interactions from genome sequences. *Science*, 285:751–753, 1999.

6. F. Pazos and A. Valencia. Similarity of phylogenetic trees as indicator of protein-protein interaction. *Protein Eng.*, 9(14):609–614, 2001.

7. R. Jansen, H. Yu, D. Greenbaum, Y. Kluger, N. J. Krogan, S. Chung, A. Emili, M. Snyder, J. F. Greenblatt, and M. Gerstein. A Bayesian networks approach for predicting protein-protein interactions from genomic data. *Science*, 302(5644):449–453, 2003.

8. T. Akutsu, S. Miyano, and S. Kuhara. Algorithms for identifying Boolean networks and related biological networks based on matrix multiplication and fingerprint function. *J. Comput. Biol.*, 7(3–4):331–343, 2000.

9. T. Chen, H. L. He, and G. M. Church. Modeling gene expression with differential equations. *Pac. Symp. Biocomput.*, 29–40, 1999.

10. J. Tegner, M. K. S. Yeung, J. Hasty, and J. J. Collins. Reverse engineering gene networks: integrating genetic perturbations with dynamical modeling. *Proc. Natl. Acad. Sci. U S A*, 100(10):5944–5949, May 2003.

11. T. S. Gardner, D. Bernardo, D. Lorenz, and J. J. Collins. Inferring genetic networks and identifying compound mode of action via expression profiling. *Science*, 301(5629):102–105, 2003.

12. K.-C. Chen, T.-Y. Wang, H.-H. Tseng, C.-Y. F. Huang, and C.-Y. Kao. A stochastic differential equation model for quantifying transcriptional regulatory network in *Saccharomyces cerevisiae*. *Bioinformatics*, 21(12):2883–2890, 2005.

13. D. Bernardo, M. J. Thompson, T. S. Gardner, S. E. Chobot, E. L. Eastwood, A. P. Wojtovich, S. J. Elliott, S. E. Schaus, and J. J. Collins. Chemogenomic profiling on a genome-wide scale using reverse-engineered gene networks. *Nat. Biotechnol.*, 23(3):377–383, 2005.

14. M. Bansal, G. Della Gatta, and D. Bernardo. Inference of gene regulatory networks and compound mode of action from time course gene expression profiles. *Bioinformatics*, 22(7):815–822, 2006.

15. N. Friedman, M. Linial, I. Nachman, and D. Pe'er. Using Bayesian networks to analyze expression data. *J. Comput. Biol.*, 7(3–4):601–620, 2000.

16. S. Tavazoie, J. D. Hughes, M. J. Campbell, R. J. Cho, and G. M. Church. Systematic determination of genetic network architecture. *Nat. Genet.*, 1999.

17. A. J. Butte, P. Tamayo, D. Slonim, T. R. Golub, and I. S. Kohane. Discovering functional relationships between RNA expression and chemotherapeutic susceptibility using relevance networks. *Proc. Natl. Acad. Sci. USA*, 97(22):12182–12186, 2000.

18. J. J. Faith, B. Hayete, J. T. Thaden, I. Mogno, J. Wierzbowski, G. Cottarel, S. Kasif, J. J. Collins, and T. S. Gardner. Large-scale mapping and validation of Escherichia coli transcriptional regulation from a compendium of expression profiles. *PLoS Biol.*, 5(1):e8, 2007.

19. Y. Yamanishi, J.-P. Vert, and M. Kanehisa. Protein network inference from multiple genomic data: a supervised approach. *Bioinformatics*, 20:i363–i370, 2004.

20. J.-P. Vert and Y. Yamanishi. Supervised graph inference. In L. K. Saul, Y. Weiss, and L. Bottou, editors. *Advances in Neural Information Processing Systems*. Vol. 17, MIT Press, Cambridge, MA, 2005, pp. 1433–1440.

21. Y. Yamanishi, J.-P. Vert, and M. Kanehisa. Supervised enzyme network inference from the integration of genomic data and chemical information. *Bioinformatics*, 21:i468–i477, 2005.

22. A. Ben-Hur and W. S. Noble. Kernel methods for predicting protein-protein interactions. *Bioinformatics*, 21(Suppl 1):i38–i46, 2005.

23. G. Biau and K. Bleakley. Statistical inference on graphs. *Statistics Decis.*, 24(2):209–232, 2006.

24. J.-P. Vert, J. Qiu, and W. S. Noble. A new pairwise kernel for biological network inference with support vector machines. *BMC Bioinform.*, 8(Suppl 10):S8, 2007.

25. K. Bleakley, G. Biau, and J.-P. Vert. Supervised reconstruction of biological networks with local models. *Bioinformatics*, 23(13):i57–i65, 2007.

26. F. Mordelet and J.-P. Vert. SIRENE: Supervised inference of regulatory networks. *Bioinformatics*, 24(16): i76–i82, 2008.

27. T. Hastie, R. Tibshirani, and J. Friedman. *The Elements of Statistical Learning: Data Mining, Inference, and Prediction*. Springer, New York, 2001.

28. C. M. Bishop. *Pattern Recognition and Machine Learning*. Springer, New York, 2006.

29. B. Schölkopf, K. Tsuda, and J.-P. Vert. *Kernel Methods in Computational Biology*. MIT Press, Cambridge, MA, 2004.

30. J.-P. Vert. Kernel methods in genomics and computational biology. In G. Camps-Valls, J.-L. Rojo-Alvarez, and M. Martinez-Ramon, editors, *Kernel Methods in Bioengineering, Signal and Image Processing*. IDEA Group, 2007.

31. P. Pavlidis, J. Weston, J. Cai, and W. S. Noble. Learning gene functional classifications from multiple data types. *J. Comput. Biol.*, 9(2):401–411, 2002.

32. G. R. G. Lanckriet, T. De Bie, N. Cristianini, M. I. Jordan, and W. S. Noble. A statistical framework for genomic data fusion. *Bioinformatics*, 20(16):2626–2635, 2004.

33. V. N. Vapnik. *Statistical Learning Theory*. Wiley, New York, 1998.

34. N. Cristianini and J. Shawe-Taylor. *An Introduction to Support Vector Machines and Other Kernel-Based Learning Methods*. Cambridge University Press, 2000.

35. B. Schölkopf and A. J. Smola. *Learning with Kernels: Support Vector Machines, Regularization, Optimization, and Beyond*. MIT Press, Cambridge, MA, 2002.

36. B. Schölkopf, J. C. Platt, J. Shawe-Taylor, A. J. Smola, and R. C. Williamson. Estimating the support of a high-dimensional distribution. *Neural Comput.*, 13:1443–1471, 2001.

37. A. Ben-Hur and W. S. Noble. Choosing negative examples for the prediction of protein-protein interactions. *BMC Bioinform.*, 7(Suppl 1):S2, 2006.

38. M. Kanehisa, S. Goto, S. Kawashima, Y. Okuno, and M. Hattori. The KEGG resource for deciphering the genome. *Nucleic Acids Res.*, 32(Database issue):D277–D280, 2004.

39. M. B. Eisen, P. T. Spellman, P. O. Brown, and D. Botstein. Cluster analysis and display of genome-wide expression patterns. *Proc. Natl. Acad. Sci. U S A*, 95:14863–14868, 1998.

40. P. T. Spellman, G. Sherlock, M. Q. Zhang, V. R. Iyer, K. Anders, M. B. Eisen, P. O. Brown, D. Botstein, and B. Futcher. Comprehensive identification of cell cycle-regulated genes of the yeast *Saccharomyces cerevisiae* by microarray hybridization. *Mol. Biol. Cell*, 9:3273–3297, 1998.

41. W.-K. Huh, J. V. Falvo, L. C. Gerke, A. S. Carroll, R. W. Howson, J. S. Weissman, and E. K. O'Shea. Global analysis of protein localization in budding yeast. *Nature*, 425(6959):686–691, 2003.

42. T. Kato, K. Tsuda, and K. Asai. Selective integration of multiple biological data for supervised network inference. *Bioinformatics*, 21(10):2488–2495, 2005.

43. K. Tsuda, S. Akaho, and K. Asai. The em algorithm for kernel matrix completion with auxiliary data. *J. Mach. Learn. Res.*, 4:67–81, 2003.

44. C. von Mering, R. Krause, B. Snel, M. Cornell, S. G. Oliver, S. Fields, and P. Bork. Comparative assessment of large-scale data sets of protein-protein interactions. *Nature*, 417(6887):399–403, 2002.

45. H. Salgado, S. Gama-Castro, M. Peralta-Gil, E. Díaz-Peredo, F. Sánchez-Solano, A. Santos-Zavaleta, I. Martínez-Flores, V. Jiménez-Jacinto, C. Bonavides-Martínez, J. Segura-Salazar, A. Martínez-Antonio, and J. Collado-Vides. RegulonDB (version 5.0): *Escherichia coli* K-12 transcriptional regulatory network, operon organization, and growth conditions. *Nucleic Acids Res.*, 34(Database issue):D394–D397, 2006.

46. A. A. Margolin, I. Nemenman, K. Basso, C. Wiggins, G. Stolovitzky, R. Dalla Favera, and A. Califano. ARACNE: an algorithm for the reconstruction of gene regulatory networks in a mammalian cellular context. *BMC Bioinform.*, 7(Suppl 1):S7, 2006.

8

SUPERVISED INFERENCE OF METABOLIC NETWORKS FROM THE INTEGRATION OF GENOMIC DATA AND CHEMICAL INFORMATION

Yoshihiro Yamanishi

Mines ParisTech - Institut Curie - Inserm U900, Paris, France

8.1 INTRODUCTION

Most biological functions involve the coordinated actions of many biomolecules such as genes, proteins, and chemical compounds, and the complexity of living systems arises as a result of such interactions. It is, therefore, important to understand the biological systems through the analysis of the relationships amongst biomolecules. The biological system can be represented by a network of proteins by using graph representation, with proteins as nodes and their functional interactions as edges. Examples of such biological networks include metabolic network, protein–protein interaction network, gene regulatory network, and signaling network. A grand challenge in recent bioinformatics and systems biology is to computationally predict such biological networks from genomic and molecular information for practical applications. Recent sequence projects and development in biotechnology have contributed to an increasing amount of high throughput genomic data for biomolecules and their

Elements of Computational Systems Biology   Edited by Huma M. Lodhi and Stephen H. Muggleton
Copyright © 2010 John Wiley & Sons, Inc.

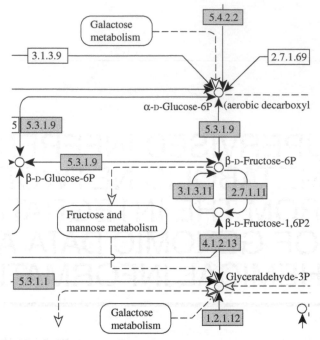

Figure 8.1   An example of the metabolic pathway in the KEGG pathway database. One box indicates an enzyme and the number in the box corresponds to the EC number. One circle indicates a chemical compound.

interactions, including amino acid sequences, gene expression data, yeast two-hybrid data, and several more. These data are useful sources from which we can computationally infer various biological networks [1–4].

In this chapter, we focus on the metabolic network, which is an important class of biological network consisting of enzymes and chemical compounds. Figure 8.1 shows an illustration of a part of the metabolic network. Recent development of pathway databases such as KEGG [5] and EcoCyc [6] enables us to analyze the current knowledge about known metabolic networks. Unfortunately, most of the organism-specific metabolic networks contain many pathway holes or missing enzymes in known pathways. Since the experimental determination of metabolic networks remains very challenging, even for the most basic organisms, there is a need to develop methods to infer the unknown parts of metabolic networks and to identify genes coding for missing enzymes in known metabolic pathways [7, 8]. Thanks to the development of homology detection tools [9, 10], enzyme genes can be easily found from fully sequenced genomes using comparative genomics [11], but it is difficult to assign them a precise biological role in a pathway.

To date, techniques for the reconstruction of metabolic networks have depended heavily on sequence homology detection [12]. A typical computational approach for reconstructing the metabolic network from the genome sequence of a certain organism is as follows:

(1) Assign enzyme commission (EC) number [13] to enzyme candidate genes by detecting sequence homology based on comparative genomics across different organisms.

(2) Obtain the information about ligands such as substrates and products, in which the enzyme genes are involved, from reaction knowledge based on the EC number.

(3) Assign each enzyme gene to appropriate positions in the metabolic pathway maps created from current biochemical knowledge for many organisms.

(4) Visualize the metabolic pathways that are specific to a target organism of interest.

However, this procedure does not always work well to reconstruct the correct metabolic pathways and tends to produce many pathway holes or missing enzymes. If we cannot detect a significant sequence homology with characterized enzyme genes in other organisms, it is impossible to identify the candidate genes for missing enzymes. This has been a cause of pathway holes or missing enzymes, as suggested in Karp [7] and Osterman and Overbeek [8].

For inferring unknown part of the metabolic pathways and finding genes of missing enzymes, there are two research directions. The first is to use genomic information such as the use of gene order information along the chromosome of bacterial genomes [14], gene fusions [15], genomic context [16], gene expression patterns [17], statistical methods [18], and multiple genomic datasets [19]. The second approach is to use the information about the chemical compounds with which the enzymes are involved. An example is the path computation approach [20], where all possible paths between two compounds are searched by losing the substrate specificity restriction. However, it has been pointed out that this system tends to produce too many candidate paths, and it is difficult to select reliable paths. It is more natural to use both genomic data and chemical information simultaneously, rather than to use each individual information source.

Recently, several supervised network inference methods with metric learning for inferring biological networks (e.g., protein network, enzyme network) have been developed in the framework of kernel methods [19, 21–23]. By supervised we mean that the reliable *a priori* knowledge about parts of the true network is used in the inference process itself. The supervised approach is a two-step process. First, a model is learned to explain the "gold standard" from available datasets. Second, this model is applied to new proteins absent from the "gold standard" in order to infer their interactions. While supervised classification is a classical paradigm in machine learning and statistics, most methods cannot be adapted directly to the network inference problem because the goal is to predict properties between proteins, not about individual proteins. A straightforward way to use supervised classification for predicting the protein network is to apply classifiers such as support vector machine (SVM) to protein pairs by creating the descriptors or kernel functions for protein pairs [24]. However, the pairwise SVM requires considerable computational resources and it suffers from a serious scalability problem. For example, the time complexity of the quadratic programming problem for the pairwise SVM is $O(n^6)$, where n is the number of proteins in the biological network, and the space complexity is $O(n^4)$, which is just for storing the kernel matrix.

In this chapter, we review recently developed metric learning algorithms for the supervised network inference. The corresponding algorithms of the previous methods are based on kernel canonical correlation analysis [19], distance metric learning [21], *em*-algorithm [22], and kernel matrix regression [23]. These algorithms are more efficient compared with the binary classification framework of protein pairs. For example, the space complexity of the metric learning algorithms is $O(n^2)$. Note that they are far more efficient than the pairwise SVM requiring $O(n^4)$ space.

This chapter also presents an attempt to infer the metabolic networks from the integration of multiple genomic data and chemical information in the framework of supervised graph inference [25]. The originality of the methods is the integration of both genomic and chemical informations describing enzymes in order to predict more biologically reliable networks. This is made possible by the introduction of chemical compatibility constraints, representing the possibility of successive chemical reactions involving candidate enzymes. These constraints are built from the chemical information encoded in the EC number [13] assigned to the enzymes. In general, these constraints enable the elimination of incompatible predicted enzyme–enzyme relations from the network predicted by the supervised network inference methods. In the experiment, we show the usefulness of the supervised method and data integration method toward the metabolic network reconstruction.

8.2 MATERIALS

8.2.1 Metabolic Network

In this study, we focus on the metabolic pathways of the yeast *Saccharomyces cerevisiae*. As a gold standard for a part of the metabolic network, we take the KEGG PATHWAY database [5]. The metabolic network is a graph, with proteins as vertices and with edges as enzyme–enzyme relations when two genes code for enzymes that catalyze successive reactions in metabolic pathways. Figure 8.1 shows an example of the metabolic network in KEGG. The resulting enzyme network, which contains 668 nodes and 2782 edges as of November 2004, is regarded as a reliable part of the global metabolic network. This network is based on biological phenomena, representing known molecular interaction networks in various cellular process.

8.2.2 Genomic Data

8.2.2.1 Gene Expression Data The gene expression data corresponding to 157 experiments, 77 from Spellman et al. [26] and 80 from Eisen et al. [27], are used. In the previous work [26], the gene expression levels of the yeast *S. cerevisiae* were observed over time in various phases in the cell cycle. In the previous work [27], the gene expression levels of the yeast *S.cerevisiae* were observed in many experimental conditions such as during the diauxic shift, the mitotic cell division cycle, sporulation, and temperature and reducing shocks. Therefore, a vector of dimension 157 is associated with each gene coding for an enzyme protein.

8.2.2.2   Protein Localization Data   The localization data were obtained from the large-scale budding yeast localization experiment [28]. This dataset describes localization information of proteins in 23 intracellular locations such as mitochondrion, Golgi, and nucleus. To each enzyme protein is, therefore, attached a string of 23 bits, in which the presence and absence of the enzyme protein in a certain intracellular location is coded as 1 and 0, respectively, across the 23 intracellular locations.

8.2.2.3   Phylogenetic Profile   Phylogenetic profiles [29] were constructed from the ortholog gene clusters in the KEGG database, which describes the sets of orthologuous proteins in 145 organisms. In this study, we focus on the organisms with fully sequenced genomes, including 11 eukaryotes, 16 archaea, and 118 bacteria. Each phylogenetic profile consists of a string of bits, in which the presence and absence of an orthologuous protein is coded as 1 and 0, respectively, across the 145 organisms.

8.2.3   Chemical Information

We obtained the information about enzyme genes from the KEGG GENES database, in which EC numbers are assigned to enzyme candidate genes. As of November 2004, the number of genes to which at least one EC number is assigned is 1120. We obtained the chemical information for the enzyme genes, such as chemical reactions, substrates, and products from their EC numbers from the KEGG LIGAND database, which stores 11,817 compounds and 6349 reactions as of November 2004. We collected organic chemical compounds that are involved in the enzymes catalyzing chemical reactions. For example, we do not take inorganic compounds (e.g., water, oxygen, and phosphate) into consideration because such compounds tend to appear in too many reactions.

8.2.4   Kernel Representation

In order to deal with the data heterogeneity and take advantage of recent works on kernel similarity functions on general data structures [30], we will assume that all the data are represented by a positive definite kernel k, that is, a symmetric function k : $\mathcal{X}^2 \to \mathbf{R}$ satisfying $\sum_{i,j=1}^{n} a_i a_j k(x_i, x_j) \geq 0$ for any $n \in \mathbf{N}$, and $(a_1, a_2, \dots, a_n) \in \mathbf{R}^n$. This operation enables us to work in a unified mathematical framework across different types of datasets.

The gold standard metabolic network consists of a graph, with enzyme genes as nodes and enzyme–enzyme relations as edges, so a natural candidate is the diffusion kernel defined as the matrix $G = \exp(-\beta H)$, where $\beta > 0$ is a parameter and L is the Laplacian matrix of the graph ($L = D - A$, where A is the adjacency matrix and D is the diagonal matrix of node connectivity) [31]. In this study, the diffusion kernel with parameter $\beta = 1$ is applied to the gold standard network data, and the resulting kernel is denoted as G.

The expression data, localization data, and phylogenetic profiles are sets of numerical vectors, so the Gaussian RBF kernel $k(x, x') = \exp(- \| x - x' \|^2 / 2\sigma^2)$ or the linear kernel $k(x, x') = x \cdot x'$ are natural candidates. In this study, the Gaussian RBF kernel with width parameter $\sigma = 5$ is applied to the expression data and phylogenetic profiles, and the resulting kernels are denoted as $K_{\exp}$ and K_{phy}, respectively. The linear kernel is applied to the localization data, and the resulting kernel is denoted as K_{loc}.

All the kernel matrices are supposed to be normalized so that the diagonal elements are all ones and centered in the feature space.

8.3   SUPERVISED NETWORK INFERENCE WITH METRIC LEARNING

To infer the metabolic gene network from genomic data, we use recently developed supervised network inference method with metric learning. For simplicity, the metabolic gene network is sometimes called gene network below.

8.3.1   Formalism of the Problem

Let us formally define the problem of the supervised network inference with metric learning. Suppose that we are given an undirected graph $\Gamma = (V, E)$, where $V = (v_1, \ldots, v_n)$ is a set of vertices and $E \subset (V \times V)$ is a set of edges. The problem is, given an additional set of vertices $V' = (v_{n+1}, \ldots, v_N)$, to infer a set of new edges $E' \subset V' \times (V + V') \cup (V + V') \times V'$ involving the additional vertices in V'.

The prediction of the metabolic network is a typical problem, which is suitable in this framework from a practical viewpoint. In this case, V corresponds to a set of genes (enzyme genes with known biological roles in pathways) and E corresponds to a set of known enzyme–enzyme relations (successively catalyzing the reactions). V' corresponds to a set of additional genes (enzyme candidate genes) and E' corresponds to a set of unknown enzyme–enzyme relations.

The prediction is performed based on available observed data about the vertices in V and V'. Suppose that the nodes $V = (v_1, \ldots, v_n)$ and $V' = (v_{n+1}, \ldots, v_N)$ are represented by $\mathcal{X} = (x_1, \ldots, x_n)$ and $\mathcal{X}' = (x_{n+1}, \ldots, x_N)$, respectively. In this study, genes belonging to $\mathcal{X}$ and $\mathcal{X}'$ are referred to as training set and prediction set, respectively. For example, genes are represented by various genomic data or experimental data such as gene expression profiles, localization profiles, and phylogenetic profiles. The question is how to predict unknown enzyme–enzyme interactions from such genomic data using the preknowledge about known enzyme–enzyme interactions.

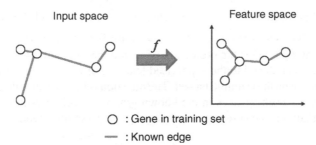

○ : Gene in training set

— : Known edge

Figure 8.2 Supervised network inference: training process. Genes in the training set are mapped onto a feature space, where interacting genes are close to each other.

8.3.2 From Metric Learning to Graph Inference

Suppose that a graph must be inferred on N points $(x_1, \ldots, x_N)$ in the Euclidean space $\mathbf{R}^d$, where the distance between the points is based on the observed data. The simplest prediction strategy is to use the data-based similarity information directly, that is, putting an edge between the points that are close to each other if the distance (dissimilarity) between the points is smaller than a fixed threshold δ. This strategy is referred to as the "direct approach" below.

The supervised graph inference problem can be formulated in the following two-step procedure:

- Map the original points to a Euclidean space through mappings $\mathbf{f} : \mathcal{X} \to \mathbf{R}^d$.
- Apply the direct approach to infer the edges between the points $\{\mathbf{f}(x), x \in \mathcal{X} + \mathcal{X}'\}$.

Figures 8.2 and 8.3 show an illustration of the procedure. The goal of this projection is to define a feature space where pairs of interacting genes have similar projection, so that it becomes possible to infer interaction from similarity in the feature space. Hence, whenever x interacts with x', we would like $\mathbf{f}(x)$ to be similar to $\mathbf{f}(x')$, which

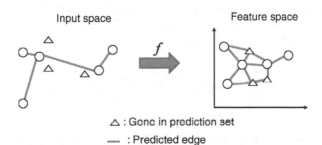

△ : Gene in prediction set

— : Predicted edge

Figure 8.3 Supervised network inference: prediction process. Genes in the prediction set are mapped onto the feature space. Then, interacting gene pairs are predicted using the nearest neighbor approach.

ideally would be fulfilled if $f^{(l)}(x)$ was close to $f^{(l)}(x')$ for each $l = 1, \ldots, d$. By the mapping, each gene x is represented by a vector $\mathbf{f}(x) = \left(f^{(1)}(x), \ldots, f^{(d)}(x) \right)^\top$, where $d < N$ and $f^{(l)}(x)$ is the projection of x onto the l-th component.

The problem is reduced to the supervised learning of $\mathbf{f}$ using the partially known graph information on the training dataset. The question is how to estimate the mapping $\mathbf{f}$, which maps adjacent vertices in the known graph to nearby positions in $\mathbf{R}^d$ such that the direct approach can recover the known graph to some extent.

8.4 ALGORITHMS FOR SUPERVISED NETWORK INFERENCE

In this section, we describe five algorithms that can be used for the problem of supervised network inference: (1) kernel canonical correlation analysis (KCCA) [19], (2) distance metric learning (DML) [21], (3) kernel matrix regression (KMR) [23], (4) penalized kernel matrix regression (PKMR) [23], and (5) kernel matrix completion with *em*-algorithm (em) [22].

8.4.1 Kernel Canonical Correlation Analysis (KCCA)

If the gene network was known beforehand, an "ideal" feature space would be a subspace defined by functions $f^{(l)}$ $(l = 1, \ldots, d)$ that vary slowly between adjacent nodes of the gene network. Such functions are usually called smooth, and it is known that the norm $\|f\|_{\mathcal{H}}$ associated with a diffusion kernel on a graph exactly quantifies this smoothness: the smoother f, the smaller $\|f\|_{\mathcal{H}}$ [32].

As a result, if the gene network was known, an ideal feature space would be defined by the projection onto the first principal directions defined by kernel PCA [33] with a diffusion kernel on the graph [31]. As the total gene network is not known beforehand, the projections onto this ideal feature space cannot be computed. Therefore, we propose to constrain it to somehow fit the ideal feature space, at least on the part of the network known beforehand.

Let K be the kernel representing the genomic information and G be the diffusion kernel derived from the known gene network. Both of them are restricted to n genes in the training set, so K and G are then $n \times n$ matrices. According to the representer theorem in the reproducing kernel Hilbert space (RKHS) [34], let us write features $f(x)$ for genomic data and $g(v)$ for graph as follows:

$$f(x) = \sum_{j=1}^{n} k(x, x_j)\alpha_j, \quad g(v) = \sum_{j=1}^{n} g(v, v_j)\beta_j, \tag{8.1}$$

where $\boldsymbol{\alpha} = (\alpha_1, \alpha_2, \ldots, \alpha_n)^\top$ and $\boldsymbol{\beta} = (\beta_1, \beta_2, \ldots, \beta_n)^\top$. Let $\|f\|$ and $\|g\|$ be the corresponding norms. In order to define a feature f such that $\|f\|$ be small, as in the spectral approach, and $\|g\|$ be small simultaneously, as in the ideal representation, we propose to use the following trick: find two functions f and g such that

$\sum_{i=1}^{n} f(x_i)^2 = 1$ and $\sum_{i=1}^{n} g(x_i)^2 = 1$ and that maximize the functional

$$\text{corr}(f, g) \times \frac{1}{\sqrt{1 + \lambda_1 ||f||^2}} \times \frac{1}{\sqrt{1 + \lambda_2 ||g||^2}}, \tag{8.2}$$

where λ_1 and λ_2 are positive regularization parameters and corr(f, g) is the correlation coefficient between f and g. The first term of this product ensures that f "fits" g on the *a priori* known part of the network, while the second and last terms ensure that $||f||$ and $||g||$ are small simultaneously. Subsequent features can be defined recursively by minimizing the same functional with additional orthogonality conditions.

The maximization problem of the functional (8.2) can be shown to be equivalent to the following generalized eigenvalue problem:

$$\begin{pmatrix} 0 & KG \\ GK & 0 \end{pmatrix} \begin{pmatrix} \alpha \\ \beta \end{pmatrix} = \rho \begin{pmatrix} (K + \lambda_1 I)^2 & 0 \\ 0 & (G + \lambda_2 I)^2 \end{pmatrix} \begin{pmatrix} \alpha \\ \beta \end{pmatrix}, \tag{8.3}$$

where I is an identity matrix, α and β are the eigenvectors associated with eigenvalue ρ. This problem is usually called KCCA [35, 36].

The features are built from the genomic data kernel k only and are expected to fit the ideal features on genes in the training set. If one now focuses on the first d solutions, we obtain a vector of features $\mathbf{f}(x) = (f^{(1)}(x), \ldots, f^{(d)}(x))^{\top}$, where each feature can now be generalized to any gene x as

$$f^{(l)}(x) = \sum_{j=1}^{n} \alpha_j^{(l)} k(x_j, x), \quad l = 1, 2, \ldots, d. \tag{8.4}$$

This is the set of features of mapped genes before inferring edges between genes.

8.4.2 Distance Metric Learning (DML)

A criterion to assess whether connected (resp. disconnected) vertices are mapped onto similar (resp. dissimilar) points in $\mathbf{R}$ is as follows:

$$R(f) = \frac{\sum_{(v,v')\in E}(f(x) - f(x'))^2 - \sum_{(v,v')\notin E}(f(x) - f(x'))^2}{\sum_{(v,v')\in V\times V}(f(x) - f(x'))^2}. \tag{8.5}$$

A small value of $R(f)$ ensures that connected vertices tend to be closer than disconnected vertices in the sense of quadratic error. The mapping f is learned by finding f, which minimizes the above criterion.

Let us denote by $f_V = (f(x_1), \ldots, f(x_n))^T \in \mathbf{R}^n$ the values taken by f on the training set. If we restrict f_V to have zero means as $\sum_{i=1}^{n} f(x_i) = 0$, then the criterion

(8.5) can be rewritten as follows:

$$R(f) = 4 \frac{f_V^\top L f_V}{f_V^\top f_V} - 2, \tag{8.6}$$

where L is the combinatorial Laplacian of the graph $\Gamma = (V, E)$.

To avoid the overfitting problem and obtain meaningful solutions, we propose to regularize the criterion (8.6) by a smoothness functional on f based on a classical approach in statistical learning [37, 38]. We assume that f belongs to the RKHS $\mathcal{H}$ defined by the kernel k on $\mathcal{X}$, and to use the norm of f as a regularization operator. Let us define by $\|f\|$ the norm of f in $\mathcal{H}$. Then, the regularized criterion to be minimized becomes:

$$R(f) = \frac{f_V^\top L f_V + \lambda \|f\|^2}{f_V^\top f_V}, \tag{8.7}$$

where λ is a regularization parameter that controls the trade-off between minimizing the original criterion (8.5) and ensuring that the solution has a small norm in the RKHS.

In order to obtain a d-dimensional feature representation of the vertices, we propose to iterate the minimization of the regularized criterion (8.7) under orthogonality constraints in the RKHS, that is, we recursively define the l-th features $f^{(l)}$ for $l = 1, \ldots, d$ as follows:

$$f^{(l)} = \mathrm{argmin}_{f \in \mathcal{H}, f \perp f^{(1)}, \ldots, f^{(l-1)}} \frac{f_V^\top L f_V + \lambda \|f\|^2}{f_V^\top f_V}. \tag{8.8}$$

Let k be the kernel on the observed dataset $\mathcal{X}$. According to the representer theorem in the RKHS [34], for any $i = 1, \ldots, d$, the solution to Eq. (8.8) has the following expansions:

$$f^{(l)}(x) = \sum_{j=1}^{n} \alpha_j^{(l)} k(x_j, x),$$

for some vector $\alpha^{(l)} = (\alpha_1^{(l)}, \ldots, \alpha_n^{(l)})^T \in \mathbf{R}^n$.

Let K be the Gram matrices of the kernel k on the set $\mathcal{X}$ such that $(K)_{ij} = k(x_i, x_j)$, $i, j = 1, \ldots, n$. The corresponding feature vector $f_V^{(l)}$ can be written in terms of $\alpha^{(l)}$ by $f_V^{(l)} = K_v \alpha^{(l)}$. The squared norm of feature $f^{(l)}$ in $\mathcal{H}_V$ is equal to $\|f^{(l)}\|^2 = \alpha^T K_v \alpha$, so the orthogonarity constraint $f^{(l)} \perp f^{(m)}$ ($l \neq m$) can be written by $\alpha^{(l)T} K_u \alpha^{(m)} = 0$.

Then, the minimization problem of $R(f)$ is equivalent to finding α which minimizes

$$R(f) = \frac{\alpha^\top K L K \alpha + \lambda \alpha^\top K \alpha}{\alpha^\top K^2 \alpha} \tag{8.9}$$

under the following orthogonality constraints: $\alpha^\top K \alpha^{(1)} = \cdots = \alpha^\top K \alpha^{(l-1)} = 0$.

Taking the differential of Eq. (8.9) with respect to α to zero, the solution of the first vectors $\alpha^{(1)}$ can be obtained as the eigenvectors associated with the smallest (nonnegative) eigenvalue in the following generalized eigenvalue problem:

$$(KLK + \lambda K)\alpha = \rho K^2 \alpha. \tag{8.10}$$

Sequentially, the solutions of vectors $\alpha^{(1)}, \ldots, \alpha^{(d)}$ can be obtained as the eigenvectors associated with d smallest (nonnegative) eigenvalues in the above generalized eigenvalue problem.

If one now focuses on the first d solutions, we obtain a vector of features $\mathbf{f}(x) = (f^{(1)}(x), \ldots, f^{(d)}(x))^{\top}$, where each feature can now be generalized to any gene x as

$$f^{(l)}(x) = \sum_{j=1}^{n} \alpha_j^{(l)} k\left(x_j, x\right), \quad l = 1, 2, \ldots, d. \tag{8.11}$$

8.4.3 Kernel Matrix Regression (KMR)

An apparent drawback of the KCCA approach is that the objective function of KCCA is different from that of correctly predicting the values of the kernel G. In particular, by computing features g for the node v, the notion of similarity between nodes is changed, although in this issue, we do not want to change the similarity space for the graph. We want instead to change the object–object similarity space only for genomic data object x to make it fit the object–object similarity space with the node v in the graph. In this section, we propose a variant of the regression model based on the underlying features in the RKHS by modifying the idea of KCCA.

The ordinary regression model between an explanatory variable $x \in \mathcal{X}$ and a response variable $y \in \mathbf{R}$ can be formulated as follows:

$$y = h(x) + \epsilon, \tag{8.12}$$

where $h : \mathcal{X} \to \mathbf{R}$ and ϵ is a noise term. By analogy, we propose to regard $(x, x') \in \mathcal{X} \times \mathcal{X}$ as an explanatory variable and $g(v, v') \in \mathbf{R}$ as a response variable in our context. Assuming the underlying feature $\mathbf{f}(x) \in \mathbf{R}^d$ in the RKHS, we formulate a variant of the regression model as follows:

$$g(v, v') = h(x, x') + \epsilon = \mathbf{f}(x)^{\top} \mathbf{f}(x') + \epsilon, \tag{8.13}$$

where $h : \mathcal{X} \times \mathcal{X} \to \mathbf{R}$. We refer to this model as kernel matrix regression (KMR) model. We note that imposing h to be of the form $h(x, x') = \mathbf{f}(x)^{\top} \mathbf{f}(x')$ for some feature $\mathbf{f} : \mathcal{X} \to \mathbf{R}^d$ ensures that the regression function is positive definite.

Following a classical approach in kernel methods, we consider features in the RKHS of the kernel K that possess an expansion of the form:

$$f(x) = \sum_{j=1}^{n} k(x, x_j) w_j, \tag{8.14}$$

where $\mathbf{w} = (w_1, w_2, \ldots, w_n)^\top$ is a weight vector and n is the number of objects in the training set. When d different features are considered, we express them by a feature vector as $\mathbf{f}(x) = (f^{(1)}(x), f^{(2)}(x), \ldots, f^{(d)}(x))^\top$.

In order to represent the set of features for all the objects, we define feature score matrices $F_t(x) = [\mathbf{f}(x_1), \ldots, \mathbf{f}(x_n)]^\top$ for the training set and $F_p(x) = [\mathbf{f}(x_{n+1}), \ldots, \mathbf{f}(x_N)]^\top$ for the test set. Let K_{tt} be a kernel matrix for the training set itself as $(K_{tt})_{ij} = k(x_i, x_j), i, j = 1, \ldots, n$, and K_{pt} be a kernel matrix for the prediction set against the training set as $(K_{pt})_{ij} = k(x_i, x_j), i = n + 1, \ldots, N, j = 1, \ldots, n$. In the matrix form, we can actually compute the feature score matrices as $F_t = K_{tt}W$ for the training set and $F_p = K_{pt}W$ for the prediction set, where $W = [\mathbf{w}^{(1)}, \mathbf{w}^{(2)}, \ldots, \mathbf{w}^{(d)}]$.

Here, we want to find the $n \times d$ weight matrix W such that $F_t F_t^\top$ fits G as much as possible. If we set $A = WW^\top$, this problem can be replaced by finding A, which minimizes the difference between G and $F_t F_t^\top$. It means that, this enables us to avoid considerable computational burden for computing W itself, even if d is infinite. Therefore, we attempt to find $A(= WW^\top)$, which minimizes

$$L = \| G - K_{tt} A K_{tt}^\top \|_F^2, \tag{8.15}$$

where $\| \cdot \|_F$ indicates the Frobenius norm. We can rewrite the above equation in the trace form as

$$L = \text{tr} \left\{ (G - K_{tt} A K_{tt}^\top)(G - K_{tt} A K_{tt}^\top)^\top \right\}. \tag{8.16}$$

Taking a differential of L with respect to A and setting to zero, the solution is analytically obtained by

$$A = WW^\top = K_{tt}^{-1} G_{tt} K_{tt}^{-1}.$$

Then, the weight matrix W can be computed as follows:

$$W = K_{tt}^{-1} G^{1/2}. \tag{8.17}$$

If one now focuses on the first d solutions, we obtain a vector of features $\mathbf{f}(x) = (f^{(1)}(x), \ldots, f^{(d)}(x))^\top$, where each feature can now be generalized to any gene x as

$$f^{(l)}(x) = \sum_{j=1}^{n} w_j^{(l)} k\left(x_j, x\right), \quad l = 1, 2, \ldots, d. \tag{8.18}$$

8.4.4 Penalized Kernel Matrix Regression (PKMR)

Here, we consider introducing the idea of regularization in the KMR method in the previous section. To do so, we attempt to find $A(= WW^\top)$, which minimizes the following penalized loss function:

$$L = \| G - K_{tt} A K_{tt} \|_F^2 + \lambda \text{PEN}(A), \tag{8.19}$$

where λ is a regularization parameter and $\text{PEN}(A)$ is a penalty term for A defined as follows. Each positive semidefinite matrix A can be expanded as $A = \sum_{l=1}^{d} \mathbf{w}^{(l)} \mathbf{w}^{(l)\top}$. To each $\mathbf{w}^{(l)}$ is associated a feature $f^{(l)} : \mathcal{X} \to \mathbf{R}$ by (8.14), whose norm in the RKHS of K is given by:

$$\| f^{(l)} \|_{\text{RKHS}}^2 = \sum_{i,j=1}^{n} w_i^{(l)} w_j^{(l)} k(\mathbf{x}_i, \mathbf{x}_j) = \text{tr}(\mathbf{w}^{(l)} \mathbf{w}^{(l)\top} K).$$

To enforce regularity of the global mapping f, we therefore define the following penalty for A:

$$\text{PEN}(A) = 2 \sum_{l=1}^{d} \| f^{(l)} \|_{\text{RKHS}}^2 = 2 \sum_{l=1}^{d} \text{tr}(\mathbf{w}^{(l)} \mathbf{w}^{(l)\top} K_{tt}) = 2\text{tr}(A K_{tt}).$$

In this case, the optimization problem is reduced to finding A, which minimizes

$$L = \text{tr} \left\{ (G - K_{tt} A K_{tt}^\top)(G_{tt} - K_{tt} A K_{tt}^\top)^\top \right\} + 2\lambda \text{tr} \{A K_{tt}\}. \tag{8.20}$$

Taking a differential of L with respect to A and setting to zero, the solution of the above penalized optimization problem is obtained by

$$A = K_{tt}^{-1}(G - \lambda K_{tt}^{-1}) K_{tt}^{-1}.$$

We note that the justification for the penalty used is only valid for positive semidefinite matrices, which will be obtained at least for small enough λ. Then, the weight matrix W can be computed as follows:

$$W = K_{tt}^{-1}(G_{tt} - \lambda K_{tt}^{-1})^{1/2}. \tag{8.21}$$

If one now focuses on the first d solutions, we obtain a vector of features $\mathbf{f}(x) = (f^{(1)}(x), \ldots, f^{(d)}(x))^\top$, where each feature can now be generalized to any gene x as

$$f^{(l)}(x) = \sum_{j=1}^{n} w_j^{(l)} k(x_j, x), \quad l = 1, 2, \ldots, d. \tag{8.22}$$

8.4.5 Relationship with Kernel Matrix Completion and *em*-algorithm

It is possible to tackle the supervised network inference problem from the viewpoint of the kernel matrix completion. In this section, we explain how the kernel matrix completion can be used for the supervised network inference problem and discuss the relationship between the kernel matrix regression and the *em* algorithm.

Let k and g be symmetric positive definite kernels defined on an explanatory variable x and response variable y, respectively. When we compute the kernel matrix for the explanatory variable x, we obtain an $N \times N$ kernel matrix K, where $(K)_{ij} = k(x_i, x')$ $(1 \leq i, j \leq N)$, x_i belongs to a set $\mathcal{X}$, and N is the number of all objects. On the other hand, when we compute the kernel matrix for the response variable y, we obtain an $N \times N$ kernel matrix G, where $(G)_{ij} = g(y_i, y_j)$ $(1 \leq i, j \leq n)$, y_i belongs to a set $\mathcal{Y}$, and n is the number of available objects $(n < N)$. Note that G contains in fact missing values for all entries $(G)_{ij}$ with $\max(i, j) > n$. We want to estimate the missing part of G using full Gram matrix K, taking into account a form of correlation between the two kernels.

In this study, we express each kernel matrix by splitting the matrix into four parts. We denote by K_{tt} (resp. G_{tt}) the $n \times n$ kernel matrix for the training set versus itself, K_{pt} (resp. G_{pt}) the $(N - n) \times n$ kernel matrix for the prediction set versus the training set, and K_{pp} (resp. G_{pp}) the $(N - n) \times (N - n)$ kernel matrix for the prediction set versus itself:

$$K = \begin{pmatrix} K_{tt} & K_{pt}^\top \\ K_{pt} & K_{pp} \end{pmatrix}, \qquad G = \begin{pmatrix} G_{tt} & G_{pt}^\top \\ G_{pt} & G_{pp} \end{pmatrix}. \tag{8.23}$$

Note that K_{pt} and K_{pp} are known, while G_{pt} and G_{pp} are unknown. The goal is to predict G_{pt} and G_{pp} from K and G_{tt}. In this case, we can predict the potential edges involving the prediction set by putting an edge between the points that are close to each other if estimated response kernel similarity between the points is larger than a fixed threshold δ.

If the KMR model is used for the kernel matrix completion problem, missing part of G can be estimated as follows.

Prediction set versus training set:

$$\hat{G}_{pt} = F_p F_t^\top = K_{pt} K_{tt}^{-1} G_{tt}. \tag{8.24}$$

Prediction set versus prediction set:

$$\hat{G}_{pp} = F_p F_p^\top = K_{pt} K_{tt}^{-1} G_{tt} K_{tt}^{-1} K_{pt}^\top. \tag{8.25}$$

Toward the supervised network inference with the kernel matrix completion, the use of the *em* algorithm based on information geometry has been proposed [22]. In their work, the kernel matrix completion problem is defined as finding missing entries that minimize the Kullback–Leibler divergence between the resulting completed matrix and a spectral variant of the full matrix. Because of space limitation, the details of the explanation about this method is not shown in this chapter. For more details, see the original paper [22].

It is interesting to observe that the final algorithms between *em* and KMR are very similar. The *em* algorithm results in the following equations for estimating the incomplete parts $\hat{G}_{pt}$ and $\hat{G}_{pp}$:

Prediction set versus training set:

$$\hat{G}_{pt} = K_{pt} K_{tt}^{-1} G_{tt}. \tag{8.26}$$

Prediction set versus test set:

$$\hat{G}_{pp} = K_{pp} + K_{pt} K_{tt}^{-1} K_{pt}^{\top} + K_{pt} K_{tt}^{-1} G_{tt} K_{tt}^{-1} K_{pt}^{\top}. \tag{8.27}$$

We note that the $\hat{G}_{pt}$ of the *em* algorithm is equivalent to that of the kernel matrix regression. On the other hand, the $\hat{G}_{pp}$ of the *em* algorithm is not equivalent to that of the kernel matrix regression. It differs by $K_{pp} + K_{pt} K_{tt}^{-1} K_{pt}^{\top}$. This stems from the difference of the geometry space between the two methods. The *em* algorithm is based on the information geometry, while the proposed KMR is based on the Euclidean geometry.

8.5 DATA INTEGRATION

8.5.1 Genomic Data Integration

Suppose that we use $P \geq 1$ sorts of heterogeneous genomic data as predictors to infer the metabolic network, and that they are represented by P kernels $K_1, \ldots, K_P$. The function K_p measures the similarity of enzyme genes with respect to the p-th dataset. A simple data integration is obtained by creating a new kernel as the sum of the kernels as $K = \sum_{p=1}^{P} K_p$. The usefulness of this procedure has already been proved [19, 39]. We can go further in this strategy by considering weighted sums of kernels of the form $K = \sum_{p=1}^{P} w_p K_p$, where w_p represents the weight associated with the p-th dataset for predicting metabolic networks. Intuitively, the weight of a dataset should be related to the relevance of the dataset for predicting metabolic networks.

Therefore, the essential problem is how to determine the weight w_p in the integration process. In this study, we propose to take the weights $(w_1, \ldots, w_P)$ proportional to an estimation of prediction accuracy of the corresponding dataset (e.g., ROC scores -0.5), obtained from experiments on each individual datasets [25]. More complex algorithm can be imagined to automatically determine the weight in the integration of heterogeneous data through kernel operation (e.g., convex optimization).

8.5.2 Chemical Compatibility Network

Following the definition of EC numbers [13], we focus on the first three digits in the EC number because the fourth digit in the EC number is just a serial number [40]. If the first three digits in the EC numbers are the same between two enzymes, we merge all compounds involved with the EC numbers into a list of compounds. If two enzymes share at least one compound across their compound lists, there is a possibility that the two enzymes catalyze successive chemical reactions in metabolic networks. We refer to this property as chemical compatibility in this study.

It should be pointed out that keeping only the first three digits of EC numbers is also a protection against annotation errors resulting from homology-based EC number annotation. Indeed, the prediction of the chemical reaction type (corresponding to the first three numbers) has a higher accuracy than the prediction of the fourth number, so the information of the fourth digit is not used in our approach.

We regard the chemical compatibility between two enzyme genes as a possible enzyme–enzyme relation or successive chemical reactions in metabolic networks. Using the chemical compatibilities among all enzyme genes, we constructed a graph, with enzymes as nodes and chemical compatibilities as edges. The numbers of nodes and edges of the resulting graph are 1120 and 40,4853, respectively. Obviously, most enzyme–enzyme relations in this network are not likely to correspond to biologically meaningful enzyme–enzyme relations (or biological phenomena). However, this simple constraint already enables to disregard roughly one-third of the 627,760 possible edges between 1120 nodes.We refer to this network as the chemical compatibility network.

8.5.3 Incorporating Chemical Constraint

For each network inference method, we present two approaches to integrate the chemical information contained in the chemical compatibility network, which we refer to as preintegration and postintegration, respectively [25].

The preintegration strategy consists of considering the chemical compatibility network as an additional source of information about the enzyme genes, encode it into a kernel similarity measure, and use it as an additional component when kernels are integrated through sum or weighted convex combination. Since the data structure of the chemical compatibility network is a graph, a candidate of the kernel is the diffusion kernel [31]. In this study, the diffusion kernel with parameter $\beta = 0.01$ is applied to the chemical compatibility network, and the resulting kernel is denoted as K_{che}. The rationale behind this approach is to try to enforce some chemical constraint in the kernel itself, without strictly enforcing all constraints. Indeed, the absence of an edge between two genes in the chemical compatibility network can be due to the absence of an EC number assignment, in which case, a lack of an edge in the chemical compatibility should not be strictly enforced as strong evidences for the presence of an edge stem from other sources of data.

To the contrary, the postintegration strategy gives a dominant role to the chemical constraints by strictly enforcing them. It consists of first performing the normal network inference without chemical information, followed by the selection among predicted edges of those that fulfill the chemical constraint, namely, the ones that are present in the chemical compatibility network. With this method, all edges of the resulting graph necessarily fulfill the chemical constraints.

8.6 EXPERIMENTS

We performed a series of experiments to test the performance of different methods: KCCA, DML, KMR, PKMR, and *em*-algorithm on the problem of reconstructing the gold standard metabolic network. As a baseline method, we also applied the direct approach, that is, to predict an edge between two genes x and y when the similarity value $k(x, y)$ is large enough. In the case of the KCCA, we set the regularization parameters λ_1 and λ_2 as 0.1 and 0.1, respectively, and we used 30 features. In the case of the PKMR, the regularization parameter λ is set to 0.1.

As a measure of the performance, we used the area under the ROC curve (AUC) score [41], because the performance depends on the threshold given in advance. The ROC curve is defined as a function of the true-positive rates against the false-positive rates based on several threshold values. "True positive" means that the predicted gene pairs are actually present in the gold standard network, while "false positive" means that the predicted gene pairs are absent in the gold standard network. The curves can be computed for the direct approach by just inferring the global gold standard network. The supervised methods require the knowledge of a part of the network in the training process. We, therefore, evaluated them with the following 10-fold cross-validation procedure: The set of all nodes is split in 10 subsets of roughly equal size, each subset is taken apart in turn to perform the training with 90 percent of the nodes, and the prediction concerns the edges that involve the nodes in the subset taken apart during training.

Table 8.1 summarizes the experiments performed. For each method, we tested both the pre- and the postintegration strategies to take into account the chemical constraints. The comparison results are reported in Tables 8.2 and 8.3. The direct methods seem to catch little information to recover the metabolic network from the datasets. The use of the constraint of chemical compatibility seems to have effects of refining the network predicted by the direct approaches in all the cases. However, these methods are unpractical in actual applications because of their high false-positive rate against true-positive rate at any threshold.

In contrast, the supervised network inference methods seem to catch information to recover the gold standard metabolic network. We observe that the use of the supervised learning significantly improves the prediction accuracy in all cases. Especially, KML, PKML, and *em*-method seem to work well. We observe slight differences between five supervised methods when individual kernels are used. The phylogenetic profile kernel significantly outperforms both the expression and the localization kernel with the KCCA method, while it is roughly at the level of the expression kernel and above the localization kernel with the DML method, for example. More importantly, we observe that the preintegration of chemical constraint has little influence on the accuracy, while the postintegration strategy consistently improves the ROC score in all cases. Finally, we observe a significant improvement when kernels are combined with weights.

The overall best result (0.871) is obtained by the PKMR method in conjunction with a weighted integration of all genomic datasets, combined with the chemical constraints using the postintegration strategy. The comparison of these experimental results highlights the accuracy improvements resulting from the use of supervised approach, the weighted integration of multiple datasets, and the use of the chemical constraint.

Since we confirmed the validity of the supervised method by the cross-validation experiments, we finally conducted a comprehensive prediction of a global network

Table 8.1 List of experiments for each network inference method with chemical preprocessing and postprocessing

	Preprocessing		Postprocessing	
Data	Predictor kernel	Data	Predictor kernel	Chemical constraint
Expression	K_{exp}	Expression	K_{exp}	Postintegration
Localization	K_{loc}	Localization	K_{loc}	Postintegration
Phylogenetic profile	K_{phy}	Phylogenetic profile	K_{phy}	Postintegration
Chemical compatibility	K_{che}	Integration	$K_{exp}+K_{loc}+K_{phy}$	Postintegration
Integration	$K_{exp}+K_{loc}+K_{phy}$	Weighted integration	$w_1 K_{exp} + w_2 K_{loc} + w_3 K_{phy}$	Postintegration
Integration with	$K_{exp}+K_{loc}+K_{phy}+K_{che}$			
Weighted integration	$w_1 K_{exp} + w_2 K_{loc} + w_3 K_{phy} + w_4 K_{che}$			

Table 8.2   AUC score (area under the ROC curves) for different supervised network inference methods when the chemical information is integrated with the preprocessing

Method	Direct	KCCA	DML	KMR	PKMR	*em*
Expression	0.502	0.639	0.706	0.701	0.706	0.711
Localization	0.561	0.567	0.577	0.561	0.577	0.540
Phylogenetic profile	0.567	0.747	0.707	0.702	0.707	0.714
Chemical compatibility	0.539	0.750	0.592	0.582	0.592	0.582
Integration	0.574	0.804	0.809	0.829	0.831	0.827
Integration with chem.	0.586	0.800	0.803	0.821	0.827	0.822
Weighted integration	0.595	0.809	0.818	0.838	0.852	0.841

for all enzyme candidate proteins (1120 enzymes in this study) of the yeast. The predicted network enabled us not only to make new biological inferences about unknown enzyme–enzyme relations, but also to identify genes coding for missing enzymes in known metabolic pathways. We take YJR137C as a target protein, for example. The detailed function of this protein was not clear as of starting this work, although the first two digits of EC number was known as EC:1.8.-,-. In the predicted network, this protein is connected to the enzyme proteins YPR167C (EC:1.8.4.8) and YGR012W (EC:2.5.1.47) in sulfur metabolism shown in Figure 8.4. We can guess that the target protein might be functionally related to these enzymes. Recently, there has been a report that this protein is annotated as EC:1.8.1.2 according to the MIPS database, where EC:1.8.1.2 is known to have successive reactions with EC:1.8.4.8 and EC:2.5.1.47, for example, according to the sulfur metabolism in the KEGG pathway database. Of course, such inference can be applied to other enzyme candidate proteins.

8.7   DISCUSSION AND CONCLUSION

In this chapter, we present five algorithms for supervised network inference with metric learning and show application for reconstructing the metabolic network. It should be pointed out that in this supervised framework, different networks can be inferred from the same data by changing the partial network used in the learning step.

Table 8.3   AUC score (area under the ROC curves) for different supervised network inference methods when the chemical information is integrated with the postprocessing

Method	Direct	KCCA	DML	KMR	PKMR	*em*
Expression	0.571	0.688	0.741	0.723	0.731	0.740
Localization	0.624	0.626	0.640	0.611	0.620	0.612
Phylogenetic profile	0.629	0.779	0.764	0.778	0.774	0.767
Chemical compatibility	–	–	–	–	–	–
Integration	0.628	0.819	0.817	0.843	0.862	0.846
Integration with chem.	–	–	–	–	–	–
Weighted integration	0.642	0.822	0.820	0.852	0.871	0.859

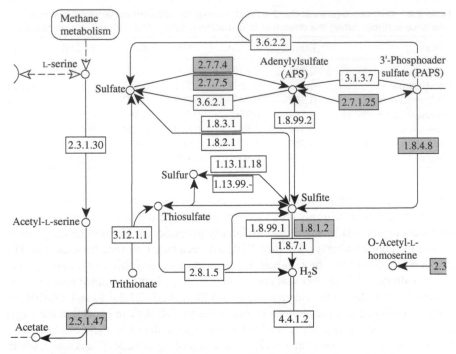

Figure 8.4   Sulfur metabolism of the yeast in the KEGG pathway database.

For example, these methods can be applied to not only metabolic network but also gene regulatory network and protein–protein interaction network. Another strength of this method is the possibility to naturally integrate heterogeneous data. Experimental results confirmed that this integration is beneficial for the prediction accuracy of the method. Moreover, other sorts of genomic data can be integrated, as long as kernels can be derived from them. As the list of kernels for genomic data keeps increasing fast [30], new opportunities might be worth investigating.

We also present two strategies to integrate multiple genomic data and chemical information toward reconstructing the metabolic network. One strategy (pre-processing) amounts to considering the chemical constraints as another genomic dataset, while the second strategy (postprocessing) operates as a filter on the predicted edges to strictly enforce chemical constraints. The cross-validation experiments showed that the methods, in particular, the postintegration strategy combined with supervised learning on weighted linear combinations of kernels, improved the prediction accuracy to a large extent. In this study, we focused on the first three digits in the EC numbers assigned to the enzyme candidate genes and created a chemical compatibility network to look for biochemically possible edges. However, this process tends to produce too many possible enzyme–enzyme relations, similar to the path computation method, so we might need to develop a method to reduce the candidates of possible enzyme–enzyme relations. One possibility is to eliminate cofactors (coenzymes), such as NAD(P)+ and ATP because they tend to appear in too many reactions, although the definition of a cofactor is a very difficult problem.

The methods presented in this chapter have been successfully used in practical applications. One application is the prediction of missing enzyme genes in the metabolic network for the bacteria *Pseudomonas aeruginosa* from the integration of gene position along the chromosome, phylogenetic profiles, and EC number information [42]. In their work, they attempted to predict several missing enzyme genes in order to reconstruct the lysine degradation pathway and identified genes for putative 5-aminovalerate aminotransferase (EC: 2.6.1.48) and putative glutarate semialdehyde dehydrogenase (EC: 1.2.1.20). To verify the prediction experimentally, they conducted biochemical assays and examined the activity of the products of the predicted genes in a coupled reaction and observed that the predicted gene products catalyzed the expected reactions.

Another application is the extraction of functionally related genes to the response of nitrogen deprivation in cyanobacteria *Anabaena* sp. *PCC 7120* from microarray data, phylogenetic profiles, and gene orders on the chromosome [43]. They confirmed the validity of the prediction result from the viewpoint of protein domains and functional motifs that are known to be related with nitrogen metabolism. They successufully obtained a set of candidate genes related with nitrogen metabolism, which can be depicted as extensions of existing KEGG pathways.

Recently, we developed a Web server named GENIES (GEne Network Inference Engine based on Supervised analysis), which is freely available and enables us to carry out most algorithms for supervised gene network inference on the Web (http://www.genome.jp/tools/genies/). It is possible that the users can upload their own datasets and carry out the gene network inference using the methods presented in this chapter.

REFERENCES

1. H. Toh and K. Horimoto. Inference of a genetic network by a combined approach of cluster analysis and graphical Gaussian modeling. *Bioinformatics*, 18:287–297, 2002.

2. M. W. Covert, E. M. Knight, J. L. Reed, M. J. Herrgard, and B. O. Palsson. Integrating high-throughput and computational data elucidates bacterial networks. *Nature*, 429:92–96, 2004.

3. Z. Hu, J. Mellor, J. Wu, T. Yamada, D. Holloway, and C. Delisi. Visant: data-integrating visual framework for biological networks and modules. *Nucleic Acids Res.*, 33:W352–W357, 2005.

4. C. von Mering, M. Huynen, D. Jaeggi, S. Schmidt, P. Bork, and B. Snel. String: a database of predicted functional associations between proteins. *Nucleic Acids Res.*, 31:258–261, 2003.

5. M. Kanehisa, M. Araki, S. Goto, M. Hattori, M. Hirakawa, M. Itoh, T. Katayama, S. Kawashima, S. Okuda, T. Tokimatsu, and Y. Yamanishi. Kegg for linking genomes to life and the environment. *Nucleic Acids Res.*, 36(Database issue):D480–484, 2008.

6. I. M. Keseler, J. Collado-Vides, S. Gama-Castro, J. Ingraham, S. Paley, I. T. Paulsen, M. Peralta-Gil, and P. D. Karp. Ecocyc: a comprehensive database resource for *Escherichia coli*. *Nucleic Acids Res.*, 33(Database issue):D334–337, 2005.

7. P. D. Karp. Call for an enzyme genomics initiative. *Genome Biol.*, 5:401, 2004.

8. A. Osterman and R. Overbeek. Missing genes in metabolic pathways: a comparative genomics approach. *Curr. Opin. Chem. Biol.*, 7:238–251, 2003.

9. T. F. Smith and M. S. Waterman. Identification of common molecular subsequences. *J. Mol. Biol.*, 147:195–197, 1981.

10. S. F. Altschul, W. Gish, W. Miller, E. Myers, and D. J. Lipman. Basic local alignment search tool. *J. Mol. Biol.*, 215:403–410, 1990.

11. S. E. Brenner, C. Chothia, and T. J. P. Hubbard. Assessing sequence comparison methods with reliable structurally identified distant evolutionary relationships. *Proc. Natl. Acad. Sci. USA*, 95:6073–6078, 1998.

12. H. Bono, H. Ogata, S. Goto, and M. Kanehisa. Reconstruction of amino acid biosynthesis pathways from the complete genome sequence. *Genome Res.*, 8:203–210, 1998.

13. A. J. Barrett, C. R. Canter, C. Liebecq, G. P. Moss, W. Saenger, N. Sharon, K. F. Tipton, P. Vnetianer, and V. F. G. Vliegenthart. *Enzyme Nomenclature*. Academic Press, San Diego, CA, 1992.

14. R. Overbeek, M. Fonstein, M. D'Souza, G. D. Pusch, and N. Maltsev. The use of gene clusters to infer functional coupling. *Proc. Natl. Acad. Sci. USA*, 96:2896–2901, 1999.

15. A. J. Enright, I. Iliopoulos, N. C. Kyrpides, and C. A. Ouzounis. Protein interaction maps for complete genomes based on gene fusion events. *Nature*, 402:25–26, 1999.

16. M. Huynen, B. Snel, W. Lathe, and P. Bork. Predicting protein function by genomic context: quantitative evaluation and qualitative inferences. *Genome Res.*, 10:1204–1210, 2000.

17. P. Kharchenko, D. Vitkup, and G. M. Church. Filling gaps in a metabolic network using expression information. *Bioinformatics*, 20:449–453, 2004.

18. M. L. Green and P. D. Karp. A bayesian method for identifying missing enzymes in predicted metabolic pathway databases. *BMC Bioinform.*, 5:76, 2004.

19. Y. Yamanishi, J. P. Vert, and M. Kanehisa. Protein network inference from multiple genomic data: a supervised approach. *Bioinformatics*, 20(Suppl 1):i363–i370, 2004.

20. S. Goto, H. Bono, H. Ogata, W. Fujibuchi, T. Nishioka, K. Sato, and M. Kanehisa. Organizing and computing metabolic pathway data in terms of binary relations. *Pacific Symp. Biocomput.*, 2:175–186, 1996.

21. J.-P. Vert and Y. Yamanishi. Supervised graph inference. *Advances in Neural Information and Processing System*, 2005, pp. 1433–1440.

22. T. Kato, K. Tsuda, and K. Asai. Selective integration of multiple biological data for supervised network inference. *Bioinformatics*, 21:2488–2495, 2005.

23. Y. Yamanishi and J. P. Vert. Kernel matrix regression. In *Proceedings of the 12th International Conference on Applied Stochastic Models and Data Analysis*, 2007.

24. A. Ben-Hur and W. S. Noble. Kernel methods for predicting protein-protein interactions. *Bioinformatics*, 21(Suppl 1):i38–i46, 2005.

25. Y. Yamanishi, J. P. Vert, and M. Kanehisa. Supervised enzyme network inference from the integration of genomic data and chemical information. *Bioinformatics*, 21(Suppl 1): i468–i477, 2005.

26. P. T. Spellman, G. Sherlock, M. Q. Zhang, V. R. Iyer, K. Anders, M. B. Eisen, P. O. Brown, D. Botstein, and B. Futcher. Comprehensive identification of cell cycle-regulated genes of the yeast *Saccharomyces cerevisiae* by microarray hybridization. *Mol. Biol. Cell.*, 9:3273–3297, 1998.

27. M. B. Eisen, P. T. Spellman, O. B. Patrick, and D. Botstein. Cluster analysis and display of genome-wide expression patterns. *Proc. Natl Acad. Sci. USA*, 95:14863–14868, 1998.

28. W. K. Huh, J. V. Falvo, C. Gerke, A. S. Carroll, R. W. Howson, J. S. Weissman, and E. K. O'Shea. Global analysis of protein localization in budding yeast. *Nature*, 425:686–691, 2003.

29. M. Pellegrini, E. M. Marcotte, M. J. Thompson, D. Eisenberg, and T. O. Yeates. Assigning protein functions by comparative genome analysis: protein phylogenetic profiles. *Proc. Natl Acad. Sci. USA*, 96:4285–4288, 1999.

30. B. Schölkopf, K. Tsuda, and J. P. Vert. *Kernel Methods in Computational Biology*. MIT Press, 2004.

31. R. I. Kondor and J. Lafferty. Diffusion kernels on graphs and other discrete input. In *Proceedings of International Conference on Machine Learning (ICML 2002)*, 2002, pp. 315–322.

32. J.-P. Vert and M. Kanehisa. Graph-driven features extraction from microarray data using diffusion kernels and kernel cca. *Advances in Neural Information and Processing System*, 2003, 1425–1432.

33. B. Scholkopf, A. J. Smola, and K.-R. Muller. Nonlinear component analysis as a kernel eigenvalue problem. *Neural Comput.*, 10:1299–1319, 1998.

34. J. Shawe-Taylor and N. Cristianini. *Kernel Methods for Pattern Analysis*. Cambridge University Press, 2004.

35. S. Akaho. A kernel method for canonical correlation analysis. In *International Meeting of Psychometric Society (IMPS)*, 2001.

36. F. R. Bach and M. I. Jordan. Kernel independent component analysis. *J. Mach. Learning Res.*, 3:1–48, 2002.

37. G. Wahba. *Splines Models for Observational Data: Series in Applied Mathematics*. SIAM, Philadelphia, PA 1990.

38. F. Girosi, M. Jones, and T. Poggio. Regularization theory and neural networks architectures. *Neural Comput.*, 7:219–269, 1995.

39. Y. Yamanishi, J. P. Vert, A. Nakaya, and M. Kanehisa. Extraction of correlated gene clusters from multiple genomic data by generalized kernel canonical correlation analysis. *Bioinformatics*, 19 (Suppl 1):i323–i330, 2003.

40. M. Kotera, Y. Okuno, M. Hattori, S. Goto, and M. Kanehisa. Computational assignment of the ec numbers for genomic-scale analysis of enzymatic reactions. *J. Am. Chem. Soc.*, 126:16487–16498, 2004.

41. M. Gribskov and N. L. Robinson. Use of receiver operating characteristic (roc) analysis to evaluate sequence matching. *Comput. Chem.*, 20:25–33, 1996.

42. Y. Yamanishi, H. Mihara, M. Osaki, H. Muramatsu, N. Esaki, T. Sato, Y. Hizukuri, S. Goto, and M. Kanehisa. Prediction of missing enzyme genes in a bacterial metabolic network: reconstruction of the lysine-degradation pathway of pseudomonas aeruginosa. *FEBS J.*, 274:2262–2273, 2007.

43. S. Okamoto, Y. Yamanishi, S. Ehira, S. Kawashima, K. Tonomura, and M. Kanehisa. Prediction of nitrogen metabolism-related genes in anabaena by kernel-based network analysis. *Proteomics*, 7:900–909, 2006.

9

INTEGRATING ABDUCTION AND INDUCTION IN BIOLOGICAL INFERENCE USING CF-INDUCTION

Yoshitaka Yamamoto

Department of Informatics, The Graduate University for Advanced Studies, Chiyoda-ku, Tokyo, Japan

Katsumi Inoue

Department of Informatics, The Graduate University for Advanced Studies, Chiyoda-ku, Tokyo, Japan
National Institute of Informatics, Chiyoda-ku, Tokyo, Japan

Andrei Doncescu

LAAS-CNRS, Avenue du Colonel Roche, Toulouse, France

9.1 INTRODUCTION

The newly emerging field of systems biology has been developed toward precise understanding of the whole mechanism of living cells and organisms. Metabolism is one of the essential biological systems oriented in this field. It is organized in a complex network of interconnected reactions, called a metabolic pathway [1], and its whole behavior results from individual properties of reactions and global properties of the network organization. An important key for understanding this whole

Elements of Computational Systems Biology   Edited by Huma M. Lodhi and Stephen H. Muggleton
Copyright © 2010 John Wiley & Sons, Inc.

metabolic system lies in regulatory mechanism on activities of enzymes catalyzing chemical reactions involved in metabolism. Metabolic flux analysis (MFA) [2, 3] is a methodology for quantitatively analyzing those enzymatic activities. The flux of a reaction, defined by the rate of the reaction, can be regarded as an effective value for indicating the activity of a certain enzyme catalyzing the reaction. There are two kinds of approaches for computing a flux distribution over the reactions. The first approach uses kinetics of chemical reactions and models the time-series changes of fluxes [4]. These dynamic behaviors can be represented as coupled nonlinear differential equations. The second approach introduces a steady-state approximation to the first approach and reconstructs a prior set of equations into the linear formalization by considering the stoichiometry of the chemical reactions [5]. In general, the equations in both approaches cannot be analytically solved because there are a large number of intracellular metabolites involved in the chemical reactions. The fluxes of these reactions cannot be experimentally observed. Thus, the nonlinear equations are underdetermined. This problem is usually managed in such a way that the equations are numerically simulated *in silico* with several kinds of approximating constraints. Indeed, elementary mode analysis [6] and extreme pathways analysis [7] have been previously proposed in the second approach and introduce some relevant optimization functions with respect to the cellular growth maximization or the energy consumption minimization. However, even if these approximation methods are utilized, a large-scale metabolic pathway cannot be solved only with these methods due to huge computational costs.

Our long-term goal is to identify master reactions whose fluxes are relatively high in a metabolic pathway [8]. It is a crucial feature of flux distributions that reactions with fluxes spanning several orders of magnitude coexist under the same conditions [9]. Whereas most metabolic reactions have low fluxes, the overall behavior of metabolism is dominated by several reactions with very high fluxes. Therefore, we can divide activities of enzyme reactions into two kinds of states, that is, an activated state and a nonactivated state. If we could know which chemical reactions are in an activated or a nonactivated state, it would be helpful to solve the equations using the previously proposed MFA techniques. Because we can reconstruct a prior set of equations into more simplified ones as the nonactivated reactions with low fluxes can be ignored.

In this work, we focus on a logic-based approach that enables us to estimate possible reaction states in a metabolic pathway. Our approach introduces the logical viewpoint with respect to causal relations between states of the enzymatic activity influencing a reaction and concentration changes of metabolites involved in the reaction. Based on these causal relations, we quantitatively estimate possible states of enzyme reactions that logically explain the concentration changes of measurable metabolites obtained from experiments. Computation for this estimation is based on inductive logic programming (ILP) [10], which is a machine learning technique. ILP studies inductive learning with a relational representation in first-order predicate logic. The main task of ILP is to find hypotheses that logically explain a set of observations with respect to a background theory. In this ILP setting, we can obtain possible states of enzyme reactions as a hypothesis that logically explains the concentration changes of the measurable metabolites with a background theory. In this chapter, we use CF-induction [11] that is one of the ILP techniques for realizing this task.

CF-induction has a unique feature that can integrate inductive and abductive inferences, preserving its soundness and completeness for finding hypotheses in full clausal logic. While both inductive and abductive inferences are used to find hypotheses that account for given observations, their use in applications is quite different. Abduction is applied for finding specific explanations (causes) of observations obtained by using the current background theory. On the other hand, induction is applied for finding general rules that hold universally in the domain but are missing in the background theory. In our problem, an explanation obtained by abduction corresponds to an estimation of enzyme reaction states. If a background theory is complete with respect to the regulatory mechanism of enzymatic activities, then possible reaction states could be computed only using abduction. However, since background theories are incomplete, in general, it is necessary to find such missing rules that represent some unknown control mechanisms using induction. Therefore, it could be a crucial advantage if we could analyze metabolic pathways using both abductive and inductive inferences in CF-induction. We show how CF-induction can work for both estimating possible reaction states and completing missing causal relations using several examples.

The rest of this chapter is organized as follows. Section 9.2 first explains notions of metabolic pathways and a basic approach for MFA in brief and than introduces the logical model representing the causal relations between enzymatic activities and concentration changes of metabolites. Section 9.3 first introduces the ILP setting for representing the logical formalizations of these relations and than explains the procedure of CF-induction in order to show how it can realize both abduction and induction. Section 9.4 shows experimental results obtained by applications of CF-induction for estimation of possible reaction states from given observations. The examples include the metabolic network of pyruvate as well as simple topology of a metabolic pathway. Section 9.5 discusses related work. Section 9.6 concludes this paper.

9.2 LOGICAL MODELING OF METABOLIC FLUX DYNAMICS

9.2.1 Metabolic Pathways

Whereas cells have different morphologies and structures and the fact that their roles in the different organisms are varied, their basic functionality is the same. One of those basic activities of cells is to insure their own survival. Its whole activity can be summarized in the two points. First, cells need to find the necessary energy for its activity. This energy is mainly obtained by degradation of mineral or organic molecules. Second, cells need to manufacture simple molecules necessary for their survival. The former is called catabolism and the latter anabolism. These two great activities are regrouped under the name of metabolism and result from a great number of mechanisms and biochemical reactions. Most of these reactions, unfolding in a cell, are catalyzed by special molecules called enzymes. Such a large amount of data on

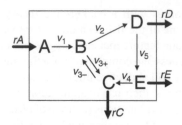

Figure 9.1   System of mass balance.

metabolism is represented as a network [1], called a metabolic pathway, and has been stored and maintained in a large-scale database such as KEGG [12].

Recently, the study of metabolic pathways has become increasingly important to exploit an integrated, systemic approach for simulating or optimizing cellular properties or phenotypes. One of these significant properties is a metabolic flux defined as the rate of a biochemical reaction, which can be very often utilized to improve production of metabolites in industry [2]. One basic but powerful approach to understand the steady-state fluxes is metabolite flux balancing, which is based on the stoichiometric model of the biochemical reactions. Figure 9.1 represents simple topology of a metabolic pathway in a cell, which consists of five metabolites A, B, C, D, and E, and six reactions, each of which connects two certain metabolites. Each flux is placed on the corresponding reaction in Figure 9.1. Although the concentrations of A, C, D, and E are experimentally measurable, the concentration of B cannot be measured. Hence, B is the intracellular metabolite. Based on the enzyme kinetics, the dynamic behavior of the flux of an enzyme reaction can be represented as the following differential equation:

$$\frac{dC_X}{dt} = v_{\text{in}} - v_{\text{out}} - \mu C_X, \tag{9.1}$$

where C_X is the concentration of a metabolite X, v_{in} (resp. v_{out}) is the sum of fluxes of reactions for producing (resp. consuming) X, and μC_X represents the growth rate of biomass in a cell. If all the metabolites are in the steady state, the left term of Eq. (9.1) must be zero, since there are no time-series changes of the concentrations, and also, it can be assumed that the dilution of components due to biomass growth (corresponding to the last term of Eq. (9.1)) is neglected [3]. This fact means that for each metabolite X, the fluxes consuming X are balanced with the ones producing X in the steady state. Metabolic flux balancing is based on this simple notion. For example, its balancing in Figure 9.1 can be represented as the following linear equations:

$$v_1 = rA, \qquad rD + v_5 = v_2, \qquad rE + v_4 = v_5,$$

$$v_2 + v_{3+} = v_{3-} + v_1, \qquad rC + v_{3-} = v_{3+} + v_4. \tag{9.2}$$

Then, we can analyze the flux distribution based on Eq. (9.2) with the measurable fluxes rA, rC, rD, and rE. In general, these equations cannot be deterministically solved as the number of unknown values such as $v_1, \ldots, v_5$ corresponding to the fluxes of intracellular enzyme reactions becomes larger than the number of known values corresponding to measurable fluxes. The previously proposed methods such as elementary mode analysis and extreme pathway analysis use optimization functions in order to solve the equations. Those introduced functions are usually constructed by assuming the cellular growth maximization or the energy consumption minimization. However, in the case of a large-scale metabolic pathway, we cannot solve the flux distribution with these approximation methods due to huge computational cost.

In this work, we propose a new approach that enables us to reduce the complexity of a given metabolic pathway. One essential feature of enzymatic activities is that all the activities are not necessarily on the same level. There exist enzymes whose activities are about 100 or 1000 times higher than other enzymes. This fact allows us to assume whether each enzyme reaction is in a relatively activated state or not. Then, if we could estimate which enzyme reactions are in an activated or a nonactivated state, we could simplify the prior metabolic pathway by ignoring those reactions in the nonactivated state, which are estimated to have low fluxes. The smaller the target pathway, the smaller the number of unknown values in the equations obtained from the pathway. It implies that the possibility of solving the equations with the previously proposed approximation methods. In our approach, we introduce a logical model that represents causal relations between enzyme reaction states and concentration changes of metabolites. Based on the logical model, we estimate possible states that can explain the observations, which are experimentally observed. In the following, we focus on those causal relations in enzyme reactions.

9.2.2   Regulation of Enzymatic Activities

The cellular metabolic system has a sophisticated mechanism for dynamically controlling the activities of enzymes to meet the needs of a cell. This regulatory mechanism can be represented as causal relations between enzymatic activities and concentration changing of metabolites. Here, we consider two simple metabolic pathways: First one consists of two reactions with three metabolites and second one consists of one reaction with two metabolites. Note that in the following figures we describe activated and nonactivated reactions as (back) circles and slashes over arrows corresponding to reactions, respectively. And also, a upward (resp. downward) arrow represents the increase (resp. decrease) in a metabolite concentration.

Figure 9.2 corresponds to the metabolic pathway consisting of three metabolites X, Y, and Z, and two reactions. Figure 9.2 shows that if the concentration of Y tends to be increasing at some time, provided that the state of enzyme reaction $Y \rightarrow X$ (resp. $X \rightarrow Z$) is in an activated (resp. nonactivated) state, then the concentration

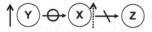

Figure 9.2   The first relation between reaction states and concentration changes of metabolites.

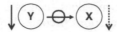

Figure 9.3   The second relation between reaction states and concentration changes of metabolites.

of X will also change to be increasing. This causal relation is a rational assumption based on Eq. (1.1). Assume that the increase in concentration of X is observed, which is denoted by a dotted arrow in the figures. Then, it will be possible to estimate the states of the concentration change of Y and two reactions, so that the estimated states cause this concentration change of X. One possible case is that the concentration of Y increases, the reaction $Y \rightarrow X$ is activated and the reaction $X \rightarrow Z$ is not activated. This is because X produced from Y cannot be consumed for generates Z.

Next, we consider Figure 9.3, which represents a metabolic pathway consisting of two metabolites X and Y, and one reaction. Figure 9.3 shows that even if the reaction $Y \rightarrow X$ is activated, the concentration of X must decrease as far as the concentration of Y decreases. Accordingly, if we observe that the concentration of X decreases, we can assume the concentration of Y decreases, and the reaction $Y \rightarrow X$ is activated as one possible case.

As we see in the above, consideration of these causal relations enables us to estimate possible reaction states that explain the concentration changes of measurable metabolites. Two causal relations shown in Figures 9.2 and 9.3 are not sufficient for explaining all the possible cases. In other words, there exist cases that we cannot estimate possible reaction states using these causal relations only. Although it will be possible to assume other causal relations *a priori*, however, it must be crucially difficult to enumerate the complete causal relations corresponding to the whole regulatory mechanism on enzymatic activities. This problem brings the necessity to complete the current causal relations for estimation in some cases. Hence, we need to simultaneously realize these two tasks, that is, an estimation of possible reaction states and completion of missing causal relations.

9.3   CF-INDUCTION

In this section, we explain the procedure of CF-induction to show how it can be used for solving our problem.

9.3.1   Inductive Logic Programming

First, we review the notion and terminology used for ILP [13] in order to represent our problem into the logical setting of ILP. A literal is an atom or the negation of an atom. A clause is the disjunction of literals and is often denoted by the set of literals. A clause $\{A_1, \ldots, A_m, \neg B_1, \ldots, \neg B_n\}$, where A_i and $\neg B_j$ are positive and negative atoms, respectively, is also written as $A_1 \vee \cdots \vee A_m \leftarrow B_1 \wedge \cdots \wedge B_n$. Any variable in a clause is assumed to be universally quantified at the front. A definite clause is a clause that contains only one positive literal. A negative clause is a clause that contains only negative literals. A Horn clause is a definite clause or a negative clause; otherwise it is non-Horn. The length of a clause is the number of literals it contains. A unit clause is a clause with length 1. A clausal theory is a finite set of clauses that can be identified with the conjunction of the clauses. A clausal theory is full if it contains non-Horn clauses. When Σ is a clausal theory, the complement of Σ, denoted by $\overline{\Sigma}$, is defined as a clausal theory obtained by translating $\neg\Sigma$ into CNF using a standard translation procedure [13].

Let S and T be clausal theories. S logically implies T, denoted as $S \models T$, if and only if for every interpretation I such that S is true under I, T is also true under I. We call $\models$ the entailment relation. For a clausal theory Σ, a consequence of Σ is a clause entailed by Σ. We denote by $Th(\Sigma)$ the set of all consequences of Σ.

Let C and D be two clauses. C subsumes D, denoted $C \succeq D$, if there is a substitution θ such that $C\theta \subseteq D$. C properly subsumes D if $C \succeq D$ but $D \not\succeq C$. For a clausal theory Σ, $\mu\Sigma$ denotes the set of clauses in Σ not properly subsumed by any clause in Σ.

In the logical setting of ILP, a background theory and observations are given as inputs and represented as clausal theories. Let B and E be a background theory and observations, respectively. Then, the task of ILP [11] is to find a clausal theory H such that

$$B \wedge H \models E, \tag{9.3}$$

where $B \wedge H$ is consistent. We call such a clausal theory H as a hypothesis with respect to B and E. If no confusion arises, a "hypothesis with respect to B and E" will simply be called a "hypothesis." If H consists of only literals, we especially call H as an abductive explanation.

EXAMPLE 9.1

Assume the following background theory B and observations E:

$$B = \{linked\_to(a, b),$$
$$can\_reach(X, Y) \leftarrow can\_reach(X, Z) \wedge linked\_to(Z, Y)\}.$$
$$E = \{can\_reach(a, c)\}.$$

We denote capital and small letters in the formulas as variables and particular objects, respectively. B is represented with the following two predicates: The predicate $linked\_to(X, Y)$ means that a node X is directly linked to a node Y, and the predicate $can\_reach(X, Y)$ means that a node X can reach a node Y, that is, there is a path from X to Y. B consists of the information on the connection of a network and an incomplete definition of the predicate $can\_reach(X, Y)$. Since only B cannot logically explain the observations E, we need some hypotheses that complete the prior background theory. Suppose the following clausal theory:

$$H_1 = \{can\_reach(a, b), linked\_to(b, c)\}.$$

Then, H_1 is an abductive explanation since $B \wedge H_1 \models E$, $B \wedge H_1$ is consistent and H_1 consists of literals. Next, suppose the following clausal theory H_2:

$$H_2 = \{can\_reach(X, Y) \leftarrow linked\_to(X, Y), linked\_to(b, c)\}.$$

H_2 is also a hypothesis, since $B \wedge H_2 \models E$ and $B \wedge H_2$ is consistent. Whereas both H_1 and H_2 imply an extensional linkage from the node b to the node c, H_2 completes a missing definition of the predicate $can\_reach(X, Y)$.

Given incomplete rules in the prior background theory such as the one in this example, we need not only abductive inference but also inductive inference. Our problem also needs two types of inferences. The abductive problem is to estimate possible reaction states that logically explain the observations with the prior background theory. The inductive problem is to find causal rules that are missing in the background theory.

We represent our problem in the ILP setting. The metabolic pathway topology in Figure 9.1 can be represented as the following clausal theory T consisting of facts:

$$T = \{reac(a, b), reac(b, d), reac(d, e), reac(e, c), reac(b, c), reac(c, b)\},$$

where the literal $reac(X, Y)$ means that there is a reaction between the substrate X and the product Y. Along with the logical representation of topology, we formalize the causal relations in Figures 9.2 and 9.3 as the following two clauses (9.4) and (9.5), respectively:

$$con(X, up) \leftarrow reac(Y, X) \wedge reac(X, Z)$$
$$\wedge \, con(Y, up) \wedge act(Y, X) \wedge \neg act(X, Z), \tag{9.4}$$

$$con(X, down) \leftarrow reac(Y, X)$$
$$\wedge \, con(Y, down) \wedge act(Y, X), \tag{9.5}$$

where the literal $con(X, up)$ (resp. $con(X, down)$) means that the concentration of the metabolite X increases (resp. decreases), and the literal $act(X, Y)$ means that the reaction $X \rightarrow Y$ is activated. Note that both (9.4) and (9.5) are non-Horn clauses.

In the ILP setting of our problem, the background theory B consists of the above logical formulae. Along with B, observations E are given as concentration changes of measurable metabolites obtained from experimental results. Using these two inputs B and E, we need to compute hypotheses that not only estimate possible reaction states but also complete missing causal relations in B. In this chapter, we use CF-induction for these two tasks, that is, estimation and completion, which is one of the ILP techniques and can realize both abductive and inductive inferences.

9.3.2   Abduction and Induction in CF-induction

Computation of CF-induction is based on inverse entailment (IE) [14]. By the principle of IE, Eq. (9.3) is logically equivalent to find a consistent hypothesis H such that

$$B \wedge \neg E \models \neg H. \tag{9.6}$$

IE is the basis of many successful Horn clause systems such as Progol [14, 15], which have been used in real application domains.

Recently, IE methods have been developed for full clausal theories to enable the solution of more complex problems in richer knowledge representation formalisms. One such method is CF-induction [11], which has two important benefits: Unlike some related systems, such as FC-HAIL [16], CF-induction is complete for finding full clausal hypotheses; and unlike other related systems, such as the residue procedure [17], CF-induction can exploit language bias to focus the procedure on some relevant part of the search space specified by the user.

The principle of CF-induction is based on the notion of characteristic clauses, which represents "interesting" consequences of a given problem for users [18]. Each characteristic clause is constructed over a subvocabulary of the representation language called a production field. A production field $\mathcal{P}$ is defined as a pair $\langle \mathbf{L}, Cond \rangle$, where $\mathbf{L}$ is a set of literals closed under instantiation and $Cond$ is a certain condition to be satisfied, for example, the maximum length of clauses, the maximum depth of terms, and so on. When $Cond$ is not specified, $\mathcal{P}$ is simply denoted as $\langle \mathbf{L} \rangle$. A clause C belongs to $\mathcal{P} = \langle \mathbf{L}, Cond \rangle$ if every literal in C belongs to $\mathbf{L}$ and C satisfies $Cond$. For a set Σ of clauses, the set of consequences of Σ belonging to $\mathcal{P}$ is denoted $Th_{\mathcal{P}}(\Sigma)$. Then, the characteristic clauses of Σ with respect to $\mathcal{P}$ are defined as:

$$Carc(\Sigma, \mathcal{P}) = \mu Th_{\mathcal{P}}(\Sigma).$$

Note that $Carc(\Sigma, \mathcal{P})$ can, in general, include tautological clauses [18].

When a new clause F is added to a clausal theory, some consequences are newly derived with this additional information. The set of such clauses that belong to the production field is called new characteristic clauses. Formally, the new characteristic clauses of F with respect to Σ and $\mathcal{P}$ are defined as:

$$NewCarc(\Sigma, F, \mathcal{P}) = Carc(\Sigma \cup \{F\}, \mathcal{P}) - Carc(\Sigma, \mathcal{P}).$$

In the following, we assume the production field $\mathcal{P} = \langle \mathbf{L}, max\_length \rangle$, where $\mathbf{L}$ is a set of literals reflecting an inductive bias whose literals are the negations of those literals we wish to allow in hypothesis clauses and max_length is the maximum length of clauses in the complements of those hypotheses we wish to find. When no inductive bias and conditions are considered, $\mathcal{P}$ is just set to $\langle \mathcal{L} \rangle$, where $\mathcal{L}$ is the set of all literals in the first-order language. We say H is a hypothesis with respect to B, E, and $\mathcal{P}$ if and only if H is a hypothesis with respect to B and E and satisfies the following two conditions:

(1) For every literal L appearing in H, its complement $\overline{L}$ is in **L**.
(2) The maximum length of the clauses in the complement of H is less than or equal to *max_length*.

Then, it holds that for any hypothesis H with respect to B, E, and $\mathcal{P}$,

$$B \wedge \overline{E} \models Carc(B \wedge \overline{E}, \mathcal{P}) \models \neg H; \qquad (9.7)$$

$$B \models Carc(B, \mathcal{P}) \not\models \neg H. \qquad (9.8)$$

The two formulae above follow from the principle of IE and the definition of characteristic clauses. In particular, Formula (9.7) implies that we can use characteristic clauses to construct intermediate bridge formulae for IE. Formula (9.8) ensures the consistency of the hypothesis and background theory. As explained in Inoue [11], this can always be ensured by including at least one clause from $NewCarc(B, \overline{E}, \mathcal{P})$ in an intermediate bridge formula [11], which is defined as a clausal theory satisfying the following conditions:

(1) Each clause $C_i \in CC$ is an instance of a clause in $Carc(B \wedge \overline{E}, \mathcal{P})$.
(2) At least one $C_i \in CC$ is an instance of a clause from $NewCarc(B, \overline{E}, \mathcal{P})$.

Let B, E be clausal theories and $\mathcal{P}$ be a production field. Then, it is known that for any hypothesis H with respect to B, E, and $\mathcal{P}$, there exists a bridge formula CC with respect to B, E, and $\mathcal{P}$ such that $H \models \neg CC$ [11].

This fact shows that any hypothesis can be computed by constructing and generalizing the negation $\neg CC$ of a set of characteristic clauses CC. In CF-induction, a bridge formula CC is first selected. Then, a clausal theory F is obtained by skolemizing $\neg CC$ and translating it to CNF. Finally, H is obtained by applying a series of generalizers to F under the constraint that $B \wedge H$ is consistent. Many such generalizers have been proposed such as reverse skolemization [19] (converting Skolem constants/functions to existentially quantified variables), anti-instantiation (replacing ground subterms with variables), anti-weakening (adding some clauses), anti-subsumption (dropping some literals from a clause), inverse resolution [20] (applying the inverse of the resolution principle), and Plotkin's least generalization [21]. Using those generalizers, CF-induction computes hypotheses in the following procedure:

Step 1. Compute $Carc(B \wedge \overline{E}, \mathcal{P})$;
Step 2. Construct a bridge formula CC;
Step 3. Convert $\neg CC$ into the CNF formula F;
Step 4. H is obtained by a generalizer to F under the constraint that $B \wedge H$ is consistent.

EXAMPLE 9.2

Recall Example 9.1. Let the background theory B and observations E be the same as in Example 9.1. We show how CF-induction computes the hypotheses H_1 and H_2 in Example 9.1. Suppose the following production field $\mathcal{P}$:

$$\mathcal{P} = \langle \{linked\_to(X, Y), \neg linked\_to(X, Y), \neg can\_reach(X, Y)\},$$
$$max\_length = 2 \rangle.$$

Then, $NewCarc(B, \overline{E}, \mathcal{P})$ and $Carc(B \wedge \overline{E}, \mathcal{P})$ are as follows:

$$NewCarc(B, \overline{E}, \mathcal{P}) = \{\neg can\_reach(a, c),$$
$$\leftarrow can\_reach(a, Z) \wedge linked\_to(Z, c),$$
$$\leftarrow can\_reach(a, a) \wedge linked\_to(b, c)\},$$
$$Carc(B \wedge \overline{E}, \mathcal{P}) = \{linked\_to(a, b)\} \cup NewCarc(B, \overline{E}, \mathcal{P}) \cup Taut,$$

where $Taut$ denotes the tautological clauses in $Carc(B \wedge \overline{E}, \mathcal{P})$. Let CC_1 be the clausal theory $\{\leftarrow can\_reach(a, b) \wedge linked\_to(b, c)\}$. Since the clause in CC_1 is an instance of the clause $\leftarrow can\_reach(a, Z) \wedge linked\_to(b, Z)$ in $NewCarc(B, \overline{E}, \mathcal{P})$, CC_1 is a bridge formula. The clausal theory F_1 obtained by converting $\neg CC_1$ into the CNF formula is

$$\{can\_reach(a, b), linked\_to(b, c)\}.$$

F_1 is the same as the abductive explanation H_1 in Example 9.1. Since $B \wedge F_1 \models E$ and $B \wedge F_1$ are consistent, F_1 is a hypothesis with respect to B and E. Note that the complement of each literal in F_1 belongs to $\mathcal{P}$ and the length of the clause in $\overline{F_1}$ is 2, which is equal to max_length in $\mathcal{P}$. Hence, F_1 is a hypothesis with respect to B, E, and $\mathcal{P}$.

Next, let CC_2 be the following clausal theory:

$$\{\leftarrow can\_reach(a, b) \wedge linked\_to(b, c), linked\_to(a, b)\}.$$

Since CC_2 includes an instance of a clause in $NewCarc(B, \overline{E}, \mathcal{P})$, CC_2 is also a bridge formula. The clausal theory F_2 obtained by converting $\neg CC_2$ into the CNF formula is as follows:

$$F_2 = \{can\_reach(a, b) \leftarrow linked\_to(a, b), \tag{9.9}$$
$$linked\_to(b, c) \leftarrow linked\_to(a, b)\}. \tag{9.10}$$

Assume that we apply both a dropping and an anti-instantiation generalizers in such a way that the terms a and b appearing in the clause (9.9) are replaced by variables X

and Y, respectively, and also the literal $linked\_to(a, b)$ in the clause (9.10) is dropped. Then, the following clausal theory F_2' is constructed:

$$F_2' = \{can\_reach(X, Y) \leftarrow linked\_to(X, Y), linked\_to(b, c)\}.$$

Since $B \land F_2' \models E$ and $B \land F_2'$ are consistent, F_2' is a hypothesis with respect to B and E. Note that the complement of each literal in F_2' belongs to $\mathcal{P}$ and the maximum length of the clauses in $\overline{F_2'}$ is 2, which is equal to max_length in $\mathcal{P}$. Hence, F_2' is also a hypothesis with respect to B, E, and $\mathcal{P}$. F_2' is the same as H_2 completing a missing definition of the predicate $can\_reach(X, Y)$.

As we see in the above example, abductive explanations can be computed without any applications of generalizers in CF-induction. Let H be an abductive explanation with respect to a background theory B, observations E, and a production field $\mathcal{P}$. H is minimal if no proper subconjunction H' of H satisfies $B \land H' \models E$. The set of minimal abductive explanations with respect to B, E, and $\mathcal{P}$ is the set of formulas, each of which is the negation of a clause in $NewCarc(B, \overline{E}, \mathcal{P})$ [18].

In contrast with abductive computation, computing inductive hypotheses in CF-induction needs some generalizers in CF-induction when they include variables.

9.4 EXPERIMENTS

In this section, we show what kinds of hypotheses the current implementation of CF-induction can find using two examples. The simple pathway in the first example corresponds to Figure 9.1, and the metabolic pathway of pyruvate is used in the second example.

9.4.1 A Simple Pathway

Define a background theory B as follows:

$$B = T \cup \{con(a, up), (9.4), (9.5),$$
$$\leftarrow con(X, up) \land con(X, down)\}, \tag{9.11}$$

where the rule (9.11) means that concentrations of any metabolites cannot be up and down at the same time. Note here that $con(a, up)$ can be regarded as an input signal to the metabolic system. So it is put into B. In the following figures, concentration changes, which are observed and included in B, are represented as dotted bold arrows. Here, we assume the measurable concentration changes as follows:

$$E = \{con(d, up), con(c, down), con(e, down)\}.$$

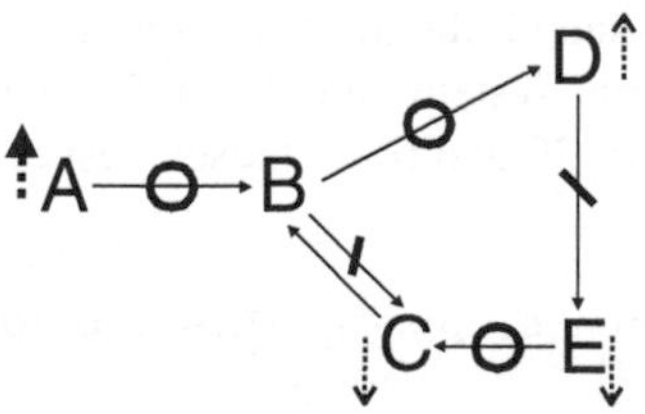

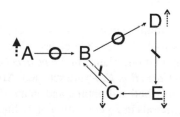

Figure 9.4   The first hypothesis H_1.

As a hypothesis with respect to B and E, the following clausal theory is considered:

$$H_1 = \{con(e, down) \leftarrow \neg act(d, e) \wedge act(e, c),$$

$$act(a, b), act(e, c), act(b, d), \neg act(b, c), \neg act(d, e)\}.$$

Figure 9.4 shows the reaction states in H_1. According to H_1, although the reactions $A \to B$, $B \to D$, and $E \to C$ are activated, the reactions $B \to C$ and $D \to E$ are not activated. This estimation of reaction states is realized using abduction. On the other hand, we cannot explain the reason why the concentration of E decreases only with abductive hypotheses. However, CF-induction outputs a new rule worth considering as an answer, that is, "the concentration of E decreases if the reaction $D \to E$ is not activated and the reaction $E \to C$ is activated."

As another hypothesis, the following clausal theory can also be considered:

$$H_2 = \{con(X, down) \leftarrow \neg act(Y, X) \wedge con(Y, up),$$

$$act(a, b), act(b, d), \neg act(b, c), \neg act(d, e)\}.$$

Figure 9.5 shows the states of reactions in H_2. Compared with H_1, the rule for explaining the concentration change of E is more general, and also H_2 does not say whether the reaction E–C is activated or not. These two hypotheses can be computed using the current implementation of CF-induction. Let a production field $\mathcal{P}$ be as follows:

$$\mathcal{P} = \langle\{con(X, Y), \neg con(X, Y), \neg act(X, Y), act(X, Y)\},$$

$$max\_length = 6\rangle.$$

Figure 9.5   The second hypothesis H_2.

Here, we set the maximum search depth for computing the characteristic clauses in CF-induction as 4. The current system outputs the following $NewCarc(B, \overline{E}, \mathcal{P})$ and $Carc(B \wedge \overline{E}, \mathcal{P})$ consisting of 30 and four clauses, respectively:

```
NewCarc:
(1)[-con(c,down),-con(b,up),-act(b,d),act(d,e),-con(e,down)]
                        ...
(9)[-con(e,down),-act(e,c),-act(a,b),act(b,c),-act(b,d),act(d,e)]
                        ...
(30)[-con(c,down),-con(d,up),-con(e,down)]

 Carc:
(1)[-con(_0,up),-con(_0,down)]  (2)[con(a,up)]
(3)[con(_0,_1),-con(_0,_1)]  (4)[-act(_0,_1),act(_0,_1)]
```

We construct a bridge formula CC_1 in such a way that both instances of the fourth clause in $Carc(B \wedge \overline{E}, \mathcal{P})$ and the ninth clause in $NewCarc(B, \overline{E}, \mathcal{P})$ are manually selected.

```
CC:[
[-con(e,down),-act(e,c),-act(a,b),act(b,c),-act(b,d),act(d,e)],
[-act(d,e),act(d,e)],  [-act(e,c),act(e,c)]]
```

The system automatically computes the clausal theory F_1 obtained by converting $\neg CC_1$ into the CNF formula.

```
-CC:[
[con(e,down),act(d, e),-act(e, c)],  [act(e,c),act(d,e)],
[act(a,b),act(d,e),-act(e,c)],  [-act(b,c),act(d,e),-act(e,c)],
[act(b,d),act(d,e),-act(e,c)],  [-act(d,e),act(e,c)],
[-act(d,e),-act(e,c)]]
```

Third, we apply a dropping generalizer to F_1 in such a way that relevant nine literals in F_1 consisting of 18 literals are dropped. Then, the clausal theory corresponding to H_1 is constructed. Last, the system performs the consistency checking of H_1. Since $H_1 \wedge B$ is consistent, it successfully outputs H_1.

```
Hypothesis:[
[con(e,down),act(d,e),-act(e,c)],  [act(e,c)],
[act(a,b)],  [-act(b,c)],
[act(b,d)],  [-act(d,e)]]
```

Next, we change the maximum search depth to 6. Then, $NewCarc(B, \overline{E}, \mathcal{P})$ (resp. $Carc(B \wedge \overline{E}, \mathcal{P})$) increases to 137 (resp. 84) clauses. We construct another bridge formula CC_2 in such a way that one clause in $NewCarc(B, \overline{E}, \mathcal{P})$, two clauses, and two instances of a clause in $Carc(B \wedge \overline{E}, \mathcal{P})$ are selected. After converting $\neg CC_2$ into the CNF formula F_2, we apply both a dropping and an anti-instantiation generalizers to F_2 in such a way that 15 literals in F_2 consisting of 27 literals are dropped and four ground terms are replaced by variables. Then, the clausal theory corresponding to H_2 is constructed.

Table 9.1   Performance of abductive explanations in CF-induction

	Test data ($depth = 6$, $max\_length = 6$)		
	$\{con(c, down)\}$	$\{con(d, up)\}$	$\{con(e, down)\}$
N_H	21	22	22
N_P	8	2	7
Ratio (%)	38	9	32
Time (ms)	6915	11,360	10,751

Both H_1 and H_2 need inductive inference to be constructed. In general, it becomes necessary to apply inductive inference for completing missing causal relations in our problem. Along with this completion task, inductive inference will be necessary to find efficient hypotheses that have high predictive accuracy to unknown observations. Table 9.1 shows the performance of abductive explanations obtained by CF-induction. As we mentioned in the previous section, each minimal abductive explanation is the negation of a clause in $NewCarc(B, \overline{E}, \mathcal{P})$. Then, we evaluate the performance of these minimal abductive explanations based on a leave-one-out strategy [22]. First, we select one clause C in observations E as a test example. Second, for each clause D in $NewCarc(B, \overline{E - \{C\}}, \mathcal{P})$, we check whether or not $\overline{D}$ is consistent with B and $B \wedge \overline{D} \models \{C\}$, that is, $\overline{D}$ can also explain the test example $\{C\}$. N_H and N_P in Table 9.1 denote the number of minimal abductive explanations with respect to B, $E - \{C\}$, and $\mathcal{P}$ and the number of those explanations that can also explain the test example $\{C\}$. In this experiment, CF-induction can actually compute such abductive explanations that accurately predict an unseen observation (test example) for each case. However, we notice that the ratio of N_P to N_H is not so high in Table 9.1. It shows that few explanations may succeed with the prediction of an unseen example, whereas most of them cannot. This fact, thus, makes both abductive and inductive inferences necessary for improving the predictive accuracy of hypotheses.

9.4.2   A Metabolic Pathway of Pyruvate

Next, we consider the metabolic pathway of pyruvate (see Figure 9.6). The logical representation of topology in Figure 9.6 is as follows:

$$T' = \{terminal(ethanol), reac(pyruvate, acetylcoa),$$

$$reac(pyruvate, acetaldehyde), reac(glucose, glucosep),$$

$$reac(glucosep, pyruvate), reac(acetaldehyde, acetate),$$

$$reac(acetate, acetylcoa), reac(acetaldehyde, ethanol)\},$$

where the predicate $terminal(X)$ means that there is no reaction where X is consumed. If the metabolite X is terminated and the reaction, where X is produced, is activated, then the concentration of X must increase. However, this consequence cannot be derived only using the previous causal rule (9.4), which concerns with the concentration

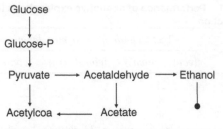

Figure 9.6   Metabolic pathway of pyruvate.

increase of a metabolite. Thus, we construct the following new causal rules obtained by incorporating the concept of "*terminal*" with the rule (9.4):

$$blocked(X) \leftarrow reac(X, Z) \wedge \neg act(X, Z), \tag{9.12}$$

$$blocked(X) \leftarrow terminal(X), \tag{9.13}$$

$$con(X, up) \leftarrow reac(Y, X) \wedge act(Y, X) \wedge blocked(X), \tag{9.14}$$

where the predicate $blocked(X)$ means that metabolite X cannot be consumed. Define a background theory B as follows:

$$B = T' \cup \{(9.12), (9.13), (9.14), con(glucose, up)\}.$$

Next, we input the following observations E:

$$E = \{con(ethanol, up), con(pyruvate, up)\}.$$

Then, the following clausal theories H_3 and H_4 are considerable as hypotheses with respect to B and E.

$$H_3 = \{act(glucosep, pyruvate),$$

$$\neg act(pyruvate, acetylcoa), act(acetaldehyde, ethanol)\}.$$

$$H_4 = \{con(Y, up) \leftarrow act(X, Y) \wedge con(X, up),$$

$$act(glucosep, pyruvate), act(acetaldehyde, ethanol),$$

$$act(pyruvate, acetaldehyde), act(glucose, glucosep)\}.$$

Figures 9.7 and 9.8 show the states of reactions in H_3 and H_4, respectively. Compared with H_3, H_4 includes a new general rule concerning the mechanism of how concentrations of metabolites increase. Both H_3 and H_4 can be generated using CF-induction. Let a production field $\mathcal{P}$ be as follows:

$$\mathcal{P} = \langle \{con(X, Y), \neg con(X, Y), \neg act(X, Y), act(X, Y)\},$$

$$max\_length = 6 \rangle.$$

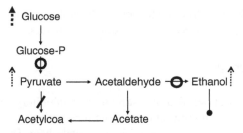

Figure 9.7   The first hypothesis H_3.

We set the maximum search depth as 4. Then, the system of CF-induction computes $NewCarc(B, \overline{E}, \mathcal{P})$ consisting of six clauses and $Carc(B \wedge \overline{E}, \mathcal{P})$ consisting of three clauses as follows:

```
NewCarc:
(1)[-act(acetaldehyde,ethanol),-con(pyruvate,up)]
(2)[-con(ethanol,up),-act(glucosep,pyruvate),
    act(pyruvate,acetylcoa)]
(3)[-con(ethanol,up),-act(glucosep,pyruvate),
    act(pyruvate,acetaldehyde)]
(4)[-act(acetaldehyde,ethanol),-act(glucosep,pyruvate),
    act(pyruvate,acetylcoa)]
(5)[-act(acetaldehyde,ethanol),-act(glucosep,pyruvate),
    act(pyruvate,acetaldehyde)]
(6)[-con(ethanol,up),-con(pyruvate,up)]

Carc:
(1)[con(glucose,up)]
(2)[-act(_0,_1),act(_0,_1)]
(3)[con(_0,_1),-con(_0,_1)]
```

Since H_3 is an abductive explanation, there exists a clause C in $NewCarc(B, \overline{E}, \mathcal{P})$ such that $\neg C$ is a subconjunction of H_3. Indeed, the fourth clause in $NewCarc(B, \overline{E}, \mathcal{P})$ is the one corresponding to $\neg H_3$. Hence, a bridge formula for finding H_3 can be constructed with only one clause. Moreover, no generalizers are necessary to generate H_3. On the other hand, a bridge formula for finding H_4 can be constructed with the first and fifth clauses in $NewCarc(B, \overline{E}, \mathcal{P})$, and the first clause, four instances of the second clause, and one instance of the third clause in

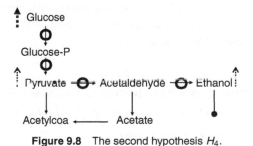

Figure 9.8   The second hypothesis H_4.

$Carc(B \wedge \overline{E}, \mathcal{P})$. After constructing this bridge formula, CF-induction can output H_4 using both a dropping and an anti-instantiation generalizers.

9.5   RELATED WORK

Tamaddoni-Nezhad et al. studied an estimation of inhibitory effects on metabolic pathways using ILP [23]. Inhibition of enzyme functions plays an important role on dynamically controlling enzymatic activities on metabolism. They have also introduced the logical modeling of metabolic pathways and firstly showed the possibility of application of ILP to qualitatively analyze metabolic pathways with their logical model on inhibitory effects to concentration changes of metabolites. Here, we refer to three points as the difference compared with their work.

The first point is the difference of main goal that we try to solve using ILP. Our long-term goal is a more precise modeling of the flux distribution corresponding to dynamics on enzymatic activities. Previously proposed techniques in MFA that quantitatively analyze the flux distribution can have the limitation of those applications to a large-scale metabolic pathway. Using ILP, we can estimate possible reaction states in metabolic pathways, which enable us to reconstruct the prior pathway into more simplified one by removing enzyme reactions with low fluxes. In other words, we intend to reduce the complexity of a given metabolic pathway. In contrast, they have focused on the inhibitory effects of particular toxins affected to objects to be examined, which are used as drugs.

The second point is the difference of ILP techniques applied to problems. They have used Progol5.0 [15], which is one of the successful ILP systems and can also compute both inductive and abductive hypotheses. Compared with Progol5.0, CF-induction preserves the soundness and completeness for finding hypotheses and can use not only Horn but also non-Horn clauses in the knowledge representation formalisms. Tamaddoni-Nezhad et al. [23] have evaluated the predictive accuracy of both abductive explanations and inductive hypotheses obtained by Progol5.0 in the metabolic pathway consisting of 76 enzyme reactions and 31 metabolites. The dataset of this metabolic pathway is available on their Web site. Then, it will be interesting to evaluate the hypotheses obtained by CF-induction using the dataset. Note that in an initial experiment with this dataset, CF-induction computes 66 abductive explanations, including the unique output of Progol5.0 when we set the maximum search depth as 5 and put the maximum length of a production field as 15. The following example is concerning an inductive hypothesis introduced in Tamaddoni-Nezhad et al. [23]. We show how CF-induction can compute the same inductive hypothesis as the one obtained by Progol5.0 using the next example.

EXAMPLE 9.3

Define a background theory B and an observation E to be as follows:

$$B = \{con(X, up) \leftarrow reac(X, Y, Z) \wedge inh(X, Y, Z),$$
$$reac(s, e, p), class(e, c)\},$$
$$E = con(s, up).$$

The predicate $reac(X, Y, Z)$ includes the new term Y, which denotes an enzyme catalyzing the reaction $X \rightarrow Z$. The predicate $inh(X, Y, Z)$ means that the reaction between a substrate X and a product Z, catalyzed by an enzyme Y, is inhibited. Note that those reactions that are inhibited might be regarded as nonactivated reactions. However, the activated state does not necessarily always correspond to the noninhibited state because there are other factors that cause the nonactivated state. We, thus, distinguish the inhibited state from the nonactivated state. Along with the predicate $inh(X, Y, Z)$, the predicate $class(X, Y)$ is newly introduced. It means that an enzyme X belongs to an enzyme class Y.

Tamaddoni-Nezhad et al. [23] introduced the following inductive hypothesis H:

$$H = inh(s, X, p) \leftarrow class(X, c).$$

Suppose the following production field:

$$\mathcal{P} = \langle \{inh(X, Y, Z), \neg inh(X, Y, Z), class(X, Y)\} \rangle.$$

$NewCarc(B, \overline{E}, \mathcal{P})$ and $Carc(B \wedge \overline{E}, \mathcal{P})$ are computed as follows:

$$NewCarc(B, \overline{E}, \mathcal{P}) = \{\neg inh(s, e, p), \neg con(s, up)\},$$

$$Carc(B \wedge \overline{E}, \mathcal{P}) = \{class(e, c), \neg inh(s, e, p)\}.$$

Let a bridge formula CC be the clausal theory $\{\neg inh(s, e, p), class(e, c)\}$. Then, the clausal theory F is obtained by translating $\neg CC$ into CNF as follows:

$$F = inh(s, e, p) \leftarrow class(e, c).$$

If we apply an anti-instantiation generalizer to F in such a way that the ground term e appearing in F is replaced with the variable X, then the hypothesis H can be generated.

The process of computing the above inductive hypothesis can be sketched in Figure 9.9. This hypothesis is constructed using an abductive explanation. Hence, it is necessary to generate abductive explanations in advance for constructing inductive hypotheses. Indeed, Progol5.0 first computes an abductive explanation and second finds the inductive hypothesis using the abductive explanation. In other words, Progol5.0 performs abduction and induction processes, step by step. On the other hand,

---

B: $con(X, up) \leftarrow reac(X, Y, Z) \wedge inh(X, Y, Z), \quad reac(s, e, p), \quad class(e, c)$

E: $con(s, up)$

_____

(abduction) $\quad inh(s, e, p)$

_____

(induction) $\qquad\qquad inh(s, X, p) \leftarrow class(X, c)$

Figure 9.9 Integrating abduction and induction for finding hypotheses.

CF-induction can realize them with one process. This difference of those mechanisms for integrating abduction and induction is the last and crucial point. In our problem setting, we need to not only estimate possible reaction states but also complete missing causal relations in the prior background. CF-induction can realize these two tasks simultaneously using both abduction and induction.

There are several works that have been studied on applications of ILP techniques to biology [24, 25]. King et al. showed that hypothesis-finding techniques can help to reduce the experimental costs for predicting the functions of genes in their project called robot scientist [24]. Besides, Zupan et al. have developed a system based on abduction, which enables us to find new relations from experimental genetic data for completing the prior genetic networks [25].

9.6 CONCLUSION AND FUTURE WORK

We have studied a logic-based method for estimating possible states of enzyme reactions. Since this method can help us to understand which enzyme reactions are activated, it can be potentially used in MFA in that it is important for optimizing or improving production and identifying master reactions that have high fluxes. In this work, we have showed how CF-induction can realize not only estimation of possible reaction states but also completion of the current causal relations.

On the other hand, it is still far from our long-term goal that we construct a new technique integrating our logic-based analysis with previously proposed MFA methods. As an important work, we point out the necessity of realizing an efficient search algorithm, which enables CF-induction to automatically find relevant hypotheses. Although CF-induction has several theoretical merits, it cannot necessarily be accomplished as a sophisticated inductive system that automatically computes the hypotheses users wish to obtain. We intend to address this issue by considering the notion of compression that other ILP systems have introduced. Other important future work is the evaluation of the estimated reaction states that CF-induction computes. In our current project [8], we intend to use statistical relational leaning techniques to evaluate those estimations that are computed by CF-induction. Besides, it will be interesting that we actually compute the flux distribution from the simplified equations constructed by removing the estimated reactions with low fluxes and compare it with the result of other MFA techniques.

ACKNOWLEDGMENTS

This research is in part supported by both the Japan Science and Technology Agency (JST) and Centre National de la Recherche Scientifique (CNRS, France) under the 2007–2009 Strategic Japanese-French Cooperative Program "Knowledge-based Discovery in Systems Biology," and by 2008–2011 JSPS Grant-in-Aid Scientific Research (A) (No. 20240016). The authors would like to thank the anonymous reviewers for giving us useful and constructive comments. We are grateful to Professor

Hidetomo Nabeshima for a lot of help at implementing CF-induction. We would also like to present our sincere thanks to Professors Taisuke Sato and Yoshitaka Kameya for useful discussions and comments on the topics in this paper.

REFERENCES

1. Y. Deville, D. Gilbert, J. van Helden, and S. J. Wodak. An overview of data models for the analysis of biochemical pathways. *Brief. Bioinform.*, 4:246–259, 2003.

2. G. Stephanopoulos, A. Aristidou, and J. Nielsen. *Metabolic Engineering*, Academic Press, 1998.

3. K. Schugerl and K. H. Bellgardt. *Bioreaction Engineering: Modeling and Control*, Springer, 2000.

4. P. Mendes and D. B. Kell. Non-linear optimization of biochemical pathways: applications to metabolic engineering and parameter estimation. *Bioinformatics*, 14:869–883, 1998.

5. A. Varma and B. O. Palsson. Metabolic flux balancing: basic concepts, scientific and practical use. *Nat. Biotechnol.*, 12:994–998, 1994.

6. S. Schuster, D. A. Fell, and T. Dandekar. A general definition of metabolic pathways useful for systematic organization and analysis of complex metabolic networks. *Nat. Biotechnol.*, 18:326–332, 2000.

7. C. H. Schilling, D. Letscher, and B. O. Palsson. Theory for the systemic definition of metabolic pathways and their use in interpreting metabolic function from a pathway-oriented perspective. *Theor. Biol.*, 203:229–248, 2000.

8. A. Doncescu, K. Inoue, and T. Sato, Hypothesis-finding in systems biology. *The ALP Newslett.*, 21(1–3), 2008.

9. E. Almaas, B. Kovács, T. Vicsek, Z. N. Oltvai, and A. N. Barabási. Global organization of metabolic fluxes in the bacterium *Escherichia coli. Nature*, 427(6977):839–843, 2004.

10. N. Lavrač and S. Džeroski. *Inductive Logic Programming: Techniques and Applications*, Ellis Horwood, 1994.

11. K. Inoue. Induction as consequence finding. *Machine Learn.*, 55(2):109–135, 2004.

12. M. Kanehisa and S. Goto. KEGG: Kyoto encyclopedia of genes and genomes. *Nucleic Acids Res.*, 28:27–30, 2000.

13. S. Nienhuys-Cheng and R. de Wolf. *Foundations of Inductive Logic Programming, Lecture Notes in Computer Science*, vol. 1228, Springer, 1997.

14. S. H. Muggleton. Inverse entailment and Progol. *New Generat. Comput.*, 13(3–4):245–286, 1995.

15. S. H. Muggleton and C. H. Bryant. Theory completion using inverse entailment. In *Proceedings of the 10th International Conference on Inductive Logic Programming, Lecture Notes in Artificial Intelligence*, Vol 1886, Springer, 2000, pp. 130–146.

16. O. Ray and K. Inoue. Mode directed inverse entailment for full clausal theories. In *Proceedings of the 17th International Conference on Inductive Logic Programming, Lecture Notes in Artificial Intelligence*, Vol 4894, Springer, 2007, pp. 225–238.

17. A. Yamamoto. Hypothesis finding based on upward refinement of residue hypotheses. *Theoret. Computer Sci.*, 298:5–19, 2003.

18. K. Inoue. Linear resolution for consequence finding. *Artificial Intelligence*, 56(2–3):301–353, 1992.

19. P. T. Cox and T. Pietrzykowski. A complete, nonredundant algorithm for reversed skolemization. *Theoret. Computer Sci.*, 28(3):239–261, 1984.

20. S. H. Muggleton and W. L. Buntine. Machine invention of first order predicates by inverting resolution. In *Proceedings of the 5th International Conference on Machine Learning*, 1988, pp. 339–352.

21. G. D. Plotkin. A further note on inductive generalization. *Machine Intelligence*, 6:101–124, 1971.

22. M. Bramer. *Principles of Data Mining*, Springer, 2007.

23. A. Tamaddoni-Nezhad, R. Chaleil, and S. H. Muggleton. Application of abductive ILP to learning metabolic network inhibition from temporal data. *Machine Learning*, 65(1–3): 209–230, 2006.

24. R. D. King, K. E. Whelan, F. M. Jones, P. G. Reiser, C. H. Bryant, S. H. Muggleton, D. B. Kell, and S. G. Oliver. Functional genomic hypothesis generation and experimentation by a robot scientist. *Nature*, 427(6971):247–252, 2004.

25. B. Zupan, J. Demsar, I. Bratko, P. Juvan, J. A. Halter, A. Kuspa, and G. Shaulsky. GenePath: a system for automated construction of genetic networks from mutant data. *Bioinformatics*, 19:383–389, 2003.

10

ANALYSIS AND CONTROL OF DETERMINISTIC AND PROBABILISTIC BOOLEAN NETWORKS

Tatsuya Akutsu

Kyoto University, Kyoto, Japan

Wai-Ki Ching

The University of Hong Kong, Hong Kong, China

10.1 INTRODUCTION

Analyses of genetic networks are important topics in computational systems biology. For that purpose, mathematical models of genetic networks are needed, and thus various models have been proposed or utilized, which include Bayesian networks, Boolean networks (BNs), and probabilistic BN, ordinary and partial differential equations, and qualitative differential equations [1]. Among them, a lot of studied have been done on the BN. BN is a very simple model [2]: Each node (e.g., gene) takes either 0 (inactive) or 1 (active), and the states of nodes change synchronously according to regulation rules given as Boolean functions. Although such binary expression is very simple, BN is considered to retain meaningful biological information contained in the real continuous domain gene expression patterns. Furthermore, a lot of theoretical studies have been done on the distribution of length and number of attractors for

Elements of Computational Systems Biology Edited by Huma M. Lodhi and Stephen H. Muggleton
Copyright © 2010 John Wiley & Sons, Inc.

randomly generated BNs with average indegree K, where an attractor corresponds to a steady state of a cell. However, exact results have not yet been obtained.

In 2002, probabilistic Boolean network (PBN) was proposed as a stochastic extension of BN [3]. Although only one Boolean function is assigned to each node in a BN, multiple Boolean functions can be assigned to each node in a PBN, and one Boolean function is selected randomly per each node and per each time step. After its invention, various aspects of PBN have been studied. Among them, control of PBNs is quite important [4] because one of the important challenges of systems biology is to establish a control theory of biological systems [5, 6]. Since biological systems contain highly nonlinear subsystems and PBNs are highly nonlinear systems, development of control methods for PBNs may be a small but important and fundamental step toward establishment of control theory for biological systems.

Based on the above discussions, in this chapter we focus on BNs and PBNs. In particular, we focus on computational aspects of identification of steady states and finding of control actions for both BNs and PBNs. We give a brief introduction of these models and review works on the following problems.

BN-ATTRACTOR   *Given a BN, identify all singleton attractors and cyclic attractors with short period.*

BN-CONTROL   *Given a BN, an initial state, and a desired state, find a control sequence of external nodes leading to the desired state.*

PBN-STEADY   *Given a PBN, find the steady-state distribution.*

PBN-CONTROL   *Given a PBN along with cost function and its initial state, find a sequence of control actions with the minimum cost.*

As mentioned above, attractors in a BN correspond to steady states. Therefore, we discuss two problems on two models with focusing on the works mainly done by the authors and their colleagues.

10.2   BOOLEAN NETWORK

As mentioned in Section 10.1, BN is a model of genetic networks [2]. Although BN was proposed in 1960s, extensive studies have been done on BN.

A BN $G(V, F)$ consists of a set $V = \{v_1, \ldots, v_n\}$ of nodes and a list $F = (f_1, \ldots, f_n)$ of Boolean functions. Each node corresponds to a gene and takes either 0 (gene is not expressed) or 1 (gene is expressed) at each discrete time t. The state of node v_i at time t is denoted by $v_i(t)$, where the states on nodes change synchronously according to given regulation rules. A Boolean function $f_i(v_{i_1}, \ldots, v_{i_k})$ with inputs from specified nodes $v_{i_1}, \ldots, v_{i_k}$ is assigned to each node, where it represents a regulation rule for node v_i. We use $IN(v_i)$ to denote the set of input nodes $v_{i_1}, \ldots, v_{i_k}$ to v_i. Then, the state of node v_i at time $t + 1$ is determined by

$$v_i(t + 1) = f_i(v_{i_1}(t), \ldots, v_{i_{k_i}}(t)).$$

Here, we let

$$\mathbf{v}(t) = [v_1(t), \ldots, v_n(t)],$$

which is called a gene activity profile (GAP) at time t or a (global) state of BN at time t. We also write $v_i(t + 1) = f_i(\mathbf{v}(t))$ to denote the regulation rule for v_i. Furthermore, we write

$$\mathbf{v}(t + 1) = \mathbf{f}(\mathbf{v}(t))$$

to denote the regulation rule for the whole BN. We define the set of edges E by

$$E = \{(v_{i_j}, v_i) | v_{i_j} \in IN(v_i)\}.$$

Then, $G(V, E)$ is a directed graph representing the network topology of a BN. An edge from v_{i_j} to v_i means that v_{i_j} directly affects the expression of v_i. The number of input nodes to v_i (i.e., $|IN(v_i)|$) is called the indegree of v_i. We use K to denote the maximum indegree of a BN, which plays an important role in analysis of BNs.

An example of BN is given in Figure 10.1. In this example, the state of node v_1 at time $t + 1$ is determined by the state of node v_2 at time t. The state of node v_2 at time $t + 1$ is determined by the logical AND of the state of v_1 and the negation (i.e., logical NOT) of the state of v_3 at time $t + 1$. The state of node v_3 at time $t + 1$ is determined by AND of the state of node v_1 and NOT of the state of node v_2 at time t. We use $x \wedge y$, $x \vee y$, $x \oplus y$, $\bar{x}$ to denote logical AND of x and y, logical OR of x and y, exclusive OR of x and y, and logical NOT of x, respectively.

The dynamics of a BN can be well-described by a state transition diagram shown in Figure 10.2. For example, an edge from 101 to 001 means that if GAP of BN is $[1, 0, 1]$ at time t, GAP of BN becomes $[0, 0, 1]$ at time $t + 1$. From this diagram, it is seen that if $\mathbf{v}(0) = [1, 0, 1]$, GAP changes as:

$$[1, 0, 1] \Longrightarrow [0, 0, 1] \Longrightarrow [0, 0, 0] \Longrightarrow [0, 0, 0] \Longrightarrow \cdots$$

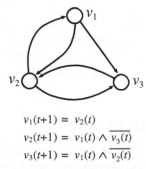

$$v_1(t+1) = v_2(t)$$
$$v_2(t+1) = v_1(t) \wedge \overline{v_3(t)}$$
$$v_3(t+1) = v_1(t) \wedge \overline{v_2(t)}$$

Figure 10.1   Example of a Boolean network.

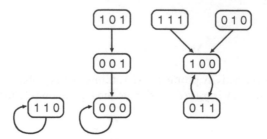

Figure 10.2   State transition diagram for BN in Figure 10.1.

and the same GAP $[0, 0, 0]$ is repeated after $t = 1$. It is also seen that if BN begins from $\mathbf{v}(0) = [1, 1, 1]$, $[1, 0, 0]$, and $[0, 1, 1]$ are repeated alternatively after $t = 0$. These kinds of sets of repeating states are called attractors, each of which corresponds to a directed cycle in a state transition table. The number of elements in an attractor is called the period of the attractor. An attractor with period 1 is called a singleton attractor, which corresponds to a fixed point. An attractor with period greater than 1 is called a cyclic attractor. In the BN of Figure 10.1, there are three attractors: $\{[0, 0, 0]\}$, $\{[1, 1, 0]\}$, $\{[1, 0, 0], [0, 1, 1]\}$, where the first and second ones are singleton attractors and the third one is a cyclic attractor with period 2.

10.3 IDENTIFICATION OF ATTRACTORS

Since attractors in a BN are biologically interpreted so that different attractors correspond to different cell types [2], extensive studies have been done for analyzing the number and length of attractors in randomly generated BNs with average indegree K. Starting from [2], a fast increase in the number of attractors has been seen [7–9]. Although there is no conclusive result on the mean length of attractors, it has been studied by many researches [2, 8]. Recently, several studies have been done for on efficient identification of attractors [10–13], whereas it is known that finding a singleton attractor (i.e., a fixed point) is NP-hard [13, 14]. Devloo et al. developed a method using transformation to a constraint satisfaction problem [10]. Garg et al. developed a method based on binary decision diagrams (BDDs) [11]. Irons developed a method that makes use of small subnetworks [12]. However, theoretical analysis of the average case time complexity was not performed in these works. We recently developed algorithms for identifying singleton attractors and small attractors and analyzed the average case time complexities [13]. In this section, we overview our results on the identification of attractors.

10.3.1 Definition of BN-ATTRACTOR

As mentioned in the previous section, starting from an initial GAP, a BN will eventually reach a set of global states called an attractor. Recall that attractors correspond to directed cycles in a state transition diagram, and there are two types of attractors:

singleton attractors (i.e., attractors with period 1) and cyclic attractors (i.e., attractors with period greater than 1). The set of all GAPs that eventually evolve into the same attractor is called the basin of attraction. Different basins of attraction correspond to different connected components in the state transition diagram, and each connected component contains exactly one directed cycle.

In this chapter, the attractor identification problem (BN-ATTRACTOR) is defined as a problem of enumerating all attractors for a given BN. However, it is very difficult to find attractors with long periods. Thus, we focus on identification of singleton attractors and identification of attractors with period at most given threshold p_{max}. That is, we enumerate all singleton attractors or all attractors with period at most p_{max}. This problem is referred as BN-ATTRACTOR-p_{max} in this chapter. The singleton attractor identification problem corresponds to BN-ATTRACTOR-1.

10.3.2 Basic Recursive Algorithm

We can identify all attractors if a state transition diagram is given. However, the size of the diagram is $O(2^n)$, since there are 2^n nodes in the diagram. Thus, the naive approach using a state transition diagram takes at least $O(2^n)$ time. Furthermore, if the regulation rules are given as $v_i(t + 1) = v_i(t)$ for all i, the number of singleton attractors is 2^n. Thus, $O(2^n)$ time is required in the worst case if all the singleton attractors are to be identified. On the other hand, it is known that the average number of singleton attractors is 1 regardless of the number of genes n and the maximum indegree K [15]. Based on these facts, we developed a series of algorithms for BN-ATTRACTOR-1 and BN-ATTRACTOR-p_{max} with short period p_{max} [13], each of which examines much smaller number of states than 2^n in the average case. In this section, we review the basic version of our developed algorithms, which is referred to as the basic recursive algorithm.

In the basic recursive algorithm, a partial GAP (i.e., profile with m ($< n$) genes) is extended one by one toward a complete GAP (i.e., singleton attractor), according to a given gene ordering (i.e., a random gene ordering). If it is found that a partial GAP cannot be extended to a singleton attractor, the next partial GAP is examined. The pseudocode of the algorithm is given below, where this procedure is invoked with $m = 1$.

Algorithm 10.1

```
BasicRecursive (v,m):
  if m = n + 1
  then Output [v₁(t), v₂(t),..., vₙ(t)],  return;
  for b = 0 to 1 do
    Vₘ(t) := b;
    if it is found that f_j(v(t)) ≠ v_j(t) for some j ≤ m
    then  continue
    else  BasicRecursive(v,m + 1);
  return.
End pseudo-code.
```

At the m-th recursive step, the states of the first $m - 1$ genes (i.e., a partial GAP) are already determined. Then, the algorithm extends the partial GAP by letting $v_m(t) = 0$. If either $v_j(t + 1) = v_j(t)$ holds or the value of $v_j(t + 1)$ is not determined for each $j = 1, \ldots, m$, the algorithm proceeds to the next recursive step. That is, if there is a possibility that the current partial GAP can be extended to a singleton attractor, it goes to the next recursive step. Otherwise, it extends the partial GAP by letting $v_m(t) = 1$ and executes a similar procedure. After examining $v_m(t) = 0$ and $v_m(t) = 1$, the algorithm returns to the previous recursive step. Since the number of singleton attractors is small in most cases, it is expected that the algorithm does not examine many partial GAPs with large m. The average case time complexity is estimated as follows [13].

Assume that we have tested the first m out of n genes, where $m \geq K$. For all $i \leq m$, $v_i(t) \neq v_i(t + 1)$ holds with probability

$$P(v_i(t) \neq v_i(t + 1)) = 0.5 \cdot \frac{\dbinom{m}{k_i}}{\dbinom{n}{k_i}} \approx 0.5 \cdot \left(\frac{m}{n}\right)^{k_i} \geq 0.5 \cdot \left(\frac{m}{n}\right)^{K},$$

where we assume that Boolean functions of k_i ($< K$) inputs are selected at random uniformly. If $v_i(t) \neq v_i(t + 1)$ holds for some $i \leq m$, the algorithm cannot proceed to the next recursive level. Therefore, the probability that the algorithm examines the $(m + 1)$th gene is no more than

$$[1 - P(v_i(t) \neq v_i(t + 1))]^m = \left[1 - 0.5 \cdot \left(\frac{m}{n}\right)^{K}\right]^m.$$

Thus, the number of recursive calls executed for the first m genes is at most

$$f(m) = 2^m \cdot \left[1 - 0.5 \cdot \left(\frac{m}{n}\right)^{K}\right]^m.$$

Here, we let

$$s = \frac{m}{n} \quad \text{and} \quad F(s) = [2^s \cdot (1 - 0.5 \cdot s^K)^s]^n = [(2 - s^K)^s]^n.$$

Then, the average case time complexity is estimated by computing the maximum value of $F(s)$. Although an additional $O(nm)$ factor is required, it can be ignored, since $O(n^2 a^n) \ll O((a + \epsilon)^n)$ holds for any $a > 1$ and $\epsilon > 0$.

Recall that our purpose of the analysis is to estimate the average case time complexity as a function of n. Thus, we only need to compute the maximum value of the function $g(s) = (2 - s^K)^s$, which can be obtained by a simple numerical calculation for fixed K. Then, the average case time complexity of the algorithm can be estimated as $O((\max(g))^n)$. The average case time complexities for $K = 2, \ldots, 8$ are obtained

Table 10.1   Theoretically estimated average case time complexities of basic, outdegree-based, and BFS-based algorithms for the singleton attractor detection problem [13]

K	2	3	4	5	6	7	8
Basic	1.35^n	1.43^n	1.49^n	1.53^n	1.57^n	1.60^n	1.62^n
Outdegree based	1.19^n	1.27^n	1.34^n	1.41^n	1.45^n	1.48^n	1.51^n
BFS based	1.16^n	1.27^n	1.35^n	1.41^n	1.45^n	1.50^n	1.53^n

Source: [13]

as in the first row of Table 10.1. From the table, it is seen that for small K, the basic recursive algorithm is much faster than the naive algorithm that takes at least $O(2^n)$ time. That is, the basic recursive algorithm does not examine all GAPs in the average case.

We obtained variants of this basic recursive algorithm by sorting nodes according to various orderings before invoking the recursive procedure [13]. In particular, we used the orderings of nodes according to the outdegree and breadth-first search (BFS). For these algorithms, we obtained theoretical estimates of the average case time complexity (see Table 10.1). Since some approximations were included in our theoretical analyses, we also performed computational experiments. As a result, good agreements were observed. We also extended the basic recursive algorithm for identifying cyclic attractors with short period [13]. Although the extended algorithm is not efficient compared with those in Table 10.1, it still works in $o(2^n)$ time in the average case, and the result of computational experiment suggested that it is actually faster than the naive algorithm for small K.

10.3.3   On the Worst Case Time Complexity of BN-ATTRACTOR

We have considered the average case time complexity in the above discussion. It is also very important to consider the worst case time complexity. As mentioned above, there exist 2^n attractors in the worst case and thus the identification problem takes $\Omega(2^n)$ time in the worst case. However, it may be possible to develop an $o(2^n)$ time algorithm if we consider the singleton attractor detection problem (i.e., decide whether or not there exists a singleton attractor). It has been shown that the detection problem can be solved in $o(2^n)$ time for constant K by a reduction to the satisfiability problem for CNF (conjunctive normal form) [16]. It has also been shown that the detection problem can be solved in $o(2^n)$ time for general K if Boolean functions are restricted to AND/OR of literals [16]. However, no $o(2^n)$ time algorithm is known for more general cases. Therefore, development of such an algorithm is left as an open problem.

10.4   CONTROL OF BOOLEAN NETWORK

As mentioned in Section 10.1, development of control theory/methods for biological systems is important, since biological systems are complex and contain highly nonlinear subsystems, and, thus, existing methods in control theory cannot be directly applied to control of biological systems. Since BNs are highly nonlinear systems, it is reasonable to try to develop methods for control of BNs.

In 2003, Datta et al. proposed a dynamic programming algorithm for finding a control strategy for PBN [4], from which many extensions followed [17–20]. In their approach, it is assumed that states of some nodes can be externally controlled, and the objective is to find a sequence of control actions with the minimum cost that leads to a desirable state of a network. Their approach is based on the theory of Markov chains and makes use of the classical technique of dynamic programming. Since BNs are special cases of PBNs, their methods can also be applied to control of BNs. However, it is required in their methods to handle exponential size matrices, and, thus, their methods can only be applied to small biological systems. Therefore, it is reasonable to study how difficult it is to find control strategies for BNs. We showed that finding control strategies for BNs is NP-hard [21]. On the other hand, we showed that this problem can be solved in polynomial time if BN has a tree structure. In this section, we review these results along with the essential idea of Datta et al. [4].

10.4.1 Definition of BN-CONTROL

In this subsection, we review a formal definition of the problem of finding control strategies for BNs (BN-CONTROL) [21].

In BN-CONTROL, we modify the definition of BN in order to introduce control nodes (see also Figure 10.3). We assume that there are two types of nodes: internal nodes and external nodes, where internal nodes correspond to usual nodes (i.e., genes) in BN and external nodes correspond to control nodes. Let a set V of $n + m$ nodes be $V = \{v_1, \ldots, v_n, v_{n+1}, \ldots, v_{n+m}\}$, where $v_1, \ldots, v_n$ are internal nodes and $v_{n+1}, \ldots, v_{n+m}$ are external nodes. For convenience, we also use x_i to denote an external node v_{n+i}. We let $\mathbf{v}(t) = [v_1(t), \ldots, v_n(t)]$ and $\mathbf{x}(t) = [x_1(t), \ldots, x_m(t)]$. Then, the state of each internal node $v_i(t + 1)$ $(i = 1, \ldots, n)$ is determined by

$$v_i(t + 1) = f_i(v_{i_1}(t), \ldots, v_{i_{k_i}}(t)),$$

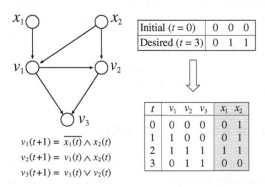

$$v_1(t+1) = \overline{x_1(t)} \wedge x_2(t)$$
$$v_2(t+1) = v_1(t) \wedge x_2(t)$$
$$v_3(t+1) = v_1(t) \vee v_2(t)$$

Figure 10.3   Example of BN-CONTROL.

where each v_{i_k} is either an internal node or an external node. Thus, the dynamics of a BN is described as

$$\mathbf{v}(t + 1) = \mathbf{f}(\mathbf{v}(t), \mathbf{x}(t)),$$

where $\mathbf{x}(t)$s are determined externally.

Suppose that the initial states of internal nodes $\mathbf{v}^0$ at time $t = 0$ and the desired states of internal nodes $\mathbf{v}^M$ at time $t = M$ are given. Then, the problem is to find a sequence of 0–1 vectors $\langle \mathbf{x}(0), \ldots, \mathbf{x}(M) \rangle$, which leads the BN from $\mathbf{v}(0) = \mathbf{v}^0$ to $\mathbf{v}(M) = \mathbf{v}^M$. There may not exist such a sequence. In such a case, "none" should be the output.

An example of BN-CONTROL is given in Figure 10.3. In this example, $\mathbf{v}^0 = [0, 0, 0]$ and $\mathbf{v}^M = [0, 1, 1]$ are given as an input (along with BN), where $M = 3$. Then, the following is computed as a desired control sequence:

$$\langle \mathbf{x}(0) = [0, 1], \ \mathbf{x}(1) = [0, 1], \ \mathbf{x}(2) = [1, 1], \ \mathbf{x}(3) = [0, 0] \rangle,$$

where $\mathbf{x}(3)$ is not relevant.

10.4.2   Dynamic Programming Algorithms for BN-CONTROL

In this subsection, we review two dynamic programming algorithms: one is a simplified version of the algorithm for PBNs [4], the other one is developed for BNs with tree structures. The former one can be applied to all types of BNs but takes exponential time. The latter one works in polynomial time but can only be applied to BNs having tree structures.

First, we review the former one [4]. We use a table $D[a_1, \ldots, a_n, t]$, where each entry takes either 0 or 1. Here, $D[a_1, \ldots, a_n, t]$ takes 1 if there exists a control sequence $\langle \mathbf{x}(t), \ldots, \mathbf{x}(M) \rangle$, which leads to the desired state $\mathbf{v}^M$ beginning from the state $\mathbf{a} = [a_1, \ldots, a_n]$ at time t. This table is computed from $t = M$ to $t = 0$ by using the following procedure:

$$D[a_1, \ldots, a_n, M] = \begin{cases} 1, & \text{if } [a_1, \ldots, a_n] = \mathbf{v}^M, \\ 0, & \text{otherwise}, \end{cases}$$

$$D[a_1, \ldots, a_n, t - 1] = \begin{cases} 1, & \text{if there exists } (\mathbf{b}, \mathbf{x}) \text{ such that } D[b_1, \ldots, b_n, t] = 1 \\ & \text{and } \mathbf{b} = \mathbf{f}(\mathbf{a}, \mathbf{x}), \\ 0, & \text{otherwise}, \end{cases}$$

where $\mathbf{b} = [b_1, \ldots, b_n]$. Then, there exists a desired control sequence if and only if $D[a_1, \ldots, a_n, 0] = 1$ holds for $\mathbf{a} = \mathbf{v}^0$. Once the table is constructed, a desired control sequence can be computed using the the standard traceback technique in dynamic programming.

In this method, the size of table $D[a_1, \ldots, a_n, t]$ is clearly $O(M \cdot 2^n)$. Moreover, we should examine pairs of $O(2^n)$ internal states and $O(2^m)$ external states for each time t. Thus, it requires $O(M \cdot 2^{n+m})$ time, excluding the time for calculation of Boolean functions. Therefore, this algorithm is an exponential time algorithm.

Next, we review the latter one [21]. This algorithm can only be applied to BNs, in which the network has a tree structure (i.e., $G(V, E)$ is connected and there is no cycle). Since the algorithm is a bit complicated, we show here a simple algorithm for the case in which the network has a rooted tree structure (i.e., all paths are directed from leaves to the root). Although dynamic programming is also used here, it is used in a significantly different way from the above.

We define a table $S[v_i, t, b]$ as below, where v_i is either an internal node or an external node in a BN, t is a time step, and b is a Boolean value (i.e., 0 or 1). Here, $S[v_i, t, b]$ takes 1 if there exists a control sequence (up to time t) that makes $v_i(t) = b$.

$$
S[v_i, t, 1] = \begin{cases} 1, & \text{if there exists } \langle \mathbf{x}(0), \ldots, \mathbf{x}(t) \rangle \text{ such that } v_i(t) = 1, \\ 0, & \text{otherwise.} \end{cases}
$$

$$
S[v_i, t, 0] = \begin{cases} 1, & \text{if there exists } \langle \mathbf{x}(0), \ldots, \mathbf{x}(t) \rangle \text{ such that } v_i(t) = 0, \\ 0, & \text{otherwise.} \end{cases}
$$

Then, $S[v_i, t, 1]$ can be computed by the following dynamic programming procedure.

$$
S[v_i, t+1, 1] = \begin{cases} 1, & \text{if there exists } [b_{i_1}, \ldots, b_{i_k}] \text{ such that } f_i(b_{i_1}, \ldots, b_{i_k}) = 1 \\ & \text{holds and } S[v_{i_j}, t, b_{i_j}] = 1 \text{ holds for all } j = 1, \ldots, k, \\ 0, & \text{otherwise.} \end{cases}
$$

$S[v_i, t, 0]$ can be computed in a similar way. It should be noted that each leaf is either a constant node (i.e., an internal node with no incoming edges) or an external node. For a constant node, either $S[v_i, t, 1] = 1$ and $S[v_i, t, 0] = 0$ hold for all t, or $S[v_i, t, 1] = 0$ and $S[v_i, t, 0] = 1$ hold for all t. For an external node, $S[v_i, t, 1] = 1$ and $S[v_i, t, 0] = 1$ hold for all t. Since the size of table $S[v_i, t, b]$ is $O((n + m)M)$, this dynamic programming algorithm works in polynomial time, where we assume that the value of each Boolean function can be computed in polynomial time. A desired control sequence can also be obtained from the table in polynomial time using the traceback technique. In order to extend this algorithm to BNs with general tree structures, other procedures are required. Since these procedures are a bit complicated, we omit details. Interested readers are referred to Akutsu et al. [21].

10.4.3   NP-hardness Results on BN-CONTROL

We have shown two dynamic programming algorithms for BN-CONTROL. However, the general version takes exponential time and can only be applied to small size BNs (e.g., BNs with at most 20–30 nodes). Therefore, it is reasonable to ask whether or not there exists a polynomial time algorithm. However, we have shown that the problem

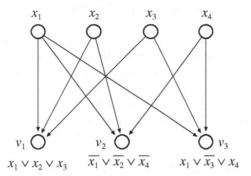

Figure 10.4 Example of reduction from 3SAT to BN-CONTROL.

is NP-hard [21], which means it is impossible (under the assumption of P ≠ NP) to develop a polynomial time algorithm for the general case.

The proof is done by using a simple reduction from 3SAT to BN-CONTROL. Let $y_1, \ldots, y_N$ be Boolean variables (i.e., 0–1 variables). Let $c_1, \ldots, c_L$ be a set of clauses over $y_1, \ldots, y_N$, where each clause is a disjunction (logical OR) of at most three literals. Then, 3SAT is a problem of asking whether or not there exists an assignment of 0–1 values to $y_1, \ldots, y_N$, which satisfies all the clauses (i.e., the values of all clauses are 1).

From an instance of 3SAT, we construct a BN as follows (see also Figure 10.4). We let the set of nodes $V = \{v_1, \ldots, v_L, x_1, \ldots, x_N\}$, where each v_i corresponds to c_i and each x_j corresponds to y_j. Suppose that $f_i(y_{i_1}, \ldots, y_{i_3})$ is a Boolean function assigned to c_i in 3SAT. Then, we assign $f_i(x_{i_1}, \ldots, x_{i_3})$ to v_i in the BN. Finally, we let $M = 1$, $\mathbf{v}^0 = [0, 0, \ldots, 0]$, and $\mathbf{v}^M = [1, 1, \ldots, 1]$. For example, an instance of 3SAT $\{y_1 \vee y_2 \vee y_3, \overline{y_1} \vee \overline{y_2} \vee \overline{y_4}, y_1 \vee \overline{y_3} \vee y_4\}$ is transformed into the instance of BN-CONTROL shown in Figure 10.4. Then, it is easy to see that the above is a polynomial time reduction, which completes the proof.

It is also shown in Akutsu et al. [21] that the control problem remains NP-hard even for BNs having very restricted network structures. In particular, it is shown that it remains NP-hard if the network contains only one control node and all the nodes are OR or AND nodes (i.e., there is no negative control). However, it is unclear whether the control problem is NP-hard or can be solved in polynomial time if a BN contains a fixed number of directed cycles or loops (it is unclear even for the case of two cycles). Deciding the complexity of such a special case is left as an open problem.

Although we have shown negative results, NP-hardness does not necessarily mean that we cannot develop algorithms, which work efficiently in most practical cases. Recently, Langmund and Jha proposed a method using techniques from the field of model checking and applied it to a BN model of embryogenesis in *Drosophila melanogaster* with 15,360 Boolean variables [22]. Such an approach might be useful and thus should be studied further.

10.5 PROBABILISTIC BOOLEAN NETWORK

In a BN, one regulation rule (one Boolean function) is assigned to each node, and thus transition from $\mathbf{v}(t)$ to $\mathbf{v}(t+1)$ occurs deterministically. However, real genetic networks do not necessarily work deterministically. It is reasonable to assume that real genetic networks work stochastically by means of the effects of noise and elements other than genes. To introduce noise into a BN, the noisy Boolean network was proposed in Akutsu et al. [23]. Soon after, PBN was introduced by Shmulevich et al. [3], and since many studies have been done on PBNs [24]. In this section, we briefly review the definition of PBN.

PBN is an extension of BN. The difference between BN and PBN is only that in a PBN, for each vertex v_i, instead of having only one Boolean function, there are a number of Boolean functions (predictor functions) $f_j^{(i)} (j = 1, 2, \ldots, l(i))$ to be chosen for determining the state of gene v_i. The probability of choosing $f_j^{(i)}$ is $c_j^{(i)}$, where $c_j^{(i)}$ should satisfy the following:

$$0 \leq c_j^{(i)} \leq 1 \quad \text{and} \quad \sum_{j=1}^{l(i)} c_j^{(i)} = 1 \quad \text{for} \quad i = 1, 2, \ldots, n.$$

Let f_j be the jth possible realization,

$$f_j = (f_{j_1}^{(1)}, f_{j_2}^{(2)}, \ldots, f_{j_n}^{(n)}), \quad 1 \leq j_i \leq l(i), \quad i = 1, 2, \ldots, n.$$

The probability of choosing such a realization in an independent PBN (the selection of the Boolean function for each gene is independent) is given by

$$p_j = \prod_{i=1}^{n} c_{j_i}^{(i)}, \quad j = 1, 2, \ldots, N,$$

where $N = \prod_{i=1}^{n} l(i)$ is the maximum possible number of different realizations of BNs.

An example of PBN is given in Figure 10.5. Suppose that GAP of PBN at time t is $[0, 0, 0]$. If $(f_1^{(1)}, f_1^{(2)}, f_1^{(3)})$ is selected with probability $0.8 \times 0.7 = 0.56$, GAP at time $t+1$ is still $[0, 0, 0]$. Similarly, if $(f_1^{(1)}, f_2^{(2)}, f_1^{(3)})$ is selected with probability $0.8 \times 0.3 = 0.24$, GAP at time $t+1$ is still $[0, 0, 0]$. On the other hand, if $(f_2^{(1)}, f_1^{(2)}, f_1^{(3)})$ is selected with probability $0.2 \times 0.7 = 0.14$ or $(f_2^{(1)}, f_2^{(2)}, f_1^{(3)})$ is selected with probability $0.2 \times 0.3 = 0.06$, GAP at time $t+1$ becomes $[1, 0, 0]$. Therefore, we have the following transition probabilities:

$$\text{Prob}(\mathbf{v}(t+1) = [0, 0, 0] \mid \mathbf{v}(t) = [0, 0, 0]) = 0.8,$$

$$\text{Prob}(\mathbf{v}(t+1) = [1, 0, 0] \mid \mathbf{v}(t) = [0, 0, 0]) = 0.2,$$

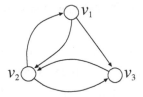

	Boolean function	Probability
$f_1^{(1)}$	$v_1(t{+}1) = v_2(t)$	0.8
$f_2^{(1)}$	$v_1(t{+}1) = \overline{v_2(t)}$	0.2
$f_1^{(2)}$	$v_2(t{+}1) = v_1(t) \wedge \overline{v_3(t)}$	0.7
$f_2^{(2)}$	$v_2(t{+}1) = v_3(t)$	0.3
$f_1^{(3)}$	$v_3(t{+}1) = v_1(t) \wedge \overline{v_2(t)}$	1.0

Figure 10.5   An example of PBN.

where the probabilities of the other transitions from $[0, 0, 0]$ are 0. For another example, the (nonzero) transition probabilities from $[0, 0, 1]$ are as follows:

$$\text{Prob}(\mathbf{v}(t+1) = [0, 0, 0] \mid \mathbf{v}(t) = [0, 0, 1]) = 0.56,$$

$$\text{Prob}(\mathbf{v}(t+1) = [0, 1, 0] \mid \mathbf{v}(t) = [0, 0, 1]) = 0.24,$$

$$\text{Prob}(\mathbf{v}(t+1) = [1, 0, 0] \mid \mathbf{v}(t) = [0, 0, 1]) = 0.14,$$

$$\text{Prob}(\mathbf{v}(t+1) = [1, 1, 0] \mid \mathbf{v}(t) = [0, 0, 1]) = 0.06.$$

The transition probabilities of a PBN can be represented by using $2^n \times 2^n$ matrix A. For each $\mathbf{a} = [a_1, \ldots, a_n] \in \{0, 1\}^n$, let

$$id(\mathbf{a}) = 2^{n-1}a_n + 2^{n-2}a_{n-1} + \cdots + 2a_2 + a_1 + 1.$$

Then, A is defined by

$$A_{ij} = \text{Prob}(\mathbf{v}(t+1) = \mathbf{b} \mid \mathbf{v}(t) = \mathbf{a}),$$

where $i = id(\mathbf{b})$ and $j = id(\mathbf{a})$. For example, the transition matrix of the PBN of Figure 10.5 is as follows:

$$
\begin{pmatrix}
0.8 & 0.56 & 0.2 & 0.14 & 0 & 0 & 0.06 & 0.14 \\
0 & 0 & 0 & 0 & 0.24 & 0.56 & 0 & 0 \\
0 & 0.24 & 0 & 0.06 & 0 & 0 & 0.14 & 0.06 \\
0 & 0 & 0 & 0 & 0.56 & 0.24 & 0 & 0 \\
0.2 & 0.14 & 0.8 & 0.56 & 0 & 0 & 0.24 & 0.56 \\
0 & 0 & 0 & 0 & 0.06 & 0.14 & 0 & 0 \\
0 & 0.06 & 0 & 0.24 & 0 & 0 & 0.56 & 0.24 \\
0 & 0 & 0 & 0 & 0.14 & 0.06 & 0 & 0
\end{pmatrix}.
$$

For example, the first column of this matrix represents the transition probabilities from $[0, 0, 0]$. The second column represents the transition probabilities from $[0, 0, 1]$. As seen from this matrix, the dynamics of a PBN can be understood in the context of a standard Markov chain. Thus, the techniques developed in the field of Markov chain can be applied to PBNs, as explained in the following sections.

10.6   COMPUTATION OF STEADY STATES OF PBN

10.6.1   Exact Computation of PBN-STEADY

A PBN is characterized by its steady-state distribution. To compute this probability distribution, an efficient matrix-based method has been developed in Zhang et al. [25]. The method can be used to analyze the sensitivity of the steady-state distribution in a PBN to the change of input genes, connections between genes, and Boolean functions. It is a matrix-based method (a deterministic method) that can solve the steady-state probability distribution more accurately than Markov chain Monte-Carlo (MCMC) method (a probabilistic method). In fact, an MCMC method has been proposed in Shmulevich et al. [26] to estimate the steady-state distribution of a PBN. In the MCMC method, it regards a PBN as a Markov chain. Then, by simulating the underlying Markov chain for a sufficiently long time (in steady state), one can get the approximation of the steady state probability distribution. It can be successfully used only if we are sufficiently confident that the system has evolved to its steady state.

The main idea of the matrix-based method is two-fold. The method consists of two steps: an efficient method for generating the transition probability matrix of the underlying PBN and the power method for computing the steady-state probability distribution. To generate the transition probability matrix A efficiently, one has to take advantage of the sparsity of the matrix. Given a state i, if a specific Boolean function can lead it to a state j, then A_{ji} will have a value corresponding to the probability of this BN. If another BN also can lead i to j, then the probability will be greater by the probability corresponding to the BN. When comparing to the method in Shmulevich et al. [3], which has a complexity of about $O(N2^{2n})$, the proposed matrix-based method is of $O(N2^n)$. Once the transition probability matrix is generated to solve for the steady state distribution of a PBN, an iterative method, the power method, is employed for this duty. Actually, power method is used for solving the largest eigenvalue in modulus (the dominant eigenvalue) and its corresponding eigenvector of a square matrix. We remark that if the underlying Markov chain of the PBN is irreducible, then the maximum eigenvalue of the transition probability matrix is one and the modulus of the other eigenvalues are less than one. Moreover, the eigenvector corresponding to the maximum eigenvalue is the steady state distribution vector. In the power method, given an initial vector $\mathbf{x}^{(0)}$, one has to compute $\mathbf{x}^{(k)} = A\mathbf{x}^{(k-1)}$ until $\|\mathbf{x}^{(k)} - \mathbf{x}^{(k-1)}\|_\infty < \epsilon$ satisfying some given tolerance ϵ. Here, $\mathbf{x}^{(k)}$ is the kh approximate of the steady state distribution. It is to be noted $\mathbf{x}^{(k)}$ is not an n-dimensional 0–1 vector, but a 2^n-dimensional real vector. The main computational cost of the power method comes from the matrix–vector multiplications. The convergence rate of the power method depends on the ratio of $|\lambda_2/\lambda_1|$, where λ_1 and λ_2 are, respectively, the largest and the second largest eigenvalue of the matrix A.

10.6.2 Approximate Computation of PBN-STEADY

The problem of computing the steady-state distribution of a PBN is a problem of huge size when the number of genes n increases. Ching et al. [27] an proposed approximation method for computing the steady-state distribution of a PBN based on neglecting some BNs with very small probabilities during the construction of the transition probability matrix. One actually observes that in many realizations of a PBN, a large number of BNs have very small chance of being chosen. In fact, this was shown mathematically in Ching et al. [27] under some reasonable assumptions. Therefore, the proposed approximation method is to consider only those BNs with probability greater than a given threshold. Suppose the steady-state probability vector of the original transition matrix $\tilde{A}x = x$ is X. There are n_0 Boolean networks being removed whose corresponding transition matrices are $(A_1, A_2, \ldots, A_{n_0})$ and their probability of being chosen are given by $p_1, p_2, \ldots, p_{n_0}$, respectively. Then, after the removal of these n_0 Boolean networks and making a normalization, one can obtain a perturbed transition probability matrix $\hat{A}$. Suppose that the corresponding steady state distribution vector satisfying the linear system $\hat{A}x = x$ is $\hat{X}$, then it is shown in Ching et al. [27] that

$$E\left(\|\tilde{A}\hat{X} - \hat{X}\|_\infty\right) < (p_1 + p_2 + \cdots + p_{n_0})(2 + 2n)\|\hat{X}\|_\infty.$$

If $\|X\|_\infty$ is equal to or very close to $\|\hat{X}\|_\infty$, one can see

$$E\left(\frac{\|\tilde{A}\hat{X} - \hat{X}\|_\infty}{\|X\|_\infty}\right) < (p_1 + p_2 + \cdots + p_{n_0})(2 + 2n).$$

Here, $\|\mathbf{X}\|_\infty = \max_i\{|X_i|\}$. Numerical experiments in Ching et al. [27] indicate that the approximation method is efficient and effective. Moreover, the approximation method can be extended to the case of context-sensitive PBN.

10.7 CONTROL OF PROBABILISTIC BOOLEAN NETWORKS

In this section, we review the control problem and methods on PBN introduced in Datta et al. [4].

In BN-CONTROL, we introduced external nodes into the standard BN. For control of PBN (PBN-CONTROL), we generalize the concept of external nodes. We assume that the transition matrix depends on m bit control inputs $\mathbf{x} \in \{0, 1\}^m$, and the matrix is represented as $A(\mathbf{x})$.

As in the case of BN-CONTROL, we assume that the initial state $\mathbf{v}(0)$ is given. However, instead of considering only one desired state, we consider the cost of the final state. We use $C_M(\mathbf{v})$ to denote the cost of GAP $\mathbf{v}$ at time $t = M$. Furthermore, we consider the cost of application of control $\mathbf{x}$ to GAP $\mathbf{v}$ at time t, which is is denoted by $C_t(\mathbf{v}, \mathbf{x})$. Then, the total cost for control sequence $X = \langle \mathbf{x}(0), \mathbf{x}(1), \cdots, \mathbf{x}(M-1) \rangle$ is defined by

$$J_X(\mathbf{v}(0)) = E \left[\sum_{t=0}^{M-1} C_t(\mathbf{v}(t), \mathbf{x}(t)) + C_M(\mathbf{v}(M)) \right],$$

where $E[\cdots]$ means the expected cost when PBN transits according to the transition probabilities given by $A(\mathbf{x})$. Then, PBN-CONTROL is defined as a problem of finding a control sequence X that minimizes $J_X(\mathbf{v}(0))$.

10.7.1 Dynamic Programming Algorithm for PBN-CONTROL

As in BN-CONTROL, PBN-CONTROL can be solved by using dynamic programming [4]. In order to apply dynamic programming, we need to define a table. Here, we define $J_t^*(\mathbf{v})$ to be the minimum cost of the optimal control sequence, in which PBN starts from GAP $\mathbf{v}$ at time t. Then, $J_t^*(\mathbf{v})$ is a table of size $2^n \times (M + 1)$ because there exist 2^n possible GAPs. The elements of the table are filled from $t = M$ to $t = 0$, and the desired minimum cost is given by $J_t^*(\mathbf{v}(0))$.

For the case of $t = M$, the following clearly holds:

$$J_M^* = C_M(\mathbf{v}).$$

Next, we assume that we have already obtained the minimum cost $J_{t+1}^*(\mathbf{u})$ beginning from GAP $\mathbf{u}$ at time $t + 1$. Then, it is not difficult to see that $J_t^*(\mathbf{v})$ can be computed by:

$$J_t^*(\mathbf{v}) = \min_{\mathbf{x}} E \left[C_t(\mathbf{v}, \mathbf{x}) + J_{t+1}^*(\mathbf{u}) \right]$$

$$= \min_{\mathbf{x}} \left[C_t(\mathbf{v}, \mathbf{x}) + \sum_{j=1}^{2^n} A_{ij}(\mathbf{x}(t)) \cdot J_{t+1}^*(\mathbf{u}) \right],$$

where $i = id(\mathbf{u})$, $j = id(\mathbf{v})$, and the minimum is taken over $\mathbf{x} \in \{0, 1\}^m$. Once this table is constructed, we can obtain an optimal control sequence by applying the traceback technique.

Datta et al. demonstrated the usefulness of this dynamic programming algorithm by means of application to simulation of a small network including WNT5A gene, which is known to be related to Melanoma [4].

10.7.2 Variants of PBN-CONTROL

Dougherty et al. have proposed several extensions of PBN-CONTROL along with their algorithms. The major extensions are as follows.

- *Imperfect information case* [17]. In PBN-CONTROL, it is assumed that states of all genes are available. However, in many real cases, states of only a limited number of genes are available. Thus, Datta et al. proposed a control strategy that can be used when perfect information about states of genes is not available.
- *Context sensitive PBN* [19]. In a PBN, regulation rules change at every time step. However, it is not plausible that regulation rules change so frequently. Therefore, PBN is extended to the context-sensitive PBN, in which change of regulation rules only occurs with probability q. Besides, in order to cope with noise, it is also assumed that there is a random gene perturbation at each time for each node with probability p. Pal et al. gave a control strategy for this extension of PBN.
- *Infinite horizon control* [20]. In PBN-CONTROL, we considered finite horizon control: The target time step is given in advance and the scores for short periods are taken into account. However, it may be more appropriate in some cases to consider long range behavior of cells. Therefore, Pal et al. formulated the infinite horizon control of PBNs and proposed some methods to solve the problem.
- *Application of Q-learning* [18]. As mentioned before, almost all of the methods for control of general BNs and PBNs take exponential time. Furthermore, control problems have been proven to be NP-hard. However, we still need efficient methods. Faryabi et al. applied Q-learning to find a sequence of control actions. Here, Q-learning is a reinforcement learning method. Their proposed method has two advantages: (1) the method has a polynomial update time and (2) the method is model-free, that is, it is not needed to give $A(\mathbf{x})$ in advance. However, it seems that an exponential number of samples are needed to obtain meaningful results.

We have also developed variants of PBN-CONTROL as below.

10.7.2.1 *Integer Programming Model for Control of PBNs*   Ng et al. [28] proposed a discrete linear control model taking into considerations the following network dynamics:

$$\mathbf{x}(k + 1) = \alpha_k A\mathbf{x}(k) + \beta_k B\mathbf{u}(k). \tag{10.1}$$

Here, $\mathbf{x}(k)$ is the state probability distribution at time k and is a 2^n-dimensional real vector. The matrix A is the one-step transition probability matrix for representing the network dynamics. The matrix B is the control transition matrix. The two parameters α_k and β_k are nonnegative, such that $\alpha_k + \beta_k = 1$ and β_k represents the intervention strength of the control in the network. The vector $\mathbf{u}(k)$ is the control vector on the states, with $u_i(k)$, $i = 1, 2, \ldots, m$ taking on the binary values 0 or 1. It can be set in each column to represent the transition from one specific state to another on a particular gene. Through the control matrix B, the controls are effectively transferred to different possible states in the captured PBN. We note that $u_i(k) = 1$ means that the active control is applied at the time step k, while $u_i(k) = 0$ means that the control is not applied. If there are m possible controls at each time step, then the matrix B is of the size $2^n \times m$. Starting from the initial state probability distribution $\mathbf{x}(0)$, one may apply the controls $\mathbf{u}(0), \mathbf{u}(1), \ldots, \mathbf{u}(T - 1)$ to drive the probability distribution of the genetic network to some desirable state probability distribution at each time step in a period of T. The discrete control problem can be formulated as an integer programming (IP) model and be efficiently solved by LINGO software.

10.7.2.2 Control of PBNs with Hard Constraints

A control model for PBNs with hard constraints has been proposed in Ching et al. [29]. The control model differs from those mentioned above in the assumption that only a finite number of controls or interventions are allowed. The control problem can be considered as a discrete time control problem. Beginning with an initial probability distribution $\mathbf{x}_0$, the PBN evolves according to two possible transition probability matrices A_0 and A_1. Without any external control, it is assumed that the PBN evolves according to a fixed transition probability matrix A_0. However, when a control is applied, the PBN will then evolve according to another transition probability matrix A_1 with more favorable steady states, but it will return back to A_0 again when no more control is applied to the network. The maximum number of controls that can be applied during the finite investigation period T (finite horizon) is K where $K \leq T$. The objective here is to find an optimal control policy such that state of the network is close to a target state vector $\mathbf{z}$. The vector $\mathbf{z}$ can be a unit vector (a desirable state) or a probability distribution (a weighted average of desirable states). To facilitate our discussion, we define the following state probability distribution vectors $\mathbf{x}(i_k i_{k-1} \cdots i_1) = P_{i_k} \cdots P_{i_1} \mathbf{x}_0$ to represent all the possible network state probability distribution vectors up to time k. Here, $i_1, \ldots, i_k \in \{0, 1\}$ and $\sum_{j=1}^{k} i_j \leq K$ and $i_k i_{k-1} \cdots i_1$ is a Boolean string of size k. We then define

$$U(k) = \left\{ \mathbf{x}(i_k i_{k-1} \ldots i_1) : i_1, \ldots, i_k \in \{0, 1\} \quad \text{and} \quad \sum_{j=1}^{k} i_j \leq K \right\}$$

to be the set containing all the possible state probability vectors up to time k. Two mathematical formulations for the optimal control problem are proposed. The first one is to minimize the terminal distance with the target vector $\mathbf{z}$, that is,

$$\min_{\mathbf{x}(i_T i_{T-1} \cdots i_1) \in U(T)} ||\mathbf{x}(i_T i_{T-1} \cdots i_1) - \mathbf{z}||_2. \tag{10.2}$$

The second one is to minimize the overall average of the distances of the state vectors $\mathbf{x}(i_t \ldots i_1)$ $(t = 1, 2, \ldots, T)$ to the target vector $\mathbf{z}$, that is,

$$\min_{\mathbf{x}(i_T i_{T-1} \cdots i_1) \in U(T)} \frac{1}{T} \sum_{t=1}^{T} ||\mathbf{x}(i_t \cdots i_1) - \mathbf{z}||_2. \tag{10.3}$$

Both problems can be solved by using the principle of dynamic programming.

10.8 CONCLUSION

In this chapter, we have overviewed two fundamental problems, analysis of steady states, and control, on two basic models (BN and PBN) of genetic networks, with focus on the authors' works. Although BNs and PBNs may be too simple as a model of genetic networks, some of the results are meaningful. At least, the negative NP-hardness results should still hold for more general models. Since biological networks are considered to contain highly nonlinear subnetworks like BNs and PBNs, the negative results suggest difficulty of computation of steady states and optimal control actions for real networks.

In order to apply the reviewed methods to real biological networks, there are several challenges. One of the important challenges is to break the barrier of time complexity. Almost all of the reviewed algorithms take exponential time and thus can only be applied to small size subnetworks. Besides, all the problems are NP-hard. However, NP-hardness does not necessarily mean that we cannot develop efficient algorithms for real instances. Thus, the development of practically fast algorithms is left as an important future work.

Another important challenge is to combine BNs and/or PBNs with continuous linear and/or nonlinear models. In BNs and PBNs, gene expression levels are simplified into either 0 or 1. Of course, it seems not difficult to extend models and algorithms, so that a fixed number of gene expression levels are treated. However, such discrete models would still be insufficient. It seems that negative feedback loops without oscillation, which are quite popular in linear systems and real biological subnetworks, are hardly expressed by using such discrete models as BNs and PBNs. It also seems that some parts of biological systems are well-represented by continuous models, and some other parts are well-represented by discrete models. Besides, rigorous theories and useful methods have been developed in the fields of linear control and nonlinear control. Therefore, development of a hybrid mathematical model that combines BN/PBN with continuous models and development of analysis and control methods on such a model are important challenges, which may lead to the ultimate goal of computational systems biology.

ACKNOWLEDGMENTS

The work by TA was supported in part by Systems Genomics from MEXT, Japan. The work by WKC was supported in part by HKRGC Grant No. 7017/07P, HKUCRGC Grants, HKU Strategy Research Theme fund on Computational Sciences, Hung Hing Ying Physical Research Sciences Research Grant, National Natural Science Foundation of China Grant No. 10971075 and Guangdong Provincial Natural Science Grant No. 9151063101000021.

REFERENCES

1. H. D. Jong. Modeling and simulation of genetic regulatory systems: a literature review. *J. Comput. Biol.,* 9: 67–103, 2002.

2. S. A. Kauffman. *The Origins of Order: Self-organization and Selection in Evolution,* Oxford University Press, New York, 1993.

3. I. Shmulevich, E. R. Dougherty, S. Kim, and W. Zhang. Probabilistic boolean networks: a rule-based uncertainty model for gene regulatory networks. *Bioinformatics,* 18:261–274, 2002.

4. A. Datta, A. Choudhary, M. L. Bittner, and E. R. Dougherty. External control in markovian genetic regulatory networks. *Mach. Learn.,* 52:169–191, 2003.

5. H. Kitano. Computational systems biology. *Nature,* 420:206–210, 2002.

6. H. Kitano. Cancer as a robust system: implications for anticancer therapy. *Nat. Rev. Cancer,* 4:227–235, 2004.

7. S. Bilke and F. Sjunnesson. Number of attractors in random boolean networks. *Phys. Rev. E,* 72:016110, 2005.

8. B. Drossel, T. Mihaljev, and F. Greil. Number and length of attractors in a critical kauffman model with connectivity one. *Phys. Rev. Lett.,* 94:088701, 2005.

9. B. Samuelsson and C. Troein. Superpolynomial growth in the number of attractors in kauffman networks. *Phys. Rev. Lett.,* 90:098701, 2003.

10. V. Devloo, P. Hansen, and M. Labbé. Identification of all steady states in large networks by logical analysis. *Bull. Math. Biol.,* 65:1025–1051, 2003.

11. A. Garg, I. Xenarios, L. Mendoza, and G. DeMicheli. An efficient method for dynamic analysis of gene regulatory networks and in silico gene perturbation experiments. *Lect. Notes Comput. Sci.,* 4453:62–76, 2007.

12. D. J. Irons. Improving the efficiency of attractor cycle identification in Boolean networks. *Physica D,* 217:7–21, 2006.

13. S-Q. Zhang, M. Hayashida, T. Akutsu, W-K. Ching, and M. K. Ng. Algorithms for finding small attractors in boolean networks. *EURASIP J. Bioinform. Syst. Biol.,* 2007:20180, 2007.

14. M. Milano and A. Roli. Solving the safistiability problem through Boolean networks. *Lect. Notes Artifi. Intell.,* 1792:72–93, 2000.

15. A. Mochizuki. An analytical study of the number of steady states in gene regulatory networks. *J. Theor. Biol.,* 236:291–310, 2005.

16. T. Tamura and T. Akutsu. An improved algorithm for detecting a singleton attractor in a boolean network consisting of AND/OR nodes. In *Proceedings of the 3rd International Conference on Algebraic Biology,* 216–229, 2008.

17. A. Datta, A. Choudhary, M. L. Bittner, and E. R. Dougherty. External control in Markovian genetic regulatory networks: the imperfect information case. *Bioinformatics,* 20:924–930, 2004.

18. B. Faryabi, A. Datta, and E. R. Dougherty. On approximate stochastic control in genetic regulatory networks, *IET Syst. Biol.,* 1:361–368, 2007.

19. R. Pal, A. Datta, M. L. Bittner, and E. R. Dougherty. Intervention in context-sensitive probabilistic Boolean networks. *Bioinformatics,* 21:1211–1218, 2005.

20. R. Pal, A. Datta, M. L. Bittner, and E. R. Dougherty. Optimal infinite-horizon control for probabilistic Boolean networks. *IEEE Trans. Signal Process.* 54:2375–2387, 2006.

21. T. Akutsu, M. Hayashida, W-K. Ching, and M. K. Ng. Control of Boolean networks: hardness results and algorithms for tree-structured networks. *J. Theor. Biol.,* 244:670–679, 2007.

22. C. J. Langmead and S. K. Jha. Symbolic approaches for finding control strategies in Boolean networks. In *Proceedings of 6th Asia-Pacific Bioinformatics Conference,* Imperial College Press, 2008, pp. 307–319.

23. T. Akutsu, S. Miyano, and S. Kuhara. Inferring qualitative relations in genetic networks and metabolic pathways. *Bioinformatics,* 16:727–734, 2000.

24. I. Shmulevich and E. R. Dougherty. *Genomic Signal Processing,* Princeton University Press, 2007.

25. S-Q. Zhang, W-K. Ching, M. K. Ng, and T. Akutsu. Simulation study in probabilistic boolean network models for genetic regulatory networks. *Int. J. Data Mining Bioinform.,* 1:217–240, 2007.

26. I. Shmulevich, I. Gluhovsky, R. F. Hashimoto, E. R. Dougherty, and W. Zhang. Steady-state analysis of genetic regulatory networks modeled by probabilistic Boolean networks. *Comp. Funct. Genomics,* 4:601–608, 2003.

27. W-K. Ching, S-Q. Zhang, M. K. Ng, and T. Akutsu. An approximation method for solving the steady-state probability distribution of probabilistic Boolean networks. *Bioinformatics,* 23:1511–1518, 2007.

28. M. K. Ng, S-Q. Zhang, W-K. Ching, and T. Akutsu. A control model for markovian genetic regulatory networks. *Transactions on Computational Systems Biology,* 36–48, 2006.

29. W-K. Ching, S-Q. Zhang, Y. Jiao, T. Akutsu, and S. Wong. Optimal finite-horizon control for probabilistic Boolean networks with hard constraints. *Proc. International Symposium on Optimization and Systems Biology,* 21–28, 2007.

11

PROBABILISTIC METHODS AND RATE HETEROGENEITY

Tal Pupko and Itay Mayrose

Department of Cell Research and Immunology, George S. Wise Faculty of Life Sciences, Tel Aviv University, Tel Aviv, Israel

11.1 INTRODUCTION TO PROBABILISTIC METHODS

Evolutionary forces such as mutation, drift, and to a certain extent selection are stochastic in their nature. It is thus not surprising that probabilistic models of sequence evolution quickly became the workhorse of molecular evolution research. The long, ongoing effort to accurately model sequence evolution stems from two different needs. The first is that of evolutionary biologists: Models of sequence evolution allow us to test evolutionary hypotheses and to reconstruct phylogenetic trees and ancestral sequences [1–3]. The second is that of bioinformaticians and system biologists— probabilistic/evolutionary methods are critical components in numerous applications. For example, the construction of similarity networks is based upon all-against-all homology searches. Each pairwise evaluation is done using tools such as Blast and Blat [4, 5], which rely on evolutionary models. Additional examples include gene finding and genome annotation [6], alignment algorithms [7, 8], detecting genomic regions of high and low conservation [9, 10], prediction of transcription-factor binding sites [11], function prediction [12], and protein networks analysis [13, 14]. In this chapter, we describe how probabilistic models are used to study

Elements of Computational Systems Biology   Edited by Huma M. Lodhi and Stephen H. Muggleton
Copyright © 2010 John Wiley & Sons, Inc.

substitution rates, that is, the rate at which mutations become fixed in the population. We focus on the variation of substitution rates among sequence positions (spatial variation). Our goal is to provide the needed mathematical and conceptual aspects of modeling rate variation in sequence evolution.

11.2 SEQUENCE EVOLUTION IS DESCRIBED USING MARKOV CHAINS

We start with a very simplified model of sequence evolution through which we introduce basic principles of probabilistic evolutionary models. After describing the model, we discuss its shortcomings as the motivation for the use of more complicated, yet more realistic models.

Consider a sequence of length 100 base pairs. The model assumes that each nucleotide is equally likely to appear, and that all substitutions from one state to another have the same fixation probabilities. Specifically, we assume that the nucleotide at each position is randomly drawn with equal probabilities: $\pi_A = \pi_G = \pi_C = \pi_T = 1/4$. Once the first sequence is drawn, we let it evolve through generations. In any given generation, each nucleotide can change with a very small probability p. If a change occurs, the new nucleotide is drawn with equal probabilities $(1/3)$. Although this model is clearly oversimplified, various questions regarding the evolutionary process can be addressed. For example, does the sequence composition change over time (what will be the character distribution after many generations)? What is the substitution rate (what will be the distribution of the number of changes per generation per position)? What is the probability that nucleotide A is replaced with nucleotide C after t generations? Fortunately, these computational questions can be answered, once we describe the evolutionary process at each position as a discrete Markov chain [15], summarized by the following matrix:

$$
P = \begin{array}{c} \\ A \\ C \\ G \\ T \end{array}
\begin{array}{cccc}
A & C & G & T
\end{array}
\left[
\begin{array}{cccc}
1-p & p/3 & p/3 & p/3 \\
p/3 & 1-p & p/3 & p/3 \\
p/3 & p/3 & 1-p & p/3 \\
p/3 & p/3 & p/3 & 1-p
\end{array}
\right].
$$

The term $P_{ij}(t)$ denotes the probability that character i will end up being character j after t generations. From the theory of Markov chains, this value is $[P^t]_{ij}$. that is, the i, j entry in matrix P, which is raised to the power of t. From the equality of the transition probabilities among all characters, it is clear that after a long time, the average nucleotide frequency of each nucleotide remains $1/4$ (this is formally termed the stationary distribution). Finally, the number of generations until a substitution occurs (the waiting time of the process) is geometrically distributed with parameter p.

Our first extension of this model is to switch from a discrete time scale (measured in generations) to a continuous time scale (measured in years). This is biologically reasonable because generations are seldom synchronized nor do they have a fixed length. This generalization is standard in Markov process theory—instead of assuming that the waiting times are geometrically distributed, we now assume that they are exponentially distributed. Such an assumption leads to a continuous time Markov process. The heart of the model is the instantaneous rate matrix Q. In this matrix, the diagonal values are related to the waiting time of each character, that is, the waiting time of character i is exponentially distributed with parameter $-q_{ii}$ (where q_{ij} is the entry of row i and column j of the Q matrix). Given that a substitution has occurred, the probability that i changes to j is given by $-q_{ij}/q_{ii}$. Furthermore, the number of substitutions from character i to character j in a small time interval dt is $q_{ij} \times$ dt. For the model described above, the Q matrix is:

$$
Q = \begin{array}{c} \\ A \\ C \\ G \\ T \end{array}
\begin{array}{cccc}
A & C & G & T \\
\left[\begin{array}{cccc}
-3\alpha & \alpha & \alpha & \alpha \\
\alpha & -3\alpha & \alpha & \alpha \\
\alpha & \alpha & -3\alpha & \alpha \\
\alpha & \alpha & \alpha & -3\alpha
\end{array}\right] .
\end{array}
$$

In this matrix, α is referred to as the instantaneous rate between any two states. Higher values of α specify a process in which more substitutions occur in each time interval. The substitution probabilities can be obtained by exponentiating the Q matrix.

Specifically, $P_{ij}(t)$, the probability that character i will end up being character j after t time units equals $[e^{Qt}]_{ij}$. The model described by the matrix Q above is termed the JC model after its developers [16], who also provided explicit formulae for $P_{ij}(t)$, eliminating the need for matrix exponentiations:

$$
P_{ij}(t) = \frac{1 - e^{-4\alpha t}}{4} \qquad P_{ii}(t) = \frac{1 + 3e^{-4\alpha t}}{4} . \tag{11.1}
$$

An important characteristic of the JC model is that it is time reversible: $\pi_x P_{xy}(t) = \pi_y P_{yx}(t)$. Explicitly, the probability of the event "start with x and evolve to y" is equal to the probability of the event "start with y and evolve to x." This implies that $\pi_x Q_{xy} = \pi_y Q_{yx}$. Note, however, that time reversibility does not impose the Q matrix to be symmetric.

For any continuous time Markov process, the expected number of character transitions in t time units is the summation over all nondiagonal entries:

$$
d = \sum_i \sum_{j \neq i} \pi_i Q_{ij} t. \tag{11.2}
$$

For the JC model, this is simply: $d = 3\alpha t$.

11.2.1 Estimating Pairwise Distances

We next show how the JC model is used to estimate the distance between two given sequences. Consider the sequence ACCA evolving through time to ACCG. We know that at least one substitution has occurred, but if we consider backward and multiple substitutions, it is possible that various other substitutions have occurred. Using likelihood calculations, we can estimate the number of substitutions that have occurred. The likelihood of observing the two sequences above is the probability of starting with ACCA multiplied by the replacement probabilities. Assuming site independence, the likelihood is

$$L(t, \alpha) = \pi_A P_{AA}(t) \times \pi_C P_{CC}(t) \times \pi_C P_{CC}(t) \times \pi_A P_{AG}(t), \tag{11.3}$$

$$L(t, \alpha) = \left(\frac{1}{4}\right)^4 \left(\frac{1 - e^{-4\alpha t}}{4}\right) \left(\frac{1 + 3e^{-4\alpha t}}{4}\right)^3. \tag{11.4}$$

As α and t are usually unknown, one can estimate their values by maximizing the likelihood function. Since the two parameters always appear in the form of $\alpha \times t$, it is clear that one cannot evaluate each parameter separately. In fact, in all evolutionary models, the parameters of the rate matrix Q and time appear as such multiplications. However, if the product $\alpha \times t$ is estimated, d above can thus be estimated. The α parameter is usually set to a fixed value of $1/3$ and by doing so $d = 3\alpha t = t$, and thus optimizing t is equivalent to optimizing d. In other words, in this setting, one can think of t not as time measured in years, but rather as evolutionary time measured in substitutions per site. In fact, for all evolutionary models, d is always set equal to t and the equation above becomes:

$$d = \sum_i \sum_{j \neq i} \pi_i q_{ij} t = \sum_i \sum_{j \neq i} \pi_i q_{ij} d = d \sum_i \sum_{j \neq i} \pi_i q_{ij} \tag{11.5}$$

$$\Rightarrow \sum_i \sum_{j \neq i} \pi_i q_{ij} = 1.$$

Thus, by normalizing Q so that the average instantaneous rate is one, it is ensured that in a branch of length t, we expect that the average number of substitutions across all sites will also be t.

For the JC model, a closed-form formula for the distance d that maximizes the likelihood can be obtained [17]:

$$\hat{d} = -\frac{3}{4} \ln\left(1 - \frac{4}{3}\hat{p}\right), \tag{11.6}$$

where $\hat{p}$ is the proportion of sites, which differ between the two compared sequences. In the example above, $\hat{p} = 0.25$ and thus $\hat{d} \cong 0.3$. Notably, for more complicated models, no such closed-form formula exists, and the distance estimate is obtained by numerically maximizing the likelihood function.

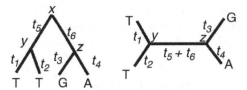

Figure 11.1   A rooted tree (left) and an unrooted tree (right) and their associated branch lengths. The assignment for one position of the sequence is shown.

11.2.2   Calculating the Likelihood of a Tree

The JC model, although an extreme oversimplification of the evolutionary process, is already very powerful. For example, given a set of sequences from various organisms, one can estimate the number of substitutions that have occurred between each sequence pair. Given these distance estimates, a phylogenetic tree can easily be reconstructed, for example, using the neighbor joining (NJ) method [18].

Given the model, one can compute the likelihood of a given tree, that is, the probability of observing the sequence data given the tree topology (T), the branch lengths (t), and the model (M). The likelihood for the rooted tree in Figure 11.1 is:

$$P(\text{data} \mid T, t, M)$$
$$= \sum_{x,y,z=\{ACGT\}} \pi_x P_{x \to y}(t_5) P_{x \to z}(t_6) P_{y \to T}(t_1) P_{y \to T}(t_2) P_{z \to G}(t_3) P_{z \to A}(t_4).$$

$$(11.7)$$

This is the likelihood of a single position. The likelihood of the entire dataset is achieved by assuming that all positions are conditionally independent:

$$P(\text{data} \mid T, t, M) = \prod_{i=1}^{N}(D_i \mid T, t, M), \qquad (11.8)$$

N is the sequence length and D_i are the data represented by column i of the alignment. Using this computation, we can go over many trees and rank them according to their likelihood. The maximum-likelihood (ML) tree reconstruction method chooses the tree with the highest likelihood score. In practice, the number of possible trees is enormous, and thus, available tree reconstruction programs use heuristic search strategies, rather than calculate the likelihood of all possible trees [19].

11.2.2.1   *Rooted versus Unrooted Trees*   When constructing phylogenetic trees, we would ultimately like to obtain a rooted tree, a tree in which one node, called the root, specifies the common ancestor of all sequences. In such a tree, the directionality of time is defined. However, in most tree-reconstruction methods, including those that employ likelihood computations, only unrooted trees can be

obtained. When the likelihood is computed using a time-reversible model, the position of the root does not affect the likelihood score.

For any time reversible model, the likelihood of the position shown in Figure 11.1 is:

$$P(\text{data} \mid T, t, M) = \tag{11.9}$$

$$\sum_x \sum_y \sum_z \pi_x P_{x \to y}(t_5) P_{x \to z}(t_6) P_{y \to T}(t_1) P_{y \to T}(t_2) P_{z \to G}(t_3) P_{z \to A}(t_4) =$$

$$\sum_z \sum_y \pi_y P_{y \to T}(t_1) P_{y \to T}(t_2) P_{z \to G}(t_3) P_{z \to A}(t_4) \sum_x P_{y \to x}(t_5) P_{x \to z}(t_6) =$$

$$\sum_z \sum_y \pi_y P_{y \to T}(t_1) P_{y \to T}(t_2) P_{z \to G}(t_3) P_{z \to A}(t_4) P_{y \to z}(t_5 + t_6).$$

The second line is obtained from the reversibility property and the third line from the Chapman–Kolmogorov equation ($P^{t_1+t_2} = P^{t_1} P^{t_2}$). Thus, the likelihoods for the rooted and unrooted trees are the same, where for the unrooted tree in Figure 11.1, the likelihood is computed after the root is arbitrarily set to node y. Felsenstein [20] developed an efficient postorder tree traversal algorithm to compute the likelihood of an unrooted tree.

11.2.3 Extending the Basic Model

While the JC model paved the way to probabilistic analysis of sequence data, it assumes biologically unrealistic assumptions, which may lead to erroneous conclusions:

(1) The substitutions probabilities as well as the initial character probabilities are assumed to be identical for all character states.

(2) All positions are assumed to evolve under exactly the same process.

(3) All positions are assumed to evolve independently of each other.

A great deal of research was devoted to develop computationally feasible models, which alleviate these unrealistic assumptions. Regarding the first assumption, the introduction of several parameters in the substitution matrix resulted in a nested series of models such as the K2P model that assumes unequal rates of transition and transversion [21], the F81 model that allows any value for the nucleotide frequencies [20] and the most general time reversible model, GTR, in which a parameter is assumed for each substitution type [22].

When analyzing amino acid sequences, there are 190 different types of substitutions. If a parameter is assumed for each such substitution type, a large number of parameters should be estimated afresh for each protein dataset analyzed. Estimating such large number of parameters from a small dataset is likely to result in large errors associated with each estimated parameter and in over fitting of the model to the data [23]. For this reason, researchers have evaluated amino acid matrices from a large set of aligned amino acid sequences (often, the entire protein sequence databank). Using

these matrices, one can compute the likelihoods of a given multiple sequence alignment of protein sequences without optimizing any parameter of the Q matrix. The first
such empirical matrix was developed by Dayhoff et al. [24]. When more data became
available, updated matrices were computed, such as the JTT matrix [25] and the WAG
matrix [26]. Since mitochondrial and chloroplast proteins evolve under genetic codes
different from nuclear proteins, empirical amino acid substitution matrices were also
estimated for mitochondrial proteins [27] and for chloroplast proteins [28].

11.3 AMONG-SITE RATE VARIATION

When examining a multiple sequence alignment, such as that presented in Figure 11.2,
it is typical that some positions vary more than others. There are two explanations

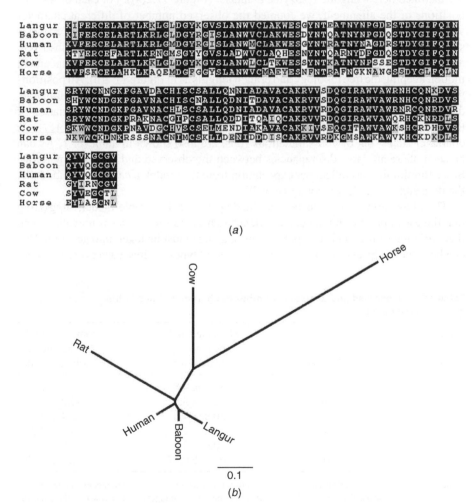

(a)

(b)

Figure 11.2 Multiple sequence alignment and a phylogenetic tree of six lysozyme c sequences.
Data from Yang et al. [29].

for this observation. The first is that these variations result from the stochastic nature of amino acid substitutions. Meaning, all positions evolve under the same stochastic process, but some positions experienced more substitutions than others simply by chance. An alternative explanation is the existence of an additional layer of variation caused by differences in the evolutionary process among positions. Two indications favor the second explanation. The first is based on biological knowledge. It is widely accepted that the intensity of purifying selection varies across protein positions. For example, positions that are associated with the active site of enzymes are under strong purifying selection compared to the remaining protein sites. These positions will thus exhibit little sequence variation relative to the other positions among analyzed sequences.

The second argument in favor of the second hypothesis is statistical in nature and is illustrated here using the lysozyme c dataset (Figure 11.2(a)). For each of the 128 positions of the alignment, we counted the observed number of different character states. In Table 11.1, we present the number of positions in which a single character state is observed, the number of positions in which two character states are observed, and so on. We next simulated sequences according to the JTT amino acid replacement model, keeping the tree topology and branch lengths as in Figure 11.2(b). All positions were simulated under the same evolutionary process, implying a homogenous rate distribution among all positions (see below). The average and standard deviation of the number of positions in the simulated alignments for which there are $1, \ldots, 6$ character states, out of 100 simulations runs, are also shown in Table 11.1. As can be seen, there are large discrepancies between the observed and simulated patterns. Since the simulations reflect our expectation from the model, it can be concluded that the data and the model do not agree well.

The above arguments illustrate the inadequacy of the simple model, suggesting that the assumption of homogenous stochastic process for all sites is unrealistic and that variation of the stochastic process among sites must be taken into account. This can be achieved by assuming that there are several types of sites, each evolving under

Table 11.1   Observed and simulated number of character states in the lysozyme c dataset*

Number of character states	Observed	Simulated under homogenous rate distribution	Simulated under among-site rate variation model
1	46	33.9 ± 4.8	44.1 ± 5.3
2	44	56.7 ± 5.5	43.0 ± 5.3
3	29	30.4 ± 4.5	28.4 ± 4.9
4	8	6.4 ± 2.2	10.6 ± 3.3
5	1	0.6 ± 0.8	1.9 ± 1.4
6	0	0.03 ± 0.17	0.13 ± 0.37

* The quantile gamma discretization technique with four rate categories was used to model among site rate variation (see section 4). The log-likelihood of the data under the homogenous model was −1044, and the log-likelihood of the among-site rate variation was −1035.8, with an ML estimate of $\alpha = 1.3$.

a different stochastic process. Since our focus is on the variation in the number of substitutions, we assume that these types differ in their waiting times. If process A is identical to process B except that all waiting times of A are halved, then the Q matrix of process A is simply twice the Q matrix of process B. Thus, sites are characterized by Q matrices differing from each other up to a multiplication factor, which is termed the evolutionary rate of the process. The most straightforward model accounting for among-site rate variation is to assume that all sequence positions have the same substitution matrix, Q, with each site characterized by its own evolutionary rate. Thus, site i is characterized by the matrix $Q \times r_i$, where r_i is the evolutionary rate of site i. Recall that for a process M characterized by a rate matrix Q, $P_{ij}(t \mid M) = [e^{Q \times t}]_{ij}$. Thus, for a site with a process M' characterized by an evolutionary rate r_i, the substitution probabilities become $P_{ij}(t \mid M') = [e^{(Q \times r_i) \times t}]_{ij} = [e^{Q \times (r_i \times t)}]_{ij} = P_{ij}(r_i \times t \mid M)$. This implies that when computing the likelihood of a site with a rate r, instead of multiplying the Q matrix by r, the likelihood can be obtained simply by multiplying all the branches by r and using the original Q. Since the branch lengths are indicative of the average number of substitutions, this implies that a site with an evolutionary rate of 2 experiences on average twice as many substitutions as a site with an evolutionary rate of 1.

A common approach to model rate heterogeneity among sites is to assume that there are K possible rate categories $(r^{(1)}, \ldots, r^{(K)})$ with associated probabilities $(p^{(1)}, \ldots, p^{(K)})$. The rates and their associated probabilities are collectively termed θ. The rate of site i (r_i) can be any one of these K possible rates, according to their associated probabilities. Formally, a distribution Ω over the possible evolutionary rates is assumed, and the rate r_i is in fact a random variable drawn from Ω.

When computing the likelihood of position i, we usually do not know the actual value of r_i, and we thus need to consider all possible rate assignments:

$$P(D_i \mid T, t, M, \theta) = \sum_{k=1}^{K} p^{(k)} P(D_i \mid T, t, M, r^{(k)}). \tag{11.10}$$

Recall that in the homogenous rate model, we normalized Q so that the average number of substitutions along a branch of length t equals t (see Eq. (11.5)). This equality still holds for heterogeneous rate models, but now, the average number of substitutions along a branch of length t equals $\sum_{k=1}^{K} \sum_i \sum_{i \neq j} \pi_i q_{ij} r^{(k)} t p^{(k)}$. Equating this expression to t, we obtain:

$$\sum_{k=1}^{K} \sum_i \sum_{i \neq j} \pi_i q_{ij} t r^{(k)} p^{(k)} = t \quad \Rightarrow$$

$$\sum_{k=1}^{K} r^{(k)} p^{(k)} \sum_i \sum_{i \neq j} \pi_i q_{ij} = 1 \quad \Rightarrow \tag{11.11}$$

$$\sum_{k=1}^{K} r^{(k)} p^{(k)} = 1.$$

The third line is obtained from the second line because Q is normalized. We conclude that in order for the branch lengths to indicate the average number of substitutions per site, the weighted average over all rates, that is, the expected rate, must be 1.

11.4 DISTRIBUTION OF RATES ACROSS SITES

The model described above assumes that each site is assigned a specific rate from a predefined rate distribution. The challenge is to find a distribution that balances between the number of free parameters and its flexibility to model a range of datasets that differ in their among-site rate variation pattern. One option is to assign each site its own rate ($r_1, \ldots, r_N$). This model requires $N - 1$ parameters to be inferred (since the average rate is constrained to equal 1). This is, however, a model very rich in parameters. When so many parameters are inferred, there is a high probability that the model overfits the data, unless a very large number of sequences are available [30]. The error associated with each parameter is also very large in such cases. Thus, it is desirable to search for a model with significantly less parameters, which still captures the inherent variability of rates among sites. For example, one can *a priori* assume the existence of three rate categories $\{r^{(1)}, r^{(2)}, r^{(3)}\}$ with associated probabilities $\{p^{(1)}, p^{(2)}, p^{(3)}\}$. In this case, $\theta = \{r^{(1)}, r^{(2)}, r^{(3)}, p^{(1)}, p^{(2)}, p^{(3)}\}$, and the likelihood of the data can be computed using Eq. (11.10). In most cases, the parameters are unknown and can be inferred using ML: $\theta = \text{argmax} P(D_i \mid T, t, M, \theta)$. Since $\sum_i p^{(i)} = 1$ and $\sum_k p^{(k)} r^{(k)} = 1$, this requires optimizing four parameters (or in general $2K - 2$; K being the number of categories). While significantly fewer parameters are inferred in this model, for small values of K, the model tends not to represent the entire repertoire of rates, while for large values of K, there are many parameters and the model tends to overfit the data. It is possible to reduce the number of parameters by approximately half, by either fixing all rate probabilities to be equal or to set the rates to fixed values and optimize only their probabilities. Susko et al. [31] applied the latter with 101 rates in the range of [0, 10]. This variant still estimates dozens of free parameters, which is usually justified only for extremely large datasets. Fortunately, models were suggested in which a large repertoire of rates are allowed, yet the number of parameters is relatively very small. These models take advantage of classical continuous distributions.

11.4.1 The Gamma Distribution

Yang [32] suggested using the continuous gamma distribution to model among-site rate variation. In this model, it is assumed that the rate at each site is independently sampled from a gamma distribution. This distribution has two parameters: a shape parameter, α, and a scale parameter, β. A variable R is gamma distributed, denoted by $R \sim \Gamma(\alpha, \beta)$, if its density function is

$$g(r; \alpha, \beta) = \frac{\beta^\alpha}{\Gamma(\alpha)} e^{-\beta r} r^{\alpha-1}. \tag{11.12}$$

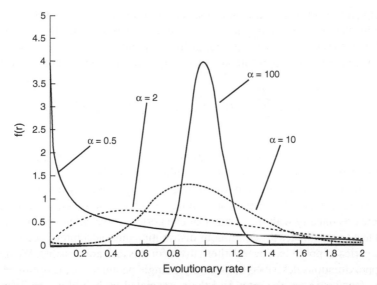

Figure 11.3   The gamma distribution. The α parameter specifies the distribution shape. When α is close to zero, the distribution is L-shaped, whereas high α values correspond to a bell-shaped distribution.

The mean of the gamma distribution is α/β and the variance is α/β^2. Since the mean of the rate distribution should equal 1, β is fixed so that $\beta = \alpha$. Hence, the shape of the gamma distribution is determined by a single positive parameter, α, which is indicative of rate variation. When $\alpha = 1$, the gamma distribution reduces to the exponential distribution with parameter 1. When α is higher than 1, the distribution is bell-shaped suggesting little rate heterogeneity. In the case of $\alpha < 1$, the distribution is highly skewed and is L-shaped, which indicates high levels of rate variation. This flexibility makes the distribution suitable for accommodating different levels of rate variation in different datasets (Figure 11.3). To compute the likelihood of site i, L_i, under a continuous gamma distribution, the following expression is computed:

$$L_i = \int_0^\infty P(D_i \mid T \times r)g(r; \alpha, \alpha)dr \qquad (11.13)$$

Here, $T \times r$ indicates a tree topology as in T, in which all branches are multiplied by the factor r. The α parameter is optimized by maximizing the likelihood of the entire dataset:

$$\alpha = \text{argmax} \prod_{i=1}^{N} L_i \qquad (11.14)$$

While it is possible to compute the likelihood under this continuous gamma distribution for pairwise sequences [33], no polynomial algorithm is available to compute the likelihood of a tree (three or more sequences). In order to avoid this computational difficulty, the continuous gamma distribution is approximated by a discrete one. Accordingly, the actual range of $r(0, \infty)$ is divided into C rate categories, such that the integral in Eq. (11.13) is approximated by a weighted sum over a set of discrete rates:

$$L_i \simeq \sum_{j=1}^{C} P(D_i \mid T, t, M, r^{(j)}) p^{(j)}, \tag{11.15}$$

where $(r^{(1)}, \ldots, r^{(C)})$ are representative rates and $(p^{(1)}, \ldots, p^{(C)})$ are the corresponding rate probabilities. These rates and probabilities should be chosen so as to approximate the desired gamma distribution most accurately. Naturally, the more discrete categories are used, the better the approximation will be. However, the computation time increases linearly with the number of categories. The challenge is thus to use a method that approximates the continuous distribution most accurately, yet uses as few rate categories as possible. Several alternatives for this task are possible. We note that in all approximations described below, only a single parameter, α, is optimized from the data. Once α is set, the rates and their associated probabilities are determined according to the numerical approximation procedure. The various approximation techniques differ in this numerical procedure.

11.4.2 Numerical Approximation of the Continuous Gamma Distribution

The discrete gamma distribution, as suggested by Yang [34], is by far the most widely used method to account for among-site rate variation and is implemented in most available phylogenetic programs. In this "Quantile" method, the rates are chosen such that all categories have an equal weight of $1/K$. Two alternatives for such a discritization of the gamma distribution were suggested in Yang [34]. In the first alternative, the mean of each category is used to represent all the rates within that category. For a category i with boundaries a and b, the average rate is:

$$r^{(i)} = K \int_a^b r g(r; \alpha, \alpha) dr. \tag{11.16}$$

The inner boundaries (the boundaries besides 0 and ∞) are calculated as the $(1/K, 2/K, \ldots, K-1/K)$ quantiles of the gamma distribution. In the second alternative, the medians are used to represent each discrete rate category. In this case, the representative rates, $(r^{(1)}, \ldots, r^{(K)})$ are calculated as the $(1/2K, 3/2K, \ldots, 2K-1/2K)$ quantiles of the gamma distribution. In this case, the rates have to be normalized so that the average over all rates is 1. We note that Yang [34] recommended using the mean rather than the median discretization method.

A second approximation was suggested by Felsenstein [30] and is based on the generalized Laguerre quadrature technique. In this approach, both the rates and their associated probabilities that give the best fit to the continuous distribution are searched for (unlike the quantile approximation, in which only optimal rates are determined). For implementation details, see Mayrose et al. [35]. The quadrature method seems to better approximate the continuous gamma distribution compared to the quantile approximation, since the likelihood of the tree is less sensitive to the exact number of rate categories. It, thus, seems that using the quadrature method can be more economical in terms of the number of discrete categories used, which results in reduced computation time.

In both discretization techniques detailed above, because the gamma distribution depends on the α parameter, different values of α specify a different set of discretized rates. Thus, the terms $P(D_i \mid T, t, M, r^{(j)})$ are recomputed over and over during the process of α optimization, thus rendering it computationally expensive. Susko et al. [31] devised an alternative procedure, in which the rate categories $(r^{(1)}, \ldots, r^{(K)})$ are set to predefined fixed values, and only their associated probabilities are allowed to vary when different α values are considered during optimization. In this approximation, the expensive computations of $P(D_i \mid T, t, M, r^{(j)})$ are computed only once during optimization for all α values considered. Thus, for a fixed tree and a fixed Q matrix, a larger number of rate categories can practically be used, resulting in more accurate approximations.

Using the techniques to model rate variation described above, we can now evaluate, using simulations, the fit of among-site rate variation models to the observed number of character states observed in each position for the lysozyme c data. As can be seen in Table 11.1, using a discrete gamma model provides a significant better fit to the data compared with the homogeneous model. Moreover, to statistically compare between the fits of the two models to the lysozyme c data, the corresponding log-likelihoods are compared using the likelihood ratio test statistic (for details about model selection, see Yang [3]). Using this test, the among-site rate variation model fits the lysozyme c data significantly better than the homogeneous model (P value $<10^{-4}$).

11.4.3 Alternative Rate Distributions

In a multiple sequence alignment, some sites are extremely conserved, showing no variation across the entire set of sequences analyzed. If these sites are abundant, it might be that the gamma distribution will either capture the rate of these slowly evolving sites or the fast evolving sites, but not both. In other words, the gamma distribution might not be flexible enough to capture the distribution of evolutionary rates in real sequences. Susko et al. [31] devised a statistical test that evaluates the fit of the gamma distribution to real sequence data. In five out of the 13 datasets tested, the gamma distribution was rejected. Their analysis showed that the gamma distribution mainly failed to fit positions evolving with high rates.

Inching toward more flexible rate distributions, Gu et al. [36] suggested the gamma + invariant model. In this model, the rate distribution is composed of a gamma distribution, which is augmented with an additional rate category in which the rate equals zero. The probability of this category is an additional free parameter estimated from the data. Adding this parameter often significantly increases the fit of the model to the data. Although the gamma + invariant model is intuitively very appealing, the estimates of the model parameters are highly sensitive to taxon sampling [37, 38]. In addition, the high correlation between the proportion of the invariable sites and the gamma shape parameter indicates model inadequacy [37].

Kosakovsky Pond and Frost [39] developed a hierarchical approach, which allows generating rate distributions based on three parameters. In their method, a beta distribution (with two parameters) determines the quantiles (the boundaries of the rate categories) of an underlying distribution (e.g., a one parameter gamma distribution). The representative rate of each category is then computed as the posterior expectation of the underlying rate distribution in that interval. Notably, the two parameters of the beta distribution only define the form of the discretization, while the form of the underlying continuous distribution stays the same. This technique significantly increases the flexibility of the underlying rate distribution, resulting in a better fit of the model to real datasets.

We have previously suggested modeling the distribution of evolutionary rates by a mixture of gamma distributions [35]. The models assume the existence of a few gamma distributions, each with its own set of parameters. These parameters, as well as the probability of each gamma distribution, are estimated using ML from the data. By choosing the number of gamma components, a range of distributions with growing expressiveness with corresponding increase in the number of parameters is considered. The model can thus accommodate a multimodal rate distribution unlike the gamma and the log-normal distributions that are always unimodal. The strength in this approach is that when more data are available, more flexible rate distributions can easily be obtained.

While the gamma distribution is by far the most commonly used, several other rate distributions were suggested. The log-normal rate distribution was first suggested by Olsen [40] for pairwise distances and was discussed in Felsenstein [30]. No large-scale comparison was performed to test which of these two distributions better reflect rate variation in sequence data. As stated in Felsenstein [30], in essence, any continuous distribution on the interval $(0, \infty)$ may be appropriate to model among-site rate variation, and the log normal and the gamma distributions are simply the two best known distributions on this interval.

The approaches described above assume a specific underlying rate distribution, from which the rate at each site is sampled. A different approach for modeling rate variation among sites was suggested in Huelsenbeck and Suchard [41]. They have developed a Bayesian nonparametric method in which sites are partitioned to rate classes, that is, some sites are assigned to rate class 1, some to rate class 2, and so on. The novelty in their method is that the sites are partitioned to rate classes not in a deterministic way, but rather many possible partitions are considered, that is, the partitioning is itself a random variable with a Dirichlet process prior. The posterior distribution of rates, partitions, and other parameters are then inferred using a Markov chain Monte Carlo (MCMC) approach.

Morozov et al. [42] have also developed a method to model among-site rate variation without assuming an underlying rate distribution. In their method, either Fourier or wavelet models are applied to account for among-site rate variation. They have shown that using such a modeling approach improved the fit of the model to the data compared with the standard gamma approach. Clearly, more studies are needed to elucidate how such models influence tree reconstruction and site-specific rate estimation (see Section 11.5).

11.5 SITE-SPECIFIC RATE ESTIMATION

The heterogeneous rate models described above aimed at presenting a better description of the evolutionary process. These models were found to be an important component when predicting functional sites and regions in DNA and protein sequences. This task is achieved by estimating site-specific evolutionary rates. The assumption here is that the degree to which a site is free to vary depends on its functional (and structural) importance; a site that plays an essential role, such as the one within the active site of an enzyme, is unlikely to change over evolutionary time and will have a low evolutionary rate.

Detecting conserved regions in DNA and protein sequences is of central importance to various bioinformatics methods and is widely used to direct molecular biology experiments. Examples include the detection of active sites [43], the detection of splicing regulatory elements [44] and of promoters [45], and the prediction of three-dimensional structures [46]. Previous approaches for detecting conserved evolutionary regions were not based on probabilistic models, but rather on counting or entropy techniques (reviewed in Valdar [47]). Most of these methods ignore the phylogenetic tree and do not allow any parameters to be learnt from the data analyzed, thus implicitly making the unrealistic assumption that all sequence data evolve under the same stochastic process. Evolutionary biologists equate conservation and low rate of evolution. It is this observation that places the problem of conservation estimation in the realm of probabilistic evolutionary models. This placement benefits the field of conservation inference with the set of built-in tools that come with evolutionary models such as its statistical robust nature of inference.

Given a fixed phylogenetic tree and its associated branch lengths, site-specific rates can be inferred based on the ML paradigm [10, 48]. The most likely rate of site i is the one that maximizes the site's likelihood: $r_i = \text{argmax} P(D_i \mid T, t, M, r)$. Pupko et al. [10] have shown that the ML rate inference method outperforms the nonprobabilistic maximum parsimony approach: It enabled detecting conserved protein–protein interacting domains that were undetected by the parsimony approach.

Bayesian inference of site-specific evolutionary rates is an alternative to the ML framework [49, 50]. In this case, a prior distribution over the rates is assumed. Using Bayes theorem, we can calculate the posterior probability density of rate, r, at site i:

$$P(r_i = r \mid D_i, T, \alpha) = \frac{P(D_i \mid r, T)p(r \mid \alpha)}{\int_{r'=0}^{\infty} P(D_i \mid r', T)p(r' \mid \alpha)\mathrm{d}r'}, \tag{11.17}$$

where $P(D_i \mid r, T)$ is computed as explained above. $p(r \mid \alpha)$ is the prior distribution over the rates. As stated above, evaluating the denominator cannot be computed efficiently and so a discrete approximation is used:

$$P(r_i = r^{(j)} \mid D_i, T, \alpha) \simeq \frac{P(D_i \mid r^{(j)}, T)p(r^{(j)} \mid \alpha)}{\sum_{k=1}^{K} P(D_i \mid r^{(k)}, T)p(r^{(k)} \mid \alpha)}, \tag{11.18}$$

$p(r^{(j)} \mid \alpha)$ is the prior distribution of category j and K is the number of discrete categories. The site-specific estimate in such a case is the expectation over the posterior rate distribution:

$$E(r_i \mid D_i, T, \alpha) \simeq \sum_{j=1}^{K} r^{(j)} P(r^{(j)} \mid D_i, T, \alpha). \tag{11.19}$$

Confidence intervals around estimated rates can also be extracted from the posterior rate distribution [51]. Using simulations, we have previously shown that a discrete gamma prior provides more accurate rate estimations compared to the ML approach [49].

This Bayesian approach is an empirical one, since the prior is determined, in part, by the data. Specifically, the α parameter of the gamma prior distribution is estimated using ML based on the entire dataset and is considered as "true" for the rate estimation step. The tree topology and its associated branch lengths are also assumed to be given or inferred prior to the rate estimation. However, it is often the case that a large uncertainty exists regarding the tree topology, branch lengths, and model parameters (such as α). We have previously developed a full Bayesian approach that uses MCMC methodology to integrate over the space of all possible trees and model parameters [52]. This comprehensive evolutionary approach was shown to outperform methods that are based only on a single tree. However, the increase in rate estimation accuracy comes at the expense of running time.

11.6   TREE RECONSTRUCTION USING AMONG-SITE RATE VARIATION MODELS

Estimating the phylogeny underlying the evolution of a set of sequences is the most common use of probabilistic evolutionary models. Numerous studies (e.g., [53]) have shown that tree reconstruction using either the ML or the closely related Bayesian approach outperforms classical approaches such as the maximum parsimony [54] or distance-based methods (e.g., neighbor joining [17]). When reconstructing the tree using either the ML or the Bayesian paradigms, an underlying model of sequence evolution is always assumed, and all early models shared the assumption of homogeneous rate across sites. Following the realization that the homogeneous rate assumption is unrealistic, the impact of this oversimplified assumption on tree reconstruction accuracy was evaluated.

The importance of accounting for among-site rate variation in tree reconstruction was demonstrated in Sullivan and Swofford [55]. They have shown that ignoring rate variation can lead to systematic errors in tree inference. For example, rodent monophyly is rejected with a high bootstrap value when rate variation among sites is ignored, while the opposite is concluded when among-site rate variation is integrated. Supporting the observation that ignoring among-site rate variation can mislead phylogeny inference, Silberman et al. [56] found that deep branching position of rapidly evolving lineages might be an artifact of long branch attraction, especially when among-site rate heterogeneity is ignored.

Sullivan and Swofford [57] have conducted a simulation study to evaluate the impact of ignoring among-site rate variation on tree reconstruction. They showed that when data are simulated under among-site rate variation and analyzed using models that assume rate homogeneity, not only is the performance of the reconstruction algorithms poor, but also, for some tree topologies, the performance decreases with increased sequence length. This indicates that ignoring among-site rate variation can lead the reconstruction method to converge to the wrong tree topology, even when ample data are available.

In tree reconstruction under the ML paradigm, one searches the tree topology and its associated set of branch lengths that maximize the probability of the data given the model. However, as discussed above, the model includes various parameters that should also be optimized. In an exhaustive search, it is required to find the most likely set of tree topology, branch lengths, and model parameters. For example, when the rate is assumed to be gamma distributed, the most likely estimate of alpha should be evaluated for each tree topology, together with its most likely branch lengths. However, optimizing alpha afresh for each tree topology is computationally expensive and infeasible even when a moderate number of sequences are analyzed. This stems from the exponential dependency between the number of sequences and the number of tree topologies. Yang [34] suggested that for the gamma distribution, parameters would be stable across tree topologies. This claim was refined in Sullivan et al. [58]. They have shown that if the parameters are estimated from trees in which the bipartitions that are strongly supported by the data are maintained, then the estimates are relatively accurate. Thus, a successive-approximation approach was suggested in Sullivan et al. [59]. In this approach, an initial tree is first reconstructed (e.g., using neighbor joining) and the parameters are then estimated using this tree topology and remain fixed during the next tree topology search. Once the best tree is found, model parameters are estimated again and the search is repeated using these newly optimized parameters. The search ends when the same tree topology is obtained in two successive iterations. This approach was shown to perform well on both real and simulated data.

The situation is more complicated when distance-based methods are used to infer the tree topology. Distance methods are fast relative to either the ML or the maximum parsimony tree search criteria and are often used when the number of sequences is in the order of hundreds or thousands. While it is clear that ignoring rate variation in distance-based methods is inadequate and can lead to erroneous inferred trees, accounting for among-site rate variation in such methods is not trivial. One approach would be to optimize rate variation parameters for each pair of sequences independently. However, the variability of rates in a protein is generally common to all sequences across a given multiple sequence alignment. Thus, there is no reason to estimate the rate parameters for each pair of sequences separately. Moreover, such estimation of many parameters from scant data is likely to result in high errors. Thus, a preferable approach would be to use all sequences simultaneously in order to estimate the rate parameters globally. Such estimation, however, requires knowledge of the tree topology and branch lengths, which are the target of the optimization rather than its input. An iterative process of optimization, first suggested in Silberman [56], is an obvious solution: First, distances are estimated assuming no rate variation (or an arbitrary set of parameters, e.g., $\alpha = 1$ for the gamma distribution). Following this initial pairwise distance estimation, a tree is constructed, the parameters are reestimated, and the process is repeated until convergence is obtained. We have shown that such an approach outperforms tree reconstruction when either among-site rate variation is ignored or when the α parameter of the gamma distribution is estimated for each pair of sequences [60].

In Ninio et al. [60], we have suggested two alternatives for the iterative distance approach described above. In the first, site-specific rates are estimated using the posterior mean approach (Section 11.5 above). These site-specific rates are then used when pairwise distances are computed. One potential problem with this alternative is that a parameter is evaluated for each site, which can lead to high errors in rate estimation that in turn can reduce the accuracy of distance estimation. To overcome this potential problem, we suggested accounting for the uncertainties in site-specific rate estimation. This is done by computing a posterior rate distribution for each site. This posterior rate distribution (rather than the single rate estimate) is used when computing the pairwise distances. We have shown that these alternatives significantly increase the accuracy of distance estimation and the performance of distance-based tree reconstruction.

11.7 DEPENDENCIES OF EVOLUTIONARY RATES AMONG SITES

All of the models described above share one recurrent shortcoming: They assume that the rate at each site is independently drawn from the same rate distribution, and thus no spatial correlation among rates exists. However, biological intuition dictates that positions within the same sequence region evolve at similar rates, which typify the structural and functional importance of the region as a whole. In other words, it is unrealistic to assume that the posterior distribution of the rate at site i is not influenced by the rate at site $i - 1$.

Spatial correlation can be accounted for simply by using a sliding window approach [61]. Yang [29] and Felsenstein and Churchill [62] suggested model-based approaches, which take into account a correlation between the evolutionary rates at adjacent nucleotides by using a hidden Markov model (HMM). These models have been shown to provide a better fit for DNA data and may improve site-specific rate inference [62]. While some regions clearly display autocorrelation of rates, this might not hold for all sequence regions. The protein's three-dimensional structure and function result from complex interactions between amino acids, which are not linearly proximate. For instance, the catalytic site of an enzyme is often composed of sites that are distant in the linear sequence of the protein. Thus, the level of correlation between the evolutionary rates of these linearly distant sites may be stronger than the correlation between the linear adjacent sites. We have previously proposed a model that allows adjacent rates to be correlated at certain regions of the protein and independent at other regions. We have shown that such a model better captures among-site rate variation than the standard HMM [63].

While HMMs impose a unidirectional flow of information (i.e., site n depends on site $n - 1$), Markov random fields allow the rate at each site to depend on the rate of the site before and after it simultaneously. Such a model was developed to account for dependencies among codon positions [64, 65]. When the three-dimensional structure of a protein is available, rate dependencies between amino acid sites that are in close proximity in space should be taken into account. Such dependencies can be incorporated into a graph, where an edge between two positions represents dependency. The distance between each two vertices in the graph represents the proximity of the corresponding residues in three-dimensional. This kind of representation may facilitate the use of powerful computational tools from the field of graph theory for inferring conserved regions in proteins.

11.8 RELATED WORKS

The concepts and tools developed to account for among-site rate variation were applied, extended, and modified to fit a host of related data and computational tasks. Here, we briefly review some of these extensions.

In a similar manner to the problem of tree reconstruction, among-site rate variation was also shown to be important for reconstruction of ancestral sequences. In this problem, one searches for the set of characters in the internal nodes of the tree that maximizes the probability of the data. We note that while for phylogeny reconstruction the likelihood is computed by summing over all possible character assignments to the internal nodes, in ancestral sequence reconstruction, a single set of character states that maximizes the probability of the data is searched for. Moreover, when reconstructing ancestral states—the tree topology and branch lengths are first computed and are then considered "fixed" for the character reconstruction step. The impact of model assumptions, including among-site rate variation on ancestral state reconstruction, was recently discussed in detail (see [66]) and hence will not be elaborated here. We only note that among-site rate variation is critical for obtaining accurate estimates of the probabilities of each ancestral character state, mainly in fast evolving sites.

While the approach presented in Section 11.5 allows determining site-specific evolutionary rates, the obtained estimates are relative to the sequence being studied. For example, a site-specific rate of 0.5 indicates a site twice as conserved relative to the average conservation across all positions in that protein. When the goal is to compare conservation scores across different sequences, or when one wishes to test if a specific site evolves under purifying, neutral, or positive Darwinian selection, it is meaningless to compare these relative rates. For such tasks, the most common approach is to contrast the ratio of nonsynonymous (K_a) to synonymous (K_s) substitutions [67–72].

Early probabilistic-based methods to compute K_a/K_s ratios were shown to be superior to simple counting methods. However, these methods did not account for the heterogeneity of the evolutionary selection pressure among protein sites. In Nielsen and Yang [73] and in Yang et al. [72], Bayesian models were developed that account for such selection heterogeneity. In these models, a prior distribution of the K_a/K_s ratio is assumed. To this end, a similar methodology that was developed for among-site rate variation is applied to model K_a/K_s variation. In the latter, codon sequences are analyzed, while in the former nucleotides or amino acids are usually analyzed.

Similar to the development of models, which account for spatial correlation of evolutionary rates in proteins, it was also recently recognized that better estimates of K_a/K_s ratio can be obtained if spatial correlations in K_a rates are accounted for. Furthermore, it was realized that K_s rates also vary substantially among sites [74]. This is explained, for example, by purifying selection exerted on some synonymous sites in order to maintain mRNA stability. Indeed, Pond and Muse [75] have developed a probabilistic model that takes K_s variation into account. In their model, the K_a and the K_s rates are assumed to be sampled independently from an underlying distribution such as gamma. We have extended this model to allow both the K_a and the K_s to vary among sites and to correlate with the related K_a and K_s rates of adjacent sites. This was achieved by assuming two independent HMMs across the sequence—one for K_a and one for K_s. We have shown that such a model better fits biological data and is more conservative in inferring positive Darwinian selection [76].

Finally, the methodology developed to account for among-site rate variation, while describing the evolution of single characters such as amino acids and codons, was extended to model rate variation of larger units, for example, genes and introns. In such approaches, a site corresponds to a single genomic locus, and gene or intron presence and absence are modeled by the characters "1" and "0," respectively. Since the evolutionary rate distribution over different loci is not homogeneous, a gamma prior distribution over the locus rate is assumed. This approach was used, for example, in Cohen et al. [77] to model the evolution of gene presence and absence across genomes, and in Carmel et al. [78] to study the dynamics of intron gains and losses. These extensions demonstrate the applicability and importance of rate variation models as a general tool in bioinformatics and genome research.

REFERENCES

1. D. Graur and W. H. Li. *Fundamentals of Molecular Evolution*. Sinauer Associates, Sunderland, MA, 2000.

2. S. Whelan, P. Liò, and N. Goldman. Molecular phylogenetics: state-of-the-art methods for looking into the past. *Trends. Genetics*, 17(5):262–272, 2001.

3. Z. Yang. *Computational Molecular Evolution*. Oxford University Press, Oxford, 2006.

4. S. F. Altschul, T. L. Madden, A. A. Schaffer, J. Zhang, Z. Zhang, W. Miller, and D. J. Lipman. Gapped BLAST and PSI-BLAST: a new generation of protein database search programs. *Nucleic Acids Res.*, 25(17):3389–3402, 1997.

5. W. J. Kent, et al. BLAT—the BLAST-like alignment tool. *Genome Res.*, 12(4):656–664, 2002.

6. G. D. Stormo. Gene-finding approaches for eukaryotes. *Genome Res.*, 10(4):394–397, 2000.

7. K. Katoh and H. Toh. Recent developments in the MAFFT multiple sequence alignment program. *Brief. Bioinform.*, 9(4):286–298, 2008.

8. M. A. Larkin, G. Blackshields, N. P. Brown, R. Chenna, P. A. McGettigan, H. McWilliam, F. Valentin, I. M. Wallace, A. Wilm, R. Lopez, et al. Clustal W and Clustal X version 2.0. *Bioinformatics*, 23(21):2947, 2007.

9. D. Boffelli, J. McAuliffe, D. Ovcharenko, K. D. Lewis, I. Ovcharenko, L. Pachter, and E. M. Rubin. Phylogenetic Shadowing of primate sequences to find functional regions of the human genome. *Science*, 299(5611):1391–1394, 2003.

10. T. Pupko, R. E. Bell, I. Mayrose, F. Glaser, and N. Ben-Tal. Rate4Site: an algorithmic tool for the identification of functional regions in proteins by surface mapping of evolutionary determinants within their homologues. *Bioinformatics*, 18(90001):71–77, 2002.

11. A. M. Moses, D. Y. Chiang, D. A. Pollard, V. N. Iyer, and M. B. Eisen. MONKEY: identifying conserved transcription-factor binding sites in multiple alignments using a binding site-specific evolutionary model. *Genome Biol.*, 5(12):R98, 2004.

12. M. Landau, I. Mayrose, Y. Rosenberg, F. Glaser, E. Martz, T. Pupko, and N. Ben-Tal. ConSurf 2005: the projection of evolutionary conservation scores of residues on protein structures. *Nucleic Acids Res.*, 33:W299–W302, 2005.

13. B. E. Engelhardt, M. I. Jordan, K. E. Muratore, and S. E. Brenner. Protein molecular function prediction by Bayesian phylogenomics. *PLoS Comput. Biol.*, 1(5):e45, 2005.

14. M. A. Huynen, B. Snel, C. Mering, and P. Bork. Function prediction and protein networks. *Curr. Opin. Cell Biol.*, 15(2):191–198, 2003.

15. S. M. Ross. *Stochastic Processes*, 2nd edition. Wiley, New York, 1996.

16. T. H. Jukes and C. R. Cantor. Evolution of protein molecules. *Mamm. Protein Metab.*, 3:21–132, 1969.

17. N. Saitou. Property and efficiency of the maximum likelihood method for molecular phylogeny. *J. Mol. Evol.*, 27(3):261–273, 1988.

18. N. Saitou and M. Nei. The neighbor-joining method: a new method for reconstructing phylogenetic trees. *Mol. Biol. Evol.*, 4(4):406–425, 1987.

19. J. Felsenstein. *Inferring Phylogenies*, Sinauer Associates, Sunderland, MA, 2004.

20. J. Felsenstein. Evolutionary trees from DNA sequences: a maximum likelihood approach. *J. Mol. Evol.*, 17(6):368–376, 1981.

21. M. Kimura. A simple method for estimating evolutionary rates of base substitutions through comparative studies of nucleotide sequences. *J. Mol. Evol.*, 16(2):111–120, 1980.

22. F. Rodriguez, J. L. Oliver, A. Marin, and J. R. Medina. The general stochastic model of nucleotide substitution. *J. Theor. Biol.*, 142(4):485–501, 1990.

23. D. Posada. MODELTEST: testing the model of DNA substitution. *Bioinformatics*, 14(9):817–818, 1998.

24. M. O. Dayhoff, R. M. Schwartz, and B. C. Orcutt. A model of evolutionary change in proteins. *Atlas Protein Seq. Struct.*, 5(Suppl 3):345–352, 1978.

25. D. T. Jones, W. R. Taylor, and J. M. Thornton. The rapid generation of mutation data matrices from protein sequences. *Bioinformatics*, 8(3):275–282, 1992.

26. S. Whelan and N. Goldman. A general empirical model of protein evolution derived from multiple protein families using a maximum-likelihood approach. *Mol. Biol. Evol.*, 18(5):691–699, 2001.

27. J. Adachi. Model of amino acid substitution in proteins encoded by mitochondrial DNA. *J. Mol. Evol.*, 42(4):459–468, 1996.

28. J. Adachi, P. J. Waddell, W. Martin, and M. Hasegawa. Plastid genome phylogeny and a model of amino acid substitution for proteins encoded by chloroplast dna. *J. Mol. Evol.*, 50(4):348–358, 2000.

29. Z. Yang. A space-time process model for the evolution of DNA Sequences. *Genetics*, 139(2):993–1005, 1995.

30. J. Felsenstein and G. A. Churchill. Taking variation of evolutionary rates between sites into account in inferring phylogenies. *J. Mol. Evol.*, 53(4):447–455, 2001.

31. E. Susko, C. Field, C. Blouin, and A. J. Roger. Estimation of rates-across-sites distributions in phylogenetic substitution models. *Syst. Biol.*, 52(5):594–603, 2003.

32. Z. Yang. Maximum-likelihood estimation of phylogeny from DNA sequences when substitution rates differ over sites. *Mol. Biol. Evol.*, 10(6):1396–1401, 1993.

33. L. Jin and M. Nei. Limitations of the evolutionary parsimony method of phylogenetic analysis. *Mol. Biol. Evol*, 7(1):82–102, 1990.

34. Z. Yang. Maximum likelihood phylogenetic estimation from DNA sequences with variable rates over sites: approximate methods. *J. Mol. Evol.*, 39(3):306–314, 1994.

35. I. Mayrose, N. Friedman, and T. Pupko. A gamma mixture model better accounts for among site rate heterogeneity. *Bioinformatics*, 21(90002), 2005.

36. X. Gu. Maximum likelihood estimation of the heterogeneity of substitution rate among nucleotide sites. *Mol. Biol. Evol.*, 12(4):546–557, 1995.

37. J. Sullivan, D. L. Swofford, and G. J. P. Naylor. The effect of taxon sampling on estimating rate heterogeneity parameters of maximum-likelihood models. *Mol. Biol. Evol.*, 16(10):1347, 1999.

38. Z. Yang. Among-site rate variation and its impact on phylogenetic analyses. *Trends Ecol. Evol.*, 11(9):367–372, 1996.

39. S. L. Kosakovsky Pond and S. D. W. Frost. A simple hierarchical approach to modeling distributions of substitution rates. *Mol. Biol. Evol.*, 22(2):223–234, 2005.

40. G. J. Olsen. Earliest phylogenetic branchings: comparing rRNA-based evolutionary trees inferred with various techniques. *Cold Spring Harb. Symp. Quant. Biol.*, 52:825–37, 1987.

41. J. P. Huelsenbeck and M.A. Suchard. A nonparametric method for accommodating and testing across-site rate variation. *Syst. Biol.*, 56(6):975–987, 2007.

42. P. Morozov, T. Sitnikova, G. Churchill, F. J. Ayala, and A. Rzhetsky. A new method for characterizing replacement rate variation in molecular sequences application of the Fourier and wavelet models to Drosophila and mammalian proteins. *Genetics*, 154(1):381–395, 2000.

43. R. A. George, R. V. Spriggs, G. J. Bartlett, A. Gutteridge, M. W. MacArthur, C. T. Porter, B. Al-Lazikani, J. M. Thornton, and M. B. Swindells. Effective function annotation through catalytic residue conservation. *Proc. Nat. Acad. Sci. USA*, 102(35):12299, 2005.

44. A. Goren, O. Ram, M. Amit, H. Keren, G. Lev-Maor, I. Vig, T. Pupko, and G. Ast. Comparative analysis identifies exonic splicing regulatory sequencesthe complex definition of enhancers and silencers. *Mol. Cell*, 22(6):769–781, 2006.

45. D. C. King, J. Taylor, L. Elnitski, F. Chiaromonte, W. Miller, and R. C. Hardison. Evaluation of regulatory potential and conservation scores for detecting cis-regulatory modules in aligned mammalian genome sequences. *Genome Res.*, 15(8):1051, 2005.

46. S. J. Fleishman, V. M. Unger, and N. Ben-Tal. Transmembrane protein structures without X-rays. *Trends Biochem. Sci.*, 31(2):106–113, 2006.

47. W. S. J. Valdar. Scoring residue conservation. *Proteins Struct. Funct. Bioinform.*, 48(2):227–241, 2002.

48. R. Nielsen. Site-by-site estimation of the rate of substitution and the correlation of rates in mitochondrial DNA. *Syst. Biol*, 46(2):346–353, 1997.

49. I. Mayrose, D. Graur, N. Ben-Tal, and T. Pupko. Comparison of site-specific rate-inference methods for protein sequences: empirical Bayesian methods are superior. *Mol. Biol. Evol.*, 21(9):1781–1791, 2004.

50. Z. Yang and T. Wang. Mixed model analysis of DNA sequence evolution. *BIOMETRICS*, 51:552–552, 1995.

51. E. Susko, Y. Inagaki, C. Field, M. E. Holder, and A. J. Roger. Testing for differences in rates-across-sites distributions in phylogenetic subtrees. *Mol. Biol. Evol.*, 19(9):1514–1523, 2002.

52. I. Mayrose, A. Mitchell, and T. Pupko. Site-specific evolutionary rate inference: taking phylogenetic uncertainty into account. *J. Mol. Evol.*, 60(3):345–353, 2005.

53. M. K. Kuhner and J. Felsenstein. A simulation comparison of phylogeny algorithms under equal and unequal evolutionary rates. *Mol. Biol. Evol*, 11(3):459–468, 1994.

54. W. M. Fitch. Toward defining the course of evolution: minimum change for a specific tree topology. *Syst. Zool.*, 20(4):406–416, 1971.

55. J. Sullivan and D. L. Swofford. Are guinea pigs rodents? The importance of adequate models in molecular phylogenetics. *J. Mamm. Evol.*, 4(2):77–86, 1997.

56. J. D. Silberman. Phylogeny of the genera Entamoeba and Endolimax as deduced from small-subunit ribosomal RNA sequences. *Mol. Biol. Evol.*, 16(12):1740–1751, 1999.

57. J. Sullivan and D. L. Swofford. Should we use model-based methods for phylogenetic inference when we know that assumptions about among-site rate variation and nucleotide substitution pattern are violated? *Syst. Biol.*, 50(5):723–729, 2001.

58. J. Sullivan, K. E. Holsinger, and C. Simon. The effect of topology on estimates of among-site rate variation. *J. Mol. Evol.*, 42(2):308–312, 1996.

59. J. Sullivan, Z. Abdo, P. Joyce, and D. L. Swofford. Evaluating the performance of a successive-approximations approach to parameter optimization in maximum-likelihood phylogeny estimation. *Mol. Biol. Evol.*, 22(6):1386–1392, 2005.

60. M. Ninio, E. Privman, T. Pupko, and N. Friedman. Phylogeny reconstruction: increasing the accuracy of pairwise distance estimation using Bayesian inference of evolutionary rates. *Bioinformatics*, 23(2):e136, 2007.

61. M. A. Fares, S. F. Elena, J. Ortiz, A. Moya, and E. Barrio. A sliding window-based method to detect selective constraints in protein-coding genes and its application to RNA viruses. *J. Mol. Evol.*, 55(5):509–521, 2002.

62. J. Felsenstein. A hidden Markov model approach to variation among sites in rate of evolution. *Mol. Biol. Evol.*, 13(1):93–104, 1996.

63. A. Stern and T. Pupko. An evolutionary space-time model with varying among-site dependencies. *Mol. Biol. Evol.*, 23(2):392–400, 2006.

64. E. Schadt and K. Lange. Codon and rate variation models in molecular phylogeny. *Mol. Biol. Evol.*, 19(9):1534–1549, 2002.

65. E. E. Schadt, J. S. Sinsheimer, and K. Lange. Applications of codon and rate variation models in molecular phylogeny. *Mol. Biol. Evol.*, 19(9):1550–1562, 2002.

66. D. A. Liberles. Ancestral sequence reconstruction, Oxford University Press, Oxford, NY, 2007.

67. N. Goldman and Z. Yang. A codon-based model of nucleotide substitution for protein-coding DNA sequences. *Mol. Biol. Evol.*, 11(5):725–736, 1994.

68. L. D. Hurst. The Ka/Ks ratio: diagnosing the form of sequence evolution. *Trends Genet.*, 18(9):486–487, 2002.

69. S. V. Muse and B. S. Gaut. A likelihood approach for comparing synonymous and nonsynonymous nucleotide substitution rates, with application to the chloroplast genome. *Mol. Biol. Evol.*, 11(5):715–724, 1994.

70. M. Nei and T. Gojobori. Simple methods for estimating the numbers of synonymous and nonsynonymous nucleotide substitutions. *Mol. Biol. Evol.*, 3(5):418–426, 1986.

71. Z. Yang and R. Nielsen. Mutation-selection models of codon substitution and their use to estimate selective strengths on codon usage. *Mol. Biol. Evol.*, 25(3):568–579, 2008.

72. Z. Yang, R. Nielsen, N. Goldman, and A. M. K. Pedersen. Codon-substitution models for heterogeneous selection pressure at amino acid sites. *Genetics*, 155(1):431–449, 2000.

73. R. Nielsen and Z. Yang. Likelihood models for detecting positively selected amino acid sites and applications to the HIV-1 envelope gene. *Genetics*, 148(3):929–936, 1998.

74. J. V. Chamary, J. L. Parmley, L. D. Hurst, et al. Hearing silence: non-neutral evolution at synonymous sites in mammals. *Nat. Rev. Genet.*, 7(2):98–108, 2006.

75. S. K. Pond and S. V. Muse. Site-to-site variation of synonymous substitution rates. *Mol. Biol. Evol.*, 22(12):2375–2385, 2005.

76. I. Mayrose, A. Doron-Faigenboim, E. Bacharach, and T. Pupko. Towards realistic codon models: among site variability and dependency of synonymous and non-synonymous rates. *Bioinformatics*, 23(13):i319, 2007.

77. O. Cohen, N. D. Rubinstein, A. Stern, U. Gophna, and T. Pupko. A likelihood framework to analyze phyletic patterns. *Philos. Trans. R. Soc. B.* 363:3903–3911, 2008.

78. L. Carmel, I. B. Rogozin, Y. I. Wolf, and E. V. Koonin. Patterns of intron gain and conservation in eukaryotic genes. *BMC Evol. Biol.*, 7:192, 2007.

IV

GENOMICS
AND COMPUTATIONAL
SYSTEMS BIOLOGY

VI

GENOMICS
AND COMPUTATIONAL
SYSTEMS BIOLOGY

12

FROM DNA MOTIFS TO GENE NETWORKS: A REVIEW OF PHYSICAL INTERACTION MODELS

Panayiotis V. Benos

*Departments of Computational Biology and Biomedical Informatics,
School of Medicine, University of Pittsburgh, Pittsburgh, PA, USA*

Alain B. Tchagang

*Department of Computational Biology, School of Medicine,
University of Pittsburgh, Pittsburgh, PA, USA*

12.1 INTRODUCTION

Understanding the interactions between biomolecules within a cell and between cells and their environment is one of the major challenges in computational biology. Although every cell in an organism contains the same genetic material, its expression profile depends on the tissue type, developmental stage, and the extracellular signals it receives at the given point in time. Cells exert various ways to regulate the expression of their genes. Chromatin structure, for example, can make large parts of the genome transcriptionally silent or potentially active. Also, posttranscriptional and posttranslational mechanisms can influence the amount and the activity of the available proteins and noncoding genes in a cell. The best studied mechanism for gene expression control, however, is the transcription regulation at the individual

Elements of Computational Systems Biology   Edited by Huma M. Lodhi and Stephen H. Muggleton
Copyright © 2010 John Wiley & Sons, Inc.

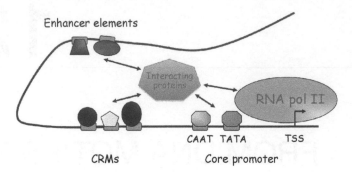

Figure 12.1   Schematic representation of a typical eukaryotic promoter. The transcription start site (TSS), the core promoter, and the enhancer elements are depicted.

gene level. Transcription factor (TF) proteins recognize short DNA "signals" (typically 6–15 base pairs long) in the vicinity of the genes' transcription start sites (TSSs) and enhance or suppress their expression. These DNA signals are commonly referred to as transcription-factor binding sites (TFBSs) or—more general—as *cis*-regulatory elements. A broad classification of the role of these regulatory elements can be done on the basis of their distance from the gene's TSS (Figure 12.1). The region located in the first 300–500-bp upstream of the TSS constitutes the core promoter of the gene and frequently contains binding sites for general TFs, like the TATA-box and the CAAT-box. Core promoters are relatively conserved regions across all vertebrates [1, 2]. Farther upstream are located the TF binding sites that are responsible for the gene's expression specificity (i.e., when and where the gene is expressed). The timely and tissue-specific expression of all genes is crucial for the cell itself and the organism as a whole. Expression is usually regulated by sets of TFs, whose binding sites are closely located in the genome, and the TFs themselves can directly interact with each other. These sets of sites are known as *cis*-regulatory modules (CRMs.) CRMs can be found few kilobases around the TSS. Finally, in complex eukaryotic organisms, some TF target sequences can be found tens of thousands of bases away from the TSS. These regions are usually called enhancers, and their main role is to fine-tune genes' regulation, usually through protein–protein interactions. Figure 12.1 presents some of the features of a typical eukaryotic promoter.

TF genes interact with each other either directly (i.e., by forming protein complexes) or indirectly (i.e., by regulating each other's expression). TFs act individually (as monomers) or in complexes (as homo- or hetero-multimers). This creates a network of interactions that characterizes a cell's response to a particular stimulus. Focusing only on TF genes, one can construct the network of all regulatory interactions. Figure 12.2 shows some of the simple components of the TF interaction networks that have been observed [3]. Reverse engineering refers to the traditional mathematical inverse problem, which is to infer the gene regulatory circuit (network topology) from gene expression data. Genes can be represented as nodes in a graph, where edges represent the direct interactions between genes. There are two broad classes of reverse-engineering algorithms for gene regulatory networks [4]: those based on

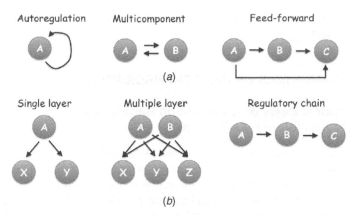

Figure 12.2   Network components. Regulatory network components are presented with respect to their interactions (a) or the layers of the signal transduction (b). Data from Alon [3] and Lee et al. [48].

the "physical interactions" that aim at identifying interactions among transcription factors and their target genes (gene-to-sequence) and those based on the "influence interactions" that try to relate the expression of a gene to the expression of the other genes in the cell (gene-to-gene).

A number of approaches have been developed for modeling regulatory networks. A broad taxonomical organization suggests four major methodological categories for these approaches. The first includes optimization methods based on the maximization of a high-dimensional objective function associated with different network topologies such as Bayesian networks [5, 6] or chain functions [7]. An objective function used frequently is the log-likelihood of the network topology given the observed data. The second category includes a variety of regression techniques to fit the observed data to an empirical *a priori* model of the underlying biochemical interactions [8–10]. A third group includes integrative bioinformatics approaches that combine data from a number of independent clues, such as known protein–protein and protein–DNA interactions (from databases or literature), expression data, or DNA binding motifs [11–13]. The fourth category includes statistical/information theoretical methods [14, 15], which define two-way or higher order probabilistic measures of gene correlation to distinguish potential interactions from background noise. Models of gene regulatory networks can also be divided according to the representation of the network states (discrete vs. continuous), the nature of the data (static vs. dynamic over time or different conditions), the representation of gene associations (qualitative vs. quantitative), the dependencies between genes (linear vs. nonlinear), the nature of the model (deterministic vs. stochastic), and the location of the genes in the cells (nonspatial vs. spatial).

This chapter focuses on the "physical interaction" networks. First, we will give an overview of the physical basis of transcription regulation and the representation of the regulatory DNA patterns. Then, we will survey some of the physical interaction algorithms for reverse engineering of gene expression data. The coverage of the algorithms is not exhaustive and is biased toward what we believe are the more practical methods. We attempt to cover at least one method from each class of algorithms of this broad category.

12.2   FUNDAMENTALS OF GENE TRANSCRIPTION

12.2.1   Physical Basis of Transcription Regulation and Representation of DNA Patterns

Each TF recognizes a set of DNA binding sites with high affinity. It usually achieves this by placing one or more α-helices in the major groove of the DNA. The specific DNA target recognition results from the molecular contacts (hydrogen bonds, electrostatic interactions, etc.) between the amino acids and the DNA bases. Contacts from and to the backbone of the protein or DNA also contribute to the overall binding affinity (how strongly a target sequence is bound), although their contribution to binding specificity (how more strongly a sequence is bound compared to a random sequence) is generally assumed to be secondary [16]. Sometimes, nonbase-specific DNA interactions contribute to the target recognition. This is usually referred in the literature as "indirect readout." An example is the *CAP* (or *CPR*) protein, which bends the DNA upon binding. In this case, in addition to the specific base–amino acid contacts, the overall sequence of the DNA target needs to have some degree of "bendability," thus restricting further the repertoire of tolerated changes.

Preferred binding sites of a TF can be discovered and verified by *in vitro* target selection experiments (e.g., SELEX [17] or protein-binding microarrays [18]) or by biochemical analysis of the upstream regions of its known target genes. The length and the number of optimal targets vary, depending on the TF in question. For example, *c-myc* oncogene in mammals and Ultrabiothorax (*Ubx*) gene in *Drosophila* have a very restricted set of targets (CACGTG and ATTA, respectively), whereas the pattern of p53 is more degenerate (Figure 12.3). There are many ways to represent the TF binding preferences [19], but the most popular so far has been proven to be the position-specific scoring matrices (PSSMs) or position weight matrices (PWMs.)

PSSM models are $4XL$ weight matrices, where L is the length of the DNA binding motif (the single targets of most TFs are of a given length L, which is a characteristic of the TF). To generate a PSSM model, the known sites of a given TF are aligned and a $4XL$ frequency table is calculated. Column I in this table consists of the four base frequencies at position I of the alignment. The PSSM model typically consists of the log-likelihood ratios of the observed frequencies against the background frequency of the corresponding base. We note that the average log-likelihood ratio in each position is the relative entropy, formally defined as:

$$\mathrm{RH}(I) = \sum_{b=A}^{T} f(b,\,I) \ \ln\frac{f(b,\,I)}{P_{\mathrm{ref}}(b)}, \tag{12.1}$$

where $f(b,I)$ is the estimated frequency of base b at position I of the pattern and $P_{\mathrm{ref}}(b)$ is background frequency of base b (e.g., in the genome). Averaging over all

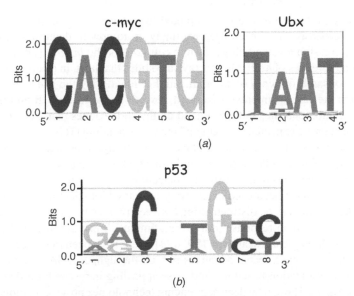

(a)

(b)

Figure 12.3 Types of DNA patterns. *Ubx* and *c-myc* have very restricted repertoire of binding sites (a), whereas *p53* targets are more degenerate (b).

L positions, we obtain the average relative entropy of the motif. A number of motif finding algorithms identify patterns that maximize either the overall log-likelihood of the motif or its relative entropy.

There is an interesting theoretical interpretation of the PSSM models. Through a Boltzmann theory perspective, a PSSM model can be viewed as the average binding specificity of a TF protein to its DNA targets. There are examples in the literature that show that the PSSM score is in agreement with binding energy measurements [20]. One general assumption of the PSSM models is the position independence, that is, the observed base frequencies in one position are independent of the frequencies in any other position. According to the thermodynamic model, this corresponds to energetic additivity, that is, each base position contributes independently of the others to the total binding energy. Energetic additivity is a simplification of the physical properties of the TF–DNA interactions and it does not hold in general [21, 22]. However, in practice, it has been found to be a good approximation in modeling binding affinities [23]. In addition, additive models require a significantly smaller number of parameters. These two properties have made additive models very useful and contributed to their popularity.

12.2.2 High-Throughput Data: Microarrays, Deep Sequencing, ChIP-chip, and ChIP-seq

The last couple of decades have seen the emergence of new technologies that revolutionized the biological research. Large-scale sequencing has now advanced to the point of sequencing millions of bases per day. This allows the genome sequencing of a small organism (e.g., a bacterium) to be completed in few weeks. Also, gene expression arrays or microarrays have been used routinely up to now to determine simultaneously the expression levels of all genes in a cell [24], or the *in vitro* [18] and *in vivo* [25] DNA preferences of a TF. Microarrays are slides that host, in an orderly fashion, probes of thousands of genes of an organism. For identifying the genes' expression, mRNA from the cells of interest is isolated, reverse transcribed, PCR amplified, labeled with a fluorochrome, and hybridized on the slide. Genes that are expressed in the sampled cells are expected to "light up" the corresponding probes in the array. The higher the number of mRNA copies in the cell, the strongest the signal is expected to be. However, problems related to cross-hybridization as well as technical biases can make the hybridization signals sometimes inaccurate for quantitative modeling. That said, microarrays have been used extensively in many biological applications, from cell type classification (e.g., distinguishing between two types of cancer) to modeling the dynamics of cells in response to a given stimulus. Since the first application of microarrays in biological research in 1995 [24], there have been many technological improvements. However, recent advances in high-throughput DNA sequencing tend to make the hybridization-based methods less appealing in research for determining genes' expression. These new deep sequencing technologies provide a unique opportunity for measuring genes' expression with an unprecedented accuracy [26]. They can produce hundreds of thousands of 200-bp reads in one run, which leads to an unbiased and more accurate measurement of the expression of all genes in the genome, known and novel, protein coding and noncoding, and small and large. In addition, they avoid problems of cross-hybridization and probe selection that made the microarray data less robust. Most gene network modeling algorithms use microarray data as their primary source of information, although they can be easily adapted to accommodate other gene expression measurements.

Chromatin immunoprecipitation (ChIP) [25] is a biochemical procedure for capturing genomic regions that are associated *in vivo* with a protein of interest, for example, a TF. Briefly, proteins are cross-linked onto the DNA with formaldehyde; cells are lysed and sonicated to fractionate the genomic DNA; the protein–DNA complexes are precipitated with an antibody against the protein of interest; cross-links are reversed, and DNA fragments are purified, amplified, and labeled with a fluorochrome and hybridized on specific microarrays. These arrays contain probes for the promoters of the genes in an organism or the whole genome ("tiling arrays"). Many physical interaction algorithms can use information from ChIP-microarray (or ChIP-chip) experiments to guide the TF–gene associations. But, like with the measurement of gene expression data, the measuring of the *in vivo* protein–DNA interactions has benefited from the advancement of direct sequencing methods. Instead of hydridizing the precipitated DNA to a microarray, one can now directly deep sequence it (ChIP-seq), resulting in a finer mapping of the genomic locations where the TF binds.

The effect of the high-throughput technologies in biological research is profound. Because of the fact that vast amount of data can be generated quickly, the research philosophy has now shifted from the traditional reductionist approach that dominated the research efforts in the past (i.e., studying the parts in the hope they will ultimately reveal the whole) to a truly holistic approach that puts the systems biology in the center.

12.3 PHYSICAL INTERACTION ALGORITHMS

Physical interaction algorithms are those reverse-engineering algorithms that aim at identifying interactions among TFs and their target genes (gene-to-sequence interactions). Microarray measurements, of course, do not necessarily reflect the transcription factor activities (TFAs) in all cases, since posttranscriptional and posttranslational modifications may play an important role for determining the activity of a TF. Nevertheless, for practical purposes, all physical network algorithms focus on the TFAs that can be deduced from microarray data.

Practically, physical interaction algorithms have two goals. One is to identify the genes regulated by a TF (or a set of TFs). In other words, they aim to reconstruct the connectivity structure and weights of the network. Second, they aim to reconstruct the activity profile of each TF from the gene expression data. An advantage of this strategy, compared to influence interaction algorithms, is that it reduces the dimensionality of the problem by analyzing only the interactions between TFs and their putative target genes (instead of all-against-all). It also enables the use of genome sequence data ("static data"), in combination with gene expression data ("dynamic data"), in order to enhance the sensitivity and specificity of the predicted interactions. The limitation of this approach is that it can only describe the regulatory control exercised by TFs.

Some physical interaction algorithms depend on the prediction of sets of coregulated genes, while others construct a more general model without such assumptions. Some of the algorithms represent regulatory activities as a function of the mRNA measurements, while others treat the regulatory activities as hidden variables. Finally, some of the algorithms can model complex *cis*-regulatory logic of multiple interacting TFs binding closely located DNA targets (*cis*-regulatory modules or CRMs). In the following, we will review four classes of physical interaction algorithms: the clustering-based approaches, the regression-based models, the network component analysis methods, and the factor analysis methods.

12.3.1 Basic Definitions

Throughout this chapter, we assume that we are given a set of N genes, $G = \{g_1, \ldots, g_n, \ldots, g_N\}$, and an $N \times M$ gene expression matrix, Z. We also assume that the gene expression values are normalized to correct for systematic or technical biases. The gene expression matrix, Z, may consist of time series gene expression data of the N genes in M time points $T = \{t_1, \ldots, t_m, \ldots, t_M\}$ (or simply $T = \{1, \ldots, m, \ldots, M\}$), or steady-state measurements of the N genes under M different conditions $C = \{c_1, \ldots, c_m, \ldots, c_M\}$. In the former case, we will try to model the gene expression that dynamically changes with time, while in the latter, we will try to predict relationships by analyzing steady-state gene expression levels in various conditions. In all cases, z_{nm} represents the expression level of gene n in condition or time point m.

The term "identifiable network" refers to a network that (1) Eq. (12.2) (see below) has an essentially unique solution under certain constrains and (2) it can be distinguished from another network characterized by these constraints.

12.3.2 Problem Formulation

Given the $N \times M$ gene expression data Z as defined before, all physical network algorithms but the clustering-based approaches aim at decomposing Z as a product of two matrices, plus some residual terms:

$$Z = XY + E, \tag{12.2}$$

where X is an $N \times L$ connectivity matrix (also known as the factor-loading matrix). Each column in X describes the strength of interaction between one of the L transcription factors and the N potential gene targets. The entries of X can either be binary (0 or 1) or numeric (e.g., from ChIP-chip data), with a zero value indicating no physical binding between a transcription factor and a target. Y is an $L \times M$ matrix that represents the TFAs of the L transcription factors for each of the M samples. It is a vector of L hidden variables also known as factors. Finally, E is an $N \times M$ matrix containing error terms. In practical applications, the number L of factors is always smaller than or equal to the number N of observed variables. So, the problem can be formulated as: given the gene expression data, Z, identify X and Y that best represent the data.

12.3.2.1 *Identifiability Problems*   The decomposition of the matrix Z into two matrices X, Y, and the residual term E according to Eq. (12.2) is an inverse problem whose solution is, in general, not uniquely defined unless further assumptions on the matrices X or Y are made. In order to show this, let us consider a nonsingular $L \times L$ matrix Q. Furthermore, let us define $X_1 = XQ$ and $Y_1 = Q^{-1}Y$. By inserting the nonsingular matrix Q into Eq. (12.2) defined above, we obtain $Z - E = XQQ^{-1}Y = (XQ).(Q^{-1}Y) = X_1 Y_1$. This clearly shows that Z cannot be uniquely decomposed unless further assumptions are either made on the connectivity matrix X, on the TFAs matrix Y, or on both X and Y.

Classical dimensional reduction algorithms such as principal component analysis (PCA) or independent component analysis (ICA) will identify a connectivity matrix X such that the reconstructed TFA matrix Y verifies orthogonality or statistical independence criteria, respectively. In the case of gene regulatory networks, such assumptions are not biologically meaningful. For example, the statistical criterion in the case of ICA lacks biological explanations. Therefore, physical interaction algorithms aim at finding a mathematical decomposition that makes no statistical assumptions and that at the same time will incorporate prior biological knowledge into the decomposition.

12.3.3 Clustering-Based Approaches

Clustering-based approaches are trying to identify the TFs that control the expression of certain genes. Assuming that genes that are controlled by the same TFs will show similar expression patterns, the clustering-based approaches first group genes based on their expression profiles. Then, the promoters of the genes in each cluster are analyzed for common *cis*-regulatory signals. Figure 12.4 presents the workflow diagram of these methods.

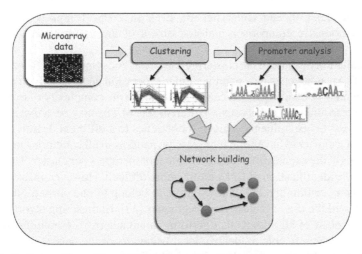

Figure 12.4 Schematic representation of the methodology followed by the clustering-based approaches for reconstructing TF–DNA relationships.

Algorithm 12.1 General Clustering-Based Approach

Input:

- X = gene expression data
- Upstream DNA sequence of each gene

Output:

- Set of clusters
- Potential binding sites of each cluster.

Begin

- Identify co-expressed genes using a clustering algorithm.
- Identify the overrepresented motifs in each cluster using a motif-finding algorithm.

End Begin

Clustering-based approaches were introduced by Tavazoie et al. [27]. They used the k-means algorithm with the Euclidean distance metric to cluster the gene expression profiles. However, other clustering methods can also be used. For a recent survey of approaches using different clustering algorithms, we refer the reader to Xu et al. [28]. Note that some of the approaches described in Xu et al. [28] have been developed specifically for dealing with time series data (long or short) or steady-state data in multiple conditions, while others are more general.

For DNA motif finding, Tavazoie et al. used the AlignACE algorithm [29]. Again, there are a number of alternative algorithms one can use, reviewed recently by Das and Dai [30] and GuhaThakurta [31]. In 2005, Tompa et al. [32] performed an extensive comparison and assessment of the performance of 14 motif finders.

One limitation of some of the clustering-based methods (including Tavazoie's et al. method [27]) is that genes may exhibit similar expression patterns only in a subset of the time points or conditions. This can be attributed to the complexity of transcription regulation (especially in eukaryotes). Different sets of TFs may be active at different conditions and hence influence a given set of genes to a different degree. Requiring the genes of a cluster to have similar expression patterns in all conditions makes more tight clusters at the expense of a reduced number of members per cluster. This, in turn, will make the identification of DNA motifs more difficult. However, instead of using a clustering algorithm that only allows genes to belong to one cluster, other groups have suggested the use of biclustering techniques [33]. Biclustering algorithms refer to a distinct class of algorithms that perform simultaneous row–column clustering, and they are generally able to identify local behaviors of the dataset analyzed [34]. One advantage of biclustering algorithms is that genes may be grouped together in one subset of conditions (or time points), and grouped together with other genes in a different subset of conditions (or time points). Allowing participation in more than one cluster increases the number of genes per cluster, but retaining homogeneous clusters with respect to the TFs that might regulate their expression. On the other hand, biclustering algorithms require, in general, a larger number of samples, which might not be always available.

Beer and Tavazoie presented in 2004 [35] an extension to the original Tavazoie et al. algorithm [27]. After clusters and DNA motifs have been identified, the method proceeds with an enrichment step, in which each motif is used to scan the promoters of all genes (not only those belonging to the specific cluster where the motif originated) to predict more putative targets. Various characteristics of the targets (e.g., orientation, spacing, order, etc.) are converted to binary variables and used as an input (parent nodes) to a Bayesian network model. The parent nodes are then evaluated in their ability to predict expression data based on a greedy, iterative procedure. In each iteration, the best predictor is added to the model until convergence. The authors showed that this method performs better than the original Tavazoie et al. [27] and comparable to REDUCE [36] (see below).

Clustering-based approaches have been extensively exploited for analyzing microarray data. In the above, we only discuss some representative examples. Other examples include the work of Segal et al. [37, 38] in which they used the expectation-maximization (EM) algorithm (see below) on probabilistic graphical models to identify the optimal number of clusters and associated motifs that best explain the expression data. GRAM [39] is another cluster-based algorithm, in which the resulting clusters contain genes that are coexpressed (based on gene expression data) and associated with the same set of TFs (based on ChIP-chip data). Notably, a number of studies reported that the use of ChIP-chip data in the place of motif predictions significantly improves the performance of the clustered-based algorithms [40, 41].

12.3.4   Sequence- or ChIP-Based Regression Methods

Sequence- or ChIP-based regression algorithms model TFAs as hidden variables and try to infer them from gene expression data in combination with DNA sequence data and/or ChIP-chip data.

12.3.4.1   *Sequence-Based Linear Regression*   Bussemaker and Siggia [36] presented REDUCE, an algorithm that predicts binding motifs from microarray and promoter (sequence) data without the need for clustering. The justification for this approach is that with the exception of ribosomal and few other gene categories, most other genes do not belong to clusters of reasonable size to allow for efficient motif detection. REDUCE reports statistically significant patterns (oligomers, individual or in pairs with fixed spacing and combinations of those) in the promoters of the genes that affect gene expression. Its major assumption is additivity of the contributions of the DNA motifs to the overall (log)expression of the downstream gene. One of the advantages of this method is that it has no adjustable parameters. Motifs are reported on the basis of their user-defined P value cutoff. Below, we outline the main steps of the REDUCE algorithm of Bussemaker and Siggia [36].

Algorithm 12.2a   REDUCE algorithm [36]

Input:
  - Z = Gene expression data
  - Upstream DNA sequence of each gene

Output:
  - X = Number of occurrence of a given motif
  - Y = Transcription factor activity (TFA) profiles

Begin
  - Generate a set of motifs using all possible combinations of nucleotides up to length 7.
  - For each experiment, construct a smaller set (number of motifs ≪ number of genes), which contains motifs that significantly correlate with the expression data.
  - Divide the motifs into several classes of related and overlapping motifs.
  - Use the forward selection procedure to find one representative for each class.
  - Then, check the independent and linear contributions of the significant motifs to the log expression level.
  - Compute an activity value for every significant motif.
  - For each significant set of motifs in an experiment, construct a TFA profile.

End Begin

As we mentioned above, the REDUCE model assumes additivity of the contributions of the DNA binding motifs defined as [36]:

$$Z_n = Z_0 + \sum_{m \in M} Y_m X_{mn}, \qquad (12.3)$$

where Z_0 is the baseline expression level of gene n (in terms of $\log_2$ ratio of two cell populations), and Z_n is the observed (log)ratio of expression. X_{mn} is the number of occurrences of motif m in the regulatory region (analogous to a quantitative measure of connectivity) and Y_m is the best PSMM score obtained in the upstream sequences (analogous to TFA). The model accounts for both activator and repressor TF proteins (positive and negative values of Y_m, respectively).

REDUCE performs multivariate linear regression to estimate the TFAs (Y_m in Eq. (12.3). There are a number of extensions and improvements of this algorithm published in the following years [42, 43]. Also, Conlon et al. [44] developed another algorithm based on the same idea. Genes are initially ranked according to their expression level; motifs are identified in their promoters using program MDscan [45] with a library of PSSM models; linear regression is performed between PSSM scores and expression levels to remove insignificant motifs; finally, sets of motifs (CRMs) are identified with stepwise regression.

12.3.4.2 Multivariate Least Squares Regression Another regression-based algorithm is MA-Networker, which was developed by Gao et al. [46]. Unlike the sequence-based approaches that use sequence analysis to infer TFAs, MA-networker does so by using ChIP-chip data. MA-Networker first constructs a set of significant TFs using a backward selection algorithm. Unlike forward selection that REDUCE uses (adding one model at a time), the backward selection algorithm of Gao et al. [46] starts by fitting a model with all the variables of interest. Next, the least significant variable is dropped in each round, as long as it is not significant at a chosen critical level. Then, the algorithm continues by iteratively refitting reduced models and applying the same rule until all remaining variables are statistically significant. MA-Networker iteratively removes TFs that have insignificant P values based on the F-test.

Algorithm 12.2b   MA-Networker [46]

```
Input:
    -   Z = Gene expression data
    -   X = ChIP-chip data
Output:
    -   Y = Transcription factor activity (TFA) profile
Begin
    -   Construct a set of significant TFs using backward
        selection. This is done by iteratively removing
        TFs, which have insignificant  p-values based on the
        F-test.
```

- Construct a TFA profile for each TF using microarray and ChIP-chip data.

End Begin

The multivariate regression model used to obtain the transcription factor activity profiles is given by:

$$Z_{gt} = Z_{g0} + \sum_f Y_{ft} X_{fg}, \tag{12.4}$$

where Z_{gt} represents the mRNA expression log-ratio of gene g in condition or time point t, Z_{g0} represents a baseline expression log-ratio of gene g, X_{fg} represents the ChIP log-ratio for TF f and the promoter region of gene g, and Y_{ft} the inferred activity of TF f at condition or time point t. The unknown parameter Y_{ft} is found by minimizing the error between model and experimental data.

12.3.4.3 Partial Least Squares Regression   The approach proposed by Boulesteix and Strimmer [47] used partial least squares (PLS) regression to infer TFAs from gene expression data and DNA–protein binding experiments (ChIP-chip). PLS is an extension of multiple linear regression model. This method allows the detection of functional interactions between TFs. In addition, Boulesteix and Strimmer [47] showed that their method was able to detect false-positive calls in the ChIP-chip data. It also attempts to predict whether a TF enhances or represses the transcription of its target genes.

One of the advantages of the PLS method is that it performs well with small samples, even if the predictors (TFAs) are nonindependent. However, it strongly depends on availability of extensive ChIP-chip datasets, which are currently available only for yeast [48]. Below, the main steps of the *PLS* algorithm are highlighted.

Algorithm 12.2c   PLS Algorithm [47]

Input:

- Z = Gene expression data
- X = ChIP-chip data

Output:

- Y = Transcription factor activity (TFA) matrix.

Begin

1. Center X and Z to column mean zero, resulting in matrices X_1 and Z_1; scale the input matrices to unit variance.

2. Using the linear dimension reduction $T = X_1 R$, the L predictors in X_1 are mapped onto $K \le rank(X_1) \le min(L, N)$ latent components in T (an $N \times K$ matrix).

3. Assuming the model $Z_1 = TQ' + E$, Z_1 is regressed by ordinary least squares against the latent components T (also known as X-scores) to obtain the loadings Q (a $M \times K$ matrix), that is, $Q = Z_1'T(T'T)^{-1}$.

4. The PLS estimate of the coefficients Y_1 in $Z_1 = X_1 Y_1 + E$ is computed from estimates of the weight matrix R and the Z-loadings Q via $Y_1 = RQ'$.

5. The coefficients **Y** for the original $Z = XY + E$ are computed by rescaling **Y_1**.

End Begin

The PLS algorithm was validated using synthetic data, as well as real biological data (the *Escherichia coli* data from the Kao et al. study [49]). It was found to be as good as the original NCA algorithm [50] that we discuss below, but it has the advantage that it can be applied to any arbitrary topology.

12.3.5 Network Component Analysis Methods

Network component analysis (NCA) is a technique for inferring the dynamics of regulatory networks. NCA relies on predefined biological constrains in the connectivity structure of the network to restrict the decomposition solution space. NCA algorithm was pioneered by Liao et al. [50], and it was later generalized by Tran et al. [51]. More recently, Chang et al. [52] proposed a fast version of the network component analysis (FastNCA) framework.

12.3.5.1 Network Component Analysis Algorithm   To solve the inverse problem of Eq. (12.2), that is to recover X and Y from Z, Liao et al. [50] proposed the NCA framework, which is based on the following three constraints referred to as NCA criteria: (1) the connectivity matrix X must have full-column rank; (2) when an element in the regulatory domain is removed along with all the output elements connected to it, the connectivity matrix of the resulting network is still of full-column rank; and (3) the TFA matrix Y must have full-row rank. When the identifiability properties of X are true (see Section 12.3.1), then criteria (1) and (2) are verified and *NCA* decomposes the data matrix Z into matrices X and Y by minimizing E under the constraint that the network structure or the nonzero entries of the matrix X is conserved. The NCA algorithm restricts the solution space by taking advantage of the sparsity of the true biological connections and constraining matrix X with the use of zero elements in predefined positions. NCA assumes that a unique (or essentially unique) decomposition of Z to X and Y can be achieved up to a diagonal $L \times L$ matrix. Once the NCA criteria [50] for essentially unique decomposition are satisfied, NCA can find this decomposition by using bilinear optimization [51].

Algorithm 12.3a   Network Component Analysis Algorithm [50]

Input:
- Z = Gene expression data
- S_X = Set of X matrices that have zero elements in the predesignated position.

Output:
- X = Connectivity matrix
- Y = Transcription factor activities (TFA) matrix

Begin
- Initialize $X = X^{(0)}$, where $X^{(0)} \in S_X$:
- Given $X^{(0)}$, find $Y^{(1)} \in R^{LxM}$ such that $||Z - X^{(0)} Y^{(1)}||_F$ via QR factorization.
- Given $Y^{(1)}$, find $X^{(1)} \in S_X$ such that $||Z - X^{(1)} Y^{(1)}||_F$ via QR factorization.
- Repeat step 2 then 3 until the residual $||Z - X^{(n)} Y^{(n)}||_F$ is less than a specific tolerance.
- Normalize the matrices X by a diagonal matrix Q and Y by Q^{-1}.

End Begin

The normalization condition can be chosen such that the average value of a matrix entry in X is unity. A corresponding choice of such diagonal elements of Q is:

$$Q_{ll} = \frac{1}{K} \sum_{k=1}^{K} |X_{kl}|,$$ (12.5)

where K is the total number of nonzeros in the lth column of matrix X.

Liao et al. [50] biochemically validated the NCA algorithm on a network of seven solutions of three hemoglobin genes. Absorbance spectra measurements were used as the primary source of data. Liao et al. [50] found that NCA outperforms PCA and ICA.

12.3.5.2 Generalized Network Component Analysis
NCA described above is developed based on assigning constraints only to the connectivity matrix X. In many biological networks, the criteria for essential uniqueness [50] that the NCA method assume cannot be satisfied. The generalized NCA (*gNCA*) [51] method extends the standard NCA, so that constraints can be imposed on both the connectivity matrix X and the regulatory signal matrix Y, thus restricting further the search space. The authors used time series microarray data from *E. coli* (wild-type strain and an *arcA* deletion strain grown on glucose minimum medium) to test their method, although they did not verify their predictions afterwards.

Algorithm 12.3b   Generalized Network Component Analysis Algorithm [51]

Input:

- Z = Gene expression data

- S_X = Set of X matrices that have zero elements in the predesignated position.

- S_Y = Set of Y matrices that have zero elements in the predesignated position.

Output:

- X = Connectivity matrix

- Y = TFA matrix

Begin

- Given $X^{(0)}$; find $Y^{(1)} \in S_Y$ such that $||Z - X^{(0)} Y^{(1)}||_F$ is minimum by using QR factorization.

- Given $Y^{(1)}$; find $X^{(1)} \in S_X$ such that $||Z - X^{(1)} Y^{(1)}||_F$ by using QR factorization.

- Repeat step 2 then 3 until the residual $||Z - X^{(n)} Y^{(n)}||_F$ is less than a tolerance.

- Finally, the matrices X and Y are normalized by a chosen scaling matrix Q.

End Begin

Tran et al. [51] emphasized that in the *gNCA* framework the distinguishability of a given biological network from others need to be tested. A potential drawback of the bilinear optimization scheme used in the *gNCA* framework is that multiple local minima may exist. This problem can be addressed by running the algorithm multiple times with different initializations. Stable solutions are those that appear frequently. A technical potential problem is that noninvertible matrices may destabilize the numerical algorithm and result in physically unreasonable solutions [51]. In order to address this problem, Tran et al. redefine the optimization objective function using the Tikhonov regulation method (NCA-r).

12.3.5.3 Fast Network Component Analysis   The standard NCA algorithm, as described above, has two potential limitations: It is computationally unstable and can be trapped in local minima. The NCA-r algorithm with Tikhonov regularization [51] addresses mainly the first issue. The recently developed FastNCA algorithm [52] is based on matrix factorization and projection, and it attempts to account for both issues.

Indeed, it was shown by Chang et al. [52] that FastNCA provides a much faster analytical solution than NCA and NCA-r without having the above limitations. In particular, it is one order of magnitude faster than NCA and two orders of magnitude faster than NCA-r. Also, they showed that in the case of random Gaussian noise, K can be chosen as $K = L$ (see Algorithm 12.3c), with good performance and superior computational efficiency. Finally, Chang et al. [52] showed that FastNCA is not sensitive to either (small) inaccuracies of the initially defined network structure or correlations between input signals. In real cell cycle microarray data, they found FastNCA to predict the activities of cell cycle regulators at levels comparable to the semi-quantitative data obtained by Lee et al. [48]. The major disadvantage of FastNCA and the original NCA algorithms is that they only work well on networks that are NCA compliant. That is, the three NCA criteria (as they stated above) must be strictly satisfied. The FastNCA algorithm is summarized below.

Algorithm 12.3c   Fast Network Component Analysis Algorithm [52]

Input:
  - Z = Gene expression data,

Output:
  - X = Connectivity matrix
  - Y = TFA matrix

Begin
  - Perform a rank-K Eckart-Young_Mirsky (*EYM*) approximation of Z by singular values decomposition (*SVD*) as $Z_K = U_K\Sigma_K V_K^T$, and let $W = U_K$.
  - Estimation of X
    - For l = 1 to L
      - Re-order rows of W so that the lth column of X has the structure $x_l = \begin{bmatrix} x'_l \\ 0 \end{bmatrix}$.
      - Partition $W = \begin{bmatrix} W_c \\ W_r \end{bmatrix}$ conformally with this structure.
      - Do SVD for W_r, and get the last $K - L + 1$ right singular vectors. Denoted as a matrix v_0.
      - Compute the x'_l = the first left singular vector of $W_c v_0 v_0^T$.
  - Estimate the TFA matrix by: $Y = (X^T X)^{-1} X^T Z_K$.

End Begin

12.3.6 Factor Analysis Methods

Factor analysis (FA) methods treat the expression data as the observed variables that can be explained by (fewer) hidden variables, the TFAs. Unlike NCA and some regression algorithms, FA methods do not rely heavily on any knowledge of the connectivity matrix. The fact that FA algorithms try to reconstruct both the connectivity matrix and the TFAs makes the task more difficult. To enforce sparsity in the connectivity matrix, FA methods utilize matrix rotation (e.g., orthogonal rotation), while Bayesian FA methods do so by the incorporation of appropriate priors. The error terms, E (see Eq. (12.2), in FA models are assumed to be multivariate, normally distributed with zero mean, so the expression values, A, are also multivariate, normally distributed. Next, we review some of the FA algorithms.

12.3.6.1   *FA Parameters* In the FA models, the TFA profiles (factors) are assumed to be normally distributed with mean zero and covariance matrix Σ_y. It has been proposed by many groups [53–55] that setting the TFA covariance matrix to be equal to the identity matrix (I_K) can solve the network's identifiability problem (i.e., an essentially unique solution exists, see above). Other solutions for the TFA covariance matrix have been suggested, including Sabatti and James [56] $\Sigma y = \sigma_y^2 I_K$ (with σ_y being a constant value), and West [57] suggesting the more general prior $\Sigma_y = \text{diag}(\sigma_{y1}^2, \ldots, \sigma_{y2}^2)$. A detail presentation of many FA methods can be found in the Pournara and Wernisch review article [58].

The main differences between the existing FA models lie in the assignment of the prior distribution of the connectivity matrix, X, and its covariance matrix. In order to enforce sparsity on the connectivity matrix, Tipping [59], initially, and Fokoue [60], later, suggested independent normal priors on each element of X and gamma prior on the X's covariance matrix [58]. West [57], on the other hand, suggested a mixture prior on the elements of X to tackle the same problem.

12.3.6.2   *FA Optimization Algorithms and Implementation Details* Various strategies have been implemented in the context of FA algorithms long before their application in microarray data. For example, Hinton et al. developed an EM algorithm for FA models applied to image processing [61] and an exact EM algorithm for mixtures of FAs [53]. More recently, Utsugi and Kumagai [54] suggested a Gibbs sampler for mixtures of FAs.

The first time FA algorithms were applied in biological data was with the work of West in 2003 [57]. They used MCMC Bayesian FA approach to analyze breast cancer gene expression data. Sabatti and James [56] recently followed the same idea, but information about the connectivity matrix is provided in advance. This is achieved by first run of their Vocabulon algorithm [62] to calculate the probability that a given promoter could be bound by a TF. TF binding preferences are inferred from a set of PSSM models. This is similar to the requirement of a predefined connectivity matrix that some regression [47] and NCA algorithms [50] have been used in the past.

In the following, we outline the EM algorithm of Ghahramani and Hinton [53], which consists of two steps: (1) the E-step, in which, in every iteration, the expected values and the variances of the TFAs are calculated, given the current X and covariance of X; and (2) the M-step, in which, the values of X and covariance of X are calculated, given the current values of the TFAs.

Algorithm 12.4   The EM Algorithm of Ghahramani and Hinton

Input:

- Z = Gene expression data

Output:

- X = Connectivity matrix
- Y = TFA matrix

Begin
E-step: given the current X and Ψ (covariance matrix,) for each gene n, compute the expected values and the variances of the factors:

$$E(y^n \mid z^n, X, \Psi) = Cz^n$$

$$(E(y^n(y^n)' \mid z^n, X, \Psi) = I - CA + Cz^n(z^n)'C'$$

$$C = X'(\Psi + XX')^{-1}$$

M-step: given the expected value of the factors, which calculates the values of X and Ψ.

$$X = \left(\sum_{n=1}^{N} z^n E(y^n \mid z^n X, \Psi)' \right) \left(\sum_{i=1}^{N} E(y^i(y^i)' \mid z^i X, \Psi) \right)^{-1}$$

$$\Psi = \frac{1}{N} diag \left(\sum_{n=1}^{N} z^n(z^n)' - XE(y^n \mid z^n X, \Psi)(z^n)' \right)$$

End Begin

12.4   CONCLUSION

In this chapter, we presented one major class of algorithms for modeling gene regulatory networks: the physical interaction network algorithms (for a summary, see Table 12.1). One advantage of the physical interaction network algorithms is that they model the potential effect of TF proteins to other genes. This is particularly important not only for identifying molecular interactions in the cell but also for assisting the identification of potentially crucial subnetworks, hence helping to understand the molecular processes and—subsequently—the selection of particular gene targets for drug development.

The algorithms presented here are representative of the approaches employed for the identification of interactions between TFs and genes using expression data, genomic sequence or ChIP data, and prior biological knowledge. The clustering-based

Table 12.1 Summary of the methods presented in this chapter

Algorithm class	Assumptions	Prior knowledge	Inputs	Methodology	Outputs	Algorithm implementation examples
Clustering methods	Coexpression implies coregulation	GO annotations helpful, but not necessary	Z, Upstr	(1) Data mining; (2) sequence alignment	(1) Modules; (2) statistically significant DNA motifs	[27,35]
Regression Sequence-based	The expression of a gene in a condition is the contribution of a set of regulators		Z, Upstr	Regression techniques and forward, backward, or stepwise variables selection	Y	[36,42–44]
ChIP-based		Nonconnected points in X (optional)	Z, ChIP			[46,47]
Network component analysis models and its generalization	Network is NCA compliant	Nonconnected points in X, or Y, or both	Z and the nonconnected points in X	(1) Bilinear optimization; (2) matrix factorization and projection	X, Y	[50–52]
Factor analysis models	Network is sparse	Prior biological knowledge (optional)	Z	(1) Bayesian framework; (2) matrix rotation	X, Y	[53–55,57]

Z: matrix of gene expression data; X: connectivity matrix; Y: transcription factor activities (TFA) matrix; Upstr: upstream DNA sequences (promoters); ChIP: ChIP-chip data.

approaches have been developed under the assumption that the genes that are regulated by the same set of TFs will exhibit similar expression patterns. In other words, coregulation leads to coexpression. However, in practice, all clustering-based approaches operate under the reverse assumption (coexpression implies coregulation), which is not expected to be generally true. For example, one can imagine a case where two distinct sets of TFs produce similar expression profiles for their target genes, especially when few conditions or time points are sampled. This problem can only be addressed by using external information about the biological function of the genes in a cluster. For example, one might like to partition the cluster further using pathway information (e.g., from the GO database [63]). The subclusters will then contain genes that are coexpressed and belong to the same pathway. These genes are more likely to be regulated by the same TFs.

Sequence- or ChIP-chip-based regression models try to circumvent the clustering paradigm. The REDUCE algorithm [36] and the MA-Networker [46] algorithm assume that the expression of a gene is the result of additive contributions of a set of regulators. In REDUCE, the contributions are based on the number of motif occurrences in the upstream sequence of a gene in combination with the corresponding TFAs. In MA-Networker, the contributions are based on the TFs ChIP log-ratio. In both cases, TFAs are inferred through a linear regression model, implying that the TF contributions are additive. The extent to which this assumption is true needs further investigation, especially for organisms with intricate gene regulation like the complex eukaryotes.

NCA algorithms provide an elegant way to decompose the gene regulatory networks. They require that the networks under study are "NCA compliant", that is, they satisfy the three criteria proposed by Liao et al. [50] (see above). For biological networks, this is somewhat restrictive from many aspects, but mainly because the connectivity matrix needs to be known *a priori* in order to test one of the criteria. This is not feasible for many practical applications.

FA algorithms avoid this problem by calculating concurrently both the connectivity matrix and the matrix with the TFA profiles. One of the advantages of the FA algorithms is that their way of modeling the gene networks closely resembles the nature of biological data: A number of observed variables (gene expression data) are represented by a smaller number of hidden variables (TFAs). Another advantage of the Bayesian FA algorithms, in particular, is that they can incorporate prior information or enforce sparsity of the matrix through priors. In a comparative study of five FA algorithms on simulated and real biological data, Pournara and Wernisch [58] found all five to perform similarly well. The authors demonstrated that given a sparse biological network, FA algorithms can reconstruct the TFAs in the absence of *a priori* connectivity information. They also showed that averaging the connectivity matrix values obtained from all algorithms generally improves the performance.

This chapter offers an introduction to the physical network algorithms (TF to sequence interactions) and presents few representatives of what we think are the four major categories. This presentation cannot be exhaustive. There is a plethora of algorithms developed in the past few years, and interested readers can refer to recent reviews [4, 64] for more information.

12.4.1 Future Prospects and Challenges

The existing algorithms perform reasonably well in reconstructing artificial and real data, especially those derived from simpler, unicellular organisms. However, some recent discoveries come to complicate further the network inference and challenge the efficiency of the existing algorithms. For example, it has been shown [65, 66] that the CTCF protein binds to the DNA in a sequence-specific manner and transcriptionally isolates parts of the promoter region of the genes. This will naturally complicate models that are based on TF binding site prediction to model regulatory networks. Also, the ENCODE project [67] reported that TF binding sites are present upstream as well as downstream from the genes' transcription start sites. This will definitely affect the physical interactions algorithms, as it will become necessary to extend the search space for binding motifs.

More worrisome is the fact that they found that a large part of the genome is transcribed. Although the biological role of all these transcripts is yet unknown, it is highly likely that they would need to be considered in the construction of regulatory networks in the future. microRNA (miRNA) genes, in particular, are known to play an important role in silencing other genes [68]. miRNA genes are short (22–25 nucleotides long) noncoding genes and can downregulate protein-coding genes by means of base complementarity to their mRNA transcripts [69], which leads to an acceleration in the mRNA degradation rate or blocking of translation. One miRNA gene can have many targets and multiple miRNA genes can target a mRNA.

Despite the importance of miRNAs in gene regulation, there is only one algorithm that incorporates miRNA genes in reconstructing regulatory networks [70]. This is in part due to the scarcity of high-throughput data for miRNA gene expression and in part due to the lack of knowledge about their transcription. Although many studies have shown that miRNA genes are transcribed by RNA polymerase II with mechanisms similar to those of protein-coding genes [1, 71, 72], their precise start of transcription is still unknown for the most cases. The principles behind many of the algorithms presented in this chapter, however, could easily accommodate miRNA genes once the details of their transcription become known. We should note, however, that microarray techniques cannot distinguish the protein-coding genes that are translationally repressed by miRNA genes, hence imposing another challenging problem for network modeling.

In the last 12 years since its appearence in the biological research field, microarray data transformed the way research is conducted. We have progressed from the one-gene-one-hypothesis reductionist approach to the holistic view of systems biology. Reconstructing gene regulatory networks from microarray and ChIP-chip data has met reasonable success, but the complicated biological world raises more challenges.

ACKNOWLEDGMENTS

We would like to thank Chakra Chennubhotla for critically reviewing the manuscript and an anonymous reviewer for very helpful comments. This work was supported by NIH grants 1R01LM009657 and NO1 AI-50018 and by a tobacco settlement grant from the Pennsylvania Department of Health. P.V.B. was also supported by NIH grant

1R01LM007994 and by intramural funds from the Department of Computational Biology, University of Pittsburgh and the University of Pittsburgh Cancer Institute (UPCI).

REFERENCES

1. S. Mahony, D. L. Corcoran, E. Feingold, and P. V. Benos. Regulatory conservation of protein coding and microRNA genes in vertebrates: lessons from the opossum genome. *Genome Biol.*, 8(5):R84, 2007.

2. P. Carninci, A. Sandelin, B. Lenhard, S. Katayama, K. Shimokawa, J. Ponjavic, C. A. Semple, M. S. Taylor, P. G. Engstrom, Frith M. C., et al. Genome-wide analysis of mammalian promoter architecture and evolution. *Nat. Genet.*, 38(6):626–635, 2006.

3. U. Alon. An introduction to systems biology. In *Design Principles of Biological Circuits*, Chapman & Hall/CRC, Boca Raton, FL, 2007.

4. T. S. Gardner and J. J. Faith. Reverse-engineering transcription control networks. *Phys. Life Rev.*, 2:65–88, 2005.

5. A. J. Hartemink, D. K. Gifford, T. S. Jaakkola, and R. A. Young. Using graphical models and genomic expression data to statistically validate models of genetic regulatory networks. *Pac. Symp. Biocomput.*, 422–433, 2001.

6. N. Friedman. Inferring cellular networks using probabilistic graphical models. *Science*, 303(5659):799–805, 2004.

7. I. Gat-Viks and R. Shamir. Chain functions and scoring functions in genetic networks. *Bioinformatics*, 19(Suppl 1):i108–i117, 2003.

8. A. de la Fuente, P. Brazhnik, and P. Mendes. Linking the genes: inferring quantitative gene networks from microarray data. *Trends Genet.*, 18(8):395–398, 2002.

9. T. S. Gardner, D. di Bernardo, D. Lorenz, and J. J. Collins. Inferring genetic networks and identifying compound mode of action via expression profiling. *Science*, 301(5629):102–105, 2003.

10. J. Tegner, M. K. Yeung, J. Hasty, and J. J. Collins. Reverse engineering gene networks: integrating genetic perturbations with dynamical modeling. *Proc. Natl. Acad. Sci. USA*, 100(10):5944–5949, 2003.

11. T. Ideker, V. Thorsson, J. A. Ranish, R. Christmas, J. Buhler, J. K. Eng, R. Bumgarner, D. R. Goodlett, R. Aebersold, and L. Hood. Integrated genomic and proteomic analyses of a systematically perturbed metabolic network. *Science*, 292(5518):929–934, 2001.

12. M. Steffen, A. Petti, J. Aach, P. D'Haeseleer, and G. Church. Automated modelling of signal transduction networks. *BMC Bioinform.*, 3:34, 2002.

13. M. Middendorf, A. Kundaje, C. Wiggins, Y. Freund, and C. Leslie. Predicting genetic regulatory response using classification. *Bioinformatics*, 20(Suppl 1):i232–i240, 2004.

14. A. J. Butte and I. S. Kohane. Mutual information relevance networks: functional genomic clustering using pairwise entropy measurements. *Pac. Symp. Biocomput.*, 418–429, 2000.

15. J. J. Rice, Y. Tu, and G. Stolovitzky. Reconstructing biological networks using conditional correlation analysis. *Bioinformatics*, 21(6):765–773, 2005.

16. N. M. Luscombe and J. M. Thornton. Protein-DNA interactions: amino acid conservation and the effects of mutations on binding specificity. *J. Mol. Biol.*, 320(5):991–1009, 2002.

17. C. Tuerk and L. Gold. Systematic evolution of ligands by exponential enrichment: RNA ligands to bacteriophage T4 DNA polymerase. *Science*, **249**(4968):505–510, 1990.

18. M. L. Bulyk, E. Gentalen, D. J. Lockhart, and G. M. Church. Quantifying DNA-protein interactions by double-stranded DNA arrays. *Nat. Biotechnol.*, 17(6):573–577, 1999.

19. G. D. Stormo. DNA binding sites: representation and discovery. *Bioinformatics*, 16(1):16–23, 2000.

20. P. V. Benos, A. S. Lapedes, and G. D. Stormo. Probabilistic code for DNA recognition by proteins of the EGR family. *J. Mol. Biol.*, 323(4):701–727, 2002.

21. T. K. Man and G. D. Stormo. Non-independence of Mnt repressor-operator interaction determined by a new quantitative multiple fluorescence relative affinity (QuMFRA) assay. *Nucleic Acids Res.*, 29(12):2471–2478, 2001.

22. Y. Barash, G. Elidan, N. Friedman, and T. Kaplan. Modeling dependencies in protein-DNA binding sites. In *Seventh Annual International Conference on Computational Molecular Biology (RECOMB)*, 2003.

23. P. V. Benos, M. L. Bulyk, and G. D. Stormo. Additivity in protein-DNA interactions: how good an approximation is it? *Nucleic Acids Res.*, 30(20):4442–4451, 2002.

24. M. Schena, D. Shalon, R. W. Davis, and P. O. Brown. Quantitative monitoring of gene expression patterns with a complementary DNA microarray. *Science*, 270(5235):467–470, 1995.

25. V. Orlando. Mapping chromosomal proteins in vivo by formaldehyde-crosslinked-chromatin immunoprecipitation. *Trends Biochem. Sci.*, 25(3):99–104, 2000.

26. M. R. Friedlander, W. Chen, C. Adamidi, J. Maaskola, R. Einspanier, S. Knespel, and N. Rajewsky. Discovering microRNAs from deep sequencing data using miRDeep. *Nat. Biotechnol.*, 26(4):407–415, 2008.

27. S. Tavazoie, J. D. Hughes, M. J. Campbell, R. J. Cho, and G. M. Church. Systematic determination of genetic network architecture. *Nat. Genet.*, 22(3):281–285, 1999.

28. R. Xu and D. Wunsch 2nd. Survey of clustering algorithms. *IEEE Transact. On Neural Networks*, 16(3):645–678, 2005.

29. J. D. Hughes, P. W. Estep, S. Tavazoie, and G. M. Church. Computational identification of cis-regulatory elements associated with groups of functionally related genes in Saccharomyces cerevisiae. *J. Mol. Biol.*, 296(5):1205–1214, 2000.

30. M. K. Das and H. K. Dai. A survey of DNA motif finding algorithms. *BMC Bioinform.*, 8(Suppl 7):S21, 2007.

31. D. GuhaThakurta. Computational identification of transcriptional regulatory elements in DNA sequence. *Nucleic Acids Res.*, 34(12):3585–3598, 2006.

32. M. Tompa, N. Li, T. L. Bailey, G. M. Church, B. De Moor, E. Eskin, A. V. Favorov, M. C. Frith, Y. Fu, W. J. Kent, et al. Assessing computational tools for the discovery of transcription factor binding sites. *Nat. Biotechnol.*, 23(1):137–144, 2005.

33. J. Ihmels, G. Friedlander, S. Bergmann, O. Sarig, Y. Ziv, and N. Barkai. Revealing modular organization in the yeast transcriptional network. *Nat. Genet.*, 31(4):370–377, 2002.

34. S. C. Madeira and A. L. Oliveira. Biclustering algorithms for biological data analysis: a survey. *IEEE/ACM Transact. on Comput. Biol. Bioinform.*, 1(1):24–45, 2004.

35. M. A. Beer and S. Tavazoie. Predicting gene expression from sequence. *Cell*, 117(2):185–198, 2004.

36. H. J. Bussemaker, H. Li, and E. D. Siggia. Regulatory element detection using correlation with expression. *Nat. Genet.*, 27(2):167–171, 2001.

37. E. Segal, R. Yelensky, and D. Koller. Genome-wide discovery of transcriptional modules from DNA sequence and gene expression. *Bioinformatics*, 19(Suppl 1):i273–i282, 2003.

38. E. Segal, M. Shapira, A. Regev, D. Pe'er, D. Botstein, D. Koller, and N. Friedman. Module networks: identifying regulatory modules and their condition-specific regulators from gene expression data. *Nat. Genet.*, 34(2):166–176, 2003.

39. Z. Bar-Joseph, G. K. Gerber, T. I. Lee, N. J. Rinaldi, J. Y. Yoo, F. Robert, D. B. Gordon, E. Fraenkel, T. S. Jaakkola, and R. A. Young, et al. Computational discovery of gene modules and regulatory networks. *Nat. Biotechnol.*, 21(11):1337–1342, 2003.

40. K. Lemmens, T. Dhollander, T. De Bie, P. Monsieurs, K. Engelen, B. Smets, J. Winderickx, B. De Moor, and K. Marchal. Inferring transcriptional modules from ChIP-chip, motif and microarray data. *Genome Biol.*, 7(5):R37, 2006.

41. X. Xu, L. Wang, and D. Ding. Learning module networks from genome-wide location and expression data. *FEBS Lett.*, 578(3):297–304, 2004.

42. S. Keles, M. van der Laan, and M. B. Eisen. Identification of regulatory elements using a feature selection method. *Bioinformatics*, 18(9):1167–1175, 2002.

43. E. Wang and E. Purisima. Network motifs are enriched with transcription factors whose transcripts have short half-lives. *Trends Genet.*, 21(9):492–495, 2005.

44. E. M. Conlon, X. S. Liu, J. D. Lieb, and J. S. Liu. Integrating regulatory motif discovery and genome-wide expression analysis. *Proc. Natl. Acad. Sci. USA*, 100(6):3339–3344, 2003.

45. X. S. Liu, D. L. Brutlag, and J. S. Liu. An algorithm for finding protein-DNA binding sites with applications to chromatin-immunoprecipitation microarray experiments. *Nat. Biotechnol.*, 20(8):835–839, 2002.

46. F. Gao, B. C. Foat, and H. J. Bussemaker. Defining transcriptional networks through integrative modeling of mRNA expression and transcription factor binding data. *BMC Bioinform.*, 5:31, 2004.

47. A. L. Boulesteix and K. Strimmer. Predicting transcription factor activities from combined analysis of microarray and ChIP data: a partial least squares approach. *Theor. Biol. Med. Model.*, 2:23, 2005.

48. T. I. Lee, N. J. Rinaldi, F. Robert, D. T. Odom, Z. Bar-Joseph, G. K. Gerber, N. M. Hannett, C. T. Harbison, C. M. Thompson, I. Simon, et al. Transcriptional regulatory networks in Saccharomyces cerevisiae. *Science*, 298(5594):799–804, 2002.

49. K. C. Kao, Y. L. Yang, R. Boscolo, C. Sabatti, V. Roychowdhury, and J. C. Liao. Transcriptome-based determination of multiple transcription regulator activities in *Escherichia coli* by using network component analysis. *Proc. Natl. Acad. Sci. USA*, 101(2):641–646, 2004.

50. J. C. Liao, R. Boscolo, Y. L. Yang, L. M. Tran, C. Sabatti, and V. P. Roychowdhury. Network component analysis: reconstruction of regulatory signals in biological systems. *Proc. Natl. Acad. Sci. USA*, 100(26):15522–15527, 2003.

51. L. T. Tran, C. G. Knight, R. V. O'Neill, and E. R. Smith. Integrated environmental assessment of the Mid-Atlantic region with analytical network **process**. *Envir. Monit. Assess.*, 94(1–3):263–277, 2004.

52. C. Chang, Z. Ding, Y. S. Hung, and P. C. Fung. Fast network component analysis (FastNCA) for gene regulatory network reconstruction from microarray data. *Bioinformatics*, 24(11):1349–1358, 2008.

53. Z. Ghahramani and G. E. Hinton, The EM algorithm for mixtures of factor analyzers. Technical Report CRG-TR-96-1, University of Toronto, Toronto, 1997.

54. A. Utsugi and T. Kumagai. Bayesian analysis of mixtures of factor analyzers. *Neural Comput.*, 13(5):993–1002, 2001.

55. E. Fokoue, Stochastic determination of the intrinsic structure in Bayesian factor analysis Vol. 2004. SAMSI, Research Triangle Park, NC, 2004.

56. C. Sabatti and G. M. James. Bayesian sparse hidden components analysis for transcription regulation networks. *Bioinformatics*, 22(6):739–746, 2006.

57. M. West. Bayesian factor regression models in the "Large p, Small n" paradigm. *Bayesian Statistics*, 7:733–742, 2003.

58. I. Pournara and L. Wernisch. Factor analysis for gene regulatory networks and transcription factor activity profiles. *BMC Bioinform.*, 8:61, 2007.

59. M. Tipping. Sparse Bayesian learning and the relevance vector machine. *J. Machine Learning Res.*, 1:211–244, 2001.

60. E. Fokoue, P. Goel, and D. Sun, A prior for consistent estimation for the relevance vector machine, Vol. 2004. SAMSI, Research Triangle Park, NC, 2004.

61. G. E. Hinton, P. Dayan, and M. Revow. Modelling the manifolds of images of handwritten digits. *IEEE Trans. Neural Networks*, 8:65–74, 1997.

62. C. Sabatti, L. Rohlin, K. Lange, and J. C. Liao. Vocabulon: a dictionary model approach for reconstruction and localization of transcription factor binding sites. *Bioinformatics*, 21(7):922–931, 2005.

63. M. A. Harris, J. Clark, A. Ireland, J. Lomax, M. Ashburner, R. Foulger, K. Eilbeck, S. Lewis, B. Marshall, C. Mungall, et al. The Gene Ontology (GO) database and informatics resource. *Nucleic Acids Res.*, 32(Database issue):D258–D261, 2004.

64. H. J. Bussemaker, B. C. Foat, and L. D. Ward. Predictive modeling of genome-wide mRNA expression: from modules to molecules. *Annu. Review Biophys. Biomol. Struct.*, 36:329–347, 2007.

65. H. Xi, H. P. Shulha, J. M. Lin, T. R. Vales, Y. Fu, D. M. Bodine, R. D. McKay, J. G. Chenoweth, P. J. Tesar, T. S. Furey, et al. Identification and characterization of cell type-specific and ubiquitous chromatin regulatory structures in the human genome. *PLoS Genet.*, 3(8):e136, 2007.

66. S. Renaud, D. Loukinov, Z. Abdullaev, I. Guilleret, F. T. Bosman, V. Lobanenkov, and J. Benhattar. Dual role of DNA methylation inside and outside of CTCF-binding regions in the transcriptional regulation of the telomerase hTERT gene. *Nucleic Acids Res.*, 35(4):1245–1256, 2007.

67. E. Birney, J. A. Stamatoyannopoulos, A. Dutta, R. Guigo, T. R. Gingeras, E. H. Margulies, Z. Weng, M. Snyder, E. T. Dermitzakis, R. E. Thurman, et al. Identification and analysis of functional elements in 1% of the human genome by the ENCODE pilot project. *Nature*, 447(7146):799–816, 2007.

68. J. C. Carrington and V. Ambros. Role of microRNAs in plant and animal development. *Science*, 301(5631):336–338, 2003.

69. P. Maziere and A. J. Enright. Prediction of microRNA targets. *Drug Discov. Today*, 12(11–12):452–458, 2007.

70. R. Shalgi, D. Lieber, M. Oren, and Y. Pilpel. Global and local architecture of the mammalian microRNA-transcription factor regulatory network. *PLoS Comput. Biol.*, 3(7):e131, 2007.

71. Y. Lee, M. Kim, J. Han, K. H. Yeom, S. Lee, S. H. Baek, and V. N. Kim. MicroRNA genes are transcribed by RNA polymerase II. *Embo J*, 23(20):4051–4060, 2004.

72. X. Cai, C. H. Hagedorn, and B. R. Cullen. Human microRNAs are processed from capped, polyadenylated transcripts that can also function as mRNAs. *RNA*, 10(12):1957–1966, 2004.

13

THE IMPACT OF WHOLE GENOME *IN SILICO* SCREENING FOR NUCLEAR RECEPTOR-BINDING SITES IN SYSTEMS BIOLOGY

Carsten Carlberg and Merja Heinäniemi

Life Sciences Research Unit, University of Luxembourg, Luxembourg

13.1 INTRODUCTION

Each individual human gene is under the control of a large set of transcription factors that can bind upstream and downstream of its transcription start site (TSS) [1]. These sites typically arrange into collections of neighboring sites, the so-called modules or enhancers. Modules of transcription factors that act on focused genomic regions have been shown to be far more effective than individual factors on isolated locations and can act from large distances up to hundreds of thousands of base pairs. In an ideal case, such transcription factor modules can be identified by parallel and comparative analysis of their binding sites. Here, bioinformatics approaches can be of great help, in case they can predict the actions of the transcription factors precisely enough [2].

Elements of Computational Systems Biology Edited by Huma M. Lodhi and Stephen H. Muggleton
Copyright © 2010 John Wiley & Sons, Inc.

13.2 NUCLEAR RECEPTORS

Nuclear receptors (NRs) form a superfamily with 48 human members, of which most have the special property to be ligand-inducible [3, 4]. This property has attracted interest in the NR family as possible therapeutical targets. NRs are the best characterized representatives of approximately 3000 different mammalian proteins that are involved in transcriptional regulation in human tissues [5]. NRs modulate genes that affect processes as diverse as reproduction, development, inflammation, and general metabolism. They were first recognized as the receptors for the steroid hormones estradiol (ER α and β), progesterone (PR), testosterone (AR), cortisol (GR), and aldosterol (MR) for thyroid hormones (TR α and β) and for the biologically active forms of the fat-soluble vitamins A and D, all-*trans* retinoic acid (RAR α, β, and γ), and $1\alpha,25$-dihydroxyvitamin D_3 (VDR). This group of 12 NRs constitutes the classic endocrine NR subgroup. They can be defined functionally as being able to bind their specific ligand with a K_d of 1 nM or less [3]. The 36 remaining NRs are structurally related to the endocrine NRs but were orphans at the time of their cloning because neither their ligands nor their physiological functions were initially known [6]. During the past 17 years, however, natural and synthetic ligands have been identified for nearly half of these receptors. They now form the group of adopted orphan NRs [7]. Interestingly, most of the latter group of NRs have as their natural ligands dietary components, such as lipids or exogenously derived compounds, which are encountered in the micro- to millimolar concentration range. Subsequently, these receptors have activation thresholds (in terms of K_d) in the same molar range. This functionally separates them from the endocrine receptors. The current model of NR signaling is schematically depicted in Figure 13.1.

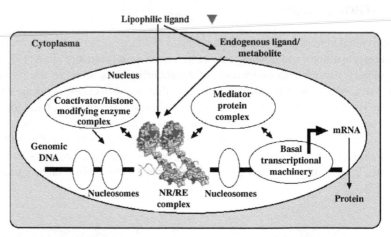

Figure 13.1 *Molecular mechanism of NR action.* NRs interact with discrete sequences in the proximity of genes to modulate transcription, a process that is governed by chromatin status and the availability of ligand and coregulators.

13.2.1 NRs as a Link between Nutrition Sensing and Inflammation Prevention

The interrelation of NRs, their diet-derived ligands, and metabolizing enzymes is a central issue in the new discipline nutrigenomics, which is the study of the impact of nutrient-derived compounds on the genome. It also encompasses the effects of food on physiological functions such as resistance to external assault from opportunistic pathogens [8]. For example, both nutritional overload and undernourishment have implications for immune function, and consequently, metabolism and immunity are closely linked [9]. Starvation and malnutrition can suppress immune function and increase susceptibility to infections, whereas obesity is associated with a state of aberrant immune activity and increasing risk for associated inflammatory diseases, including airway inflammation and fatty liver disease, a condition that impairs those organs' role in immunity [10].

One emerging concept in context of many diseases is the role of the immune system. Taking the nutrigenomics perspective and recognizing the lifestyle changes in the Western society, obesity can be taken as an example of a disease state characterized by a strong link with immune functions. Moreover, obesity is a strong risk factor to develop type 2 diabetes and atherosclerosis, making it one of the major health concerns of the industrialized world. In obesity, adipose tissue becomes inflamed both via infiltration by macrophages and as a result of adipocytes themselves producing inflammatory cytokines [11, 12]. Inflammation of adipose tissue is a crucial step in the development of peripheral insulin resistance [9]. In addition, in proatherosclerotic conditions, such as obesity and dyslipidemia, macrophages accumulate lipid to become foam cells in vessel wall plaques, where local inflammation is initiated. Inflammation itself is not problematic, if it is controlled and short term. During microbial infection, the inflammatory response defends the body while suppressing appetite and conserving fuel. An ill body is capable of defending itself by releasing adrenal steroids, mobilizing massive amounts of fuel, and finally suppressing inflammation once the pathogen is cleared. Concerning the latter aspect, the role of NRs is well-recognized. In fact, natural and synthetic GR ligands are used primarily as anti-inflammatory agents [13]. Other NRs, such as VDR, PPAR, RAR, and liver X receptor, also protect against inflammation. These receptors have the combined ability to manage energy and inflammation, indicating the important synergism between these two systems (Figure 13.2).

The duality between inflammatory and metabolic pathways is also highlighted by the overlapping biology and function of macrophages and adipocytes in obesity [9]. Gene expression of both cell types is highly similar; macrophages express many, if not the majority of "adipocyte" gene products, such as lipid-metabolizing and transporting proteins, while adipocytes can express many "macrophage" proteins, such as cytokines [14]. Inflammatory pathways can be initiated by extracellular mediators, such as cytokines and lipids, or by intracellular stresses, such as endoplasmic reticulum stress or excess reactive oxygen species production by mitochondria. NRs oppose these inflammatory pathways by promoting nutrient transport and metabolism

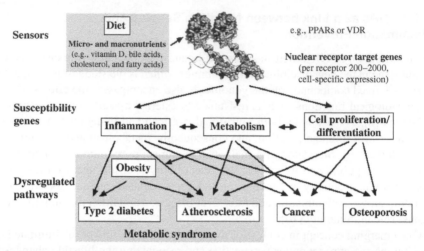

Figure 13.2 *Potential interactions of NRs with complex processes.* NR target genes regulated many physiological functions. When these pathways are dysregulated, they eventually result in disease states.

and antagonizing inflammatory activity. In conditions of overnutrition, this becomes a particular challenge.

The commonality between distinct physiologic branches suggests that the NR superfamily should be investigated by systems biology approaches as an intact functional dynamic entity. Recent studies by the NURSA consortium (www.nursa.org) have provided evidence supporting this concept. They examined the expression of all NRs in both macrophages stimulated by the stress ligands, lipopolysaccharide, and IFNγ [15] and adipocytes induced by GR and PPARγ ligands [16]. In both cases, a subset of NRs was readily detectable with some of them, for example, VDR, rising in expression levels at various time points during the induction process. This implies new, presently overlooked roles for these NRs and their ligands. Furthermore, the discovery of increases in expression of certain NRs at intermediate and late time points indicates the importance of a multitude of NRs in the proper execution of complex processes. These and other observations suggest that larger organizational principles exist on the level of transcription factors and of enzyme complexes in the nucleus, the cytoplasm, and membranes that contain NRs or their target gene products. A molecular understanding of how the NR superfamily integrates important physiological aspects will provide a conceptual basis for the treatment of complex human diseases (Figure 13.2).

13.2.2 NRs and System Biology

Until recently, approaches to diseases and gene function, in general, tended to focus on one gene at a time. In the last 10 years, high-volume research approaches have allowed scientists to grasp the total information contained within a cell concerning transcriptional activity, protein content, and metabolites. One way to monitor and

analyze these massive amounts of data is systems biology, which aims both to reduce experimental data to meaningful paradigms and also build up *in silico* testable
hypotheses [17]. However, systems biology can do more than describing generic
patterns within gene expression. The fine regulation of the NR network is specific
to each human individual and depends on the constellation of regulatory small nucleotide polymorphisms (SNPs) in his/her genome [18]. It is envisaged that some of
these regulatory SNPs will affect the binding of NRs to a subset of REs in their target
genes. This could determine an individual's susceptibility to age-related diseases such
as type 2 diabetes, atherosclerosis, cancer, and Alzheimer's disease.

Systems biology will also help to identify biomarkers (whether it be genes, proteins,
or metabolites) for the early detection of these diseases [19]. NRs are able to integrate
various central physiological actions in the human body. Therefore, NR signaling will
benefit from an analysis with systems biology methodology on the level of (i) binding
sites and changes of chromatin packaging in NR target genes, (ii) comparative mRNA
expression of NR target genes in various human tissues, (iii) analysis of key NR target
proteins and metabolites, and (iv) physiological consequences of NR signaling.

This review focuses on the PPAR subfamily of NRs studied within a Marie Curie
research training network of 14 research teams (www.uku.fi/nucsys), which is
funded by the FP6 program of the European Union.

13.3 THE PPAR SUBFAMILY

PPARs are adopted NRs that were initially described as the sensors for compounds
that induce peroxisome proliferation in rodents [20], but now they are know to be
important sensors of cellular levels of fatty acids and fatty acid derivatives that are
mainly derived from the lipoxygenase and cyclooxygenase pathways [3]. Polyunsatu-
rated fatty acids activate the three PPAR subtypes with relatively low affinity, whereas
fatty acid derivatives show more binding selectivity [21]. PPARs are prominent play-
ers in the metabolic syndrome because of their role as important regulators of lipid
storage and catabolism [22], but they also regulate cellular growth and differentiation
and, therefore, have an impact on hyperproliferative diseases such as cancer [23].
Bioinformatics approaches to identify genomic targets of PPARs and important regulatory modules with colocalizing PPREs, as they will be described below, should have
a major impact on understanding the role and potential therapeutic value of PPARs
in complex disease.

The three PPAR subtypes α, β/δ, and γ are coexpressed in numerous cell types
from either ectodermal, mesodermal, or endodermal origin, although their concentration relative to each other varies widely [24, 25]. PPARα is highly expressed in cells
that have active fatty acid oxidation capacity, including hepatocytes, cardiomyocytes,
enterocytes, and the proximal tubule cells of the kidney [26]. This PPAR subtype is
a central regulator of hepatic fatty acid catabolism and glucose metabolism. Furthermore, it potently represses the hepatic inflammatory response by downregulating the
expression of numerous genes such as various acute phase proteins. PPARα is the
molecular target for the hypolipidemic fibrates, a group of drugs that are prescribed

for their ability to lower plasma triacylglycerols and elevate plasma high-density lipoprotein levels. PPARβ/δ is expressed ubiquitously and often displays higher expression levels than PPARα and γ. It stimulates fatty acid oxidation in both adipose tissue and skeletal muscle, regulates hepatic very low density lipoprotein production and catabolism, and is involved in wound healing by governing keratinocyte differentiation [27]. PPARγ is expressed predominantly in adipose tissue and the immune system and exists as two distinct protein forms γ1 and γ2, which arise by differential TSSs and alternative splicing [26]. PPARγ is the master regulator of adipogenesis and regulates cell cycle withdrawal, as well as induction of fat-specific target genes that are involved in adipocyte metabolism [28]. PPARγ stimulates the expression of numerous genes that are involved in lipogenesis, including those for adipocyte fatty acid-binding protein, lipoprotein lipase, and fatty acid translocase. The general role for PPARγ in the regulation of lipid metabolism is underlined by the therapeutic utilization of the PPARγ ligands thiazolidinediones in obesity-linked type 2 diabetes [29].

Being transcription factors, the role that each PPAR subtype plays in different disease settings is reflected by the number and kind of target genes regulated in each tissue type. Current technologies allow researchers to address transcriptional regulation on a transcriptome-wide level using microarrays. A good example of a transcriptional approach in the PPAR field is the nutrigenomics initiative addressing PPARα target genes in liver and other metabolically active tissues [30, 31]. Integration of several microarray studies comparing wild-type and PPARα knockout mice, and high-fat diet-induced response to synthetic ligand response, identified several novel PPAR target genes functioning in hepatic lipid metabolism that had not been identified before despite much research dedicated on characterizing the role of PPARs in these pathways [32].

13.3.1 Global Datasets that Identify a Central Role for PPARs in Disease Progression

Within the field of top–down systems biology, emphasis is on network perturbations to understand disease. An important challenge will be to identify the critical networks where NRs play a role. Recently, two association studies that aimed to link gene expression profiles to clinical traits and identify underlying genetic loci suggest that a critical macrophage network is associated with clinical traits for metabolic syndrome in mouse and human [33, 34]. The mouse study identified associations of this network with glucose and insulin levels, blood pressure, aortic lesion formation, and obesity, whereas the human study focused on genetics of obesity only. PPARγ is one member of that network and the association of the expression level was validated by single gene perturbation in mouse. Furthermore, in a study of macrophage activation, where transcription factor expression profiles and target gene profiles were correlated and supported by binding site search data, PPARγ, retinoid X receptor (RXR) α, GR, and estrogen-related receptor-1 were differentially regulated [35]. The target genes found with TRANSFAC motif of PPARα–RXR (which according to our experience does not differ significantly from PPARγ-binding profile) were identified from a cluster with early and sustained induction profile, the members of which were suggested to maintain the response. In effect, such global and unbiased approaches also suggest a critical role for macrophages in determining key clinical phenotypes and an important role of PPARs in macrophage function as was already discussed earlier.

To understand more deeply the function of PPARs in cells, global binding site occupancy data will be needed to validate *in silico* predictions and to understand differences between tissues that vary on chromatin organization level. This type of data collection for transcription factors and chromatin modifications is the focus of the ENCODE project [57]. From the NR superfamily, RARα and hepatocyte nuclear factor α (HNF4α) are represented. RARα is studied in connection with neutrophil differentiation together with other transcription factors, coregulators, and histone modification in retinoic acid stimulated cells (Affymetrix chromatin immunoprecipitation (ChIP)-chip track [36]). HNF4α is studied together with other key liver transcription factors and histone 3 acetylation that marks active regions in liver cells (Uppsala ChIP track [37]). ChIP-chip data exist also for ERα [38], and it is now recognized that distal binding sites are widely used by NRs and that their arrangement into modules with other transcription factors is being explored.

13.3.2 PPAR Response Elements

An essential prerequisite for the direct modulation of transcription by PPAR ligands is the location of at least one activated PPAR protein close to the TSS of the respective primary PPAR target gene. This is commonly achieved through the specific binding of PPARs to a DNA-binding site, a so-called PPRE, and DNA looping toward the TSS [39]. In detail, the DNA-binding domain of PPARs contacts the major groove of a double-stranded hexameric DNA sequence with the optimal AGGTCA core binding sequence. PPARs bind to DNA as heterodimers with RXR [40] (Figure 13.1). PPREs are, therefore, formed by two hexameric core-binding motifs in a direct repeat orientation with an optimal spacing of one nucleotide (DR1), where PPAR occupies the 5′-motif [41]. However, characterization of PPREs from regulated gene promoters has resulted in a large collection of PPREs that deviate significantly from this consensus sequence. An extensive binding data collection for PPARs was recently published [42], where more critical deviations and well-tolerated deviations from the consensus were identified. In the following paragraphs, we will focus on the importance of binding site prediction for the systems biology approach.

13.4 METHODS FOR *IN SILICO* SCREENING OF TRANSCRIPTION FACTOR-BINDING SITES

Statistically, a NR core-binding motif, such as RGKTSA (R = A or G, K = G or T, S = C or G), should be found, on average, in every 256 bp of genomic DNA. Furthermore, dimeric assemblies of such hexamers should show up as direct repeats every 65,536 bp and as everted repeats every 32,768 bp in a random sequence. Therefore, an *in silico* screen of the human genome would identify for every NR on an average of 50,000–100,000 putative REs. Since NR proteins have an abundance of at most a few thousand molecules per cell, a biologically realistic number of NR target genes per cell should be closer to this number. If we also consider the fact that many NR target genes appear to have more than one functional RE for any given NR, it could be expected that the real number of NR target genes in any cell type is much less than the number of NR molecules. These calculations make it obvious that not every putative NR-binding site is used in nature in any cell at any given time. Further background on the bioinformatics of NRs is summarized by Danielsen [43].

The specificity of PPARs for their binding sites allows constructing a model to describe the PPRE properties that can be used to predict potential binding sites in genomic sequences. For this, the PPAR-binding preference, often expressed as position weight matrix (PWM), has to be described on the basis of experimental data such as series of gel shift assays with a large number of natural binding sites [44–47]. However, PPAR–RXR heterodimers do not only recognize a pair of the consensus-binding motifs AGGTCA, but also a number of variations to it. Independent of the individual PWM description, this leads to a prediction of PPREs every 1000–10,000 bp of genomic sequence. This probably contains many false-positive predictions, which are mainly due to scoring methodology and the limitations that are imposed by the available experimental data. For example, the quantitative characteristics of a transcription factor, that is, its relative binding strength to a number of different binding sites, are neglected in a position frequency matrix, where simply the total number of observations of each nucleotide is recorded for each position. Moreover, in the past, there was a positional bias of transcription factor-binding sites upstream in close vicinity to the TSS. This would be apparent from the collection of identified PPREs but is in contrast with a multigenome comparison of NR-binding site distribution [48] and other reports on wide-range associations of distal regulatory sites [49]. Genome-wide approaches for the identification of NR REs and NR target genes are reviewed by Tavera-Mendoza et al. [50].

Internet-based software tools, such as TRANSFAC [51], screen DNA sequences with databases of matrix models. One approach used PWMs to describe the binding preferences of PPARs using all published PPREs [52]. The accuracy of such methods can be improved by taking the evolutionary conservation of the binding site and that of the flanking genomic region into account. Moreover, cooperative interactions between transcription factors, that is, regulatory modules, can be taken into account by screening for binding site clusters. The combination of phylogenetic footprinting and PWM searches applied to orthologous human and mouse gene sequences reduces the rate of false predictions by an order of magnitude but leads to some reduction in sensitivity [53]. Recent studies suggest that a surprisingly large fraction of regulatory sites may not be conserved but yet are functional, which suggests that sequence conservation revealed by alignments may not capture some relevant regulatory regions [54].

In effect, these approaches and tools are still insufficient, and there has to be a focus on the creation of bioinformatics resources that include more directly the biochemical restrains to regulate gene transcription. One important aspect is that most putative REs are covered by nucleosomes, so that they are not accessible to the respective transcription factor. This repressive environment is found in particular for those sequences that are either contained within interspersed sequences, are located isolated from transcription factor modules or lie outside of insulator sequences marking the border of chromatin loops [55]. This perspective strongly discourages the idea that isolated, simple PPREs may be functional *in vivo*. In turn, this idea implies that the more transcription factor-binding sites a given promoter region contains and the more of these transcription factors are expressed, the higher is the chance that the chromatin on this area of the promoter becomes locally opened.

The PAZAR information mall [56] is a tertiary database that is build on the resource of a multitude of secondary databases and provides a computing infrastructure for the creation, maintenance, and dissemination of regulatory sequence annotation. The unambiguous identification of the chromosome location for any given transcription factor-binding site using genomic coordinates allows to link the results from "big biology" projects, such as ENCODE [57], and other whole genome scans for histone modification and transcription factor association. Unfortunately, so far, only a few boutiques have been opened inside the PAZAR framework. In order to benefit from binding site predictions, it is still necessary to explore dedicated resources. For example, the well-known regulator of cell cycle progression, the transcription factor p53, has an own dedicated database (p53FamTaG) for integration of gene expression and binding site data [58].

13.5 BINDING DATASET OF PPREs AND THE CLASSIFIER METHOD

A general requirement for systems biology approaches is the existence of coherent and informative quantitative datasets. Approaches for NR RE predictions have been based on a collection of disparate binding data and in general lack quantitative comparison of different experimental results. To combine evidence from several publications for an efficient binding model has challenges, thus creating a demand for a coherent binding dataset. The recently published classifier method [42] used the *in vitro* binding preferences of the three PPAR subtypes on a panel of 39 systematic single nucleotide variations of the consensus DR1-type PPRE (AGGTCAAAGGTCA) [59] as an experimental dataset. Since then, similar datasets have been created for other transcription factors [60]. One way to utilize such a data type is to create an affinity matrix as was chosen for p53. However, initial trials to correlate binding strength of a multiple variant dataset to matrix scores were discouraging and an alternative more empirical, approach was chosen. The single nucleotide variants were sorted into three classes, where in class I the PPAR subtypes are able to bind the sequence with a strength of 75 ± 15 percent of that of the consensus PPRE, in class II with 45 ± 15 percent, and in class III with 15 ± 15 percent. Although the overall binding pattern of the three PPAR subtypes showed no major differences, some variations gave rise to a PPAR subtype-specific classification. Additional 130 DR1-type PPREs were sorted on the basis of counting increasing number of variations from the consensus and taking into account the single nucleotide variant binding strength. Those variants that alone decrease the binding only modestly (class I) could be combined with even three deviations from consensus still resulting in more than 20 percent binding relative to consensus. Other combinations resulted in faster loss of binding detailed in

11 categories, where such combinations still resulted in more than 1 percent relative binding. The *in silico* binding strength predictions of PPAR–RXR heterodimers were confirmed by gel shift assays for the six PPREs of the *uncoupling protein 3* gene and showed a deviation of less than 15 percent, outperforming the affinity matrix and weight matrix that were created using the same datasets.

The main advantage, when comparing the classifier to PWM methods, is a clear separation between weak PPREs and those of medium and strong strength [42]. For the discovery of potential binding sites, this is extra information that could be especially of interest in processes considered context dependent, for example, for PPREs that reside in genomic context of transcription factor modules. Predicting the strength of PPAR binding can be a predictor of how prominent effect this receptor can have on a target gene. For example, if binding is easily competed by other transcription factors, the effect may not manifest in most tissues or it may manifest only in tissues expressing all transcription factors of a module containing the PPRE. As an example of the latter case, the insulin-like growth factor binding protein 1 gene has a weak PPRE located inside a well-conserved area (suggesting the presence of other transcription factor-binding sites) and was only in liver responsive to PPAR ligands [59]. In contrast, genes with strong PPREs, such as carnitine palmitoyltransferase 1A and angiopoietin-like 4, are PPAR responsive in many tissues (Heinäniemi et al., unpublished data).

13.6 CLUSTERING OF KNOWN PPAR TARGET GENES

The data added by binding strength analysis and by covering a larger regulatory region ($\pm$10 kB) was examined with all 38 human genes that are known to be primary PPAR targets together with their mouse ortholog. The clustering by predicted binding strength and evolutionary conservation of their PPREs resulted in four groups [42]. In general, clusters I–II contain genes that are well-conserved between human and mouse. Cluster I contains genes that carry multiple conserved PPREs, while genes in cluster II have only one or two strong or medium conserved PPRE in human, which are found in comparable strength and location in the mouse. Cluster III contains genes that have strong or medium PPREs in one species that are conserved only as weak PPREs in the other species. Finally, cluster IV contains more than 25 percent of all tested genes, which have the common property that they carry one or more PPREs, but none of them is conserved. These examples suggest that regulation of target gene can survive turnover of binding sites and might even benefit from it.

The clustering analysis indicated some useful features for whole genome PPRE screens. The presence of strong PPREs or more several medium strength PPREs within the 20 kB surrounding the annotated TSS of a gene was a strong indication for a PPAR target gene. In this way, 28 out of the 38 human genes would have been identified as PPAR targets. Similarly, for 29 of these 38 genes, the analysis of their murine ortholog would have come to the same conclusion. A combination of these two criteria (passing the threshold in either the human or mouse ortholog) would have identified 37 out of the 38 genes as PPAR targets. In this approach, full alignment is not required, just preservation of what could be called PPAR-binding potential.

The more strong PPREs a gene has accumulated, the smaller the chances are that given all 250 human tissues, none of these sites would get accessible or be built into a regulatory module with other transcription factor-binding sites.

13.6.1 A Look at PPREs in their Genomic Context: Putative Target Genes and Binding Modules

In the paper described above, the gene-dense human chromosome 19 (63.8 MB, 1445 known genes) and its syntenic mouse regions (956 genes have known orthologs) were selected for an *in silico* screening based on the above explained criteria, that is, both species were investigated for medium and strong PPREs (based on a PPARγ prediction) [42]. Interestingly, 20 percent of genes of chromosome 19 contain a colocalizing strong PPRE, and additional 4 percent have more than two medium PPREs or a proximal medium PPRE. Experimentally, a complete evaluation of the selectivity of any such screen is complicated by the restricted expression profiles of the predicted genes, which prevents simple readouts from individual target tissues. When requiring the detection in human and mouse, 12.1 percent of genes from chromosome 19 were predicted as PPAR targets. As has been outlined in the previous discussion, a binding site screen will gain more power, when it can be integrated with other genomic screens, both experimental and bioinformatics. In a vision for future of targeting regulatory modules with colocalizing PPREs, a PPRE track provided by bioinformatics approaches can be compared against evidence of other regulatory modules provided by conservation analysis and screens for other transcription factors (Figure 13.3). Experimental data comparing regulation in a disease state versus normal cells can be visualized in the same context to detect overlap in functional binding sites. Given the high interest of the scientific community to better characterize binding profiles of different transcription factors and the improved experimental techniques to detect genome-wide binding events, such additional tracks combined with a PPRE-binding track could be available in near future. Importantly, these datasets will motivate studies that aim to integrate the knowledge with systems biology methodology in order to model NR function in healthy versus disease state in various human tissues.

13.7 CONCLUSION

The identification of genes showing a primary response to NRs and their ligands, the so-called NR regulome, can be used as a prediction of their therapeutic potential as well as their possible side effects. Methods incorporating both experimental- and informatics-derived evidence to arrive at a more reliable prediction of NR targets and binding modules can bring all available data together with the aim to predict outcome in a specific context. Taking the chromosome 19 *in silico* screening trial for PPREs as an example and extrapolating the results to the whole human genome, we suggest that approximately 10 percent of all human genes (an estimate of 2000–2500 genes) have the potential to be directly regulated by a specific NR by their RE content within 10-kB distance to their TSS. Translated to regulatory modules that colocalize

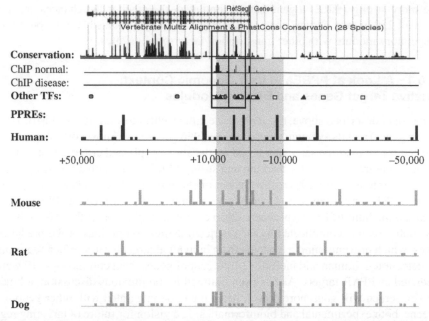

Figure 13.3   The superimposition of the PPRE tracks on other genome-wide datasets can reveal promising PPRE-containing binding modules for targeted therapy via PPAR activation. In this imaginary setting, transcription factor 1 (black triangles) is known to be one main regulator of the hypothetical gene X, and this regulation is altered in diabetes. Transcription factor 2 (represented by white squares) synergistically activates gene X but is lost in insulin-resistant beta cells. ChIP data comparing normal and disease state-binding profiles for this transcription factor reveal two main regulatory modules under normal conditions and a weaker binding in insulin-resistant samples due to loss of transcription factor 2. Combining these datasets with knowledge of PPAR binding and target genes will create hypothesis about their potential role in this disease setting. The gene is characterized by high enrichment of strong PPREs in several species providing strong evidence that PPARs can regulate this gene. A colocalizing PPRE in module 2 could enable PPARs to replace ranscription factor 2 in this module and to restore strong activation of the gene.

with REs, an even larger number of genomic regions could be targeted by a given NR. In conclusion, in this chapter, we have addressed the identification of direct targets using genomic sequences and binding data. In parallel, we have discussed the potential of looking for NR REs inside regulatory modules foreseeing that in future, very likely, the emphasis will shift from target genes to target regulatory modules to alter a physiological response and from individual genes to whole genome response.

ACKNOWLEDGMENTS

Grants (all to C.C.) from the University of Luxembourg, the Academy of Finland, the Finnish Cancer Organization, the Juselius Foundation, and the EU (Marie Curie RTN NucSys) supported our research.

REFERENCES

1. S. Sperling. Transcriptional regulation at a glance. *BMC Bioinform.*, 8 (Suppl 6):S2, 2007.

2. S. J. Jones. Prediction of genomic functional elements. *Annu. Rev. Genomics Hum. Genet.*, 7:315–338, 2006.

3. A. Chawla, J. J. Repa, R. M. Evans, and D. J. Mangelsdorf. Nuclear receptors and lipid physiology: opening the X-files. *Science*, 294:1866–1870, 2001.

4. Nuclear-Receptor-Committee: a unified nomenclature system for the nuclear receptor, superfamily. *Cell*, 97:161–163, 1999.

5. J. M. Maglich, A. Sluder, X. Guan, Y. Shi, D. D. McKee, K. Carrick, K. Kamdar, T. M. Willson, and J. T. Moore. Comparison of complete nuclear receptor sets from the human, Caenorhabditis elegans and Drosophila genomes. *Genome Biol.*, 2: RESEARCH0029, 2001.

6. V. Giguere. Orphan nuclear receptors: from gene to function. *Endocr. Rev.*, 20:689–725, 1999.

7. R. Mohan and R. A. Heyman. Orphan nuclear receptor modulators. *Curr. Top. Med. Chem.*, 3:1637–1647, 2003.

8. M. Müller and S. Kersten. Nutrigenomics: goals and strategies. *Nat. Rev. Genet.*, 4:315–322, 2003.

9. K. E. Wellen and G. S. Hotamisligil. Inflammation, stress, and diabetes. *J. Clin. Invest.*, 115:1111–1119, 2005.

10. G. S. Hotamisligil. Inflammation and metabolic disorders. *Nature*, 444:860–867, 2006.

11. P. Dandona, A. Aljada, and A. Bandyopadhyay. Inflammation: the link between insulin resistance, obesity and diabetes. *Trends Immunol.*, 25:4–7, 2004.

12. W. Khovidhunkit, M. S. Kim, R. A. Memon, J. K. Shigenaga, A. H. Moser, K. R. Feingold, and C. Grunfeld. Effects of infection and inflammation on lipid and lipoprotein metabolism: mechanisms and consequences to the host. *J. Lipid Res.*, 45:1169–1196, 2004.

13. T. Rhen and J. A. Cidlowski. Antiinflammatory action of glucocorticoids: new mechanisms for old drugs. *N. Engl. J. Med.*, 353:1711–1723, 2005.

14. K. E. Wellen, R. Fucho, M. F. Gregor, M. Furuhashi, C. Morgan, T. Lindstad, E. Vaillancourt, C. Z. Gorgun, F. Saatcioglu, and G. S. Hotamisligil. Coordinated regulation of nutrient and inflammatory responses by STAMP2 is essential for metabolic homeostasis. *Cell*, 129:537–548, 2007.

15. G. D. Barish, M. Downes, W. A. Alaynick, R. T. Yu, C. B. Ocampo, A. L. Bookout, D. J. Mangelsdorf, and R. M. Evans. A nuclear receptor atlas: macrophage activation. *Mol. Endocrinol.*, 19:2466–2477, 2005.

16. M. Fu, T. Sun, A. L. Bookout, M. Downes, R. T. Yu, R. M. Evans, and D. J. Mangelsdorf. A nuclear receptor atlas: 3T3-L1 adipogenesis. *Mol. Endocrinol.*, 19:2437–2450, 2005.

17. S. Bornholdt. Systems biology. Less is more in modeling large genetic networks. *Science*, 310:449–451, 2005.

18. T. Pastinen and T. J. Hudson. Cis-acting regulatory variation in the human genome. *Science*, 306:647–650, 2004.

19. J. R. Idle and F. J. Gonzalez. Metabolomics. *Cell Metab.*, 6:348–351, 2007.

20. I. Issemann and S. Green. Activation of a member of the steroid hormone receptor superfamily by peroxisome proliferators. *Nature*, 347:645–650, 1990.

21. G. Krey, O. Braissant, F. L'Horset, E. Kalkhoven, M. Perroud, M. G. Parker, and W. Wahli. Fatty acids, eicosanoids, and hypolipidemic agents identified as ligands of peroxisome proliferator-acitvated receptors by coactivator-dependent receptor ligand assay. *Mol. Endocrinol.*, 11:779–791, 1997.

22. T. M. Willson, P. J. Brown, D. D. Sternbach, and B. R. Henke. The PPARs: from orphan receptors to drug discovery. *J. Med. Chem.*, 43:527–550, 2000.

23. L. Michalik, B. Desvergne, and W. Wahli. Peroxisome-proliferator-activated receptors and cancers: complex stories. *Nat. Rev. Cancer*, 4:61–70, 2004.

24. L. Michalik, B. Desvergne, C. Dreyer, M. Gavillet, R. N. Laurini, and W. Wahli. PPAR expression and function during vertebrate development. *Int. J. Dev. Biol.*, 46:105–114, 2002.

25. A. L. Bookout, Y. Jeong, M. Downes, R. T. Yu, R. M. Evans, and D. J. Mangelsdorf. Anatomical profiling of nuclear receptor expression reveals a hierarchical transcriptional network. *Cell*, 126:789–799, 2006.

26. J. P. Vanden Heuvel. The PPAR resource page. *Biochim. Biophys. Acta.*, 1771:1108–1112, 2007.

27. L. Michalik, B. Desvergne, and W. Wahli. Peroxisome proliferator-activated receptors beta/delta: emerging roles for a previously neglected third family member. *Curr. Opin. Lipidol.*, 14:129–135, 2003.

28. S. Heikkinen, J. Auwerx, and C. A. Argmann. PPARgamma in human and mouse physiology. *Biochim. Biophys. Acta.*, 1771:999–1013, 2007.

29. J. Lehmann, L. B. Moore, T. A. Smith-Oliver, W. O. Wilkison, T. M. Willson, and S. A. Kliewer. An antidiabetic thiazolidinedione is a high affinity ligand for peroxisome proliferator-activated receptor g (PPARg). *J. Biol. Chem.*, 270:12953–12956, 1995.

30. M. Bunger, G. J. Hooiveld, S. Kersten, and M. Müller. Exploration of PPAR functions by microarray technology: a paradigm for nutrigenomics. *Biochim. Biophys. Acta.*, 1771:1046–1064, 2007.

31. C. Duval, M. Müller, and S. Kersten. PPARalpha and dyslipidemia. *Biochim. Biophys. Acta.*, 1771:961–971, 2007.

32. M. Rakhshandehroo, L. M. Sanderson, M. Matilainen, R. Stienstra, C. Carlberg, P. J. de Groot, M. Müller, and S. Kersten. Comprehensive analysis of PPARalpha-dependent regulation of hepatic lipid metabolism by expression profiling. *PPAR Res.*, 2007:26839, 2007.

33. Y. Chen, J. Zhu, P. Y. Lum, X. Yang, S. Pinto, D. J. MacNeil, C. Zhang, J. Lamb, S. Edwards, and S. K. Sieberts, et al. Variations in DNA elucidate molecular networks that cause disease. *Nature*, 452:429–435, 2008.

34. V. Emilsson, G. Thorleifsson, B. Zhang, A. S. Leonardson, F. Zink, J. Zhu, S. Carlson, A. Helgason, G. B. Walters, and S. Gunnarsdottir, et al. Genetics of gene expression and its effect on disease. *Nature*, 452:423–428, 2008.

35. S. A. Ramsey, S. L. Klemm, D. E. Zak, K. A. Kennedy, V. Thorsson, B. Li, M. Gilchrist, E. S. Gold, C. D. Johnson, and V. Litvak, et al. Uncovering a macrophage transcriptional program by integrating evidence from motif scanning and expression dynamics. *PLoS Comput. Biol.*, 4:e1000021, 2008.

36. S. Cawley, S. Bekiranov, H. H. Ng, P. Kapranov, E. A. Sekinger, D. Kampa, A. Piccolboni, V. Sementchenko, J. Cheng, A. J. Williams, et al. Unbiased mapping of transcription factor

binding sites along human chromosomes 21 and 22 points to widespread regulation of noncoding RNAs. *Cell*, 116:499–509, 2004.

37. A. Rada-Iglesias, O. Wallerman, C. Koch, A. Ameur, S. Enroth, G. Clelland, K. Wester, S. Wilcox, O. M. Dovey, P. D. Ellis, et al. Binding sites for metabolic disease related transcription factors inferred at base pair resolution by chromatin immunoprecipitation and genomic microarrays. *Hum. Mol. Genet.*, 14:3435–3447, 2005.

38. J. S. Carroll and M. Brown. Estrogen receptor target gene: an evolving concept. *Mol. Endocrinol.*, 20:1707–1714, 2006.

39. S. Kersten, B. Desvergne, and W. Wahli. Roles of PPARs in health and disease. *Nature*, 405:421–424, 2000.

40. S. A. Kliewer, K. Umesono, D. J. Noonan, R. A. Heyman, and R. M. Evans. Convergence of 9-cis retinoic acid and peroxisome proliferator signalling pathways through heterodimer formation of their receptors. *Nature*, 358:771–774, 1992.

41. A. Jpenberg, E. Jeannin, W. Wahli, and B. Desvergne. Polarity and specific sequence requirements of peroxisome proliferator-activated receptor (PPAR)/retinoid X receptor heterodimer binding to DNA. A functional analysis of the malic enzyme gene PPAR response element. *J. Biol. Chem.*, 272:20108–20117, 1997.

42. M. Heinäniemi, J. O. Uski, T. Degenhardt, and C. Carlberg. Meta-analysis of primary target genes of peroxisome proliferator-activated receptors. *Genome Biol.*, 8:R147, 2007.

43. M. Danielsen. Bioinformatics of nuclear receptors. *Methods Mol. Biol.*, 176:3–22, 2001.

44. S. Mader, P. Leroy, J.- Y. Chen, and P. Chambon. Multiple parameters control the selectivity of nuclear receptors for their response elements. *J. Biol. Chem.*, 268:591–600, 1993.

45. M. Schräder, K. M. Müller, M. Becker-André, and C. Carlberg. Response element selectivity for heterodimerization of vitamin D receptors with retinoic acid and retinoid X receptors. *J. Mol. Endocrinol.*, 12:327–339, 1994.

46. M. Schräder, K. M. Müller, and C. Carlberg. Specificity and flexibility of vitamin D signalling. Modulation of the activation of natural vitamin D response elements by thyroid hormone. *J. Biol. Chem.*, 269:5501–5504, 1994.

47. M. Schräder, M. Becker-Andre, and C. Carlberg. Thyroid hormone receptor functions as monomeric ligand-induced transcription factor on octameric half-sites. Consequences also for dimerization. *J. Biol. Chem.*, 269:6444–6449, 1994.

48. X. Xie, J. Lu, E. J. Kulbokas, T. R. Golub, V. Mootha, K. Lindblad-Toh, E. S. Lander, and M. Kellis. Systematic discovery of regulatory motifs in human promoters and 3′ UTRs by comparison of several mammals. *Nature*, 434:338–345, 2005.

49. A. Barski, S. Cuddapah, K. Cui, T. Y. Roh, D. E. Schones, Z. Wang, G. Wei, I. Chepelev, and K. Zhao. High-resolution profiling of histone methylations in the human genome. *Cell*, 129:823–837, 2007.

50. L. E. Tavera-Mendoza, S. Mader, and J. H. White. Genome-wide approaches for identification of nuclear receptor target genes. *Nucl. Recept. Signal.*, 4:e018, 2006.

51. V. Matys, E. Fricke, R. Geffers, E. Gossling, M. Haubrock, R. Hehl, K. Hornischer, D. Karas, A. E. Kel, O. V. Kel-Margoulis, et al. TRANSFAC: transcriptional regulation, from patterns to profiles. *Nucleic Acids Res.*, 31.374–378, 2003.

52. D. G. Lemay and D. H. Hwang. Genome-wide identification of peroxisome proliferator response elements using integrated computational genomics. *J. Lipid Res.*, 47:1583–1587, 2006.

53. W. W. Wasserman, and A. Sandelin. Applied bioinformatics for the identification of regulatory elements. *Nat. Rev. Genet.*, 5:276–287, 2004.

54. D. T. Odom, R. D. Dowell, E. S. Jacobsen, W. Gordon, T. W. Danford, K. D. MacIsaac, P. A. Rolfe, C. M. Conboy, D. K. Gifford, and E. Fraenkel. Tissue-specific transcriptional regulation has diverged significantly between human and mouse. *Nat. Genet.*, 39:730–732, 2007.

55. J. L. Burns, D. A. Jackson, and A. B. Hassan. A view through the clouds of imprinting. *FASEB J.*, 15:1694–1703, 2001.

56. E. Portales-Casamar, S. Kirov, J. Lim, S. Lithwick, M. I. Swanson, A. Ticoll, J. Snoddy, and W. W. Wasserman. PAZAR: a framework for collection and dissemination of cis-regulatory sequence annotation. *Genome Biol.*, 8:R207, 2007.

57. ENCODE-Consortium. ENCODE (ENCyclopedia of DNA Elements) Project. *Science*, 306:636–640, 2004.

58. E. Sbisa, D. Catalano, G. Grillo, F. Licciulli, A. Turi, S. Liuni, G. Pesole, A. De Grassi, M. F. Caratozzolo, A. M. D'Erchia, et al. p53FamTaG: a database resource of human p53, p63 and p73 direct target genes combining in silico prediction and microarray data. *BMC Bioinform.*, 8 (Suppl 1):S20, 2007.

59. T. Degenhardt, M. Matilainen, K. H. Herzig, T. W. Dunlop, and C. Carlberg. The insulin-like growth factor-binding protein 1 gene is a primary target of peroxisome proliferator-activated receptors. *J. Biol. Chem.*, 281:39607–39619, 2006.

60. C. L. Wei Q. Wu, V. B. Vega, K. P. Chiu, P. Ng, T. Zhang, A. Shahab, H. C. Yong, Y. Fu, Z. Weng, et al. A global map of p53 transcription-factor binding sites in the human genome. *Cell*, 124:207–219, 2006.

14

ENVIRONMENTAL AND PHYSIOLOGICAL INSIGHTS FROM MICROBIAL GENOME SEQUENCES

Alessandra Carbone and Anthony Mathelier

Génomique Analytique, Université Pierre et Marie Curie–Paris 6,
FRE3214 CNRS-UPMC, 15 rue de l'Ecole de Médecine, 75006 Paris, France

14.1 SOME BACKGROUND, MOTIVATION, AND OPEN QUESTIONS

Life mechanisms have been addressed in microbiology with a model-organism approach that has dominated the history of biology of the past century. Today, the large availability of genomic data coming from genome sequencing and from new high-throughput technologies has changed radically the nature of investigations that are envisaged in molecular biology. For the first time, an organism and its changing environment can be considered together and in concert with a multitude of other organisms. Evolutionary hypothesis start to be tested at a large scale.

Even though the experimental power is present, our understanding of microbe–environment interactions is still in its infancy, and upcoming discoveries and advances in geomicrobiology are likely to come from all areas of this discipline. This is a particularly good time for experimentalists to interact together with bioinformaticians, biomathematicians, and biophysicists for defining new experimental questions,

Elements of Computational Systems Biology   Edited by Huma M. Lodhi and Stephen H. Muggleton
Copyright © 2010 John Wiley & Sons, Inc.

analyze large amount of data, and model phenomena that characterize the new dimension within which microbiology lives today.

Microorganisms, Genome Sequences, and Comparative Genomics. The availability of a large number of genomes provides the possibility to study biodiversity between species, within species, and even within strains by comparing what is missing and what is common at a genetic level. Satisfactory formal methods and models to study similarities within the diversity have been developed, but methods to study differences within a diversity are much harder to envisage. On the experimental level, we experience a similar situation. Interaction and back-and-forth between experimentalists and bioinformaticiens/modelers, which can direct both experiments and modeling, is demanded in such a setting.

Evolutionary questions concerning chromosomal integrity, genomic expansion, chromosomal rearrangements, mobility of genetic elements, lateral gene transfer, gene share and gene loss among strains and across species, gene creation, evolution of duplicated genes, modular gene organization, gene essentiality and chromosomal organization, and sexual proliferation are at the heart of microbiology today and they need to be addressed. In fact, any question concerning the way that noncoding information in genomes, genes, and genome architecture influence and direct the biology of the microbe, such as its virulence or adaptiveness under specific environmental conditions, constitutes a major preoccupation in the field of microbiology. Adaptive and nonadaptive processes in a cell, including genomic adaptiveness (for bacteria, viruses, and eventually eukaryotic unicellular organisms), networks adjustment under changes in environmental conditions, and modular rearrangements in genome architecture are other key questions for microbiology. Together with this, the understanding of structural and functional relations in proteins, the fate of duplicated protein sequences, and speciation via divergent evolution of duplicated genes, are also key concerns.

Microorganisms and their Organization. What information can we extract from genomes concerning the biology of the organism? Statistical analysis has lead to the identification of statistical conditions (purely based on composition and on no biological information about the life of the organism) to determine the optimal growth temperature of a bacteria, to organize bacteria with respect to their ecological niche, to determine which genes are essential for the life of a unicellular organism, to determine essential metabolic networks, among others. These results are intimately connected to the evolutionary processes that an organism has undergone and any insight into the origins of evolutionary pressures is most useful for a correct understanding of the evolutionary history of the organism. It is this history that justifies today the specificities of the organism's life.

Several types of measures that induce organismal classifications might be introduced. Some of these measures try to detect environmental organization, some other physiological similarities, and others phylogenetic proximity. Differences between phylogenetic, physiological, and environmental information lead to different classifications of the microbial world. Such organizational differences are bound to be important for the understanding of evolution. In this respect, it might be that the understanding of the metagenomic data (i.e., DNA data coming from environmental genomic analysis, corresponding to multispecies communities of organisms that usually either have not been attempted to culture or have been resistant to culturing efforts) will be possible only if these three conceptually different classification paradigms for organisms will be cleared out.

Another important paradigm for classification that has risen in these last years is induced by chromosomal rearrangements. It has been observed that it does not correspond to phylogenetic organization. What sort of biological information is associated with genome reorganization? Is it dependent on environmental pressure? Or perhaps on physiological constraints?

Microorganisms, Metagenomics, and Comparative Genomics. In recent years, it became clear that comparative genomics will soon include metagenomic data and metagenomic reconstruction of partial metabolic information for different ecological niches. This new incoming information will no doubt bring a fresh view on more classical model organisms. The study of the microbe–environment relation demands to take into consideration the fact that the 99% of the microorganisms visualized microscopically in environmental samples are not cultivated by routine techniques. This reality underlies the difficulty to make sound ecological inferences based on metabolic properties of a few cultivable species.

Even if this point should be addressed, we need to keep in mind that cultivable species propose a setting where environmental conditions and changes in environmental conditions can be tested and where the behavior of microbial populations can be modeled and analyzed. The *hemiascomycetes* (to which bakery yeast belongs), for instance, constitute a group of species that are very useful for learning because characterized by a compact genome, very different ecological niches, and an easy experimental handling of several of the species.

Microorganisms and Population Genetics. The fundamental principle underpinning microbial population dynamics is that the survival of a given individual microorganism is ultimately dependent on the metabolic activity of others in its ecosystem. In this respect, the inclusion of the view of population genetics within the approaches to genome analysis for understanding diversity of microbial communities and cultures seems necessary. The microbe–environment interaction might turn out to be entangled with population processes in microbial species, such as natural selection, demography, and migrations, and the population genetics perspectives might turn out to provide the conceptual tools for this understanding.

Microorganisms, Metabolism, and Environment. Microorganisms are intimately involved in transforming inorganic and organic compounds to meet their nutritional and energetic needs. Because the metabolic waste from one type of species nearly always provides substrate for another, there is an interdependence between species growing in close proximity to one another, or alternatively, the communities can be spatially separated and elemental cycling may take on more complex and convoluted pathways. The power of microbial communities is fundamental for life and, today, experiments can be conceived to meaningfully study microbial communities at different scales.

Questions concerning networks response to environmental changes affecting microbial eukaryotic and/or prokaryotic communities might be addressed. The functioning of regulation networks will be understood in terms of population biology and interactions (competition or collaboration) among species.

Adaptiveness is another important phenomena concerning microbial organisms interacting with their environment. It might be addressed *in silico* within the context of genetic variability for bacterial/viral species/strains based on the available data. Questions on genetic exchanges within species and across species might be also ground for interdisciplinary work.

In this chapter, we address those computer scientists and mathematicians who want to learn about some open questions on the bioinformatics of microbial organisms. We look at microbial organisms with available complete genomic sequences and demonstrate that we can read evolution signals out of them and derive meaningful biological information about an organism. The approach is not comparative. We start from a genome, realize a statistical analysis of its genes, and derive insights into the biology of the organism guided by statistical biases of codon usage. We aim to find a general method that can be applied to organisms whose genome is known but for which not much biological information is available. Results involve the formalization of microbial spaces, metabolic network comparison, minimal gene sets, host-phage adaptation, and gene chromosomal organization. One of the main motivations for this work is to search for a pool of genes that are *essential* for an organism. This question is fundamental if we think of synthesizing a genome from scratch and of attaining genome minimization conditioned by specific environmental conditions and metabolic activities [1–3].

The guideline to all results presented here is to derive insights into microbial physiology and habitat directly from genome sequences by means of a purely statistical analysis and an appropriate design of algorithms.

14.2   A FIRST STATISTICAL GLIMPSE TO GENOMIC SEQUENCES

Proteins are formed out of 20 amino acids that are coded in triplets of nucleotides, called codons. The four nucleotides (A, T, C, G) define 64 codons used in the cell. Codons are not uniformly employed in the cell, but on the contrary, certain codons are preferred and we speak about *codon bias*. There are several kinds of codon biases and some of them are linked to specific biological functions. Statistical analysis of DNA sequences and, in particular, of codon bias was performed from the moment long chunks of DNA sequences were publicly available in the early 1980s [4, 5], and the roots for these studies can be traced back to the 1960s [6, 7]. However, with the increasing number of bacterial genome sequences from a broad diversity of species, this field of research has been revivified in the last few years [8–17].

Biased codon usage may result from a diversity of factors: GC content, preference for codons with G or C at the third nucleotide position [18], a leading strand richer in $G + T$ than a lagging strand [18], horizontal gene transfer that induces chromosome segments of unusual base composition [19], and, in particular, translational bias that has been frequently noticed in fast growing prokaryotes and eukaryotes [20–25]. Three main facts support the idea of "translational impact": highly expressed genes tend to use only a limited number of codons and display a high codon bias [4, 20], preferred codons and isoacceptor tRNA content exhibit a strong positive correlation [19, 26–28], and tRNA isoacceptor pools affect the rate of polypeptide chain elongation [30, 31].

To study the effect of translational bias on gene expression, Sharp and Li [20] proposed to associate with each gene of a given genome a numerical value, called *Codon Adaptation Index or CAI* for short, which expresses its synonymous codon bias (see appendix for the definition). The idea is to compute a weight (representing relative adaptiveness) for each codon from its frequency within a chosen small pool of highly expressed genes S and combine these weights to define the $CAI(g)$ value of each gene g in the genome. For Sharp and Li, the hypothesis driving the choice of S is that, for certain organisms, highly expressed genes in the cell have highest codon bias, and these genes, made out of frequent codons, are representative for the bias. Based on this rationale, one can select a pool of ribosomal proteins, elongation factors, proteins involved in glycolysis, possibly histone proteins (in eukaryotes) and outer membrane proteins (in prokaryotes), or other selections from known highly expressed genes to form the representative set S. Then, CAI values are computed and are checked to be compatible with genes known to be highly or lowly expressed in the cell. If this is the case, then predictions are drawn with some confidence on expression levels for genes and open reading frames, even with no known homologues. Even if conceptually clear, this framework has been misused several times in the literature and incorrect biological consequences have been derived for gene expression levels of organisms that do not display a dominant translational bias, as discussed in Grocock and Sharp [32]. This confusion motivated us to search for a methodology based on a precise mathematical formulation of the problem to detect the existence of translational bias.

However, the main motivation for us came from the recognition that an increasing number of genome sequences will be available for organisms for which biological knowledge consists merely of a sketched morphological and ecological description. For these organisms, it might not be evident how to define the reference set S, nor how to identify a reliable testing set that can ensure that predictions meet a satisfiable confidence level. Still, one would like to detect if translational bias holds for these genomes and if so, to predict their gene expression levels. If not, one would like to know the origin of their dominating bias and use this information for genome comparison.

14.3 AN AUTOMATIC DETECTION OF CODON BIAS IN GENES

We proposed a simple algorithm to detect dominating synonymous codon usage bias in genomes [33]. The algorithm is based on a precise mathematical formulation of the problem that leads to use the Self-Consistent Codon Index ($SCCI$) (strongly correlated to the CAI measure in translationally biased organisms) as a *universal* measure of codon bias, which is a measure for biases of possibly different origins (and not only for translational bias, as CAI was originally introduced for). The formal definitions of $SCCI$ and CAI are given in the appendix.

The idea of the algorithm is simple. It is an iterative algorithm that at iteration $i + 1$ computes codon weights based on a set S of genes selected at iteration i, then ranks all genes with respect to their $SCCI$ value, and selects a new set S, which has half the cardinality of the set determined at iteration i (if at the ith iteration, the selected set is already constituted by the 1 percent of all genes, then the new set will also be constituted by 1 percent of genes) and whose genes score the highest. The process is repeated until 1 percent of genes have been selected and convergence is reached. At the start, S is the set of all genes.

With the set of coding sequences as a sole source of biological information, the algorithm provides a reference set S of genes that is highly representative of the dominant codon bias. This set is used to compute the $SCCI$ of genes not only for organisms whose biology is well known but also for those whose functional annotation is *not* yet available. An important application concerns the detection of a reference set characterizing translational bias that is known to correlate to expression levels in many bacteria and small eukaryotes; it detects also leading–lagging strands bias, GC-content bias, GC3 bias, and horizontal gene transfer. In general, the algorithm becomes a key tool to predict gene expression levels and to compare species. The approach has been validated on 96 slow-growing and fast-growing bacteria and archaeal genomes, *Saccharomyces cerevisiae*, *Plasmodium falciparum*, *Caenorhabditis elegans*, and *Drosophila melanogaster*.

14.4 GENOMIC SIGNATURES AND A SPACE OF GENOMES FOR GENOME COMPARISON

On the basis of this analysis, we propose a novel formal framework to interpret genomic relationships derived from entire genome sequences rather than individual loci. This space allows to analyze sets of organisms related by a common *codon bias signature* (at times, more than one kind of bias influences the same genomic sequence and the ensemble of these overlapped biases defines what we call the *signature* of a genome) [34]. We give a number of numerical criteria to infer content bias, translational bias, and strand bias for genome sequences. We show in a uniform framework that genomes of quite different phylogenetic relationship share similar codon bias; other genomes grouped together by various phylogenetic methods appear to be subdivided into finer subgroups sharing different codon bias characteristics; Archaea and Eubacteria share the same codon preferences when $AT3$ or $GC3$ bias is their dominant bias; archaeal genomes satisfying translational bias use a more sharply distinguished set of preferred codons than bacterial genomes do. Our analysis, based on 96 eubacterial and archaeal genomes, opens the possibility that this space might reflect the geometry of a prokaryotic "physiology space". If this turns out to be the case, the combination of the upcoming sequencing of entire genomes and the detection of codon bias signatures will become a valuable tool to infer information on the physiology, ecology, and possibly, ecological conditions under which bacterial and archaeal organisms evolved. For many organisms, this information would be impossible to be detected otherwise. More recently, our algorithm has been applied to more than 300 genomes and our hypothesis of environmental signature has been supported at larger scale [35].

Spaces for environmental and physiological classification represent a bacterial classification alternative to phylogeny and they are closer to the living conditions of the organism. With a growing number of genomic data available, it becomes more and more important to have new alternative organizational schemes to understand bacterial populations and the biology of single organisms within their living environment. The algorithmic idea working for bacteria should be revisited for metagenomic sequences for instance and adapted for viral genomes. On such spaces, hypotheses such as adaptability of a virus to the codon bias of its host can be checked and preliminary analysis support this hypothesis (see Section 14.8).

14.5 STUDY OF METABOLIC NETWORKS THROUGH SEQUENCE ANALYSIS AND TRANSCRIPTOMIC DATA

Genes with high codon bias describe in meaningful ways the biological characteristics of the organism and are representative of specific metabolic usage [36]. *In silico* methods exploiting this basic principle are expected to become important in learning about the lifestyle of an organism and explain its evolution in the wild. We demonstrate that besides high expressivity during fast growth or glycolytic activities, which have been very often reported, the necessity for survival under specific biological conditions has its traces in the genetic coding [36]. This observation opens the possibility to predict rare but necessary metabolic activities through genome analysis.

High expression of certain classes of genes, like those constituting the translational machinery or those involved in glycolysis, are correlated particularly well in the case of fast-growing organisms. By shifting the paradigm toward metabolic pathways, we notice that several energy metabolism pathways are correlated with high codon bias in organisms known to be driven by very different physiologies, which are not necessarily fast growing and whose genomes might be very homogeneous. More generally, we derive a classification of metabolic pathways induced by codon analysis and show that genetic coding for different organisms is tuned on specific pathways and that this is a universal fact. The codon composition of enzymes involved in glycolysis for instance, often required to be rapidly translated, is highly biased by dominant codon composition across species (this is indicated by the high CAI value of these enzymes). In fast growers, the numerical evidence is definitely far more striking than for other organisms (that is, the absolute difference between the *CAI* value of these enzymes and the average *CAI* value for genes in the genome is "large"), but even for *Helicobacter pylori*, a genome of rather homogeneous codon composition, enzymes involved in glycolytic pathways happen to be biased above average. In the same manner, one detects the crucial role of photosynthetic pathways for *Synechocystis* or of methane metabolism for *Methanobacterium*.

mRNA transcriptional levels collected during the *S. cerevisiae* cell cycle under diauxic shift [37] (here, glucose quantities decrease in the media during cell cycle and yeast goes from fermentation to aerobic respiration), have been used to analyze the yeast metabolic network in a similar spirit as done with codon analysis. A classification of metabolic pathways based on transcriptomic data has been proposed, and we show that the metabolic classification obtained through codon analysis essentially "coincides" with the one based on (a large and differentiated pool of) transcriptomic data. Such a result opens the way to explain evolutionary pressure and natural selection for organisms grown in the wild, and hopefully, to explain metabolism for slow-growing bacteria, as well as to suggest best conditions of growth in the laboratory.

It is an open question whether this kind of analysis can contribute to the reconstruction metabolic information from metagenomics data.

14.6   FROM GENOME SEQUENCES TO GENOME SYNTHESIS: MINIMAL GENE SETS AND ESSENTIAL GENES

The aim of creating a synthetic genome that, when inserted into a cell, can live and replicate, possibly producing clean energy or curbing global warming [1], recently increased the interest on the fundamental question of determining which genes are essential to a microbe.

Computational and experimental attempts tried to characterize a universal core of genes representing the minimal set of functional needs for an organism. On the basis of an increasing number of available complete genomes, comparative genomics [38–44] has concluded that the universal core contains less than 50 genes. In contrast, experiments [26, 45–57] suggest a much larger set of essential genes (certainly more than several hundreds, even under the most restrictive hypotheses) that is dependent on the biological complexity and the environmental specificity of the organism. Highly biased genes, which are generally also the most expressed in translationally biased organisms, tend to be overrepresented in the class of genes deemed to be essential for any given bacterial species. Also, all functional classes are represented by highly biased genes and within different species, highly biased genes with the same functional role need not be homologous. This association between highly biased genes and essential genes is far from perfect; nevertheless, it allows to propose a new computational method based on *SCCI* to detect to a certain extent ubiquitous genes, nonorthologous genes, environment-specific genes, genes involved in stress response, and genes with no identified function but highly likely to be essential for the cell. Most of these groups of genes cannot be identified with previously attempted computational and experimental approaches. Notice, for instance, that comparative genomics infers conclusions only for homologous genes and that certain nonhomologous highly biased genes could not be identified by this approach. Also, experiments are run under optimal living conditions for the organisms and stress response genes cannot be identified by experiments. The large spread of lifestyles and the unusually detectable functional signals characterizing translationally biased organisms suggest to use them as reference organisms to infer essentiality in other microbial species. In Carbone [58], we analyze in detail 27 organisms belonging to a large variety of phylogenetic taxa, γ and δ proteobacteria, firmicutes, actinobacteria, thermococcales, and methanosarcinales; they do not display strong GC nor AT content and are characterized by different optimal growth temperatures [34]. We also discuss the case of small parasitic genomes, and data from the analysis are compared with those from previous computational and experimental studies.

14.7 A CHROMOSOMAL ORGANIZATION OF ESSENTIAL GENES

Patterns in chromosomal locations of essential genes have been examined and large-scale features of bacterial chromosomes were derived [59] (Mathelier and Carbone, manuscript in preparation). We wanted to check whether essential genes are organized in regularly spaced groups within the genome, possibly depending on transcription regulation patterns or on common functional activities of genes in the groups. Both these possibilities explaining the distribution of genes as a product of structural periodicity are attractive. The localization of certain essential genes along structural chromosomal "faces" would have the advantage of creating spatial subregions in which essential genes could be accessed by limited diffusion of RNA polymerase or RNA polymerase fixed in factories. The solenoid model [60, 61] and the rosettes model of chromosomes have been proposed as possible functional and spatial organizations of the chromosome. The idea behind these models is to bring close in space different genes through an encoded three-dimensional genomic organization. The solenoid model organizes loops of DNA along a solenoidal three-dimensional arrangement and the rosettes model organizes DNA loops radially in a flower-like three-dimensional structure.

It has been shown that groups of genes regulated by the same transcription factors in *Escherichia coli* reveal chromosomal periodicity [61] and that evolutionarily conserved gene pairs in *E. coli* also reveal chromosomal periodicity [62]. We considered the pool of core genes detected by the methodology described above and checked whether these genes are periodically spaced or not. Genomic core's genes have to be either highly expressed or rapidly expressed and we wanted to test the hypothesis that a structured organization of their regulatory elements could help to reach fast expression. We studied on a large scale the chromosomal organization of some tens of bacterial and archaeal organisms and find that most of these genomes present periodic distribution of their core genes along their chromosome [59] (Mathelier and Carbone, manuscript in preparation). This property is not proved to hold for all microbial genomes, but, still, it generates important questions on the impact of environmental pressures, selective bias, and gene rearrangement constraints in microbes. We observe that a genome might display several significant periods on the different strands and that the amplitude of the signal can vary considerably from strand to strand and from organism to organism. We computed a period of about 33 kb between core genes on the chromosomal strands of *E. coli* with a very pronounced amplitude of the signal. This seems to indicate that a chromosomal organization is hunted to help the expression of essential genes, especially within the lagging strands. We also observed that functional grouping of core genes explains chromosomal periodicity better than shared transcription regulators.

Periods computation is based on a signal-processing parameterized model and a Fourier transform analysis. Significance of the periods is established by comparing the amplitude of this signal with a random model by generating appropriate random genomes (with the same number of genes and the same distribution of distances between pairs of adjacent genes). Further investigations on the impact of structural organization on transcription mechanisms of bacterial organisms need to be addressed.

14.8 VIRAL ADAPTATION TO MICROBIAL HOSTS AND VIRAL ESSENTIAL GENES

The notion of SCCI and the algorithmic approach used to study bacterial species have been recently used to analyze viral genomes and adaptation to their host [63]. Size and diversity of bacteriophage population asks for methodologies to quantitatively study the landscape of phage differences. Statistical approaches are confronted with small genome sizes forbidding significant single-phage analysis and comparative methods analyzing full-phage genomes represent an alternative to difficult interpretation due to Lateral Gene Transfer, which creates a mosaic spectrum of related phage species. On the basis of a large-scale codon bias analysis of 116 DNA phages hosted by 11 translationally biased bacteria belonging to different phylogenetic families, we observe that phage genomes are almost always under codon selective pressure imposed by translationally biased hosts and propose a classification of phages with translationally biased hosts that is based on adaptation patterns.

The codon bias measure used in the analysis is the SCCI. Namely, SCCI values reflect codon composition of phage genes relative to host codon composition and provide a numerical index of the advantage taken by phage genes once translated in the host environment. This advantage is expected to be higher when phage gene codon composition is biased toward host codon composition. Through our computational method based on SCCI, we compare phages sharing homologous proteins, possibly accepted by different hosts, and observe that throughout phages, independently from the host, capsid genes appear to be the most affected by host translational bias. For coliphages, genes involved in virion morphogenesis, host interaction, and ssDNA binding are also affected by adaptive pressure. If phage genomes were to contain a pool of essential genes, these functional classes could suggest appropriate candidate genes. Adaptation significantly affects long and small phages. We analyze in more details the *Microviridae* phage space to illustrate the potentiality of the approach. Surprisingly, we can reconstruct the phylogenetic tree of the large phage pool defined around phage $\phi X174$ [47] using exclusively codon bias information. Also, the adaptation analysis of the set of *Microviridae* phages defined around phage $\phi MH2K$ shows that phage classification based on adaptation does not reflect bacterial phylogeny. This result highlights that adaptation patterns in phages might be profitably used to unravel the intricate mosaic of phage speciation.

The numerical finding provided by this and future studies of phage–host coevolution will hopefully be useful in clarifying the role of phages as therapeutic agents against bacteria [65] and in organizing metagenomic data.

14A.1 APPENDIX

14A.1.1 Some Comments on the Mathematical Methods

In this text, a coding sequence is represented by a 64-dimensional vector whose entries correspond to the 64 relative codon frequencies in the sequence. Recall that the frequency of a codon i in a sequence g is the number of occurrences of i in g (where g is intended to be split in consecutive nonoverlapping triplets corresponding to amino acid decomposition), and that the *relative frequency* of i in g is the frequency of i in g divided by the number of codons in g. For each vector representing a coding sequence, the sum of its entries must equal 1. Hence, a coding sequence is a point in the 64-dimensional space $[0 \cdots 1]^{64}$, where no special assumption is made on the space nor on the coordinate system.

For each genome sequence G and some set of coding sequences S in G, *codon bias* is measured with respect to its synonymous codon usage. Given an amino acid j, its synonymous codons might have different frequencies in S; if $x_{i,j}$ is the number of times the codon i for the amino acid j occurs in S, then one associates to i a *weight* $w_{i,j}$ relative to its sibling of maximal frequency y_i in S

$$w_{i,j} = \frac{x_{i,j}}{y_j}.$$

A codon with maximal frequency in S is called preferred among its sibling codons. $SCCI$ associated to g in G, is a value in $[0, 1]$, defined as

$$SCCI(g) = \left(\prod_{k=1}^{L} w_k \right)^{1/L}$$

where L is the number of codons in the gene and w_k is the weight of the kth codon gene sequence. Genes with $SCCI$ value close to 1 are made by highly frequent codons.

When the reference set S is predefined to be a set of highly expressed genes in the organism, then the index issued by the $SCCI$ formula corresponds to the known *Codon Adaptation Index* introduced by Sharp and Li [20]. The computation of the reference set S in the definition of $SCCI$ is based on a pure statistical analysis of all genes in a genome and does not rely on biological knowledge of the organism. This allows us to compute weights for organisms of unknown lifestyle.

The name $SCCI$ was employed for the first time by Carbone [58], while in Carbone [33] and Carbone and Madden [36] the notion is called CAI, even though it does not exclusively refer to codon adaptation. Notice that CAI is always employed with a manual and explicit choice of S, while the formula $SCCI$ (i.e., CAI parameterized with S) turns out to be a universal measure to study codon bias. Codon weights, reference set S, and $SCCI$ values are calculated with the program CAIJava [33], available at www.ihes.fr/~carbone/data.htm.

All results cited in this review are obtained using very simple mathematical and algorithmic notions that are fully described in Carbone [33], Willenbrock et al. [34], and Carbone and Madden [36]. The statistical analysis and numerical thresholds we propose are realized in a 64-dimensional codon space. Multivariance statistical methods have been employed as visualization tools, but none of the formal results or the biological conclusions are inferred from the three-dimensional projections. Both space of genes and space of organisms in 64 dimensions and distances between organisms are defined as ℓ_1-distances.

14A.1.2 Complete Genomes Available

In June 2008, 2623 viruses (of which 495 are phages), 56 eukaryotes, 53 archaea, and 729 bacteria are completely sequenced and present in the NCBI database at the address http://www.ncbi.nlm.nih.gov/sites/entrez?db=genome.

REFERENCES

1. J. C. Venter, S. Levy, T. Stockwell, K. Remington and A. Halpern. A massive parallelism, randomness and genomic advances. *Nat. Genet.*, 33:219–227, 2003.

2. C. Zimmer. Genomics. Tinker, tailor: Can Venter stitch together a genome from scratch?, *Science*, 299:1006–1007, 2003.

3. H. O. Smith, C. A. Hutchison, III, C. Pfannkoch, and C. Venter. Generating a synthetic genome by whole genome assembly: AX174 bacteriophage from synthetic oligonucleotides. *Proc. Natl. Acad. Sci. USA*, 100:15440–15445, 2003.

4. R. Grantham, C. Gautier, M. Gouy, R. Mercier, and A. Pave. Codon catalog usage and the genome hypothesis. *Nucl. Acids Res.*, 8:r49–r62, 1980.

5. K. S. Wada, R. Aota, F. Tsuchiya, T. Ishibashi, T. Gojobori, and T. Ikemura. Codon usage tabulated from GenBank genetic sequence data. *Nucl. Acids Res.*, 18 (Suppl):2367–2411, 1990.

6. N. Sueoka. On the genetic basis of variation and heterogeneity of DNA base composition. *Proc. Natl. Acad. Sci. USA*, 48:582–592, 1962.

7. E. Zuckerkandl, and L. Pauling. Molecules as documents of evolutionary history. *J. Theor. Biol.*, 8:357–366, 1965.

8. E. V. Koonin, and M. Y. Galperin. Prokaryotic genomes: The emerging paradigm of genomebased microbiology. *Curr. Opin. Genet. Dev.*, 7:75–7763, 1997.

9. J. Lin, and M. Gerstein. Whole-genome trees based on the occurrence of folds and orthologs: implications for comparing genomes on different levels. *Genome Res.*, 10:808–818, 2000.

10. J. P. Radomski, and P. P.Slonimski. Genomic style of proteins: Concepts, methods and analysis of ribosomal proteins from 16 microbial species. *FEMS Microbiol. Rev.*, 25:425–435, 2001.

11. R. D. Knight, S. J. Freeland, and L. F. Landweber. A simple model based on mutation and selection explains trends in codon and amino-acid usage and GC composition within and across genomes. *Genome Biol.*, 2, 2001, at http://genomebiology.com/2001/2/4/research/0010.

12. T. Sicheritz-Pontén and S. G. E. Andersson. A phylogenomic approach to microbial evolution. *Nucl. Acids Res.*, 29:545–552, 2001.

13. V. Daubin, M. Gouy, and G. Perrière. A phylogenetic approach to bacterial evidence of a core of genes sharing a comon history. *Genome Res.*, 12:1080–1090, 2002.

14. J. Lin, D. Qian, P. Bertone, R. Das, N. Echols, A. Senes, B. Stenger, and M. Gerstein. GeneCensus: Genome comparisons in terms of metabolic pathway activity and protein family sharing. *Nucl. Acids Res.*, 30:4574–4582, 2002.

15. J. R. Lobry and D. Chessel. Internal correspondence analysis of codon and amino-acid usage in thermophilic bacteria. *J. Appl. Genet.*, 44:235–261, 2003.

16. R. Sandberg, C. I. Bränden, I. Ernberg, and J. Cöster. Quantifying the species-specificity in genomic signatures, synonymous codon choice, amino-acids usage and G+C content. *Gene*, 311:35–42, 2003.

17. R. Jansen, H. J. Bussemaker, and M. Gerstein, Revisiting the codon adaptation index from a whole-genome prespective: Analyzing the relationship between gene expression and codon occurrence in yeast using a variety of models. *Nucl. Acids Res.*, 31:2242–2251, 2003.

18. B. Lafay, A. T. Lloyd, M. J. McLean, K. M. Devine, P. M. Sharp, and K. H. Wolfe. Proteome composition and codon usage in spirochaetes: species-specific and DNA strand-specific mutational biases. *Nucl. Acids Res.*, 27:1642–1649, 1999.

19. I. Moszer, E. P. C. Rocha, and A. Danchin. Codon usage and lateral gene transfer in *Bacillus subtilis*. *Curr. Opin. Microbiol.*, 2:524–528, 1999.

20. P. M. Sharp and W.-H. Li. The codon adaptation index: a measure of directional synonymous codon usage bias, and its potential applications. *Nucl. Acid Res.*, 15:1281–1295, 1987.

21. P. M. Sharp, T. M. F. Tuohy, and K. R. Mosurski. Codon usage in yeast: Cluster analysis clearly differentiate highly and lowly expressed genes. *Nucl. Acids Res.*, 14:8207–8211, 1986.

22. C. Médigue, T. Rouxel, P. Vigier, A. Hénaut, and A. Danchin. Evidence for horizontal gene transfer in *Escherichia coli* speciation. *J. Mol. Biol.*, 222:851–856, 1991.

23. D. C. Shields and P. M. Sharp. Synonymous codon usage in *Bacillus subtilis* reflects both traditional selection and mutational biases. *Nucl. Acids Res.*, 15:8023–8040, 1987.

24. P. M. Sharp, E. Cowe, D. G. Higgins, D. C. Shields, K. H. Wolfe, and F. Wright. Codon usage patterns in *Escherichia coli*, *Bacillus subtilis*, *Saccharomices pombe*, *Drosophila melanogaster* and *Homo sapiens*: a review of the considerable within-species diversity. *Nucl. Acids Res.*, 16:8207–8211, 1988.

25. M. Stenico, A. T. Loyd, and P. M. Sharp. Codon usage in *Caenorhabditis elegans*: delineation of translational selection and mutational biases. *Nucl. Acid Res.*, 22:2437–2446, 1994.

26. T. Ikemura. Codon usage and tRNA content in unicellular and multicellular organisms. *Mol. Biol. Evol.*, 2:13–34, 1985.

27. J. L. Bennetzen and B. D. Hall. Codon selection in yeast. *J. Biol. Chem.*, 257:3026–3031, 1982.

28. M. Bulmer. Coevolution of codon usage and transfer RNA abundance. *Nature*, 325:728–730, 1987.

29. M. Gouy and Ch. Gautier. Codon usage in bacteria: Correlation with gene expressivity. *Nucl. Acids Res.*, 10:7055–7070, 1982.

30. S. Varenne, J. Buc, R. Lloubès, and C. Lazdunski. Translation is a non-uniform process. Effect of tRNA availability on the rate of elongation of nascent polypeptide chains. *J. Mol. Biol.*, 180:549–576, 1984.

31. R. H. Buckingham, and H. Grosjean. The accuracy of mRNA–tRNA recognition. In *Accuracy in Molecular Processes: Its Control and Relevance to Living Systems.* T. B. L. Kirkwood, R. Rosenberger, and D. J. Galas, editors. Chapman & Hall Publishers, London, 1986, pp. 83–126.

32. R. J. Grocock and P. M. Sharp. Synonymous codon usage in *Pseudomonas aeruginosa* PA01. *Gene*, 289:131–139, 2002.

33. A. Carbone, A. Zinovyev, and F. Képès. Codon Adaptation Index as a measure dominating codon bias. *Bioinformatics*, 19:2005–2015, 2003.

34. A. Carbone, F. Képès, and A. Zinovyev, Microbial codon bias and the organisation microorganisms in codon space. *Mol. Biol. Evol.*, 22(3):547–561, 2004.

35. H. Willenbrock, C. Friis. A. S. Friis, and D. W. Ussery. An environmental signature for 323 microbial genomes based on codon adaptation indices. *Genome Biol.*, 7:R114, 2006.

36. A. Carbone and D. Madden. Insights on the evolution of metabolic networks from data and sequence analysis. *J. Mol. Evol.*, 61:456–469, 2005.

37. J. L. DeRisi, V. R. Iyer, and P. O. Brown. Exploring the metabolic and genetic control expression on a genomic scale. *Science*, 278:680–686, 1997.

38. A. R. Mushegian and E. V. Koonin. A minimal gene set for cellular life derived by comparison of complete bacterial genomes. *Proc. Nat. Acad. Sci. USA*, 93:10268–10273, 1996.

39. K. S. Makarova, L. Aravind, M. Y. Galperin, N. V. Grishin, R. L. Tatusov, Y. I. Wolf, and E. V. Koonin. Comparative genomics of the archaea (euryarchaeota): Evolution of conserved protein families, the stable core, and the variable shell. *Genome Res.*, 9:608–628, 2003.

40. C. L. Nesbø, Y. Boucher, and W. F. Doolittle. Defining the core of non-transferable prokaryotic genes: The euryarchaeal core. *J. Mol. Evol.*, 53:340–350, 2001.

41. J. K. Harris, S. T. Kelley, G. B. Spiegelman, and N. R. Pace. The genetic core of the universal ancestor. *Genome Res.*, 13:407–412, 2003.

42. J. R. Brown, C. J. Douady, M. J. Italia, W. E. Marshall, and M. J. Stanhope. Universal trees based on large combined protein sequence data sets. *Nat. Genet.*, 28:281–285, 2001.

43. E. V. Koonin. Comparative genomics, minimal gene sets and the last common ancestor. *Nat. Rev. Microbiol.*, 1:127–136, 2003.

44. R. L. Charlebois and W. F. Doolittle. Computing prokaryotic gene ubiquity: Rescuing the core from extinction. *Genome Res.*, 14:2469–2477, 2004.

45. K. Kobayashi, S. D. Ehrlich, A. Albertini, G. Amati, K. K. Andersen, M. Arnaud, K. Asai, S. Ashikaga, S. Aymerich, P. Bessieres, et al. Essential *Bacillus subtilis* genes. *Proc. Natl. Acad. Sci. USA*, 100:4678–4683, 2003.

46. C. A. Hutchison, S. N. Peterson, S. R. Gill, R. T. Cline, O. White, C. M. Fraser, H. O. Smith, and J. C. Venter. Global transposon mutagenesis and a minimal *Mycoplasma* genome. *Science*, 286:2165–2169, 1999.

47. J. I. Glass, N. Assad-Garcia, N. Alperovich, S. Yooseph, M. R. Lewis, M. Maruf, C. A. Hutchison III, H. O. Smith, and J. C. Venter. Essential genes of a minimal bacterium. *Proc. Nat. Acad. Sci. USA*, 103:425–430, 2006.

48. B. J. Akerley, E. J. Rubin, V. L. Novick, K. Amaya, N. Judson, and J. J. Mekalanos. A genome-scale analysis for identification of genes required for growth or survival of *Haemophilus influenzae*. *Proc. Nat. Acad. Sci. USA*, 99:966–971, 2002.

49. S. Y. Gerdes, M. D. Scholle, J. M. Campbell, G. Balazsi, E. Ravasz, M. D. Daugherty, A. L. Somera, N. C. Kyrpides, I. Anderson, M. S. Gelfand, A. Bhattacharya, et al. Experimental determination and system level analysis of essential genes in *Escherichia coli* MG1655. *J. Bacteriol.*, 185:5673–5684, 2003.

50. M. Hashimoto, T. Ichimura, H. Mizoguchi, K. Tanaka, K. Fujimitsu, K. Keyamura, T. Ote, T. Yamakawa, Y. Yamazaki, H. Mori, T. Katayama, and J. Kato. Cell size and nucleoid organization of engineered *Escherichia coli* cells with a reduced genome. *Mol. Microbiol.*, 55:137–49, 2005.

51. N. R. Salama, et al. Global transposon mutagenesis and essential gene analysis of *Helicobacter pylori*. *J. Bacteriol.*, 186:7926–7935, 2004.

52. Y. Ji, et al. Identification of critical staphylococcal genes using conditional phenotypes generated by antisense RNA. *Science*, 293:2266–2269, 2001.

53. R. A. Forsyth, et al. A genome-wide strategy for the identification of essential genes in *Staphylococcus aureus*. *Mol. Microbiol.*, 43:1387–1400, 2002.

54. J. A. Thanassi, et al. Identification of 113 conserved essential genes using a high-throughput gene disruption system in *Streptococcus pneumoniae*. *Nucl. Acids Res.*, 30:3152–3162, 2002.

55. E. A. Winzeler, et al. Functional characterization of the *S. cerevisiae* genome by gene deletion and parallel analysis. *Science*, 285:901–906, 1999.

56. G. Giaever, et al. Functional profiling of the *Saccharomyces cerevisiae* genome. *Nature*, 418:387–391, 2002.

57. R. S. Kamath, et al. Systematic functional analysis of the *Caenorhabditis elegans* genome using RNAi. *Nature*, 421:231–237, 2003.

58. A. Carbone. Computational prediction of genomic functional cores specific to different microbes. *J. Mol. Evol.*, 63(6):733–746, 2006.

59. A. Mathelier and A. Carbone. Chromosomal periodicity and positional networks of genes in *Escherichia coli*. Submitted manuscript, 2009.

60. F. Képès and C. Vaillant. Transcription-based solenoidal model of chromosomes. *Complexus*, 1:171–180, 2003.

61. F. Képès. Periodic transcriptional organization of the *E. coli* genome. *J. Mol. Biol.*, 340:957–964, 2004.

62. M. A. Wright, P. Krarchenko, G. M. Church, and D. Segré. Chromosomal periodicity of evolutionary conserved gene pairs. *Proc. Natl. Acad. Sci. USA*, 104:10559–10564, 2007.

63. A. Carbone. Codon bias is a major factor explaining phage evolution in translationally biased hosts. *J. Mol. Evol.* Online Feb 20, 2008.

64. D. R. Rokyta, C. L. Burch, S. B. Caudle, and H. A. Wichman. Horizontal gene transfer and the evolution of microvirid coliphage genomes. *J. Bacteriol.*, 188:1134–1142, 2006.

65. W. C. Summers. Bacteriophage therapy. *Annu. Rev. Microbiol.*, 55:437–451, 2001.

V

SOFTWARE TOOLS FOR SYSTEMS BIOLOGY

15

ALI BABA: A TEXT MINING TOOL FOR SYSTEMS BIOLOGY

Jörg Hakenberg

Computer Science and Engineering, Arizona State University, Tempe, AZ, USA

Conrad Plake

Biotechnological Centre, Technische Universität Dresden, Dresden, Germany

Ulf Leser

Knowledge Management in Bioinformatics, Humboldt-Universität zu Berlin, Berlin, Germany

15.1 INTRODUCTION TO TEXT MINING

Text mining is the process of automatically deriving information from text (as opposed to data mining that works on structured data). This process starts with accessing the relevant literature and ends with extracting the desired pieces of information. Access mostly is provided by Web-based search tools, the best known of which is PubMed [1]. PubMed currently contains citations from close to 18 million publications in the biomedical domain (biology, biochemistry, medicine, and related fields), from approximately 5200 journals, since 1865. Up to 4000 citations (abstract and bibliographical information) are added to PubMed per day, which necessitates automated means to efficiently handle searches for high-quality information.

Elements of Computational Systems Biology   Edited by Huma M. Lodhi and Stephen H. Muggleton
Copyright © 2010 John Wiley & Sons, Inc.

Text mining falls into several tasks, most of which depend on each other, but few of which have been sufficiently solved. The first task is information retrieval (IR): given a user's query, find the (most) relevant documents containing the keywords or, even better, providing an answer to the question the user actually has in mind. The later part is also called question answering (QA), where the task is not only to find relevant documents but also to extract the answer to the query from them. Information retrieval is often solved by keyword queries, as in PubMed [1], which returns the most recent abstracts containing the query. PubMed goes a step farther, expanding the initial set of keywords to related terms: a search for "cancer" will also find abstracts that mention neoplasms instead of cancer. Another related task is text summarization, which aims to summarize one or multiple documents with respect to a certain problem. An example is Entrez Gene [2], a database of genes, which contains a short summary for every entry, describing known functions, implications in diseases, and so on of the gene or the gene's products. These summaries are currently all manually compiled from various publications studying the gene and significant efforts are under way to automatize this curation process.

The next groups of tasks for text mining relates to information extraction; the most prominent is named entity recognition (NER), referring to the search for genes, proteins, diseases, drugs, and so on, mentioned in a text (we will call these biomedical entities in the remainder). In addition, instead of only recognizing that a name refers to a particular class of entities, entity mention normalization (EMN) tries to actually identify the entity, usually by searching a reference to a database. For instance, consider the name $p53$, which may stand for a large number of different yet orthologous genes; the task for EMN is to pick, when $p53$ appears in a text, the correct one of these genes by identifying a corresponding database entry, for instance in Entrez Gene. Only then can the right set of additional information (function, species, sequence, etc.) become available to the user. Word sense disambiguation (WSD), on the other hand, tries to tell apart entities of different kinds that share the same name; *cancer* mostly refers to a disease, but in some contexts, it also refers to the genus of various crab species. Once entities are recognized, classified, and properly resolved, relation mining (RM) searches for evidence for associations between them, such as protein–protein interactions or gene–disease associations.

In the biological domain, an abundance of data of various types, degrees of detail, and quality is available. Much of these are stored in curated databases, that is, databases whose content is maintained by human experts. Among these databases, some store information on single types of biomedical objects, such as proteins (e.g., UniProt [3]), genes (e.g., NCBI Entrez Gene [2]), and drugs (e.g., DrugBank [4]); or on associations between these, such as protein–protein interactions (IntAct [5], MINT [6], etc.), drug–protein and target–disease relations (TTD [7] etc.), or metabolic pathways and other processes (e.g., KEGG [8]). The curation process for most of these databases relies on trained experts extracting supportive information from scientific publications and updating the database accordingly. Far from being able to deliver off-the-shelf solutions for handling such curation automatically, research in text mining currently focuses on aiding database curators and researchers in biology, medicine, and interdisciplinary fields, who search for single, specific, and accurate pieces of information in literature collections. With novel high-throughput data generation techniques, manual curation is not sufficient any longer [9]. A second focus of text mining research is to help in the interpretation of high-throughput screens such as gene expression or RNA interference screens, which typically generate large clusters of genes with somehow similar behavior. Identifying relationships within such clusters such as protein interactions or shared function is important to gain deeper insights. Text mining can also serve directly to cluster genes by phenotype [10]. In Lage et al. [11], for example, candidate genes for diseases are identified by clustering genes based on phenotype terminology extracted from a database with text mining. In addition to search and curation, knowledge extracted from the literature, combined with knowledge from databases, helps generating hypotheses, which can then be further verified. Examples for improving protein function prediction with results from text mining are given in Gabow et al. [12] and Groth et al. [10].

With ALI BABA, we provide means to efficiently search and browse PubMed citations, extract basic information, and link these to additional information available from relevant databases [13]. The basic idea behind ALI BABA is to display the contents of a collection of PubMed abstracts as a graph, that is, biomedical entities are nodes, and connections between those refer to potential associations, for example, interactions between proteins. ALI BABA, therefore, parses abstracts selected by the user for proteins, diseases, enzymes, and so on, and searches for potential relationships. The resulting graph should be understood as a summary of all abstracts, restricted to molecular biology entities and their associations. Figure 15.1 shows an example of such a graph, which resulted from 20 abstracts for the query "glutamate metabolism." Clicking on nodes and edges accesses the original text that contains them (see lower right panel in the figure). Each node is linked to one or more entries in a relevant biological databases; for instance, proteins are linked to UniProt and drugs to either DrugBank or MeSH.

In the remainder of this chapter, we will present the ALI BABA tool, starting with examples relevant to systems biology. We describe the functionality of ALI BABA from a user's perspective in Section 15.2. In Section 15.3, we give an overview of the techniques underlying ALI BABA and present quantitative assessments of the core techniques. We conclude the chapter with a discussion of related tools and future perspectives for biomedical text mining.

From the Web page `http://alibaba.informatik.hu-berlin.de/`, users launch ALI BABA via Java Web Start.[1] Installation instructions for this environment can be found on the Web page, although it is nowadays available on most systems by default. The Web page also provides a manual, further information, answers to frequently asked questions, as well as additional examples. As a convention for this chapter, we will write user queries to ALI BABA enclosed in double quotations marks

---

[1] Java Runtime Environment 1.5 or higher has to be installed previously.

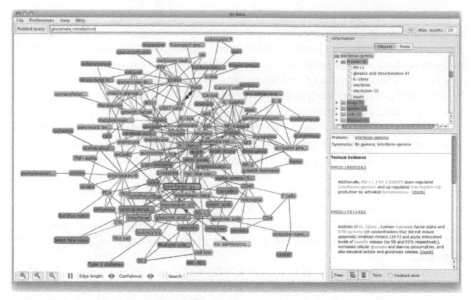

Figure 15.1   Ali Baba graph resulting from a query for "glutamate metabolism." Highlighted is the protein "interferon–gamma." Associated proteins and cells can be seen in the `Object` panel (upper right), with the supporting evidence being shown in the `Text` panel (lower right).

("query"), entities such as genes and diseases in italics (*Dickkopf*), and actions a user can take as well as items in ALI BABA in teletype (`File` menu).

15.2   ALI BABA AS A TOOL FOR MINING BIOLOGICAL FACTS FROM LITERATURE

In this section, we demonstrate how to use ALI BABA to find answers to typical questions in systems biology and biomedical research. In the former area, typical questions one may want to answer refer to the formation of protein complexes, the regulation of gene expression, signaling cascades, metabolic pathways, or genetic linkage of diseases. Clinicians might seek for explanations of symptoms or for new therapies and drugs for diseases. We have chosen the following two examples for showing how to use ALI BABA:

- Which proteins are involved in the activation or recognition mechanism for PmrD?
- What are the risk factors of treating G6PD-deficient malaria patients with primaquine?

As a third example, we will show how to combine the known pathway for Wnt signaling from KEGG with a graph representing latest findings for the protein *Dickkopf* from the literature.

15.2.1   Which Proteins are Involved in the Activation or Recognition Mechanism for PmrD?

To find an answer, we first have to translate this question into the PubMed query language. In this case, we formulate the query as "PmrD (activation OR recognition)" and enter it into ALI BABA's query field located at the top of the application window. This results in a graph of nodes (representing entities) in different colors connected by edges (representing interactions and other associations) displayed on the large main panel—the Graph view (Figure 15.2). Pressing the F9 key or the Play/Pause button on the bottom of the application window toggles the animation of the graph on or off.

In the upper righthand panel (Objects), all entities are shown as a tree, sorted by their categories (protein, drug); each category has its unique color that is used throughout the ALI BABA application—proteins in green, diseases in pink, cells in light blue, tissues in orange, drugs in brown, and species in blue. The number in brackets next to each category name tells us how many instances of this category were found in the PubMed result. A left click with the mouse on the node for *PmrD* in the graph also opens this protein in the tree and shows the different categories its direct neighbors in the graph belong to: proteins, drugs, species and so on. These categories contain objects that are related to *PmrD*. In the lower right panel, all sentences from the PubMed abstracts that mention protein *PmrD* are shown in the Text view. Opening a category below *PmrD* in the tree and clicking on one of the objects listed shows all sentences from the abstracts that are evidence for a relation between this object and *PmrD*. The same effect can be seen when clicking on the edge between the two objects in the graph.

Proteins related to *PmrD* are *PhoP*, *PhoQ*, *ugd*, *PmrA*, and *PmrB*.[2] Reading the text snippets, we can quickly verify that each of the proteins is indeed involved in either activation or recognition of *PmrD* or closely related to it. Figure 15.2 (top) shows all proteins found in the texts. The selected node *PmrD* is highlighted with a blue and its direct neighbor nodes with a red border showing the answer to the question also graphically.

15.2.2   What are the Risk Factors of Treating G6PD-Deficient Malaria Patients with Primaquine?

Figure 15.2 (bottom) shows the resulting graph for the PubMed query "primaquine malaria g6pd deficiency." The graph shows a connection between *G6PD* (deficiency), *vivax malaria* (patients), and their treatment with *primaquine*. The risk factors *hemolytic anemia/hemolysis* and *methemoglobinemia* are directly connected to *G6PD* and *primaquine*. Other nodes in the graph present more information on studied populations, the viral origin, infected cells, and information on the disease. Each object recognized by ALI BABA is linked to an appropriate external resource or database. In the upper part of the Text view, objects selected in either the graph or tree are

---

[2]PubMed result from March 2008. This may change as new documents are added to PubMed every day.

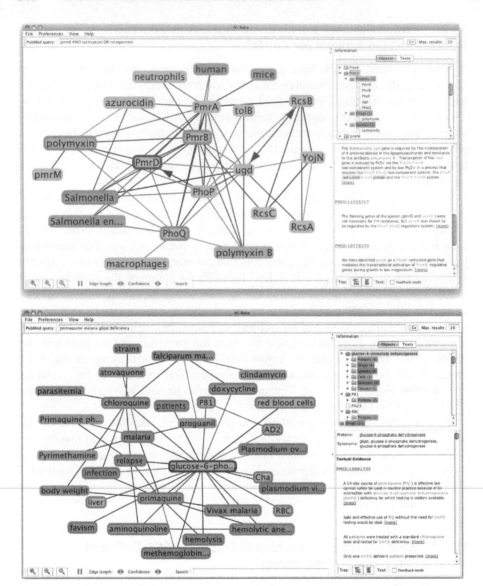

Figure 15.2   Top: The result for the PubMed query "PmrD (activation OR recognition)" as shown by ALI BABA. The selected node *PmrD* is framed in blue and all its direct neighbors in red. Bottom: The graph for query "primaquine malaria g6pd deficiency" (see text).

shown by name and by all synonyms encountered in the abstracts. A mouse click on one of the names opens the database entry page for this particular object in the web browser. We select the node *primaquine* and click on its name, appearing as a link in the `Text view`, which brings us to its entry page in DrugBank, a comprehensive database that combines drug data and drug target information. We follow the same procedure for the protein *G6PD* and the disease *hemolytic anemia*, which opens the UniProt/SwissProt page and the entry page from the Medical Subject Headings of the National Library of Medicine, respectively. The three pages together with the network and annotated texts in ALI BABA offer a lot of background information on this particular question. ALI BABA can thus serve as a starting point for information retrieval in biology and biomedicine.

15.2.3 The Wnt Signaling Pathway

The Wnt signaling pathway is a complex network of proteins well known for their roles in embryogenesis and cancer, but also involved in normal physiological processes in adult animals [14]. To load the pathway for the first time, we open the File menu and select `Update KEGG files`. After the update process is complete, we go to the File menu again and select `Open KEGG file`. In the next dialog, all available pathways are shown. The list is downloaded directly from the KEGG server and is, therefore, always up-to-date. Note that the list needs to be downloaded only once or when significant changes in KEGG are expected. Selecting, for instance, the Wnt signaling pathway will display the corresponding graph. KEGG pathways have a distinct layout that helps to get a better overview on the network. To view the pathway in its original presentation, as known from KEGG, we open the `View menu` and choose the `Coordinates layout`.

Figure 15.3 (top) shows the resulting Wnt signaling pathway of protein interactions. One of the proteins involved is *Dickkopf*, which functions as an inhibitor of the Wnt signaling pathway. The literature contains many references to this protein. From January to March 2008, about 30 articles have been published already that mention *Dickkopf* or one of its synonyms. To append a graph for *Dickkopf* from the literature to the Wnt signaling pathway from KEGG, we enable the option `Append queries` from the `Preferences menu` and then enter the query "dickkopf." The result is shown in Figure 15.3 (bottom). The appended graph does not come with distinct layout and is thus just scrambled around the upper left of the pathway, but we can see clearly many new relations for protein *Dickkopf* and other proteins from the pathway. Furthermore, textual evidences are added to some of the pathway proteins and relations as they were found in the abstracts. This can be repeated with other queries to PubMed, although the resulting network will quickly become too complex to oversee. For such cases, users may either use the various `Display filter` options or simply go to the `View` menu and switch to `Tree View only`, which hides the graph and shows only the tree (that contains the same information as the graph) and the texts.

15.3 COMPONENTS AND USAGE OF ALI BABA

In this section, we describe in detail the different components of ALI BABA, their usage, and the features they offer. The components are sorted by Views, Navigation, Filters, Storage and retrieval, and the Graph editor.

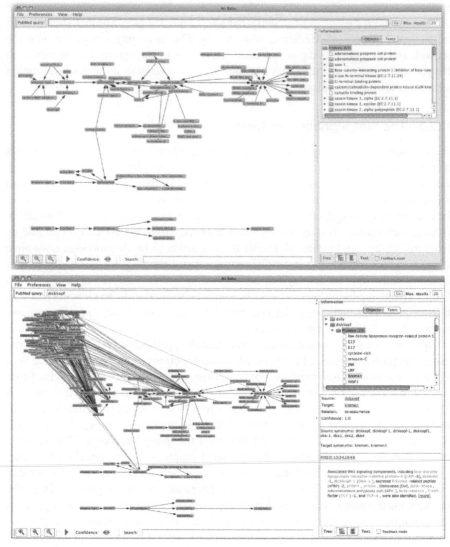

Figure 15.3 Top: The Wnt signaling pathway loaded into ALI BABA and presented using the original KEGG layout. Bottom: A graph from the literature for query "dickkopf" appended to the Wnt signaling pathway. Most of these appended texts discuss entities (upper left) related to *Dickkopf* and *catenin beta-1*, as indicated by the large number of edges toward either protein. Textual evidence for such relations can be viewed in the right panel after selecting an entity node from the graph.

15.3.1 Views

The application window of ALI BABA is divided into three sections and the PubMed query bar at the top. The left main section is the Graph view that displays PubMed and KEGG networks graphically with nodes representing objects and edges representing associations between two objects. Nodes come in different colors for the different categories they belong to proteins (green), cells (light blue), diseases (pink), drugs (brownish), tissues (orange), and species (blue). Metabolic pathways from KEGG contain also compounds (grey) and reactions (pink). The right-hand side of the application window is divided into a `Tree view` that displays all nodes and interconnections and a `Text view` that primarily displays annotated abstracts and text snippets that are evidence for selected objects and relations. On top of the `Tree view` are two tabs labeled *Objects* and *Texts*. Selection of the `Texts` tab shows the list of articles that matched the query in the original PubMed result order instead of the objects tree. After selection of an article, the complete abstract is shown in the `Text view` below.

In the `View menu`, users can select between a `graph only` view, a `tree (and text) only` view, or both (default). The `View menu` also offers to choose between different layouts for displaying the graph. By default, the force feedback layout is applied that tries to arrange nodes with a maximal distance to each other, only bounded by the length of the edges. The maximum `edge length` can be altered using the slider in the bottom panel. The `Radial layout` applies a circular arrangement of nodes around a selected node in the middle. The `Coordinates layout` lets the user define the arrangement of nodes by clicking on a node and dragging it around with the mouse or shows a predefined layout as in case of KEGG graphs.

15.3.2 Navigation

Navigation of the network in ALI BABA is always possible using either the graph or the tree. A click on a node in the graph scrolls to and opens the corresponding node in the tree, whereas a double-click on a node in the tree highlights the corresponding node in the graph with a blue frame and its direct neighbors with a red frame. To move around in the graph, press and hold the left mouse button. To zoom in or out of the graph, either use the mouse wheel or the `magnifier icons` on the bottom left. For complex networks, it can be very difficult to find a node by looking at the graph alone. To assist the user, we placed another search field on the bottom of the graph view that highlights all nodes that match the entered string. Nodes that represent objects whose name or one of its synonyms contain the entered character string will appear larger than others. Nodes in the tree are sorted by category and alphabetically within categories.

The `Text view` on the right-hand side primarily shows sentences related to the currently selected node or edge. Next to each sentence is a link called more. A click on the link shows the complete abstract. At the end of each abstract is a list of resolved abbreviations found in the text (if any) and the link `Show related abstracts as new graph`, which operates on the Related Articles feature of PubMed and initiates a new query that results in a new graph. When the `append query` option is enabled (`Preferences menu`), the new graph is added to the current one. The `Text view` does not only show the annotated abstracts but also contains links to PubMed (as PubMed ID) and to external databases for selected objects. Proteins link to UniProt, diseases, tissues, and cells link to the Medical Subject Headings of the National Library of Medicine, drugs link to DrugBank, and species to the NCBI taxonomy.

15.3.3 Filters

ALI BABA provides many ways to filter networks. This reduces complexity and helps to focus on certain aspects of the network. The types of categories shown by ALI BABA can be configured in the `Filter Preferences` dialog (located in the `Prefer-ences` menu). By default, all categories are selected; deselecting, e.g., the category "drugs" will hide all nodes in the graph and tree that refer to drugs. Users only interested in proteins and protein interactions can deselect all categories but proteins, as was shown for the *PmrD* example in Figure 15.2.

Nodes of an extracted graph from the literature usually differ in their number of neighbors. Some nodes are hubs, that is, they are directly connected to many other nodes. There are also nodes that do not have a single neighbor and are thus isolated. ALI BABA offers to filter nodes by their degree, that is, their number of direct neighbors in the graph. In the `Filter preferences`, users can select the checkbox for the node degree filter. This will bring up an additional slider below the graph view. Moving the slider from left to right increases the degree threshold and hides nodes with a lower degree. For example, moving the slider one step to the right from its very left position will hide all isolated nodes in the graph. Moving the slider to the left will show these nodes again.

Two directly connected nodes have a distance of one, as the shortest path between them contains one edge. Computing the neighborhood of a node that is reachable within a certain distance offers another convenient way to filter networks. The graph layout `Path length` hides all nodes with a distance to a selected node above a chosen limit. Enabling this layout mode from the View menu will show a text box containing the currently active limit next to the confidence slider on the bottom. A mouse click on the up-arrow to the left of the box increases the limit, a click on the down-arrow decreases it. A click on a node in the graph afterward will only show its neighbors that are reachable within this distance.

Besides filtering by node properties, filtering edges between nodes is also possible. Use the `confidence slider` on the bottom to hide or show more edges. Moving the slider to the left lowers the confidence threshold and shows more unconfident edges between objects, while moving the slider to the right increases the threshold and removes edges with a lower confidence value. Please refer to the next section on how confidence values for edges are computed.

Many terms in the biomedical domain are ambiguous. For example, the term *adhesion* can refer to the pathological process or the biological process of cell adhesion. The term *cancer* can refer to a disease or the crab. To help text mining systems distinguish between the different meanings of an ambiguous term, training data is needed to learn about the classification problem. ALI BABA offers a `feedback mode` to let users report on falsely recognized entities. To activate the `feedback mode`, select the checkbox on the bottom of the text view. Whenever the user highlights a part of the text with the mouse (as for copy and paste), a dialog will appear that asks for correction by either selecting a new category or unmark the annotated term. The data are stored anonymously at the server and will be used to retrain the word sense disambiguation component of ALI BABA from time to time (see also next section). A better classification of ambiguous terms eventually helps to reduce graph complexity as their will be, e.g., only one node for *cancer* instead of two when ALI BABA was able to decide that all underlying texts discuss the disease and not the species.

15.3.4 Storage and Retrieval

All graphs in ALI BABA can be stored locally on the user's computer. To store or re-open a graph go to the File menu and select Save as file or Open file, respectively. Files are stored in GraphML format. Select Save as image in the File menu to save the current graph as an image. As opposed to the GraphML format, this image cannot be re-opened in ALI BABA.

ALI BABA has access to two sources of biological data, PubMed and KEGG (and provides links to many other databases for recognized entities). While networks from PubMed have to be extracted using text mining techniques, KEGG graphs can be loaded directly into ALI BABA. Kyoto Encyclopedia of Genes and Genomes (KEGG) is a bioinformatics resource aiming to completely represent the cell and the organism to enable computational prediction of higher-level cellular processes and organism behavior. We integrated KEGG into ALI BABA because of the data available on cellular pathways, which are of interest to many biologists and can serve as high-confidence building blocks for larger networks. Users of ALI BABA interested in KEGG pathways Update KEGG files from the File menu. This retrieves the data from the KEGG FTP server and stores all data needed for ALI BABA locally. Note that this might take a few minutes depending on the network's bandwidth and occupies up to 60 MB on the user's hard drive. This update process needs to be done only once or if new pathways are available.

KEGG graphs are loaded into ALI BABA by choosing Open KEGG file from the File menu. After a little delay, a dialog opens and lists all available pathways from KEGG alphabetically, first all regulatory pathways followed by all metabolic pathways. This list is always up-to-date, downloaded directly from the KEGG server, which causes the delay. For finding a specific pathway, the user can enter a part of the name into the search field below the list box.

To append a new graph to an existing one, either loaded from PubMed, from KEGG, or from a local file, users can enable the Append queries option from the Preferences menu. This way it is possible to build up networks incrementally.

15.3.5 Graph Editor

ALI BABA features a build-in editor that allows for easy manipulation or creation of graphs by the user. To add a new node to the graph, right-click with the mouse anywhere in the white space. A context menu appears with the option Add node. This dialog lets the user choose a name and category for the new node. A right–click on an existing node offers user to edit this node (change its name or category), delete it, or add a new edge starting from this node. To add an edge, a target node has to be specified from a list of all available nodes. A more convenient method to add an edge is by clicking on the source node while holding the Ctrl–key and then moving the mouse over the target node, still holding the Ctrl–key. Clicking again on the target node finally adds the edge to the graph. A right–click on an existing edge opens a context menu with the option to edit or delete it. Remember to save the graph in a local file after editing to prevent its loss.

15.4   ALI BABA's APPROACH TO TEXT MINING

ALI BABA processes PubMed abstracts using several building blocks. Most of them are arranged as subsequent components, where every component uses results from previous components. Figure 15.4 shows the main components and flow of data in ALI BABA. In this section, we want to focus on these components, rather than implementation aspects of the Web server, database, and ALI BABA's user interface (which has been discussed in the previous section). The components can be divided into three main blocks: natural language processing, named entity recognition, and relation mining, which we will discuss in the following. We finish this section by presenting evaluations of some of the components, which will help users to estimate the quality of ALI BABA's predictions.

15.4.1   Natural Language Processing

The first step in ALI BABA is to analyze each abstract with "basic" natural language processing (NLP) components. Sentence boundaries have to be detected so that subsequent components can deal with data on a sentence level. ALI BABA applies a set of heuristic rules to decide whether a period (colon, semicolon) marks a sentence

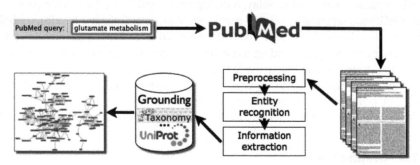

Figure 15.4   Overview of the data flow in ALI BABA. After a user submits a query, this is send to PubMed and resulting abstracts are retrieved. The abstracts are processed to find names of entities and relations between them. Grounding helps to map together identical entities that appear with different names, so that they become a single node in the resulting graph.

end or has a different meaning. An exampe for such rules is a regular expression recognizing the sequence "lower case character–period–white space–upper case character" that recognizes most sentence boundaries. In a similar way, other expressions try to deal with false positives occurring, for instance, after common abbreviations (such as "vs." and "ca."). This task is much easier in case of decimal points than, for instance, nonstandard abbreviations, which occur quite often in scientific texts. Another step in this preprocessing is *part-of-speech tagging*, that is, assigning to each word its semantic class (e.g., noun or adverb) helps for matching precompiled patterns against a sentence, which we will explain later in this section. In our case, we use the TnT–tagger [15] for this task. ALI BABA also tries to resolve abbreviations; this is necessary because most abbreviations are ambiguous and might potentially refer to a gene, trauma, or laboratory technique, like "PCR" does. Finding the correct long form then solves such issues. We use an adaptation of the algorithm presented by Schwartz and Hearst [16] to solve to map abbrevations to their long forms.

15.4.2 Named Entity Recognition and Identification

ALI BABA searches PubMed abstracts for different kinds of biomedical entities, such as proteins and diseases (see Table 15.1). Our basic approach for named entity recognition (NER) is dictionary based, that is, we compile lists of known names and synonyms of entities from various sources and match these lists against text. The main advantage of such an approach is that for each name, a database identifier is immediately available (or multiple identifiers in case of, for instance, multiple proteins sharing the same name). This helps users of ALI BABA to easily get to more information on each entity (by following a link to the underlying database entry, e.g., to KEGG). It also allows ALI BABA to map an entity that occurs with different names across multiple text to the same instance; thus, occurrences of "Fas ligand" and "CD95L" would result in a single node for this protein in the graph. The main disadvantage of dictionary-based NER comes with the immense variety names for all instances of all entity classes; by far not all variations of a name can possibly be enumerated, let alone stored in a

Table 15.1   Biomedical entities currently covered in ALI BABA, with numbers of entries and sources

Biomedical entity	Source	Number of entries
Cells	MeSH, tree A11 [17]	1074
Compound	KEGG [8]	22,635
Disease	MeSH, tree C	18,100
Drug	MeSH, tree D03–6; DrugBank [4]	14,177 + 25,698
Enzyme	KEGG	23,063
Gene/protein	UniProt/Swiss–Prot [3]	234,497
Species	NCBI Taxonomy [18]	208,143
Tissue	MeSH, tree A10	595

database (which has a different purpose than collecting spelling variations). Common variations of names can be categorized as follows:

- *orthographic*: IFN-gamma, IFN-γ; IL-1, IL1
- *morphological*: Fas ligand, Fas ligands
- *lexical*: hepatitic leukaemia, liver leukemia; tumor, tumour
- *structural*: cancer in humans, human cancers
- *acronyms/abbreviations*: FADD; TFF3
- *synonyms*: neoplasm, tumor, cancer, carcinoma
- *eponyms*: Addison's disease, Addisonian syndrome
- *paragrammatical*: (mostly typos)

There are two main strategies to deal with variations in dictionary-based approaches. The first is to compile a concise dictionary with names as gathered from the database. Recognizing names then relies on inexact string matching, for instance, using alignment to allow for some variations. The second strategy is to generate a "loose" dictionary that already includes typical deviations of spelling. We follow the second strategy. Starting with a list of terms reflecting names for entries in a biological database, we compile regular expressions that allow for variations such as plural forms, hyphenation, and capitalization. Variations for obvious abbreviations ("IFN") are introduced as well. For example, the following regular expression covers many variations of the protein names "IFN-gamma" and "CD95L," respectively:

```
(I(FN|fn)|ifn)[ \-_]?([Gg](amma)?|{gamma})s?
(CD|Cd|cd)[ \-_]?95[ \-_]?[Ll](igand)?
```

({gamma} depicting the Greek letter γ). Species often are referred to using their Latin name. Quite some possibilities for abbreviating or altering such names exist. The genus might appear with or without an initial capital and might be abbreviated using the first letter ("Mycobacterium tuberculosis," "M. tuberculosis"), and also the species might the a short form (mostly consisting of three letters, "M. tub."). In addition, the individual terms might differ in their case and number ("S. attenuatas", "S. attenuata"). Quite often, "ae" appears as "e" ("F. iinumaes," "F. iinumes"). Taken together, for instance, the name "Phaeoacremonium inflatipes" should be transformed into the regular expression

```
[Pp]([.]|ha?eoacremonium)?[ \-_]*[Ii]nflatipes .
```

We built a finite state automaton covering all expressions that we generated in the described way, using the Monq JFA package [19]. Arbitrary text is then streamed against this automaton and searching becomes linear in the length of the text.

15.4.3 Word Sense Disambiguation

Another problem for named entity recognition is ambiguity of (biomedical and common English) terms. Word sense disambiguation (WSD) is the problem of assigning to an ambiguous term in a given context its correct sense [20]; WSD can thus be seen as a classification task [21]. To approach the WSD problem for polysemy and homonymy often is based on the one-sense-per-discourse assumption [22]. This assumption says that, whenever an ambiguous term appears multiple times in the same discourse (abstract, paragraph, text, etc.), all occurrences most likely share the same sense.[3] For instance, it is not very likely to find a text that contains the term "lamb" both in the sense *species* and as an abbreviation for the *protein* "laminin subunit beta-1 precursor." Consequently, one can use the entire discourse of a term as indicator for its sense. We build on this observation by learning a model for word senses from entire texts (mostly paragraphs or scientific abstracts) containing the word sense one or multiple times. Given an ambiguous term with unknown sense within a discourse, we use an SVM to classify the term to its correct sense using the model learned before. Our strategy to automatically find a large enough training sample is to search for texts that contain a term in a given sense, plus other terms that are related to it. For instance, for an ambiguous abbreviation, we may also search for the correct long form; for protein names, we may look for known and unambiguous synonyms.

Our method immediately reaches a median success rate of 93.7% as evaluated by cross-validation on 304 terms. We also studied an extension of the training set using abstracts from different terms of the same sense; this was necessary because not for all ambiguous terms there exists enough training data. The extension takes into account training data from other terms that have the same sense. For instance, if there were no sufficient amount of examples for the term "Beta" as a *species*, we may add texts discussing other species. To improve the quality of the data, we might exploit the hierarchy given with the NCBI Taxonomy (for species), that is, searching texts that mention the family of "Amaranthaceae" that "Beta" belongs to, or even higher-ranked entries. Such a strategy not only increases the reach of our method but also improves its performance to a median success rate of 97 percent for 422 terms. Still, terms for which we cannot find at least one training example cannot be analyzed by our method.

15.4.4 Relation Mining

In ALI BABA, we employ two different strategies to search for (pairwise) associations between biomedical entities. With a cooccurrence-based method, we assume the existence of some kind of association whenever two entities (for instance, a gene and a disease) are mentioned together in a single sentence. Such strategies fail to pick up only very few instances (e.g., when they are discussed across multiple sentences), but result in incorrect assignments for all coincidental occurrences of two entities. The assumption that a cooccurrence of two entities justifies the prediction of an associations holds better for some kinds of relations than for others: genes will most often be mentioned only with diseases or with tissues when there is a real association; two proteins mentioned together, however, will not justify the prediction of a protein–protein interaction. For this later case, and also for cellular locations of proteins, we thus pursue another strategy, based on pattern recognition. Pattern

---

[3]Gale et al. [22] showed that this holds in 98% of all cases.

recognition is comparable to finding sequence motifs within proteins, as contained, for instance, in the Prosite database [23]. In our case, a motif describes a (partial) sentence typically used by authors to describe a protein–protein interaction (or subcellular location, respectively). As an example, consider the following motif (called pattern) for recognizing protein–protein interactions:

PROTEIN expression is regulated by *PROTEIN*,

which matches the sentence

"DR4 expression is regulated by NF–kappaB".

Note that for recognizing a pattern, the exact name of a protein is not important, thus we may express it using the markup *PROTEIN*: any sentence that has the name of a protein at that particular position will potentially match the pattern. In the same manner, the words "expression" and "regulated" might be replaced with other words referring to similar behavior (e.g., "activity", "inhibited"), essentially retaining the meaning of matching sentences (a protein–protein or protein–gene interaction). We may use the markup *I-NOUN* and *I-VERB-D* to refer to similar, interaction-indicating (*I*) nouns and verbs in past tense (*D*), respectively. Additionally, replacing "by" with markup for prepositions and "is" with markup for verbs results in the pattern

PROTEIN I-NOUN VB I-VERB–D PREP PROTEIN,

which matches the sentences

"IL-8 production is inhibited by IL-10" and
"CCN3 transcription is up-reglated by p53".

We have compiled sets of such patterns for both applications [24–26]. While Prosite patterns are regular expressions matching sequences (i.e., they have markup for wild cards and variable positions), we use alignment as a matching strategy to allow for variations in the sentence. For instance, it is very often the case that a determiner ("a," "the") is inserted right before a noun or nominal phrase, as is an adverb before a verb. The aforementioned pattern thus should also match the sentence

"DR4 expression is <u>negatively</u> regulated by <u>the</u> NF–kappaB."

We have shown in Hakenberg et al. [24] how large sets of patterns can be compiled automatically, especially without the need of a manually annotated training sample. To do so, we analyze groups of similar sentences that discuss protein–protein interactions by computing a *multiple sentence alignment* (see MSA in bioinformatics).

This results in consensus patterns, which can best be explained in terms of a sequence logo:[4]

weblogo.berkeley.edu

(where P refers to a protein at the given position; N to a noun in singular, S in plural; W and V to verbs in different tenses; E to a preposition; and D to a determiner.)

For both strategies, cooccurrence-based search and pattern recognition by alignment, we calculate confidence scores that estimate the reliability of a match. In the case of alignment, the confidence score is derived from the alignment score; knowing a pattern, one can compute the maximal alignment score (for a potential perfect match). A confidence score for a match with an arbitrary sentence is thus the fraction of the alignment score for this match and the maximal score. To compute confidence scores for cooccurrences of two biomedical entities, we consider the distance of the two names in a sentence as well as biomedical entities (type and number) occurring in between the two names. In general, shorter distances give a higher confidence, while many intermediate names of the same type(s) point to conjunctions and thus lower the score.

15.4.5 Evaluation of Components

Of major importance for algorithms that predict an outcome—such as the ALI BABA components that, for instance, predict that a name encountered in a text refers to a gene—are quality assessments. A standard way to evaluate different methods is to compare the predictions to a gold standard (benchmark). Such a comparison provides measures for how good a method performance is. The metrics we will use in this section to measure performance are precision, recall, and f-measure. They are all based on the predictions a method generates as compared to the benchmarked, which can be grouped as follows:

- *True positive* (TP): the method makes a prediction that is indeed correct (e.g., it predicts a gene name that indeed is a gene name).
- *False positive* (FP): the method makes a prediction that is wrong (e.g., it predicts something to be a gene name, but it is not).
- *False negative* (FN): the method misses to make a prediction (e.g., it misses a gene name).

---

[4]Created with WebLogo, available at http://weblogo.berkeley.edu/.

- *True negative* (TN): the method does not make a prediction on a certain item, which is correct (e.g., it correctly predicts that a name does not refer to a gene).

We can use these counts to estimate performance in a standardized way. The *precision* of a method states how many of the predictions are correct

$$\text{precision} = \frac{TP}{TP + FP}. \tag{15.1}$$

The *recall* measures how many of the correct instances a method has predicted

$$\text{recall} = \frac{TP}{TP + FN}. \tag{15.2}$$

The *f-measure* combines these two metrics into a harmonic mean,

$$\text{f-measure} = \frac{2 \cdot \text{precision} \cdot \text{recall}}{\text{precision} + \text{recall}}. \tag{15.3}$$

(Note that there are also formulations of the f-measure that weight precision and recall differently.)

Several standardized benchmarks exist for evaluating the performance of text mining tools in terms of precision, recall, and f-measure. Most of them handle the recognition of named entities, that is, finding mentions of proteins, and so on in a text; some cover the extraction of relations (protein–protein interactions as an example). In such benchmarks (also called *corpora* as they deal with text), positive instances are annotated by human curators and an automated text mining method is measured by comparing annotations with predictions. An overview of some benchmarks can be found in BioCreative [27].

15.4.5.1 *Named Entity Recognition for Proteins* One of the most often used benchmarks for biomedical named entity recognition of genes and proteins are the BioCreative 1 and BioCreative 2 GM data sets [28]. They consist of 15,000 sentences for training, and the actual evaluation is performed on another set of 5000 sentences. All in all, there are 6331 gene names in the evaluation set. On this set, ALI BABA achieves an f-measure of 62 percent, with a precision of 73 percent at 54 percent recall. The current bestperforming approaches achieve an f-measure of up to 88 percent [29–31], all using machine-learning strategies. However, these systems are not suitable for online-processing because classification generally is much slower than dictionary matching, and they also do not solve the EMN problem. In contrast, ALI BABA is capable of assigning UniProt IDs to proteins, enabling the user to get to more detailed background information; such a task can only be sufficiently solved using dictionaries instead of machine learning, as demonstrated in Hakenberg et al. [25, 32].

15.4.5.2 Extraction of Protein–Protein Interactions A standard bench-mark for a pipeline of subsequent text mining tasks, ultimately testing predictions of protein–protein interactions found in text, is another part of the BioCreative 2 challenge, the IPS task. The goal is to find protein–protein interactions for which a publication provides evidence for physical interactions or colocalizations [33]. In addition, systems have to provide the correct UniProt ID for each participating protein. The system we propose in Hakenberg et al. [24] achieves an f-measure of 24 percent for this joint task, with the current best system obtaining 30 percent [34]. On the SPIES corpus [34], which deals with the task of extraction of protein–protein interactions alone, we achieve an f–measure of 61%, with a precision of 75 percent at 52 percent recall.

15.5 RELATED BIOMEDICAL TEXT MINING TOOLS

PubMed is the most complete and most prominent source of literature in the biomedical domain [1]. It currently indexes about 18 million publications, with metadata on authors, journals, keywords from the MeSH terminology, and so on. Its search interface is accessed more than 2,600,000 times a day [35]. The availability of the Entrez Programming Utilities [36] and the accessibility of indexed citations in XML format highly promote research and development of text mining techniques and alternative search interfaces to PubMed. There are numerous tools available to the biomedical community that support the retrieval and browsing of publications, and tools that build on retrieval systems to extract information on biomedical entities and relations from text. Here, we present a few example tools for each type of task.

15.5.1 Document Retrieval and Summarization

GoPubMed accepts user queries and forwards them to PubMed [37]. Returned documents are sorted into the categories of the gene ontology (GO) and Medical Subject Headings (MeSH). These hierarchies can be used to navigate through the result set by showing only documents related to a selected category node. Identified GO and MeSH terms are highlighted in the text. **HubMed** offers many features to literature retrieval and browsing, such as clustering of articles in PubMed Central by their citation links or by the relatedness score computed by PubMed [38]. Connections between articles are visualized as a dynamic graph by a Java applet. It also calls the external Web service **Whatizit** [39] to identify and highlight GO terms, protein names, and drug names in text. **botXminer** imports Medline XML files into an Oracle database [40]. This allows for more advanced queries, such as proximity searches with NEAR and searches with WILDCARDs. Grouping of articles by MeSH terms, authors, keywords, chemicals, and gene symbols is also possible. Groups of articles are presented either as a hyperlinked table or as a graph image.

15.5.2 Entity Extraction

Whatizit can perform entity recognition on arbitrary text or on PubMed abstracts matching a user query [39]. It is also accessible as a Web service that can be called from other applications (e.g., see **HubMed**). It comprises many modules to recognize a wide range of different types of entities, such as proteins, diseases, drugs, organisms, GO terms, and so on. **KMedDB** searches PubMed abstracts related to different types of biochemical kinetic parameters [41]. In addition, users can filter for abstracts that also mention a certain enzyme, a chemical compound, or a species. All of the following tools for relation mining also present users with recognized entities in text.

15.5.3 Relation Mining

EBIMed performs co-occurrence analysis on PubMed abstracts [42]. It provides an overview of co-occurrences of proteins, species, drugs, and GO terms. It searches all PubMed abstracts that fit a user query and presents the resulting associations in tabular form. **iHOP** offers access to the underlying literature by means of a network of genes and proteins [43, 44]. Users access the information by searching for gene names. The result is presented as a list of relevant sentences, which can then be selected to build a network graph. Clicking on a node or an edge in the graph re-sorts all sentences and highlights the selected fact. **Chilibot** constructs relationship networks among biological concepts, genes, proteins, or drugs [45]. It can be queried with a pair of gene names or with lists of gene names and keywords. As a result, it presents relevant sentences from PubMed abstracts and a graphical network with gene and concept nodes connected by text mined relations. **Info-PubMed** helps users to find information about biomedical entities such as genes, proteins, and the interactions between them [46]. All information are presented in the form of highlighted text snippets and as a graphical network.

15.6 CONCLUSIONS AND FUTURE PERSPECTIVES

Concerning biomedical text mining in general, there have been some recent efforts that point out where the field could be headed in the near future. The BioCreative evaluation challenge, which started in 2003, brings together researchers studying various tasks in biomedical text mining (currently, named entity recognition, entity mention normalization, gene ontology–annotation of proteins, extraction of protein–protein interactions, and experimental methods) in a competition-style format [27]. In other fields of bioinformatics, similar competitions are known, among them CASP [47] and CAPRI [48], for the prediction of protein 3D structure or protein–ligand docking, respectively. These evaluations give insight into the state-of-the-art, both for researchers in text mining (What are the best performing methods; What are promising ideas?) and users from the biomedical domain (What can already be done using text mining; How reliable are text mining methods; Where to obtain them?). We see that over the last years, work on biomedical text mining has focused on extracting protein-centered information: recognition and identification of protein names (and few other types of entities such as cell types and mutations), extracting protein–protein interactions, associations of proteins with other types of entities (GO terms, mutations, diseases); but very few solutions for other, especially more advanced applications of text mining have been proposed (and some of the more basic tasks have also not been sufficiently solved). This was mainly caused by the lack of tools that yield sufficient performance on various 'basic' subtasks. Only recently (approximately since early 2007), tools have become available that solve subtasks to a degree comparable with human annotators.[5] Thus, researchers in text mining can now start to use these 'basic tools' as input for their advanced applications, instead of building such tools themselves. One initiative that provides researchers as well as potential users with a framework that brings together approaches to various tasks is the BioCreative Meta–Server project [49]. At the time of writing, roughly a dozen groups provide their tools for named entity recognition, identification, and so on, to this framework, where it can be accessed either as a search engine that annotates retrieved texts, and also through an API to include predictions as input to advanced text mining solutions.

Fundel et al. scanned 1 million Medline abstracts for protein–protein interactions with their RelEx tool, finding more than 150,000 such instances [50]. With an evaluated precision and recall of 80 percent of RelEx, one can estimate that in abstracts alone, there might be around 600,000 protein–protein interactions 'hidden' in text (with the simplified assumption that more than 4 million abstracts discuss genes and/or proteins; this estimate contains duplicate mentions). This figure is consistent with results reported for the PreBIND system [51]; according to that study, Medline contained 300,000 interactions from the three organisms human, mouse, and yeast alone. Extending the search to full text publications will further increase this estimate. Compared to amounts of interaction stored in renowned databases, among them DIP (ca. than 56,000), IntAct (ca. 105,000), and MINT (ca. 105,000), one clearly sees the necessity to provide means of accessing information contained in text. This will enable researchers to view and analyze more exhaustive information than is currently available from databases alone. In addition, depending on the database under consideration, as much as half of the data originate from large-scale, high-throughput screening assays (such as yeast two-hybrid screens and BiFC; comprising, for instance, ca. 70% of data in IntAct), which are much less reliable than small-scale experiments (for instance, co-immunoprecipitation or tandem affinity purification). Assuming that only protein–protein interactions discovered in small-scale experiments are reliable enough to be discussed in an abstract, information extraction will find specifically these high-quality data; most publications contain only verified interactions in their main body, and provide results from high-throughout screens as tables, figures, or supplementary information.

Another open topic, although it has been addressed in some recent studies, is the integration on information obtained from databases with information extracted from publications. Knowledge integration necessitates the mapping of biomedical concepts as found in a text to their respective pendants in databases. Entity mention normalization has been successfully applied to some entity types and remains open for others.

---

[5]If one considers the pairwise *inter-annotator agreement*, measured in various studies to be around 90%; for instance in Morgan et al. [53].

Especially the handling of complex terms, for instance, from the GO, has proven a difficult task; this holds both for recognition (e.g., GO concepts that labels consist of five or more words will seldom be found literally in any piece of text) and the disambiguation/normalization (consider the GO term "development," which has nine different meanings, only one referring to the sense in GO). **PolySearch** [52] is one of the first available tools that can query PubMed and various databases at the same time, resulting in an integrated view of knowledge on certain facts. While the information from databases is certainly of a higher quality than information automatically extracted from text, the most recent knowledge, with some surprising nuggets and significant new findings, might only be found in publications.

ACKNOWLEDGMENTS

The authors would like to thank Edda Klipp, Max–Planck Institute for Molecular Genetics, Berlin, and her group, in particular, Axel Kowald and Sebastian Schmeier, for fruitful discussions and collaboration. We thank Torsten Schiemann, Emre Kutbay, Kevin Arnoult, Markus Pankalla, Peter Palaga, and Quang Long Nguyen for their part in setting up and maintaining ALI BABA. We kindly acknowledge founding by the German Federal Ministry of Education and Research (BMBF) under grant contract 0312705B.

REFERENCES

1. NCBI Entrez PubMed, http://www.ncbi.nlm.nih.gov/sites/entrez/.
2. NCBI Entrez Gene, http://www.ncbi.nlm.nih.gov/sites/entrez?db=gene.
3. UniProt, http://www.uniprot.org/.
4. DrugBank, http://www.drugbank.ca/.
5. S. Kerrien, Y. Alam-Faruque, B. Aranda, I. Bancarz, A. Bridge, et al. IntAct—Open Source Resource for Molecular Interaction Data. *Nucl. Acids Res.*, 35(Database issue):D561–D565, 2007. http://www.ebi.ac.uk/intact/
6. A. Chatr-Aryamontri, A. Ceol, L. M. Palazzi, G. Nardelli, M. V. Schneider, L. Castagnoli, and G. Cesareni. MINT: The Molecular INTeraction database. *Nucl. Acids Res.*, 35(Database issue):D557–D560, 2007.
7. X. Chen, Z. L. Ji, and Y. Z. Chen. TTD: Therapeutic Target Database. *Nucl. Acids Res.*, 30(1):412–415, 2002. http://xin.cz3.nus.edu.sg/group/ttd/ttd.asp
8. M. Kanehisa and S. Goto. KEGG: Kyoto Encyclopedia of Genes and Genomes. *Nucl. Acids Res.*, 28:27–30, 2000. http://www.genome.jp/kegg/
9. W. Baumgartner, L. Fox, G. Acquaah-Mensah, K. B. Cohen, and L. Hunter. Manual curation is not sufficient for annotation of genomic databases. *Bioinformatics*, 23(13):i41–48, 2007.
10. P. Groth, B. Weiss, H–D. Pohlenz, and U. Leser. Mining phenotypes for gene function prediction. *BMC Bioinform.*, 9:136, 2008.

11. K. Lage, E. O. Karlberg, Z. M. Storling, P. I. Olason, A. G. Pedersen, et al. A human phenome–interactome network of protein complexes implicated in genetic disorders. *Nat. Biotechnol*, 25(3):309–316, 2007.

12. A. P. Gabow, S. M. Leach, W. A. Baumgartner, L. E. Hunter, and D. S. Goldberg. Improving protein function prediction methods with integrated literature data. *BMC Bioinform.*, 9:198, 2008.

13. C. Plake, T. Schiemann, M. Pankalla, J. Hakenberg, and U. Leser. Ali Baba: PubMed as a graph. *Bioinformatics,* 22(19):2444–2445, 2006.

14. D-C. Lie, S. A. Colamarino, H-J. Song, L. Dèsirè, H. Mira, A. Consiglio, E. S. Lein, S. Jessberger, H. Lansford, A. R. Dearie, and F. H. Gage. Wnt signalling regulates adult hippocampal neurogenesis. *Nature,* 437(7063):1370–1375, 2005.

15. T. Brants. TnT—A Statistical Part-of-Speech Tagger. In *Proceedings of the Applied Natural Language Processing Conference (ANLP)*, Seattle, WA, 2000.

16. A. S. Schwartz and M. A. Hearst. A simple algorithm for identifying abbreviation definitions in biomedical text. In *Proceedings of the Pacifio Symposium on Bioinformatics*, Hawaii, 2003.

17. Medical Subject Headings (MeSH). http://www.nlm.nih.gov/mesh/

18. NCBI Entrez Taxonomy. http://www.ncbi.nlm.nih.gov/sites/entrez?db=taxonomy

19. H. Kirsch, S. Gaudan, and D. Rebholz-Schuhmann. Distributed modules for text annotation and IE applied to the biomedical domain. *Int. J. Med. Info.*, 75:496–500, 2005.

20. N. Ide and J. Veronis. Word sense disambiguation: The state of the art. *Comput. Linguist.*, 24(1):1–40, 1998.

21. E. Agirre and P. Edmonds. *Word Sense Disambiguation—Algorithms and Applications*. Springer, Berlin, 2006.

22. W. A. Gale, K. W. Church, and D. Yarowsky. One sense per discourse. In *Proceedings of the HLTC*, Harriman, New York, 1992, pp. 233–237.

23. N. Hulo, A. Bairoch, V. Bulliard, L. Cerutti, B.A. Cuche, et al. The 20 years of PROSITE. *Nucl. Acids Res.*, 36(Database issue):D245–D249, 2008.

24. J. Hakenberg, M. Schroeder, and U. Leser. Consensus pattern alignment to find protein–protein interactions in text. In *Proceedings of the 2nd BioCreative Challenge Evaluation Workshop*, Madrid, Spain, 2007, pp. 213–215.

25. J. Hakenberg, C. Plake, L. Royer, H. Strobelt, U. Leser, and M. Schroeder. Gene mention normalization and interaction extraction with context models and sentence motifs. *Genome Biol.*, 9(Suppl 2):S14, 2008.

26. C. Plake, J. Hakenberg, and U. Leser. Optimizing syntax patterns for discovering protein–protein interactions. In *Proceedings of the ACM SAC, Bioinformatics Track*, Vol. 1, Santa Fe, NM, 2005, pp. 195–201.

27. BioCreative—Critical Assessment for Information Extraction in Biology. http://biocreative.sourceforge.net/

28. L. Smith, L. K. Tanabe, R. J. nee Ando, C-Ju Kuo, I-Fang Chung, et al. Overview of BioCreative II gene mention recognition. *Genome Biol.*, 9(Suppl 9):S2, 2008.

29. C-Nan Hsu, Y-Ming Chang, C-Ju Kuo, Y-Shi Lin, H-Shen Huang, and I-Fang Chung. Integrating high dimensional bi-directional parsing models for gene mention tagging. *Bioinformatics*, 24(13):i286–i294, 2008.

30. R. K. Ando. BioCreative II gene mention tagging system at IBM Watson. In *Proceedings of the 2nd BioCreative Challenge Evaluation Workshop*, Madrid, Spain, 2007, pp. 101–103.

31. R. Leaman and G. Gonzalez. BANNER: An executable survey of advances in biomedical named entity recognition. In *Proceedings of the Pacific Symposium on Bioinformatics*, Hawaii, 2008, pp. 652–663.

32. J. Hakenberg, C. Plake, R. Leaman, M. Schroeder, and G. Gonzalez. Interspecies normalization of gene mentions with GNAT. *Bioinformatics*, 24(16):i126–i132, 2008.

33. M. Krallinger, F. Leitner, C. Rodriguez-Penagos, and A. Valencia. Overview of the protein–protein interaction annotation extraction task of BioCreative II. *Genome Biol.*, 9(Suppl 2):S4, 2008.

34. M. Huang, S. Din, H. Wang, and X. Zhu. Mining physical protein–protein interactions by exploiting abundant features. In *Proceedings of the 2nd BioCreative Challenge Evaluation Workshop*, Madrid, Spain, 2007, pp. 237–245.

35. J. R. Herskovic, L. Y. Tanaka, W. Hersh, and E. V. Bernstam. A day in the life of PubMed: Analysis of a typical day's query log. *J. Am. Med. Inform. Assoc.*, 14(2):212–220, 2007.

36. NCBI Entrez Programming Utilities. `http://eutils.ncbi.nlm.nih.gov/entrez/query/static/eutils_help.html`.

37. A. Doms and M. Schroeder. GoPubMed: Exploring PubMed with the Gene Ontology. *Nucl. Acid Res.*, 33(Web Server issue):W783–W786, 2005.

38. A. D. Eaton. HubMed: a web-based biomedical literature search interface. *Nucl. Acids Res.*, 34(Web Server issue):W745–W747, 2006.

39. D. Rebholz-Schuhmann, M. Arregui, S. Gaudan, H. Kirsch, and A. Jimeno. Text processing through Web services: Calling Whatizit. *Bioinformatics,* 24(2):296–298, 2008.

40. U. Mudunuri, R. Stephens, D. Bruining, D. Liu, and F. J. Lebeda. botXminer: Mining biomedical literature with a new web-based application. *Nucl. Acids Res.*, 34(Web Server issue):W748–W752, 2006.

41. KMedDB. `http://sysbio.molgen.mpg.de/KMedDB/`

42. D. Rebholz-Schuhmann, H. Kirsch, M. Arregui, S. Gaudan, M. Riethoven, and P. Stoehr. EBIMed–text crunching to gather facts for proteins from Medline. *Bioinformatics,* 23(2):e237–e244, 2007.

43. R. Hoffmann and A. Valencia. A gene network for navigating the literature. *Nat. Genet.*, 36(7):664, 2004.

44. R. Hoffmann and A. Valencia. Implementing the iHOP concept for navigation of biomedical literature. *Bioinformatics*, 21:ii252–ii258, 2005.

45. H. Chen and B. M. Sharp. Content-rich biological network constructed by mining PubMed abstracts. *BMC Bioinform.*, 5:147, 2004.

46. Info-PubMed. `http://www-tsujii.is.s.u-tokyo.ac.jp/info-pubmed/`

47. CASP—Critical Assessment of Techniques for Protein Structure Prediction. `http://predictioncenter.org/`

48. CAPRI—Critical Assessment of PRedicted Interactions. `http://www.ebi.ac.uk/msd-srv/capri/`

49. F. Leitner, M. Krallinger, C. Rodriguez-Penagos, J. Hakenberg, C. Plake, et al. Introducing meta-services for biomedical information extraction. *Genome Biol.*, 9(Suppl 2):S6, 2008. `http://bcms.bioinfo.cnio.es/`

50. K. Fundel, R. Küffner, and R. Zimmer. RelEx—relation extraction using dependency parse trees. *Bioinformatics*, 23(3):365–371, 2007.

51. I. Donaldson, J. Martin, B. de Bruijn, C. Wolting, V. Lay, et al. PreBIND and Textomy-mining the biomedical literature for protein–protein interactions using a support vector machine. *BMC Bioinform.*, 4:11, 2003.

52. PolySearch. http://wishart.biology.ualberta.ca/polysearch/

53. A. A. Morgan, Z. Lu, X. Wang, A. A. Cohen, J. Fluck, et al. Overview of BioCreative II gene normalization. *Genome Biol.*, 9(Suppl 2):S3, 2008

16

VALIDATION ISSUES IN REGULATORY MODULE DISCOVERY

Alok Mishra and Duncan Gillies

Department of Computing, Imperial College London, London, UK

16.1 INTRODUCTION

Over the last decade, many new techniques have emerged for measuring the functional activity of genes. These include measurements of individual genes through their transcriptional activity, the interaction of their products, or by *in vitro* experiments with synthesized DNA. For each measurement technique a different set of data is created, each containing information on the functioning of genes, but under differing conditions and with different degrees of experimental error. At the same time, summary information of accepted gene behavior is being collected in the form of the gene ontology database and annotation terms for individual genes. These resources represent accumulated knowledge rather than individual experimental data. Current research is being undertaken to investigate ways in which these rich but diverse sources of information about gene behavior can be combined to provide a more accurate interpretation of experimental work. The goals are two-fold. Firstly, fusing data from diverse sources can be used to stabilize the results from individual experiments. For example, microarray experiments have been generally found to produce data of high variance, and therefore require some form of regularization before results can be interpreted. Secondly, when the data are processed to infer some

Elements of Computational Systems Biology   Edited by Huma M. Lodhi and Stephen H. Muggleton
Copyright © 2010 John Wiley & Sons, Inc.

higher organization among genes, it is essential to have some form of validation of the results.

Work in molecular biology has focused both on identifying the function of individual genes and the way in which they interact in regulation processes. In nature, complex functions of living cells are carried out through the concerted activities of many genes and gene products that are organized into coregulated sets also known as regulatory modules [1]. Understanding the organization of these sets of genes will provide insights into the cellular response mechanism under various conditions. Recently, a considerable volume of data on gene activity, measured using several diverse techniques, has become widely available. By fusing these data using an integrative approach, it may be possible to unravel the regulation process at a more global level. Although an integrated model could never be as precise as one built from a small number of genes in controlled conditions, such global modeling can provide insights into higher processes in which many genes are working together to achieve a task. Various techniques from statistics, machine learning, and computer science have been employed by researchers for the analysis and combination of the different types of data in an attempt to understand the function of regulatory modules.

There are two underlying problems resulting from the nature of the available data. Firstly, each of the different data types (microarrays, DNA-binding, protein–protein interaction, and sequence data) provides a partial and noisy picture of the whole process. They need to be integrated in order to obtain an improved and reliable picture. Secondly, the amount of data that is available from each of these techniques is severely limited. To learn good models, we need considerable amounts of data. Unfortunately, data are only available for a few experiments of each type. These two problems are often cited as a reason for taking an integrative approach. However, integration will filter and obscure some of the information in the actual experimental results, and thus proper validation methods are required to test the effectiveness of any approach.

16.2 DATA TYPES

Various types of data are used to identify regulatory mechanisms. These are primarily generated by molecular biologists using experimental techniques. In most cases, a considerable amount of data processing must be applied before the results can be interpreted.

One of the most important sources of data is genome-wide measurement of mRNA expression levels carried out using microarrays. These have received considerable attention in the last 6 years and various technologies for microarray measurement have been developed [2]. Microarrays allow simultaneous measurement of the expression levels of a large number of genes. Similar expression profiles identify genes that may be controlled by a shared regulatory mechanism. An important point to note is that coregulation does not necessarily imply only positive correlation of expression values, as some of the genes might be downregulated, while others may be upregulated [3]. Processing microarray data to make different experiments as far as possible comparable is known as normalization. A good overview of techniques for normalization and analysis is provided by Quackenbush [4] and a detailled discussion of the statistical issues involved is given by Smyth [5].

Spellman was one of the microarray pioneers who studied the global expression of genes [6]. He studied both the expression variation at various time points in the yeast cell cycle, and, along with other researchers [7], the response of the yeast genes when subjected to various kinds of stress.

A second major source of data is transcription factor–DNA binding data, which is generated as a result of the chromatin immunoprecipitation (ChIP) technique, also popularly known as the ChIP–chip assay. The technique is used to determine whether proteins, including transcription factors, will bind to particular regions of the chromatin within living cells. Harbison et al. determined the global genomic occupancy of 203 transcription factors in yeast, which are all known to bind to DNA in the yeast genome [8]. Lee et al. produced a similar yeast dataset for a smaller number of transcription factors [9]. Both these researchers reported results in the form of a confidence value (statistical P value) of a transcription factor attaching to the promoter region of a gene. The reason behind using statistical techniques was to reduce the experimental errors inherent in microarray technology and to account for multiple cell populations. One of the prominent problems with such approaches is that in order to infer whether a transcription factor is attached to the promoter sequence or not, we have to choose an arbitrary artificial threshold of the P-value.

Transcription factor binding motifs are sequence patterns observed in the intergenic regions of the genome usually located upstream of the genes. They are thought to be responsible for allowing access of transcription factors to binding sites. Initial approaches to identifying these were based on first clustering genes by coexpression and then looking for common sequences in the upstream regions of the genes located in the same cluster. Kellis et al. used comparative genome analysis between three related yeast species to find these motifs [10].

Protein–protein interaction (PPI) data for human and other organisms are available as a result of advances in technologies like mass spectroscopy and yeast two-hybrid assays. There has been a tremendous growth in this type of data in the recent years.

16.3 DATA INTEGRATION

There has been a considerable volume of recent research into data integration in genetics. The methods are often specific to the formalisms used to infer dependency structures from data. Causal networks, for example, Bayesian nets, have been a popular approach to identify the gene regulatory process [11–14]. However, when applied to experimental data alone, the results were poor due to the fact that the data were, and still are, very sparse compared to the large number of variables (genes) that need to be modeled. This is typical of small sample size problems in general. Moreover, there is cyclical feedback operating in gene networks and inference networks generally only handle acyclic relationships among the variables. They need an explicit model of time to be able to deal with feedback. The overall performance of these models was not good and not many verifiable findings were made [12]. In order to improve upon the results, work was done to incorporate better prior knowledge in the Bayesian network-based modeling. Imoto et al. combined PPI, DNA binding, promoter element motifs as well as literature text mining [15]. Tanay et al. also used similar diverse datasets to build Bayesian network models [16, 17].

A more promising pragmatic approach, which we call weakly supervized module identification, did yield very good results and is still used in current research [1, 18]. The method takes a list of potential regulators and the microarray expression data as input. An initial clustering of the genes is carried out, which is then refined using an iterative procedure, based on the expectation maximization (EM) algorithm. For each cluster of genes, it searches for a regulation program that provides the best prediction of the expression profiles of genes in the module as a function of the expression of a small number of genes from the regulator set. After identifying regulation programs for all clusters, the algorithm re-assigns each gene to the cluster whose program best predicts its behavior. It iterates till convergence, refining both the regulation program and the gene partition in each iteration. To test the method, they integrated a set of regulators from the Saccharomyces Genome Database (SGD) and the Yeast Proteome Database (YPD). They obtained modules that showed significant similarity in promoter element motifs as well as in the database compiled by the Gene Ontology Consortium (2001). Despite its success, one of the biggest shortcomings of this research was that the biological prior knowledge that was incorporated was almost of an insignificant level. Only the names of transcription factors were employed by Segal. At about this time, more significant prior knowledge started becoming available in the form of ChIP–chip DNA binding data and other sources as described in an earlier section. The next step of research focused on ways of integrating these datasets in order to find gene modules.

The algorithm called Signature [19] takes a similar approach, clustering genes and conditions together using expression data. The input to the algorithm is a set of genes and, in the first step, the experimental conditions under which these genes change their expression above a threshold are chosen. In the second stage, all genes that have changed expression significantly under these conditions are selected. The consistency of the clustering result is evaluated by analyzing the recurrence of the output gene sets in their resulting modules when the input is mixed with irrelevant genes. The idea is that the results of any good algorithm should not deviate too much when slight perturbations are introduced in the data. A module is considered to be reliable if it is obtained from several distinct slightly perturbed input gene sets. Since the clusters are refined in two stages, there can be no guarantee that the results are clustered in an optimal manner. A better formulation might be to use the EM algorithm in order to maximize the objective function.

The Genetic Regulatory Modules (GRAM) algorithm uses a more strongly supervized method for discovering regulatory modules. It combines microarray expression data with DNA-binding data. DNA-binding data provide direct physical evidence of regulation and thus offer an improvement on previous work in which only indirect evidence of interaction was used for prior information [20]. Similar work was carried out by Lemmens et al. [21]. In this work, a very simple and intuitive algorithm was used to find coregulated sets of genes that have similar expression profiles, the same binding transcription factors, and a commonality of motifs. The principal difference from earlier algorithms is that where others used motif information to validate their results, Lemmens et al. used it in order to find the modules itself. All parameters, such as the cutoff for various datasets, have been chosen without much justification, and the basic idea seems very similar to the work in GRAM. Some of the comparison metrics used do not seem very sound, for example, average functional enrichment values have been calculated for the modules without normalizing to account for the size of the modules. Similarly, summary statistics like the minimum and maximum number of genes in the modules do not provide relevant information for comparing the algorithms.

Tanay et al. analyzed several diverse datasets in an attempt to reveal the modular organization of the yeast regulation system. They defined modules as groups of genes with statistically significant correlated behavior across the diverse datasets. Their algorithm is called Statistical-Algorithmic Method for Bicluster Analysis (SAMBA) and is an extensible framework that can be easily updated as new datasets become available. In their analysis, they have integrated expression, PPI, and DNA-binding datasets. The positive aspect of their approach is that it utilizes all sources of information in one uniform representation and only requires a measure of similarity of genes across a subset of properties. It also allows overlapping modules (with common genes), which is not a feature of traditional clustering algorithms. One of the limitations of their approach is that all sources of data are assigned equal weights and it is not possible to weigh them separately according to reliability or importance [16]. More recently, they analyzed more diverse datasets and focused more on the biological significance of the results, explaining them much more fully. They proposed that work should be carried out on integration across species on the basis that transcription modules are highly conserved among species.

Huang and Pan investigated clustering solutions using a K-medoids algorithm [22]. They incorporated prior knowledge by modifying the distance metric used while clustering. They clustered microarray expression data while deriving biological knowledge about the known similarity between pairs of genes from gene ontology. The authors used a shrinkage approach for the distance metric to shrink it toward zero in cases where there is strong evidence that two genes are functionally related. In a later piece of work, Pan used known functions of genes from existing biological research to assign different prior probabilities for a gene to belong to a cluster [23]. He developed an expectation maximization algorithm for this stratified mixture model.

Troyanskaya et al. developed a generic meta framework, known as Multisource Association of Genes by Integration of Clusters (MAGIC), for integration of diverse sources of data. It is called "meta" because it does not directly integrate the datasets but uses results from other techniques like clustering and combines them with other evidence [24]. Their proposed framework is based on a Bayesian network whose conditional probability tables have been built with the advice of yeast genetic experts. Given a pair of genes, it outputs the probability that they are functionally related after weighing the evidences from various sources. Evaluation of the predictions from the system was done using gene ontology data.

Most of the techniques that we have described work well for real (numerical) data but are less effective when dealing with string data, for example, gene sequences, or graph data such as protein interactions. In many cases, ad-hoc techniques have been deployed. In an approach to this problem, Lanckriet et al. proposed a framework where such diverse data could be merged in a principled manner [25]. It is based on kernel methods in which algorithms work on kernel matrices that are derived from pairwise similarity among variables using so-called kernel functions [26]. If a valid kernel function can be defined to encode the similarity between two variables, then the methods are applicable regardless of the different types of data—strings, vectorial or graphical—being used. This framework will provide a means to integrate more diverse types of data when they become available in the future. The original paper proposed the framework only for supervized learning, but extensions to unsupervised learning are possible.

16.4   VALIDATION APPROACHES

In essence, discovery of regulatory mechanisms comes down to clustering genes that show similar behavior in some context, for example, co-expression in a microarray experiment. The validation problem is to determine how good the resulting clusters are. As yet, no generally accepted method has emerged to address it. Approaches may be divided into those that are purely statistical (internal validation) and those that take into account some measure of biological significance of the clusters (external validation). The term *external* meaning that further information, not involved in the clustering process, is used for the validation. In contrast, *internal* validation uses only the data from which the clusters are derived. Those in the latter class are drawn from traditional statistical methods [27], and more recent approaches stem from studies into data mining [28].

16.4.1   Internal Validation Methods

Traditional internal methods use three criteria to validate a set of clusters: compactness, separation, and connectedness. The first two criteria have their roots in well-known statistical pattern classification work. Generally, the input data are used to create an affinity (or similarity) matrix from the measurements. Genes that are strongly correlated in the measurement space have high similarity values in the affinity matrix. Spectral clustering is then used to partition the affinity matrix. The matrix can be re-ordered so that clustered items are located together in submatrices about the diagonal. Ideally, gene pairs in each individual cluster will have high similarity values and the compactness can be measured by finding the average similarity in the submatrix corresponding to each cluster. Separation can be estimated from the affinity matrix elements outside the class submatrices. These elements represent the degree of similarity of genes belonging to different classes and should ideally be zero. These two measures validate the clusters in a manner analogous to the way in which Fisher's linear discriminant analysis finds the space where a set of classes have the smallest within-class variance (compactness) and maximal between-class variance (separation). Connectedness is a different concept that looks at the overlapping between classes. The most connected classes are those with a Gaussian distribution. Those with multimodal distributions have poorer connectedness. We can assess this by testing the nearest neighbors to a class centroid to see what proportion belong to that class. The use of these individual measures and the methods for combining them are rather heuristic in nature, and the results will be dependent on the data used.

Another important class of statistical methods that can be used to validate a clustering solution is resampling. Following this approach, bootstrap datasets are drawn from the original data by sampling with replacement. Each bootstrap set is then clustered and the resulting set of clusters is examined for consistency. Consistent clustering between the different bootstrap datasets is taken to be an indication that the clustering solution is good.

Comparision of different clustering solutions can be done using a well-established measure of cluster similarity, namely the adjusted Rand Index. Milligan and Cooper [29] carried out an extensive empirical study on several such measures and found this index effective even when comparing partitions with different numbers of clusters. The Rand index works by pairwise matching on each of the clusters that are being compared. Given two clusterings C_1 and C_2 of the same dataset, we define:

- N_{11}: the number of pairs of objects in the same cluster in both C_1 and C_2.
- N_{00}: the number of pairs of objects in different clusters in both C_1 and C_2.
- N_{01}: the number of pairs of objects in different clusters in C_1 but same cluster in C_2.
- N_{10}: the number of pairs of objects in the same cluster in C_1 but different clusters in C_2.

The Rand index is simply the fraction of items in agreement to the total

$$\frac{N_{11} + N_{00}}{N_{11} + N_{00} + N_{01} + N_{10}}. \tag{16.1}$$

When the two partitions are identical, the Rand Index is 1, whereas it reaches 0 when they have nothing in common. Unfortunately, the expected value of the Rand index for two random partitions is not zero. The adjusted Rand index corrects for this, in effect normalizing the range [30]. It takes the form

$$\frac{\text{index} - \text{randomexpectation}}{\text{maximumindex} - \text{randomexpectation}}. \tag{16.2}$$

Its maximum is bounded at 1, but it returns zero for random clusters.

Some evaluation of other statisticals methods for validating clusters in gene expression data has been carried out by Yang et al. [31].

16.4.2 Measures of Biological Significance

External measures of the quality of a clustering solution are made by using other knowledge about the functioning of the genes in a cluster. To this end, genes can tagged with labels, referred to as annotations, attributes, or terms, that give an indication of their known functions. Early attempts to create curated databases describing gene function were inconsistent in their use of terms. However, the Gene Ontology Consortium was recently formed to provide a unified description vocabulary that is generally accepted and continuously evolving [32]. An important publicly available source of genetic knowledge is the The Gene Ontology (GO) database, which provides a set of standard terms that can be used to annotate individual genes. The terms are divided into three groups corresponding to cellular components, biological processes, and molecular functions. Generally, the terms describe functionality without reference to specific conditions in which those functions are carried out. Examples of molecular function are catalytic activity, transporter activity, and binding. Genes are annotated with terms on the basis of accepted experimental evidence that may originate from many sources. The sources are also recorded, since some provide better evidence of the annotation than others. The ontology is created by a set of relations between terms. This forms a semantic network in which each node is a term and the directed arcs are the relations. The relations are *is_a* and *part_of*. For example, a nuclear chromosome *is_a* chromosome and a nucleus is *part_of* a cell, since there are other parts of a cell and not all cells have nuclei. These relations impose a partial ordering on the terms, with those at higher levels expressing more generality. A term may have multiple parents, and a constraint is that all parents of a term must be applicable to any gene annotated by that term. The descriptive power of the GO database makes it attractive for research into gene function in cell regulation. It encapsulates the *prior knowledge* of gene function that should be used when making any inference from new experimental data.

Applying the knowledge encapsulated in the GO database to cluster validation is not straightforward and is currently an active area of research. There are many terms, and in a given set of experimental data, each term may be more or less significant as a cluster discriminant. One approach to deciding the significance of a particular annotation within a cluster is to ask whether there are more genes annotated to that term than would be expected in a random cluster. For this purpose, the hypergeometric distribution has been investigated by several researchers [33–35]. The hypergeometric distribution is calculated for a particular term using

$$p = \frac{\binom{M}{x} \times \binom{N-M}{n-x}}{\binom{N}{n}}, \tag{16.3}$$

where p is the probability that if n genes are selected at random from the background set then x of them will be annotated by the term in question. N and M describe the background set of genes, N is the number and M the number annotated with the term in question. The background set of genes will in general represent all the genes involved in the experiment. Terms with high p values are less effective at discriminating classes than those with low p values.

Given a clustering solution where the genes are labeled by the GO terms that form significant discriminants for that experiment, the question of assessing the quality of that clustering solution can be looked on as a multivariate problem. Each annotation term used in the total that has been clustered can be considered a variable and each gene in a cluster will contain a binary value for that term (annotated or not), which can be organized as a binary attribute vector. Cluster quality methods based on the attribute vector have been investigated [36]. A promising approach uses information theory [37]. This method is based on calculating the mutual information between the clusters and the attributes. For each term, the number of genes annotated by that term in the cluster is counted. This forms a matrix between the clusters and the terms which can be normalized into a joint probability distribution. Calculating the Kullback–Leibler divergence of this distribution returns the mutual information between the clusters and the terms attributed to their genes. A high value of this entropy indicates a high degree of biological significance in the cluster. A low value indicates that the terms are distributed evenly among the clusters and thus the clusters do not have much biological significance. A popular quality measure is the z-score, which is computed by comparing the mutual entropy of a given partition to the expectation for random partitions.

An approach, known as Renisk's similarity, combines both statistical and topological information, and has been extensively studied [38]. In GO, the information shared by two terms is computed from the set of common ancestors. In general, the higher up in the ontology a term is, the lower the information associated with it. The objective is, therefore, to find the lowest common ancestral term and use its information content as the similarity measure. The information is equated to the negative log of the probability that a gene is annotated to that term or its descendents.

One important question to be resolved in using the GO to validate a clustering solution is the level of detail at which any of the above tests are applied. To increase the generality, terms can be replaced by their ancestors at a given level of the ontology. The higher the level to which the terms are projected, the smaller the total number of terms in any validation problem. This integrative process could offer significant advantages in reducing noise and stabilizing the results, but requires further study into how the optimal level could be found.

Some recent studies have looked into the question of combining statistical and biological validation methods [39]. A comparison of statistical and ontology-based approaches to validation was carried out by Bolshakova et al. [40], and a method for resolving differences in the results of differing validation methods has been investigated by Pihur et al. [41].

16.5 CONCLUSIONS

In modern molecular biology, there is increasingly a chain of processing steps that must be undergone before any experimental results can be interpreted. At the lowest level, microarray experiments require normalization, and at higher levels of abstraction, data fusion and integration is required to stabilize experimental results. This processing separates the scientist from the data and may introduce errors and artefacts. There is, therefore, a need for proper validation of any high-level functionality interpreted from experimental data.

GO is emerging as a powerful resource for recording accepted knowledge about gene functions in a way that allows automatic statistical testing and analysis. Validation methods have been proposed and have met with some success; however, the field is still in its infancy. The information richness of the emerging GO offers the potential for development of powerful new validation methods.

REFERENCES

1. E. Segal, M. Shapira, A. Regev, D. Pe'er, D. Botstein, D. Koller, and N. Friedman. Module networks: identifying regulatory modules and their condition-specific regulators from gene expression data. *Nat. Genet.*, 34(2):166–176, 2003.

2. A. Schulze and J. Downward. Navigating gene expression using microarrays–a technology review. *Nat. Cell. Biol.*, 3(8), 2001.

3. M. Elati, P. Neuvial, M. Bolotin-Fukuhara, E. Barillot, F. Radvanyi, and C. Rouveirol. Licorn: learning co-operative regulation networks from gene expression data. *Bioinformatics*, 23(18):2407–2414, 2007.

4. J. Quackenbush. Microarray data normalization and transformation. *Nat Genet*, 32(Suppl):496–501, 2002.

5. G. K. Smyth, Y.H. Yang, and T. P. Speed. Statistical issues in cDNA microarray data analysis. *Methods Mol. Biol.*, 224:111–136, 2003.

6. P. T. Spellman, G. Sherlock, M. Q. Zhang, V. R. Iyer, K. Anders, M. B. Eisen, P. O. Brown, D. Botstein, and B. Futcher. Comprehensive identification of cell cycle-regulated genes of the yeast *Saccharomyces cerevisiae* by microarray hybridization. *Mol. Biol. Cell.*, 9(12):3273–3297, 1998.

7. A. P. Gasch, P. T. Spellman, C. M. Kao, O. Carmel-Harel, M. B. Eisen, G. Storz, D. Botstein, and P. O. Brown. Genomic expression programs in the response of yeast cells to environmental changes. *Mol. Biol. Cell.*, 11(12):4241–4257, 2000.

8. T. H. Christopher, D. G. Benjamin, I. L.Tong, J. R. Nicola, D. M. Kenzie, W. D.Timothy, M. H. Nancy, T. Jean-Bosco , B. R. David, Y. Jane , et al. Transcriptional regulatory code of a eukaryotic genome. *Nature*, 431(7004):99–104, 2004.

9. T. I. Lee, N. J. Rinaldi, F. Robert, D. T. Odom, Z. Bar-Joseph, G. K. Gerber, N. M. Hannett, C. T. Harbison, C. M. Thompson, I. Simon, J. Zeitlinger, E. G. Jennings, H. L. Murray, D. B. Gordon, B. Ren, J. J. Wyrick, J. B. Tagne, T. L. Volkert, E. Fraenkel, D. K. Gifford, and R. A. Young. Transcriptional regulatory networks in saccharomyces cerevisiae. *Science*, 298(5594):799–804, 2002.

10. M. Kellis, N. Patterson, M. Endrizzi, B. Birren, and E. S. Lander. Sequencing and comparison of yeast species to identify genes and regulatory elements. *Nature*, 423(6937):241–254, 2003.

11. N. Friedman. Inferring cellular networks using probabilistic graphical models. *Science*, 303(5659):799–805, 2004.

12. D. Husmeier. Sensitivity and specificity of inferring genetic regulatory interactions from microarray experiments with dynamic Bayesian networks. *Bioinformatics*, 19(17):2271–2282, 2003.

13. K. Murphy and S. Mian. Modelling gene expression data using dynamic Bayesian networks. Technical report, Computer Science Division, University of California, Berkeley, CA., 1999. citeseer.ist.psu.edu/murphy99modelling.html.

14. M. Zou and S. D. Conzen. A new dynamic Bayesian network (DBN) approach for identifying gene regulatory networks from time course microarray data. *Bioinformatics*, 21(1): 71–79, 2005.

15. S. Imoto, T. Higuchi, T. Goto, K. Tashiro, S. Kuhara, and S. Miyano. Combining microarrays and biological knowledge for estimating gene networks via Bayesian networks. In *Proceedings of the 2nd Computational Systems Bioinformatics*, IEEE Computer Society, 2003, pp. 104–113.

16. A. Tanay, R. Sharan, M. Kupiec, and R. Shamir. Revealing modularity and organization in the yeast molecular network by integrated analysis of highly heterogeneous genomewide data. *Proc. Natl. Acad. Sci. USA*, 101(9):2981–2986, 2004.

17. A. Tanay, I. Steinfeld, M. Kupiec, and R. Shamir. Integrative analysis of genome-wide experiments in the context of a large high-throughput data compendium. *Mol. Syst. Biol.*, 1(1):msb4100005–E1–msb4100005–E10, 2005.

18. E. Segal, D. Pe'er, A. Regev, D. Koller, and N. Friedman. Learning module networks. *J. Machine Learn. Res.*, 6(Apr):557–588, 2005.

19. J. Ihmels, G. Friedlander, S. Bergmann, O. Sarig, Y. Ziv, and N. Barkai. Revealing modular organization in the yeast transcriptional network. *Nat. Genet.*, 31:370–377, 2002.

20. Z. Bar-Joseph, G. K Gerber, T. Ihn Lee, N. J Rinaldi, J. Y Yoo, F. Robert, D. B. Gordon, E. Fraenkel, T. S Jaakkola, R. A Young, and D. K Gifford. Computational discovery of gene modules and regulatory networks. *Nat. Biotechnol.*, 21(11):1337–1342, 2003.

21. K. Lemmens, T. Dhollander, T. De Bie, P. Monsieurs, K. Engelen, B. Smets, J. Winderickx, B. De Moor, and K. Marchal. Inferring transcriptional modules from chip-chip, motif and microarray data. *Genome Biol.*, 7(5), 2006.

22. D. Huang and W. Pan. Incorporating biological knowledge into distance-based clustering analysis of microarray gene expression data. *Bioinformatics*, 22(10):1259–1268, 2006.

23. W. Pan. Incorporating gene functions as priors in model-based clustering of microarray gene expression data. *Bioinformatics*, 22(7):795–801, 2006.

24. O. G. Troyanskaya, K. Dolinski, A. B. Owen, R. B. Altman, and D. Botstein. A Bayesian framework for combining heterogeneous data sources for gene function prediction (in *Saccharomyces cerevisiae*). *Proc. Natl. Acad. Sci. USA*, 100(14):8348–8353, 2003.

25. G. R. Lanckriet, M. Deng, N. Cristianini, M. I. Jordan, and W. S., Noble. Kernel-based data fusion and its application to protein function prediction in yeast. In *Proceedings of the Pacific Symposium on Biocomputing*, January 2004, pp. 300–311. http://psb.stanford.edu/psb-online/proceedings/psb04/.

26. J. Shawe-Taylor and N. Cristianini. *Kernel Methods for Pattern Analysis*. Cambridge University Press, 2004.

27. J. Handl, J. Knowles, and D. Kell. Computational cluster validation in post-genomic data analysis. *Bioinformatics*, 21(15):3201–3212, 2005.

28. J. Dopazo. Microarray data processing and analysis. *Methods Microarray Data Anal. II*, 43–63, 2002.

29. G. W. Milligan and M. C. Cooper. An examination of procedures for determining the number of clusters in a data set. *Psychometrika*, 50:159–179, 1985.

30. K. Y. Yeung and W. L. Ruzzo. Details of the adjusted rand index and clustering algorithms. supplement to the paper âĽžan experimental study on principal component analysis for clustering gene expression data. *Bioinformatics*, 17(17):763–774, 2001.

31. C. Yang, B. Wan, and X. Gao. Effectivity of internal validation techniques for gene clustering. In *ISBMDA*, 2006, pp. 49–59.

32. GeneOntologyConsortium. Gene ontology. *Nat. Genet.*, pp. 25–29, 2000.

33. R. Gentleman. Using go for statistical analysis. *Proceedings of COMPSTAT.* 2004, pp. 171–180.

34. E. Boyle, S. Weng, J. Gollub, H. Jin, D. Botstein, and J. Cherry. Go::termfinder-opensource software for accessing gene ontology information and finding significantly enriched gene ontology terms associated with a list of genes. *Bioinformatics*, 20(18):3710–3715, 2004.

35. S. Falcon and R. Gentleman. Using gostats to test gene lists for go term association. *Bioinformatics*, 23(2):257–258, 2007.

36. I. Gat-Viks, R. Sharan, and R. Shamir. Scoring clustering solutions by their biological relevance. *Bioinformatics*, 19(18):2381–2389, 2003.

37. F. Gibbons and F. Roth. Judging the quality of gene expression-based clustering methods using gene annotation. *Genome Res.*, 12(10):1574–1581, 2002.

38. H. Wang, F. Azuaje, O. Bodenreiderm, and J. Dopazo. Gene expression correlation and gene ontology-based similarity: an assessment of quantitative relationships. In *Proceedings of the 2004 IEEE Symposium on Computational Intelligence in Bioinformatics and Computational Biology*, 2004, pp. 25–31.

39. S. Datta and S. Datta. Validation measures for clustering algorithms incorporating biological information. In *IMSCCS (1)*, 2006, pp. 131–135.

40. N. Bolshakova, A. Zamolotskikh, and P. Cunningham. Comparison of the data-based and gene ontology-based approaches to cluster validation methods for gene microarrays. In *CBMS '06: Proceedings of the 19th IEEE Symposium on Computer-Based Medical Systems*, IEEE Computer Society. Washington, DC, USA, 2006, pp. 539–543.

41. V. Pihur, S. Datta, and S. Datta. Weighted rank aggregation of cluster validation measures: a Monte Carlo cross-entropy approach. *Bioinformatics*, 23(13):1607–1615, 2007.

17

COMPUTATIONAL IMAGING AND MODELING FOR SYSTEMS BIOLOGY

Ling-Yun Wu, Xiaobo Zhou, and Stephen T.C. Wong

The Center for Biotechnology and Informatics, The Methodist Hospital Research Institute and Department of Radiology, The Methodist Hospital Weill Cornell Medical College, Houston, Texas, USA

Conventional biological studies focus on one gene or one protein at a time. Life, however, is a complex system that is not subject such a reductionalist approach. In today's postgenomic era, biologists believe that many genes and proteins interact in various fashions and that the deciphering and modeling of interaction among them would help better reveal and understand the mechanisms of living systems [1]. The emerging field of systems biology attempts to investigate such complex biological interaction from a systems viewpoint instead of individual molecules or components. New computational techniques are much needed for this new scientific endeavor, and, in particular, imaging plays an important role of providing objective, repeatable, quantitative phenotyping measures for complementing and correlating with large-scale genotyping studies. In this chapter, we will discuss the computational imaging and modeling techniques used in systems biology studies.

Computational techniques in systems biology can be roughly categorized into two broad classes: bioinformatics and bioimage informatics. Bioinformatics in systems biology mainly focuses on the biomarker discovery, including high-throughput molecular data analysis, molecular networks reconstruction from high-throughput data,

Elements of Computational Systems Biology Edited by Huma M. Lodhi and Stephen H. Muggleton
Copyright © 2010 John Wiley & Sons, Inc.

molecular networks analysis, and so on. Bioimage informatics, on the other hand, address issues of image phenotyping, secondary screening, target validation, drug lead selection, and so on. The two classes of techniques are not necessarily orthological and are often integrated in solving complex problems. For example, Figure 17.1 exemplifies a systems biologic oriented workflow for biomarker discovery and validation, involving both bioinformatics (left) and bioimage informatics (right). The biomarker can be identified directly from the high-throughput data, such as gene microarray and mass spectrometry, as well as from the integrated molecular networks, such as gene regulatory networks, protein–protein interaction networks, and metabolic signaling networks. The molecular networks can be reconstructed from the high-throughput biological data by computational modeling means and integrated with the existing knowledge from the literatures and the databases, such as (KEGG) Kyoto Encyclopedia of Genes and Genomes and (DIP) Database of Interacting Proteins. Once we have identified certain candidate biomarkers, the next step is to validate them by biological experiments, such as knockout experiments using RNAi (RNA interference) and PCR (polymerase chain reaction). The validation provides valuable feedback for the next iteration of biomarker discovery process. The biomedical imaging provides multidimensional functional and morphologic features of biological systems under investigation and plays an important role in the biomarker validation, for example, high content screening for *in vitro* experiments and molecular imaging for *in vivo* experiments.

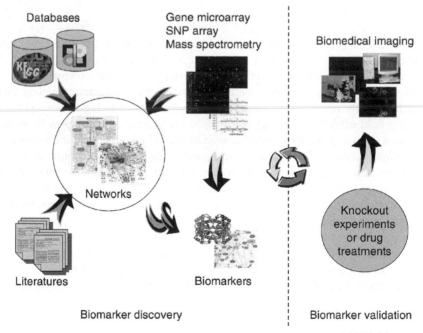

Figure 17.1   Systems biology approach that integrates bioinformatics and biomedical imaging in iterative biomarker discovery and validation.

The rest of the chapter is organized as follows. First, computational issues related to several high-throughput biotechniques and molecular networks are introduced in Section 17.1. Second, the computational issues related to biomedical imaging techniques are presented in Section 17.2. Then, more recent works on the systems biology fusing bioinformatics and biomedical imaging together are reviewed in Section 17.3. Finally, Section 17.4 provides a summary of the chapter.

17.1 BIOINFORMATICS

In this section, we briefly introduce major high-throughput biotechniques that are useful in the studies of systems biology, including techniques in genomics, proteomics, and metabonomics.

17.1.1 Gene Microarray

Gene microarray is one kind of oligonucleotide microarray used to measure simultaneously the expression levels for hundreds of thousands of genes. Gene microarray is a powerful tool in pharmaceutical and clinical research, as well as in basic biology research. It can be used to study the effects of certain treatments and diseases, as well as the regulatory relationship between genes. We can also use gene microarray to identify genes related to specific disease or phenotype by comparing gene expressions in different cells or tissues. The huge amount of data generated by gene microarray experiments is explored to answer fundamental questions about gene functions and their interdependence and hopefully to provide answers to questions like what type of disease affects a cell or which genes have strong influence on this disease.

Since there exist hundreds of thousands of coding genes while only tens or hundreds of samples in microarray data, feature reduction or gene selection is the necessary step for biomarker discovery. There are two major approaches: one is filter methods and the other is wrapper methods. Filter methods select the best features according to a reasonable criterion from prior knowledge, with the criterion independent of the real problem. Wrapper methods search through the space of possible features and evaluate each subset by running a model on the subset. Wrapper methods can be computationally expensive and have a risk of overfitting to the model. Many gene selection methods have been proposed, for example, the support vector machine method [2], the genetic algorithm [3], the perceptron method [4], Bayesian variable selection [5, 6], and the voting technique [7]. We also developed new methods in our laboratory, such as a mutual information-based method for gene and feature selection [8] and a logistic regression model based method for feature selection [9].

17.1.2 Mass Spectrometry

Mass spectrometry (MS) is one of the most important high-throughput techniques emerging in the last decade for the proteomics field. MS can be used in the protein–protein interaction detection [10, 11] and the proteomics-based biomarker selection [12, 13]. MS can also be applied to differentiate between patient samples, such as diseased from normal controls or to select patients who are most likely to benefit from a particular treatment, and, therefore, is promising in delivering early diagnosis and prognosis, as well as monitoring disease progression and treatment response. Currently, there are two leading MS techniques: surface-enhanced laser desorption ionization–time of fight (SELDI-TOF) [14, 15] and matrix-assisted laser desorption ionization–time of fight (MALDI-TOF) [16, 17]. More sophisticated MS techniques are also arising, such as inductively coupled plasma–mass spectrometry (ICP-MS) [18], nanostructure–initiator mass spectrometry (NIMS) [19]; however, the bioinformatics algorithms for these new high-throughput MS techniques are much less established.

Despite their important role in biomarker discovery, only a few published papers dealt with the preprocessing of the MS data. Most researchers obtained the peaks directly from the raw data with the software provided by the equipment vendors. Making sense out of these high-dimensional complex MS data is challenging and necessitates the use of a systematic analytic strategy. The computational proteomic issues consist of low-level processing, biomarker selection, sample classification and prediction, and protein/peptide identification. For the SELDI data, each peak may correspond to a real protein or peptide. In Yasui et al. [20], the peaks are obtained by examining whether the intensity at the point is the highest among its nearest N points neighborhood set. If it is the highest, it is then considered as a peak. To calibrate the protein m/z measurements across samples, a shift window of size 0:2 percent of the m/z is defined. Since there is much noise embedded in MS data, the detection of peaks will not be accurate.

On the other hand, MALDI data have a higher resolution than SELDI data. Each true peak corresponds to a cluster of isotopic peaks. For the baseline correction and denoizing, most methods used to handle SELDI data can be applied to process MALDI data. The undecimated discrete wavelet transform is applied to do the denoizing first in [21]. Another paper [22] uses the continuous wavelet transform. A method to detect the peaks in MALDI data is included in Yu et al. [23]. The median values within the local neighborhood are computed first and the baseline is obtained by the cubic interpolation. Then, Gaussian filter is applied to smooth the baseline-corrected data. A Gabor quadrature filter is applied to extract the envelope signal and obtain the monoisotopic peak for the isotopic peaks. At last, the local maximum search is applied to identify the peaks. The Gabor filter depends on the real data to identify the monoisotopic peak. If the intensity is not large, it may be able to smoothen the peaks. In brief, peak identification is still an open and unresolved research issue.

17.1.3 Molecular Networks and Pathways

One active research area of systems biology is the study of the interactions between the components of a biological system by interaction networks and of showing that how these interactions give rise to the function and behavior of the system [24, 25]. Many complicated systems can be represented as networks of interactions among individual components. The network properties can characterize the whole system and its individual components [26–28] at the same time; thus, they are generally able to be applied to many disciplines. Examples include social networks (e.g., scientific collaboration networks), technological networks (e.g., world wide Web and power grids), and biological networks (e.g., neural networks, cellular, and metabolic networks) [29, 30]. A network model often abstracts the components as nodes (vertices) and their relationships as edges (lines) in a graph, where the weights companying with nodes and/or edges represent the degree or constraint of the relationships [30].

There are three main molecular networks: gene regulatory networks, protein–protein interaction networks, and metabolic networks. Network modeling is the essential step in the study of biological networks, which attempts to mathematically describe the interactions among the components. The gene regulatory networks are modeled by directed and undirected graphs [31, 32], Bayesian networks [33, 34], boolean networks [35, 36], differential equations [25, 37, 38], and stochastic equations [39, 40]. The major challenge in the reconstruction of gene regulatory networks from experimental data is the dimensionality problem, that is, the number of genes far exceeds the number of conditions. A typical gene expression dataset consists of less than 100 conditions with respect to tens of thousands of genes. Therefore, the reconstruction problem is underdetermined. Some biological plausible criteria such as sparsity are introduced as constraints to solve the problem. We refer readers to Jong [31] and Gardner and Faith [41] for more detailed review. For the protein–protein interaction networks, the undirected graphs are often used. High-throughput physical protein–protein interactions are detected by yeast two hybridization system [42] and mass spectrometry [43, 44]. On the basis of the experimental datasets, a whole array of computational algorithms has been developed to infer the protein–protein interactions. For instance, there are the gene fusion (Rosetta Stone) method [45, 46], the phylogenetic profile method [47], the interaction domain pair profile method [48], the probabilistic method [49], the SVM (support vector machine)-based method [50], the LP (linear programming)-based approach [51], the association method [52], the EM algorithm [53], and the APM (assocaite probabilistic method) method [24]. An organism's metabolic system is the basic chemical system that generates essential components, such as amino acids, sugars, and lipids, and the energy required to synthesize them and to use them in creating proteins and cellular structures [54]. In recent years, several genome-scale metabolic networks for different organisms are reconstructed from the genomic data *in silico* [54–59].

Besides the three main molecular networks, there exist many other types of biological networks such as gene co-expression network [60], functional linkage network [61], protein structure network [62], protein folding network [63], protein domain interaction network, and so on. Some of them may share similar mathematical models and analysis methods, while others would need the development of new computational models and methods.

17.2 BIOIMAGE INFORMATICS OF HIGH-CONTENT SCREENING

High-content screening (HCS) is a powerful tool for simultaneously studying the response of a population of cells under a range of different chemical, genetic, or radiological perturbations in the model cell-based assays. These assays are widely used in disease diagnosis and prognosis, drug target validation, and compound lead selection. The ability to visualize, trace, and quantify cellular morphologies at high spatial and temporal resolutions is essential for the understanding of biological processes and for the development of effective therapeutic agents. Current optical microscopy techniques coupled with the large arsenal of fluorescent and other labeling methods generate a tremendous number of images that need to be processed and quantitated. However, the development of computerized tools for analyzing these images has not kept pace with the hardware development [64].

Within the bioimage informatics pipeline, we identify five top-level stages: screening and image acquisition; image processing; information/database management; data modeling and statistical analysis; and system–biology integration. In this section, we focus on the computational models and algorithms used in the image-processing stage, which includes four major steps: (1) image preprocessing; (2) cell detection, segmentation, and centerline extraction; (3) cell tracking and registration; and (4) feature extraction. We refer interested users to Zhou and Wong [65] for more details.

17.2.1   Image Pre-processing

The goal of image pre-processing is, to improve the quality of raw images prior to image segmentation and feature extraction, by employing a series of computational methods. Image pre-processing generally consists of three parts: image restoration, noise removal, and contrast enhancement [66, 67]. Image restoration often deconvolutes the degraded image from the microscope using the point spread function provided by the microscopy manufacturer [68]. Noise removal often uses a median filter to remove the pepper noise generated by CCD detectors in optical fluorescent microscopy. This median filter can preserve high-frequency information describing cell edges in high-content microscopic images. Background correction is important in microscopy image processing. Due to uneven illumination over the field of view, there can be a large variation in image intensity. A data-driven method is often implemented to remove variations in intensity [69]. In image contrast enhancement, an active contrast adjust algorithm is deployed to enhance image contrast and reduce nonuniform image intensity from uneven light illumination. Our studies indicate that nearest-neighbors deblurring filters [70, 71] work well. Blind deconvolution and maximum likelihood deconvolution methods [72] are extensively studied in the literature. They are theoretically useful, but often fail when dealing with real applications because the point spread function is generally unknown.

17.2.2   Cell Detection, Segmentation, and Centerline Extraction

After image pre-processing, the cells and their boundaries must be identified before any cell feature can be extracted. Cell or nucleus detection is an important task in biological image analysis.

17.2.2.1 Cell Detection   In recent years, successful efforts have been made in the development of image analysis methods for two-dimensional object detection. Sjostrom et al. [73] used an artificial neural network for automated cell counting. Chen et al. [74] developed a cellular image analysis method to segment, classify, and track individual cells in a living cell population. Yang and Parvin [75] detected blob objects by analyzing the Hessian matrix of each pixel. They also proposed a method based on iterative voting along the gradient direction to determine the centers of blobs [76]. Byun et al. [77] utilized the inverted Laplacian of the Gaussian for blob detection in the application of detecting nuclei in immunofluorescent retinal images.

Throughout these different kinds of detection methods, a persistent problem is over- and underdetection. An essential aspect of solving this problem is for the image segmentation step to offer "seeds" to reduce the over- and underdetection problem. There is no efficient method of detecting the local intensity maxima directly, however. Recently, we proposed a cell- and nucleus-detection method employing a Gaussian filter to generate local-intensity maxima inside the cell nuclei image map [78]. After computing the smooth-gradient vector flow field and the motion of the pixels of the cells in the smooth-gradient vector flow field, we replaced detection of the local-intensity maxima with detection of the central point of the object with the most pixels.

In three-dimensional (3D) nucleus detection, manual neuron detection and segmentation is a time-consuming task because it requires the comparison of each slice to its successive and predecessive slices in order to track the different cross-sections of each neuron. In automating this process, the first step is to develop an efficient segmentation method that can be used on each optical slice. Belien et al. [79] developed a contour-based 3D segmentation method. Their find-object algorithm examines successive images to ascertain overlapping areas. Lin et al. [80] presented an accurate 3D watershed segmentation method followed by 3D object feature selection for merging and breaking objects in confocal image stacks. Ortiz de Solorzano et al. [81], on the other hand, applied a semi-automatic method for segmentation based on watershed and morphological reconstruction followed by the analyst's classification. We recently proposed a new automated approach for accurate cell segmentation in different slices of such 3D confocal microscope images [82]. This contour-based method performs well in comparison with the well-known watershed segmentation algorithm that was introduced by Vincent and Sollie [83].

17.2.2.2 Cell Segmentation   Cell segmentation is a challenging issue in HCS because of the problem of touching spots. Generally speaking, cell segmentation can be categorized into two classes: nucleic segmentation and cytoplasm segmentation. Nucleic segmentation has been extensively studied in recent years and several automated nuclei segmentation and cytoplasm-segmentation methods have been introduced. These methods can be roughly classified into three categories: deformable models [84–86], Voronoi diagrams [87, 88], and watershed methods [74].

17.2.2.3 Neurite Centerline Extraction   Automated extraction and labeling of all the neurite segments in a fluorescence microscopy neuron image is one of the fundamental goals of neuron image processing. We observe that a neurite segment can be treated as a bright, elongated wire-like structure surrounded by a dark background. In this way, the problem can be mapped to the problem of extracting line structures from digital images, for which there are two major approaches: direct exploratory tracing algorithms [89–93] and line-pixel detection algorithms [94–97]. Given the increasing development of high-throughput screening of neuron-based assays, there is a need for the development of an automated image analysis algorithm that can extract and label neurite segments accurately and completely with minimum user intervention. Toward this end, we proposed a number of novel algorithms for automatic labeling and tracing of neurite segments in microscopy neuron images, including one that selects the starting and end points automatically and links the lines using dynamic programming techniques, and another that uses the curvilinear structure detection method [98, 99].

17.2.3 Cell Tracking and Registration

Based on the results of cell detection and segmentation, the next step is cell tracking and registration. There are many published reports on cell-tracking methods. In a review paper [100], the authors discussed five single matching algorithms frequently applied to the problem of particle tracking: the centroid method, the Gaussian fit method, the correlation method, the sum absolute difference method, and the interpolation method. In [74], we proposed an improved matching algorithm. Mean shift [101], Kalman filter [102], mutual information [103, 104], and fuzzy logic inference methods [105, 106] are also applied to cell-tracking problem. Ideally, parallel tracking can track all cells according to one objective function. In a sense, it is an optimal method, but it is computationally costly. Suppose $x_i(t)$ is the ith cell in frame t and the number of cell nuclei in frame t and $t + 1$ are m and n, respectively. We match the correspondence between nuclei at time t and $t + 1$ by computing a similarity metric $U(t) = \{u_{ij}(t)\}$, where $u_{ij}(t) = s_{ij}(t) = d_{ij}(t)$, $i = 1, 2, \ldots, m$ and $j = 1, 2, \ldots, n$, is the cosine similarity of $x_i(t)$ and $x_j(t + 1)$. $d_{ij}(t)$ is the distance of $x_i(t)$ and $x_j(t + 1)$. In this kind of method, the challenge is to find the optimal match for all cell sequences. In our recent study, a tree structure matching is applied on our subgraph [107]; that is, we search all the possible pairs locally in the subgraphs and find the pairs with highest summation of weights. After the favorite matching and local tree (FMLT) matching, we can find a group of optimal one-to-one matching.

17.2.4 Feature Extraction

After cell detection, segmentation, and tracking, a lots of cell features can be extracted from images. The basic cell feature group includes measurements of cell area, shape, size, perimeter, intensity, texture, Zernike moment, and Haralick texture. Zernike moment and Haralick texture are calculated from processed protein localization images as described by Boland et al. [108]. Zernike moments are calculated using an orthogonal basis set, that is, the Zernike polynomials, which are defined over the unit circle. On the other hand, Haralick texture features are statistics calculated on the gray level co-occurrence matrix derived from each image. Some features such as the coefficients coming wavelet transformations and time frequency transformations are also studied. We have done some preliminary investigations of the extraction of more specific features [109]. For feature extraction, additional image features specific to the different cell phenotypes, such as the spiky region, ruffling region [69], and actin acceleration region, can be identified [109]. Scientists sometimes consider features at the image level, termed image descriptors, such descriptors are usually set as the global information about the whole image, such as the mean of the cell intensity, cell area, or other descriptors.

17.3 CONNECTING BIOINFORMATICS AND BIOMEDICAL IMAGING

Information obtained from bioinformatics studies such as high-throughput genomics, proteomics, and metabonomics can be correlated with biomedical imaging to aid in the understanding of molecular interactions and disease pathways. For instance, cell-based screening assays can be used to distinguish between phenotypes and investigate interactions between signaling pathways and are useful in determining the interaction between drug candidates and target genes. Molecular imaging offers the possibility of imaging *in vivo* gene expression and protein–protein interactions. HCS can output screening hits and functional effectors. Starting from those effectors, we can study their interactions from a systems viewpoint such as that of metabolic networks. Metabolic networks can give biologists hints such as which genes/proteins/enzymes are in the pathway under study, they can then again use cellular imaging to validate them. In this section, we briefly discuss how to connect bioinformatics to biomedical imaging within systems biology framework and review some recent development of systems biology approach in this direction.

17.3.1 Cellular Networks Analysis by Using HCS

Cellular networks are composed of complexes of physically interacting macro-molecules (mainly proteins) or of dispersed biochemical activities coordinated by rapidly diffusing secondary messengers, metabolic intermediates, ions, and other small solutes. These networks can be regarded as 3D maps depicting pathways from which higher cellular functions emerge. The dynamics of molecular interactions within these reaction cascades can be assessed in a living cell by the application of fluorescence microscopy, which allows one to correlate such phenomena as cell-cycle progression, cell migration and motility, secretion, volume control and regulation of growth, and morphogenesis and cell death.

Within fluorescence microscopy, the development of genetically encoded variants of green fluorescent proteins (GFP) as tags for proteins and indicators of small solutes (Ca^2, other ions, cAMP, ATP, GTP, inositol phosphates, etc.) has revolutionized our insights into "live" biochemistry at the microscopic level, with the advantage of preserving the cells biochemical connectivity context, compartmentalization, and spatial organization [110]. This development parallels recent progress in genomics, proteomics, and metabonomics, through which functional attributes are assigned to genes and gene products by alignment to well-characterized sequences or by comparison to models. However, only a small percentage of newly identified products can presently be categorized in this manner, and further progress depends on the collection of huge amounts of experimental data from functional and microscopic imaging bioassays.

The analysis of genetically expressed GFP-based fluorochromes is destined to follow the dynamic trafficking and clustering of gene products and the study of spatial–temporal distribution patterns of small solutes in living cells kept under normal physiological conditions. HCS will add a new dimension to these studies, with an emphasis on membrane-embedded receptors, transporters and channels, the diffusivity of cytosolic enzymes, ions and small solutes (metabolites) in cytosol, endoplasmic reticulum and mitochondria, and the supermolecular assembly of signaling factors at the cell cortex and in the nucleus.

17.3.2 Gene Function Annotation by Using HCS

Biomedical imaging techniques not only are good validation tools but also provide powerful support for quantitative and large-scale biological studies, much like bioinformatics. Gene function annotation is a common task in bioinformatics. The traditional bioinformatics uses the genomics information, such as sequence similarity and gene expression profile, to prediction gene functions. Cluster analysis is a predominant means to group gene functions, and numerous publications have been dedicated to describe gene clustering analysis-based gene expression and microarray data. The pilot study of Kiger et al. [111] detected the morphological phenotypes for 160 genes. Their work suggests that it is possible to use RNAi screening to functionally characterize a large set of genes and, to identify functional modules, by grouping genes according to morphological criteria. Recently, there have been a few studies of gene function based on cellular features, image descriptors, and phenotypes [112, 113]. In these studies, it has been verified that 16 phenotype classes of the 23 defined phenotype classes are indeed implicated in specific biochemical pathways for genes of known function. It has also been shown that the strength of combined phenotypic and bioinformatics analysis can give considerable predictive information about the function of previously uncharacterized genes.

17.3.3 Association Studies with Clinical Imaging Traits

In addition to the cell-based image features described in the last subsection, there are also strong correlation between clinical phenotypic image features and gene expression profiles. Segal et al. [114] studies the correlation between the gene expression and the clinical imaging traits in primary human liver cancer. They found the dynamic imaging traits in noninvasive computed tomography (CT) are systematically correlated with the gene expression. The association map between imaging features on three-phase contrast enhanced CT scans and gene expression patterns of 28 human hepatocellular carcinomas (HCC) are created as follows. First, 32 most informative imaging traits are identified from the initial 138 distinctive imaging traits presented in one or more HCCs, based on their frequency and prominence in the data, interobserver agreement between two radiologists and independence from other traits as determined by Pearson correlation among the traits. Second, the gene expression data of 6732 genes in HCC samples are clustered into 116 gene modules. Then, each gene modules is associated with specific combinations of imaging traits. The obtained association map can be used to reconstruct the gene expression profiles from imaging traits. Combinations of 28 imaging traits can predict 78% of the gene expression profiles. On the other hand, the association map can also identify the potential biological processes underlying specific imaging traits, based on the associated gene expression profiles. This work shows the noninvasive imaging can detect the genomic activity of human liver cancer; therefore, it is promising for the delivery of personalized medicine in the near future.

Kantarci et al. [115] show another systems biology approach for disease gene discovery by integrating the genome-wide association study (GWAS) and clinical imaging. The genome regions related to the Donnai–Barrow syndrome (DBS) and facio-oculo-acoustico-renal (FOAR) are firstly identified by identity by descent (IBD) from SNP array data for four individuals with DBS in a large family. The largest region of IBD is further refined by using microsatellite markers with linkage of disequilibrium (LOD) analysis. Finally, the mutations of LRP2 gene in six families with DBS are identified and validated by magnetic resonance imaging (MRI).

17.3.4   *In Vivo* Genomics Analysis

Molecular imaging is a new development in the past decade that aims to track, monitor, and measure, in living animals, the molecular behaviors and dynamic biological processes such as metabolic activity, cell proliferation, apoptosis, receptor occupancy, reporter gene expression, and antigen modulation. *In vivo* gene expression profiling is currently a major task in molecular imaging. Unlike most early works focusing on improving the imaging techniques, such as experimental design and probe selection [116, 117], there are recent works that integrate the molecular imaging techniques with bioinformatics from the viewpoints of systems biology.

Chuquet et al. [118] analyzed the correlation between the gene expression and brain metabolic status during cerebral ischemia. The brain metabolic status in a model of focal cerebral ischemia in baboons is obtained by positron emission tomography (PET) scanning. The gene microarray experiments identify four groups of genes and the patterns are observed in each of the distinct groups. These patterns of gene expression may be used to define molecular checkpoints for the development of an ischemic infarct and a molecular definition of the penumbra.

Wu et al. [119] analyze the effects of a triple-fusion reporter gene on embryonic stem (ES) cell transcriptional profiles by molecular imaging and genomics methods. A self-inactivating lentiviral vector carrying a triple-fusion (TF) construct consisting of fluorescence, bioluminescence, and positron emission tomography (PET) reporter genes is transfected into murine ES cells. The stably transfected populations are isolated by fluorescence-activated cell sorting (FACS) analysis. Then, microarray experiment is applied to study the gene expression in nontransfected control ES cells and stably transfected ES cells. The comparison study of gene expression reveals certain increases in transcriptional variability. Further analysis using GO annotations and gene regulatory networks shows that ES–TF cells downregulated cell cycling, cell death, and protein and nucleic acid metabolism genes while upregulating homeostatic and anti-apoptosis genes. Even though the expression of TF reporter gene affects the transcription of ES cells, HCS experiments show that the reporter gene has no significant effects on ES cell viability, proliferation, and differentiation capability. Therefore, TF reporter gene may be used for tracking ES–TF cells in living subjects.

Haberkorn et al. [120] report a study to assess the effects after transfer of anti-angiogenic genes in rat hepatoma, by using fluorodeoxyglucose positron emission tomography (FDG-PET) and gene microarray. Grigsby et al. [121] present an integrative study attempting to find gene expression patterns in human cervical tumors. Molecular FDG-PET imaging is performed in patients to detect the extent of lymph nodes metastases. The tumor tissue samples are extracted and hybridized to gene microarrays. Supervised clustering of gene expression data identifies 12 statistically significant differential expressed genes out of about 12,000 between the two patient groups with different extents of regional lymph node involvement. This study identified candidate biomarkers of extent of lymph node metastases that correlated with poor survival outcome.

17.3.5   *In Vivo* Proteomics Analysis

Protein–protein interactions are involved in processes such as enzymatic activity, signal transduction, immunological recognition, and DNA replication and repair. They, therefore, are of critical importance to maintain most cellular functions. A number of qualitative or quantitative biophysical methods were developed to detect *in vitro* protein–protein interactions [42–44]. In order to monitor dynamic real-time protein–protein interactions in living cells, some novel methods based on bioimaging techniques are developed. Fluorescence resonance energy transfer (FRET) microscopy [122, 123] and FRET anisotropy [124, 125] are used to study the movement of proteins and their interactions with cellular components, as well as other more complex cellular processes such as small-molecule-messenger dynamics, and enzyme activation. Bioluminescence resonance energy transfer (BRET) is also used to monitor homodimerization of proteins [126–128]. But all these methods only work in cell culture instead of living subjects due to several drawbacks. Recently, three general methods were developed for imaging protein–protein interactions in living subjects using reporter genes: a modified mammalian two-hybrid system, a BRET system, and split reporter protein complementation and reconstitution strategies [129–131].

The discovery of targets for tissue-specific delivery of therapeutic and imaging agents *in vivo* is difficult due to the complexity of molecular environment and the inaccessibility of most cells within a tissue. Oh et al. [132] describe a systems biology approach to identify a small subset of proteins induced at the tissue–blood interface that are inherently accessible to antibodies injected intravenously. They use proteomics and bioinformatics techniques such as protein 2D gels and tandem mass spectrometry (MS/MS) to identify endothelial cell surface proteins exhibiting restricted tissue distribution and apparent tissue modulation. The expression profiling by molecular imaging with antibodies further establishes two of these proteins, aminopeptidase-P and annexin A1, as selective *in vivo* targets for antibodies in lungs and solid tumours, respectively. The discovery of targets is validated by that radio-immunotherapy to annexin A1 destroys tumors and increases animal survival.

17.3.6   *In Vivo* Genetic Analysis

Zubieta et al. [133] studied the association between the metabolism and genetic polymorphism. In their study, the μ-opioid neurotransmitter responses to a pain stressor are evaluated by PET. The effect of the val158metCOMT (cathechol-*O*-methyltransferase, one of the enzymes that metabolizes catecholamines) genotypes on μ-opioid system activation and μ-opioid receptor binding potential maps is tested by one-way analysis of variance (ANOVA). They observed significant influence of the genetic polymorphism in COMT affecting the metabolism responses to pain in human brain.

17.3.7   *In Vivo* RNAi Experiments

RNAi has become a widely used experimental tool to study gene function and appears promising for therapies based on the targeted inhibition of disease-relevant genes. The main challenge to *in vivo* RNAi application is the efficient delivery and monitoring of the RNAi-inducing molecules, such as small interfering RNAs (siRNAs) to the target tissue. The emerging molecular imaging provides a powerful noninvasive tool for tracking the delivery, monitoring the effect, and quantifying the results of the *in vivo* RNAi experiments [134, 135].

Bartlett et al. [136] use noninvasive bioluminescent imaging, with a mathematical model of siRNA delivery and function, to monitor the effects of target-specific and treatment-specific parameters on siRNA-mediated gene silencing in cells. In this study, the mathematical model is used to predict the dosing schedule required to maintain persistent silencing of target proteins with different half-lives in rapidly dividing or nondividing cells. The approach of biomedical imaging combined with mathematical modeling provides insights into siRNA delivery and function, which may be useful in clinical research applications of siRNA.

Medarova et al. [137] describe a new noninvasive imaging method for detection of siRNA delivery and silencing. They developed dual-purpose probes for *in vivo* transfer of siRNA and the simultaneous imaging of its accumulation in tumors by high-resolution MRI and near-infrared *in vivo* optical imaging (NIRF). These probes, which consisted of magnetic nanoparticles labeled with a near-infrared dye and covalently linked to siRNA molecules specific for model or therapeutic targets, were modified with a membrane translocation peptide for intracellular delivery. The authors show the feasibility of *in vivo* tracking of tumor uptake of these probes by MRI and optical imaging in two separate tumor models. These works represent the first step toward therapeutic development and application of RNAi.

17.4   SUMMARY

The rapid advance of molecular biology and bioinformatics in the past decade reveals that the biological systems are more complex than expected. By integrating different scales of relevant biological data together in a systematic model, systems biology becomes an essential method in deciphering these complex systems. The bioinformatics results of high-throughput experiments need to be validated by *in vitro* or *in vivo* experiments, where biomedical imaging techniques prove to be powerful validation tools. On the other hand, the discovery in biomedical imaging experiments in turn can provide clue or hypothesis for the subsequent biological studies.

In this chapter, we reviewed key aspects of computational modeling issues in biomedical imaging and the recent development of integrating biomedical imaging with bioinformatics in the study of systems biology. There are certainly much more computational issues of biomedical imaging need to address and explore. Applications of biomedical imaging techniques in systems biology is still in its infancy, and comprehensive integration and fusing of biomedical imaging techniques with bioinformatics and "-omics" remains a challenge. We hope that this chapter has provided the readers a good overview of key techniques and representative examples in developing biomedical imaging and modeling for systems biology.

ACKNOWLEDGMENTS

The authors would like to thank Nalan Yildirim for the discussion and valuable suggestions in preparing and writing this chapter.

REFERENCES

1. H. Kitano. Systems biology: a brief overview. *Science*, 295(5560):1662–1664, 2002.
2. A. Ben-Hur, A. Elisseeff, and I. Guyon. A stability based method for discovering structure in clustered data. *Pac. Symp. Biocomput.*, 6–17, 2002.
3. L. Li, et al. Gene selection for sample classification based on gene expression data: study of sensitivity to choice of parameters of the GA/KNN method. *Bioinformatics*, 17(12):1131–1142, 2001.
4. S. Kim, et al. Strong feature sets from small samples. *J. Comput. Biol.*, 9(1):127–146, 2002.
5. K. E. Lee, et al. Gene selection: a Bayesian variable selection approach. *Bioinformatics*, 19(1):90–97, 2003.
6. X. Zhou, X. Wang, and E. R. Dougherty. Multi-class cancer classification using multinomial probit regression with Bayesian gene selection. *Syst. Biol.* (Stevenage), 153(2):70–78, 2006.

7. T. R. Golub, et al. Molecular classification of cancer: class discovery and class prediction by gene expression monitoring. *Science*, 286(5439):531–537, 1999.

8. X. Zhou, X. Wang, and E. R. Dougherty. Nonlinear probit gene classification using mutual information and wavelet-based feature selection. *J. Biol. Syst.*, 12(3):371–386, 2004.

9. X. Zhou, K. -Y. Liu, and S. T. C. Wong. Cancer classification and prediction using logistic regression with Bayesian gene selection. *J. Biomed. Inform.*, 37(4):249–259, 2004.

10. Y. Zhao, et al. Mapping protein-protein interactions by affinity-directed mass spectrometry. *Proc. Natl. Acad. Sci. USA*, 93(9):4020–4024, 1996.

11. R. M. Ewing, et al. Large-scale mapping of human protein-protein interactions by mass spectrometry. *Mol. Syst. Biol.*, 3: 89, 2007.

12. T. Fushiki, H. Fujisawa, and S. Eguchi. Identification of biomarkers from mass spectrometry data using a "common" peak approach. *BMC Bioinform.*, 7:358, 2006.

13. X. Zhou, et al. Biomarker discovery for risk stratification of cardiovascular events using an improved genetic algorithm. In *Proceedings of IEEE/NLM Life Science Systems and Applications Workshop*, Bethesda, MD, 2006.

14. G. L. Wright Jr, et al. Proteinchip(R) surface enhanced laser desorption/ionization (SELDI) mass spectrometry: a novel protein biochip technology for detection of prostate cancer biomarkers in complex protein mixtures. *Prostate Cancer Prostatic Dis.*, 2(5/6):264–276, 1999.

15. E. F. Petricoin, et al. Use of proteomic patterns in serum to identify ovarian cancer. *Lancet*, 359(9306):572–577, 2002.

16. P. Berndt, U. Hobohm, and H. Langen. Reliable automatic protein identification from matrix-assisted laser desorption/ionization mass spectrometric peptide fingerprints. *Electrophoresis*, 20(18):3521–3526, 1999.

17. J. Hardouin. Protein sequence information by matrix-assisted laser desorption/ionization in-source decay mass spectrometry. *Mass. Spectrom. Rev.*, 26(5):672–682, 2007.

18. S. Elliott, et al. ICP-MS: when sensitivity does matter. *Spectroscopy*, 36, 2007.

19. T. R. Northen, et al. A nanostructure-initiator mass spectrometry-based enzyme activity assay. *Proc. Nat. Acad. Sci. USA*, 105(10):3678–3683, 2008.

20. Y. Yasui, et al. An automated peak identification/calibration procedure for high-dimensional protein measures from mass spectrometers. *J. Biomed. Biotechnol.*, (4):242–248, 2003.

21. J. S. Morris, et al. Feature extraction and quantification for mass spectrometry in biomedical applications using the mean spectrum. *Bioinformatics*, 21(9):1764–1775, 2005.

22. P. Du, W. A. Kibbe, and S. M. Lin. Improved peak detection in mass spectrum by incorporating continuous wavelet transform-based pattern matching. *Bioinformatics*, 22(17):2059–2065, 2006.

23. W. Yu, et al. Detecting and aligning peaks in mass spectrometry data with applications to MALDI. *Comput. Biol. Chem.*, 30(1):27–38, 2006.

24. L. Chen, et al. Inferring protein interactions from experimental data by association probabilistic method. *Proteins*, 62(4):833–837, 2006.

25. Y. Wang, et al. Inferring gene regulatory networks from multiple microarray datasets. *Bioinformatics*, 22(19):2413–2420, 2006.

26. D. J. Watts and S. H. Strogatz. Collective dynamics of "small-world" networks. *Nature*, 393(6684):440–442, 1998.

27. A. L. Barabasi and R. Albert. Emergence of scaling in random networks. *Science*, 286(5439):509–512, 1999.

28. L. H. Greene and V. A. Higman. Uncovering network systems within protein structures. *J. Mol. Biol.*, 334(4):781–791, 2003.

29. S. H. Strogatz. Exploring complex networks. *Nature*, 410(6825):268–276, 2001.

30. M. Girvan and M. E. J. Newman. Community structure in social and biological networks. *Proc. Natl. Acad. Sci. USA*, 99(12):7821–7826, 2002.

31. H. de Jong. Modeling and simulation of genetic regulatory systems: a literature review. *J. Comput. Biol.*, 9(1):67–103, 2002.

32. M. Kanehisa and S. Goto. KEGG: Kyoto Encyclopedia of Genes and Genomes. *Nucleic Acids Res.*, 28(1):27–30, 2000.

33. N. Friedman, et al. Using Bayesian networks to analyze expression data. *J. Comput. Biol.*, 7(3–4):601–620, 2000.

34. D. Pe'er, et al. Inferring subnetworks from perturbed expression profiles. *Bioinformatics*, 17(Suppl 1):S215–S224, 2001.

35. S. Liang, S. Fuhrman, and R. Somogyi. Reveal, a general reverse engineering algorithm for inference of genetic network architectures. *Pac. Symp. Biocomput.*, 18–29, 1998.

36. T. E. Ideker, V. Thorsson, and R. M. Karp. Discovery of regulatory interactions through perturbation: inference and experimental design. *Pac. Symp. Biocomput.*, 305–316, 2000.

37. P. D'Haeseleer, S. Liang, and R. Somogyi. Genetic network inference: from co-expression clustering to reverse engineering. *Bioinformatics*, 16(8):707–726, 2000.

38. M. K. S. Yeung, J. Tegnér, and J. J. Collins. Reverse engineering gene networks using singular value decomposition and robust regression. *Proc. Natl. Acad. Sci. USA*, 99(9):6163–6168, 2002.

39. A. Arkin, J. Ross, and H. H. McAdams. Stochastic kinetic analysis of developmental pathway bifurcation in phage lambda-infected *Escherichia coli* cells. *Genetics*, 149(4):1633–1648, 1998.

40. C. J. Morton-Firth and D. Bray. Predicting temporal fluctuations in an intracellular signalling pathway. *J. Theor. Biol.*, 192(1):117–128, 1998.

41. T. S. Gardner and J. J. Faith. Reverse-engineering transcription control networks. *Phys. Life Rev.*, 2(1):65–88, 2005.

42. T. Ito, et al. A comprehensive two-hybrid analysis to explore the yeast protein interactome. *Proc. Natl. Acad. Sci. USA*, 98(8):4569–4574, 2001.

43. A. Kumar and M. Snyder. Protein complexes take the bait. *Nature*, 415(6868):123–124, 2002.

44. B. Causier. Studying the interactome with the yeast two-hybrid system and mass spectrometry. *Mass. Spectrom. Rev.*, 23(5):350–367, 2004.

45. A. J. Enright, et al. Protein interaction maps for complete genomes based on gene fusion events. *Nature*, 402(6757):86–90, 1999.

46. E. M. Marcotte, et al. Detecting protein function and protein-protein interactions from genome sequences. *Science*, 285(5428):751–753, 1999.

47. M. Pellegrini, et al. Assigning protein functions by comparative genome analysis: protein phylogenetic profiles. *Proc. Natl. Acad. Sci. USA*, 96(8):4285–4288, 1999.

48. J. Wojcik and V. Schächter. Protein–protein interaction map inference using interacting domain profile pairs. *Bioinformatics*, 17(Suppl 1):S296–S305, 2001.

49. S. M. Gomez, S. H. Lo, and A. Rzhetsky. Probabilistic prediction of unknown metabolic and signal-transduction networks. *Genetics*, 159(3):1291–1298, 2001.

50. S. Dohkan, A. Koike, and T. Takagi. Improving the performance of an SVM-based method for predicting protein–protein interactions. *In Silico Biol.*, 6(6):515–529, 2006.

51. M. Hayashida, N. Ueda, and T. Akutsu. Inferring strengths of protein–protein interactions from experimental data using linear programming. *Bioinformatics*, 19(Suppl 2):ii58–ii65, 2003.

52. E. Sprinzak and H. Margalit. Correlated sequence-signatures as markers of protein–protein interaction. *J. Mol. Biol.*, 311(4):681–692, 2001.

53. M. Deng, et al. Inferring domain-domain interactions from protein–protein interactions. *Genome Res.*, 12(10):1540–1548, 2002.

54. J. Förster, et al. Genome-scale reconstruction of the *Saccharomyces cerevisiae* metabolic network. *Genome Res.*, 13(2):244–253, 2003.

55. N. C. Duarte, et al. Global reconstruction of the human metabolic network based on genomic and bibliomic data. *Proc. Natl. Acad. Sci. USA*, 104(6):1777–1782, 2007.

56. S. S. Fong, J. Y. Marciniak, and B. Ø. Palsson. Description and interpretation of adaptive evolution of *Escherichia coli* K-12 MG1655 by using a genome-scale in silico metabolic model. *J. Bacteriol.*, 185(21):6400–6408, 2003.

57. K. Sheikh, J. Förster, and L. K. Nielsen. Modeling hybridoma cell metabolism using a generic genome-scale metabolic model of Mus musculus. *Biotechnol. Prog.*, 21(1):112–121, 2005.

58. M. J. Herrgård, S. S. Fong, and B. Ø. Palsson. Identification of genome-scale metabolic network models using experimentally measured flux profiles. *PLoS Comput. Biol.*, 2(7):e72, 2006.

59. C. Francke, R. J. Siezen, and B. Teusink. Reconstructing the metabolic network of a bacterium from its genome. *Trends Microbiol.*, 13(11):550–558, 2005.

60. L. L. Elo, et al. Systematic construction of gene coexpression networks with applications to human T helper cell differentiation process. *Bioinformatics*, 23(16):2096–2103, 2007.

61. U. Karaoz, et al. Whole-genome annotation by using evidence integration in functional-linkage networks. *Proc. Natl. Acad. Sci. USA*, 101(9):2888–2893, 2004.

62. Z.-P. Liu, et al. Predicting gene ontology functions from protein's regional surface structures. *BMC Bioinform.*, 8:475, 2007.

63. F. Rao and A. Caflisch. The protein folding network. *J. Mol. Biol.*, 342(1):299–306, 2004.

64. X. Zhou and S. T. C. Wong. Informatics challenges of high-throughput microscopy. *IEEE Signal Process. Mag.*, 23(3):63–72, 2006.

65. X. Zhou and S. T. C. Wong. A primer on image informatics of high content screening. In S. A. Haney, editor, *High Content Screening*. Wiley, New York, 2008, pp. 43–84.

66. W. K. Pratt. *Digital Image Processing.* 2nd edition. Wiley, New York, 1991.

67. E. Bengtsson, B. Nordin, and F. P. Muse: a new tool for interactive image-analysis and segmentation based on multivariate-statistics. *Comput. Methods Program Biomed.*, 42(3):181–200, 1994.

68. J. R. Swedlow and M. Platani. Live cell imaging using wide-field microscopy and deconvolution. *Cell. Struct. Funct.*, 27(5):335–341, 2002.

69. J. Lindblad, et al. Image analysis for automatic segmentation of cytoplasms and classification of Rac1 activation. *Cytometry A*, 57(1):22–33, 2004.

70. D. A. Agard. Optical sectioning microscopy: cellular architecture in three dimensions. *Annu. Rev. Biophys. Bioeng.*, 13:191–219, 1984.

71. D. A. Agard, et al. Fluorescence microscopy in three dimensions. *Methods Cell Biol.*, 30:353–377, 1989.

72. P. Sarder and A. Nehorai. Deconvolution methods for 3-D fluorescence microscopy images. *IEEE Signal Process. Mag.*, 23(3):32–45, 2006.

73. P. J. Sjöström, B. R. Frydel, and L. U. Wahlberg. Artificial neural network-aided image analysis system for cell counting. *Cytometry*, 36(1):18–26, 1999.

74. X. Chen, X. Zhou, and S. T. C. Wong. Automated segmentation, classification, and tracking of cancer cell nuclei in time-lapse microscopy. *IEEE Trans. Biomed. Eng.*, 53(4):762–766, 2006.

75. Q. Yang and B. Parvin. Harmonic cut and regularized centroid transform for localization of subcellular structures. *IEEE Trans. Biomed. Eng.*, 50(4):469–475, 2003.

76. Q. Yang and B. Parvin. Perceptual organization of radial symmetries. In *Proceedings of the IEEE Computer Society Conference on Computer Vision and Pattern Recognition CVPR 2004*, Washington, DC, 2004.

77. J. Byun, et al. Quantitative analysis of immunofluorescent retinal images. In *Proceedings of the 3rd IEEE International Symposium on Biomedical Imaging: Nano to Macro*, Arlington, Virginia, 2006.

78. X. Zhou, et al. Study of CuO nanoparticle-induced cell death by high content cellular fluorescence imaging and analysis. In *Proceedings of the IEEE International Symposium on Circuits and Systems ISCAS 2007*, New Orleans, Louisiana, 2007.

79. J. A. M. Belin, et al. Confocal DNA cytometry: a contour-based segmentation algorithm for automated three-dimensional image segmentation. *Cytometry*, 49(1):12–21, 2002.

80. G. Lin, et al. A hybrid 3D watershed algorithm incorporating gradient cues and object models for automatic segmentation of nuclei in confocal image stacks. *Cytometry A*, 56(1):23–36, 2003.

81. C. O. de Solórzano, et al. Segmentation of confocal microscope images of cell nuclei in thick tissue sections. *J. Microsc.*, 193(Pt 3):212–226, 1999.

82. M. Kamali, et al. Tracking of neuron profiles and segmentation in confocal image stacks using 3D Hough transform. Harvard University Press, Boston, Massachusetts, 2006.

83. L. Vincent and P. Soille. Watersheds in digital spaces: an efficient algorithm based on immersion simulations. *IEEE Trans. Pattern Anal. Machine Intell.*, 13(6):583–598, 1991.

84. C. Zimmer, et al. Segmentation and tracking of migrating cells in videomicroscopy with parametric active contours: a tool for cell-based drug testing. *IEEE Trans. Med. Imaging*, 21(10):1212–1221, 2002.

85. N. Ray, S. T. Acton, and K. Ley. Tracking leukocytes in vivo with shape and size constrained active contours. *IEEE Trans. Med. Imaging*, 21(10):1222–1235, 2002.

86. G. Xiong, X. Zhou, and L. Ji. Automated segmentation of Drosophila RNAi fluorescence cellular images using deformable models. *IEEE Trans. Circuits Syst. I*, 53(11):2415–2424, 2006.

87. M. M. Morelock, et al. Statistics of assay validation in high throughput cell imaging of nuclear factor kappaB nuclear translocation. *Assay Drug Dev. Technol.*, 3(5):483–499, 2005.

88. T. R. Jones, A. E. Carpenter, and P. Golland. Voronoi-based segmentation of cells on image manifolds. In *Workshop on Computer Vision for Biomedical Image Applications (CVBIA)*, Springer-Verlag, Berlin, 2005.

89. A. Can, et al. Rapid automated tracing and feature extraction from retinal fundus images using direct exploratory algorithms. *IEEE Trans. Inf. Technol. Biomed.*, 3(2): 125–138, 1999.

90. J. L. Coatrieux, et al. Computer vision approaches for the three-dimensional reconstruction of coronary arteries: review and prospects. *Crit. Rev. Biomed. Eng.*, 22(1):1–38, 1994.

91. K. A. Al-Kofahi, et al. Rapid automated three-dimensional tracing of neurons from confocal image stacks. *IEEE Trans. Inf. Technol. Biomed.*, 6(2):171–187, 2002.

92. K. A. Al-Kofahi, et al. Median-based robust algorithms for tracing neurons from noisy confocal microscope images. *IEEE Trans. Inf. Technol. Biomed.*, 7(4):302–317, 2003.

93. R. Poli and G. Valli. An algorithm for real-time vessel enhancement and detection. *Comput. Methods Programs Biomed.*, 52(1):1–22, 1997.

94. C. Steger. An unbiased detector of curvilinear structures. *IEEE Trans. Pattern Anal. Machine Intell.*, 20(2):113–125, 1998.

95. A. R. Cohen, B. Roysam, and J. N. Turner. Automated tracing and volume measurements of neurons from 3-D confocal fluorescence microscopy data. *J. Microsc.*, 173(Pt 2):103–114, 1994.

96. I. Y. Y. Koh, et al. An image analysis algorithm for dendritic spines. *Neural. Comput.*, 14(6):1283–1310, 2002.

97. C. M. Weaver, et al. Automated algorithms for multiscale morphometry of neuronal dendrites. *Neural. Comput.*, 16(7):1353–1383, 2004.

98. Y. Zhang, et al. A novel tracing algorithm for high throughput imaging Screening of neuron-based assays. *J. Neurosci. Methods*, 160(1):149–162, 2007.

99. G. Xiong, et al. Automated neurite labeling and analysis in fluorescence microscopy images. *Cytometry A*, 69(6):494–505, 2006.

100. M. K. Cheezum, W. F. Walker, and W. H. Guilford. Quantitative comparison of algorithms for tracking single fluorescent particles. *Biophys J.*, 81(4):2378–2388, 2001.

101. O. Debeir, et al. Tracking of migrating cells under phase-contrast video microscopy with combined mean-shift processes. *IEEE Trans. Med. Imaging*, 24(6):697–711, 2005.

102. X. Yang, H. Li, and X. Zhou. Nuclei segmentation using marker-controlled watershed, tracking using mean-shift, and Kalman filter in time-lapse microscopy. *IEEE Trans Circuit Syst. I*, 53(11):2405–2414, 2006.

103. C. Studholme, R. T. Constable, and J. S. Duncan. Accurate alignment of functional EPI data to anatomical MRI using a physics-based distortion model. *IEEE Trans. Med. Imaging*, 19(11):1115–1127, 2000.

104. W. M. Wells, et al. Multi-modal volume registration by maximization of mutual information. *Med. Image. Anal*, 1(1):35–51, 1996.

105. E. Meijering, I. Smal, G. Danuser. Tracking in molecular bioimaging. *IEEE Signal Process. Mag.*, 23(3):46–53, 2006.

106. M. Ehrlich, et al. Endocytosis by random initiation and stabilization of clathrin-coated pits. *Cell*, 118(5):591–605, 2004.

107. X. Zhou, et al. A novel cell tracking algorithm and continuous hidden Markov model for cell phase identification. In *Proceedings of the IEEE/NLM Life Science Systems and Applications Workshop*, Bethesda MD, 2006.

108. M. V. Boland, M. K. Markey, and R. F. Murphy. Automated recognition of patterns characteristic of subcellular structures in fluorescence microscopy images. *Cytometry*, 33(3):366–375, 1998.

109. J. Wang, et al. Cellular phenotype recognition for high-content RNA interference genome-wide screening. *J. Biomol. Screen.*, 13(1):29–39, 2008.

110. R. Yuste. Fluorescence microscopy today. *Nat. Methods*, 2(12):902–924, 2005.

111. A. A. Kiger, et al. A functional genomic analysis of cell morphology using RNA interference. *J. Biol.*, 2(4):27, 2003.

112. B. Sönnichsen, et al. Full-genome RNAi profiling of early embryogenesis in *Caenorhabditis elegans*. *Nature*, 434(7032):462–469, 2005.

113. K. C. Gunsalus, et al. Predictive models of molecular machines involved in *Caenorhabditis elegans* early embryogenesis. *Nature*, 436(7052):861–865, 2005.

114. E. Segal, et al. Decoding global gene expression programs in liver cancer by noninvasive imaging. *Nat. Biotechnol.*, 25(6):675–680, 2007.

115. S. Kantarci, et al. Mutations in LRP2, which encodes the multiligand receptor megalin, cause Donnai–Barrow and facio-oculo-acoustico-renal syndromes. *Nat. Genet.*, 39(8):957–959, 2007.

116. H. R. Herschman. Molecular imaging: looking at problems, seeing solutions. *Science*, 302(5645):605–608, 2003.

117. A. C. Silva, et al. Manganese-enhanced magnetic resonance imaging (MEMRI): methodological and practical considerations. *NMR Biomed.*, 17(8):532–543, 2004.

118. J. Chuquet, et al. Matching gene expression with hypometabolism after cerebral ischemia in the nonhuman primate. *J. Cereb. Blood Flow Metab.*, 22(10):1165–1169, 2002.

119. J. C. Wu, et al. Transcriptional profiling of reporter genes used for molecular imaging of embryonic stem cell transplantation. *Physiol. Genomics*, 25(1):29–38, 2006.

120. U. Haberkorn, et al. Changes in glucose metabolism and gene expression after transfer of anti-angiogenic genes in rat hepatoma. *Eur. J. Nucl. Med. Mol. Imaging*, 34(12):2011–2023, 2007.

121. P. W. Grigsby, et al. Gene expression patterns in advanced human cervical cancer. *Int. J. Gynecol. Cancer*, 16(2):562–567, 2006.

122. J. Lippincott-Schwartz, E. Snapp, and A. Kenworthy. Studying protein dynamics in living cells. *Nat. Rev. Mol. Cell Biol.*, 2(6):444–456, 2001.

123. J. Zhang, et al. Creating new fluorescent probes for cell biology. *Nat. Rev. Mol. Cell Biol.*, 3(12):906–918, 2002.

124. T. Heyduk, et al. Fluorescence anisotropy: rapid, quantitative assay for protein-DNA and protein–protein interaction. *Methods Enzymol.*, 274 492–503, 1996.

125. R. Varma and S. Mayor. GPI-anchored proteins are organized in submicron domains at the cell surface. *Nature*, 394(6695):798–801, 1998.

126. S. Angers, et al. Detection of beta 2-adrenergic receptor dimerization in living cells using bioluminescence resonance energy transfer (BRET). *Proc. Natl. Acad. Sci. USA*, 97(7):3684–3689, 2000.

127. M. McVey, et al. Monitoring receptor oligomerization using time-resolved fluorescence resonance energy transfer and bioluminescence resonance energy transfer. The human delta -opioid receptor displays constitutive oligomerization at the cell surface, which is not regulated by receptor occupancy. *J. Biol. Chem.*, 276(17):14092–14099, 2001.

128. M. Rocheville, et al. Subtypes of the somatostatin receptor assemble as functional homo- and heterodimers. *J. Biol. Chem.*, 275(11):7862–7869, 2000.

129. T. F. Massoud, et al. Reporter gene imaging of protein–protein interactions in living subjects. *Curr. Opin. Biotechnol.*, 18(1):31–37, 2007.

130. T. F. Massoud, R. Paulmurugan, and S. S. Gambhir. Molecular imaging of homodimeric protein–protein interactions in living subjects. *FASEB J.*, 18(10):1105–1107, 2004.

131. R. Paulmurugan, et al. Molecular imaging of drug-modulated protein–protein interactions in living subjects. *Cancer Res.*, 64(6):2113–2119, 2004.

132. P. Oh, et al. Subtractive proteomic mapping of the endothelial surface in lung and solid tumours for tissue-specific therapy. *Nature*, 429(6992):629–635, 2004.

133. J.-K. Zubieta, et al. COMT val158met genotype affects mu-opioid neurotransmitter responses to a pain stressor. *Science*, 299(5610):1240–1243, 2003.

134. M. Golzio, et al. In vivo gene silencing in solid tumors by targeted electrically mediated siRNA delivery. *Gene Ther.*, 14(9):752–759, 2007.

135. O. R. Mook, et al. Evaluation of locked nucleic acid-modified small interfering RNA in vitro and in vivo. *Mol. Cancer. Ther.*, 6(3):833–843, 2007.

136. D. W. Bartlett and M. E. Davis. Insights into the kinetics of siRNA-mediated gene silencing from live-cell and live-animal bioluminescent imaging. *Nucleic Acids Res.*, 34(1):322–333, 2006.

137. Z. Medarova, et al. In vivo imaging of siRNA delivery and silencing in tumors. *Nat. Med.*, 13(3):372–377, 2007.

INDEX

Elements of Computational Systems Biology   Edited by Huma M. Lodhi and Stephen H. Muggleton
Copyright © 2010 John Wiley & Sons, Inc.

403

WILEY SERIES ON BIOINFORMATICS: COMPUTATIONAL TECHNIQUES AND ENGINEERING

Series Editors: Yi Pan and Albert Y. Zomaya

Knowledge Discovery in Bioinformatics: Techniques, Methods, and Applications / Xiaohua Hu and Yi Pan

Grid Computing for Bioinformatics and Computational Biology / Edited by El-Ghazali Talbi and Albert Y. Zomaya

Analysis of Biological Networks / Edited by Björn H. Junker and Falk Schreiber

Bioinformatics Algorithms: Techniques and Applications / Ion Mandoiu and Alexander Zelikovsky

Machine Learning in Bioinformatics / Yanqing Zhang and Jagath C. Rajapakse

Computational Systems Biology / Huma M. Lodhi and Stephen H. Muggleton